INFINITY GAUNTLET AFTERMATH

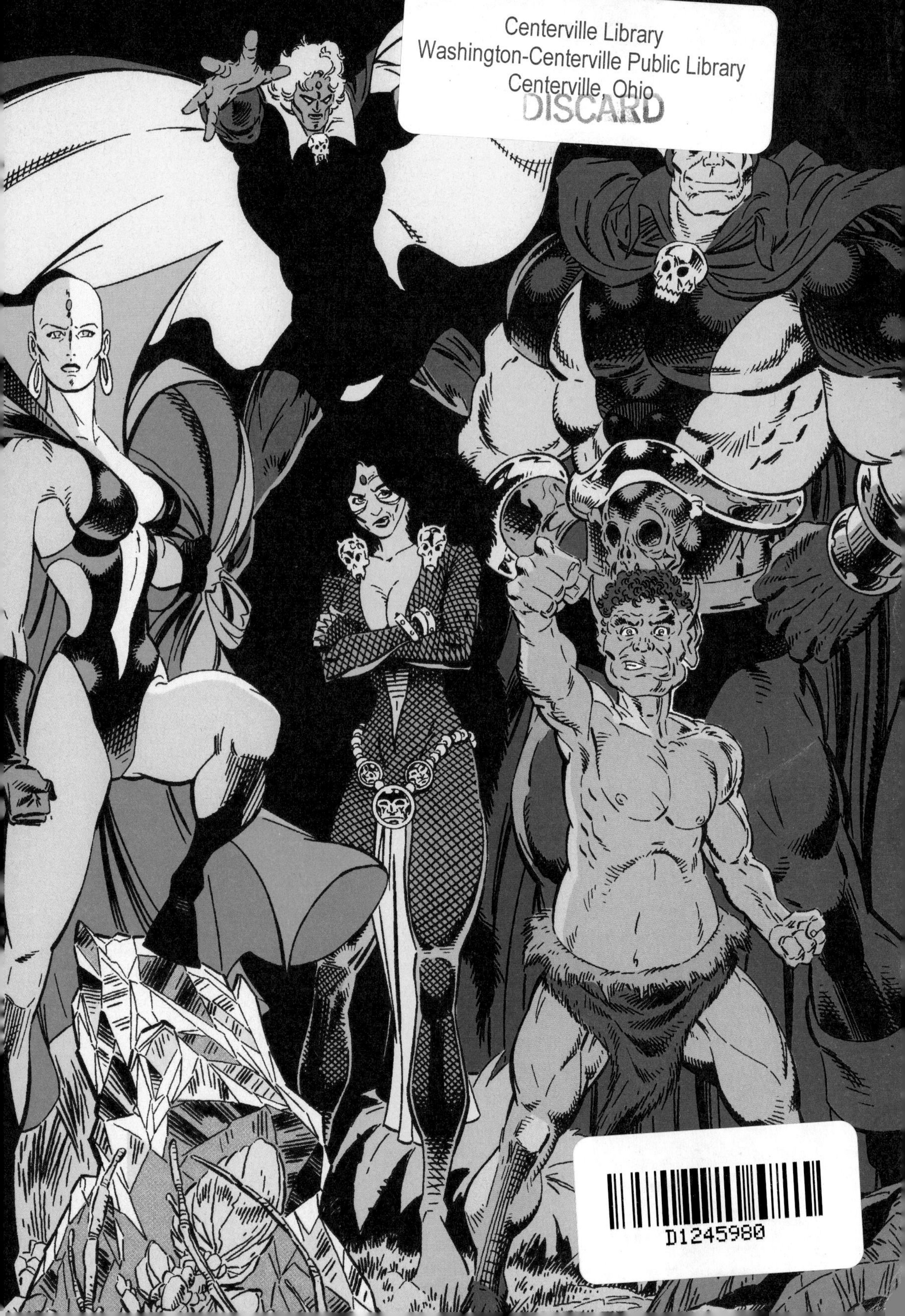

INFINITY GAUNTLET

WRITERS
RON MARZ & JIM STARLIN WITH ROY THOMAS & DANN THOMAS

PENCILERS
RON LIM, DAN LAWLIS, ANGEL MEDINA & RICK LEONARDI WITH
TODD SMITH, TOM RANEY, KARL ALTSTAETTER & KIRKWOOD
STUDIOS' STEVE CARR & DERYL SKELTON

INKERS
TOM CHRISTOPHER, JIM SANDERS III, ANDREW PEPOY,
TERRY AUSTIN & BOB ALMOND

COLORISTS
TOM VINCENT, GEORGE ROUSSOS, IAN LAUGHLIN & MARIE JAVINS

LETTERERS
KEN BRUZENAK, RICK PARKER & JACK MORELLI

ASSISTANT EDITORS
JOHN LEWANDOWSKI & BARRY DUTTER

EDITORS
CRAIG ANDERSON & MIKE ROCKWITZ

FRONT COVER ARTISTS
ANGEL MEDINA, TERRY AUSTIN & THOMAS MASON

BACK COVER ARTISTS
ANGEL MEDINA, TERRY AUSTIN & TOM SMITH

COLLECTION EDITOR
MARK D. BEAZLEY

ASSISTANT EDITORS
NELSON RIBEIRO & ALEX STARBUCK

EDITOR, SPECIAL PROJECTS
JENNIFER GRÜNWALD

SENIOR EDITOR, SPECIAL PROJECTS
JEFF YOUNGQUIST

RESEARCH & LAYOUT
JEPH YORK

PRODUCTION
COLORTEK & JOE FRONTIRRE

SVP OF PRINT
& DIGITAL PUBLISHING SALES
DAVID GABRIEL

EDITOR IN CHIEF
AXEL ALONSO

CHIEF CREATIVE OFFICER
JOE QUESADA

PUBLISHER
DAN BUCKLEY

EXECUTIVE PRODUCER
ALAN FINE

INFINITY GAUNTLET AFTERMATH. Contains material originally published in magazine form as SILVER SURFER #60-66, DR. STRANGE: SORCERER SUPREME #36, WARLOCK & THE INFINITY WATCH #1-6 and SILVER SURFER ANNUAL #5. First printing 2013. ISBN# 978-0-7851-8486-7. Published by MARVEL WORLDWIDE, INC., a subsidiary of MARVEL ENTERTAINMENT, LLC. OFFICE OF PUBLICATION: 135 West 50th Street, New York, NY 10020. Copyright © 1991, 1992 and 2013 Marvel Characters, Inc. All rights reserved. All characters featured in this issue and the distinctive names and likenesses thereof, and all related indicia are trademarks of Marvel Characters, Inc. No similarity between any of the names, characters, persons, and/or institutions in this magazine with those of any living or dead person or institution is intended, and any such similarity which may exist is purely coincidental. Printed in the U.S.A. ALAN FINE, EVP - Office of the President, Marvel Worldwide, Inc. and EVP & CMO Marvel Characters B.V.; DAN BUCKLEY, Publisher & President - Print, Animation & Digital Divisions; JOE QUESADA, Chief Creative Officer; TOM BREVOORT, SVP of Publishing; DAVID BOGART, SVP of Operations & Procurement, Publishing; C.B. CEBULSKI, SVP of Creator & Content Development; DAVID GABRIEL, SVP of Print & Digital Publishing Sales; JIM O'KEEFE, VP of Operations & Logistics; DAN CARR, Executive Director of Publishing Technology; SUSAN CRESPI, Editorial Operations Manager; ALEX MORALES, Publishing Operations Manager; STAN LEE, Chairman Emeritus. For information regarding advertising in Marvel Comics or on Marvel.com, please contact Niza Disla, Director of Marvel Partnerships, at ndisla@marvel.com. For Marvel subscription inquiries, please call 800-217-9158. Manufactured between 7/12/2013 and 8/19/2013 by R.R. DONNELLEY, INC., SALEM, VA, USA.

10 9 8 7 6 5 4 3 2 1

To win the heart of mistress Death, the mad nihilist Thanos of Titan sought the six Infinity Gems, each of which controlled a facet of the universe: time, space, power, reality, the mind and the soul. One by one Thanos confronted the gems' owners, Elders of the Universe including the Grandmaster and the Collector, and obtained their gems through cunning and trickery. He then combined all six gems on his glove, creating the Infinity Gauntlet — and gaining absolute mastery over all creation!

Thanos built a floating shrine to Death in outer space, and bestowed a grim gift upon her with a snap of his fingers — by instantly killing half the population of the universe. But within the Soul Gem, the spirit of deceased cosmic hero Adam Warlock sensed Thanos' evil. Having worn the gem on his forehead before his death, Warlock had some control over it — and was able to exit the gem's "soul world" with the spirits of his two deceased allies, Gamora and Pip the Troll. The three returned to life in new bodies, and Warlock joined the Marvel Universe's greatest heroes, including Dr. Strange and the Silver Surfer, in opposing Thanos.

Though Thanos easily bested and murdered most of Earth's champions, and even triumphed over the universe's most powerful cosmic entities, he was ultimately defeated when he shed his physical form to become a "god" — allowing Nebula, a space pirate who claimed to be Thanos' granddaughter, to yank the Infinity Gauntlet off his discarded mortal shell. Nebula used the time gem to reverse Thanos' elimination of half the universe and resurrect Earth's heroes, but she was defeated by Adam Warlock, who claimed the gauntlet's power for his own. Thanos retreated, faking his own death — and now the universe waits uneasily, hoping that Warlock will make a fairer and more benevolent ruler than Thanos…

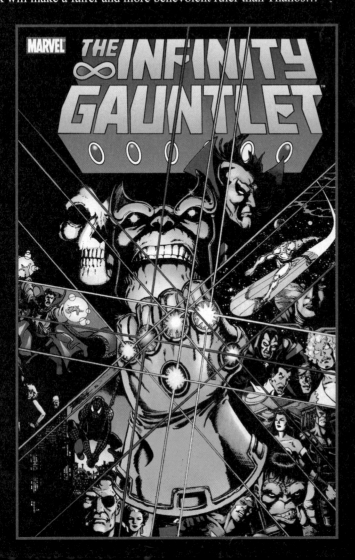

Interlude pages from *Silver Surfer* #57-59

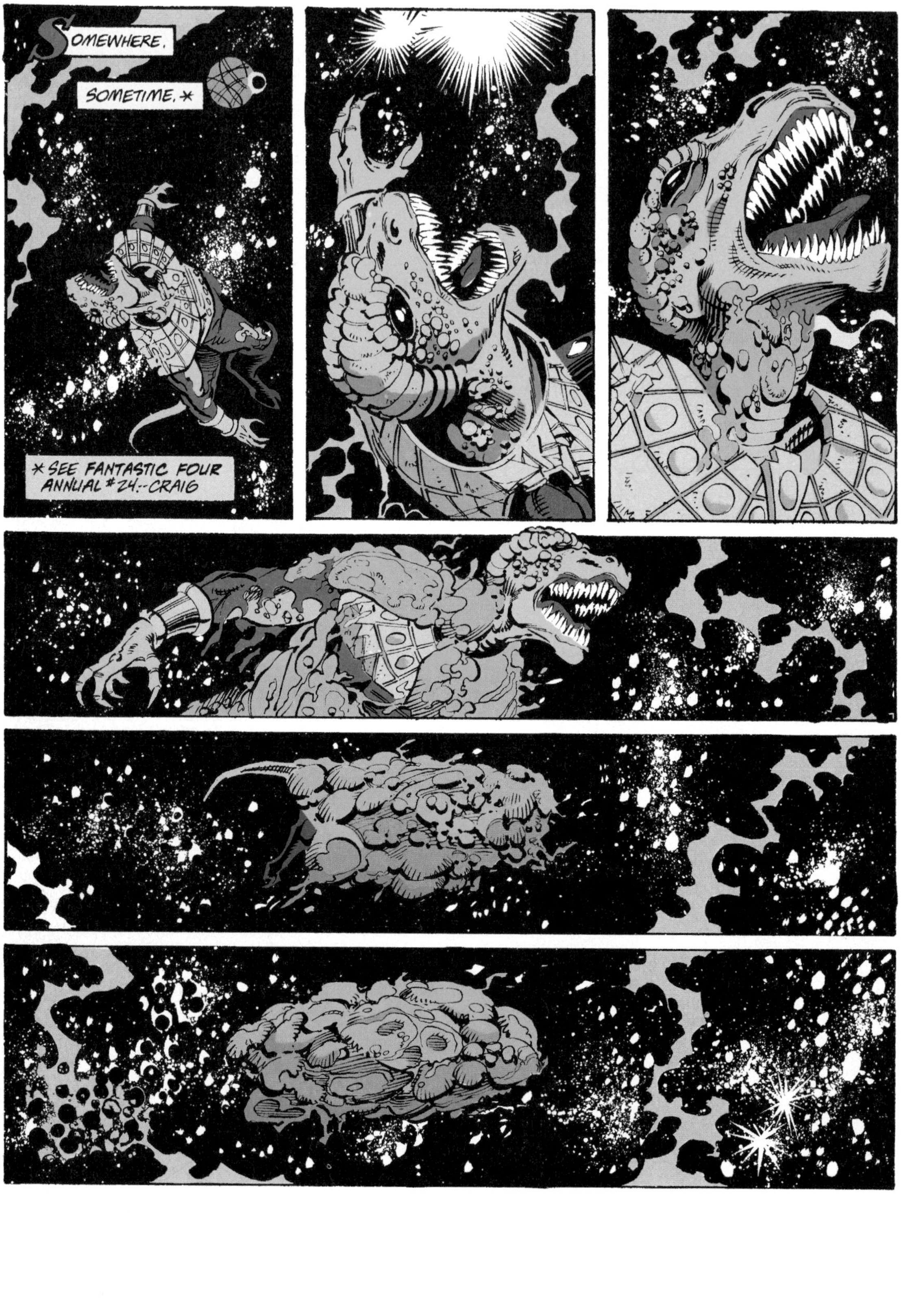
SOMEWHERE.
SOMETIME.*
*SEE FANTASTIC FOUR ANNUAL #24.--CRAIG

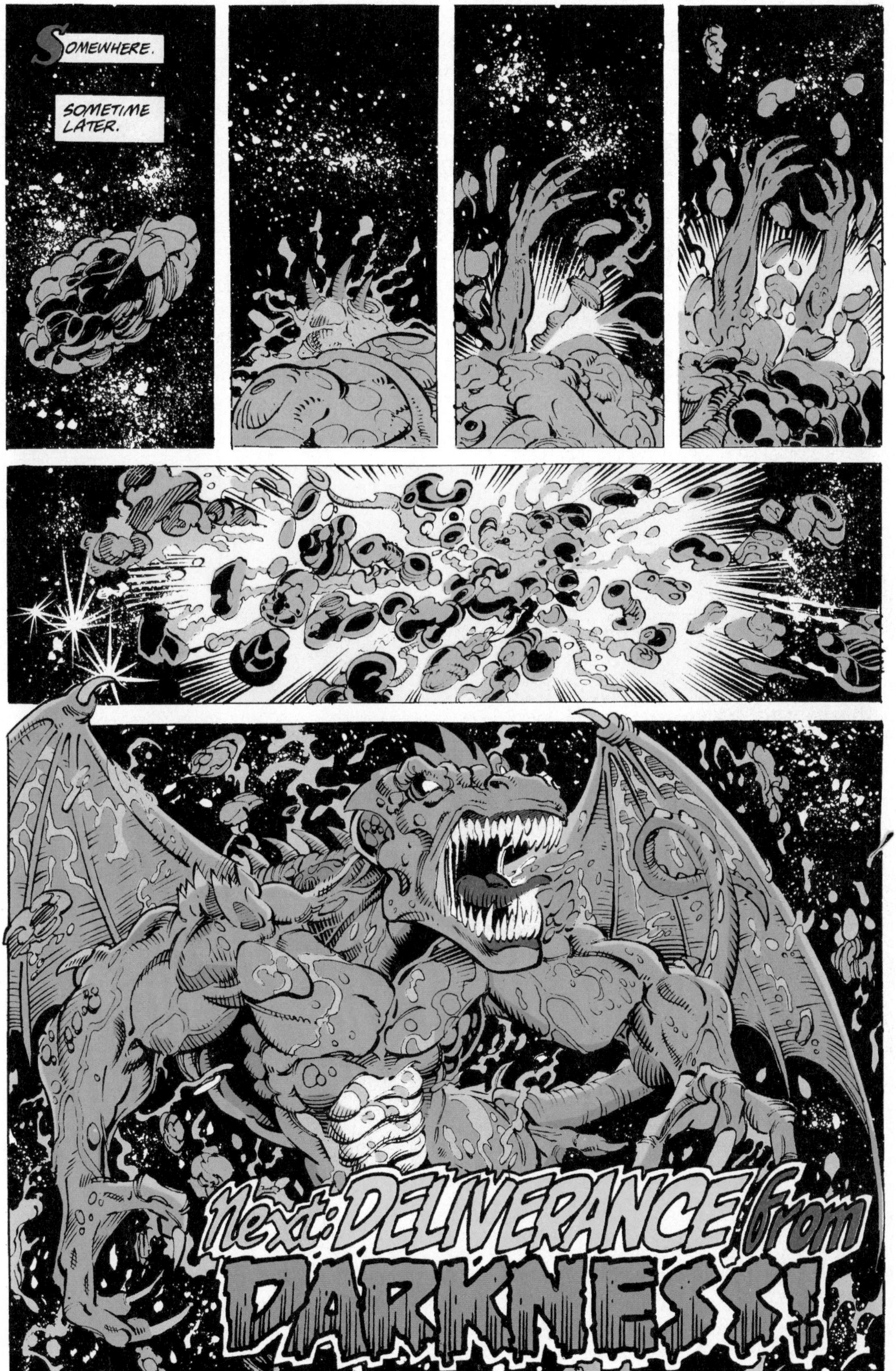
SOMEWHERE.
SOMETIME LATER.
NEXT: DELIVERANCE FROM DARKNESS!

-INTERLUDE-

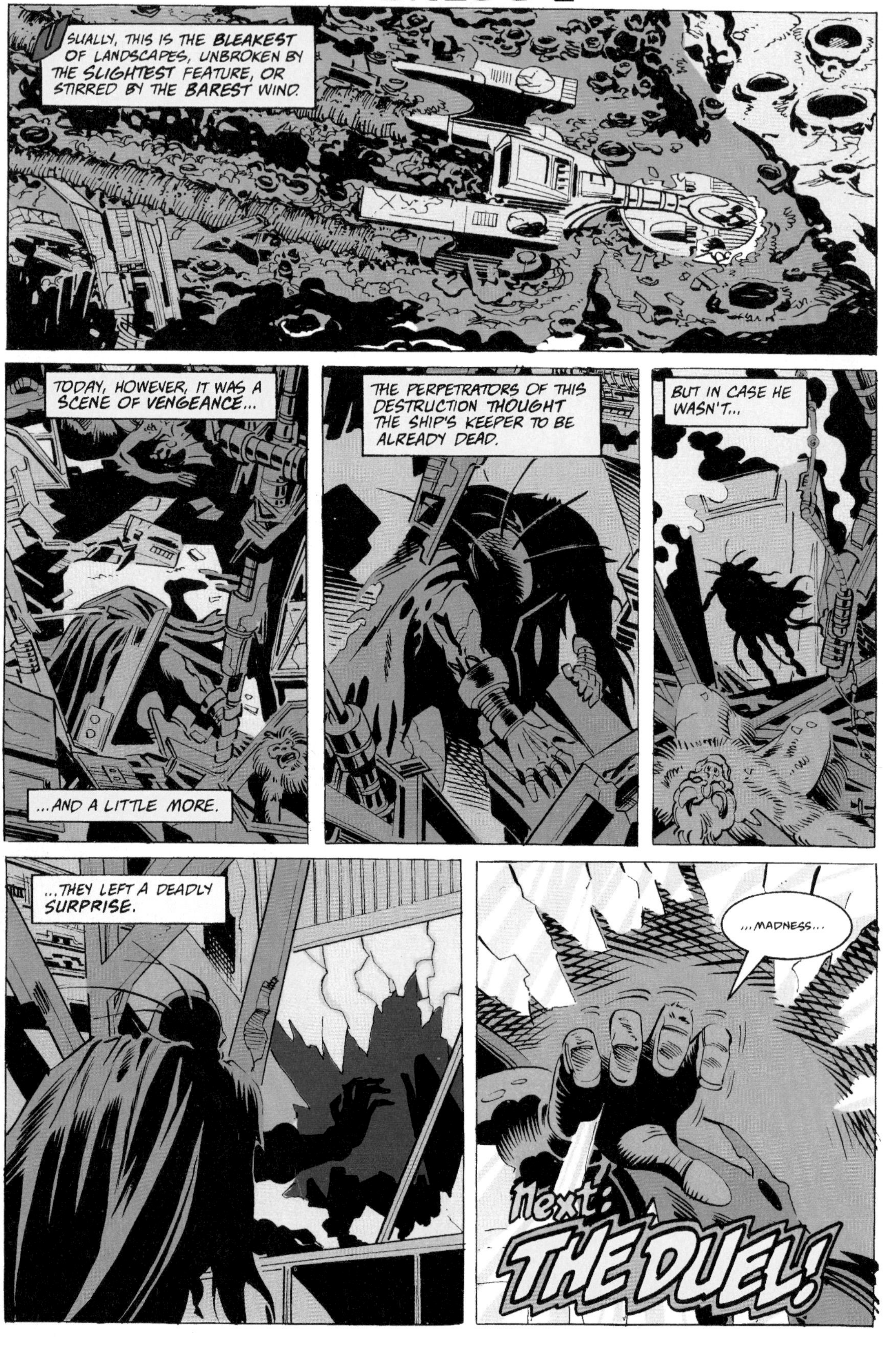
USUALLY, THIS IS THE BLEAKEST OF LANDSCAPES, UNBROKEN BY THE SLIGHTEST FEATURE, OR STIRRED BY THE BAREST WIND.
TODAY, HOWEVER, IT WAS A SCENE OF VENGEANCE...
...AND A LITTLE MORE.
THE PERPETRATORS OF THIS DESTRUCTION THOUGHT THE SHIP'S KEEPER TO BE ALREADY DEAD.
BUT IN CASE HE WASN'T...
...THEY LEFT A DEADLY SURPRISE.
...MADNESS...
next:
THE DUEL!

-INTERLUDE-

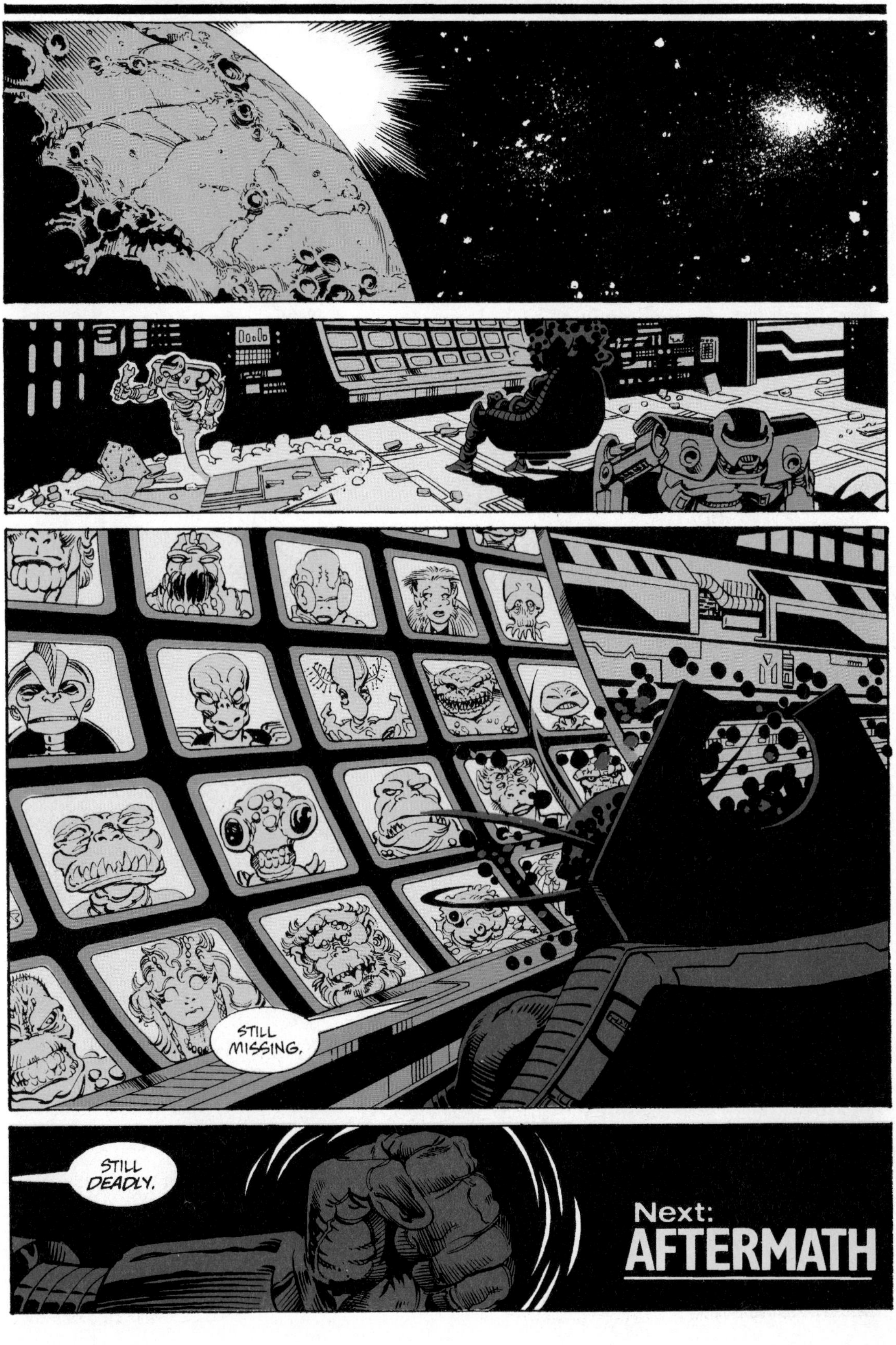
STILL MISSING.
STILL DEADLY.
Next:
AFTERMATH

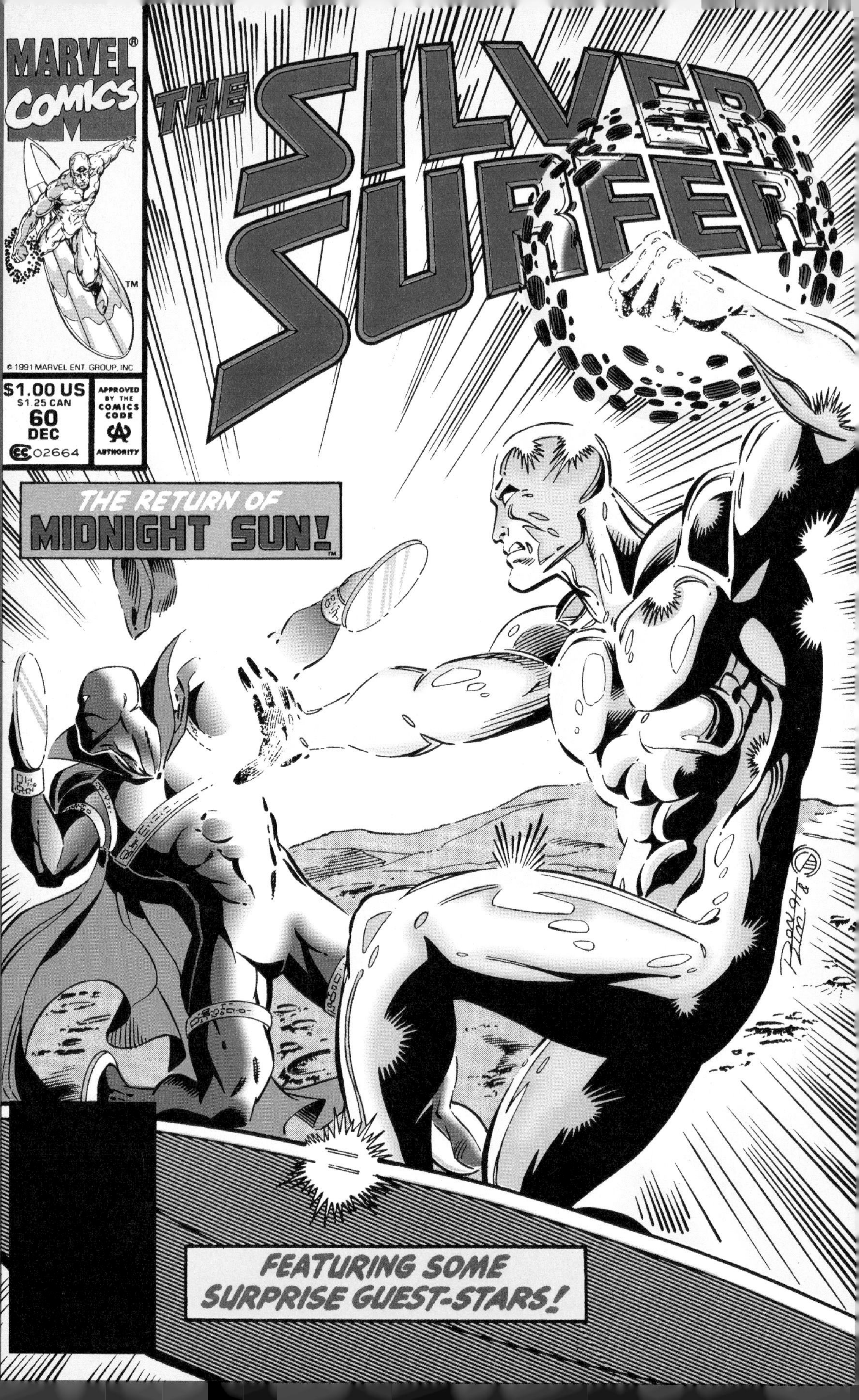
MARVEL® COMICS
THE SILVER SURFER®
© 1991 MARVEL ENT. GROUP, INC.
$1.00 US
$1.25 CAN
60
DEC
02664
APPROVED BY THE COMICS CODE AUTHORITY
THE RETURN OF MIDNIGHT SUN!™
FEATURING SOME SURPRISE GUEST-STARS!

TO SAVE HIS PLANET, NORRIN RADD SURRENDERED HIS FREEDOM TO BECOME HERALD TO THE WORLD-DEVOURING GALACTUS. COATED WITH GALACTIC GLAZE, GIVEN A SURFBOARD OBEYING HIS MENTAL COMMANDS, AND GRANTED THE POWER COSMIC, HE NOW SOARS THE UNIVERSE . A SHINING SENTINEL OF THE SPACEWAYS! STAN LEE PRESENTS . . . THE SILVER SURFER!

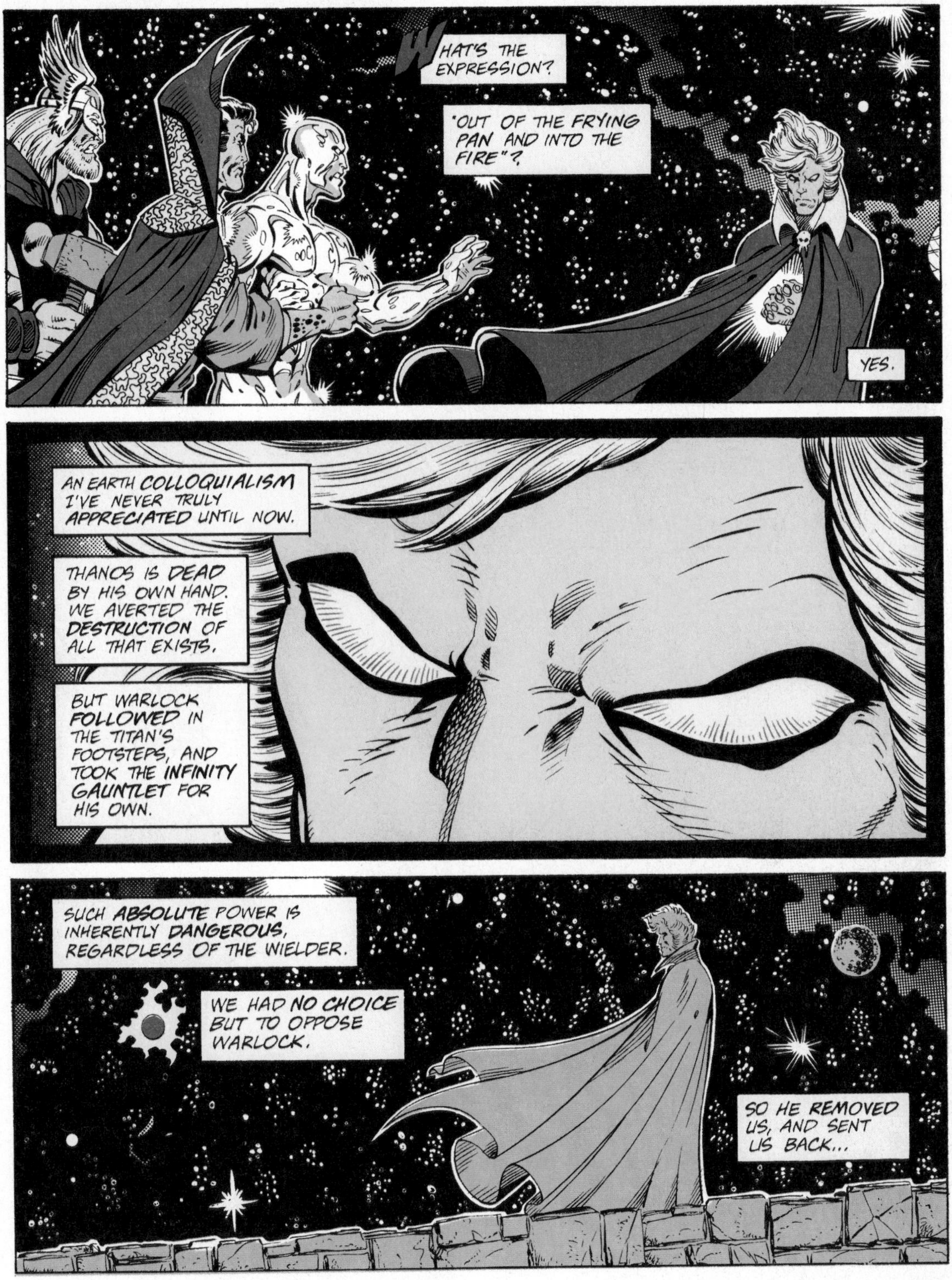

WHAT'S THE EXPRESSION?
"OUT OF THE FRYING PAN AND INTO THE FIRE"?
YES.
AN EARTH COLLOQUIALISM I'VE NEVER TRULY APPRECIATED UNTIL NOW.
THANOS IS DEAD BY HIS OWN HAND. WE AVERTED THE DESTRUCTION OF ALL THAT EXISTS.
BUT WARLOCK FOLLOWED IN THE TITAN'S FOOTSTEPS, AND TOOK THE INFINITY GAUNTLET FOR HIS OWN.
SUCH ABSOLUTE POWER IS INHERENTLY DANGEROUS, REGARDLESS OF THE WIELDER.
WE HAD NO CHOICE BUT TO OPPOSE WARLOCK.
SO HE REMOVED US, AND SENT US BACK...

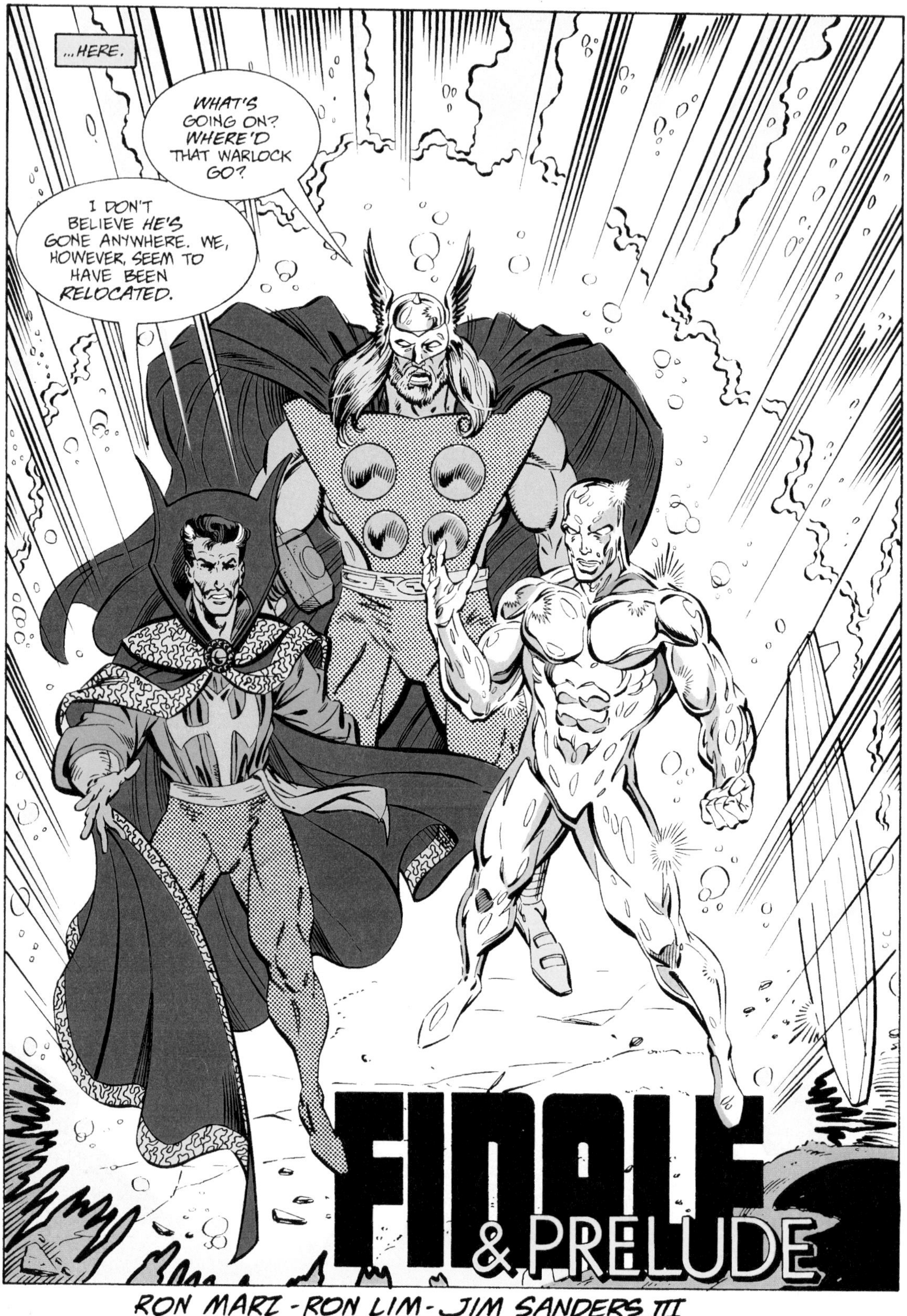
...HERE.
WHAT'S GOING ON? WHERE'D THAT WARLOCK GO?
I DON'T BELIEVE HE'S GONE ANYWHERE. WE, HOWEVER, SEEM TO HAVE BEEN RELOCATED.
FINALE & PRELUDE

RON MARZ - RON LIM - JIM SANDERS III
WRITER PENCILER INKER
KEN BRUZENAK - TOM VINCENT - CRAIG ANDERSON - TOM DeFALCO
LETTERER COLORIST EDITOR CHIEF

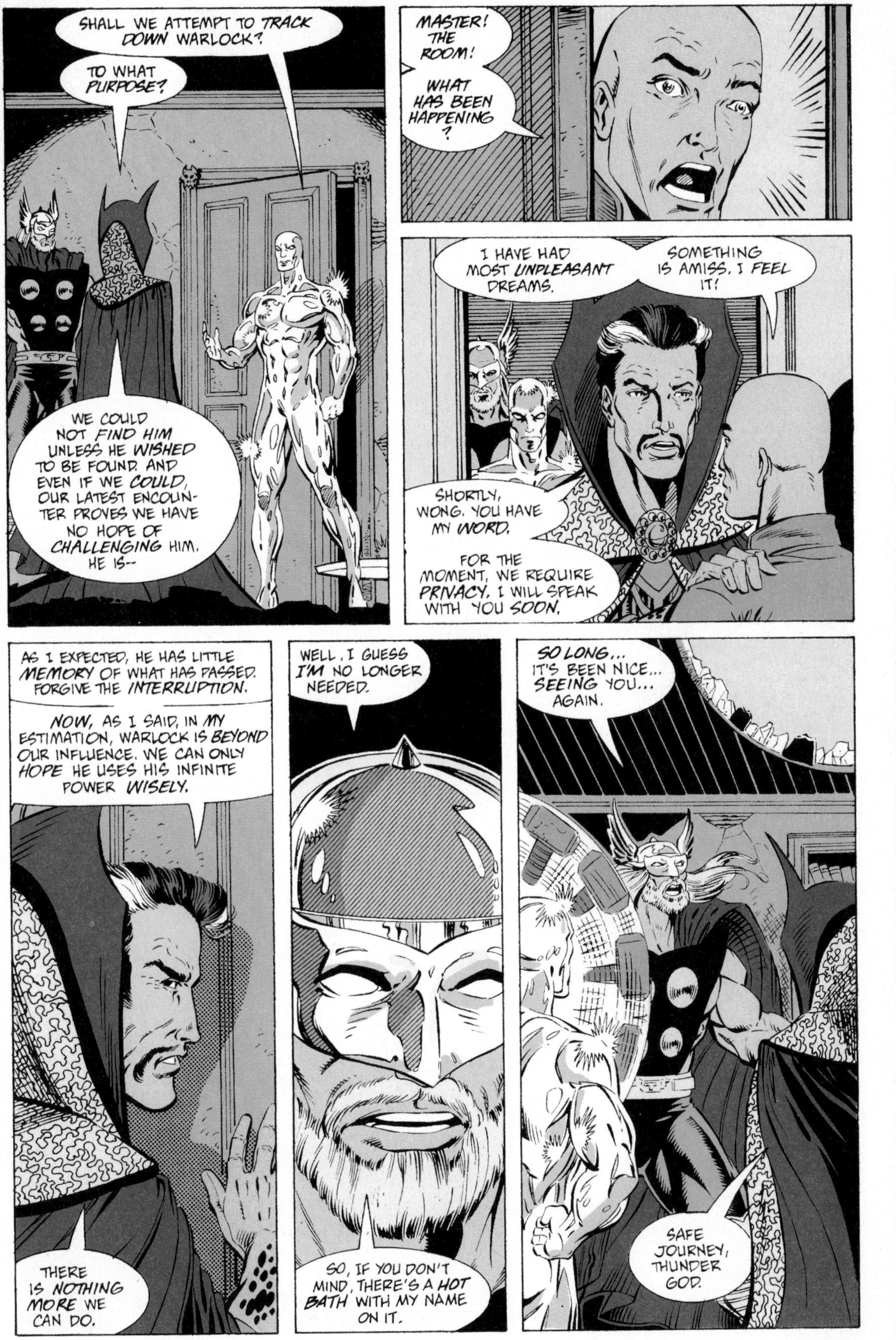

SHALL WE ATTEMPT TO TRACK DOWN WARLOCK?
TO WHAT PURPOSE?
WE COULD NOT FIND HIM UNLESS HE WISHED TO BE FOUND. AND EVEN IF WE COULD, OUR LATEST ENCOUNTER PROVES WE HAVE NO HOPE OF CHALLENGING HIM. HE IS--
MASTER! THE ROOM!
WHAT HAS BEEN HAPPENING?
I HAVE HAD MOST UNPLEASANT DREAMS.
SOMETHING IS AMISS. I FEEL IT!
SHORTLY, WONG. YOU HAVE MY WORD.
FOR THE MOMENT, WE REQUIRE PRIVACY. I WILL SPEAK WITH YOU SOON.
AS I EXPECTED, HE HAS LITTLE MEMORY OF WHAT HAS PASSED. FORGIVE THE INTERRUPTION.
NOW, AS I SAID, IN MY ESTIMATION, WARLOCK IS BEYOND OUR INFLUENCE. WE CAN ONLY HOPE HE USES HIS INFINITE POWER WISELY.
THERE IS NOTHING MORE WE CAN DO.
WELL, I GUESS I'M NO LONGER NEEDED.
SO, IF YOU DON'T MIND, THERE'S A HOT BATH WITH MY NAME ON IT.
SO LONG... IT'S BEEN NICE... SEEING YOU... AGAIN.
SAFE JOURNEY, THUNDER GOD.

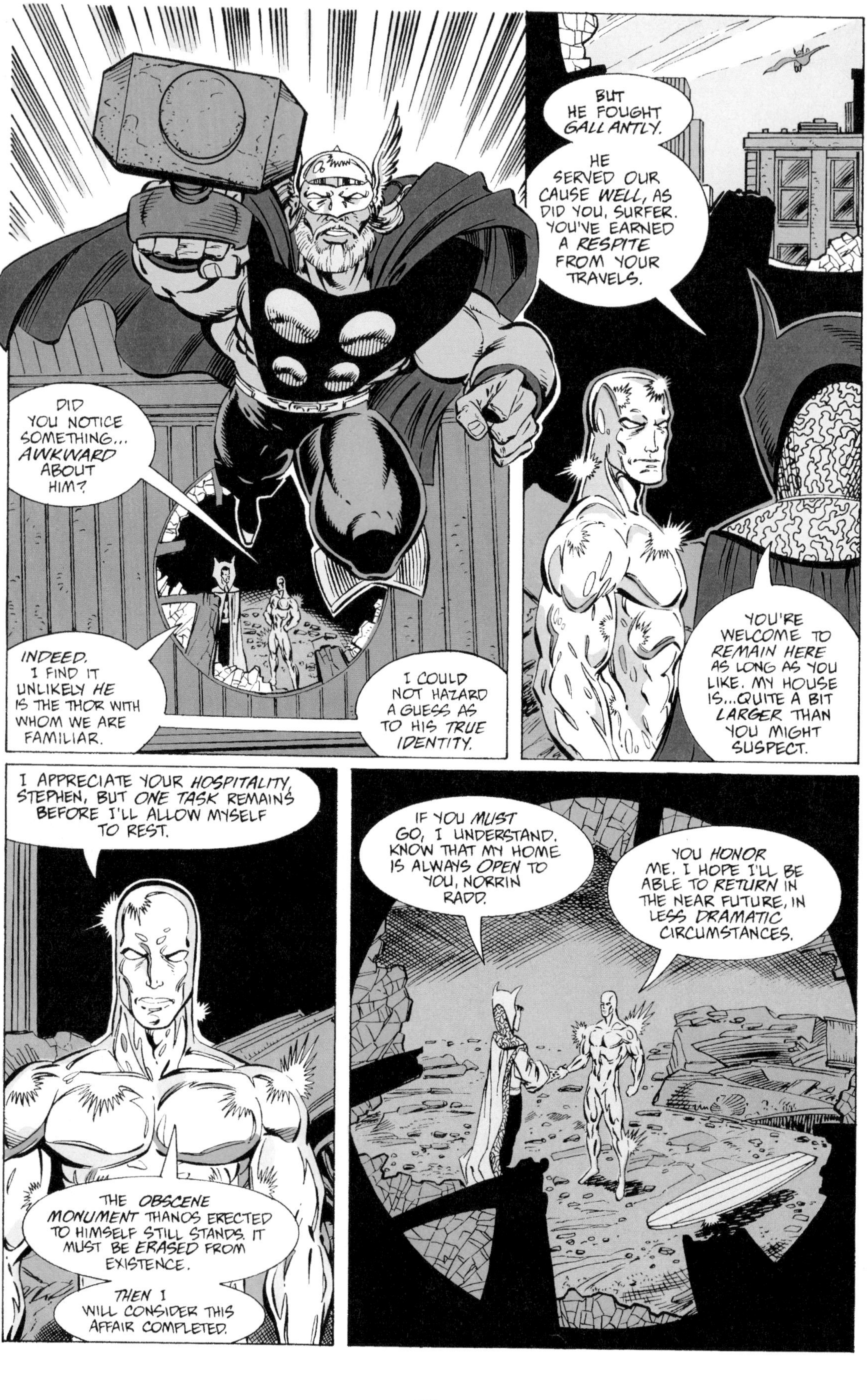
DID YOU NOTICE SOMETHING... AWKWARD ABOUT HIM?
INDEED. I FIND IT UNLIKELY HE IS THE THOR WITH WHOM WE ARE FAMILIAR.
I COULD NOT HAZARD A GUESS AS TO HIS TRUE IDENTITY.
BUT HE FOUGHT GALLANTLY.
HE SERVED OUR CAUSE WELL, AS DID YOU, SURFER. YOU'VE EARNED A RESPITE FROM YOUR TRAVELS.
YOU'RE WELCOME TO REMAIN HERE AS LONG AS YOU LIKE. MY HOUSE IS...QUITE A BIT LARGER THAN YOU MIGHT SUSPECT.
I APPRECIATE YOUR HOSPITALITY, STEPHEN, BUT ONE TASK REMAINS BEFORE I'LL ALLOW MYSELF TO REST.
THE OBSCENE MONUMENT THANOS ERECTED TO HIMSELF STILL STANDS. IT MUST BE ERASED FROM EXISTENCE.
THEN I WILL CONSIDER THIS AFFAIR COMPLETED.
IF YOU MUST GO, I UNDERSTAND. KNOW THAT MY HOME IS ALWAYS OPEN TO YOU, NORRIN RADD.
YOU HONOR ME. I HOPE I'LL BE ABLE TO RETURN IN THE NEAR FUTURE, IN LESS DRAMATIC CIRCUMSTANCES.

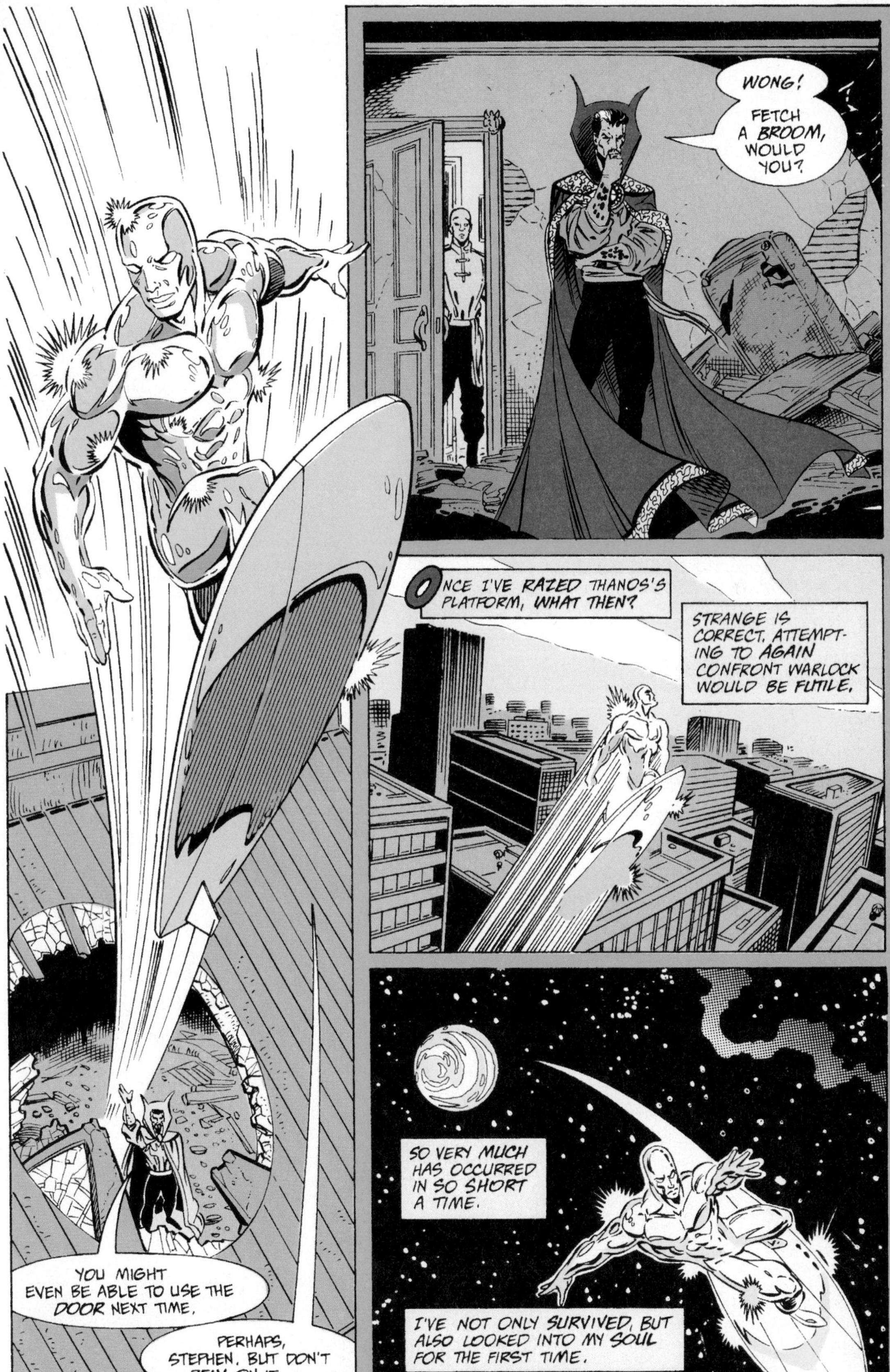
WONG! FETCH A BROOM, WOULD YOU?
ONCE I'VE RAZED THANOS'S PLATFORM, WHAT THEN?
STRANGE IS CORRECT. ATTEMPTING TO AGAIN CONFRONT WARLOCK WOULD BE FUTILE.
SO VERY MUCH HAS OCCURRED IN SO SHORT A TIME.
I'VE NOT ONLY SURVIVED, BUT ALSO LOOKED INTO MY SOUL FOR THE FIRST TIME.
YOU MIGHT EVEN BE ABLE TO USE THE DOOR NEXT TIME.
PERHAPS, STEPHEN. BUT DON'T RELY ON IT.

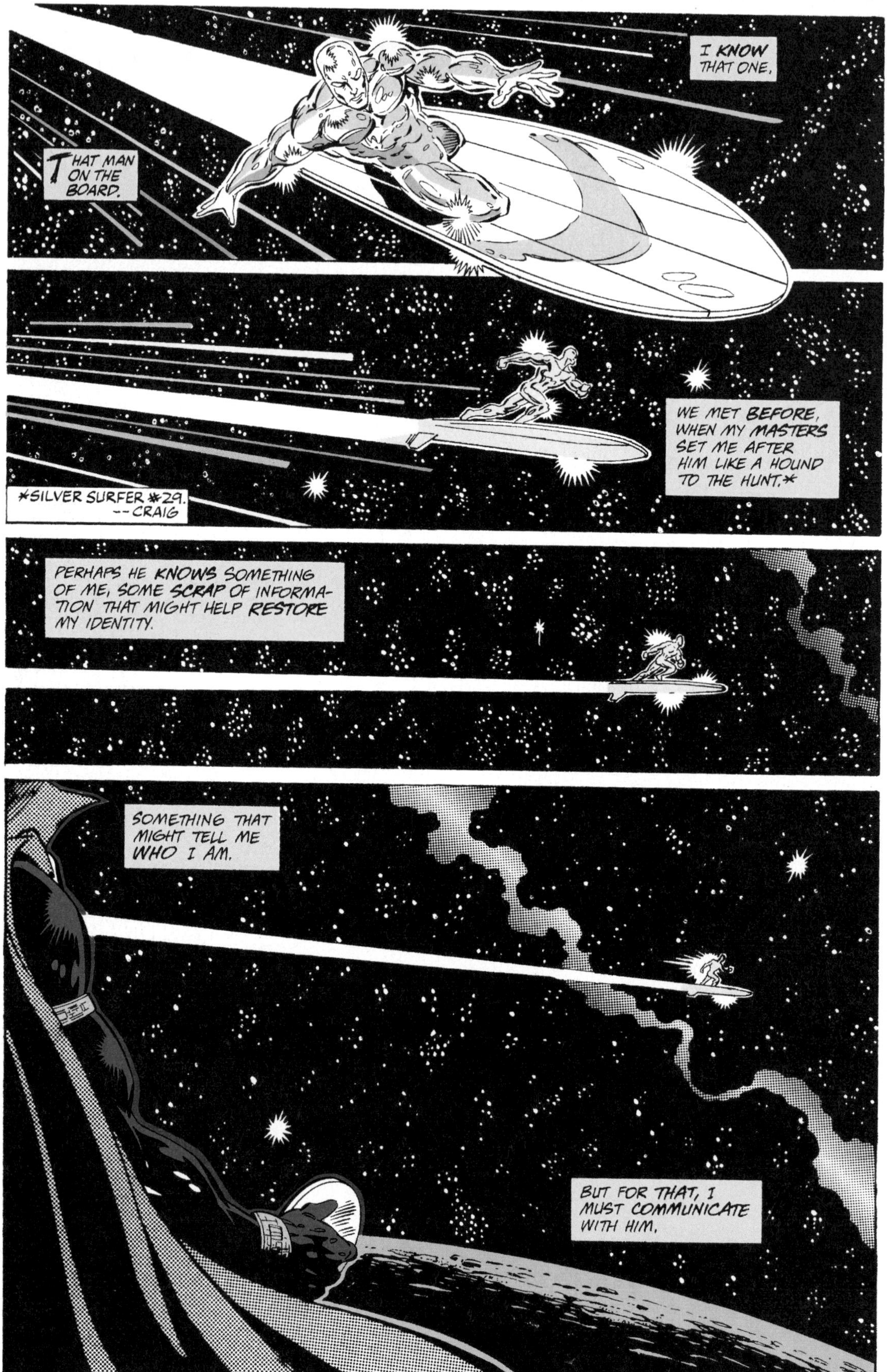
THAT MAN ON THE BOARD.
I KNOW THAT ONE.
WE MET BEFORE, WHEN MY MASTERS SET ME AFTER HIM LIKE A HOUND TO THE HUNT.*
*SILVER SURFER #29. --CRAIG
PERHAPS HE KNOWS SOMETHING OF ME, SOME SCRAP OF INFORMATION THAT MIGHT HELP RESTORE MY IDENTITY.
SOMETHING THAT MIGHT TELL ME WHO I AM.
BUT FOR THAT, I MUST COMMUNICATE WITH HIM.

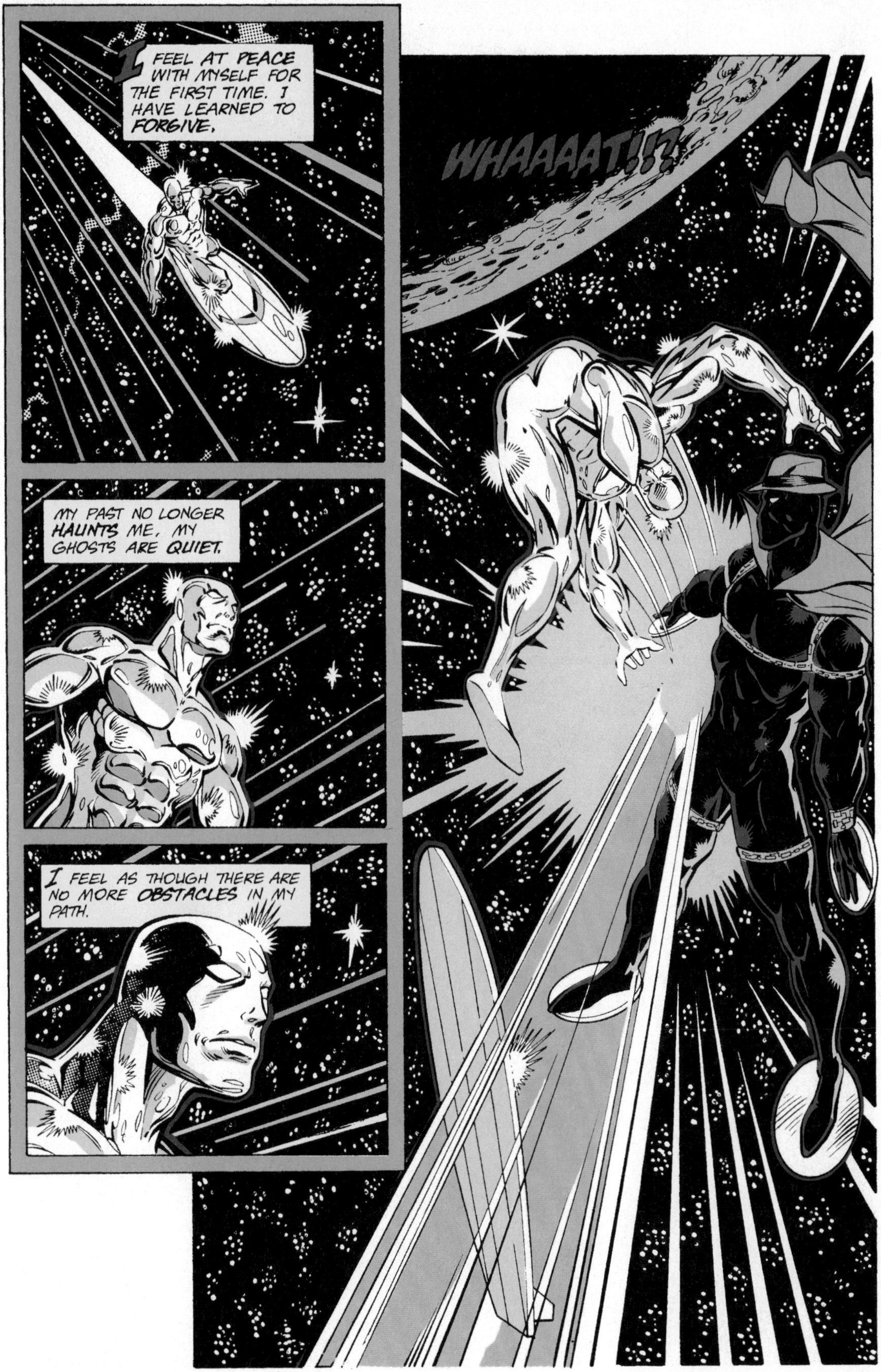
I FEEL AT PEACE WITH MYSELF FOR THE FIRST TIME. I HAVE LEARNED TO FORGIVE.
MY PAST NO LONGER HAUNTS ME. MY GHOSTS ARE QUIET.
I FEEL AS THOUGH THERE ARE NO MORE OBSTACLES IN MY PATH.
WHAAAAT!!?

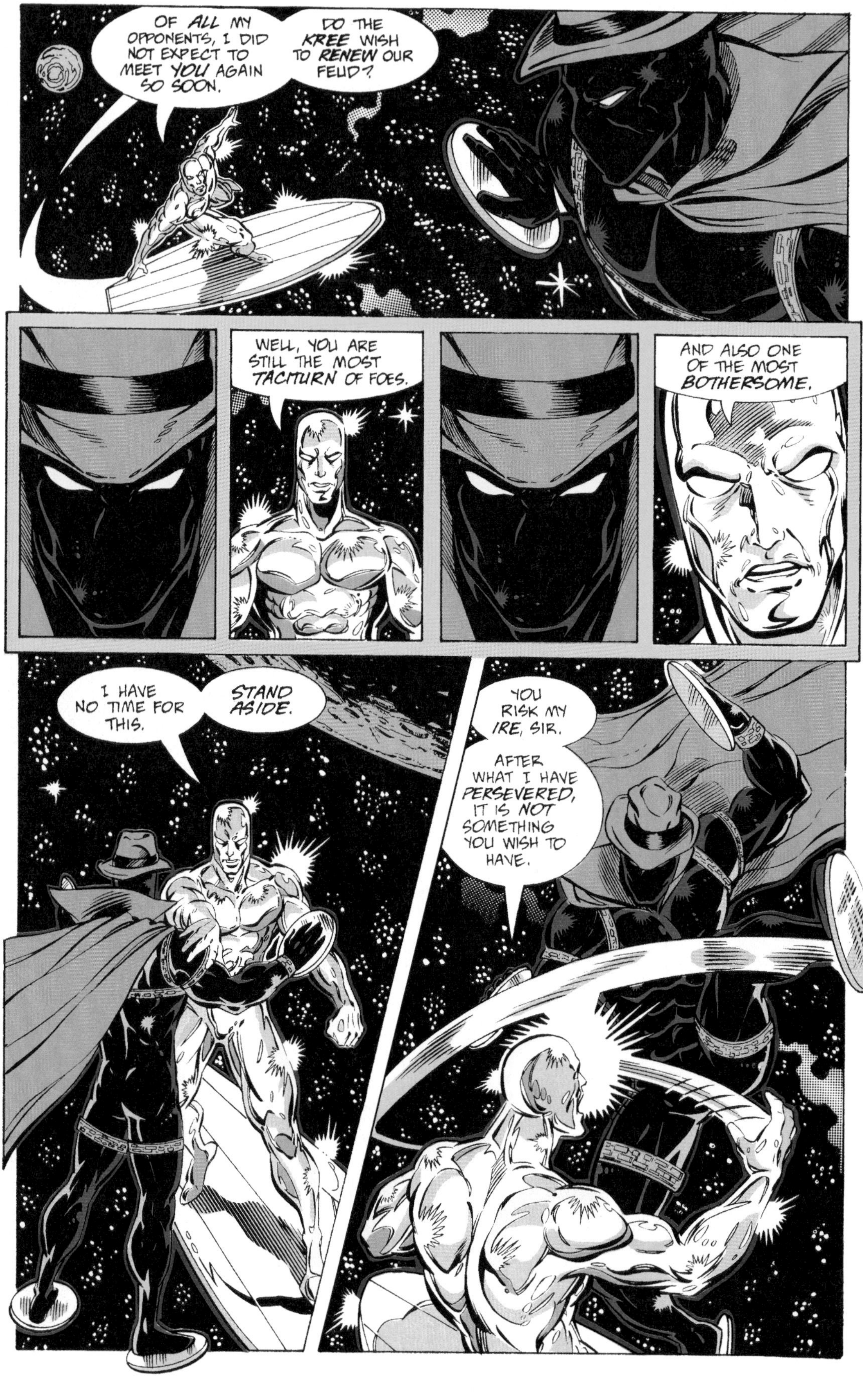
OF ALL MY OPPONENTS, I DID NOT EXPECT TO MEET YOU AGAIN SO SOON.
DO THE KREE WISH TO RENEW OUR FEUD?
WELL, YOU ARE STILL THE MOST TACITURN OF FOES.
AND ALSO ONE OF THE MOST BOTHERSOME.
I HAVE NO TIME FOR THIS.
STAND ASIDE.
YOU RISK MY IRE, SIR.
AFTER WHAT I HAVE PERSEVERED, IT IS NOT SOMETHING YOU WISH TO HAVE.

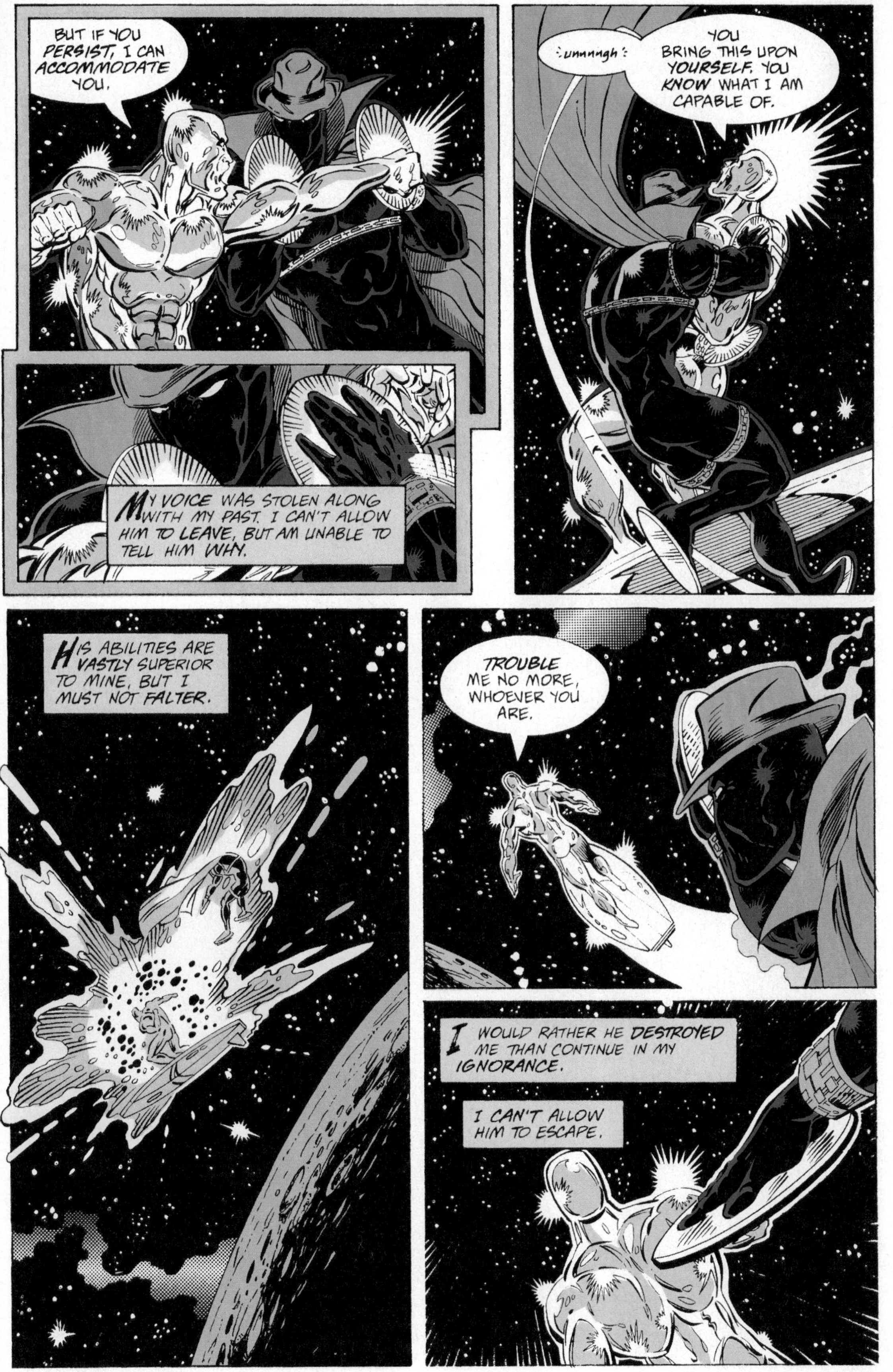

BUT IF YOU PERSIST, I CAN ACCOMMODATE YOU.
MY VOICE WAS STOLEN ALONG WITH MY PAST. I CAN'T ALLOW HIM TO LEAVE, BUT AM UNABLE TO TELL HIM WHY.
:unnnngh:
YOU BRING THIS UPON YOURSELF. YOU KNOW WHAT I AM CAPABLE OF.
HIS ABILITIES ARE VASTLY SUPERIOR TO MINE, BUT I MUST NOT FALTER.
TROUBLE ME NO MORE, WHOEVER YOU ARE.
I WOULD RATHER HE DESTROYED ME THAN CONTINUE IN MY IGNORANCE.
I CAN'T ALLOW HIM TO ESCAPE.

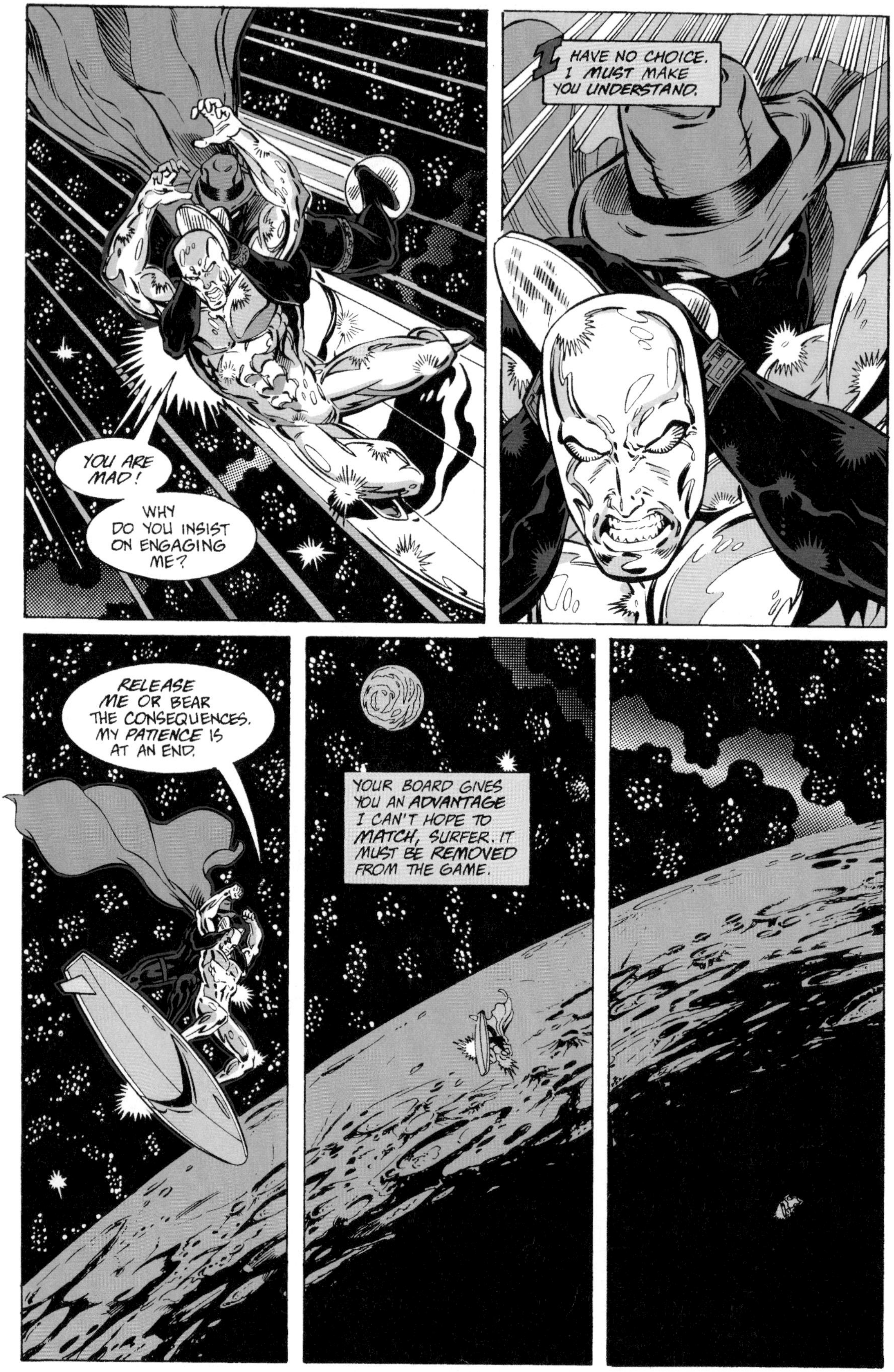
YOU ARE MAD!
WHY DO YOU INSIST ON ENGAGING ME?
I HAVE NO CHOICE. I MUST MAKE YOU UNDERSTAND.
RELEASE ME OR BEAR THE CONSEQUENCES. MY PATIENCE IS AT AN END.
YOUR BOARD GIVES YOU AN ADVANTAGE I CAN'T HOPE TO MATCH, SURFER. IT MUST BE REMOVED FROM THE GAME.

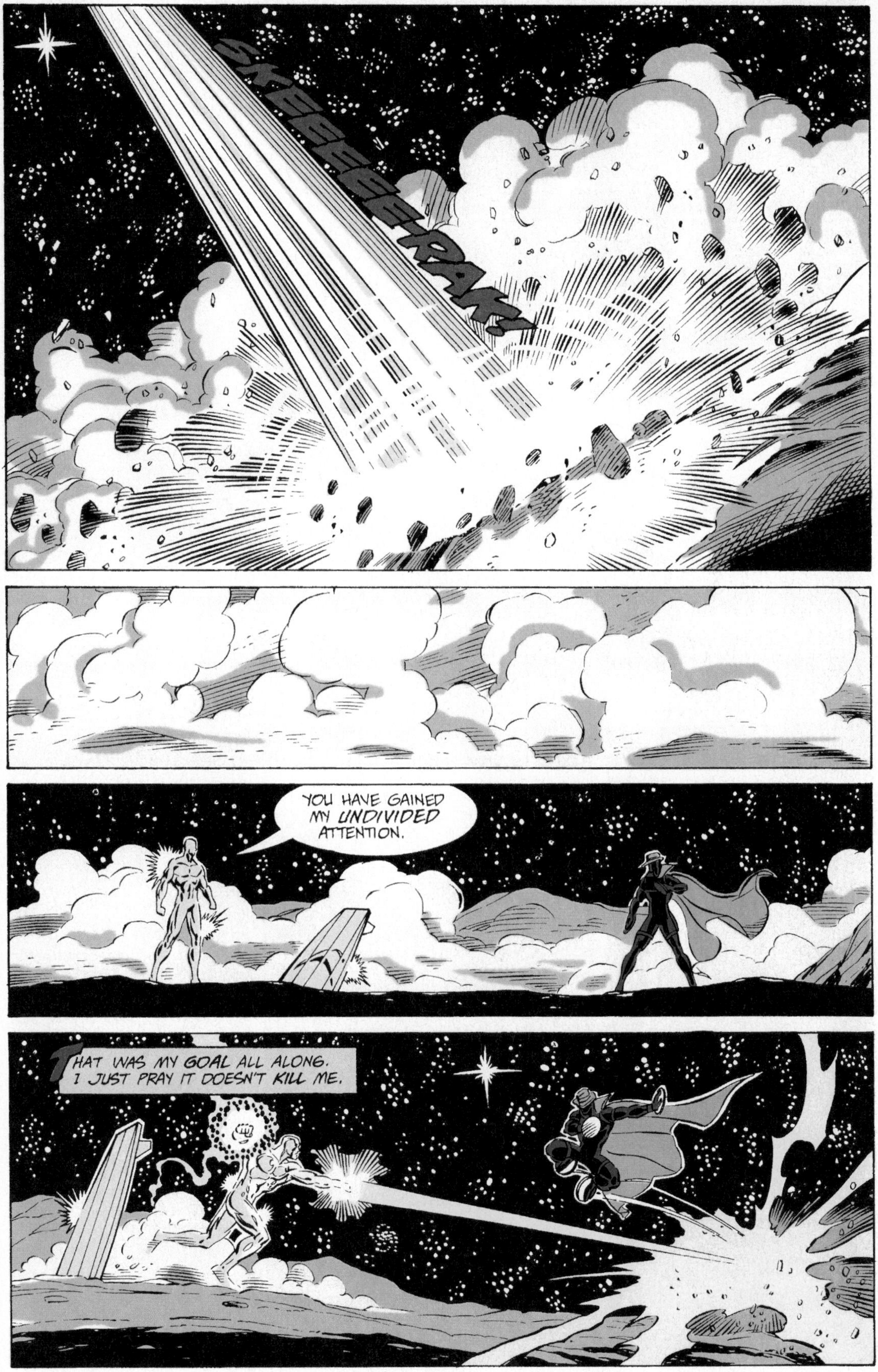
SKEEEEE-RAK!
YOU HAVE GAINED MY UNDIVIDED ATTENTION.
THAT WAS MY GOAL ALL ALONG. I JUST PRAY IT DOESN'T KILL ME.

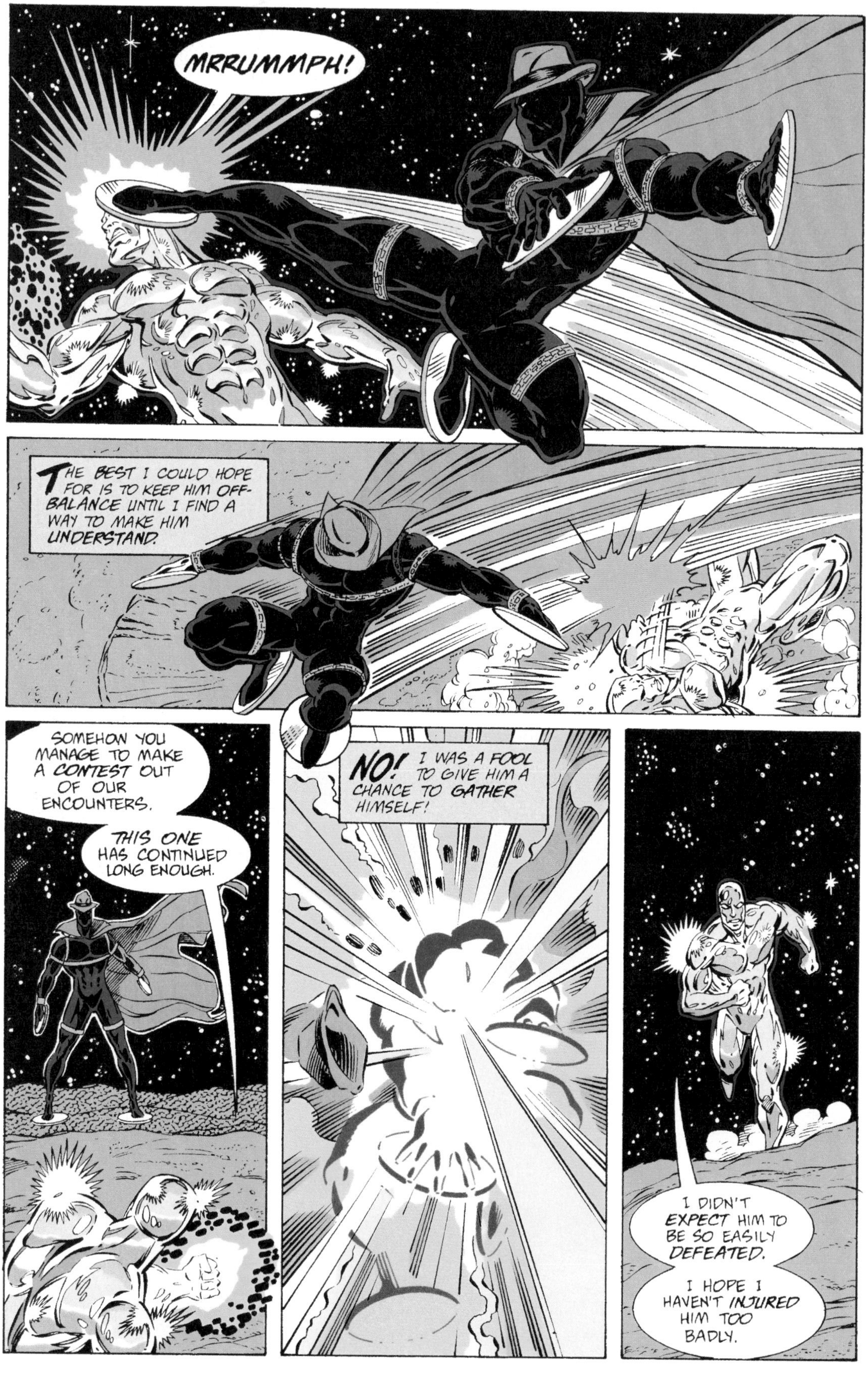
MRRUMMPH!
THE BEST I COULD HOPE FOR IS TO KEEP HIM OFF-BALANCE UNTIL I FIND A WAY TO MAKE HIM UNDERSTAND.
SOMEHOW YOU MANAGE TO MAKE A CONTEST OUT OF OUR ENCOUNTERS.
THIS ONE HAS CONTINUED LONG ENOUGH.
NO! I WAS A FOOL TO GIVE HIM A CHANCE TO GATHER HIMSELF!
I DIDN'T EXPECT HIM TO BE SO EASILY DEFEATED.
I HOPE I HAVEN'T INJURED HIM TOO BADLY.

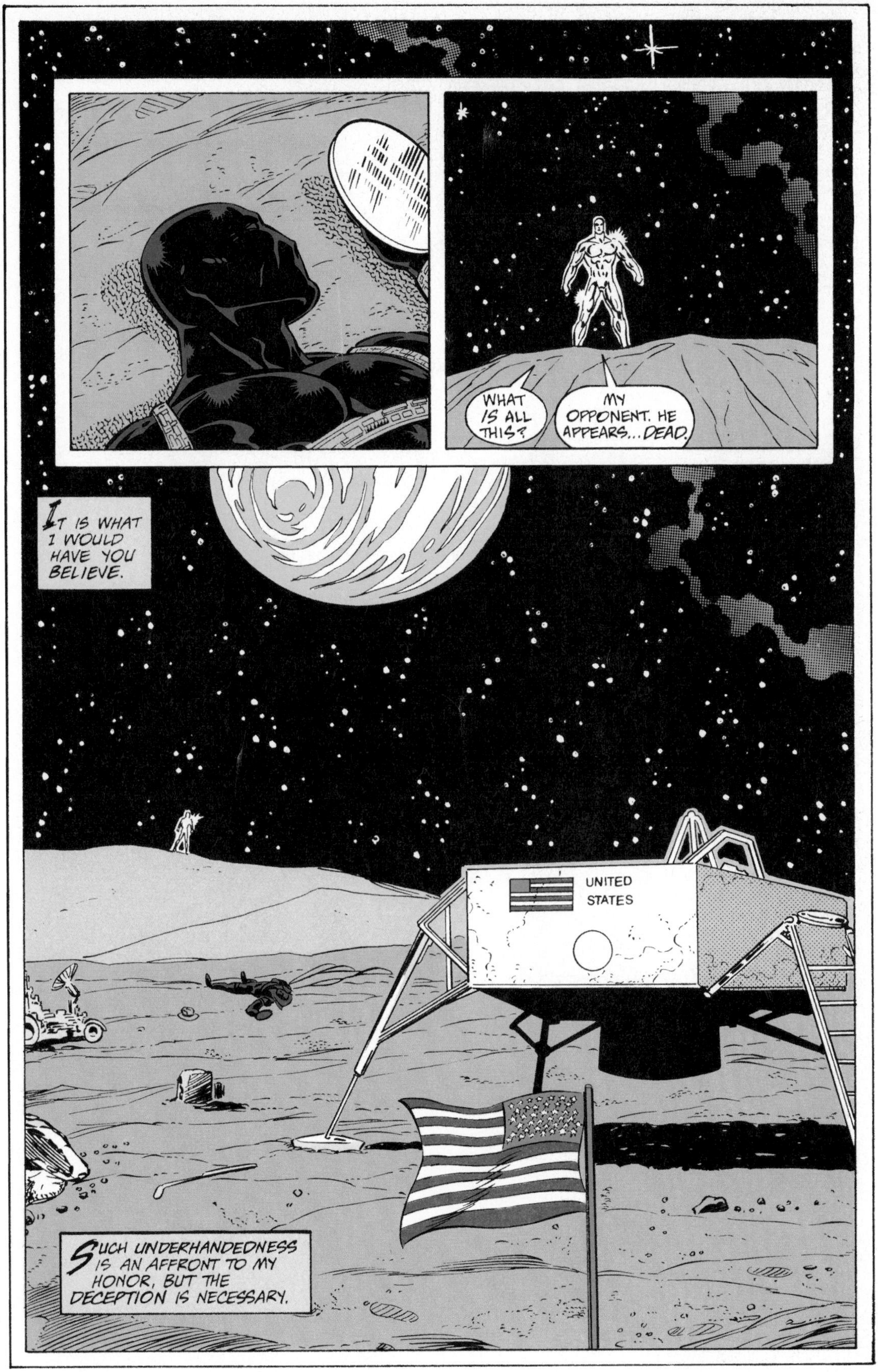
WHAT IS ALL THIS?
MY OPPONENT. HE APPEARS... DEAD.
IT IS WHAT I WOULD HAVE YOU BELIEVE.
UNITED STATES
SUCH UNDERHANDEDNESS IS AN AFFRONT TO MY HONOR, BUT THE DECEPTION IS NECESSARY.

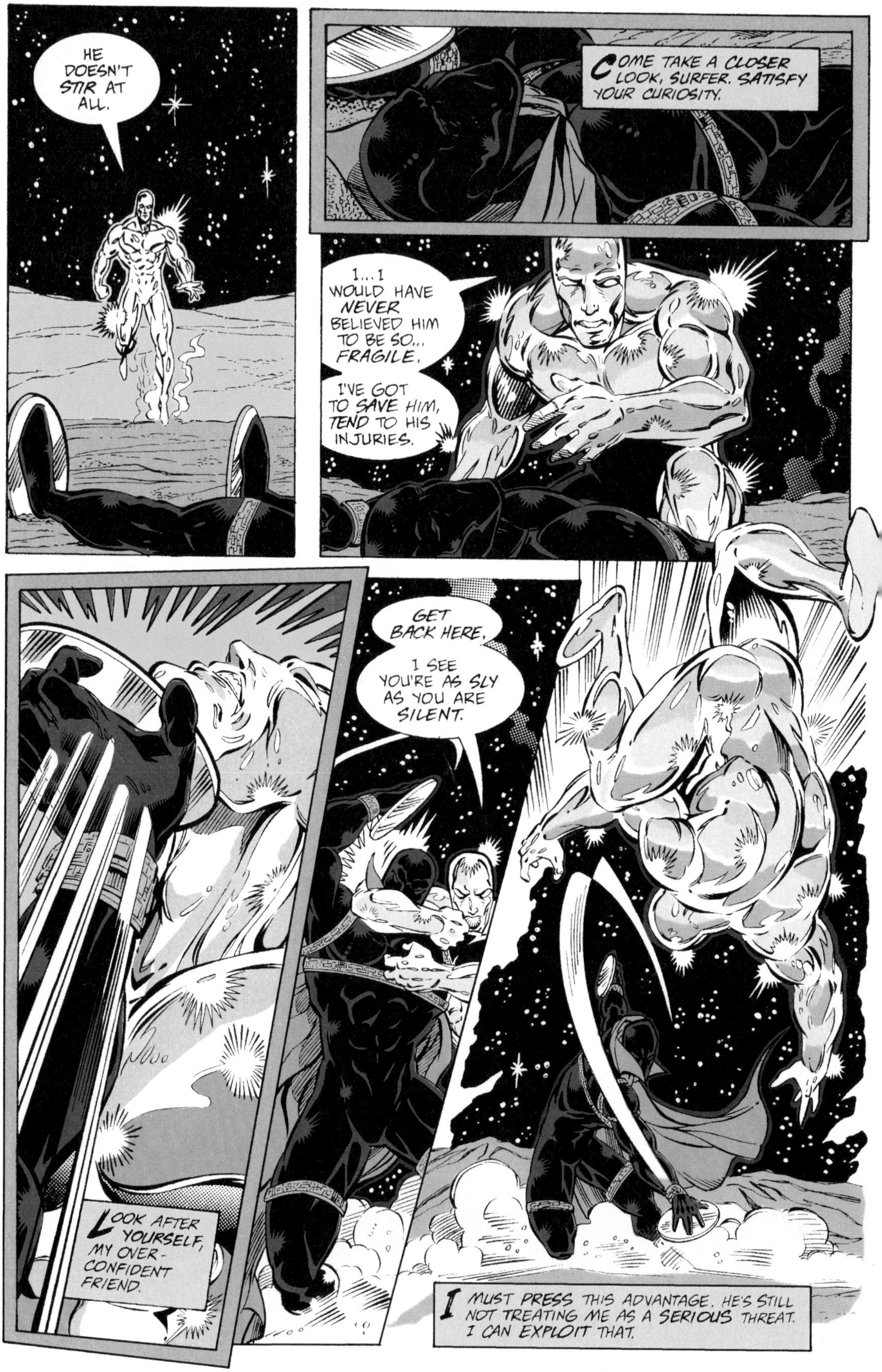
HE DOESN'T STIR AT ALL.
COME TAKE A CLOSER LOOK, SURFER. SATISFY YOUR CURIOSITY.
I... I WOULD HAVE NEVER BELIEVED HIM TO BE SO... FRAGILE.
I'VE GOT TO SAVE HIM, TEND TO HIS INJURIES.
LOOK AFTER YOURSELF, MY OVER-CONFIDENT FRIEND.
GET BACK HERE.
I SEE YOU'RE AS SLY AS YOU ARE SILENT.
I MUST PRESS THIS ADVANTAGE. HE'S STILL NOT TREATING ME AS A SERIOUS THREAT. I CAN EXPLOIT THAT.

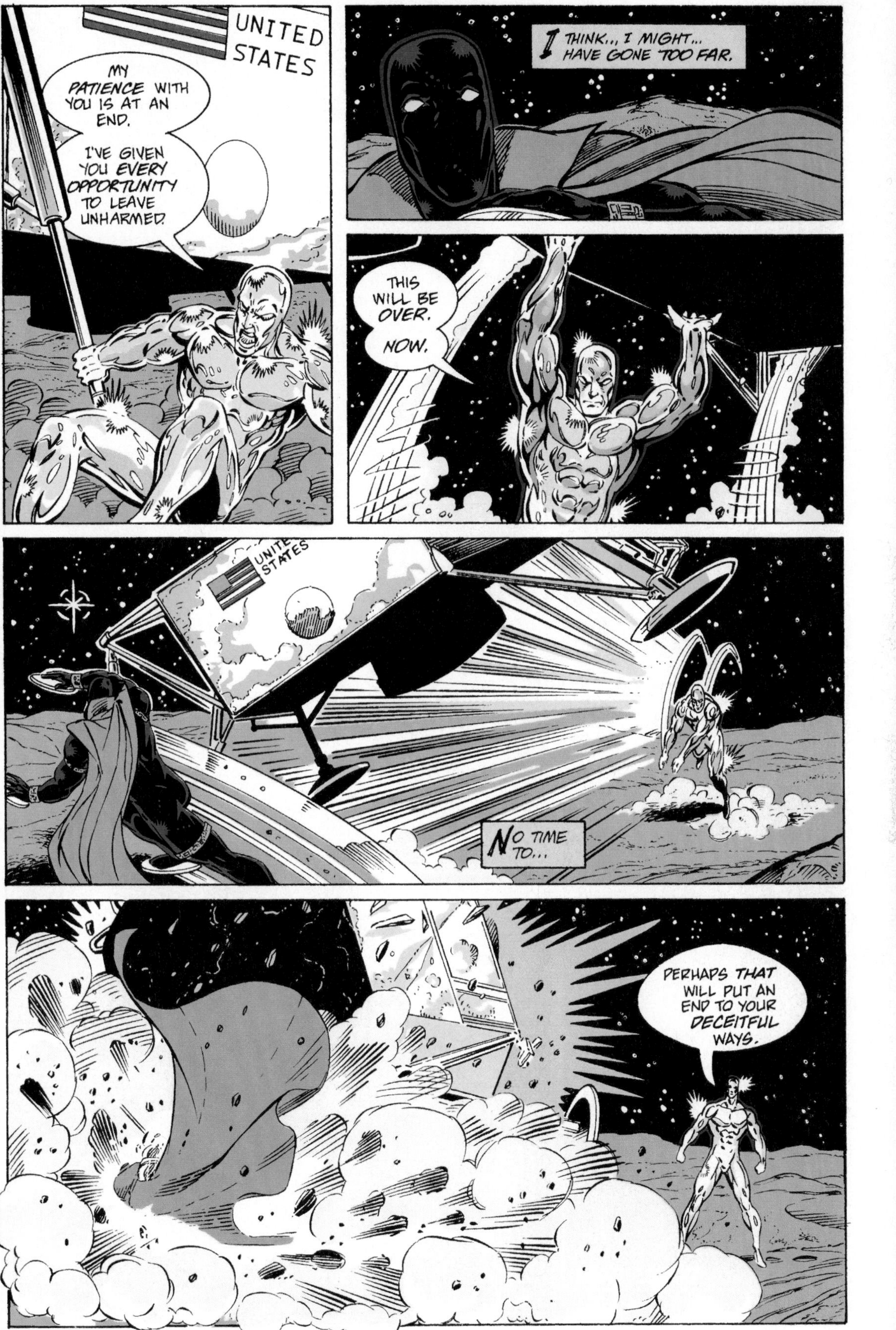
UNITED STATES
MY PATIENCE WITH YOU IS AT AN END.
I'VE GIVEN YOU EVERY OPPORTUNITY TO LEAVE UNHARMED.
I THINK.., I MIGHT... HAVE GONE TOO FAR.
THIS WILL BE OVER.
NOW.
UNITED STATES
NO TIME TO...
PERHAPS THAT WILL PUT AN END TO YOUR DECEITFUL WAYS.

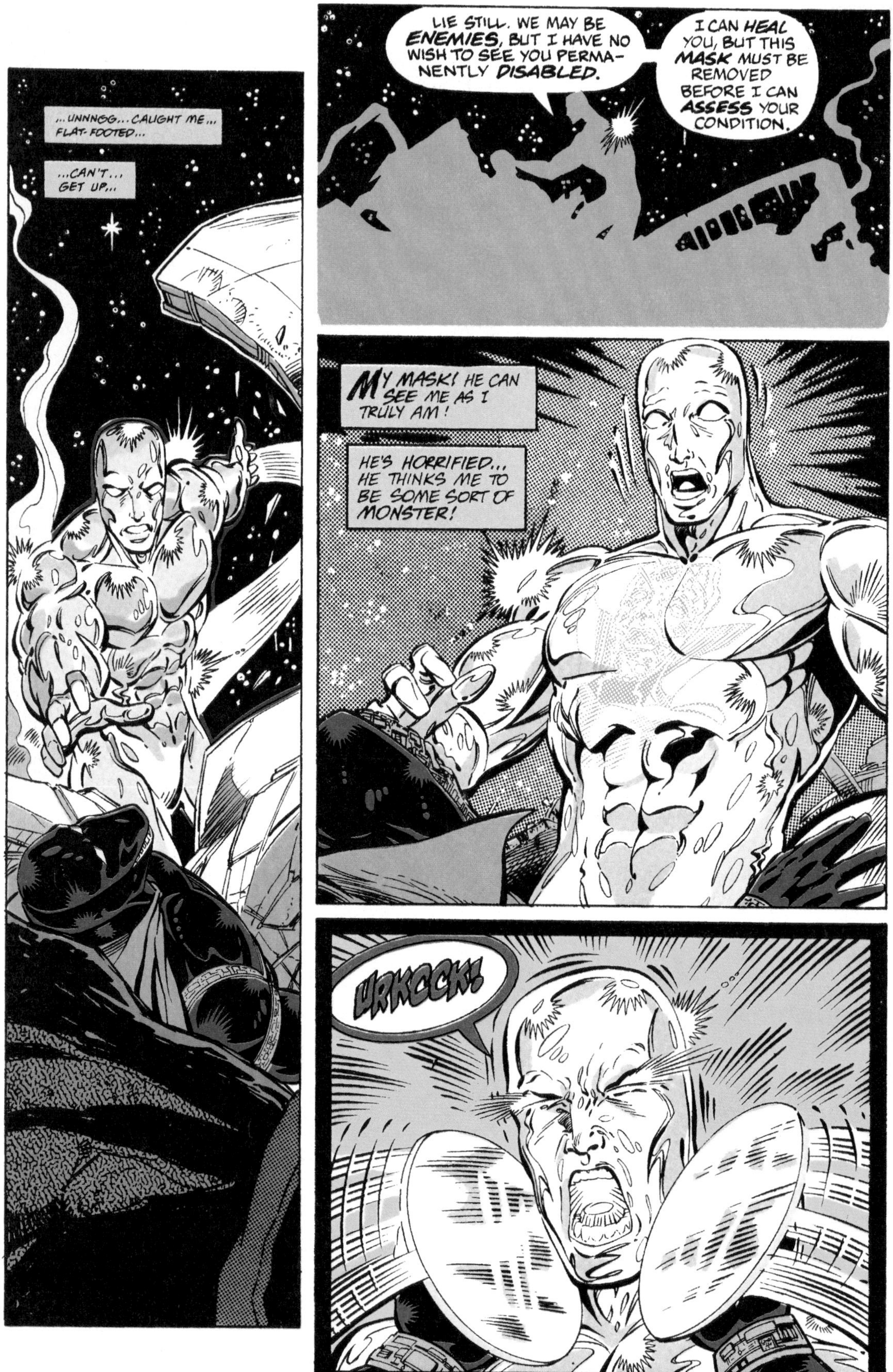

...UNNNGG...CAUGHT ME... FLAT-FOOTED...
...CAN'T... GET UP...
LIE STILL. WE MAY BE ENEMIES, BUT I HAVE NO WISH TO SEE YOU PERMA-NENTLY DISABLED.
I CAN HEAL YOU, BUT THIS MASK MUST BE REMOVED BEFORE I CAN ASSESS YOUR CONDITION.
MY MASK! HE CAN SEE ME AS I TRULY AM!
HE'S HORRIFIED... HE THINKS ME TO BE SOME SORT OF MONSTER!
URKOCK!

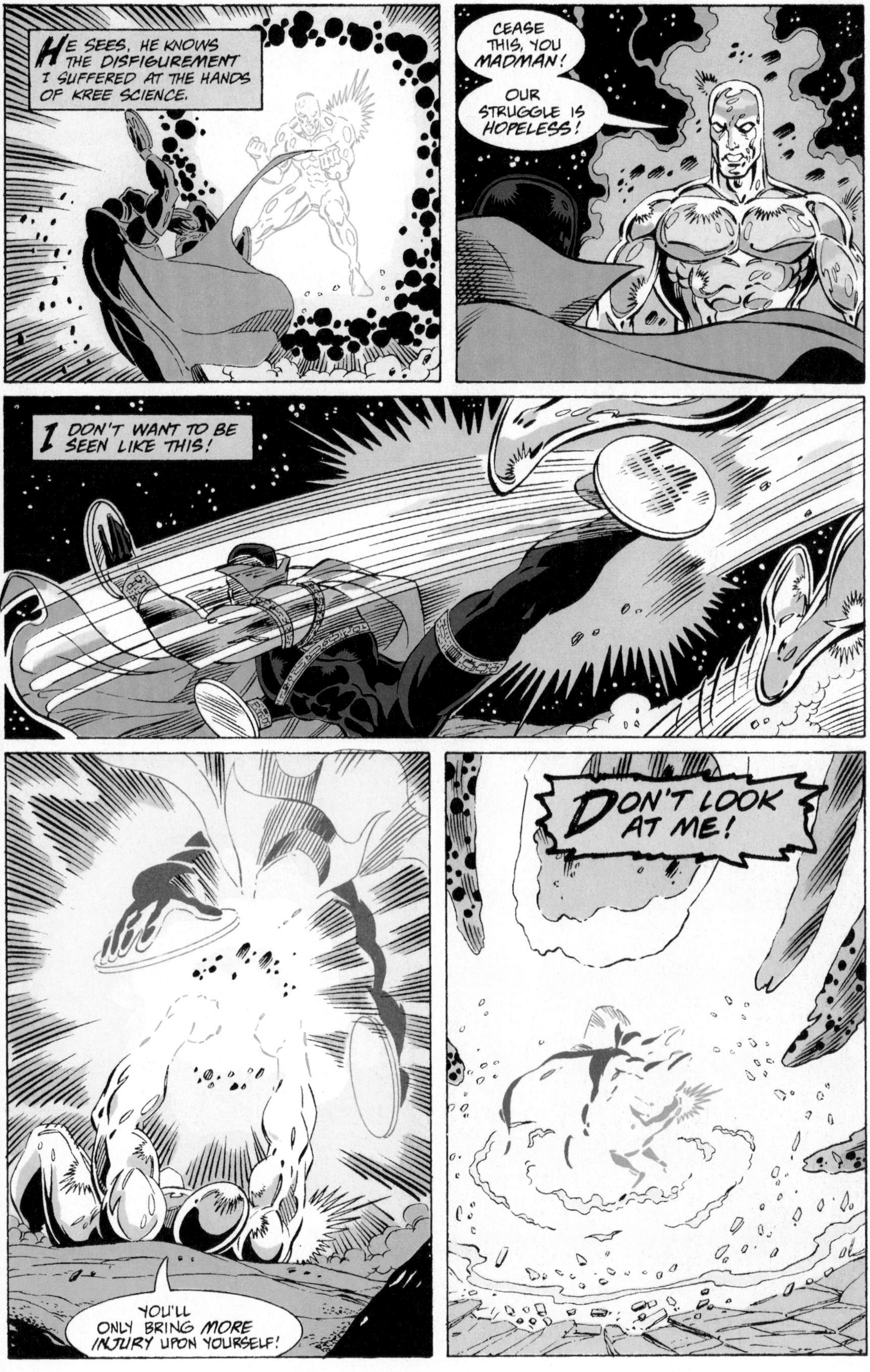
HE SEES. HE KNOWS THE DISFIGUREMENT I SUFFERED AT THE HANDS OF KREE SCIENCE.
CEASE THIS, YOU MADMAN!
OUR STRUGGLE IS HOPELESS!
I DON'T WANT TO BE SEEN LIKE THIS!
YOU'LL ONLY BRING MORE INJURY UPON YOURSELF!
DON'T LOOK AT ME!

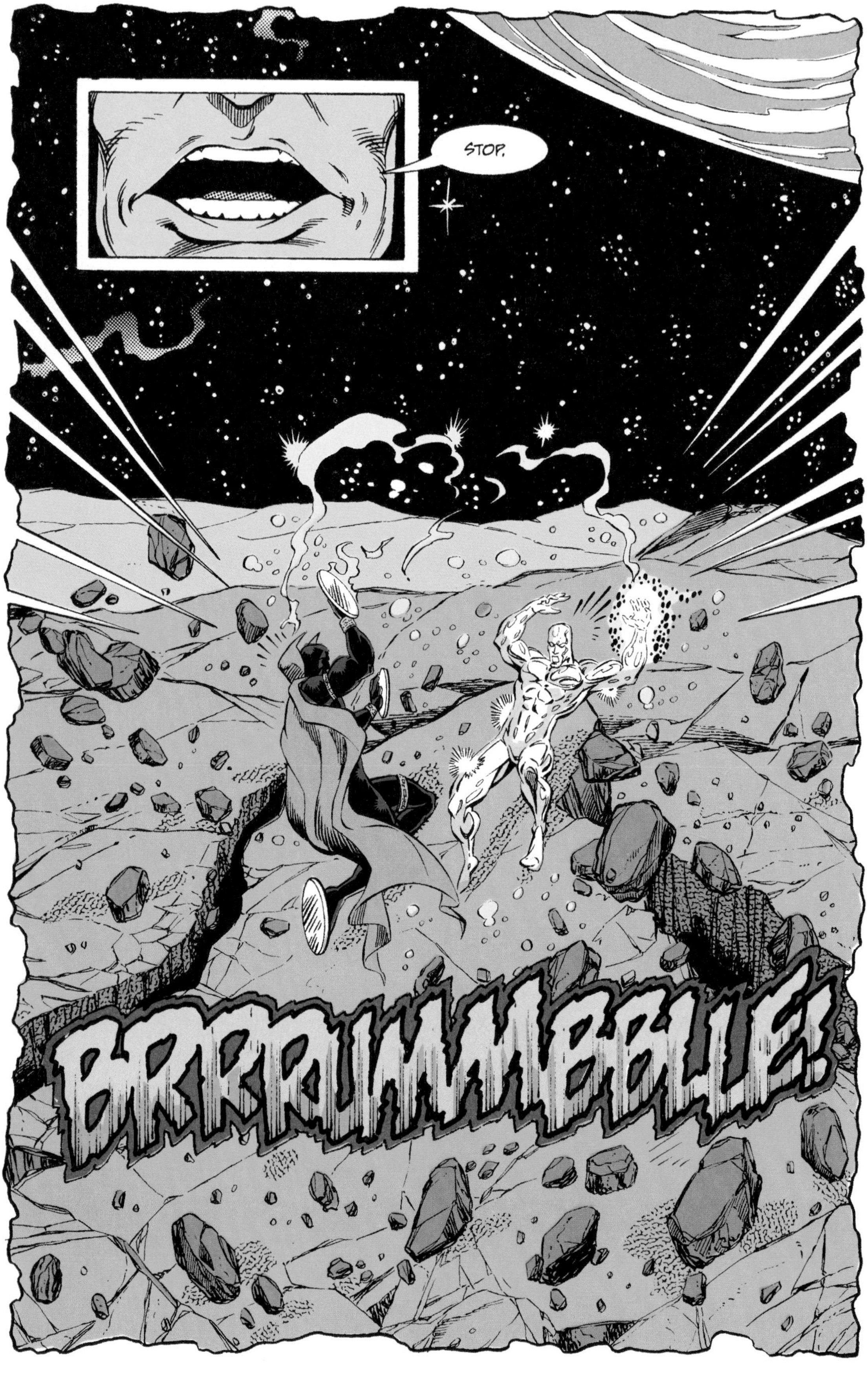
STOP.
BRRRUMMBBLLE!

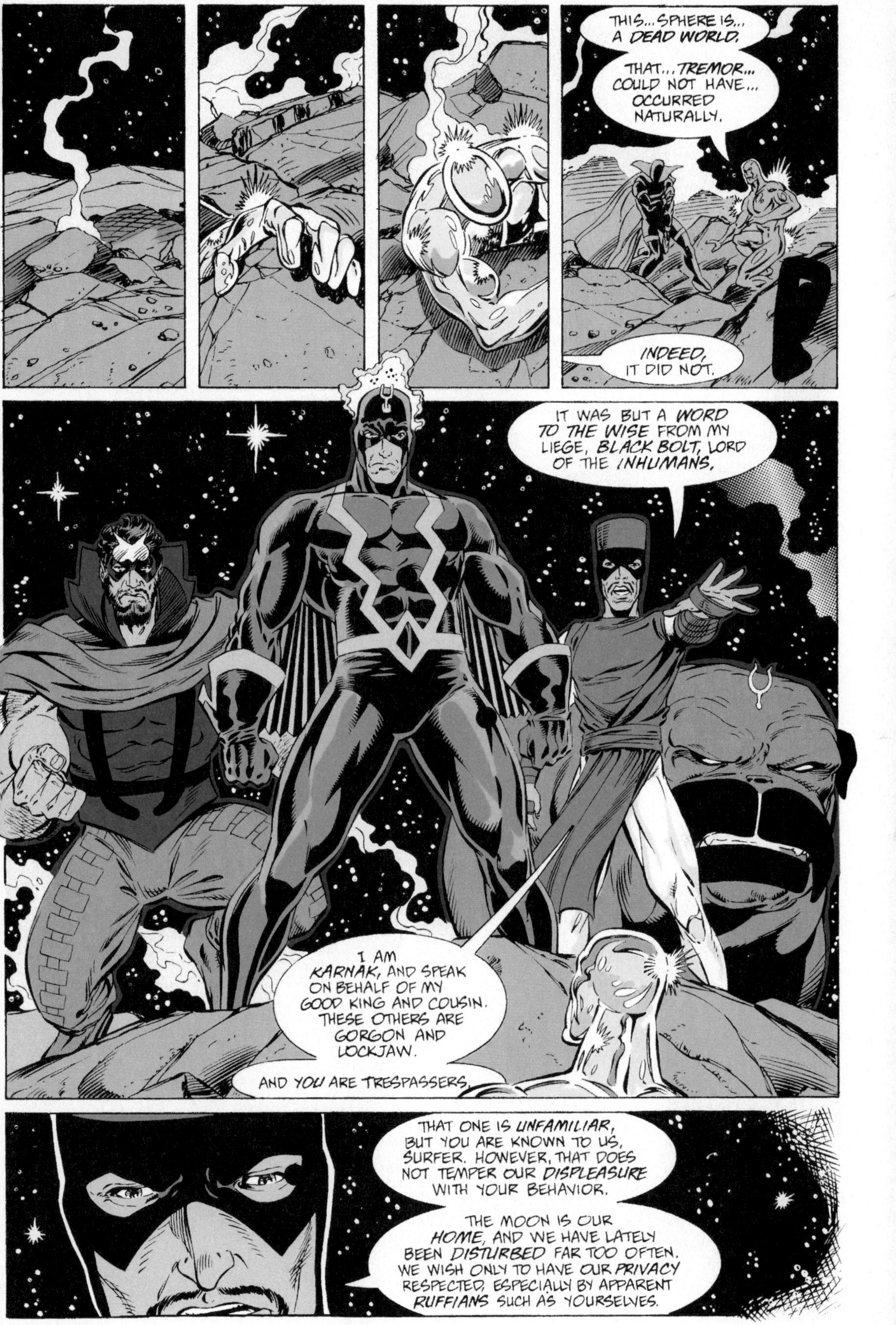
THIS... SPHERE IS... A DEAD WORLD.
THAT... TREMOR... COULD NOT HAVE... OCCURRED NATURALLY.
INDEED, IT DID NOT.
IT WAS BUT A WORD TO THE WISE FROM MY LIEGE, BLACK BOLT, LORD OF THE INHUMANS.
I AM KARNAK, AND SPEAK ON BEHALF OF MY GOOD KING AND COUSIN. THESE OTHERS ARE GORGON AND LOCKJAW.
AND YOU ARE TRESPASSERS.
THAT ONE IS UNFAMILIAR, BUT YOU ARE KNOWN TO US, SURFER. HOWEVER, THAT DOES NOT TEMPER OUR DISPLEASURE WITH YOUR BEHAVIOR.
THE MOON IS OUR HOME, AND WE HAVE LATELY BEEN DISTURBED FAR TOO OFTEN. WE WISH ONLY TO HAVE OUR PRIVACY RESPECTED, ESPECIALLY BY APPARENT RUFFIANS SUCH AS YOURSELVES.

MY HUMBLEST *APOLOGIES* TO YOU AND YOUR LORD, KARNAK, I MEANT NO *DISRESPECT*.

IT WAS NOT MY INTENTION TO *INTRUDE*. I WISHED ONLY TO RETURN TO SPACE, BUT THIS *SHADOWY FIGURE* ATTACKED ME.

I KNOW *NOTHING* OF HIM, SAVE THAT WE *BATTLED* PREVIOUSLY WHEN HE WAS AN *AGENT* OF THE KREE EMPIRE.

THAT, AND THAT HE IS SEEMINGLY *MUTE*.

I CAN TELL YOU *NO MORE*.

HE IS *NOT* MY CONCERN, SO I WILL TAKE MY LEAVE AND *INFRINGE* UPON YOUR HOSPITALITY NO LONGER.

AS YOU WISH, SURFER.

BUT WHAT WOULD YOU HAVE US *DO* WITH THIS BATTLE SCARRED *CASUALTY?*

I...UM, I DON'T KNOW.

I COULD NOT *PRESUME* TO GUESS HIS ULTIMATE GOAL.

YOUR *INDULGENCE*, FOR A MOMENT, PLEASE.

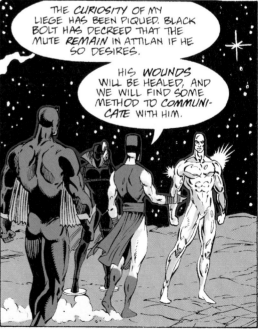

THE *CURIOSITY* OF MY LIEGE HAS BEEN PIQUED. BLACK BOLT HAS DECREED THAT THE MUTE *REMAIN* IN ATTILAN IF HE SO DESIRES.

HIS *WOUNDS* WILL BE HEALED, AND WE WILL FIND SOME METHOD TO *COMMUNICATE* WITH HIM.

28

I RESPECT YOU AS A FORMIDABLE OPPONENT, AND TRULY WISH YOU *NO HARM.*

YOU WILL *STAY* WITH THE INHUMANS?

I BID YOU *FAREWELL,* THEN, POSSIBLY WE SHALL MEET *AGAIN,* AS ALLIES RATHER THAN OPPONENTS.

*G*OODBYE TO YOU, SURFER. I NEVER MEANT TO COME INTO CONFLICT WITH YOU.

I REALIZE NOW YOU KNOW *NOTHING* OF WHO I *WAS.* WHO I AM.

PERHAPS, AMONG THESE INHUMANS, I MIGHT DISCOVER MY HUMANITY.

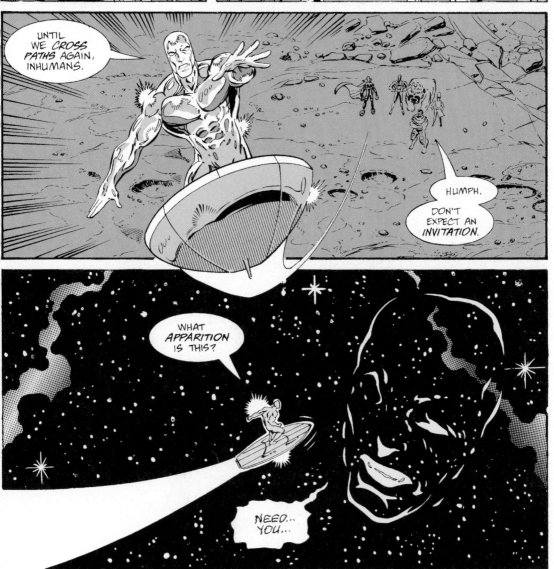

UNTIL WE *CROSS PATHS* AGAIN, INHUMANS.

HUMPH.

DON'T EXPECT AN *INVITATION.*

WHAT *APPARITION* IS THIS?

NEED... YOU...

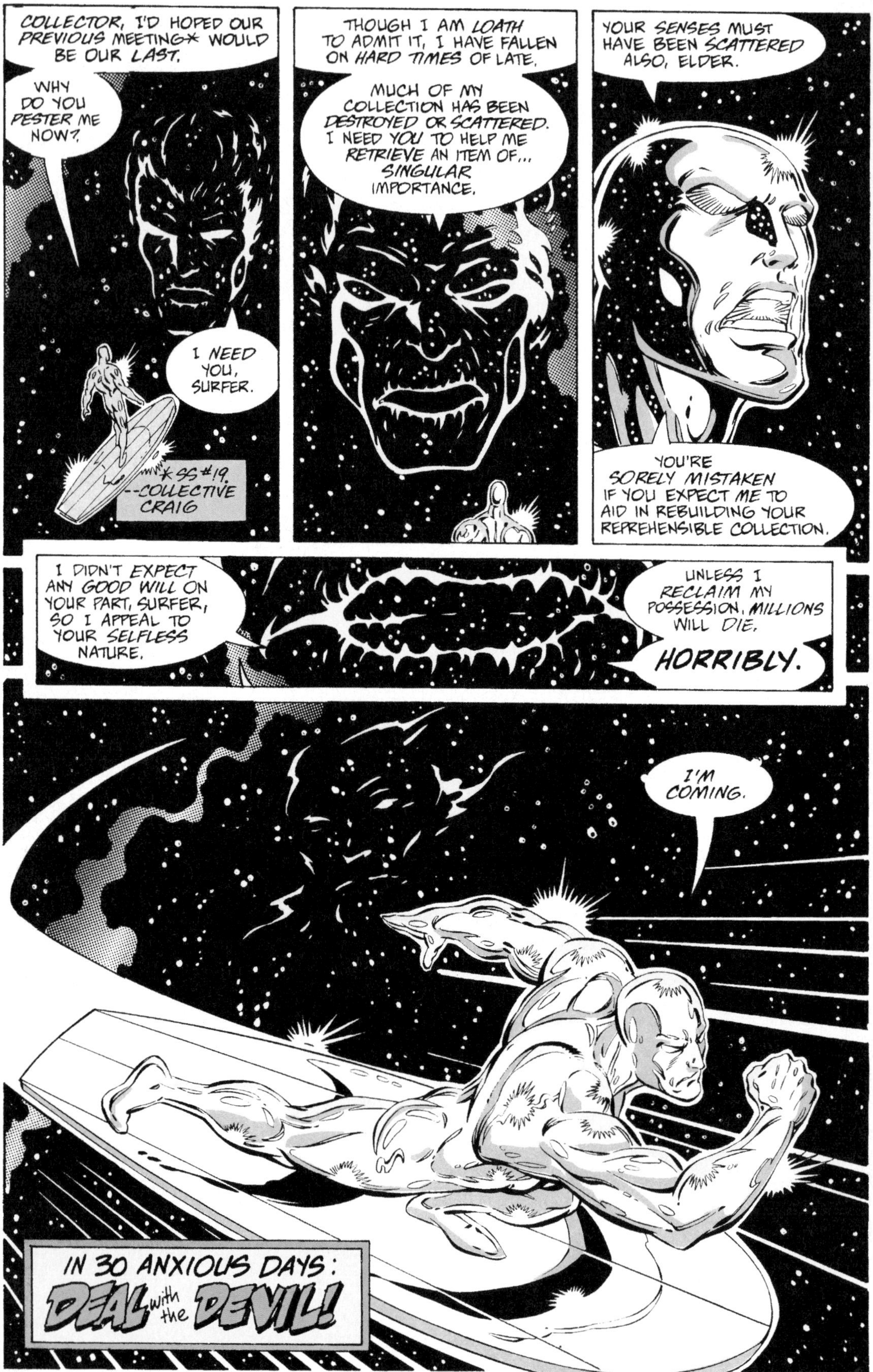
COLLECTOR, I'D HOPED OUR PREVIOUS MEETING* WOULD BE OUR LAST.
WHY DO YOU PESTER ME NOW?
I NEED YOU, SURFER.
*SS #19. --COLLECTIVE CRAIG
THOUGH I AM LOATH TO ADMIT IT, I HAVE FALLEN ON HARD TIMES OF LATE.
MUCH OF MY COLLECTION HAS BEEN DESTROYED OR SCATTERED. I NEED YOU TO HELP ME RETRIEVE AN ITEM OF... SINGULAR IMPORTANCE.
YOUR SENSES MUST HAVE BEEN SCATTERED ALSO, ELDER.
YOU'RE SORELY MISTAKEN IF YOU EXPECT ME TO AID IN REBUILDING YOUR REPREHENSIBLE COLLECTION.
I DIDN'T EXPECT ANY GOOD WILL ON YOUR PART, SURFER, SO I APPEAL TO YOUR SELFLESS NATURE.
UNLESS I RECLAIM MY POSSESSION, MILLIONS WILL DIE.
HORRIBLY.
I'M COMING.
IN 30 ANXIOUS DAYS:
DEAL with the DEVIL!

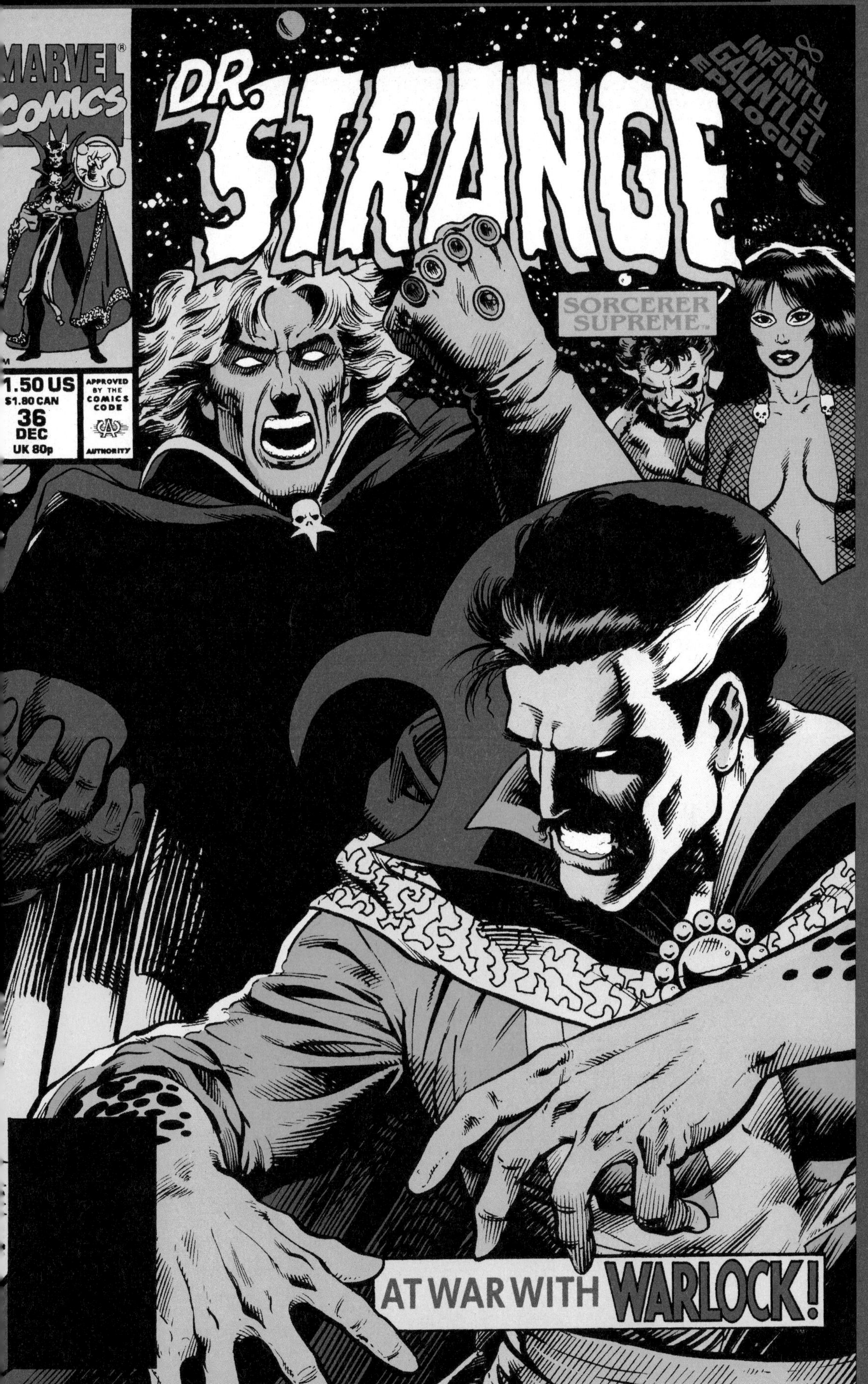
MARVEL COMICS
DR. STRANGE
AN INFINITY GAUNTLET EPILOGUE
SORCERER SUPREME
1.50 US
$1.80 CAN
36
DEC
UK 80p
APPROVED BY THE COMICS CODE AUTHORITY
AT WAR WITH WARLOCK!

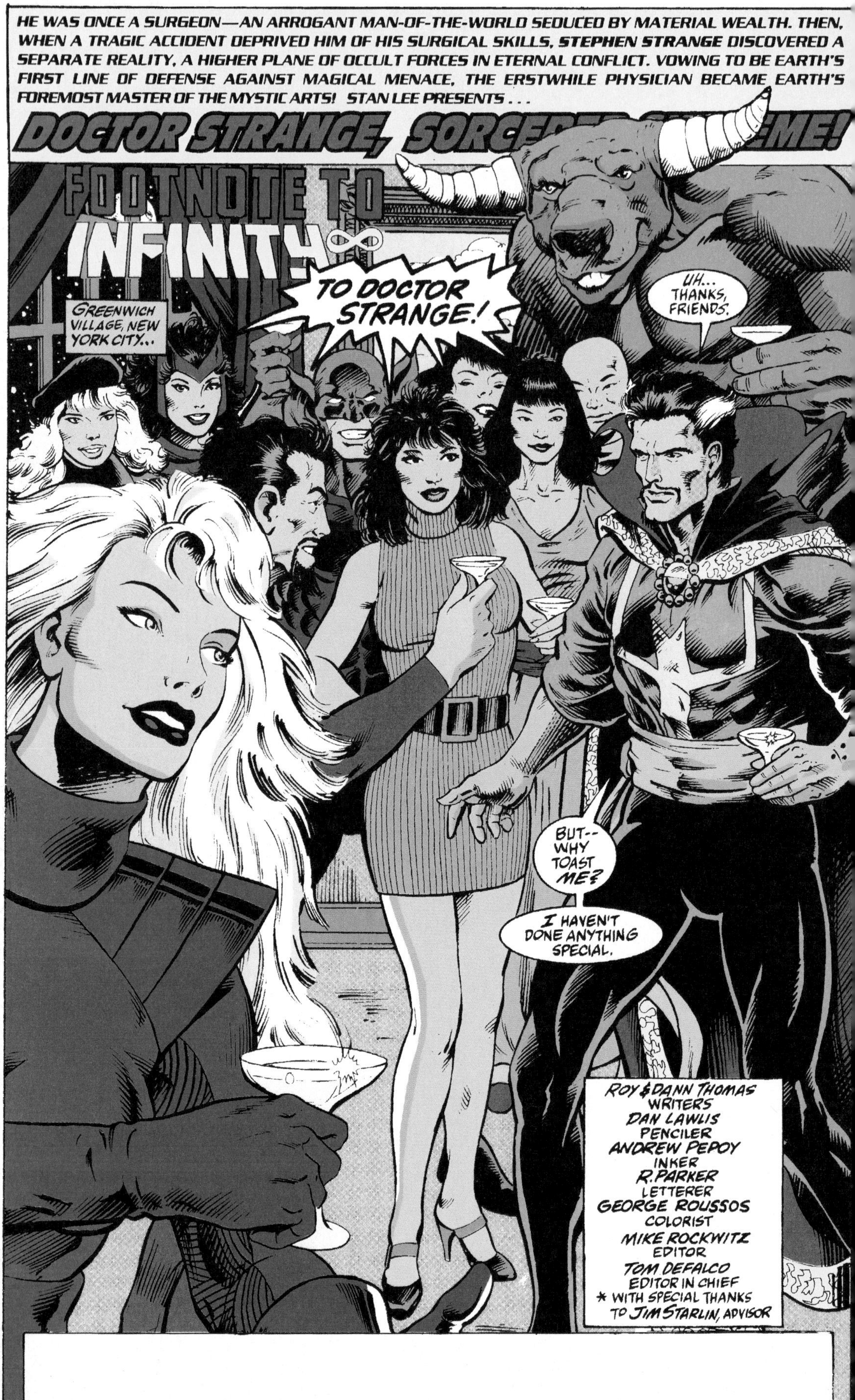

HE WAS ONCE A SURGEON—AN ARROGANT MAN-OF-THE-WORLD SEDUCED BY MATERIAL WEALTH. THEN, WHEN A TRAGIC ACCIDENT DEPRIVED HIM OF HIS SURGICAL SKILLS, STEPHEN STRANGE DISCOVERED A SEPARATE REALITY, A HIGHER PLANE OF OCCULT FORCES IN ETERNAL CONFLICT. VOWING TO BE EARTH'S FIRST LINE OF DEFENSE AGAINST MAGICAL MENACE, THE ERSTWHILE PHYSICIAN BECAME EARTH'S FOREMOST MASTER OF THE MYSTIC ARTS! STAN LEE PRESENTS . . .
DOCTOR STRANGE, SORCERER SUPREME!
FOOTNOTE TO INFINITY∞
GREENWICH VILLAGE, NEW YORK CITY...
TO DOCTOR STRANGE!
UH... THANKS, FRIENDS.
BUT-- WHY TOAST ME?
I HAVEN'T DONE ANYTHING SPECIAL.
ROY & DANN THOMAS WRITERS
DAN LAWLIS PENCILER
ANDREW PEPOY INKER
R. PARKER LETTERER
GEORGE ROUSSOS COLORIST
MIKE ROCKWITZ EDITOR
TOM DEFALCO EDITOR IN CHIEF
* WITH SPECIAL THANKS TO JIM STARLIN, ADVISOR

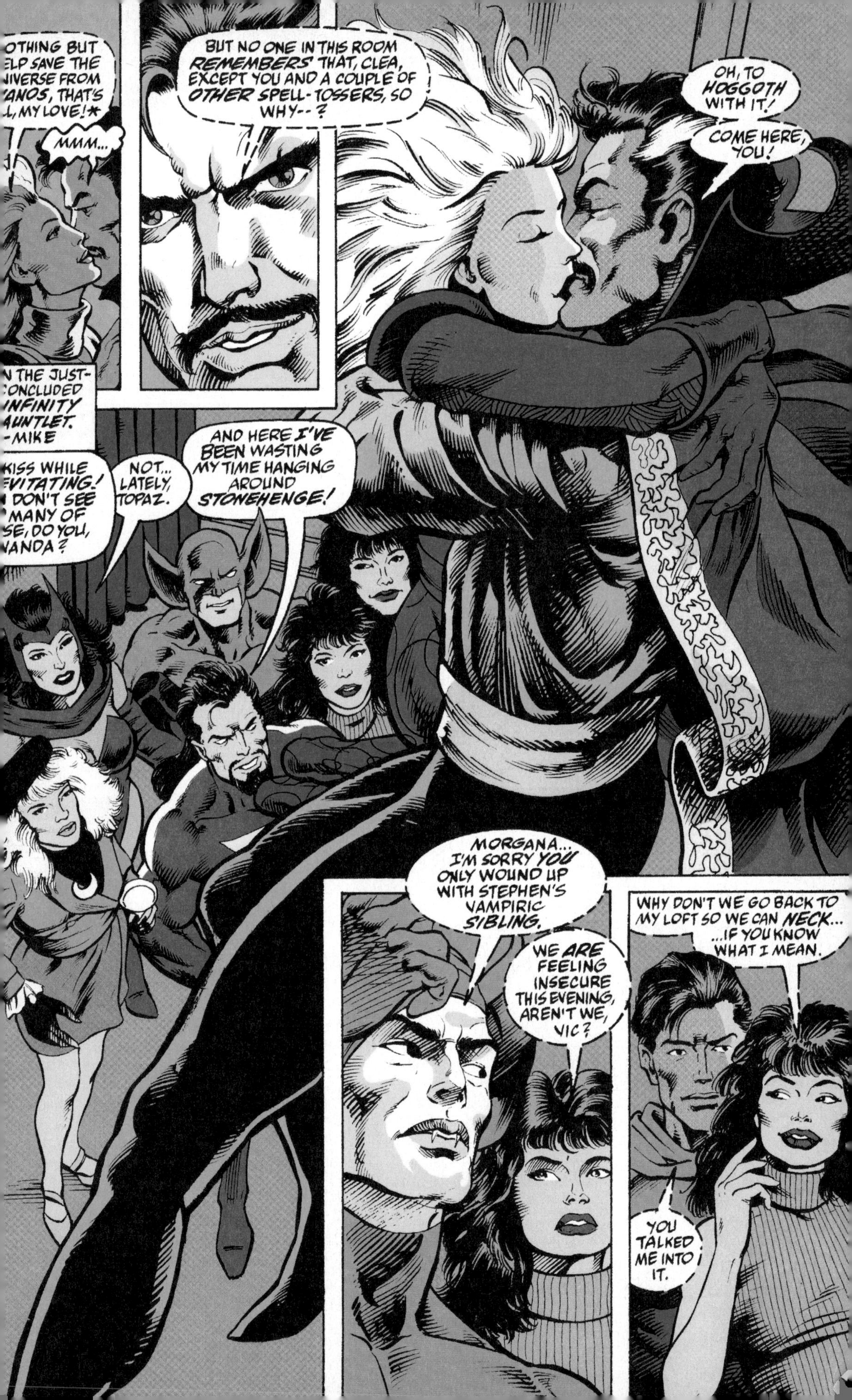

OTHING BUT ELP SAVE THE NIVERSE FROM ANOS, THAT'S L, MY LOVE!*
MMM...
BUT NO ONE IN THIS ROOM REMEMBERS THAT, CLEA, EXCEPT YOU AND A COUPLE OF OTHER SPELL-TOSSERS, SO WHY--?
OH, TO HOGGOTH WITH IT!
COME HERE, YOU!
N THE JUST-CONCLUDED INFINITY AUNTLET. -MIKE
KISS WHILE EVITATING! DON'T SEE MANY OF SE, DO YOU, ANDA?
NOT... LATELY, TOPAZ.
AND HERE I'VE BEEN WASTING MY TIME HANGING AROUND STONEHENGE!
MORGANA... I'M SORRY YOU ONLY WOUND UP WITH STEPHEN'S VAMPIRIC SIBLING.
WE ARE FEELING INSECURE THIS EVENING, AREN'T WE, VIC?
WHY DON'T WE GO BACK TO MY LOFT SO WE CAN NECK... ...IF YOU KNOW WHAT I MEAN.
YOU TALKED ME INTO IT.

VIC AND MORGANA... SNEAKING OUT... AND I'M BETTING I KNOW *WHY.*

YES... EVEN MY *KID BROTHER,* THE *UNDEAD.*

THEY'VE GOT TO LIVE THEIR *OWN* LIVES, STEPHEN.

GLAD YOU AND THE *SCARLET WITCH* COULD MAKE OUR LITTLE IMPROMPTU CELEBRATION, DRUID.

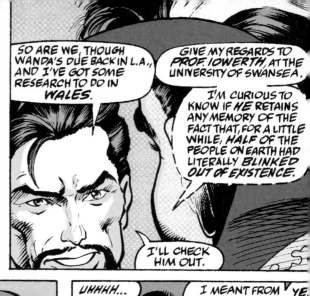

SO ARE WE, THOUGH WANDA'S DUE BACK IN L.A., AND I'VE GOT SOME RESEARCH TO DO IN *WALES.*

GIVE MY REGARDS TO *PROF. IOWERTH,* AT THE UNIVERSITY OF SWANSEA.

I'M CURIOUS TO KNOW IF *HE* RETAINS ANY MEMORY OF THE FACT THAT, FOR A LITTLE WHILE, *HALF* OF THE PEOPLE ON EARTH HAD LITERALLY *BLINKED OUT OF EXISTENCE.*

I'LL CHECK HIM OUT.

I THINK IT'S *GREAT* STEPHEN'S PROMISED TO *WORK* MORE WITH YOU, RINTRAH.

I MERELY REJOICE, SARA, THAT *YOU, WONG,* AND *IMEI* ARE SAFELY BACK.

"*BACK*"? WHY? DID WE ALL GO SOMEWHERE WE DON'T *KNOW* ABOUT?

UHHHH...

I MEANT FROM THE *INSTITUTE,* SARA.

YE... BAC... FRO... THE IN... TUT...

WE'LL BE MARRIED IN SIX MONTHS-- IN *TIBET,* THE LAND WHERE WE WERE BOTH BORN.

THAT'S WONDERFUL!

CLEA AND I WILL BE THERE-- ASSUMING WE'RE *INVITED.*

ATTENTION, EVERYONE! IMEI AND I HAVE AN ANNOUNCEMENT TO MAKE.

WE HAVE SET OUR *WEDDING DATE...*

IT WOULD NOT BE A *TRUE* WEDDING *WITHOUT YOU,* MASTER.

PLEASE, DROP THE "*MASTER*" STUFF, AT LEAST FOR TONIGHT, ALL RIGHT?

NOW, ANY OBJECTION IF I KISS THE *BRIDE-TO-BE?*

NOT FROM *ME,* DOCTOR.

GOOD. I'M A BIT *RUSTY* AT THIS, BUT-- *WHAT* IN OSHTUR'S *NAME*--?

THAT *BLINDING LIGHT*--!

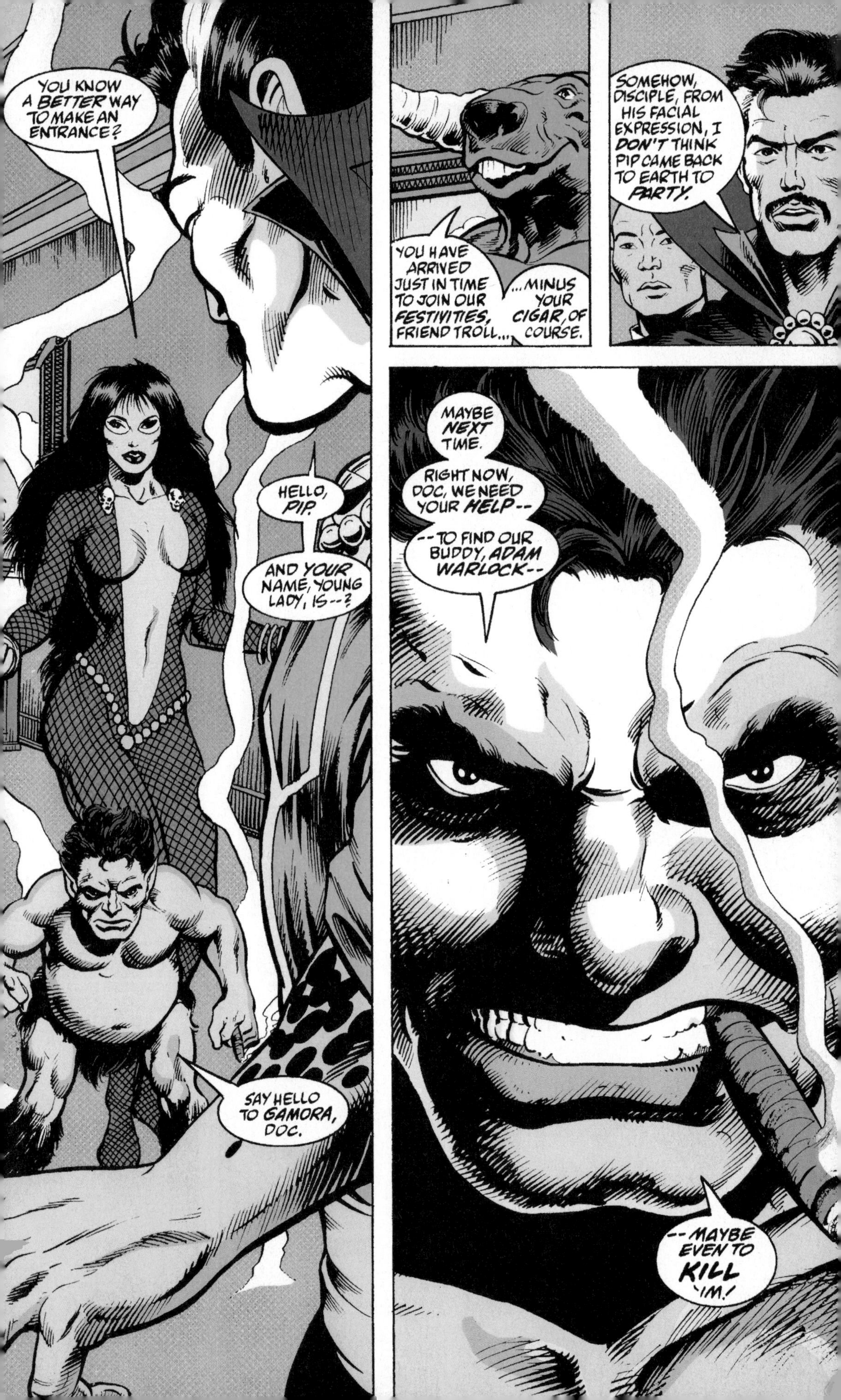

YOU KNOW A BETTER WAY TO MAKE AN ENTRANCE?
HELLO, PIP.
AND YOUR NAME, YOUNG LADY, IS--?
SAY HELLO TO GAMORA, DOC.
YOU HAVE ARRIVED JUST IN TIME TO JOIN OUR FESTIVITIES, FRIEND TROLL...
...MINUS YOUR CIGAR, OF COURSE.
SOMEHOW, DISCIPLE, FROM HIS FACIAL EXPRESSION, I DON'T THINK PIP CAME BACK TO EARTH TO PARTY.
MAYBE NEXT TIME.
RIGHT NOW, DOC, WE NEED YOUR HELP--
--TO FIND OUR BUDDY, ADAM WARLOCK--
--MAYBE EVEN TO KILL 'IM!

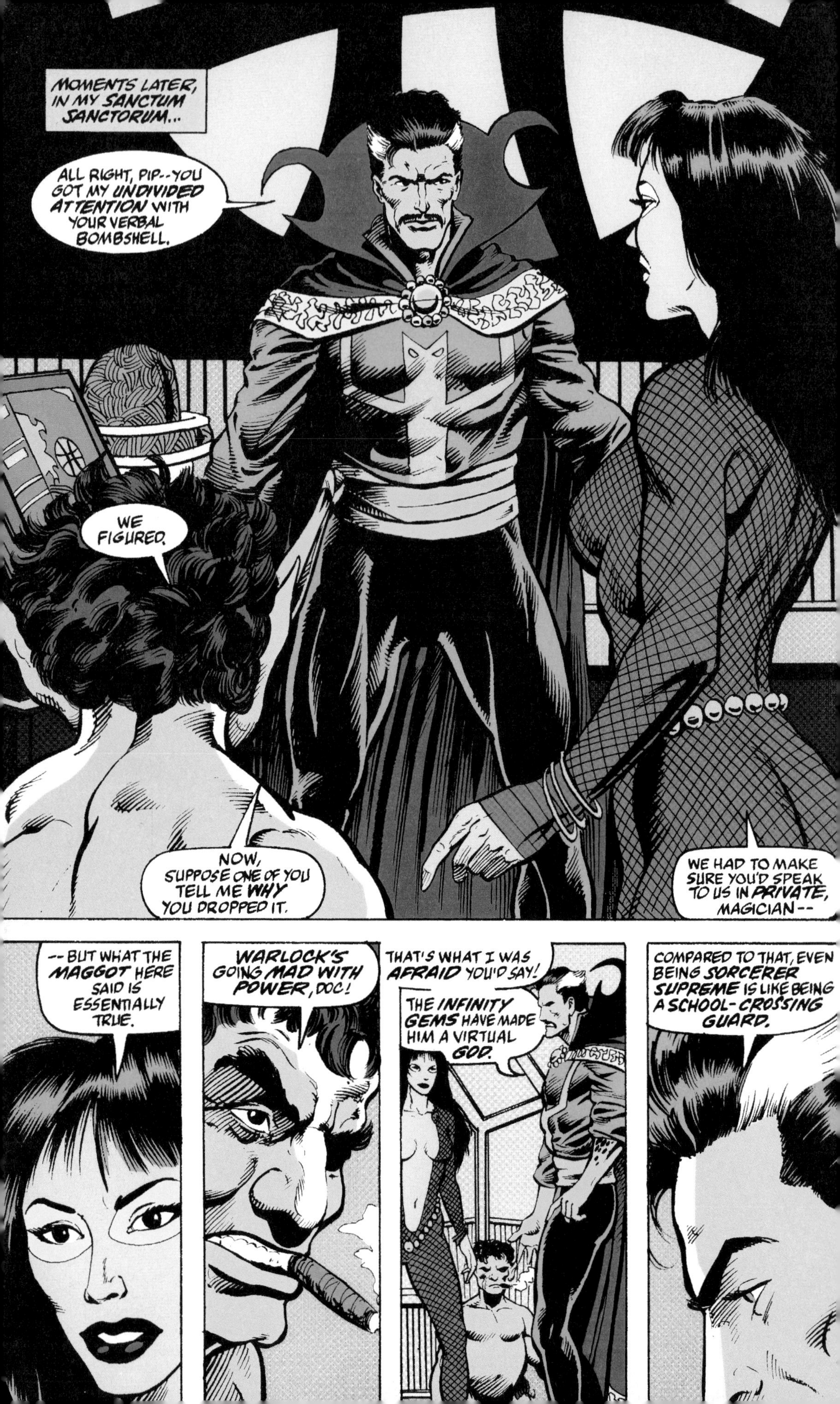
MOMENTS LATER, IN MY SANCTUM SANCTORUM...
ALL RIGHT, PIP--YOU GOT MY UNDIVIDED ATTENTION WITH YOUR VERBAL BOMBSHELL.
WE FIGURED.
NOW, SUPPOSE ONE OF YOU TELL ME WHY YOU DROPPED IT.
WE HAD TO MAKE SURE YOU'D SPEAK TO US IN PRIVATE, MAGICIAN--
--BUT WHAT THE MAGGOT HERE SAID IS ESSENTIALLY TRUE.
WARLOCK'S GOING MAD WITH POWER, DOC!
THAT'S WHAT I WAS AFRAID YOU'D SAY!
THE INFINITY GEMS HAVE MADE HIM A VIRTUAL GOD.
COMPARED TO THAT, EVEN BEING SORCERER SUPREME IS LIKE BEING A SCHOOL-CROSSING GUARD.

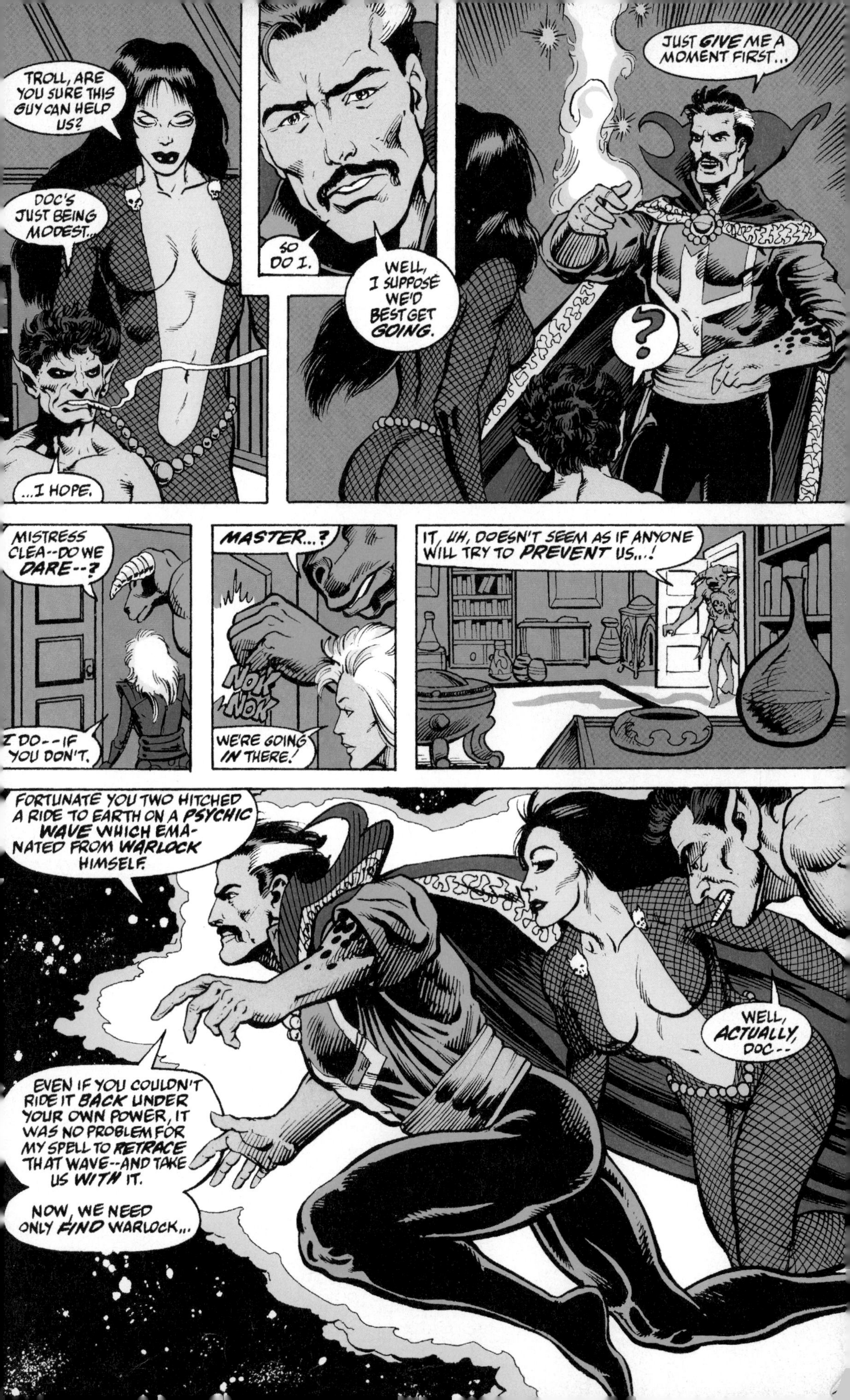
TROLL, ARE YOU SURE THIS GUY CAN HELP US?
SO DO I.
JUST GIVE ME A MOMENT FIRST...
DOC'S JUST BEING MODEST...
WELL, I SUPPOSE WE'D BEST GET GOING.
?
...I HOPE.
MISTRESS CLEA--DO WE DARE--?
I DO--IF YOU DON'T.
MASTER...?
NOK NOK
WE'RE GOING IN THERE!
IT, UH, DOESN'T SEEM AS IF ANYONE WILL TRY TO PREVENT US...!
FORTUNATE YOU TWO HITCHED A RIDE TO EARTH ON A PSYCHIC WAVE WHICH EMANATED FROM WARLOCK HIMSELF.
WELL, ACTUALLY, DOC--
EVEN IF YOU COULDN'T RIDE IT BACK UNDER YOUR OWN POWER, IT WAS NO PROBLEM FOR MY SPELL TO RETRACE THAT WAVE--AND TAKE US WITH IT.
NOW, WE NEED ONLY FIND WARLOCK...

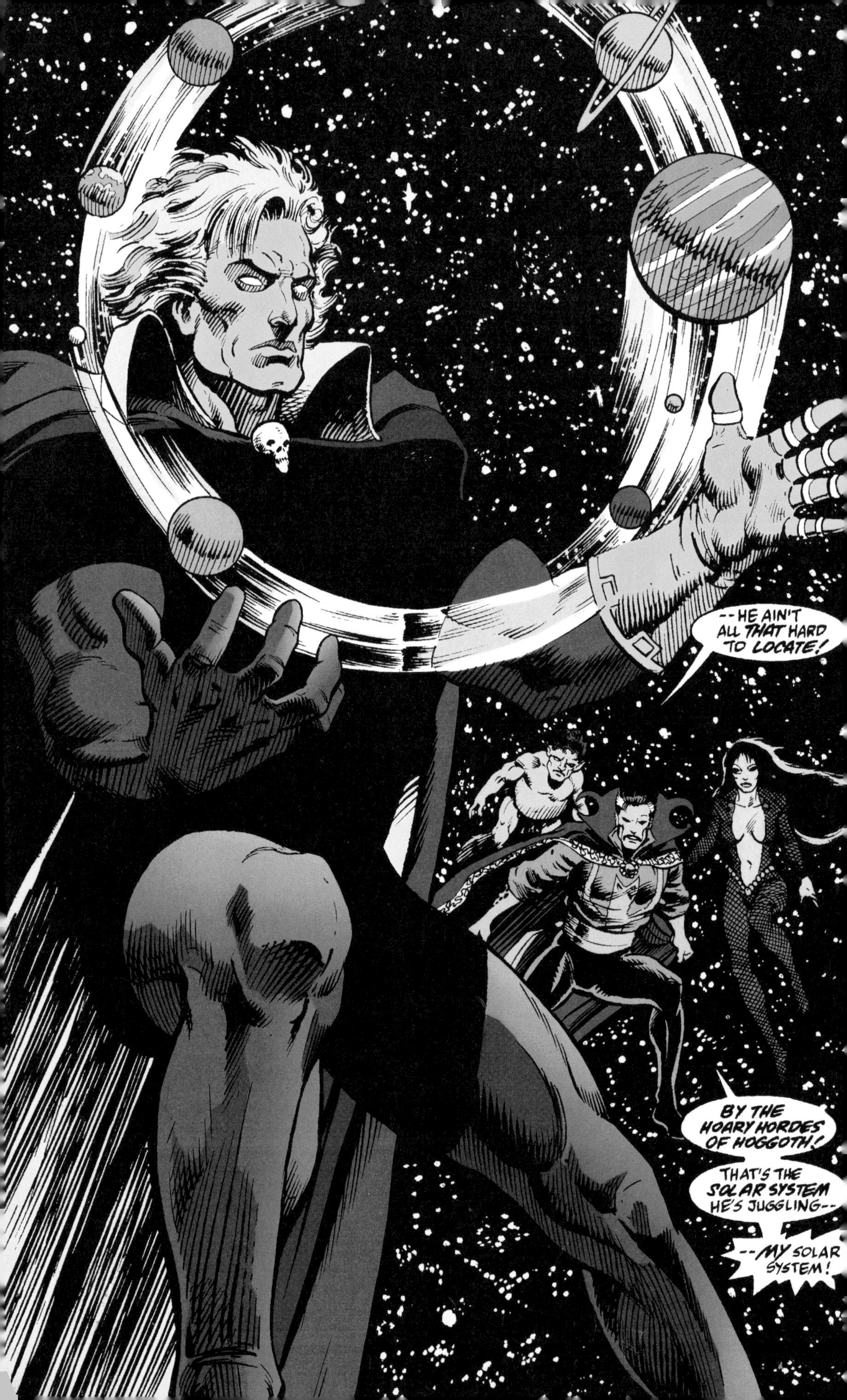
--HE AIN'T ALL THAT HARD TO LOCATE!
BY THE HOARY HORDES OF HOGGOTH!
THAT'S THE SOLAR SYSTEM HE'S JUGGLING--
--MY SOLAR SYSTEM!

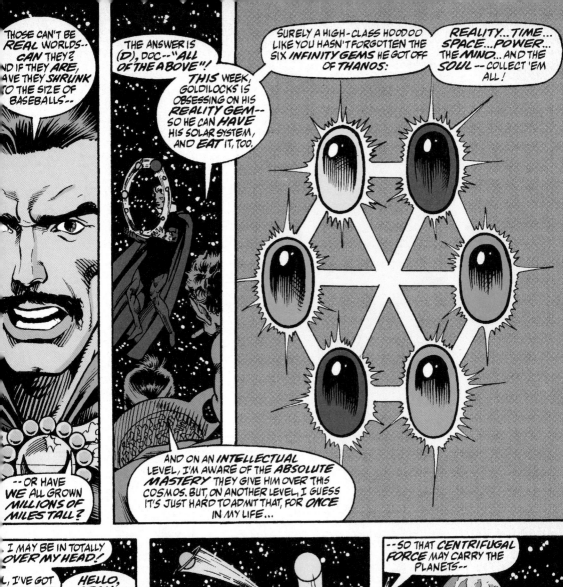

THOSE CAN'T BE *REAL* WORLDS-- ...ND IF THEY *ARE,* ...AVE THEY *SHRUNK* ...O THE SIZE OF BASEBALLS--

THE ANSWER IS *(D),* DOC-- *"ALL OF THE ABOVE"!*

THIS WEEK, GOLDILOCKS IS OBSESSING ON HIS *REALITY GEM*-- SO HE CAN *HAVE* HIS SOLAR SYSTEM, AND *EAT* IT, TOO.

SURELY A HIGH-CLASS HOODOO LIKE YOU HASN'T FORGOTTEN THE SIX *INFINITY GEMS* HE GOT OFF OF *THANOS:*

REALITY...TIME... SPACE...POWER... THE MIND... AND THE *SOUL* -- COLLECT 'EM ALL !

--OR HAVE *WE* ALL GROWN *MILLIONS* OF MILES TALL?

AND ON AN *INTELLECTUAL* LEVEL, I'M AWARE OF THE *ABSOLUTE MASTERY* THEY GIVE HIM OVER THIS COSMOS. BUT, ON ANOTHER LEVEL, I GUESS IT'S JUST HARD TO ADMIT THAT, FOR *ONCE* IN MY LIFE...

I MAY BE IN TOTALLY *OVER MY HEAD!*

...L, I'VE GOT ...HOICE BUT ...EST THE ...ATERS.

HELLO, ADAM WARLOCK.

SO, MAGE, YOU HAVE ELECTED TO STOP SPEAKING *ABOUT* ME, AND BEGIN SPEAKING *TO* ME.

IN THAT CASE, I SHALL LET *NATURAL LAW* HOLD SWAY AGAIN--

--SO THAT *CENTRIFUGAL FORCE* MAY CARRY THE PLANETS--

--BACK TO THEIR BORING *ORBITS* AROUND AN EQUALLY BORING *SUN.*

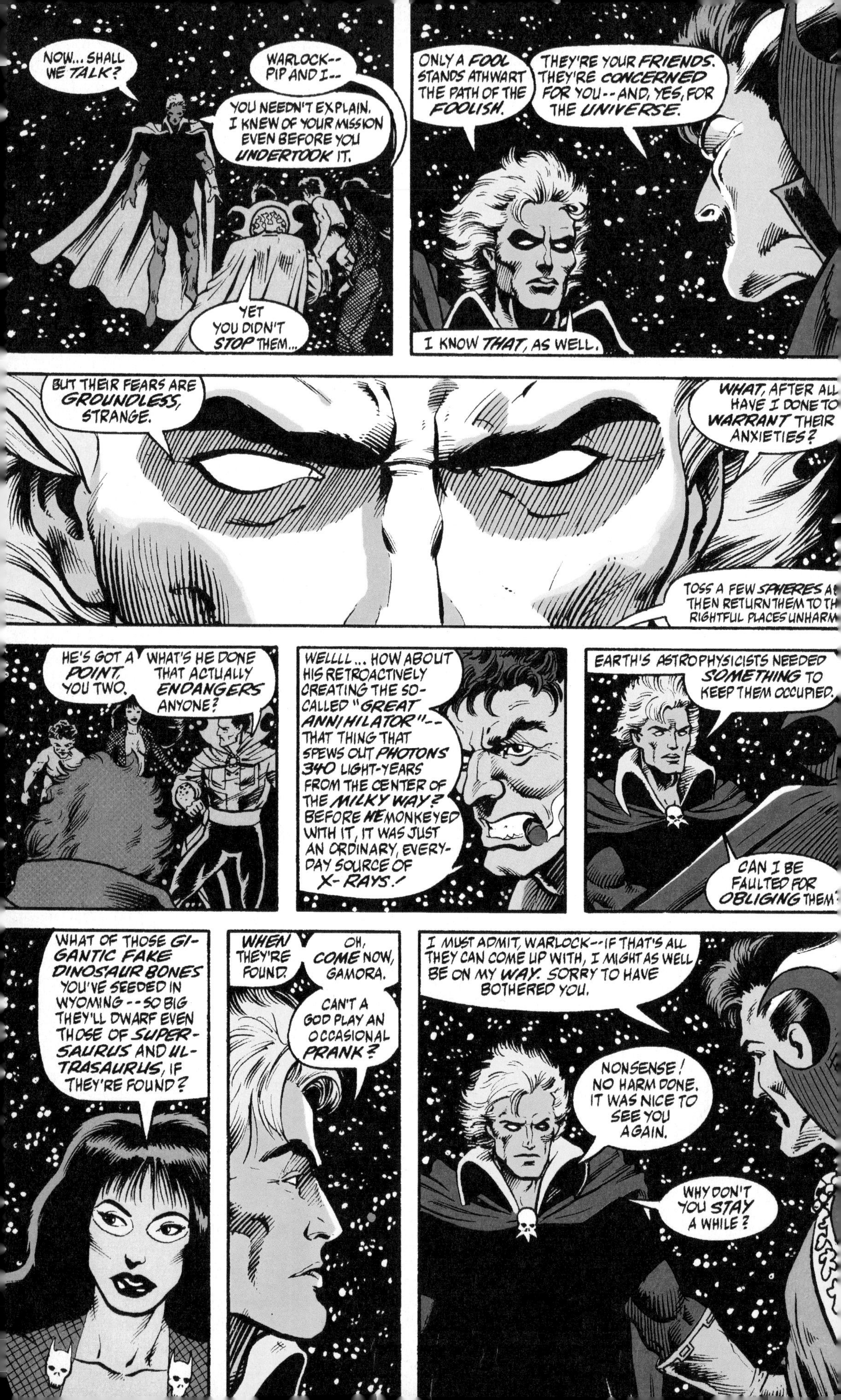
NOW... SHALL WE TALK?
WARLOCK-- PIP AND I--
YOU NEEDN'T EXPLAIN. I KNEW OF YOUR MISSION EVEN BEFORE YOU UNDERTOOK IT.
YET YOU DIDN'T STOP THEM...
ONLY A FOOL STANDS ATHWART THE PATH OF THE FOOLISH.
THEY'RE YOUR FRIENDS. THEY'RE CONCERNED FOR YOU--AND, YES, FOR THE UNIVERSE.
I KNOW THAT, AS WELL.
BUT THEIR FEARS ARE GROUNDLESS, STRANGE.
WHAT, AFTER ALL HAVE I DONE TO WARRANT THEIR ANXIETIES?
TOSS A FEW SPHERES A THEN RETURN THEM TO TH RIGHTFUL PLACES UNHARM
HE'S GOT A POINT, YOU TWO.
WHAT'S HE DONE THAT ACTUALLY ENDANGERS ANYONE?
WELLLL... HOW ABOUT HIS RETROACTIVELY CREATING THE SO-CALLED "GREAT ANNIHILATOR"-- THAT THING THAT SPEWS OUT PHOTONS 340 LIGHT-YEARS FROM THE CENTER OF THE MILKY WAY? BEFORE HE MONKEYED WITH IT, IT WAS JUST AN ORDINARY, EVERY-DAY SOURCE OF X-RAYS!
EARTH'S ASTROPHYSICISTS NEEDED SOMETHING TO KEEP THEM OCCUPIED.
CAN I BE FAULTED FOR OBLIGING THEM
WHAT OF THOSE GIGANTIC FAKE DINOSAUR BONES YOU'VE SEEDED IN WYOMING--SO BIG THEY'LL DWARF EVEN THOSE OF SUPERSAURUS AND ULTRASAURUS, IF THEY'RE FOUND?
WHEN THEY'RE FOUND.
OH, COME NOW, GAMORA.
CAN'T A GOD PLAY AN OCCASIONAL PRANK?
I MUST ADMIT, WARLOCK--IF THAT'S ALL THEY CAN COME UP WITH, I MIGHT AS WELL BE ON MY WAY. SORRY TO HAVE BOTHERED YOU.
NONSENSE! NO HARM DONE. IT WAS NICE TO SEE YOU AGAIN.
WHY DON'T YOU STAY A WHILE?

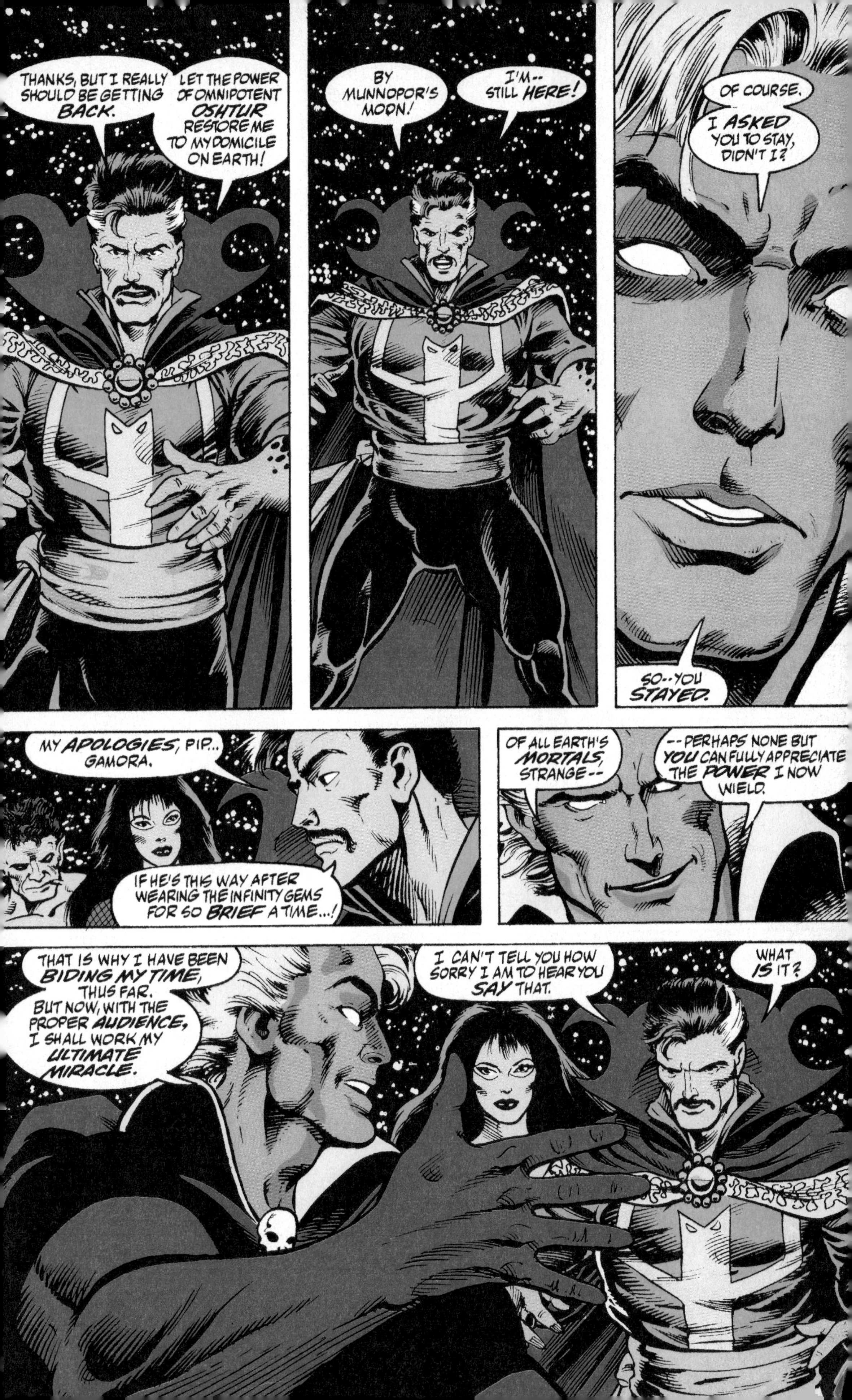
THANKS, BUT I REALLY SHOULD BE GETTING BACK.
LET THE POWER OF OMNIPOTENT OSHTUR RESTORE ME TO MY DOMICILE ON EARTH!
BY MUNNOPOR'S MOON!
I'M-- STILL HERE!
OF COURSE.
I ASKED YOU TO STAY, DIDN'T I?
SO--YOU STAYED.
MY APOLOGIES, PIP... GAMORA.
IF HE'S THIS WAY AFTER WEARING THE INFINITY GEMS FOR SO BRIEF A TIME...!
OF ALL EARTH'S MORTALS, STRANGE--
--PERHAPS NONE BUT YOU CAN FULLY APPRECIATE THE POWER I NOW WIELD.
THAT IS WHY I HAVE BEEN BIDING MY TIME, THUS FAR.
BUT NOW, WITH THE PROPER AUDIENCE, I SHALL WORK MY ULTIMATE MIRACLE.
I CAN'T TELL YOU HOW SORRY I AM TO HEAR YOU SAY THAT.
WHAT IS IT?

GOODNESS!

PARDON ME?

I SHALL SEND OUT *EMANATIONS* WHICH, IN AN INSTANT, WILL MAKE EVERY SENTIENT BEING IN THE COSMOS *GOOD* AND *NOBLE!*

HUMAN--SKRULL--KREE--SHI'AR--I WILL DRAIN THEM ALL OF SELFISH *AMBITION*, OF COMPETITIVENESS----ALL THOSE BASE TRAITS WHICH HAVE EVER LED TO *WAR* AND *STRIFE!*

ARE YOU *MAD?!*

YOU *MEAN* WELL--BUT *WITHOUT* THOSE "BASE TRAITS," AS YOU CALL THEM, MOST RACES WOULD EITHER *PERISH* FROM SHEER APATHY----OR, EVEN SURVIVING, THEIR *LIVES* WILL BECOME DULL AND ULTIMATELY *MEANINGLESS.*

DON'T TAMPER WITH THE BALANCE OF WHAT YOU PERCEIVE AS *GOOD* AND *EVIL*, WARLOCK.

EVEN WITH THOSE GEMS, YOU'RE NOT UP TO IT.

NO ONE IS.

YOU *DISAPPOINT* ME, STRANGE.

I LET P AND GAMO *SUMMON*

--SO YOU COULD BE HERE TO *WIT-NESS* -- AND *APPRECIATE.*

SOUNDS LIKE HE HAD US ON A *LONG LEASH*, PIPSQUEAK.

YOU'VE PROVED MY *POINT* FOR ME, WARLOCK.

TO BE *GOOD* IS NOT SIMPLY A SEQUENCE OF *ACTS.*

IT INCLUDES THE ABILITY TO *CHOOSE.*

I WON'T LET YOU DO THIS!

ENOUGH!

YOU WILL *RELENT*, MAGICIAN, WHEN YOU SEE WHAT I *ACCOMPLISH*--BEGINNING *NOW!*

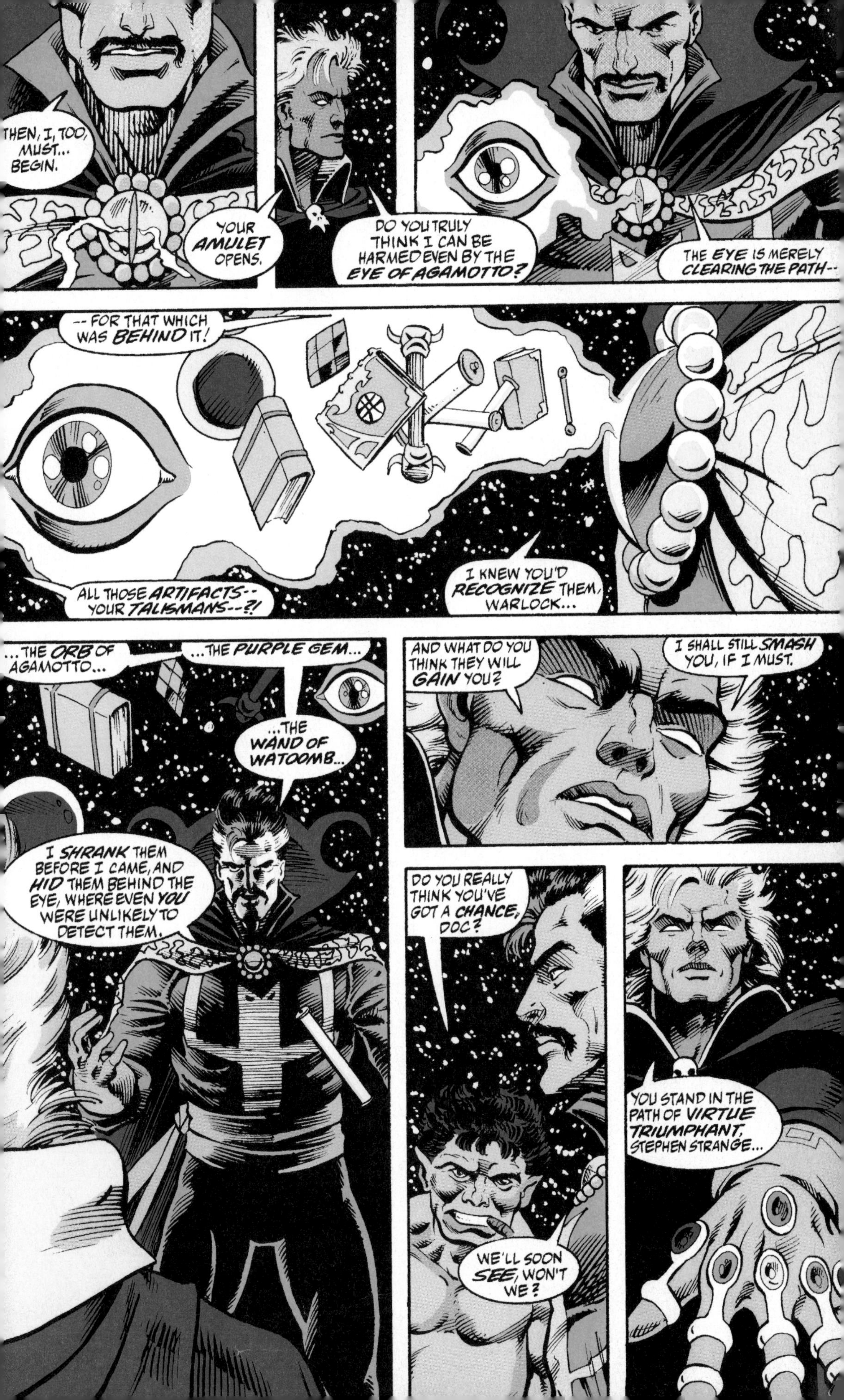
THEN, I, TOO, MUST... BEGIN.
YOUR AMULET OPENS.
DO YOU TRULY THINK I CAN BE HARMED EVEN BY THE EYE OF AGAMOTTO?
THE EYE IS MERELY CLEARING THE PATH--
--FOR THAT WHICH WAS BEHIND IT!
ALL THOSE ARTIFACTS-- YOUR TALISMANS--?!
I KNEW YOU'D RECOGNIZE THEM, WARLOCK...
...THE ORB OF AGAMOTTO...
...THE PURPLE GEM...
...THE WAND OF WATOOMB...
I SHRANK THEM BEFORE I CAME, AND HID THEM BEHIND THE EYE, WHERE EVEN YOU WERE UNLIKELY TO DETECT THEM.
AND WHAT DO YOU THINK THEY WILL GAIN YOU?
I SHALL STILL SMASH YOU, IF I MUST.
DO YOU REALLY THINK YOU'VE GOT A CHANCE, DOC?
WE'LL SOON SEE, WON'T WE?
YOU STAND IN THE PATH OF VIRTUE TRIUMPHANT, STEPHEN STRANGE...

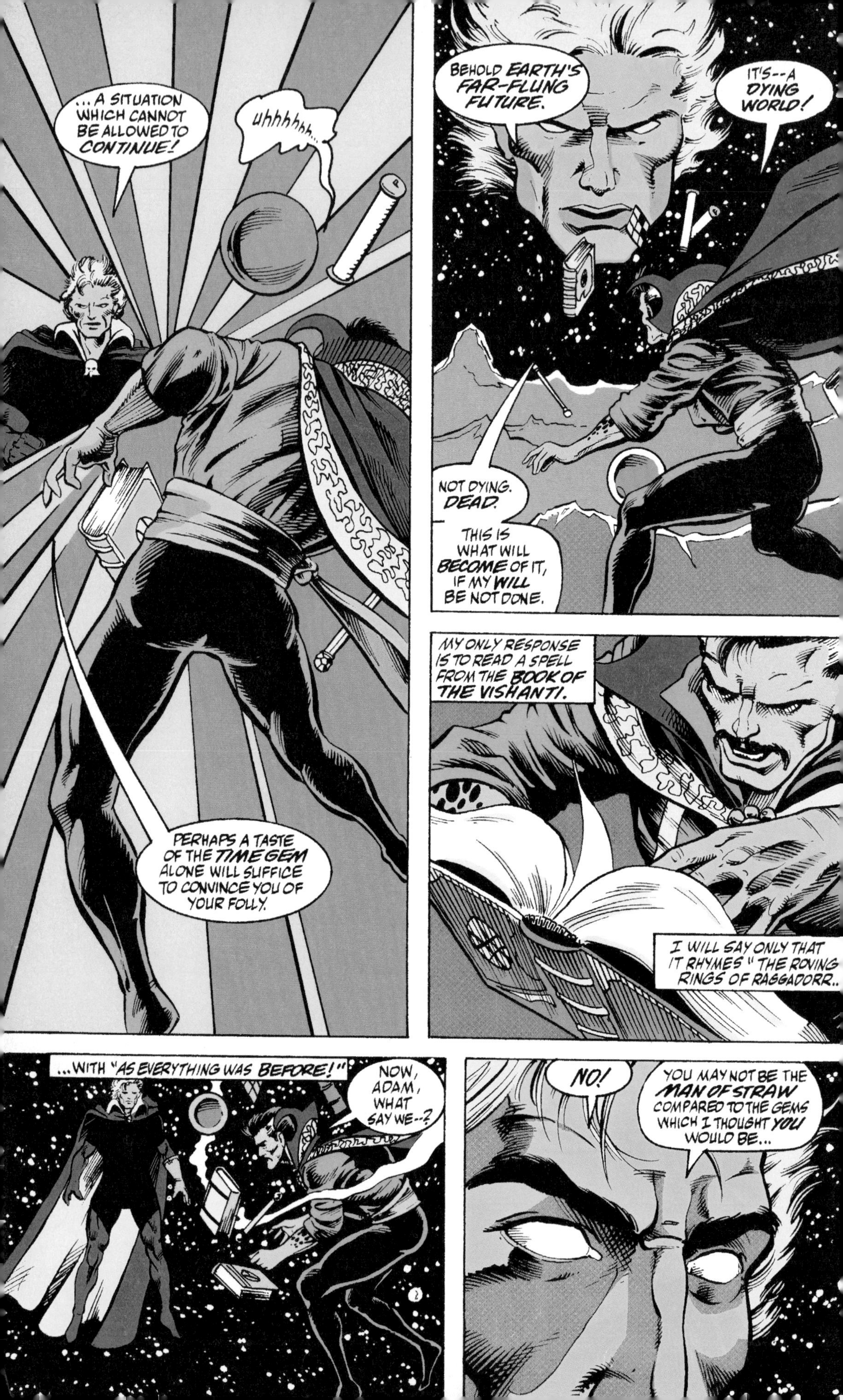

...A SITUATION WHICH CANNOT BE ALLOWED TO CONTINUE!
uhhhhhh...
PERHAPS A TASTE OF THE TIME GEM ALONE WILL SUFFICE TO CONVINCE YOU OF YOUR FOLLY.
BEHOLD EARTH'S FAR-FLUNG FUTURE.
IT'S--A DYING WORLD!
NOT DYING. DEAD.
THIS IS WHAT WILL BECOME OF IT, IF MY WILL BE NOT DONE.
MY ONLY RESPONSE IS TO READ A SPELL FROM THE BOOK OF THE VISHANTI.
I WILL SAY ONLY THAT IT RHYMES "THE ROVING RINGS OF RAGGADORR...
...WITH "AS EVERYTHING WAS BEFORE!"
NOW, ADAM, WHAT SAY WE--?
NO!
YOU MAY NOT BE THE MAN OF STRAW COMPARED TO THE GEMS WHICH I THOUGHT YOU WOULD BE...

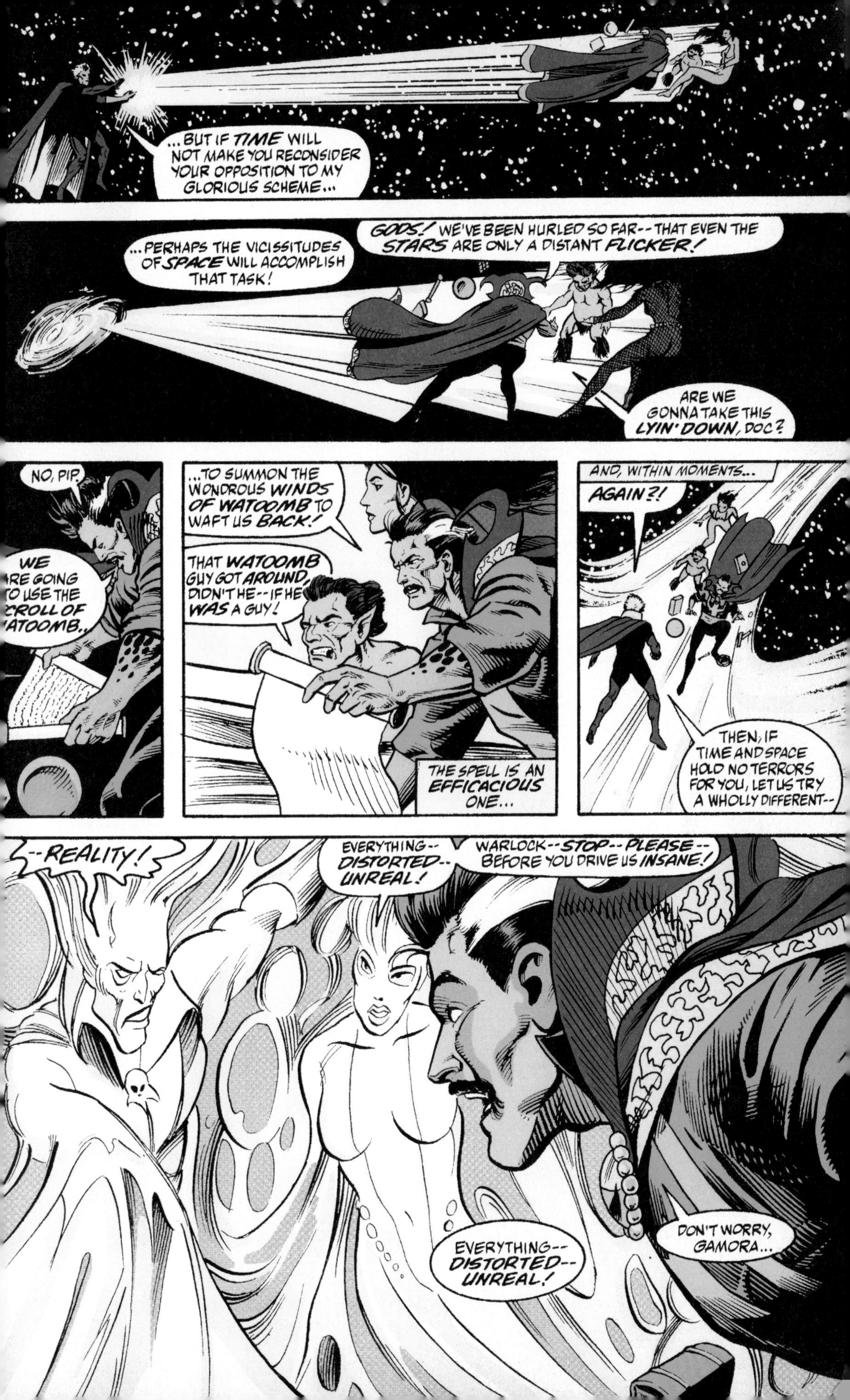
...BUT IF TIME WILL NOT MAKE YOU RECONSIDER YOUR OPPOSITION TO MY GLORIOUS SCHEME...
...PERHAPS THE VICISSITUDES OF SPACE WILL ACCOMPLISH THAT TASK!
GODS! WE'VE BEEN HURLED SO FAR-- THAT EVEN THE STARS ARE ONLY A DISTANT FLICKER!
ARE WE GONNA TAKE THIS LYIN' DOWN, DOC?
NO, PIP.
WE ARE GOING TO USE THE SCROLL OF WATOOMB...
...TO SUMMON THE WONDROUS WINDS OF WATOOMB TO WAFT US BACK!
THAT WATOOMB GUY GOT AROUND, DIDN'T HE-- IF HE WAS A GUY!
THE SPELL IS AN EFFICACIOUS ONE...
AND, WITHIN MOMENTS...
AGAIN?!
THEN, IF TIME AND SPACE HOLD NO TERRORS FOR YOU, LET US TRY A WHOLLY DIFFERENT--
--REALITY!
EVERYTHING-- DISTORTED-- UNREAL!
WARLOCK-- STOP-- PLEASE-- BEFORE YOU DRIVE US INSANE!
EVERYTHING-- DISTORTED-- UNREAL!
DON'T WORRY, GAMORA...

THE **EXPANDED ORB** OF AGAMOTTO WILL **CORRECT** YOUR SENSES, AS EASILY AS PUTTING ON A PAIR OF **GLASSES.**

THE **EYES**-- THE **EARS**-- YES--

THESE ARE AS EASILY **AUGMENTED** AS **TRICKED.**

BUT HOW DO YOU **REASON OUT** A DEFENSE--

--WHEN **REASON** ITSELF SHIFTS ITS STANCE?

THE OPERATION WAS A **SUCCESS,** DR. STRANGE. YOUR PATIENT WANTS TO **THANK** YOU.

I CAN'T BE BOTHERED. JUST BE SURE HE PAYS HIS **BILL.**

WE GOT HERE JUST IN **TIME,** JOE! CALL AN **AMBULANCE!**

BUT-- EARLIER, YOU **REFUSED** TO LET ME THANK YOU...

THAT WAS BEFORE THE **ACCIDENT** THAT ALMOST COST ME THE USE OF MY **HANDS.**

"**ALMOST**"? THAT WRECK **DID** END MY CAREER AS A SURGEON!

YOU'VE **ALTERED MY FUTURE** -- SO I **NEVER** BECOME THE ANCIENT ONE'S DISCIPLE--

--LET ALONE THE **SORCERER SUPREME!**

AND YET-- I GO ON **SAVING LIVES** -- ONLY ON A **ONE-ON-ONE** BASIS!

PERHAPS I SHOULD LA[Y] DOWN THIS AWFUL BURDEN LET SOMEC[NE] ELSE ASSU[ME] IT--MAYBE **ANTHON[Y] DRUID.**

PERHAPS...

NO, BY THE ETERNAL **VISHANTI!**

YOU'RE PLAYING TRICKS WITH MY **MIND!**

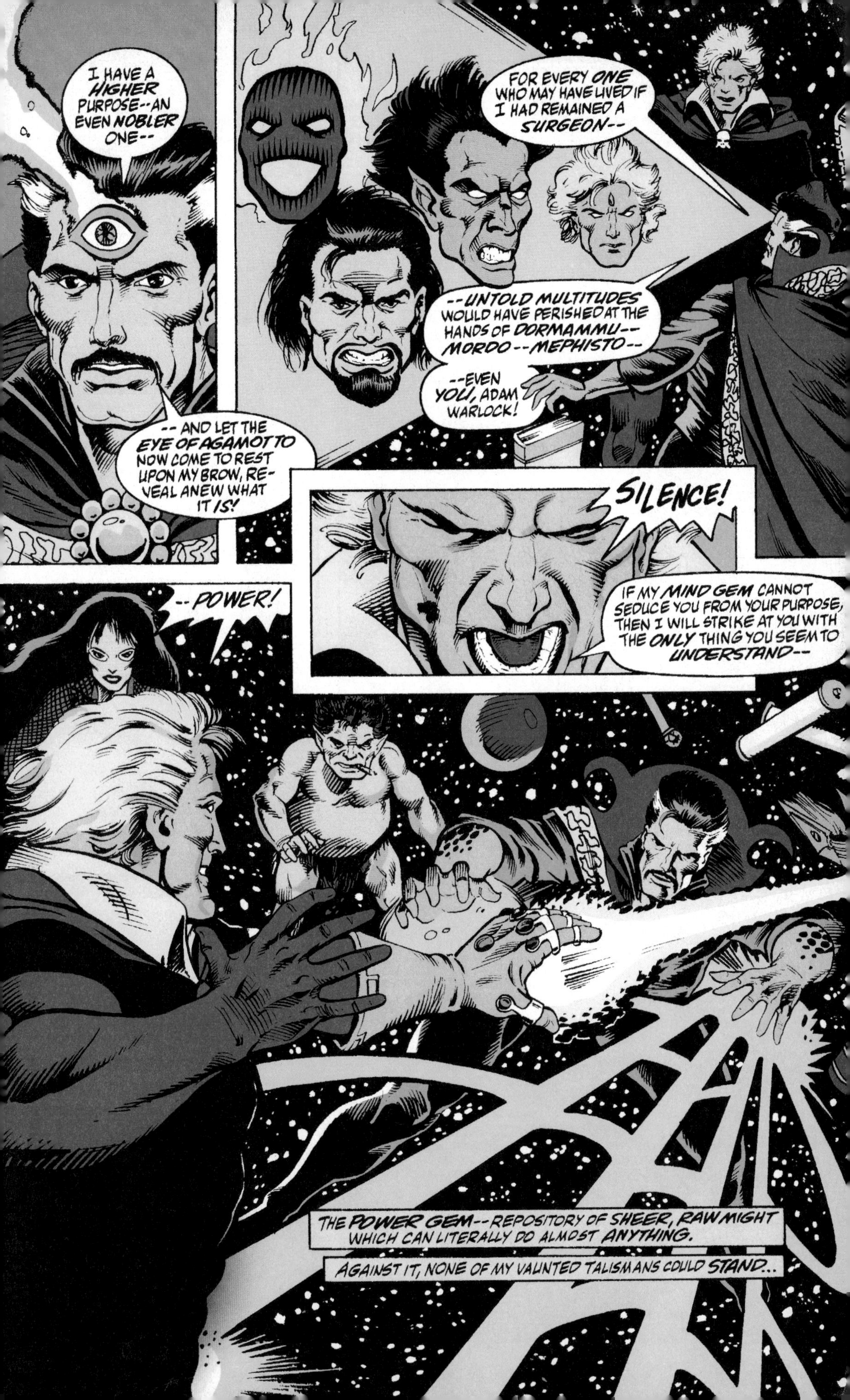

I HAVE A HIGHER PURPOSE--AN EVEN NOBLER ONE--
FOR EVERY ONE WHO MAY HAVE LIVED IF I HAD REMAINED A SURGEON--
--UNTOLD MULTITUDES WOULD HAVE PERISHED AT THE HANDS OF DORMAMMU--MORDO--MEPHISTO--
--EVEN YOU, ADAM WARLOCK!
-- AND LET THE EYE OF AGAMOTTO NOW COME TO REST UPON MY BROW, RE-VEAL ANEW WHAT IT IS!
SILENCE!
IF MY MIND GEM CANNOT SEDUCE YOU FROM YOUR PURPOSE, THEN I WILL STRIKE AT YOU WITH THE ONLY THING YOU SEEM TO UNDERSTAND--
--POWER!
THE POWER GEM--REPOSITORY OF SHEER, RAW MIGHT WHICH CAN LITERALLY DO ALMOST ANYTHING.
AGAINST IT, NONE OF MY VAUNTED TALISMANS COULD STAND...

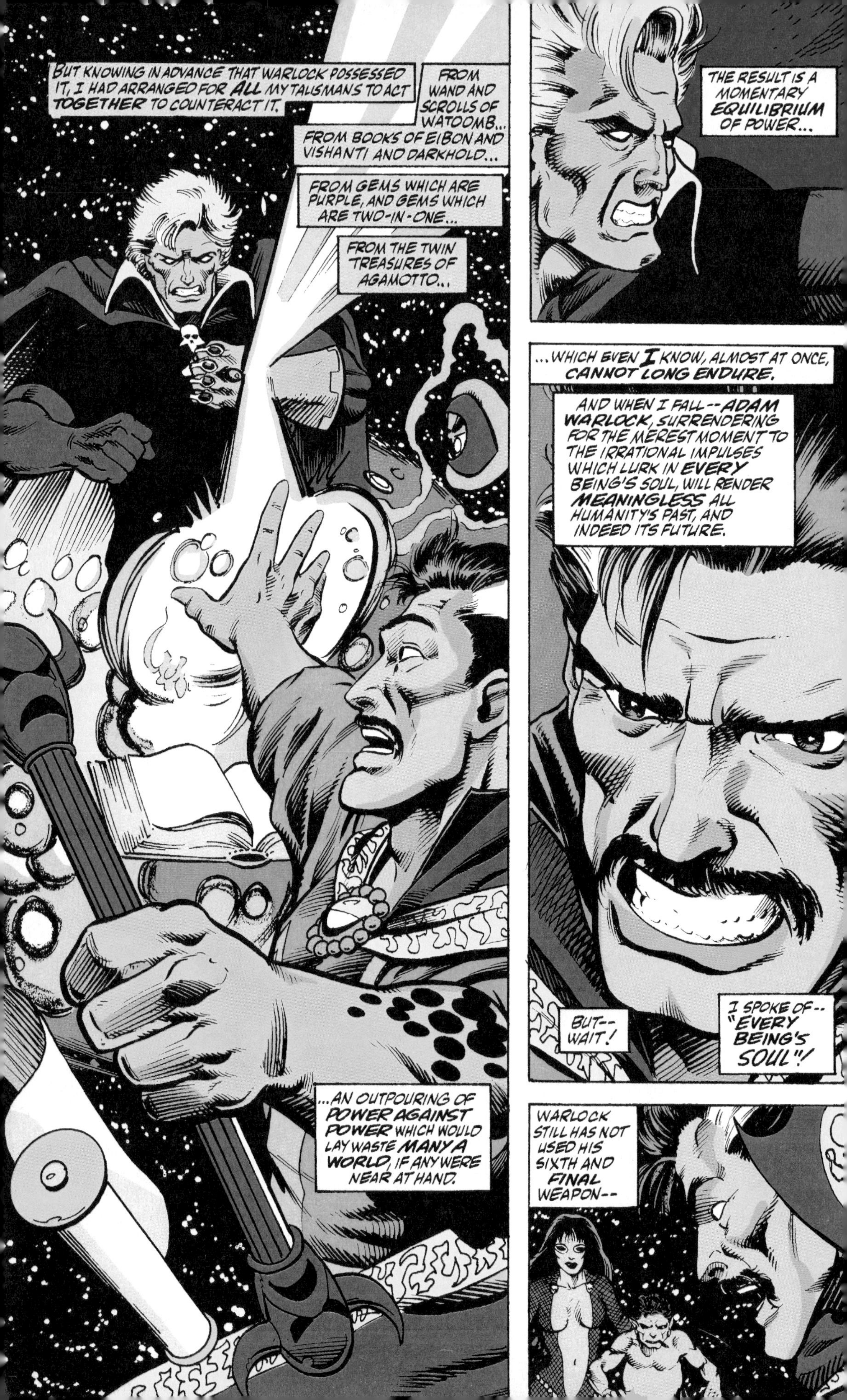

BUT KNOWING IN ADVANCE THAT WARLOCK POSSESSED IT, I HAD ARRANGED FOR ALL MY TALISMANS TO ACT TOGETHER TO COUNTERACT IT.
FROM WAND AND SCROLLS OF WATOOMB...
FROM BOOKS OF EIBON AND VISHANTI AND DARKHOLD...
FROM GEMS WHICH ARE PURPLE, AND GEMS WHICH ARE TWO-IN-ONE...
FROM THE TWIN TREASURES OF AGAMOTTO...
...AN OUTPOURING OF POWER AGAINST POWER WHICH WOULD LAY WASTE MANY A WORLD, IF ANY WERE NEAR AT HAND.
THE RESULT IS A MOMENTARY EQUILIBRIUM OF POWER...
...WHICH EVEN I KNOW, ALMOST AT ONCE, CANNOT LONG ENDURE.
AND WHEN I FALL--ADAM WARLOCK, SURRENDERING FOR THE MEREST MOMENT TO THE IRRATIONAL IMPULSES WHICH LURK IN EVERY BEING'S SOUL, WILL RENDER MEANINGLESS ALL HUMANITY'S PAST, AND INDEED ITS FUTURE.
BUT-- WAIT!
I SPOKE OF-- "EVERY BEING'S SOUL"!
WARLOCK STILL HAS NOT USED HIS SIXTH AND FINAL WEAPON--

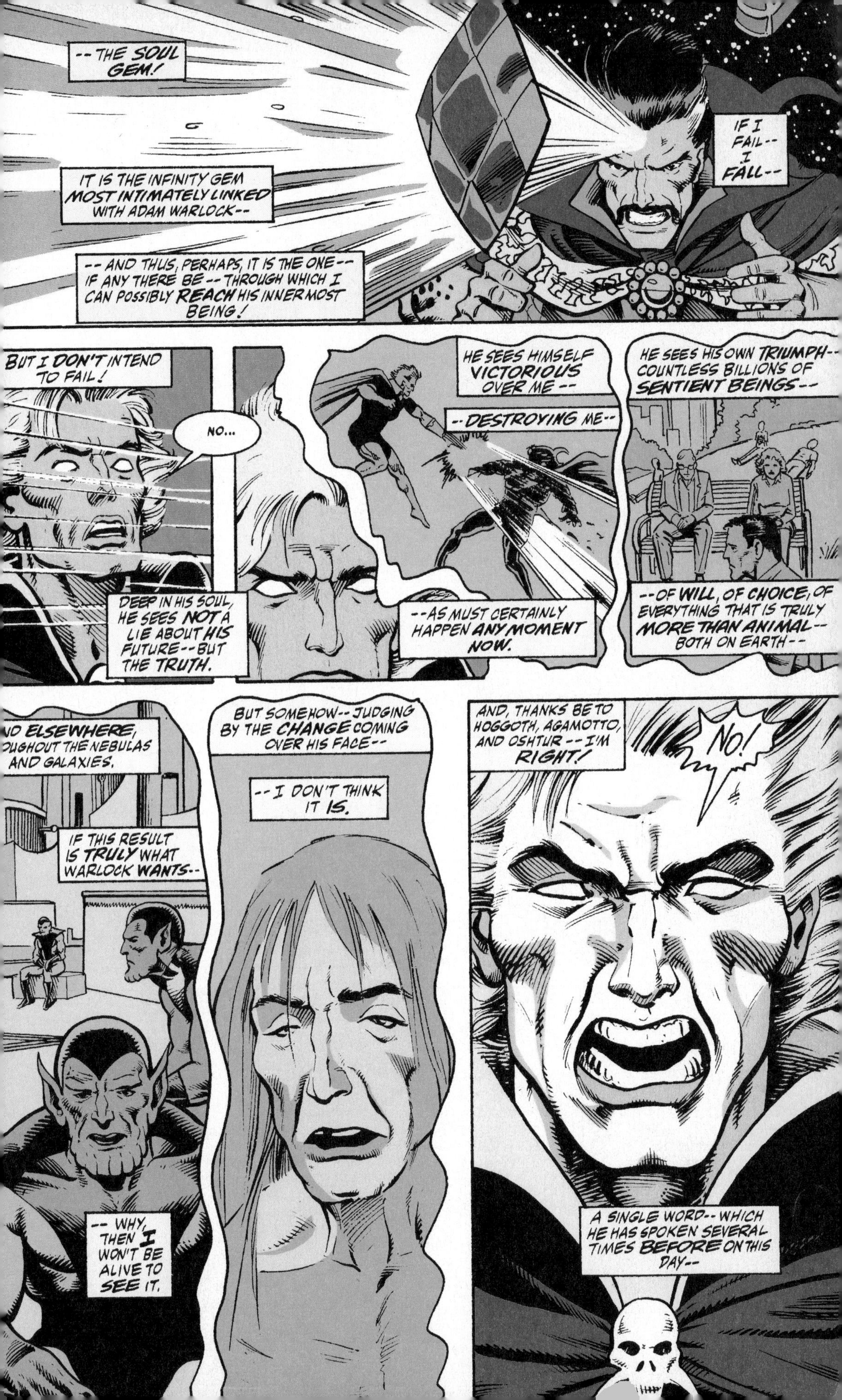
--THE SOUL GEM!
IT IS THE INFINITY GEM MOST INTIMATELY LINKED WITH ADAM WARLOCK--
--AND THUS, PERHAPS, IT IS THE ONE-- IF ANY THERE BE--THROUGH WHICH I CAN POSSIBLY REACH HIS INNERMOST BEING!
IF I FAIL-- I FALL--
BUT I DON'T INTEND TO FAIL!
NO...
DEEP IN HIS SOUL, HE SEES NOT A LIE ABOUT HIS FUTURE--BUT THE TRUTH.
HE SEES HIMSELF VICTORIOUS OVER ME--
--DESTROYING ME--
--AS MUST CERTAINLY HAPPEN ANY MOMENT NOW.
HE SEES HIS OWN TRIUMPH-- COUNTLESS BILLIONS OF SENTIENT BEINGS--
--OF WILL, OF CHOICE, OF EVERYTHING THAT IS TRULY MORE THAN ANIMAL-- BOTH ON EARTH--
ND ELSEWHERE, OUGHOUT THE NEBULAS AND GALAXIES.
IF THIS RESULT IS TRULY WHAT WARLOCK WANTS--
--WHY, THEN I WON'T BE ALIVE TO SEE IT.
BUT SOMEHOW--JUDGING BY THE CHANGE COMING OVER HIS FACE--
--I DON'T THINK IT IS.
AND, THANKS BE TO HOGGOTH, AGAMOTTO, AND OSHTUR--I'M RIGHT!
NO!
A SINGLE WORD--WHICH HE HAS SPOKEN SEVERAL TIMES BEFORE ON THIS DAY--

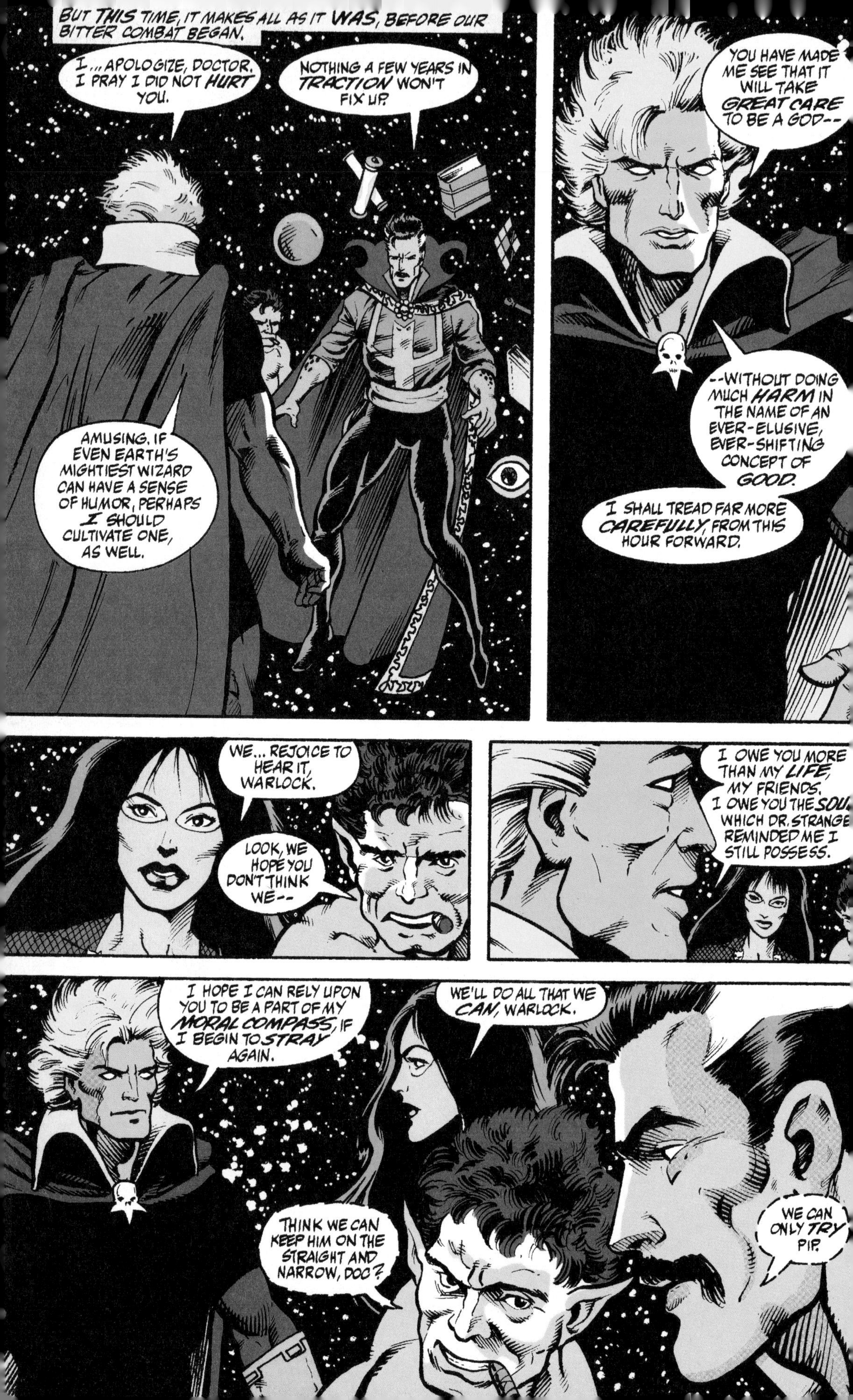
BUT THIS TIME, IT MAKES ALL AS IT WAS, BEFORE OUR BITTER COMBAT BEGAN.
I... APOLOGIZE, DOCTOR. I PRAY I DID NOT HURT YOU.
NOTHING A FEW YEARS IN TRACTION WON'T FIX UP.
AMUSING. IF EVEN EARTH'S MIGHTIEST WIZARD CAN HAVE A SENSE OF HUMOR, PERHAPS I SHOULD CULTIVATE ONE, AS WELL.
YOU HAVE MADE ME SEE THAT IT WILL TAKE GREAT CARE TO BE A GOD--
--WITHOUT DOING MUCH HARM IN THE NAME OF AN EVER-ELUSIVE, EVER-SHIFTING CONCEPT OF GOOD.
I SHALL TREAD FAR MORE CAREFULLY, FROM THIS HOUR FORWARD.
WE... REJOICE TO HEAR IT, WARLOCK.
LOOK, WE HOPE YOU DON'T THINK WE--
I OWE YOU MORE THAN MY LIFE, MY FRIENDS. I OWE YOU THE SOUL WHICH DR. STRANGE REMINDED ME I STILL POSSESS.
I HOPE I CAN RELY UPON YOU TO BE A PART OF MY MORAL COMPASS, IF I BEGIN TO STRAY AGAIN.
WE'LL DO ALL THAT WE CAN, WARLOCK.
THINK WE CAN KEEP HIM ON THE STRAIGHT AND NARROW, DOC?
WE CAN ONLY TRY, PIP.

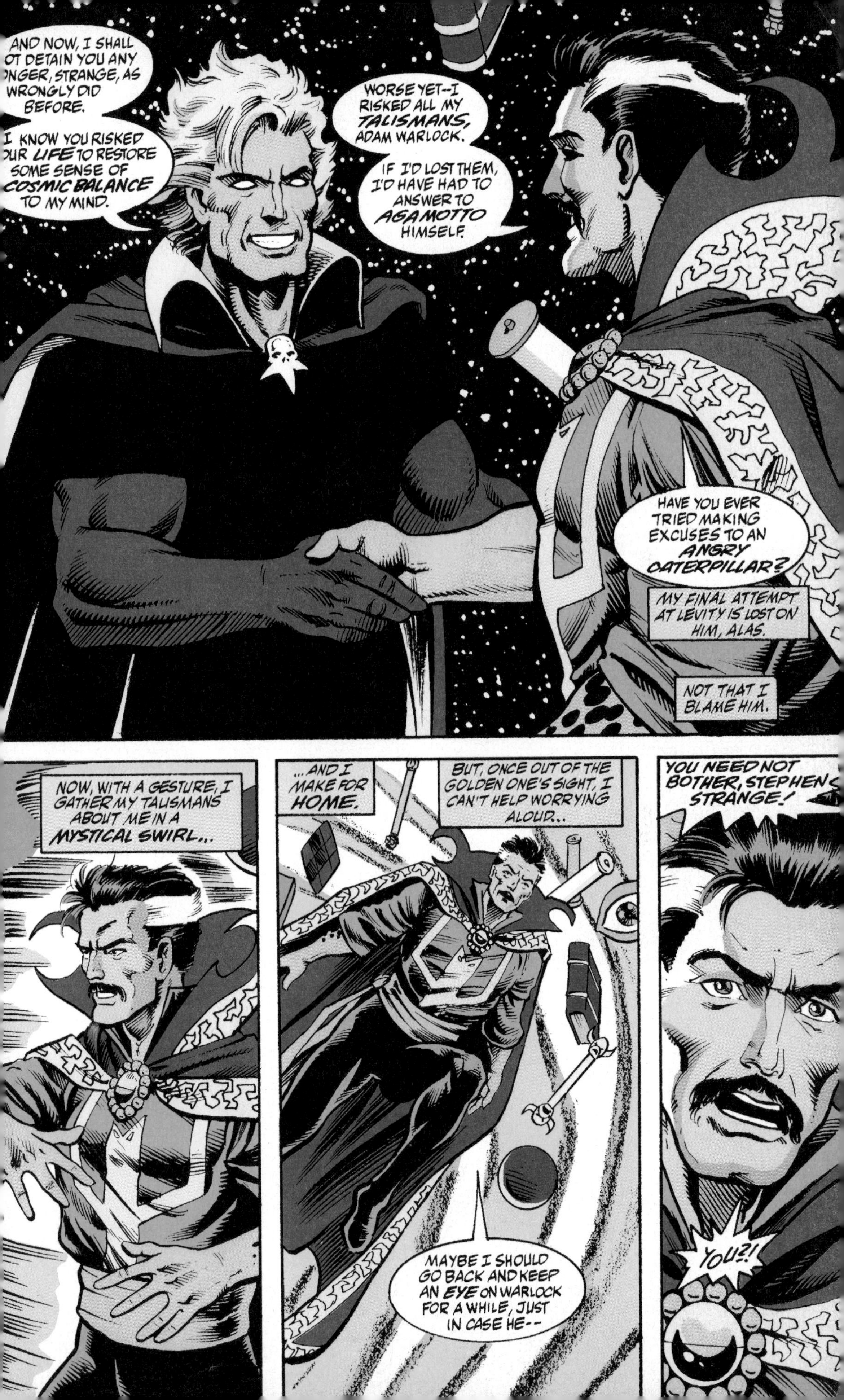
AND NOW, I SHALL OT DETAIN YOU ANY NGER, STRANGE, AS WRONGLY DID BEFORE.
I KNOW YOU RISKED UR LIFE TO RESTORE SOME SENSE OF COSMIC BALANCE TO MY MIND.
WORSE YET--I RISKED ALL MY TALISMANS, ADAM WARLOCK.
IF I'D LOST THEM, I'D HAVE HAD TO ANSWER TO AGAMOTTO HIMSELF.
HAVE YOU EVER TRIED MAKING EXCUSES TO AN ANGRY CATERPILLAR?
MY FINAL ATTEMPT AT LEVITY IS LOST ON HIM, ALAS.
NOT THAT I BLAME HIM.
NOW, WITH A GESTURE, I GATHER MY TALISMANS ABOUT ME IN A MYSTICAL SWIRL...
...AND I MAKE FOR HOME.
BUT, ONCE OUT OF THE GOLDEN ONE'S SIGHT, I CAN'T HELP WORRYING ALOUD...
MAYBE I SHOULD GO BACK AND KEEP AN EYE ON WARLOCK FOR A WHILE, JUST IN CASE HE--
YOU NEED NOT BOTHER, STEPHEN STRANGE!
YOU?!

YES, I-- **ETERNITY!**

I DARED NOT INTERVENE WHILE YOU AND ADAM WARLOCK WERE LOCKED IN BATTLE, LEST THE FATES OF **WORLDS YET UNBORN** BE AFFECTED.

BUT NOW THAT YOUR CONTEST IS ENDED, KNOW YOU **THIS**, MAGE:

I, **MYSELF** MEAN TO TAKE POSSESSION OF THE **INFINITY GEMS**, FOR THE GOOD OF **ALL THAT IS!**

BUT, IF YOU EVEN **TRY** -- THE RESULTANT STRUGGLE MIGHT WELL CAUSE EVEN MORE DAMAGE THAN **ADAM WARLOCK** COULD INFLICT ON THE COSMOS! AND-- HOW DO YOU INTEND TO **GET** THE JEWELS?

I SHALL BRING HIM TO **TRIAL** MORTAL. FAREWELLLLLL...

TRIAL? WAIT!

TOO LATE. THE ENTITY WHO IS THE **SENTIENT LIFE FORCE OF THE UNIVERSE...** IS GONE.

AND, I MUST CONFESS -- THAT'S ONE TRIAL WHERE I'D DEARLY LOVE TO BE A FLY ON THE WALL.

BUT JUST NOW...

...I'VE MORE DOWN-TO-EARTH MATTERS TO ATTEND TO.

MASTE-

I **TOLD** YOU HE WAS IN HERE, RINTRAH. WE JUST DIDN'T SEE HIM FOR A SECOND, THAT'S ALL.

IT MAY HAVE BEEN "**JUST A SECOND**" TO **YOU** TWO--

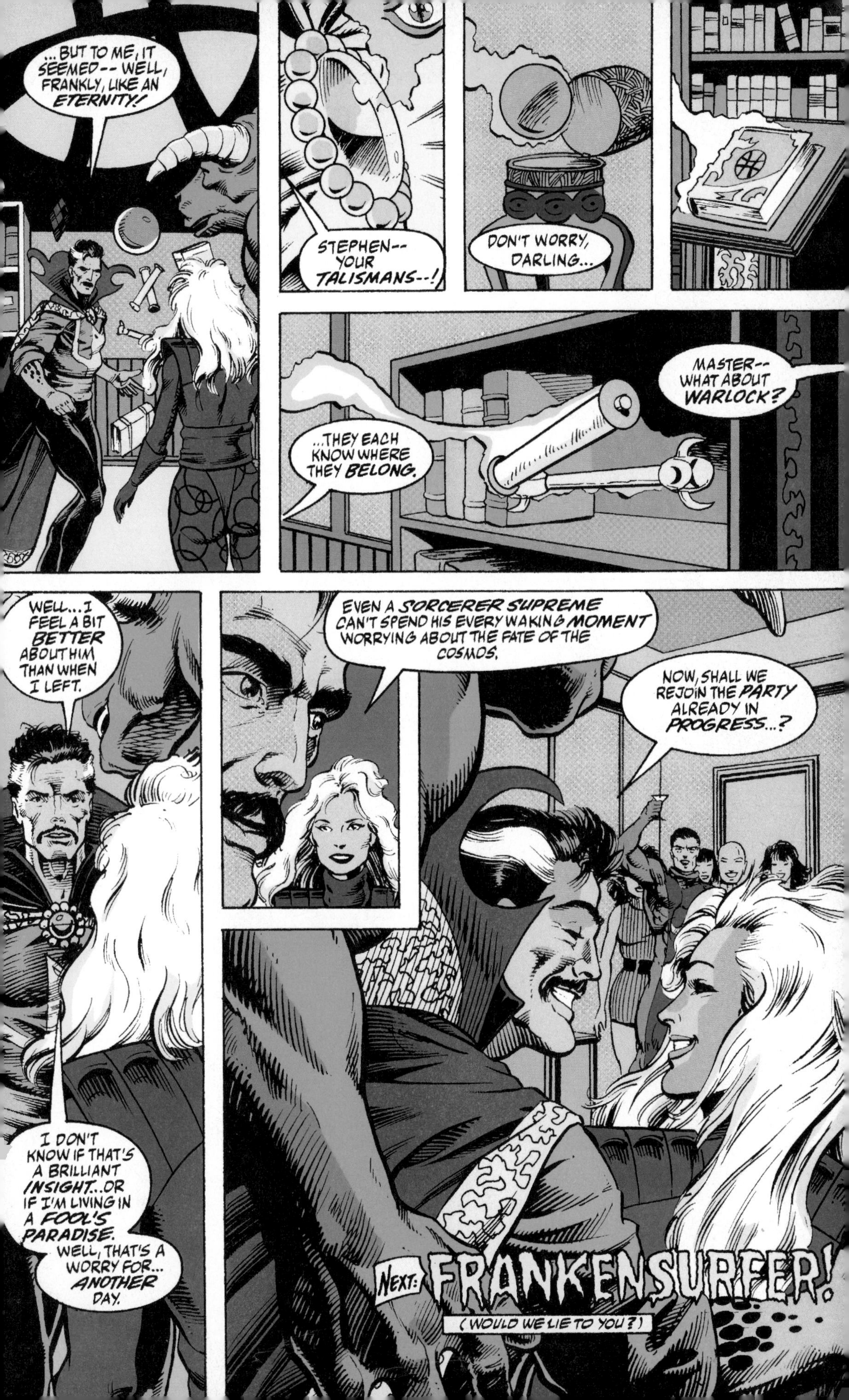
... BUT TO ME, IT SEEMED-- WELL, FRANKLY, LIKE AN ETERNITY!
STEPHEN-- YOUR TALISMANS--!
DON'T WORRY, DARLING...
...THEY EACH KNOW WHERE THEY BELONG.
MASTER-- WHAT ABOUT WARLOCK?
WELL... I FEEL A BIT BETTER ABOUT HIM THAN WHEN I LEFT.
I DON'T KNOW IF THAT'S A BRILLIANT INSIGHT...OR IF I'M LIVING IN A FOOL'S PARADISE.
WELL, THAT'S A WORRY FOR... ANOTHER DAY.
EVEN A SORCERER SUPREME CAN'T SPEND HIS EVERY WAKING MOMENT WORRYING ABOUT THE FATE OF THE COSMOS.
NOW, SHALL WE REJOIN THE PARTY ALREADY IN PROGRESS...?
NEXT: FRANKENSURFER!
(WOULD WE LIE TO YOU?)

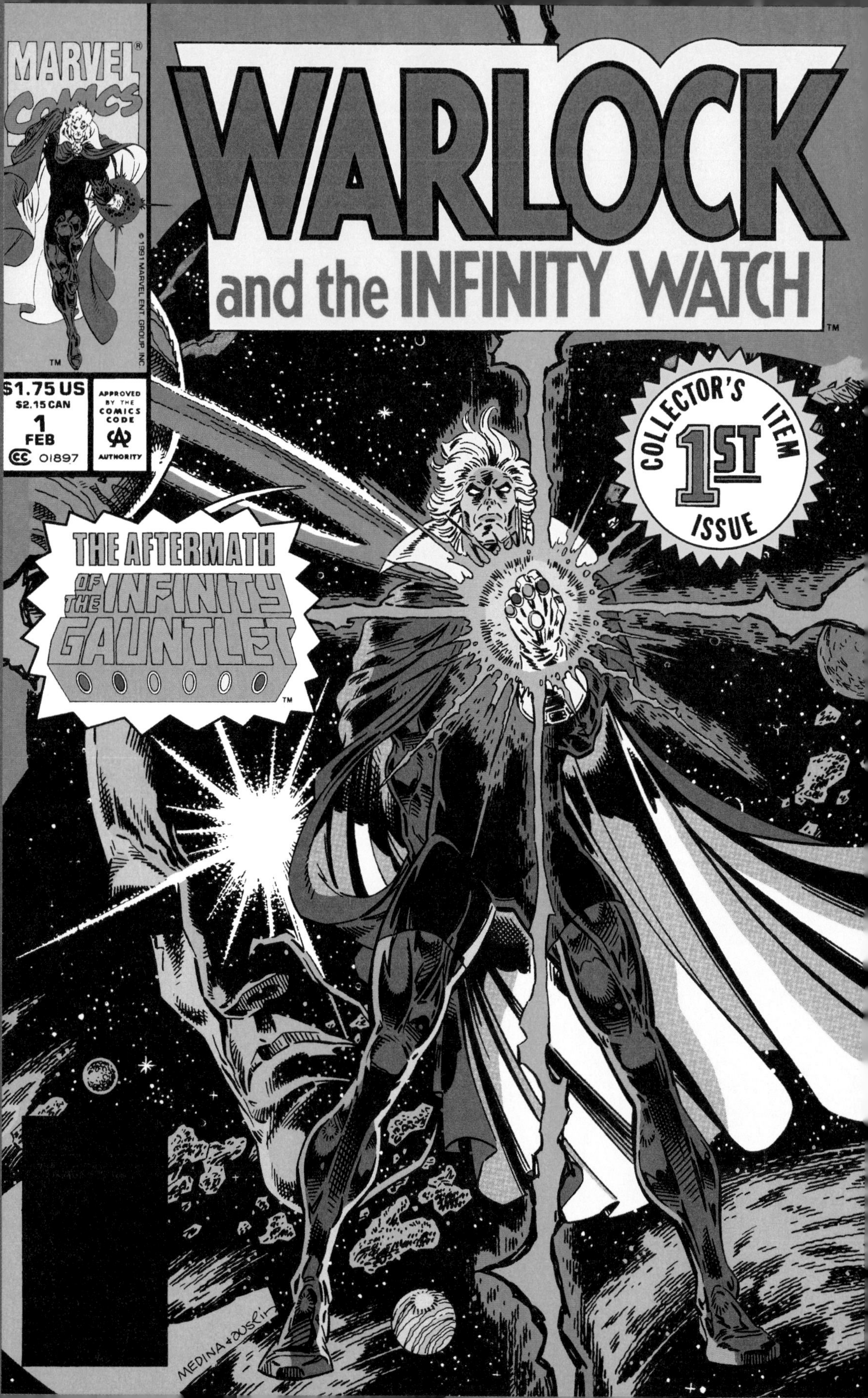
MARVEL COMICS
WARLOCK
and the INFINITY WATCH
$1.75 US
$2.15 CAN
1
FEB
01897
APPROVED BY THE COMICS CODE AUTHORITY
© 1991 MARVEL ENT. GROUP, INC.
COLLECTOR'S ITEM
1ST
ISSUE
THE AFTERMATH OF THE INFINITY GAUNTLET

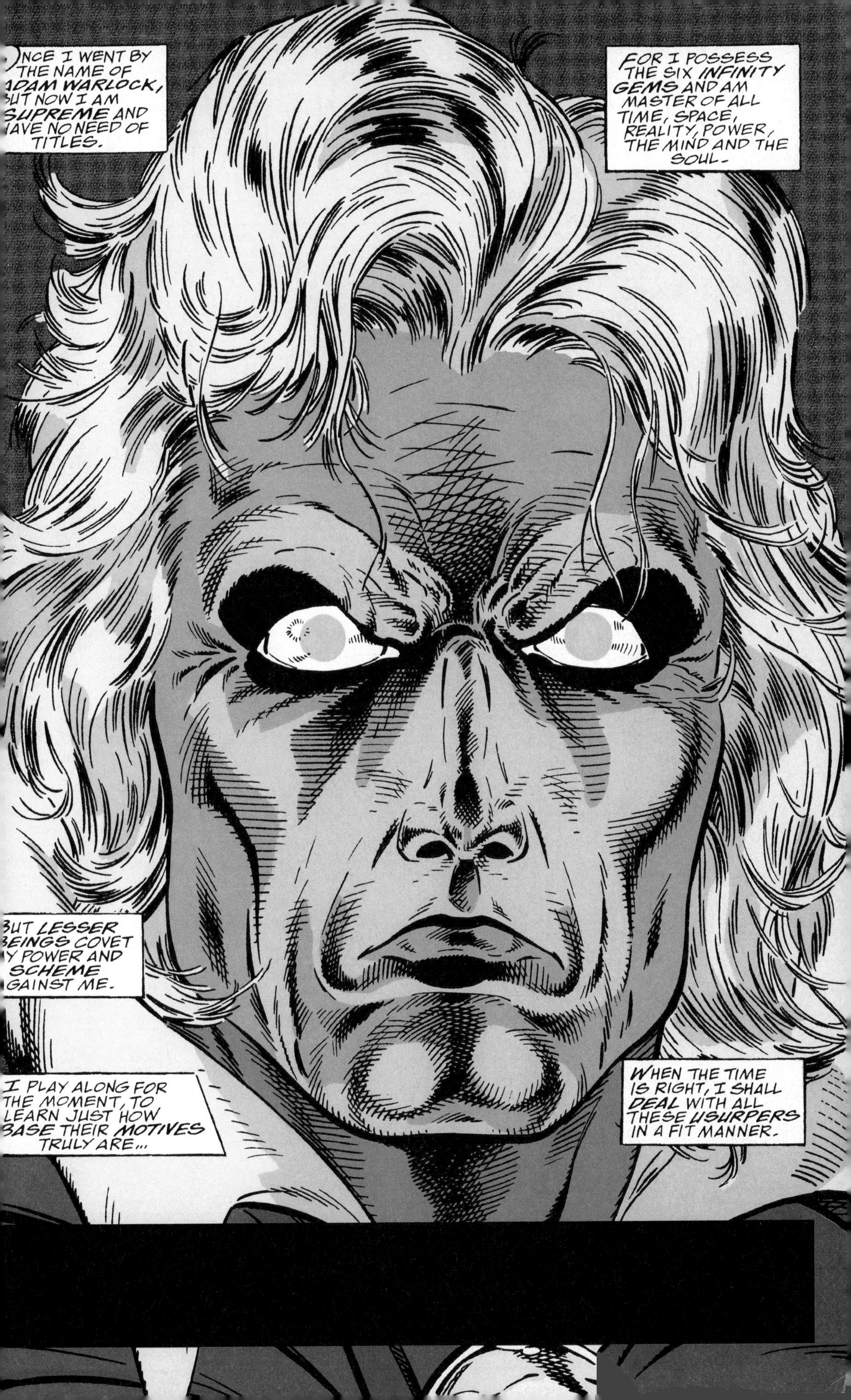
ONCE I WENT BY THE NAME OF ADAM WARLOCK, BUT NOW I AM SUPREME AND HAVE NO NEED OF TITLES.
FOR I POSSESS THE SIX INFINITY GEMS AND AM MASTER OF ALL TIME, SPACE, REALITY, POWER, THE MIND AND THE SOUL.
BUT LESSER BEINGS COVET MY POWER AND SCHEME AGAINST ME.
I PLAY ALONG FOR THE MOMENT, TO LEARN JUST HOW BASE THEIR MOTIVES TRULY ARE...
WHEN THE TIME IS RIGHT, I SHALL DEAL WITH ALL THESE USURPERS IN A FIT MANNER.
[redacted]

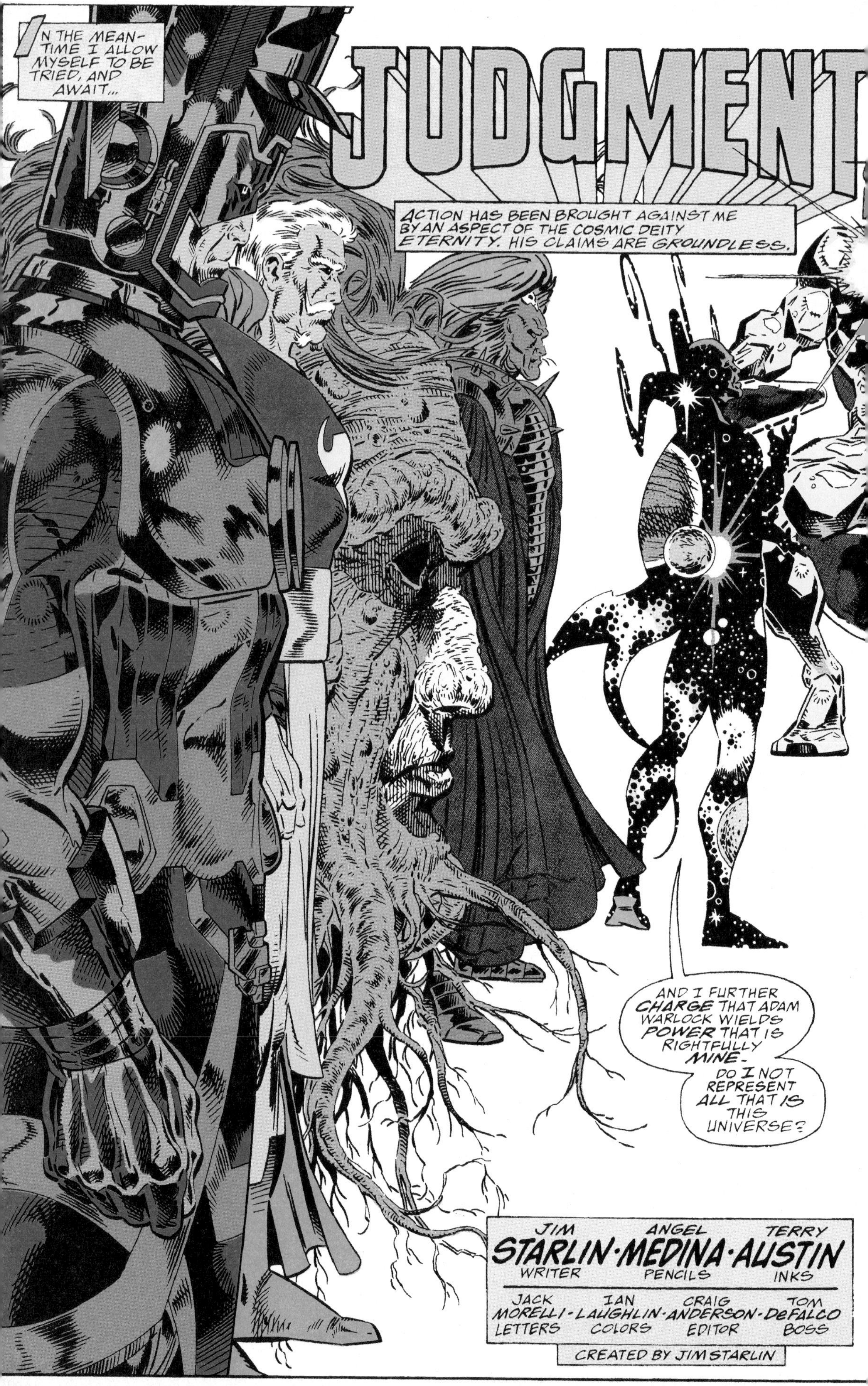
IN THE MEAN-TIME I ALLOW MYSELF TO BE TRIED, AND AWAIT...
JUDGMENT
ACTION HAS BEEN BROUGHT AGAINST ME BY AN ASPECT OF THE COSMIC DEITY ETERNITY. HIS CLAIMS ARE GROUNDLESS.
AND I FURTHER CHARGE THAT ADAM WARLOCK WIELDS POWER THAT IS RIGHTFULLY MINE-
DO I NOT REPRESENT ALL THAT IS THIS UNIVERSE?
JIM STARLIN WRITER · ANGEL MEDINA PENCILS · TERRY AUSTIN INKS
JACK MORELLI LETTERS · IAN LAUGHLIN COLORS · CRAIG ANDERSON EDITOR · TOM DeFALCO BOSS
CREATED BY JIM STARLIN

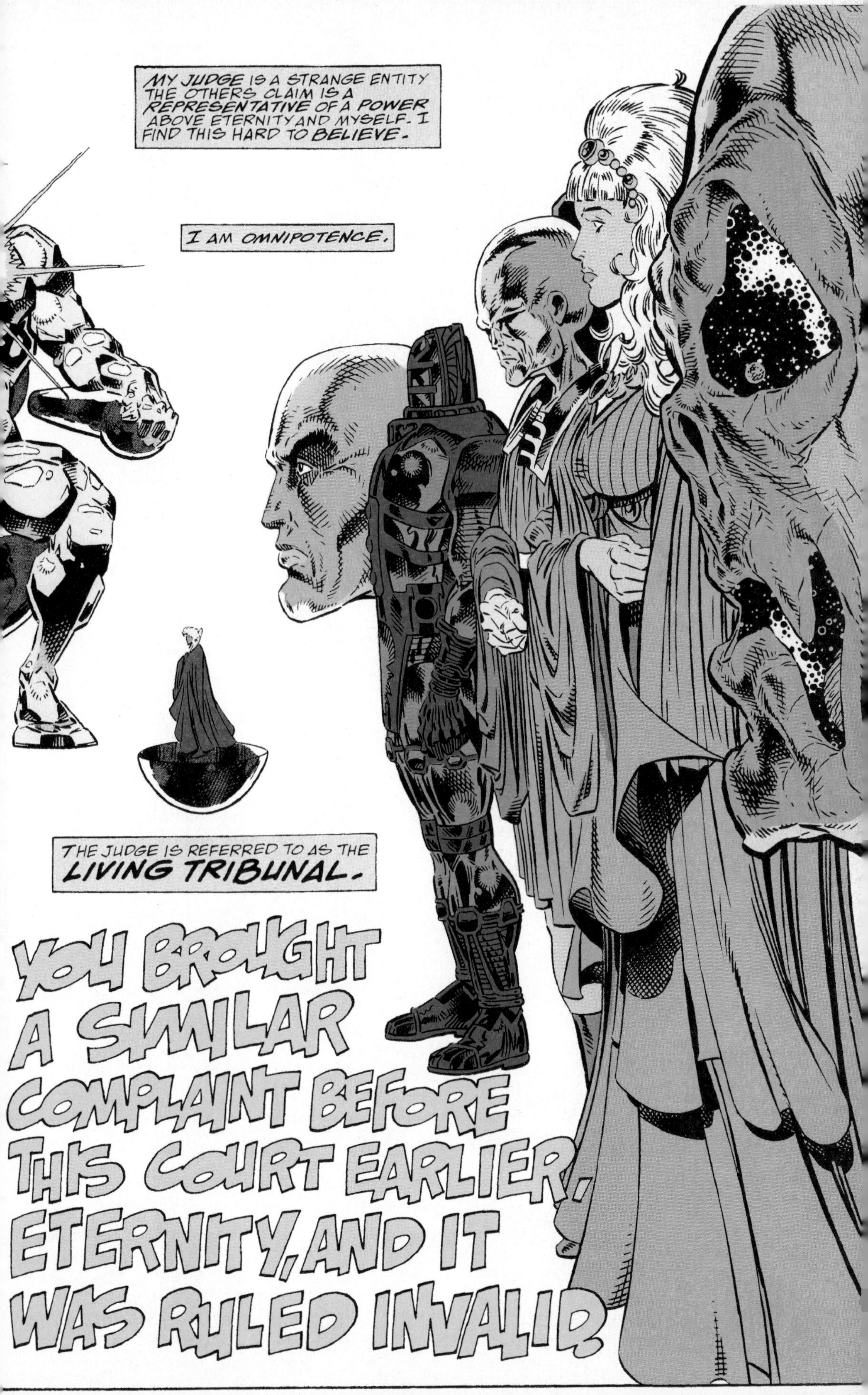
MY JUDGE IS A STRANGE ENTITY THE OTHERS CLAIM IS A REPRESENTATIVE OF A POWER ABOVE ETERNITY AND MYSELF. I FIND THIS HARD TO BELIEVE.
I AM OMNIPOTENCE.
THE JUDGE IS REFERRED TO AS THE LIVING TRIBUNAL.
YOU BROUGHT A SIMILAR COMPLAINT BEFORE THIS COURT EARLIER, ETERNITY, AND IT WAS RULED INVALID.

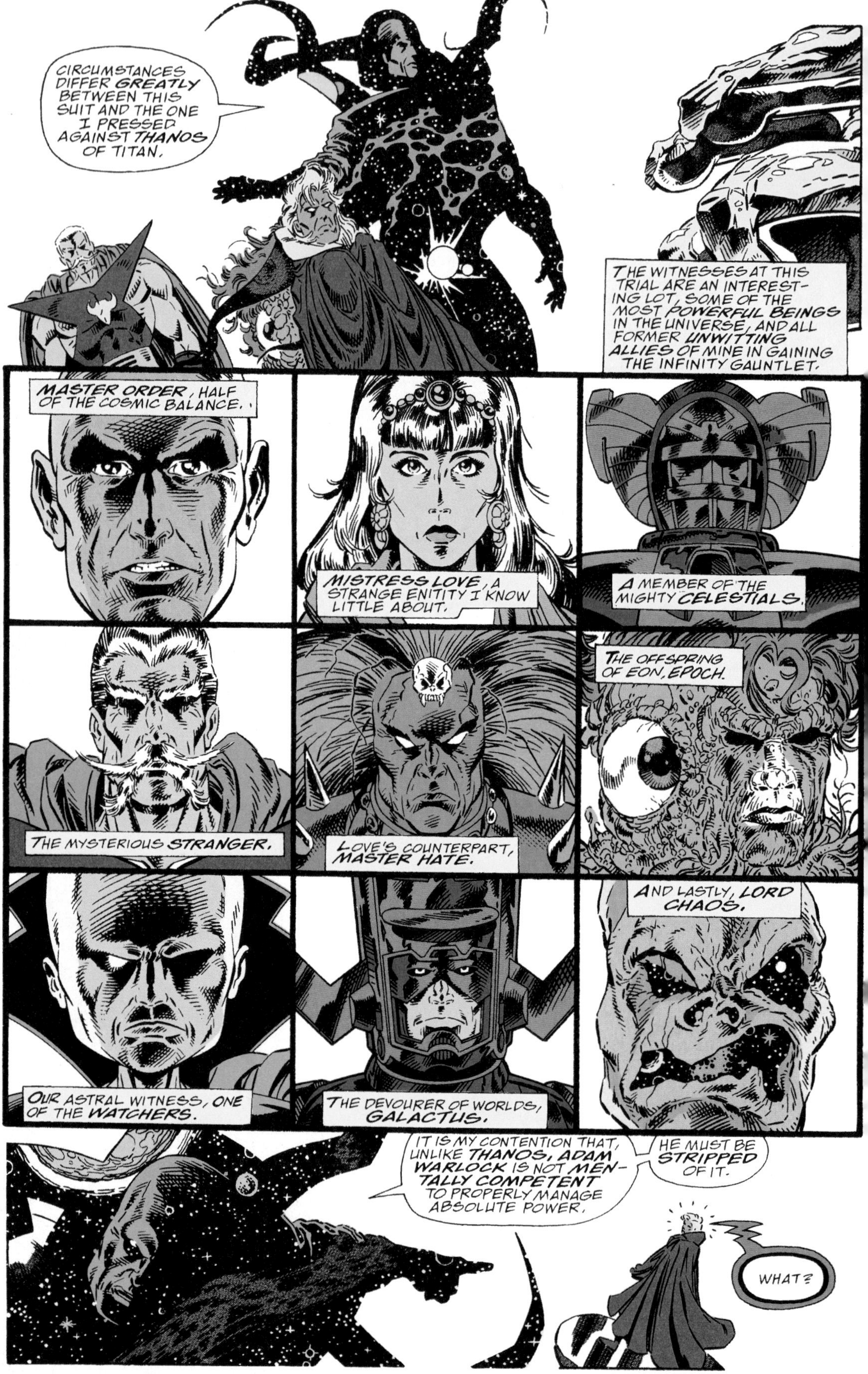
CIRCUMSTANCES DIFFER GREATLY BETWEEN THIS SUIT AND THE ONE I PRESSED AGAINST THANOS OF TITAN.
THE WITNESSES AT THIS TRIAL ARE AN INTERESTING LOT, SOME OF THE MOST POWERFUL BEINGS IN THE UNIVERSE, AND ALL FORMER UNWITTING ALLIES OF MINE IN GAINING THE INFINITY GAUNTLET.
MASTER ORDER, HALF OF THE COSMIC BALANCE.
MISTRESS LOVE, A STRANGE ENITITY I KNOW LITTLE ABOUT.
A MEMBER OF THE MIGHTY CELESTIALS.
THE MYSTERIOUS STRANGER.
LOVE'S COUNTERPART, MASTER HATE.
THE OFFSPRING OF EON, EPOCH.
OUR ASTRAL WITNESS, ONE OF THE WATCHERS.
THE DEVOURER OF WORLDS, GALACTUS.
AND LASTLY, LORD CHAOS.
IT IS MY CONTENTION THAT, UNLIKE THANOS, ADAM WARLOCK IS NOT MENTALLY COMPETENT TO PROPERLY MANAGE ABSOLUTE POWER.
HE MUST BE STRIPPED OF IT.
WHAT?

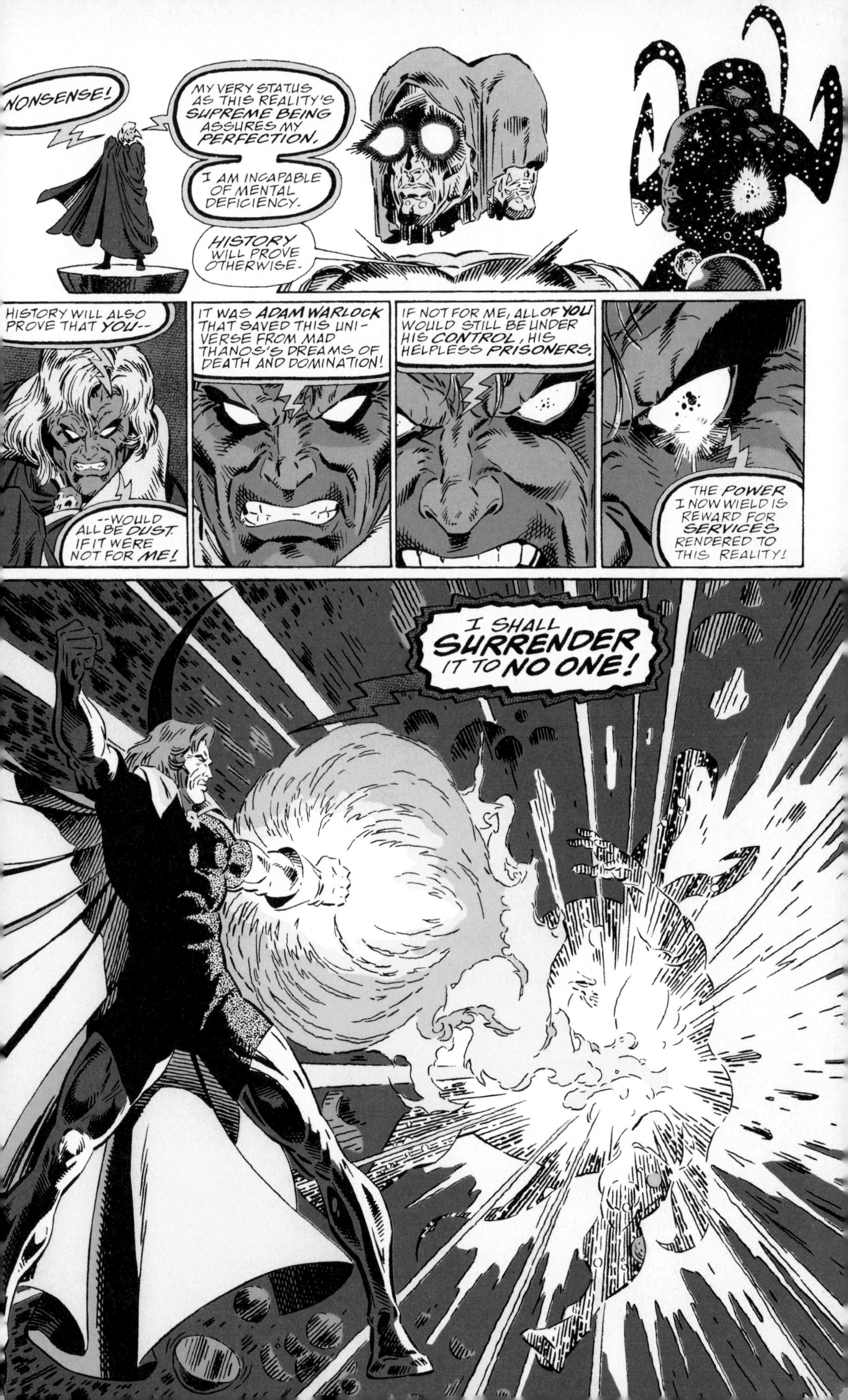
NONSENSE!
MY VERY STATUS AS THIS REALITY'S SUPREME BEING ASSURES MY PERFECTION.
I AM INCAPABLE OF MENTAL DEFICIENCY.
HISTORY WILL PROVE OTHERWISE.
HISTORY WILL ALSO PROVE THAT YOU--
--WOULD ALL BE DUST IF IT WERE NOT FOR ME!
IT WAS ADAM WARLOCK THAT SAVED THIS UNI-VERSE FROM MAD THANOS'S DREAMS OF DEATH AND DOMINATION!
IF NOT FOR ME, ALL OF YOU WOULD STILL BE UNDER HIS CONTROL, HIS HELPLESS PRISONERS.
THE POWER I NOW WIELD IS REWARD FOR SERVICES RENDERED TO THIS REALITY!
I SHALL SURRENDER IT TO NO ONE!

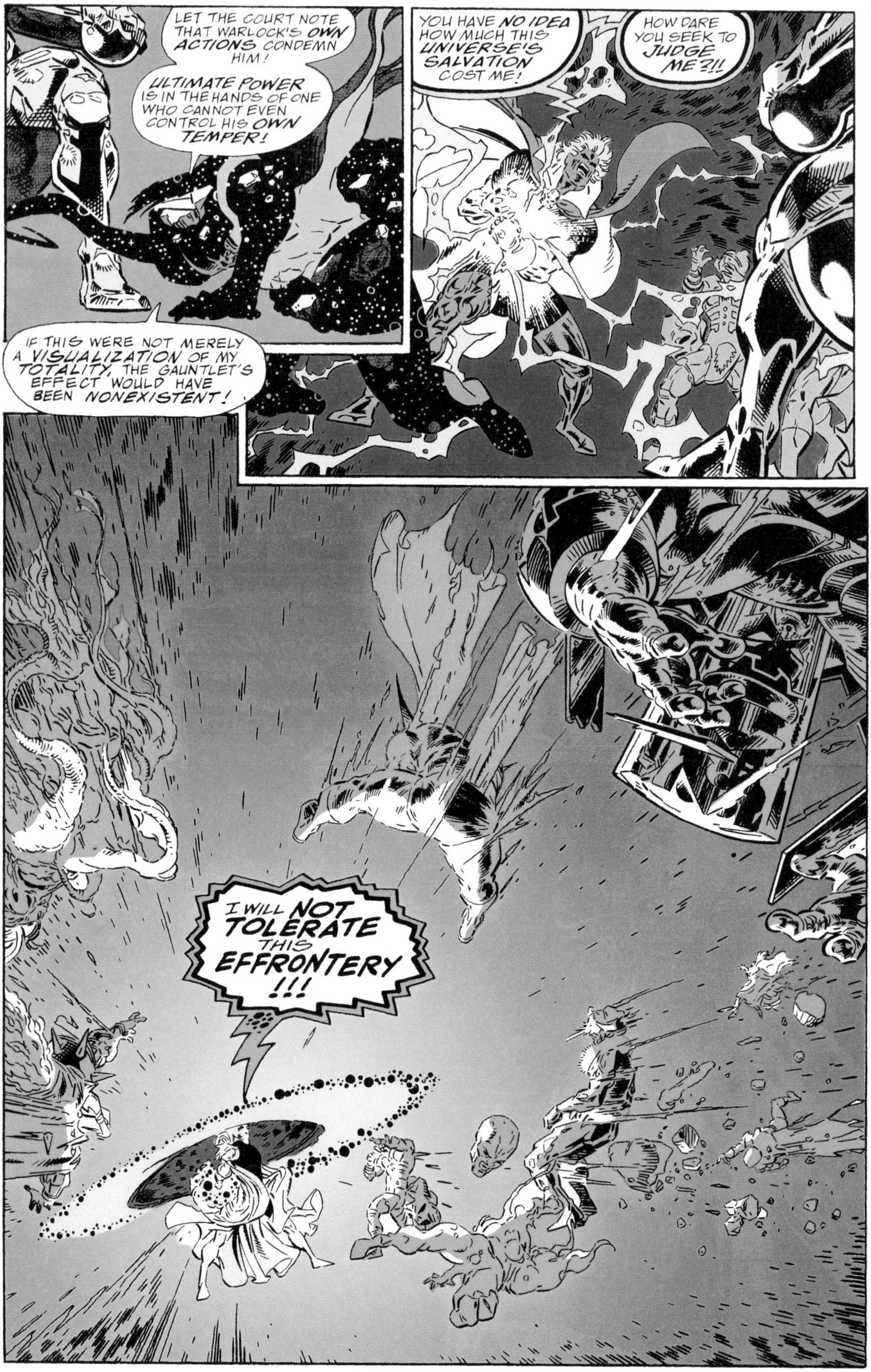
LET THE COURT NOTE THAT WARLOCK'S OWN ACTIONS CONDEMN HIM!
ULTIMATE POWER IS IN THE HANDS OF ONE WHO CANNOT EVEN CONTROL HIS OWN TEMPER!
YOU HAVE NO IDEA HOW MUCH THIS UNIVERSE'S SALVATION COST ME!
HOW DARE YOU SEEK TO JUDGE ME?!!
IF THIS WERE NOT MERELY A VISUALIZATION OF MY TOTALITY, THE GAUNTLET'S EFFECT WOULD HAVE BEEN NONEXISTENT!
I WILL NOT TOLERATE THIS EFFRONTERY!!!

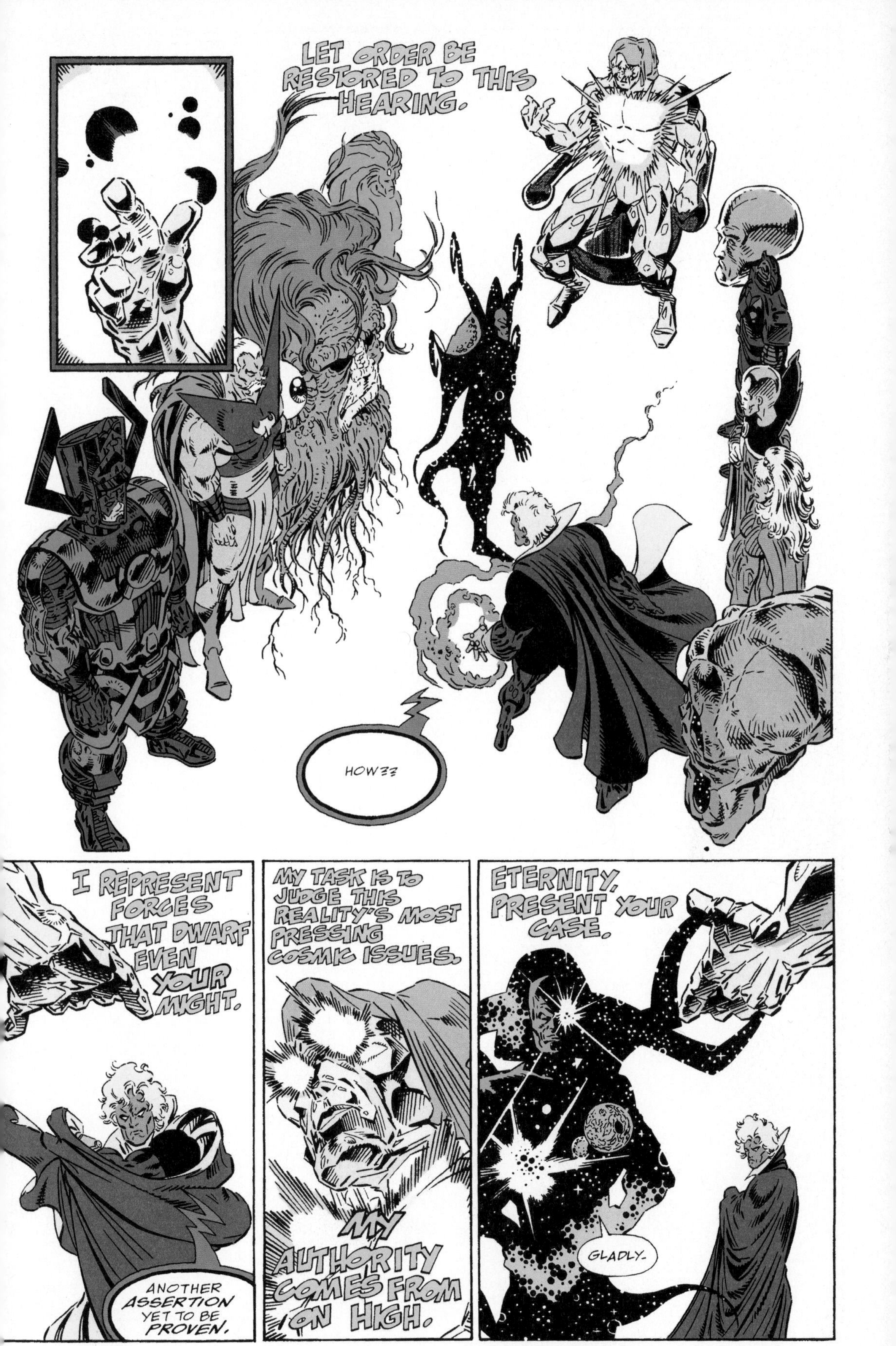
LET ORDER BE RESTORED TO THIS HEARING.
HOW??
I REPRESENT FORCES THAT DWARF EVEN YOUR MIGHT.
ANOTHER ASSERTION YET TO BE PROVEN.
MY TASK IS TO JUDGE THIS REALITY'S MOST PRESSING COSMIC ISSUES.
MY AUTHORITY COMES FROM ON HIGH.
ETERNITY, PRESENT YOUR CASE.
GLADLY.

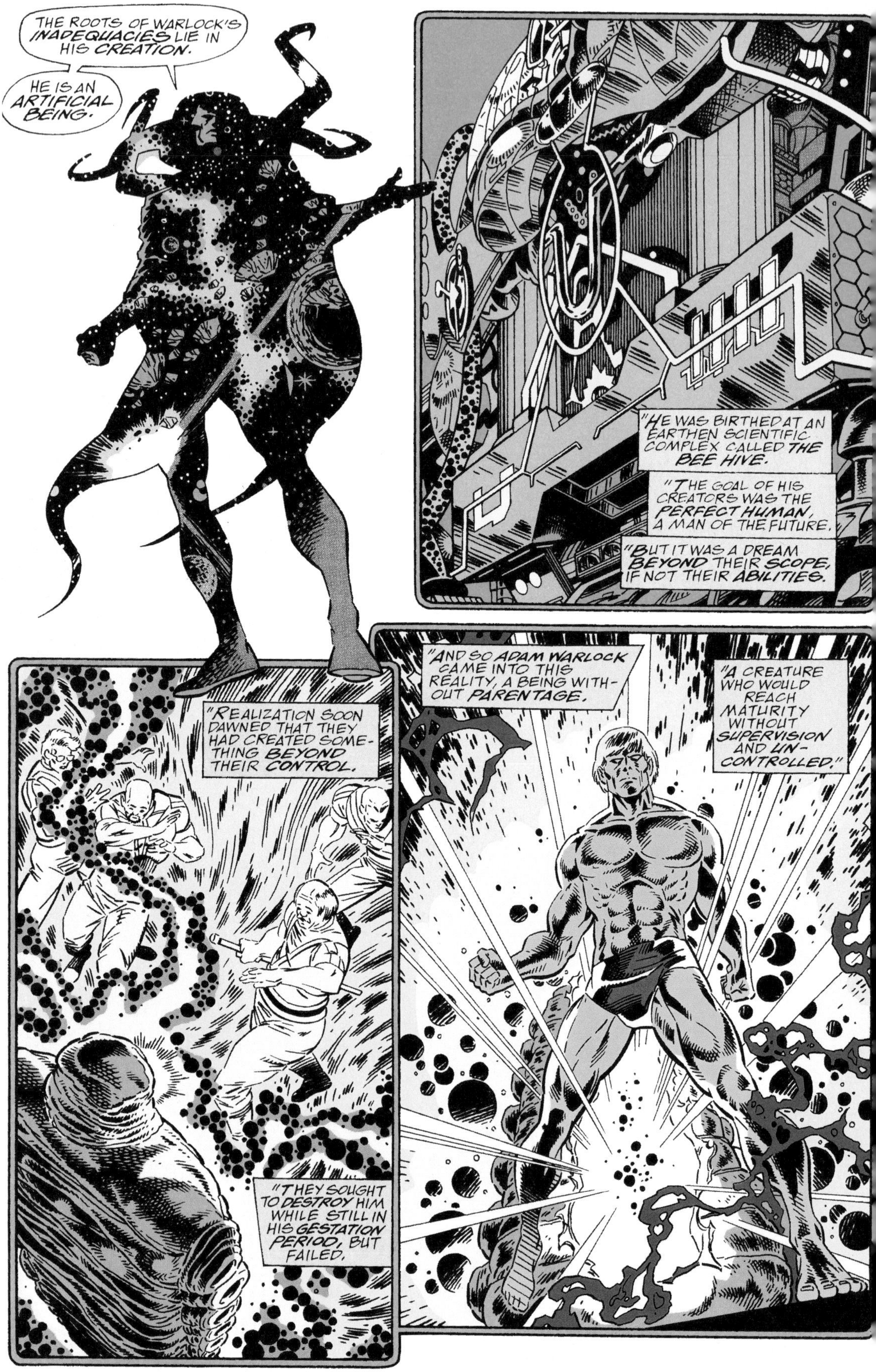
THE ROOTS OF WARLOCK'S INADEQUACIES LIE IN HIS CREATION.
HE IS AN ARTIFICIAL BEING.
"HE WAS BIRTHED AT AN EARTHEN SCIENTIFIC COMPLEX CALLED THE BEE HIVE.
"THE GOAL OF HIS CREATORS WAS THE PERFECT HUMAN, A MAN OF THE FUTURE.
"BUT IT WAS A DREAM BEYOND THEIR SCOPE, IF NOT THEIR ABILITIES.
"REALIZATION SOON DAWNED THAT THEY HAD CREATED SOMETHING BEYOND THEIR CONTROL.
"THEY SOUGHT TO DESTROY HIM WHILE STILL IN HIS GESTATION PERIOD, BUT FAILED.
"AND SO ADAM WARLOCK CAME INTO THIS REALITY, A BEING WITHOUT PARENTAGE.
"A CREATURE WHO WOULD REACH MATURITY WITHOUT SUPERVISION AND UNCONTROLLED."

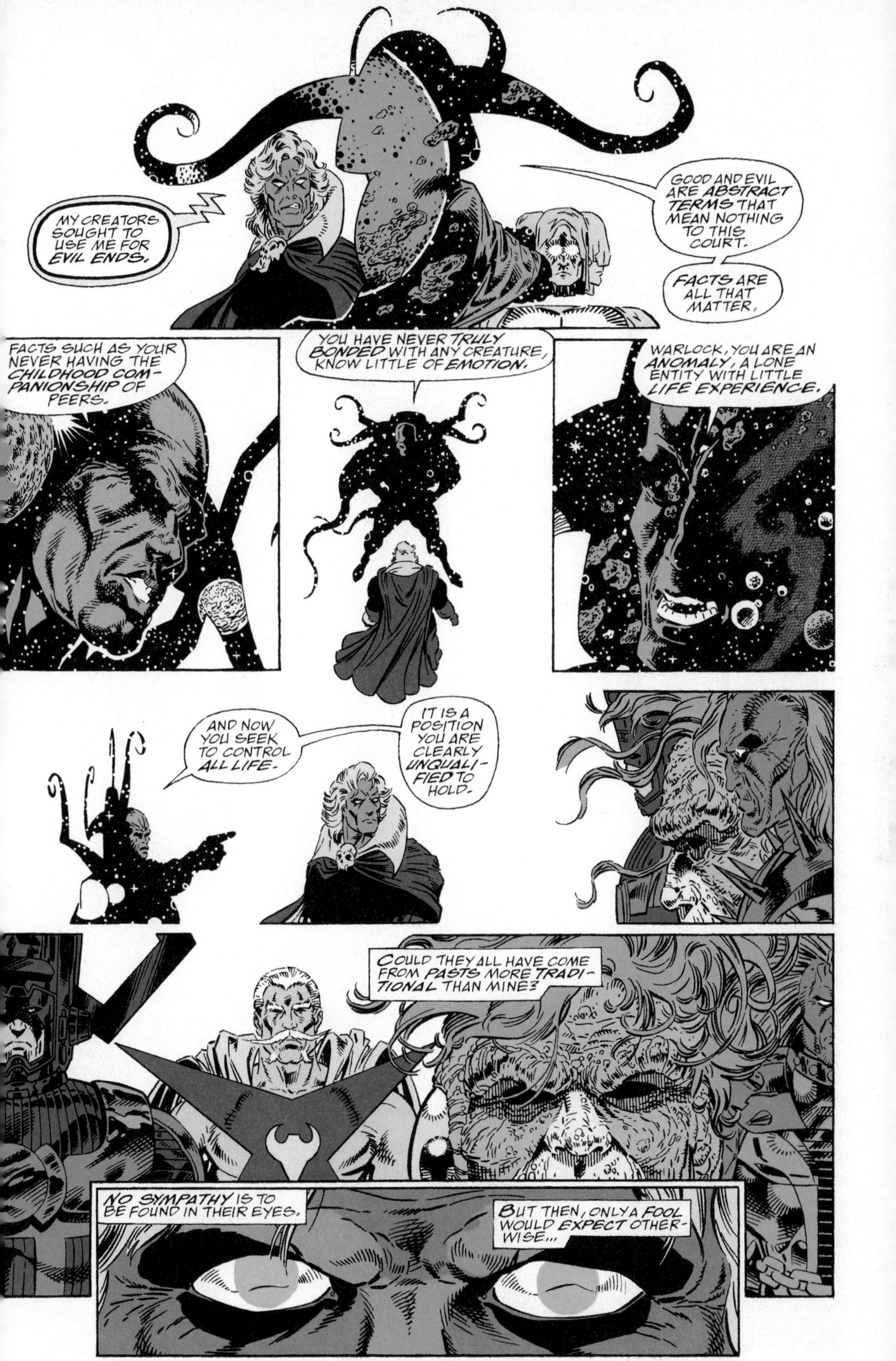
MY CREATORS SOUGHT TO USE ME FOR EVIL ENDS.
GOOD AND EVIL ARE ABSTRACT TERMS THAT MEAN NOTHING TO THIS COURT.
FACTS ARE ALL THAT MATTER.
FACTS SUCH AS YOUR NEVER HAVING THE CHILDHOOD COMPANIONSHIP OF PEERS.
YOU HAVE NEVER TRULY BONDED WITH ANY CREATURE, KNOW LITTLE OF EMOTION.
WARLOCK, YOU ARE AN ANOMALY, A LONE ENTITY WITH LITTLE LIFE EXPERIENCE.
AND NOW YOU SEEK TO CONTROL ALL LIFE.
IT IS A POSITION YOU ARE CLEARLY UNQUALIFIED TO HOLD.
COULD THEY ALL HAVE COME FROM PASTS MORE TRADITIONAL THAN MINE?
NO SYMPATHY IS TO BE FOUND IN THEIR EYES.
BUT THEN, ONLY A FOOL WOULD EXPECT OTHERWISE...

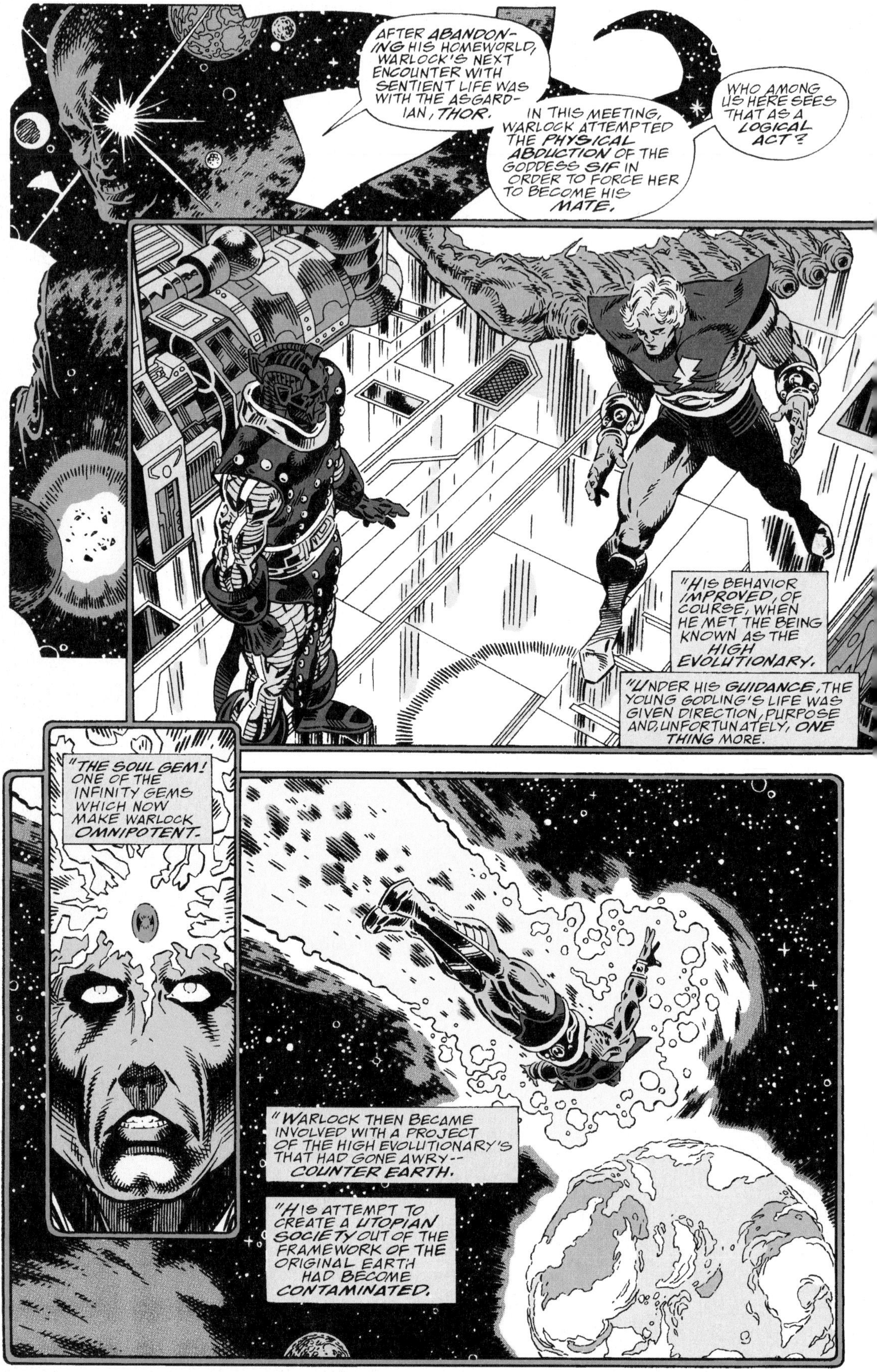

AFTER ABANDONING HIS HOMEWORLD, WARLOCK'S NEXT ENCOUNTER WITH SENTIENT LIFE WAS WITH THE ASGARDIAN, THOR.
IN THIS MEETING, WARLOCK ATTEMPTED THE PHYSICAL ABDUCTION OF THE GODDESS SIF IN ORDER TO FORCE HER TO BECOME HIS MATE.
WHO AMONG US HERE SEES THAT AS A LOGICAL ACT?
"HIS BEHAVIOR IMPROVED, OF COURSE, WHEN HE MET THE BEING KNOWN AS THE HIGH EVOLUTIONARY.
"UNDER HIS GUIDANCE, THE YOUNG GODLING'S LIFE WAS GIVEN DIRECTION, PURPOSE AND, UNFORTUNATELY, ONE THING MORE.
"THE SOUL GEM! ONE OF THE INFINITY GEMS WHICH NOW MAKE WARLOCK OMNIPOTENT.
"WARLOCK THEN BECAME INVOLVED WITH A PROJECT OF THE HIGH EVOLUTIONARY'S THAT HAD GONE AWRY-- COUNTER EARTH.
"HIS ATTEMPT TO CREATE A UTOPIAN SOCIETY OUT OF THE FRAMEWORK OF THE ORIGINAL EARTH HAD BECOME CONTAMINATED.

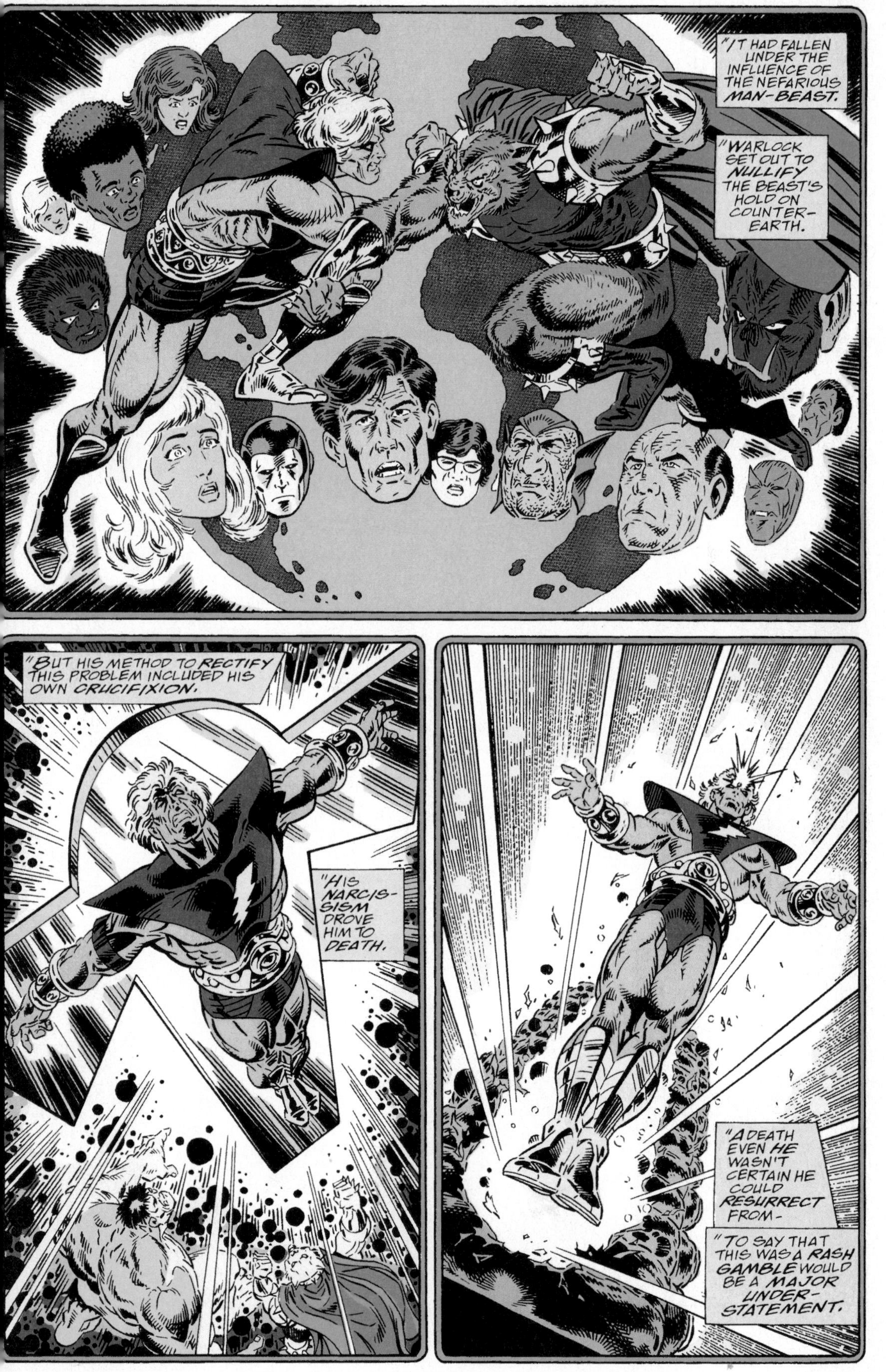
"IT HAD FALLEN UNDER THE INFLUENCE OF THE NEFARIOUS MAN-BEAST.
"WARLOCK SET OUT TO NULLIFY THE BEAST'S HOLD ON COUNTER-EARTH.
"BUT HIS METHOD TO RECTIFY THIS PROBLEM INCLUDED HIS OWN CRUCIFIXION.
"HIS NARCISSISM DROVE HIM TO DEATH.
"A DEATH EVEN HE WASN'T CERTAIN HE COULD RESURRECT FROM-
"TO SAY THAT THIS WAS A RASH GAMBLE WOULD BE A MAJOR UNDERSTATEMENT.

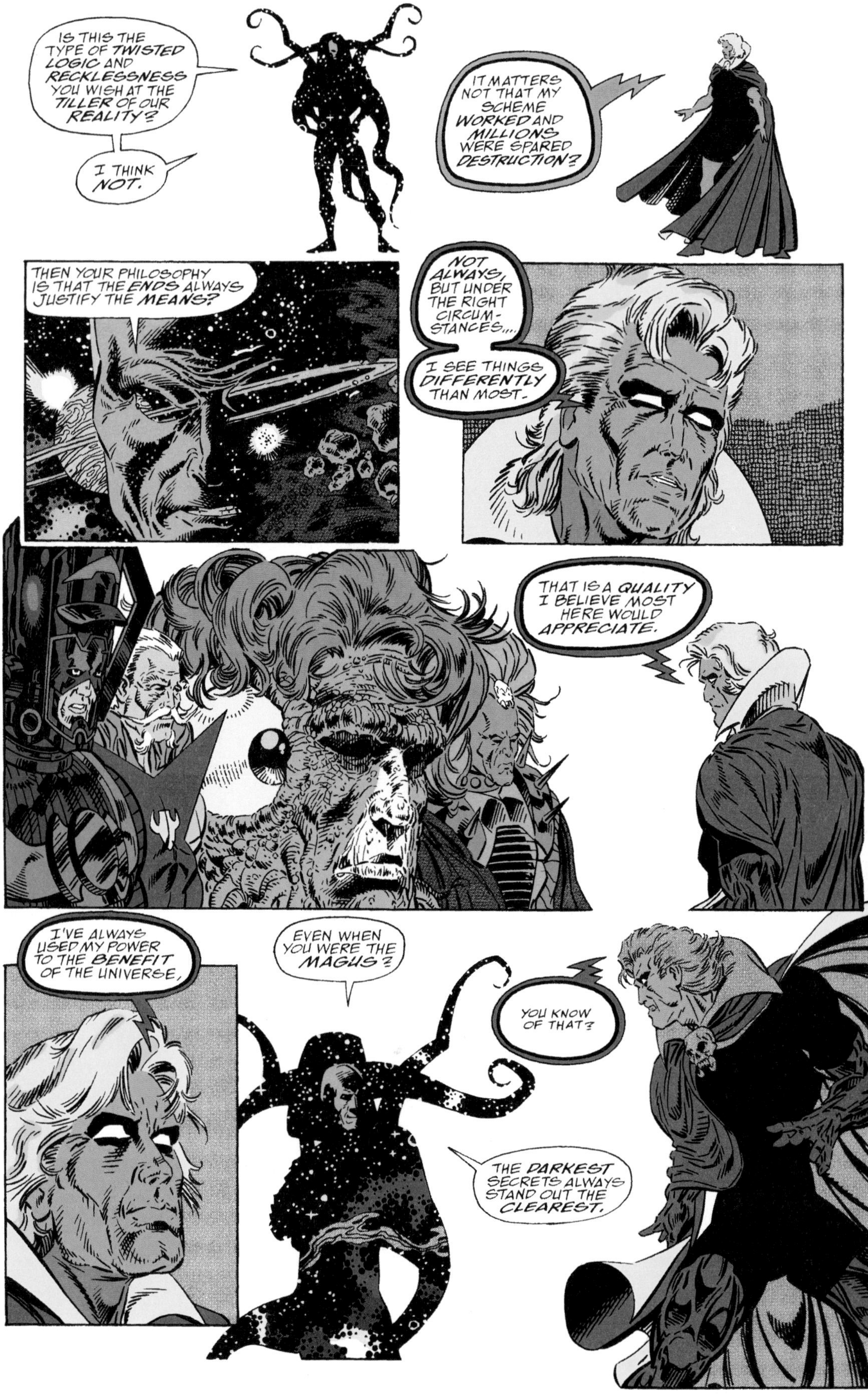
IS THIS THE TYPE OF TWISTED LOGIC AND RECKLESSNESS YOU WISH AT THE TILLER OF OUR REALITY?
I THINK NOT.
IT MATTERS NOT THAT MY SCHEME WORKED AND MILLIONS WERE SPARED DESTRUCTION?
THEN YOUR PHILOSOPHY IS THAT THE ENDS ALWAYS JUSTIFY THE MEANS?
NOT ALWAYS, BUT UNDER THE RIGHT CIRCUM-STANCES...
I SEE THINGS DIFFERENTLY THAN MOST.
THAT IS A QUALITY I BELIEVE MOST HERE WOULD APPRECIATE.
I'VE ALWAYS USED MY POWER TO THE BENEFIT OF THE UNIVERSE.
EVEN WHEN YOU WERE THE MAGUS?
YOU KNOW OF THAT?
THE DARKEST SECRETS ALWAYS STAND OUT THE CLEAREST.

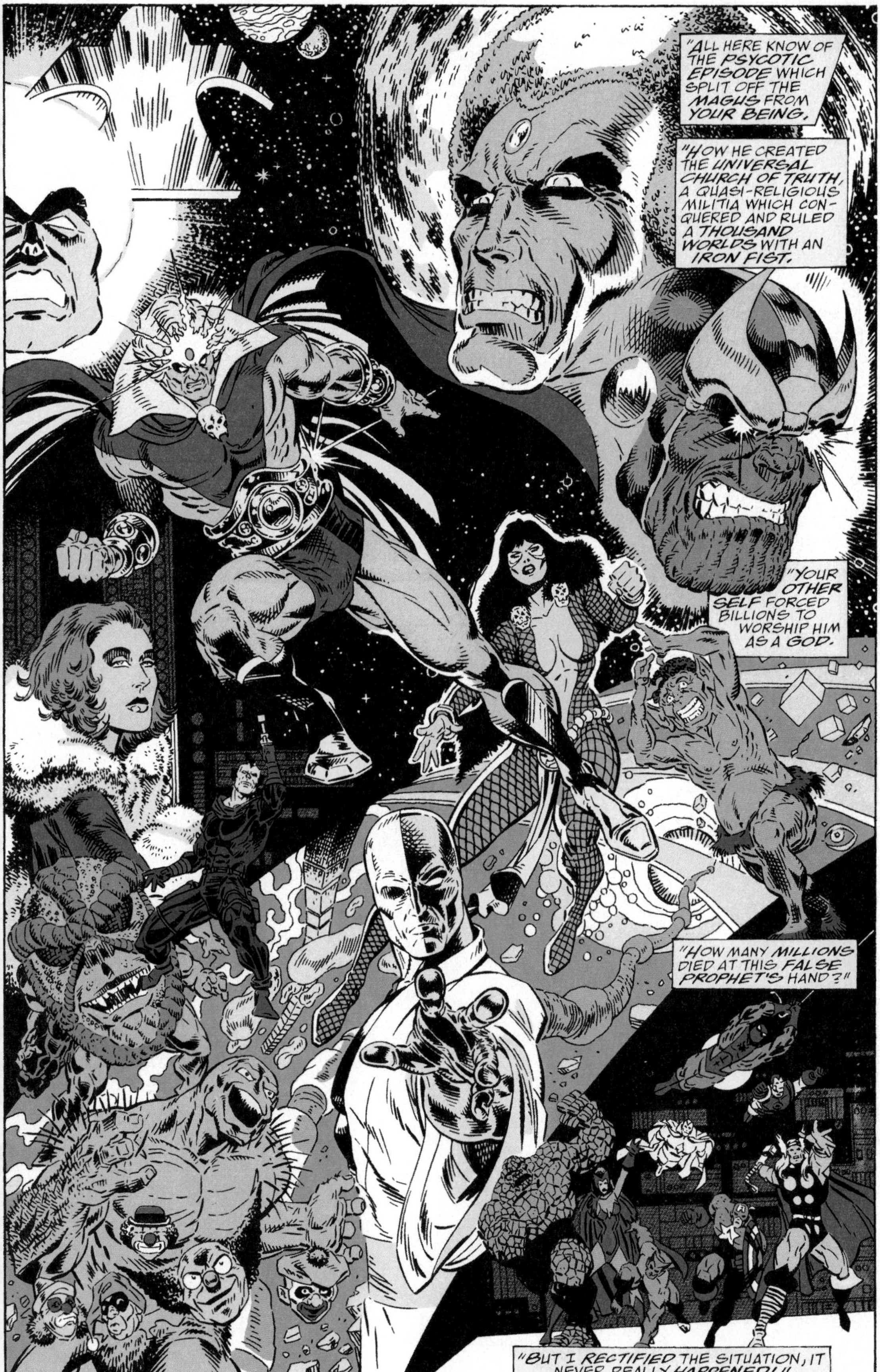
"ALL HERE KNOW OF THE PSYCOTIC EPISODE WHICH SPLIT OFF THE MAGUS FROM YOUR BEING.
"HOW HE CREATED THE UNIVERSAL CHURCH OF TRUTH, A QUASI-RELIGIOUS MILITIA WHICH CONQUERED AND RULED A THOUSAND WORLDS WITH AN IRON FIST.
"YOUR OTHER SELF FORCED BILLIONS TO WORSHIP HIM AS A GOD.
"HOW MANY MILLIONS DIED AT THIS FALSE PROPHET'S HAND?"
"BUT I RECTIFIED THE SITUATION, IT NEVER REALLY HAPPENED!"

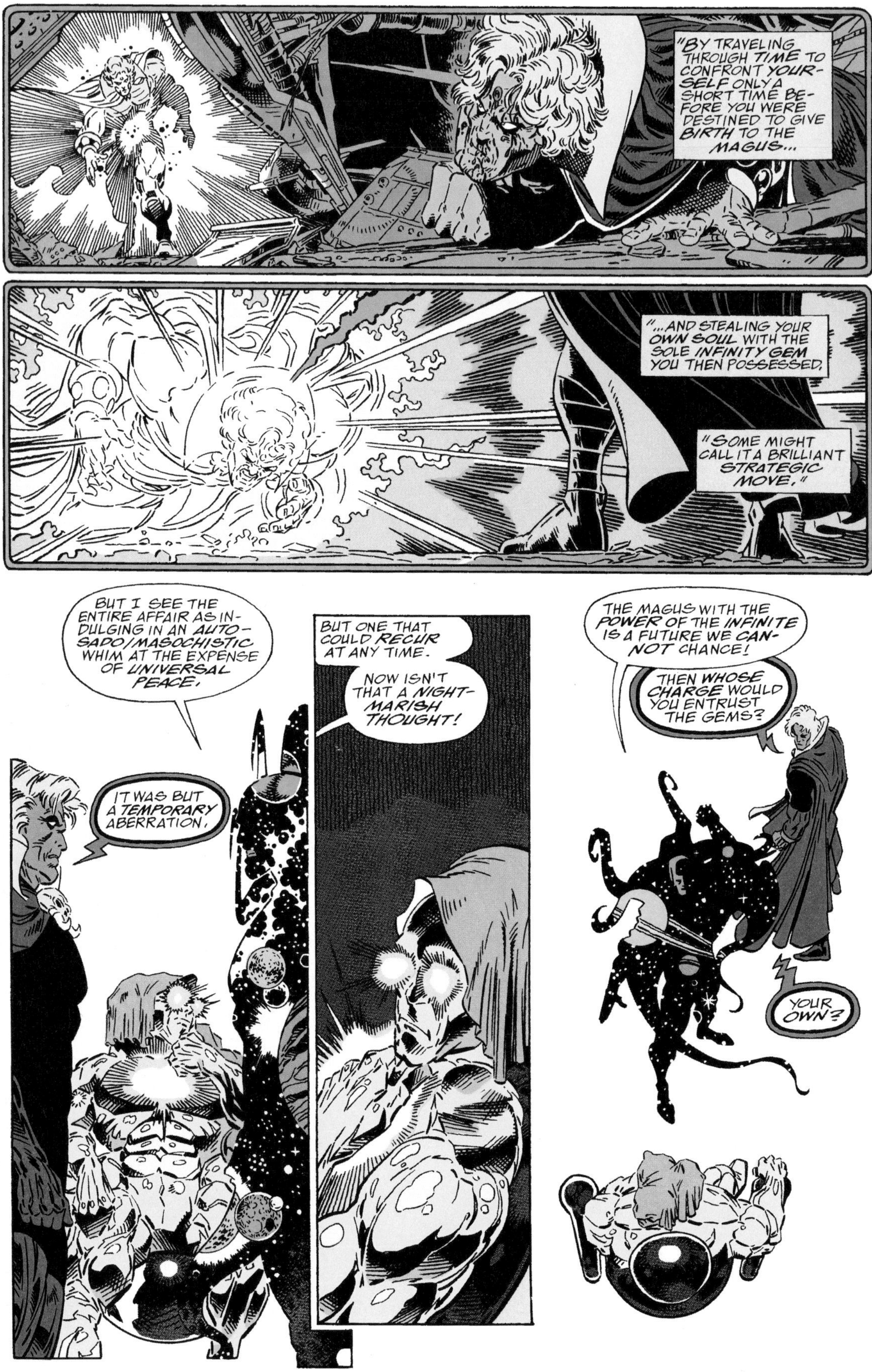
"BY TRAVELING THROUGH TIME TO CONFRONT YOURSELF ONLY A SHORT TIME BEFORE YOU WERE DESTINED TO GIVE BIRTH TO THE MAGUS...
"...AND STEALING YOUR OWN SOUL WITH THE SOLE INFINITY GEM YOU THEN POSSESSED.
"SOME MIGHT CALL IT A BRILLIANT STRATEGIC MOVE."
BUT I SEE THE ENTIRE AFFAIR AS INDULGING IN AN AUTO-SADO/MASOCHISTIC WHIM AT THE EXPENSE OF UNIVERSAL PEACE.
IT WAS BUT A TEMPORARY ABERRATION.
BUT ONE THAT COULD RECUR AT ANY TIME.
NOW ISN'T THAT A NIGHTMARISH THOUGHT!
THE MAGUS WITH THE POWER OF THE INFINITE IS A FUTURE WE CANNOT CHANCE!
THEN WHOSE CHARGE WOULD YOU ENTRUST THE GEMS?
YOUR OWN?

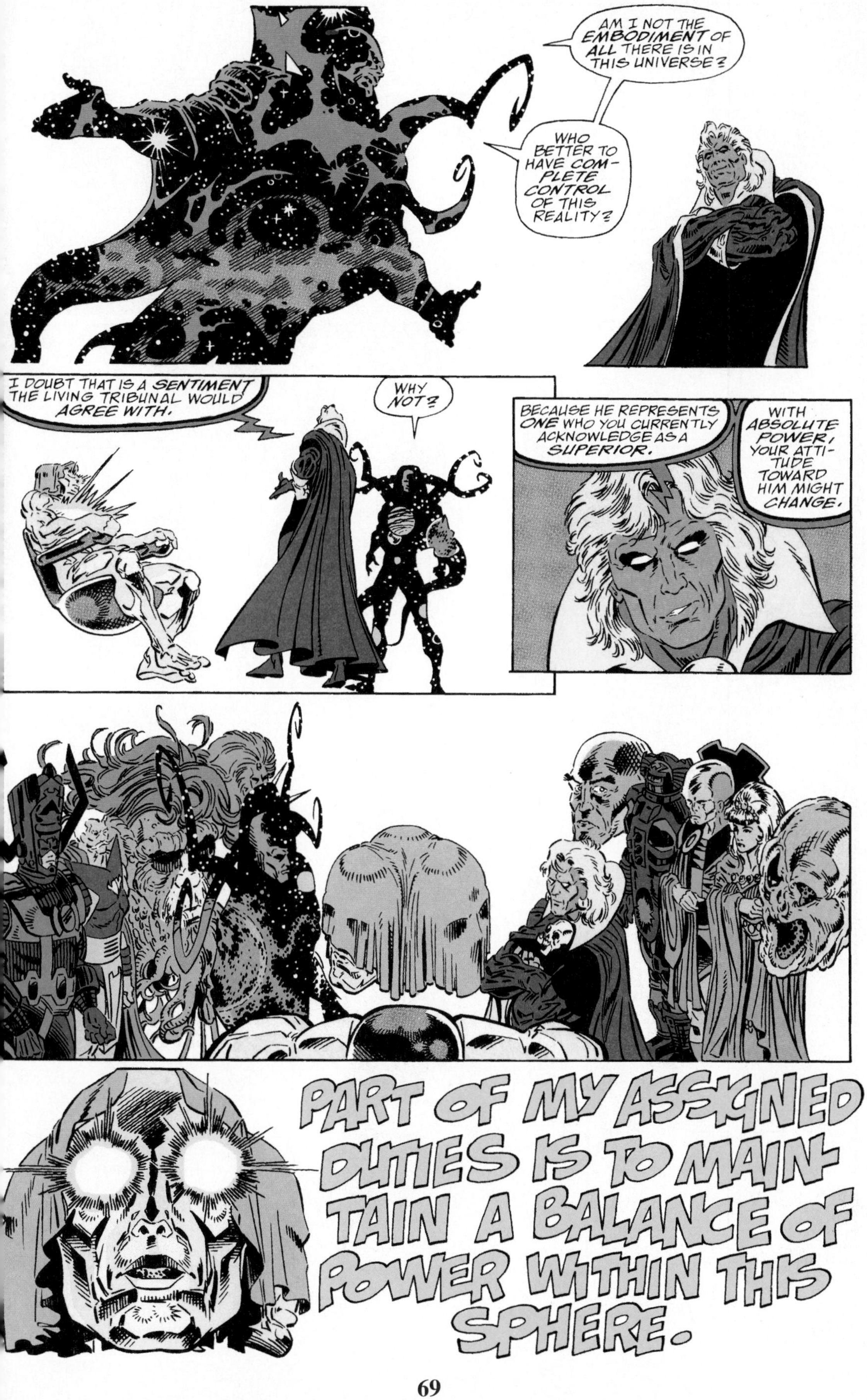
AM I NOT THE EMBODIMENT OF ALL THERE IS IN THIS UNIVERSE?
WHO BETTER TO HAVE COMPLETE CONTROL OF THIS REALITY?
I DOUBT THAT IS A SENTIMENT THE LIVING TRIBUNAL WOULD AGREE WITH.
WHY NOT?
BECAUSE HE REPRESENTS ONE WHO YOU CURRENTLY ACKNOWLEDGE AS A SUPERIOR.
WITH ABSOLUTE POWER, YOUR ATTITUDE TOWARD HIM MIGHT CHANGE.
PART OF MY ASSIGNED DUTIES IS TO MAINTAIN A BALANCE OF POWER WITHIN THIS SPHERE.

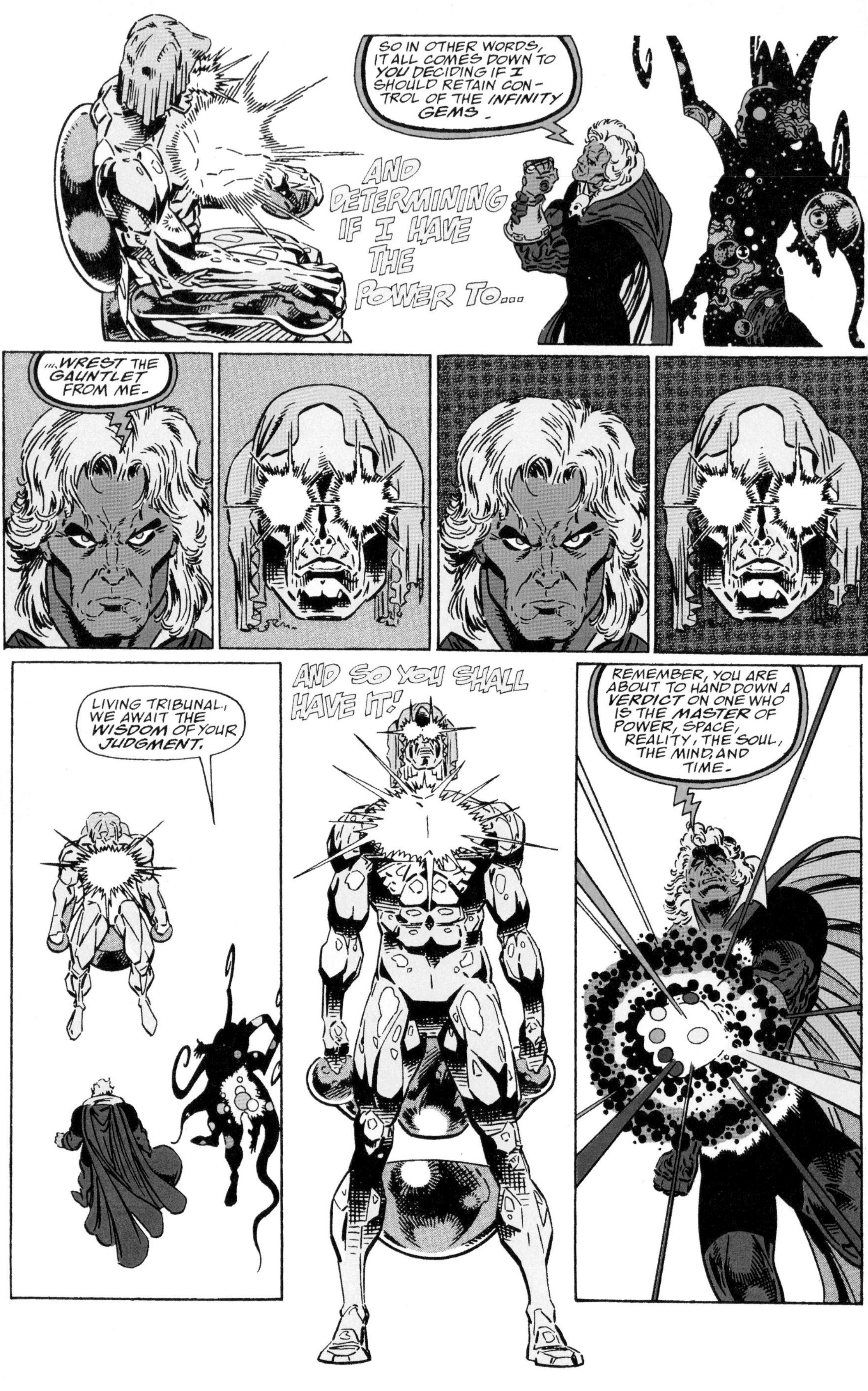

SO IN OTHER WORDS, IT ALL COMES DOWN TO YOU DECIDING IF I SHOULD RETAIN CONTROL OF THE INFINITY GEMS-
AND DETERMINING IF I HAVE THE POWER TO...
...WREST THE GAUNTLET FROM ME-
LIVING TRIBUNAL, WE AWAIT THE WISDOM OF YOUR JUDGMENT.
AND SO YOU SHALL HAVE IT!
REMEMBER, YOU ARE ABOUT TO HAND DOWN A VERDICT ON ONE WHO IS THE MASTER OF POWER, SPACE, REALITY, THE SOUL, THE MIND, AND TIME-

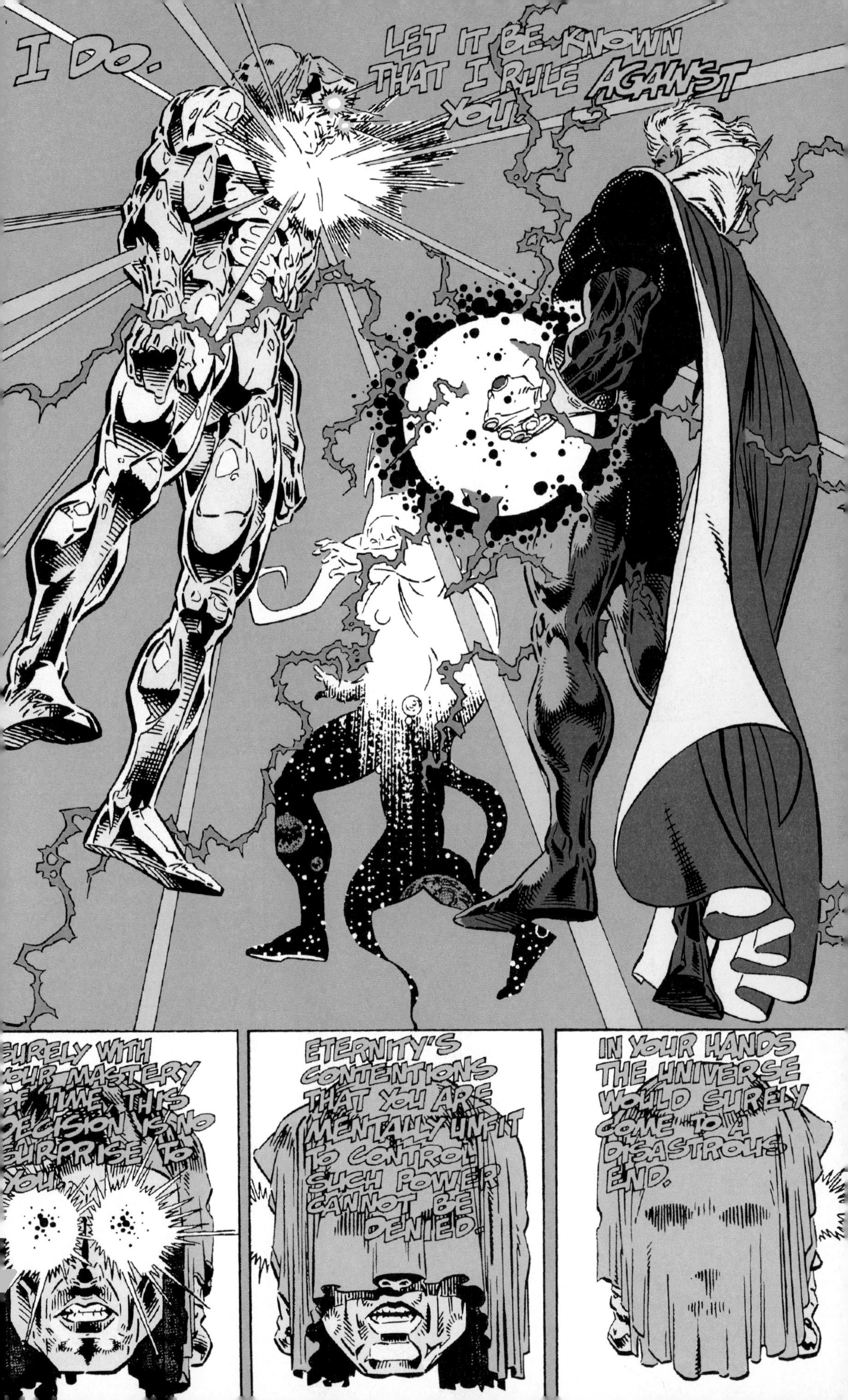
I DO.
LET IT BE KNOWN THAT I RULE AGAINST YOU.
SURELY WITH YOUR MASTERY OF TIME, THIS DECISION IS NO SURPRISE TO YOU.
ETERNITY'S CONTENTIONS THAT YOU ARE MENTALLY UNFIT TO CONTROL SUCH POWER CANNOT BE DENIED.
IN YOUR HANDS THE UNIVERSE WOULD SURELY COME TO A DISASTROUS END.

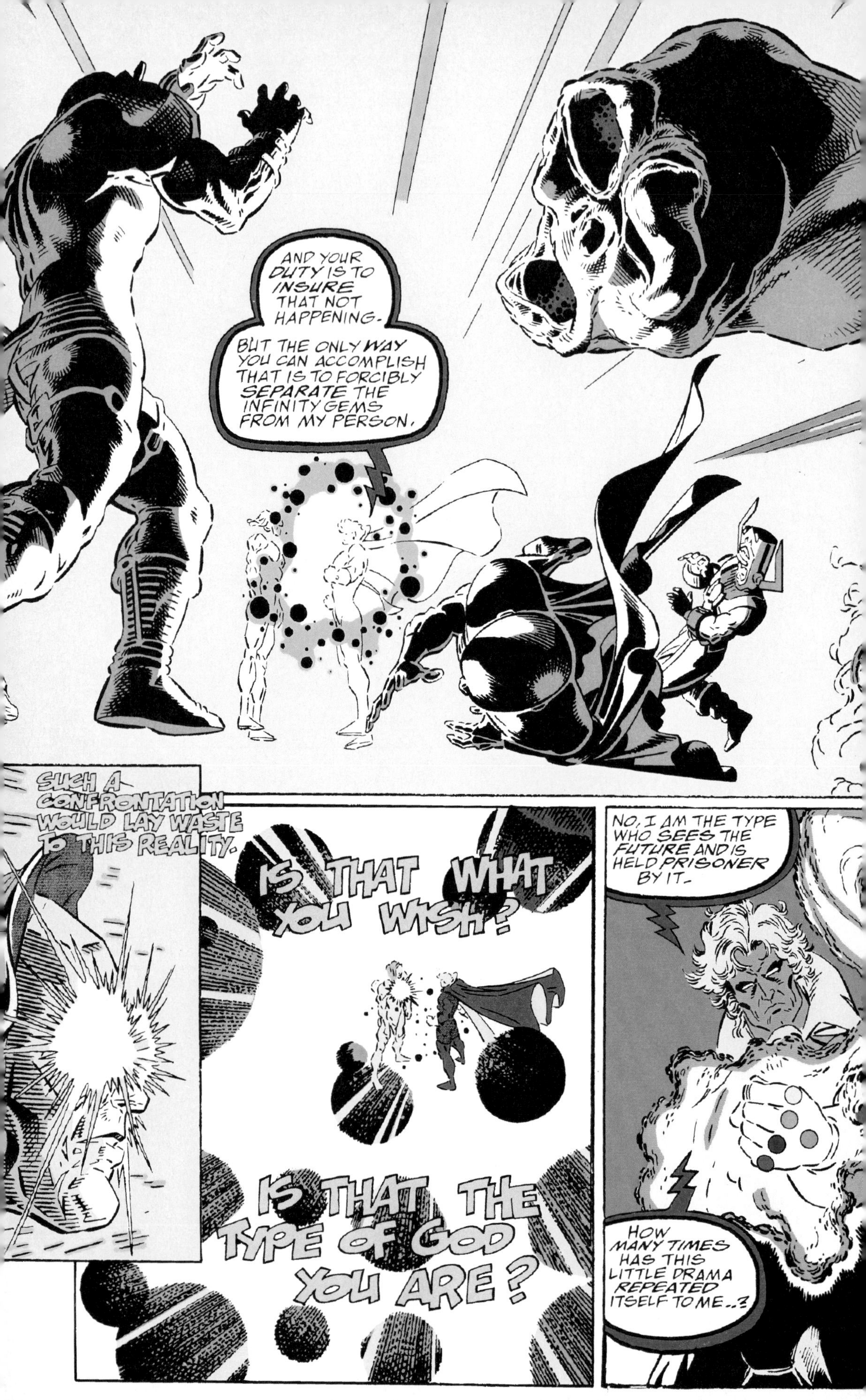
AND YOUR DUTY IS TO INSURE THAT NOT HAPPENING.
BUT THE ONLY WAY YOU CAN ACCOMPLISH THAT IS TO FORCIBLY SEPARATE THE INFINITY GEMS FROM MY PERSON.
SUCH A CONFRONTATION WOULD LAY WASTE TO THIS REALITY.
IS THAT WHAT YOU WISH?
IS THAT THE TYPE OF GOD YOU ARE?
NO, I AM THE TYPE WHO SEES THE FUTURE AND IS HELD PRISONER BY IT.
HOW MANY TIMES HAS THIS LITTLE DRAMA REPEATED ITSELF TO ME..?

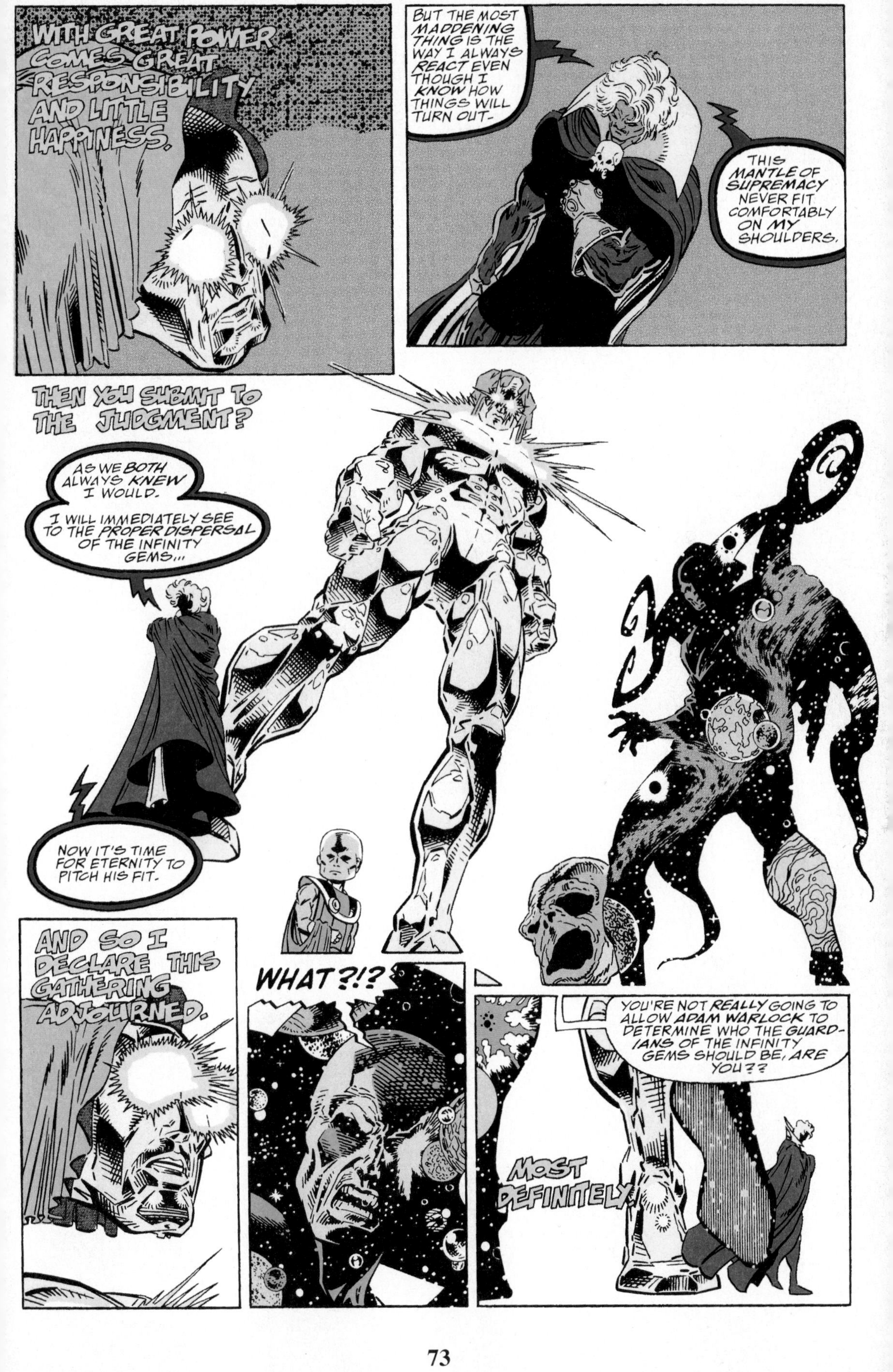
WITH GREAT POWER COMES GREAT RESPONSIBILITY AND LITTLE HAPPINESS.
BUT THE MOST MADDENING THING IS THE WAY I ALWAYS REACT EVEN THOUGH I KNOW HOW THINGS WILL TURN OUT.
THIS MANTLE OF SUPREMACY NEVER FIT COMFORTABLY ON MY SHOULDERS.
THEN YOU SUBMIT TO THE JUDGMENT?
AS WE BOTH ALWAYS KNEW I WOULD.
I WILL IMMEDIATELY SEE TO THE PROPER DISPERSAL OF THE INFINITY GEMS...
NOW IT'S TIME FOR ETERNITY TO PITCH HIS FIT.
AND SO I DECLARE THIS GATHERING ADJOURNED.
WHAT?!?
YOU'RE NOT REALLY GOING TO ALLOW ADAM WARLOCK TO DETERMINE WHO THE GUARDIANS OF THE INFINITY GEMS SHOULD BE, ARE YOU??
MOST DEFINITELY.

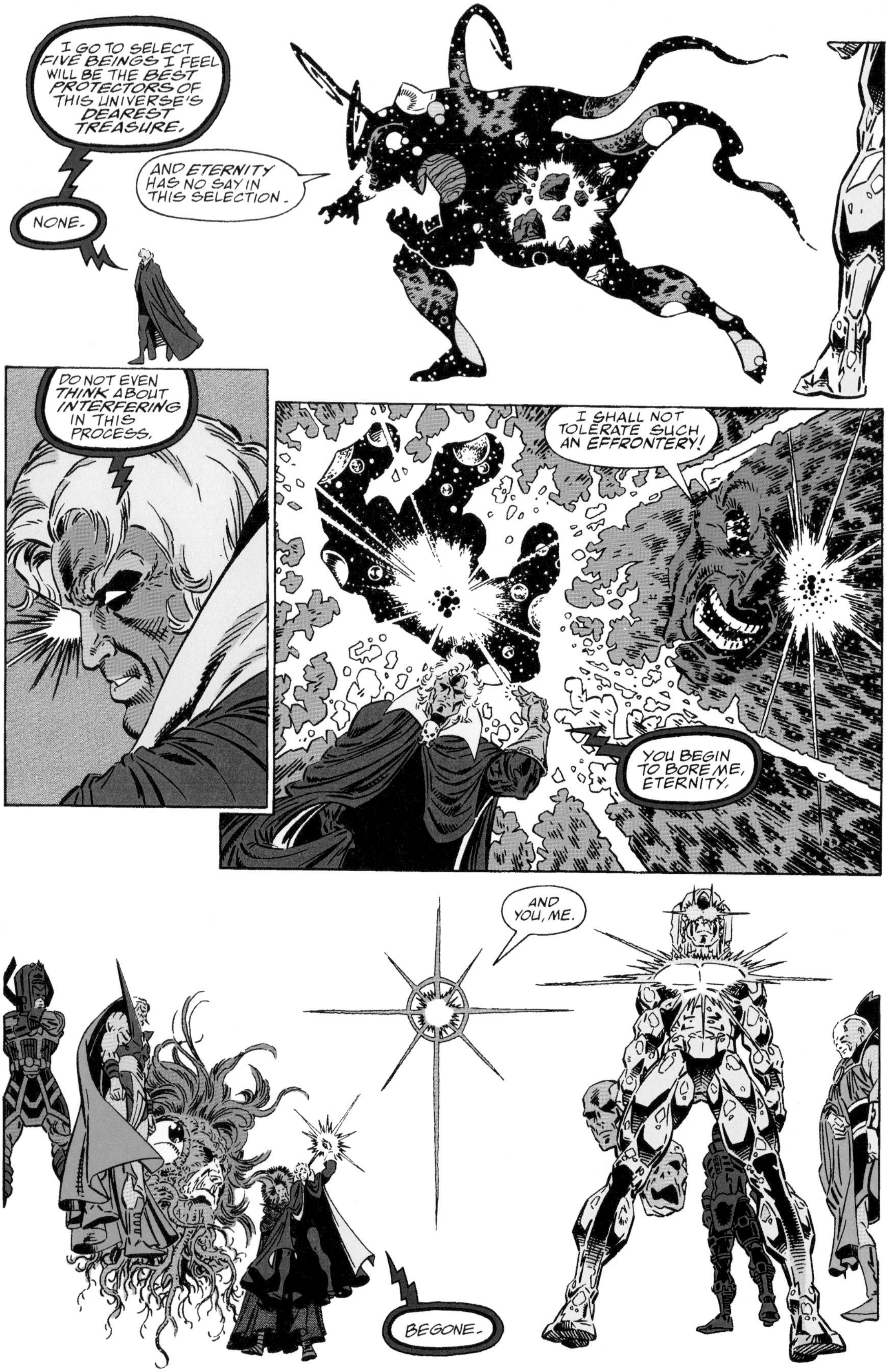
I GO TO SELECT FIVE BEINGS I FEEL WILL BE THE BEST PROTECTORS OF THIS UNIVERSE'S DEAREST TREASURE.
AND ETERNITY HAS NO SAY IN THIS SELECTION.
NONE.
DO NOT EVEN THINK ABOUT INTERFERING IN THIS PROCESS.
I SHALL NOT TOLERATE SUCH AN EFFRONTERY!
YOU BEGIN TO BORE ME, ETERNITY.
AND YOU, ME.
BEGONE.

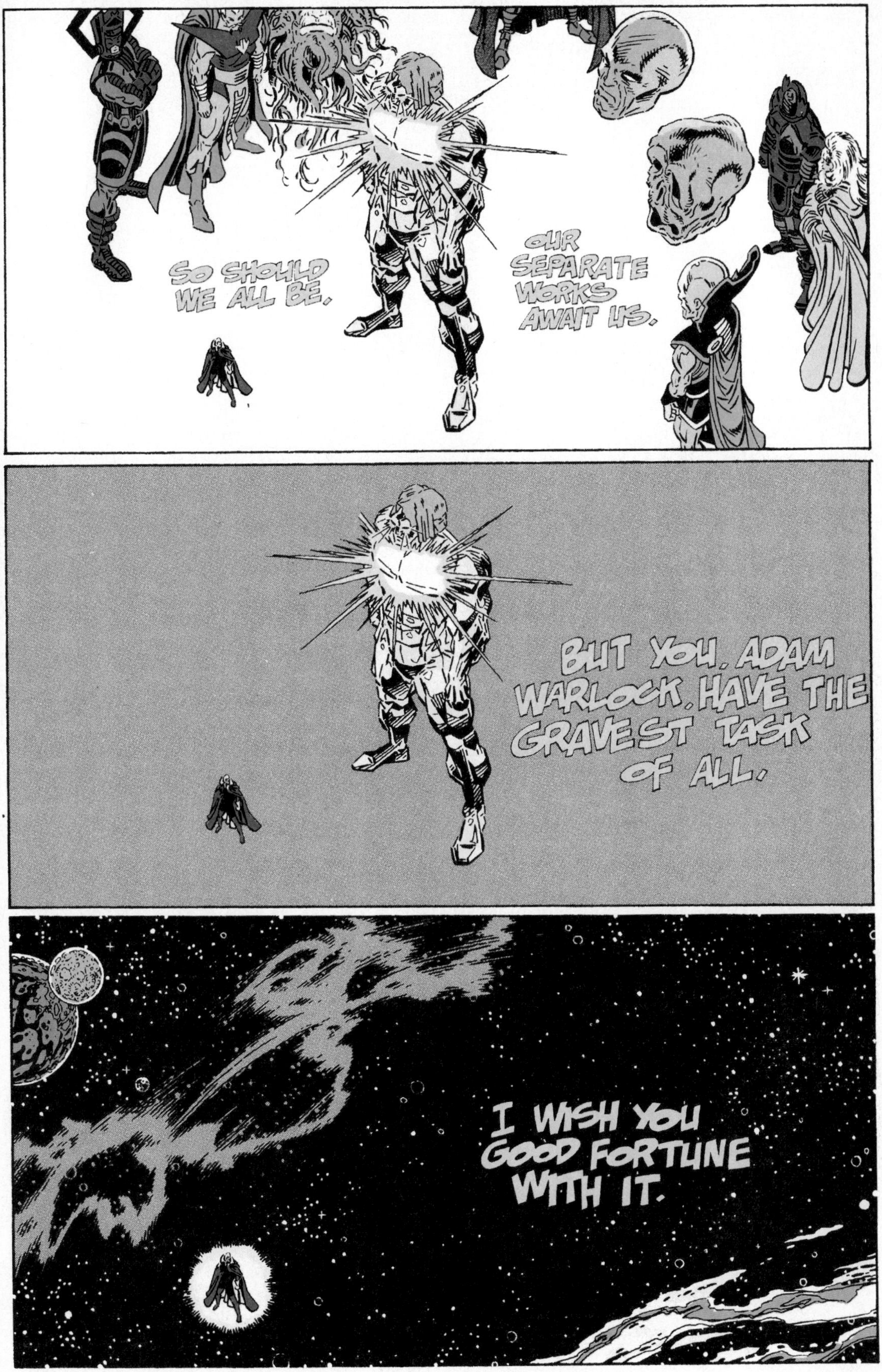
SO SHOULD WE ALL BE.
OUR SEPARATE WORKS AWAIT US.
BUT YOU, ADAM WARLOCK, HAVE THE GRAVEST TASK OF ALL.
I WISH YOU GOOD FORTUNE WITH IT.

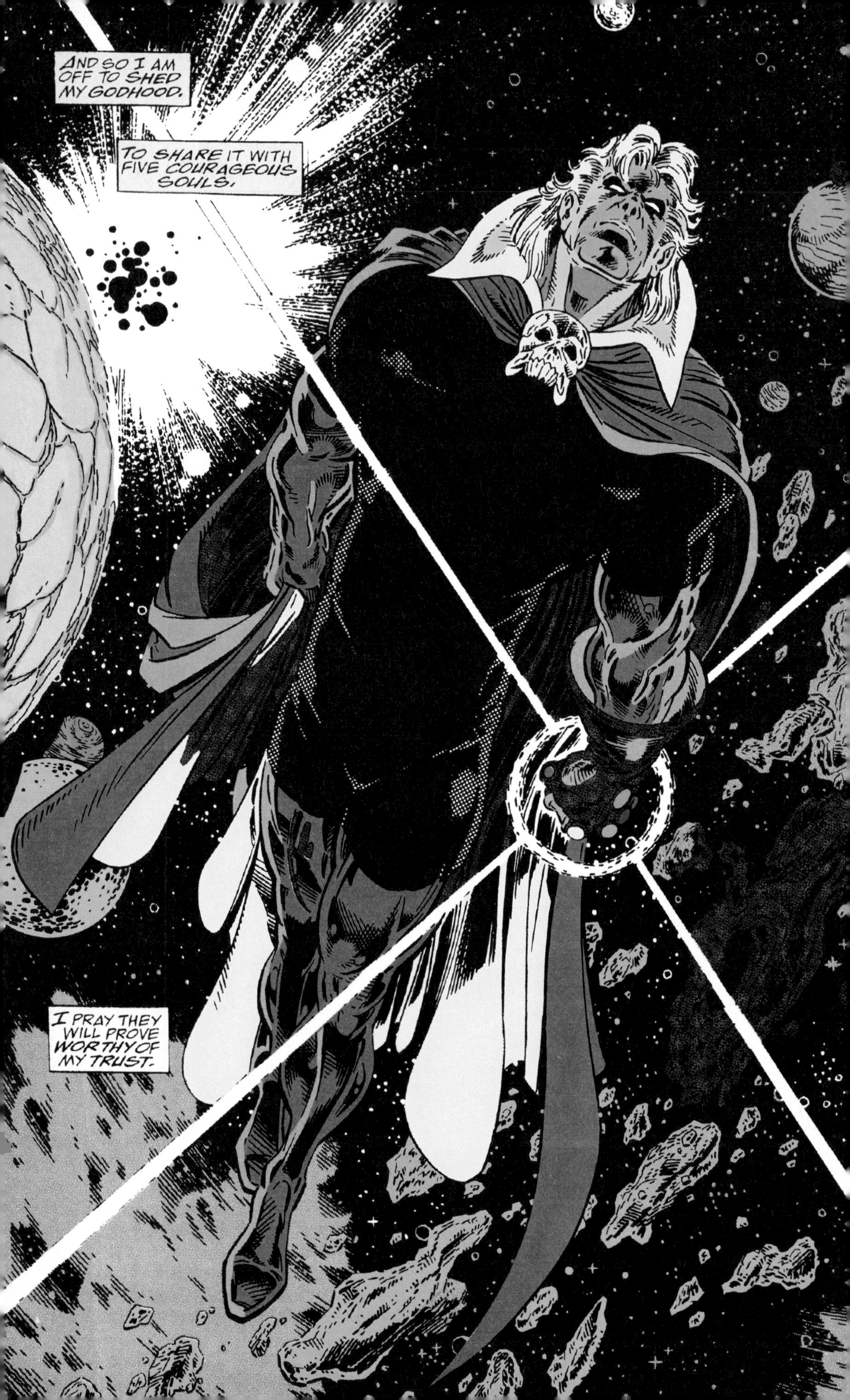
AND SO I AM OFF TO SHED MY GODHOOD.
TO SHARE IT WITH FIVE COURAGEOUS SOULS.
I PRAY THEY WILL PROVE WORTHY OF MY TRUST.

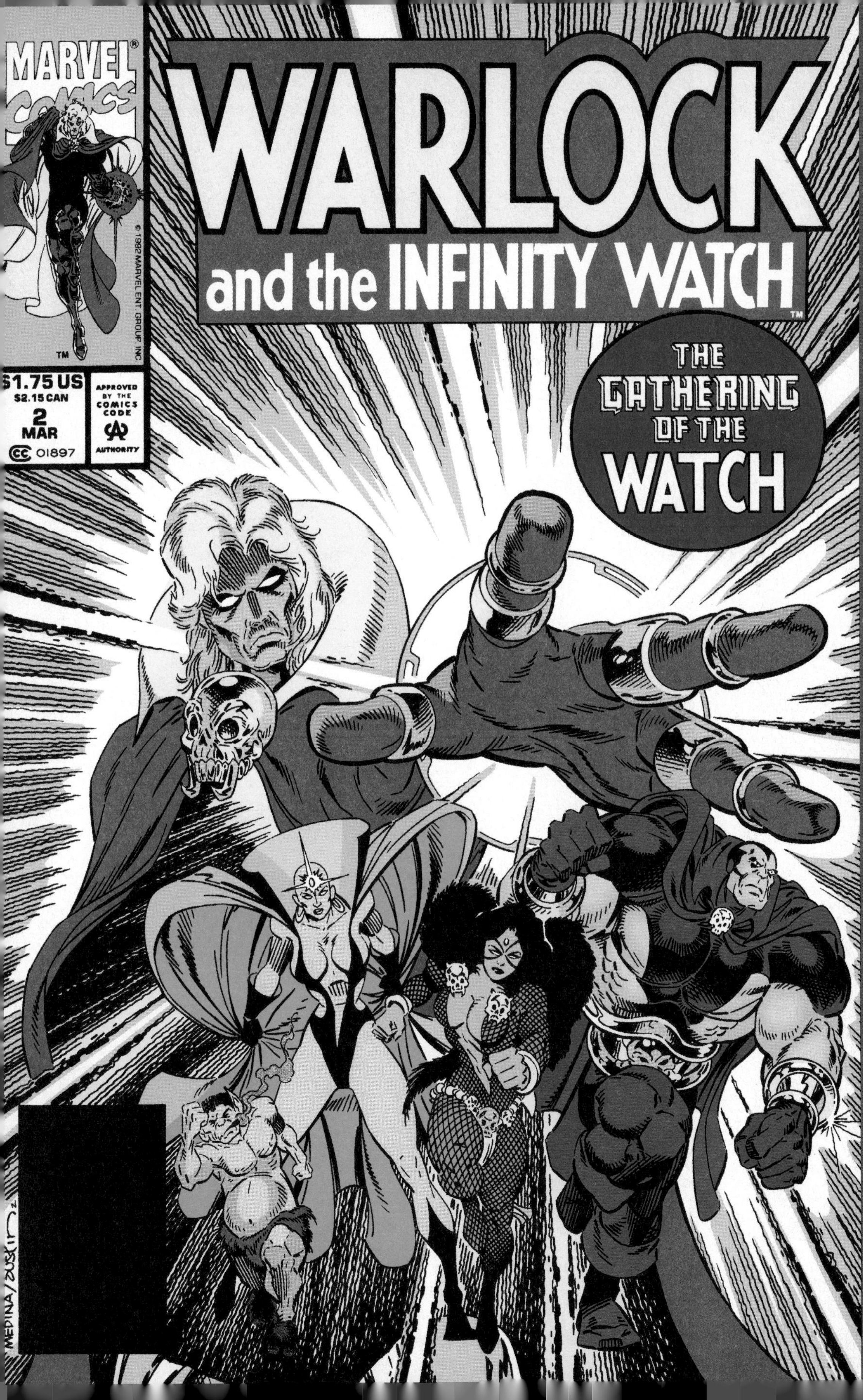
MARVEL® COMICS
WARLOCK
and the INFINITY WATCH™
© 1992 MARVEL ENT. GROUP, INC.
$1.75 US
$2.15 CAN
2
MAR
CC 01897
APPROVED BY THE COMICS CODE AUTHORITY
THE GATHERING OF THE WATCH

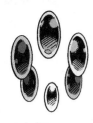

JIM
STARLIN
WRITER
ANGEL
MEDINA
PENCILS
TERRY
AUSTIN
INKS
JACK
MORELLI
LETTERS
IAN
LAUGHLIN
COLORS
CRAIG
ANDERSON
EDITOR
TOM
DeFALCO
CHIEFTAN

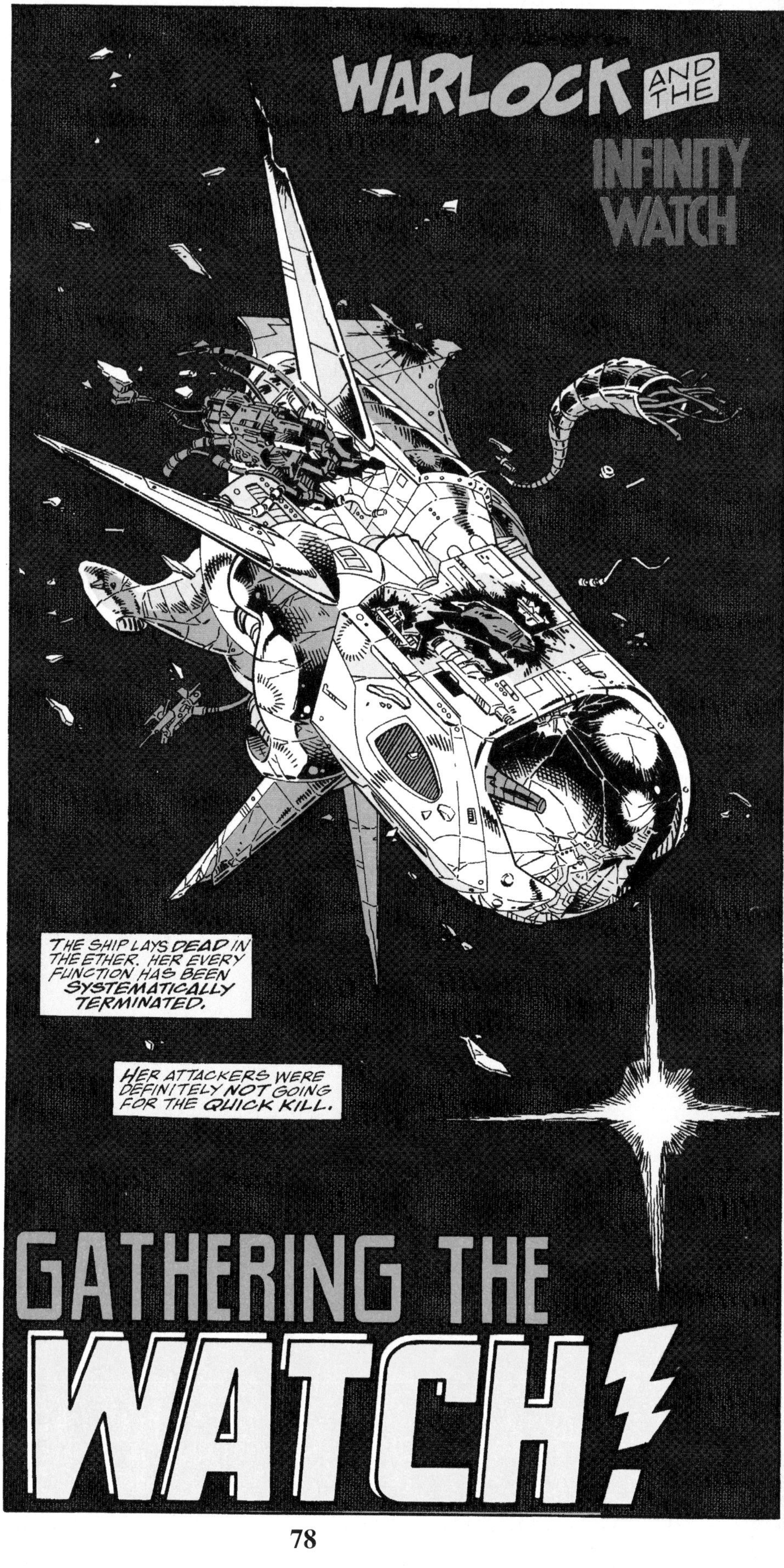
WARLOCK AND THE
INFINITY WATCH
THE SHIP LAYS DEAD IN THE ETHER. HER EVERY FUNCTION HAS BEEN SYSTEMATICALLY TERMINATED.
HER ATTACKERS WERE DEFINITELY NOT GOING FOR THE QUICK KILL.
GATHERING THE
WATCH!

THE BADOONS ENCOUNTERED THIS VESSEL JUST OUTSIDE THE STAR SYSTEM OF SOL.

THEY HAD NO COVERT DESIGNS, MERELY WISHED IDENTIFICATION ON THE STRANGE CRAFT, WHOSE PATH THEY HAD CROSSED.

BUT COMMUNICATION LED TO HARSH WORDS AND BRUISED EGOS.

CHALLENGES WERE LEVELED AND ANSWERED WITH PRECISE FIRE-POWER—

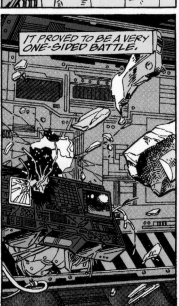

IT PROVED TO BE A VERY ONE-SIDED BATTLE.

THE CRAFT WAS QUICKLY DISABLED AND ITS SOLE PASSENGER LEFT TO FEND FOR HERSELF—

IT WAS THE KIND OF REACTION MOON-DRAGON, UNFORTUNATELY, TENDS TO BRING OUT IN PEOPLE.

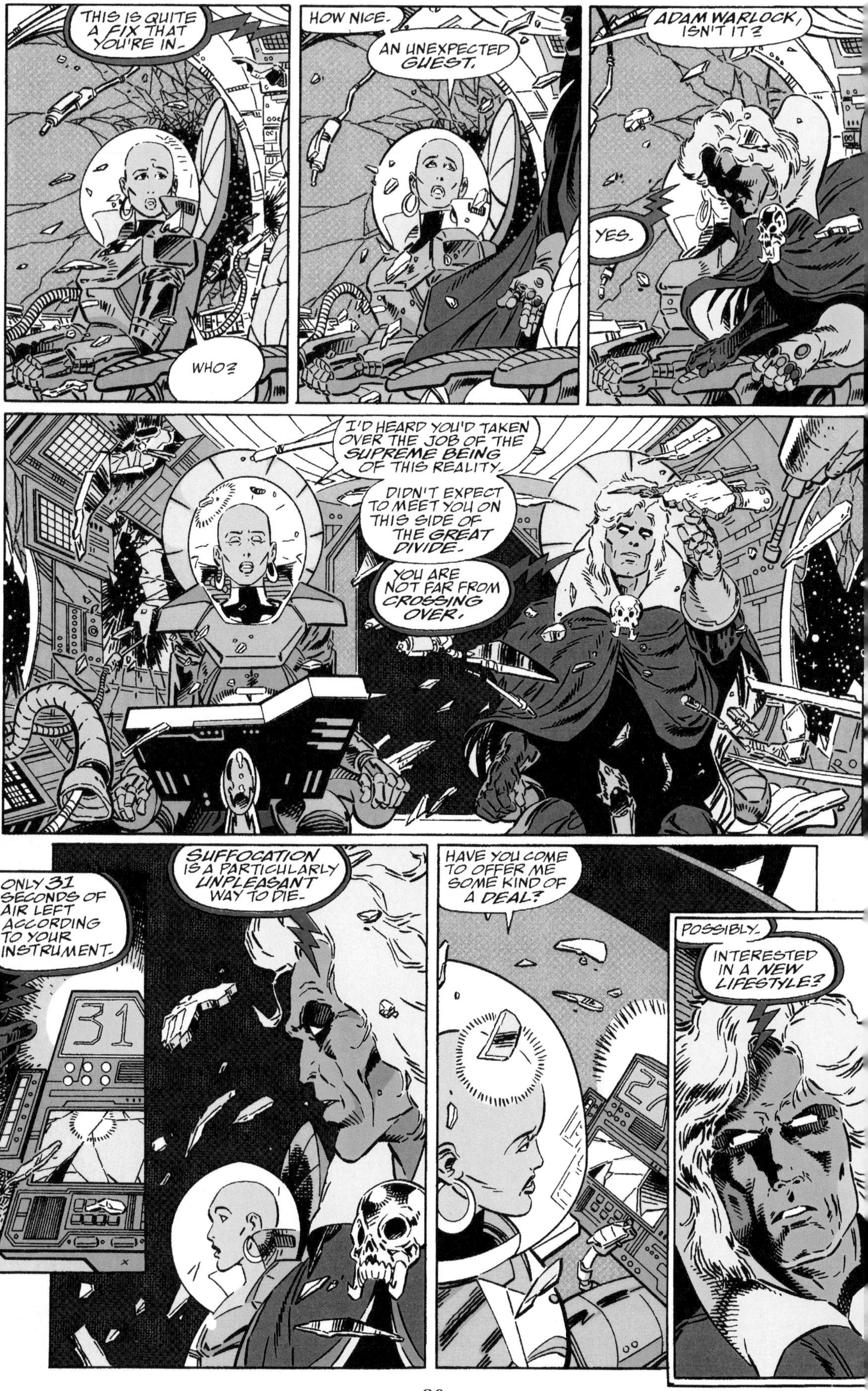
THIS IS QUITE A FIX THAT YOU'RE IN--
WHO?
HOW NICE.
AN UNEXPECTED GUEST.
ADAM WARLOCK, ISN'T IT?
YES.
I'D HEARD YOU'D TAKEN OVER THE JOB OF THE SUPREME BEING OF THIS REALITY.
DIDN'T EXPECT TO MEET YOU ON THIS SIDE OF THE GREAT DIVIDE.
YOU ARE NOT FAR FROM CROSSING OVER.
ONLY 31 SECONDS OF AIR LEFT ACCORDING TO YOUR INSTRUMENT.
31
SUFFOCATION IS A PARTICULARLY UNPLEASANT WAY TO DIE.
HAVE YOU COME TO OFFER ME SOME KIND OF A DEAL?
27
POSSIBLY.
INTERESTED IN A NEW LIFESTYLE?

MAYBE—

MY OLD ONE HASN'T WORKED OUT TOO WELL OF LATE.

IT WOULD REQUIRE SHOULDERING GREAT RESPONSIBILITY AND EARNING MY TRUST.

TRUTHFULLY, I'VE NEVER BEEN VERY GOOD WITH TRUST OR RESPONSI-BILITY.

I KNOW.

BUT I'M WILLING TO GIVE YOU A SECOND CHANCE.

WELL?

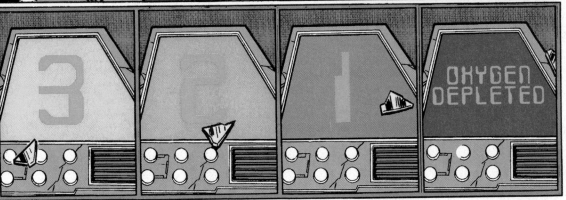

3 2 1 OXYGEN DEPLETED

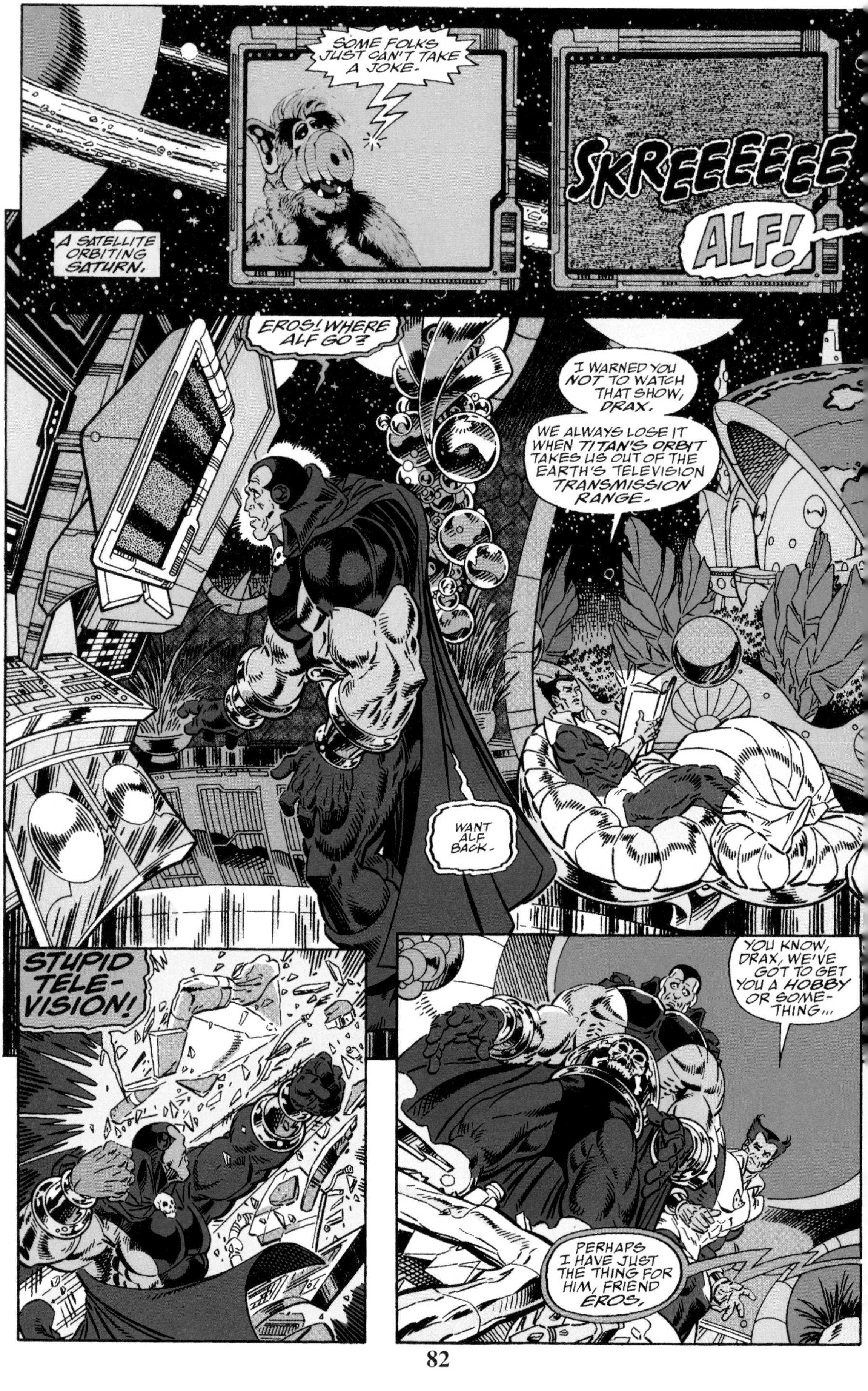
SOME FOLKS JUST CAN'T TAKE A JOKE-
SKREEEEEEE
ALF!
A SATELLITE ORBITING SATURN.
EROS! WHERE ALF GO?
I WARNED YOU NOT TO WATCH THAT SHOW, DRAX.
WE ALWAYS LOSE IT WHEN TITAN'S ORBIT TAKES US OUT OF THE EARTH'S TELEVISION TRANSMISSION RANGE.
WANT ALF BACK.
STUPID TELE-VISION!
YOU KNOW, DRAX, WE'VE GOT TO GET YOU A HOBBY OR SOME-THING...
PERHAPS I HAVE JUST THE THING FOR HIM, FRIEND EROS.

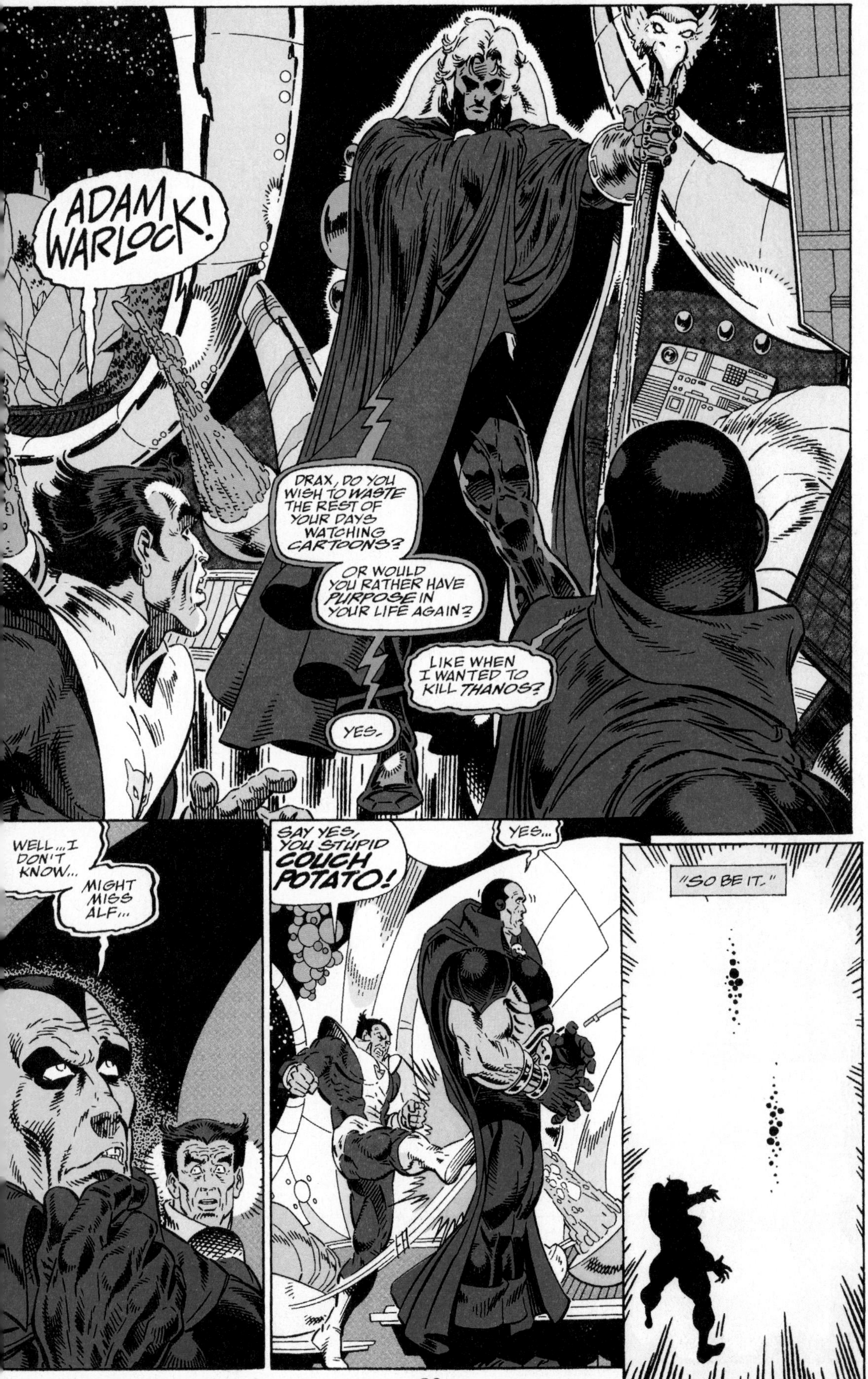
ADAM WARLOCK!
DRAX, DO YOU WISH TO WASTE THE REST OF YOUR DAYS WATCHING CARTOONS?
OR WOULD YOU RATHER HAVE PURPOSE IN YOUR LIFE AGAIN?
LIKE WHEN I WANTED TO KILL THANOS?
YES.
WELL... I DON'T KNOW...
MIGHT MISS ALF...
SAY YES, YOU STUPID COUCH POTATO!
YES...
"SO BE IT."

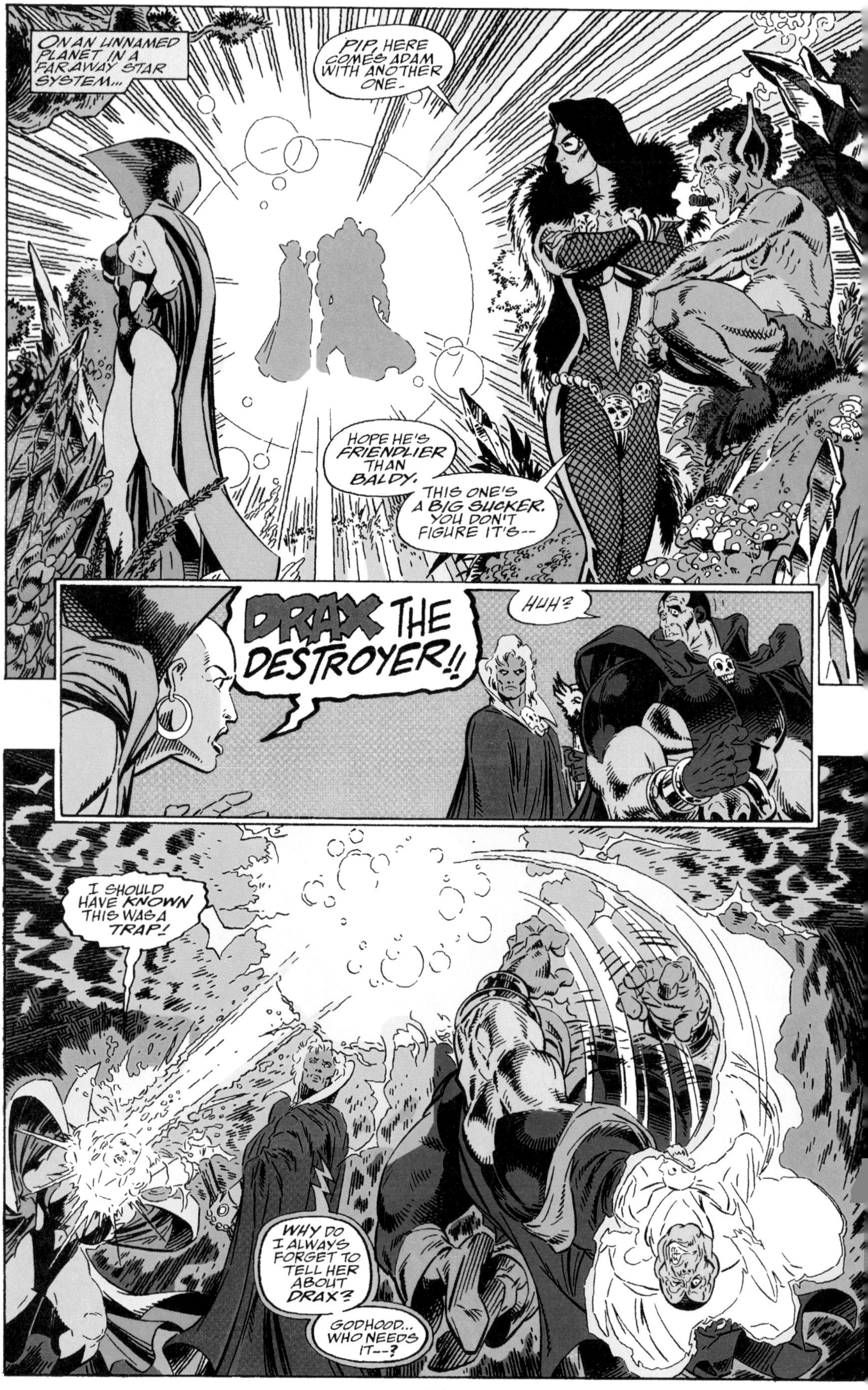
ON AN UNNAMED PLANET IN A FARAWAY STAR SYSTEM...
PIP, HERE COMES ADAM WITH ANOTHER ONE.
HOPE HE'S FRIENDLIER THAN BALDY.
THIS ONE'S A BIG SUCKER. YOU DON'T FIGURE IT'S--
DRAX THE DESTROYER!!
HUH?
I SHOULD HAVE KNOWN THIS WAS A TRAP!
WHY DO I ALWAYS FORGET TO TELL HER ABOUT DRAX?
GODHOOD... WHO NEEDS IT--?

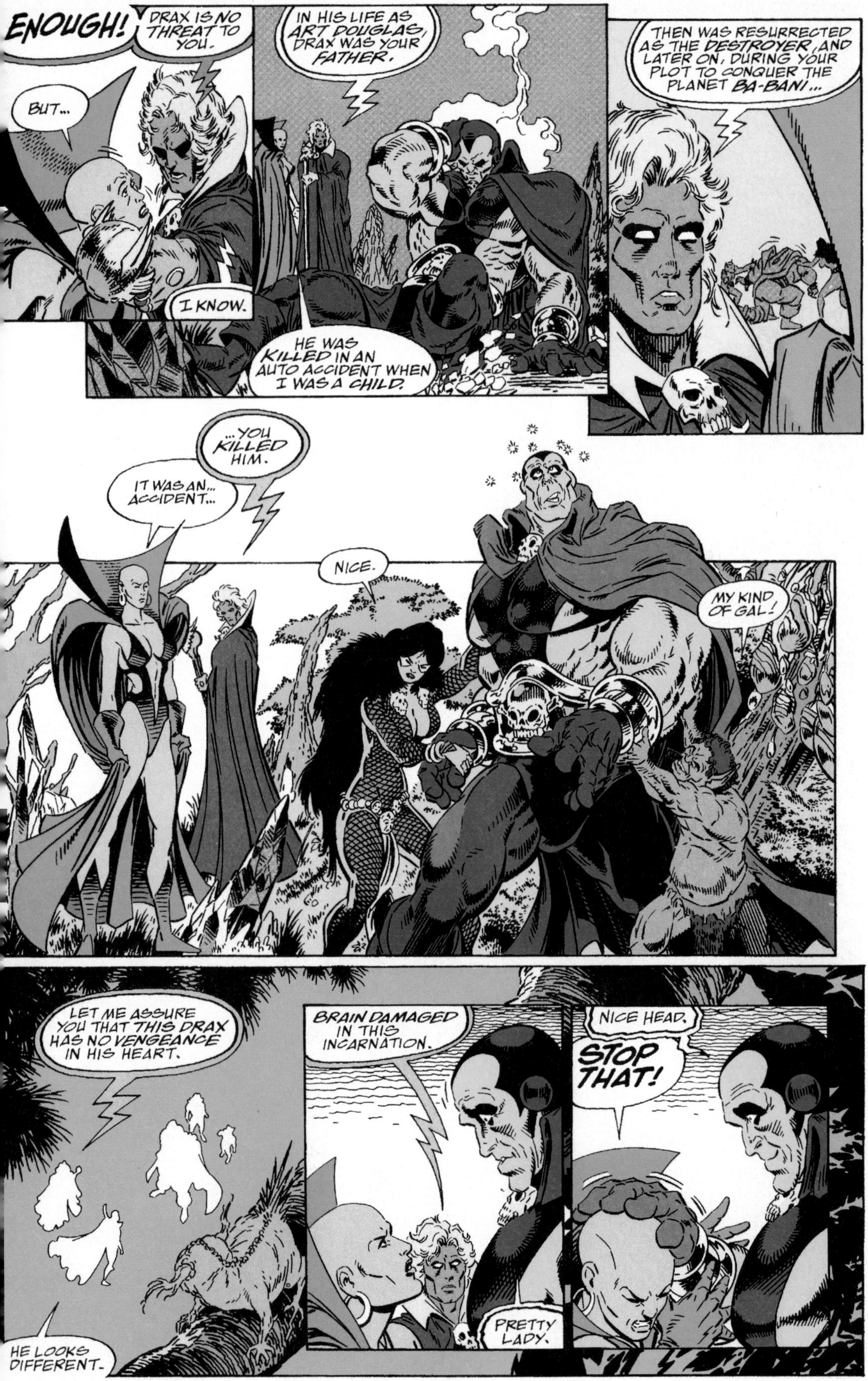

ENOUGH!
DRAX IS NO THREAT TO YOU.
BUT...
I KNOW.
IN HIS LIFE AS ART DOUGLAS, DRAX WAS YOUR FATHER.
HE WAS KILLED IN AN AUTO ACCIDENT WHEN I WAS A CHILD.
THEN WAS RESURRECTED AS THE DESTROYER, AND LATER ON, DURING YOUR PLOT TO CONQUER THE PLANET BA-BANI...
IT WAS AN... ACCIDENT...
...YOU KILLED HIM.
NICE.
MY KIND OF GAL!
LET ME ASSURE YOU THAT THIS DRAX HAS NO VENGEANCE IN HIS HEART.
HE LOOKS DIFFERENT-
BRAIN DAMAGED IN THIS INCARNATION.
PRETTY LADY.
NICE HEAD.
STOP THAT!

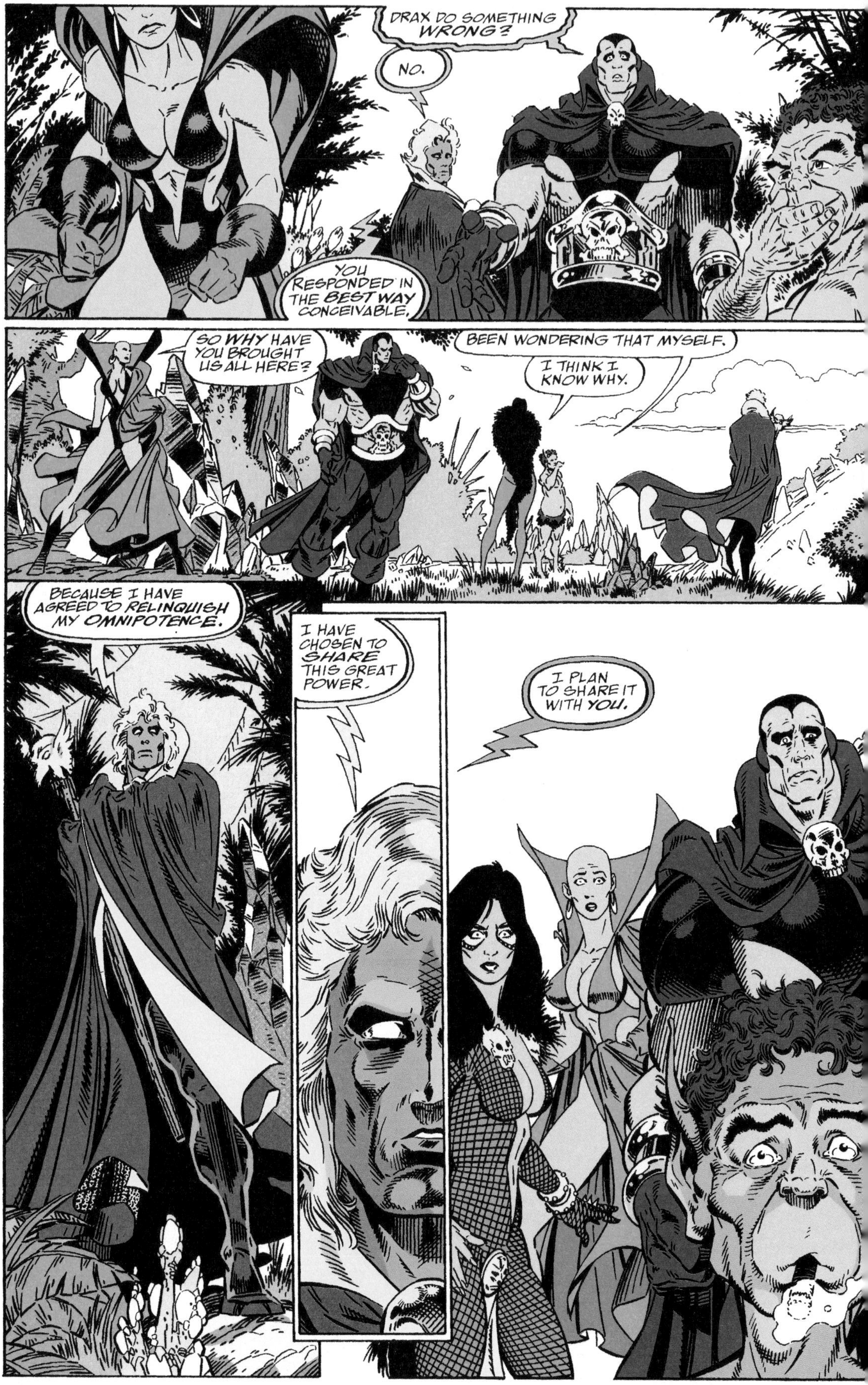
DRAX DO SOMETHING WRONG?
NO.
YOU RESPONDED IN THE BEST WAY CONCEIVABLE.
SO WHY HAVE YOU BROUGHT US ALL HERE?
BEEN WONDERING THAT MYSELF.
I THINK I KNOW WHY.
BECAUSE I HAVE AGREED TO RELINQUISH MY OMNIPOTENCE.
I HAVE CHOSEN TO SHARE THIS GREAT POWER.
I PLAN TO SHARE IT WITH YOU.

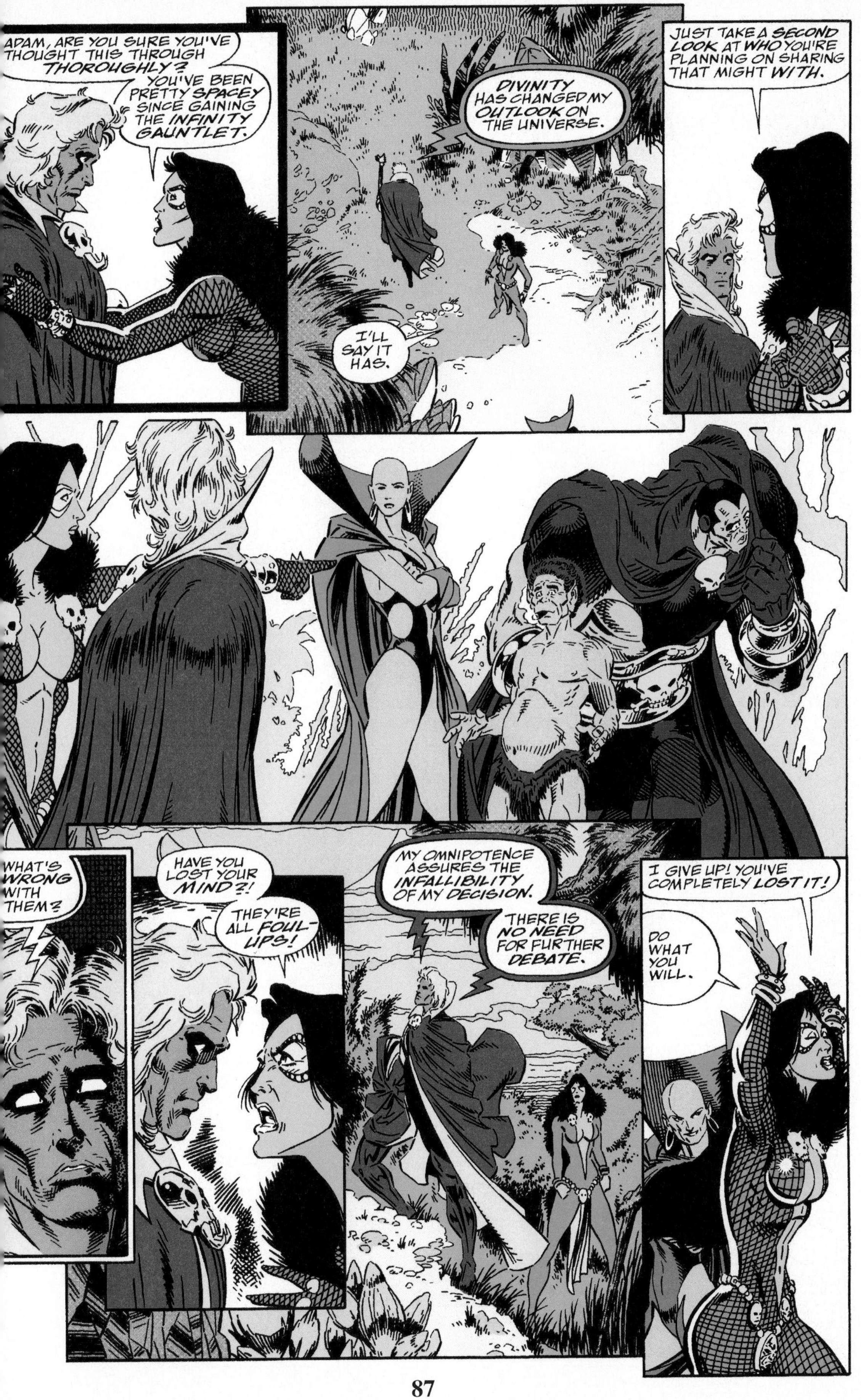
ADAM, ARE YOU SURE YOU'VE THOUGHT THIS THROUGH THOROUGHLY?
YOU'VE BEEN PRETTY SPACEY SINCE GAINING THE INFINITY GAUNTLET.
DIVINITY HAS CHANGED MY OUTLOOK ON THE UNIVERSE.
I'LL SAY IT HAS.
JUST TAKE A SECOND LOOK AT WHO YOU'RE PLANNING ON SHARING THAT MIGHT WITH.
WHAT'S WRONG WITH THEM?
HAVE YOU LOST YOUR MIND?!
THEY'RE ALL FOUL-UPS!
MY OMNIPOTENCE ASSURES THE INFALLIBILITY OF MY DECISION.
THERE IS NO NEED FOR FURTHER DEBATE.
I GIVE UP! YOU'VE COMPLETELY LOST IT!
DO WHAT YOU WILL.

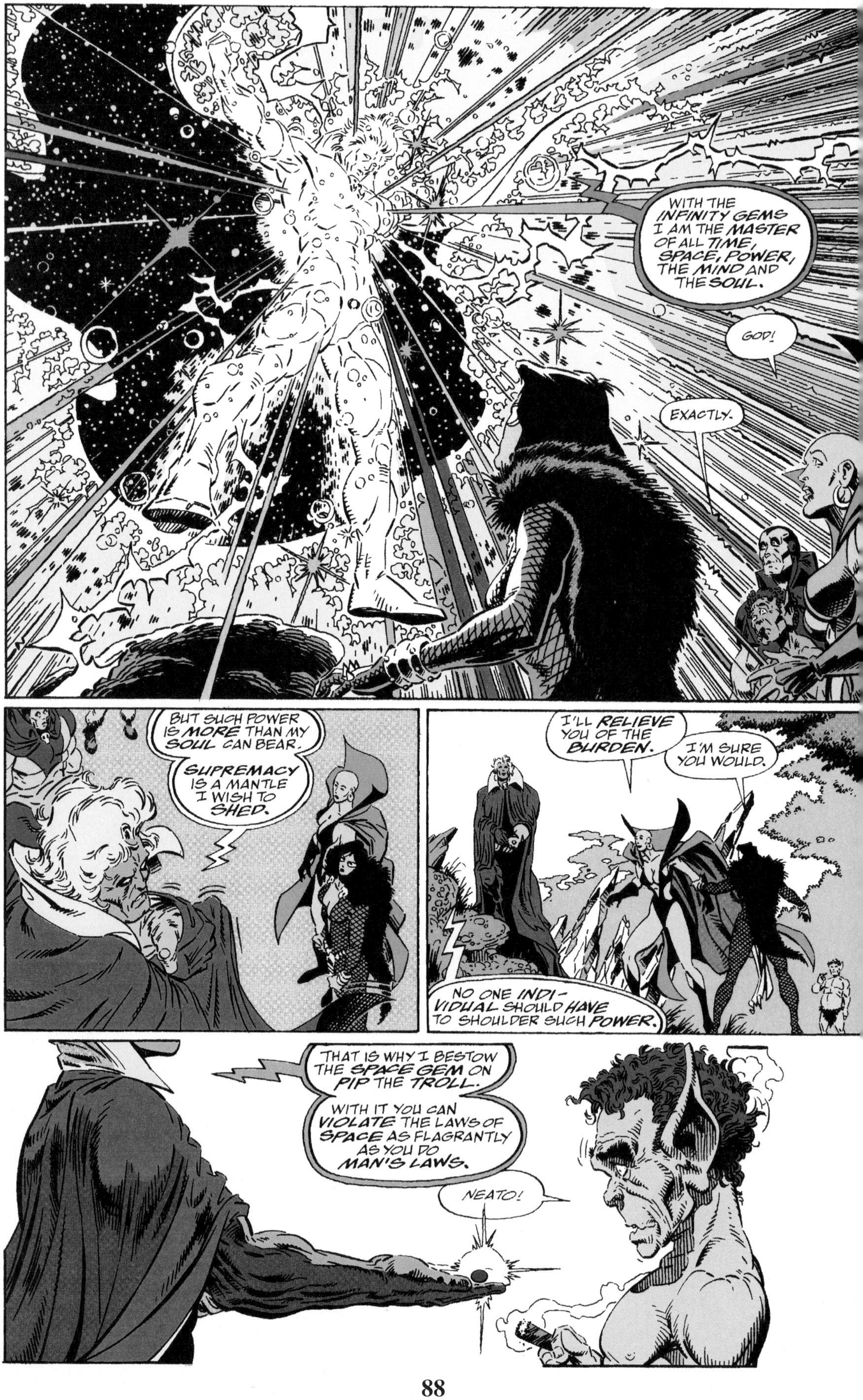
WITH THE INFINITY GEMS I AM THE MASTER OF ALL TIME, SPACE, POWER, THE MIND AND THE SOUL.
GOD!
EXACTLY.
BUT SUCH POWER IS MORE THAN MY SOUL CAN BEAR.
SUPREMACY IS A MANTLE I WISH TO SHED.
I'LL RELIEVE YOU OF THE BURDEN.
I'M SURE YOU WOULD.
NO ONE INDI-VIDUAL SHOULD HAVE TO SHOULDER SUCH POWER.
THAT IS WHY I BESTOW THE SPACE GEM ON PIP THE TROLL.
WITH IT YOU CAN VIOLATE THE LAWS OF SPACE AS FLAGRANTLY AS YOU DO MAN'S LAWS.
NEATO!

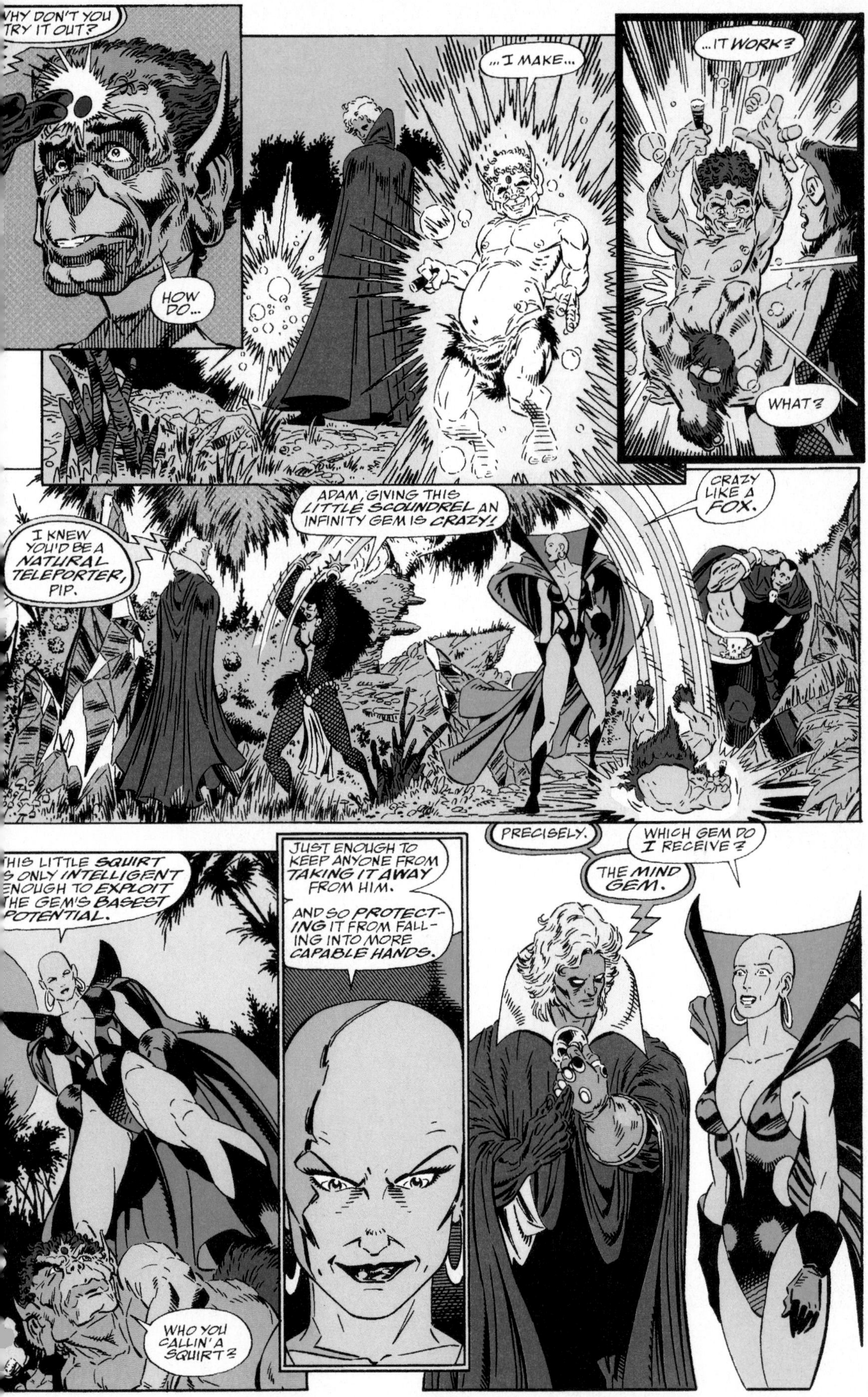
WHY DON'T YOU TRY IT OUT?
HOW DO...
...I MAKE...
...IT WORK?
WHAT?
I KNEW YOU'D BE A NATURAL TELEPORTER, PIP.
ADAM, GIVING THIS LITTLE SCOUNDREL AN INFINITY GEM IS CRAZY!
CRAZY LIKE A FOX.
THIS LITTLE SQUIRT IS ONLY INTELLIGENT ENOUGH TO EXPLOIT THE GEM'S BASEST POTENTIAL.
WHO YOU CALLIN' A SQUIRT?
JUST ENOUGH TO KEEP ANYONE FROM TAKING IT AWAY FROM HIM.
AND SO PROTECTING IT FROM FALLING INTO MORE CAPABLE HANDS.
PRECISELY.
WHICH GEM DO I RECEIVE?
THE MIND GEM.

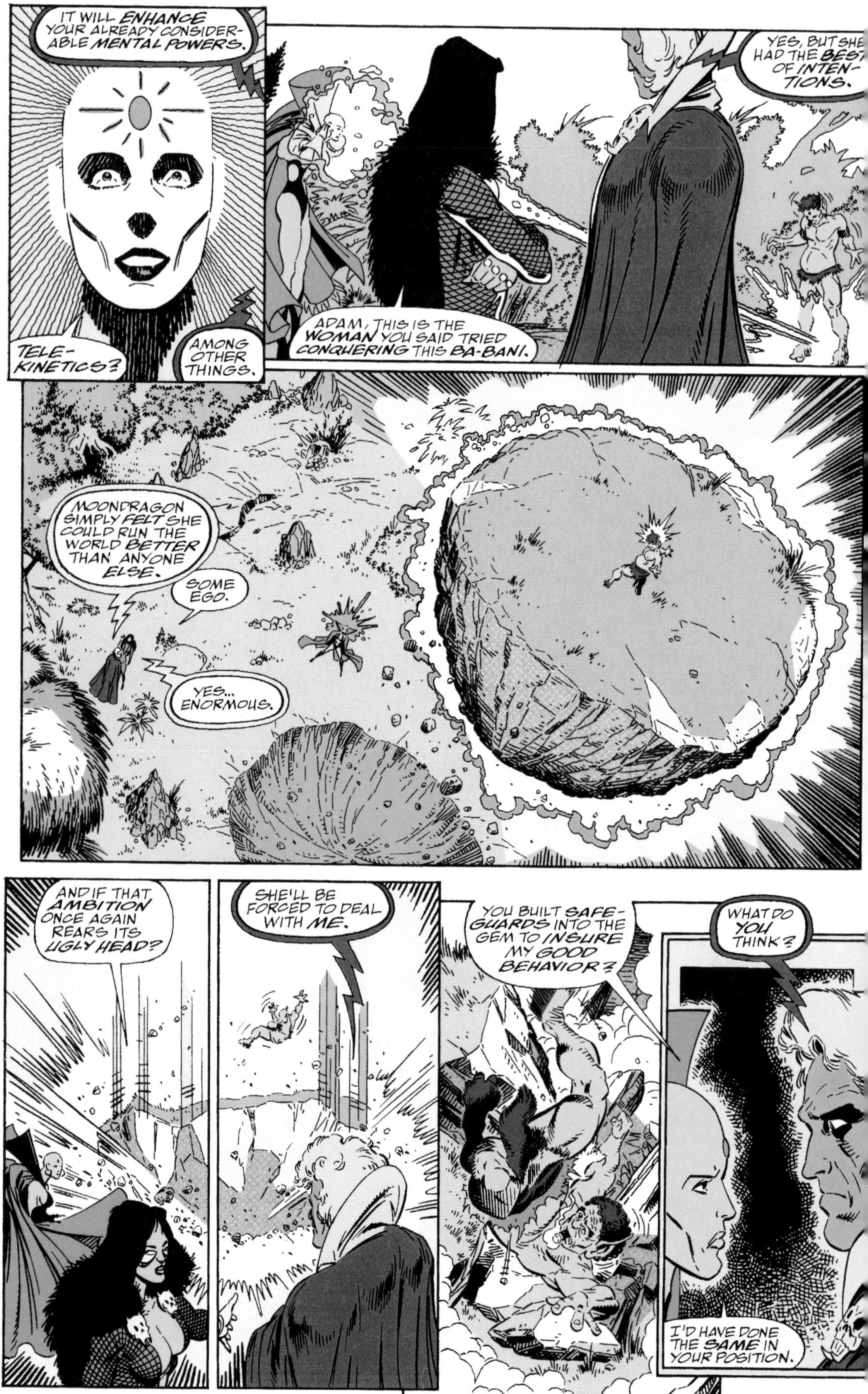
IT WILL ENHANCE YOUR ALREADY CONSIDERABLE MENTAL POWERS.
TELE-KINETICS?
AMONG OTHER THINGS.
ADAM, THIS IS THE WOMAN YOU SAID TRIED CONQUERING THIS BA-BANI.
YES, BUT SHE HAD THE BEST OF INTENTIONS.
MOONDRAGON SIMPLY FELT SHE COULD RUN THE WORLD BETTER THAN ANYONE ELSE.
SOME EGO.
YES... ENORMOUS.
AND IF THAT AMBITION ONCE AGAIN REARS ITS UGLY HEAD?
SHE'LL BE FORCED TO DEAL WITH ME.
YOU BUILT SAFEGUARDS INTO THE GEM TO INSURE MY GOOD BEHAVIOR?
WHAT DO YOU THINK?
I'D HAVE DONE THE SAME IN YOUR POSITION.

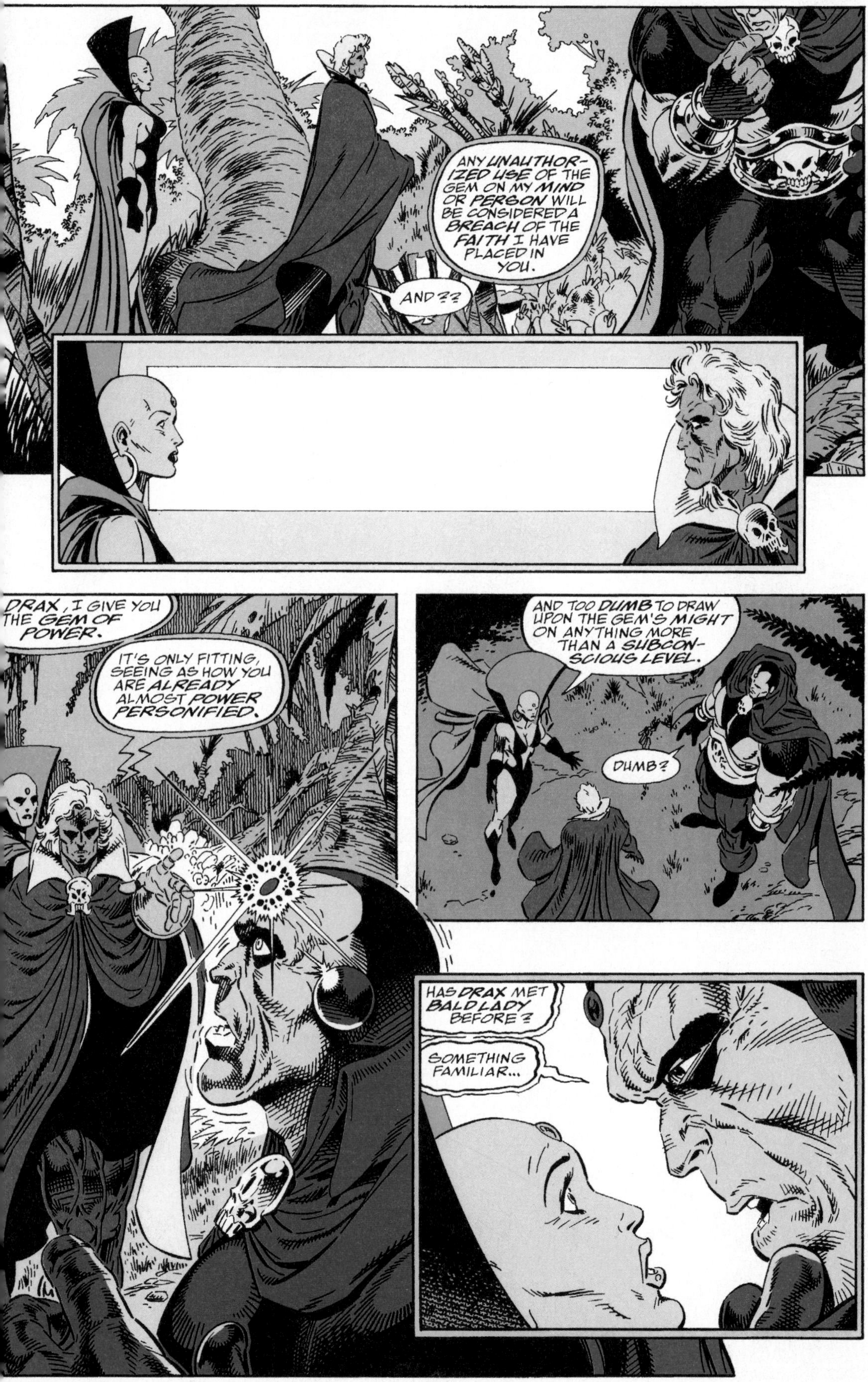
ANY UNAUTHORIZED USE OF THE GEM ON MY MIND OR PERSON WILL BE CONSIDERED A BREACH OF THE FAITH I HAVE PLACED IN YOU.
AND??
DRAX, I GIVE YOU THE GEM OF POWER.
IT'S ONLY FITTING, SEEING AS HOW YOU ARE ALREADY ALMOST POWER PERSONIFIED.
AND TOO DUMB TO DRAW UPON THE GEM'S MIGHT ON ANYTHING MORE THAN A SUBCONSCIOUS LEVEL.
DUMB?
HAS DRAX MET BALD LADY BEFORE?
SOMETHING FAMILIAR...

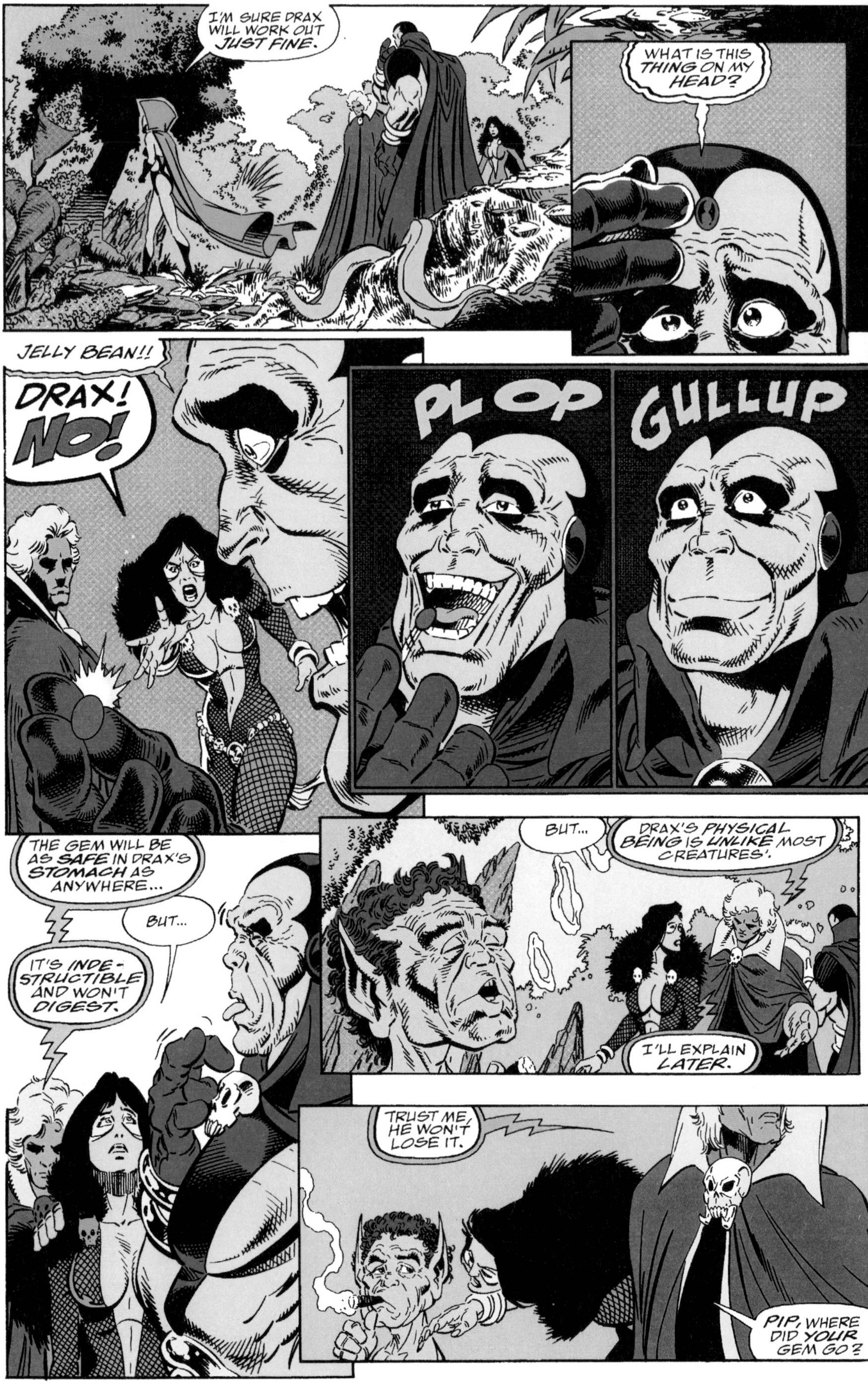
I'M SURE DRAX WILL WORK OUT JUST FINE.
WHAT IS THIS THING ON MY HEAD?
JELLY BEAN!!
DRAX! NO!
PLOP
GULLUP
THE GEM WILL BE AS SAFE IN DRAX'S STOMACH AS ANYWHERE...
BUT...
IT'S INDESTRUCTIBLE AND WON'T DIGEST.
BUT...
DRAX'S PHYSICAL BEING IS UNLIKE MOST CREATURES'.
I'LL EXPLAIN LATER.
TRUST ME, HE WON'T LOSE IT.
PIP, WHERE DID YOUR GEM GO?

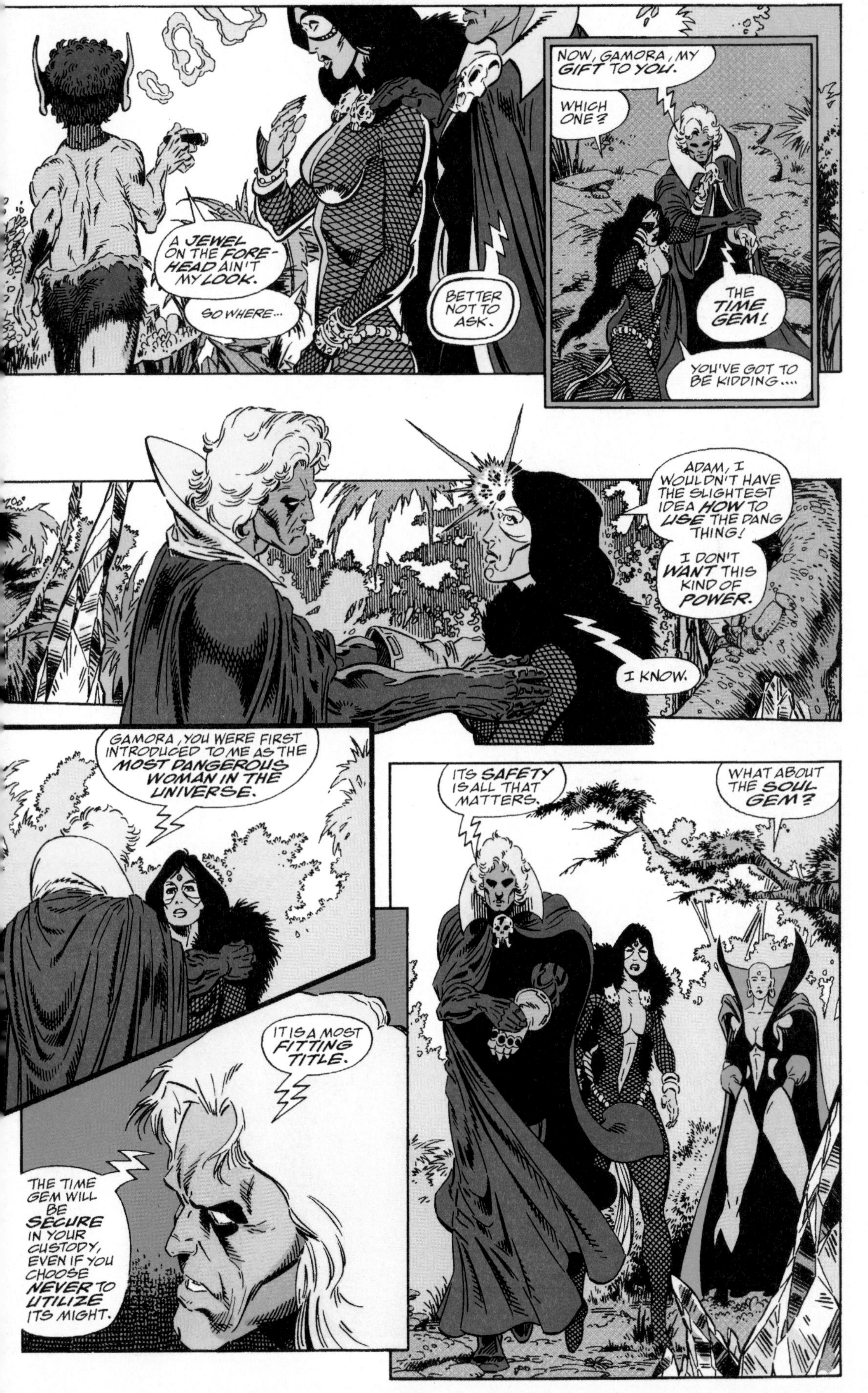
A JEWEL ON THE FOREHEAD AIN'T MY LOOK.
SO WHERE...
BETTER NOT TO ASK.
NOW, GAMORA, MY GIFT TO YOU.
WHICH ONE?
THE TIME GEM!
YOU'VE GOT TO BE KIDDING....
ADAM, I WOULDN'T HAVE THE SLIGHTEST IDEA HOW TO USE THE DANG THING!
I DON'T WANT THIS KIND OF POWER.
I KNOW.
GAMORA, YOU WERE FIRST INTRODUCED TO ME AS THE MOST DANGEROUS WOMAN IN THE UNIVERSE.
IT IS A MOST FITTING TITLE.
THE TIME GEM WILL BE SECURE IN YOUR CUSTODY, EVEN IF YOU CHOOSE NEVER TO UTILIZE ITS MIGHT.
ITS SAFETY IS ALL THAT MATTERS.
WHAT ABOUT THE SOUL GEM?

THIS BAUBLE AND I ARE *OLD FRIENDS*.

FOR BETTER OR WORSE IT STAYS WITH *ME*.

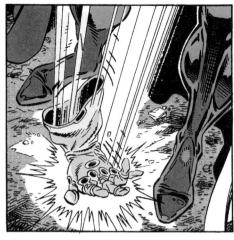

THERE WERE *SIX* INFINITY GEMS, WEREN'T THERE?

THE *REALITY GEM!*

WHERE'D IT GO?

TO A *CARETAKER* WHOSE *IDENTITY* WILL REMAIN *UNKNOWN* TO ALL BUT *ME*.

YOUR NAMELESS *ENFORCER?*

SOMEONE WHO'D *FROWN* UPON ANYONE *ATTEMPTING* TO GATHER ALL THE JEWELS FOR THEIR PERSONAL *AGGRANDIZEMENT*.

I CAN'T IMAGINE WHO...

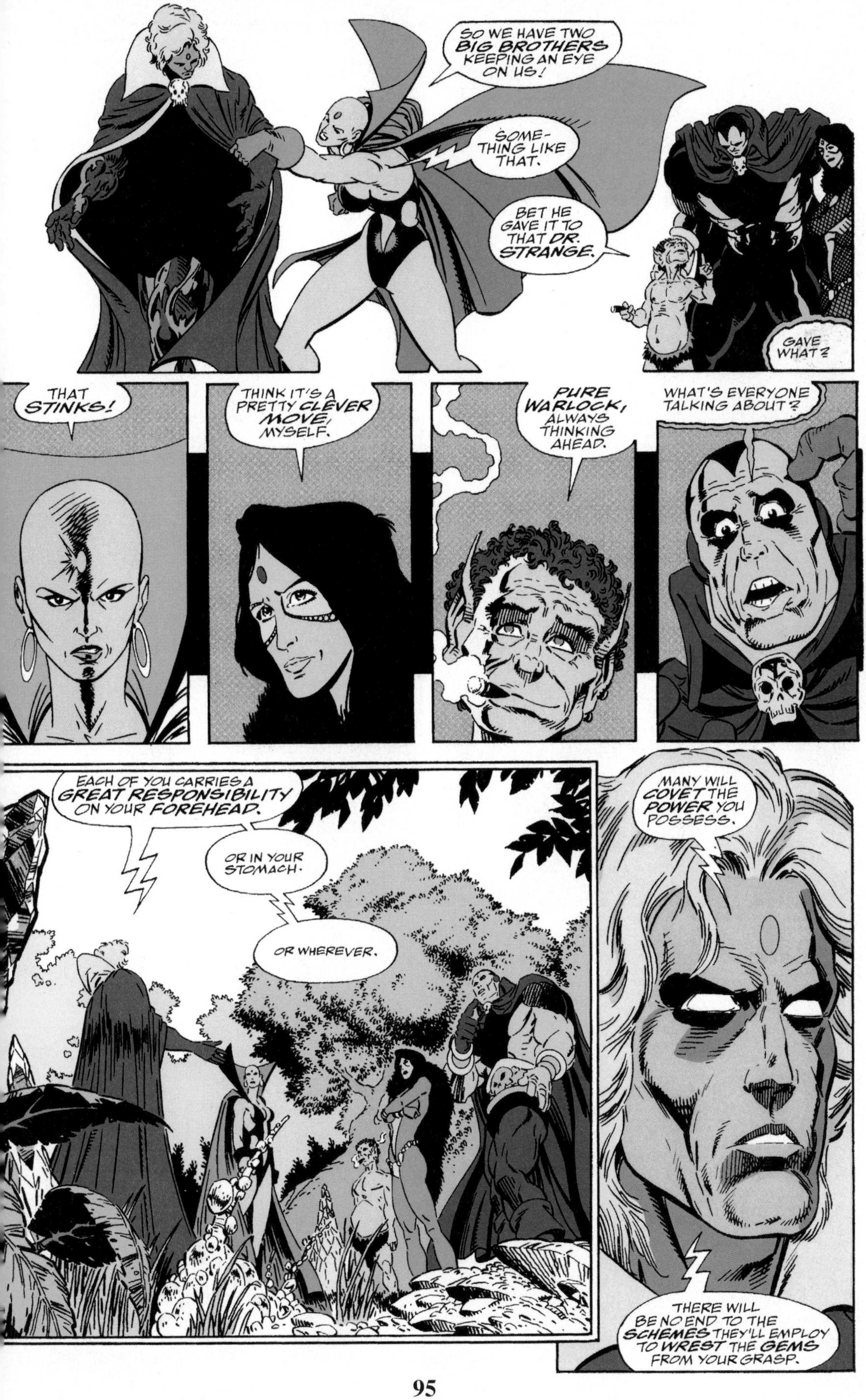
SO WE HAVE TWO BIG BROTHERS KEEPING AN EYE ON US!
SOME-THING LIKE THAT.
BET HE GAVE IT TO THAT DR. STRANGE.
GAVE WHAT?
THAT STINKS!
THINK IT'S A PRETTY CLEVER MOVE, MYSELF.
PURE WARLOCK, ALWAYS THINKING AHEAD.
WHAT'S EVERYONE TALKING ABOUT?
EACH OF YOU CARRIES A GREAT RESPONSIBILITY ON YOUR FOREHEAD.
OR IN YOUR STOMACH.
OR WHEREVER.
MANY WILL COVET THE POWER YOU POSSESS.
THERE WILL BE NO END TO THE SCHEMES THEY'LL EMPLOY TO WREST THE GEMS FROM YOUR GRASP.

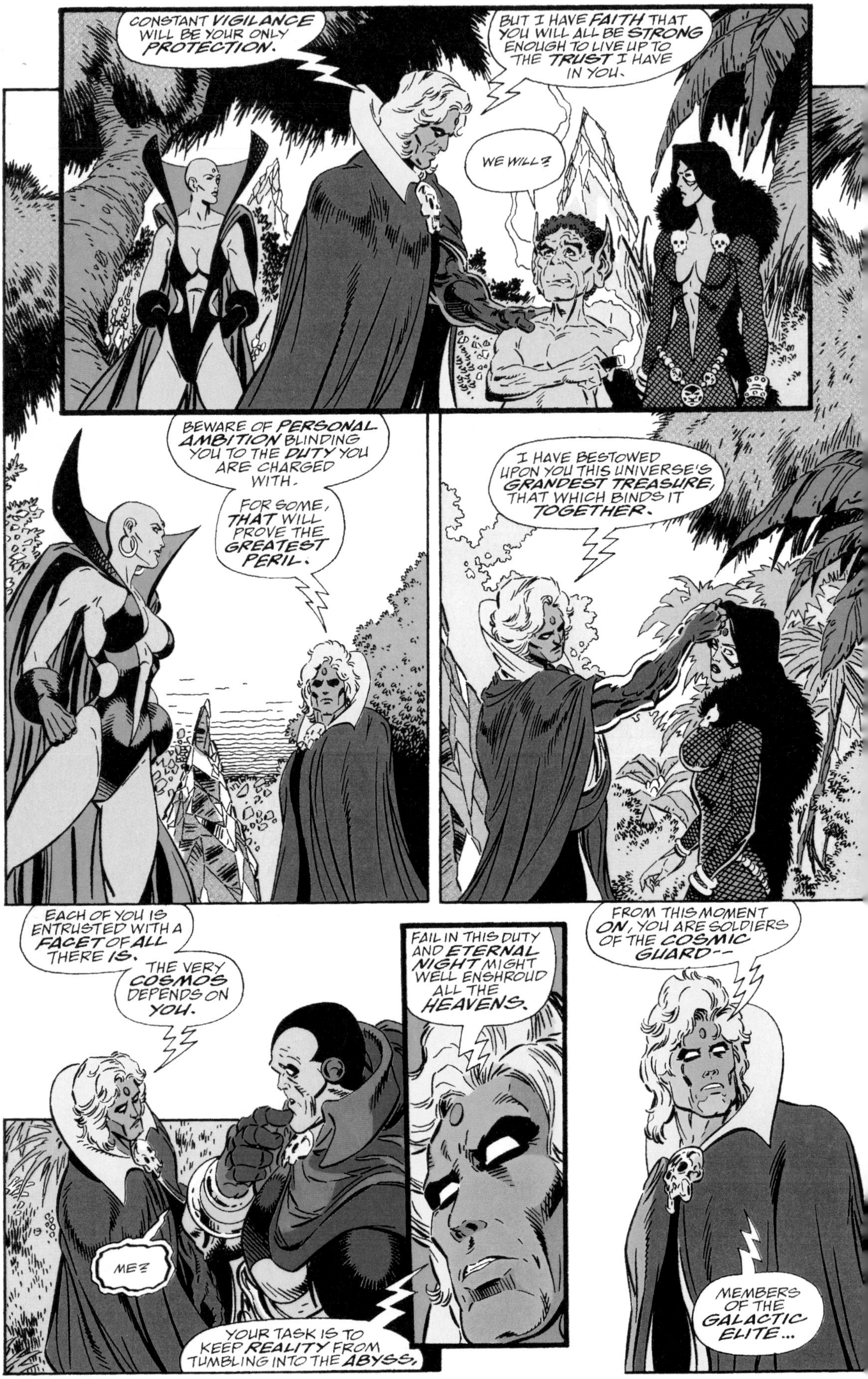
CONSTANT VIGILANCE WILL BE YOUR ONLY PROTECTION.
BUT I HAVE FAITH THAT YOU WILL ALL BE STRONG ENOUGH TO LIVE UP TO THE TRUST I HAVE IN YOU.
WE WILL?
BEWARE OF PERSONAL AMBITION BLINDING YOU TO THE DUTY YOU ARE CHARGED WITH.
FOR SOME, THAT WILL PROVE THE GREATEST PERIL.
I HAVE BESTOWED UPON YOU THIS UNIVERSE'S GRANDEST TREASURE, THAT WHICH BINDS IT TOGETHER.
EACH OF YOU IS ENTRUSTED WITH A FACET OF ALL THERE IS.
THE VERY COSMOS DEPENDS ON YOU.
ME?
YOUR TASK IS TO KEEP REALITY FROM TUMBLING INTO THE ABYSS,
FAIL IN THIS DUTY AND ETERNAL NIGHT MIGHT WELL ENSHROUD ALL THE HEAVENS.
FROM THIS MOMENT ON, YOU ARE SOLDIERS OF THE COSMIC GUARD--
MEMBERS OF THE GALACTIC ELITE...

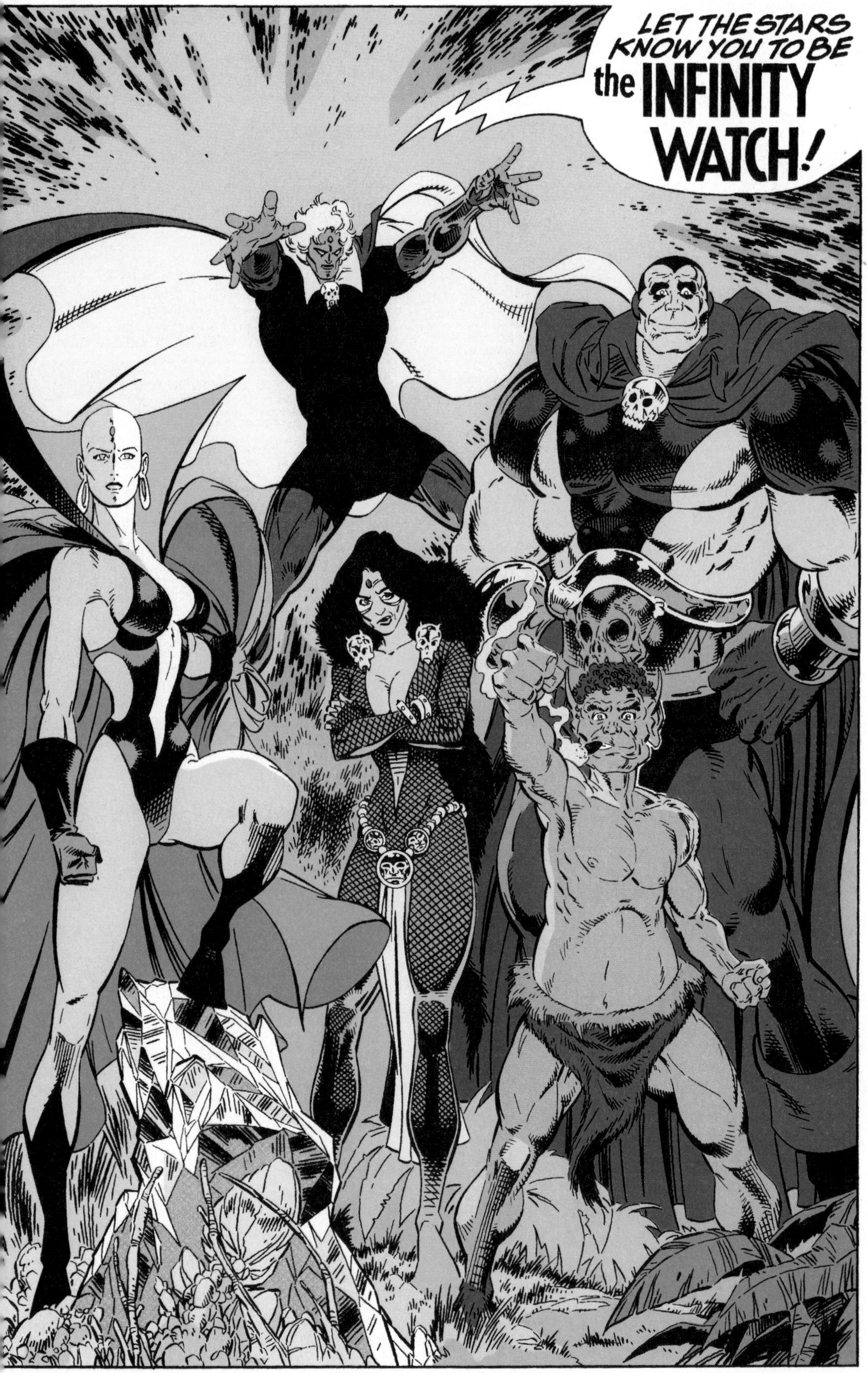
LET THE STARS KNOW YOU TO BE the INFINITY WATCH!

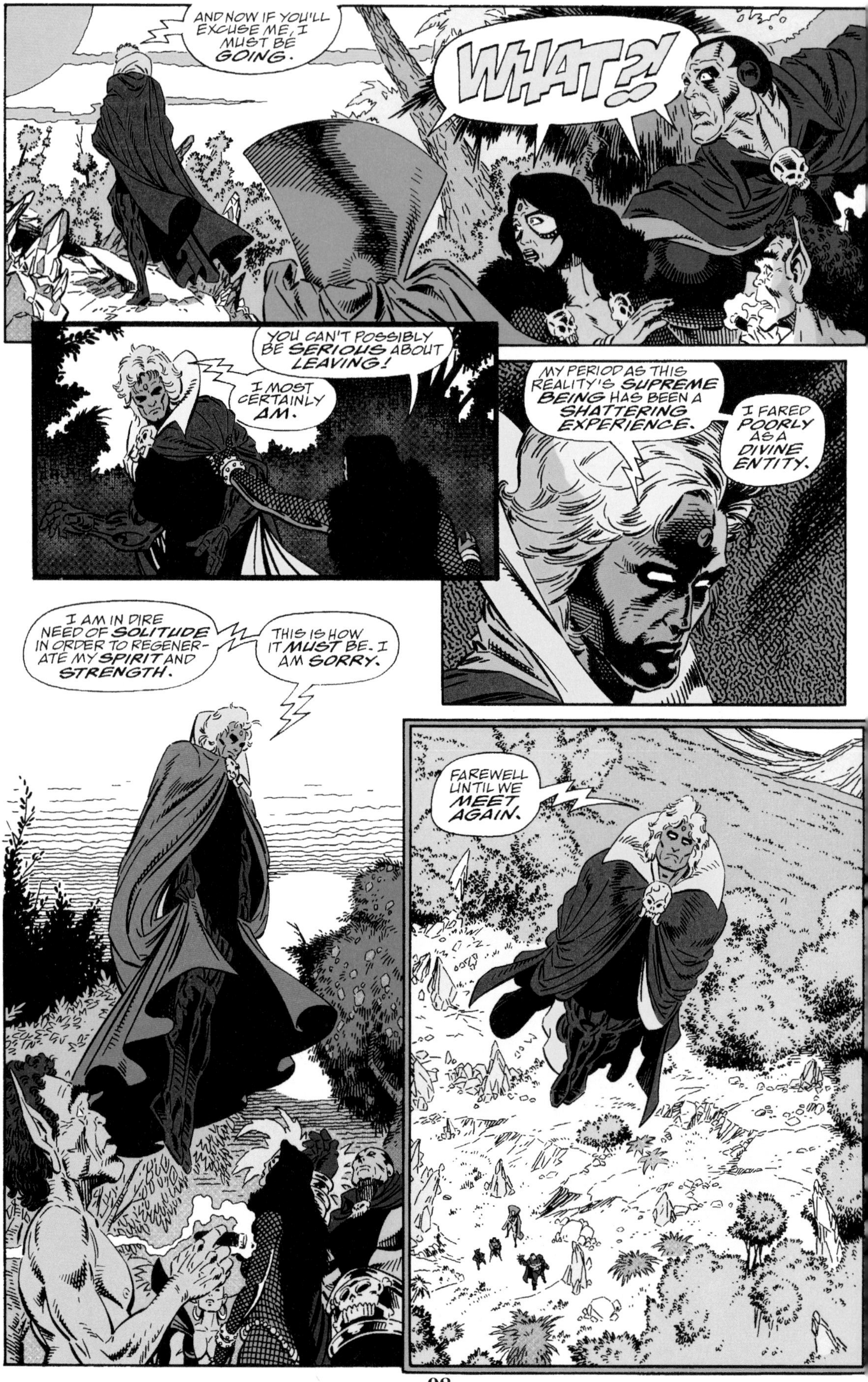

AND NOW IF YOU'LL EXCUSE ME, I MUST BE GOING.
WHAT?!
YOU CAN'T POSSIBLY BE SERIOUS ABOUT LEAVING!
I MOST CERTAINLY AM.
MY PERIOD AS THIS REALITY'S SUPREME BEING HAS BEEN A SHATTERING EXPERIENCE.
I FARED POORLY AS A DIVINE ENTITY.
I AM IN DIRE NEED OF SOLITUDE IN ORDER TO REGENERATE MY SPIRIT AND STRENGTH.
THIS IS HOW IT MUST BE. I AM SORRY.
FAREWELL UNTIL WE MEET AGAIN.

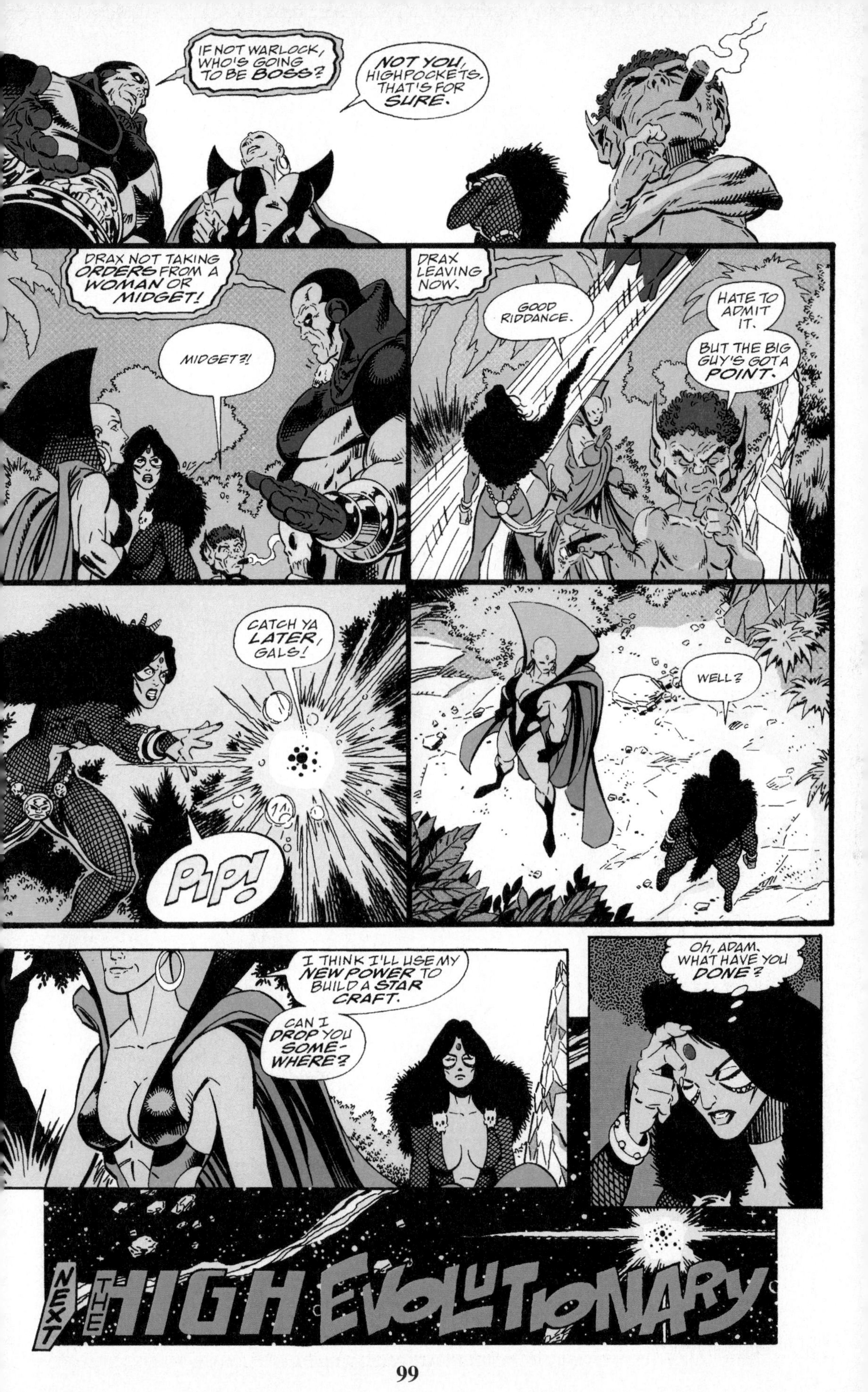
IF NOT WARLOCK, WHO'S GOING TO BE BOSS?
NOT YOU, HIGHPOCKETS. THAT'S FOR SURE.
DRAX NOT TAKING ORDERS FROM A WOMAN OR MIDGET!
MIDGET?!
DRAX LEAVING NOW.
GOOD RIDDANCE.
HATE TO ADMIT IT.
BUT THE BIG GUY'S GOT A POINT.
CATCH YA LATER, GALS!
PiP!
WELL?
I THINK I'LL USE MY NEW POWER TO BUILD A STAR CRAFT.
CAN I DROP YOU SOME-WHERE?
Oh, ADAM. WHAT HAVE YOU DONE?
NEXT THE HIGH EVOLUTIONARY

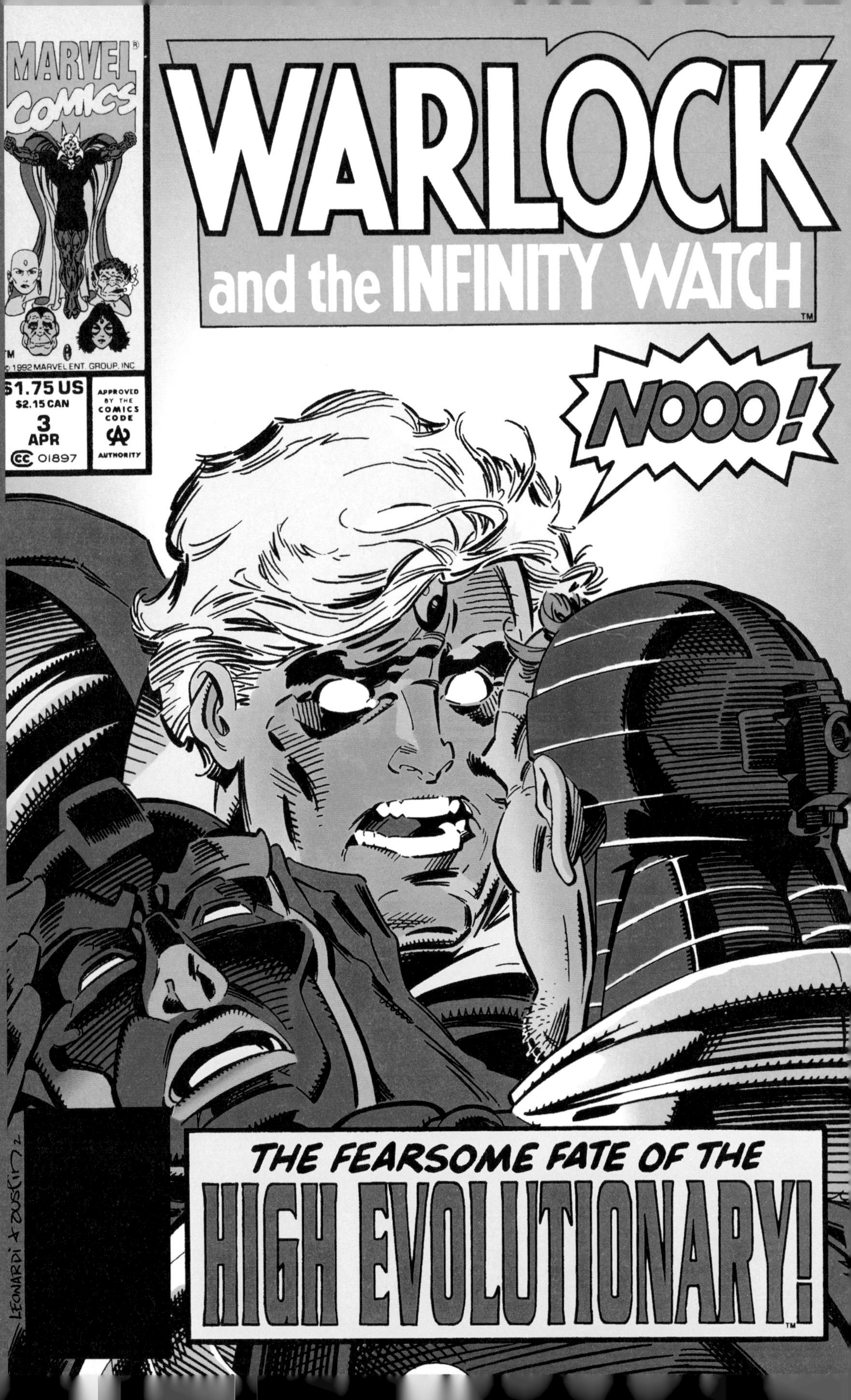
MARVEL COMICS
WARLOCK
and the INFINITY WATCH
© 1992 MARVEL ENT. GROUP, INC
$1.75 US
$2.15 CAN
3
APR
01897
APPROVED BY THE COMICS CODE AUTHORITY
NOOO!
THE FEARSOME FATE OF THE
HIGH EVOLUTIONARY!

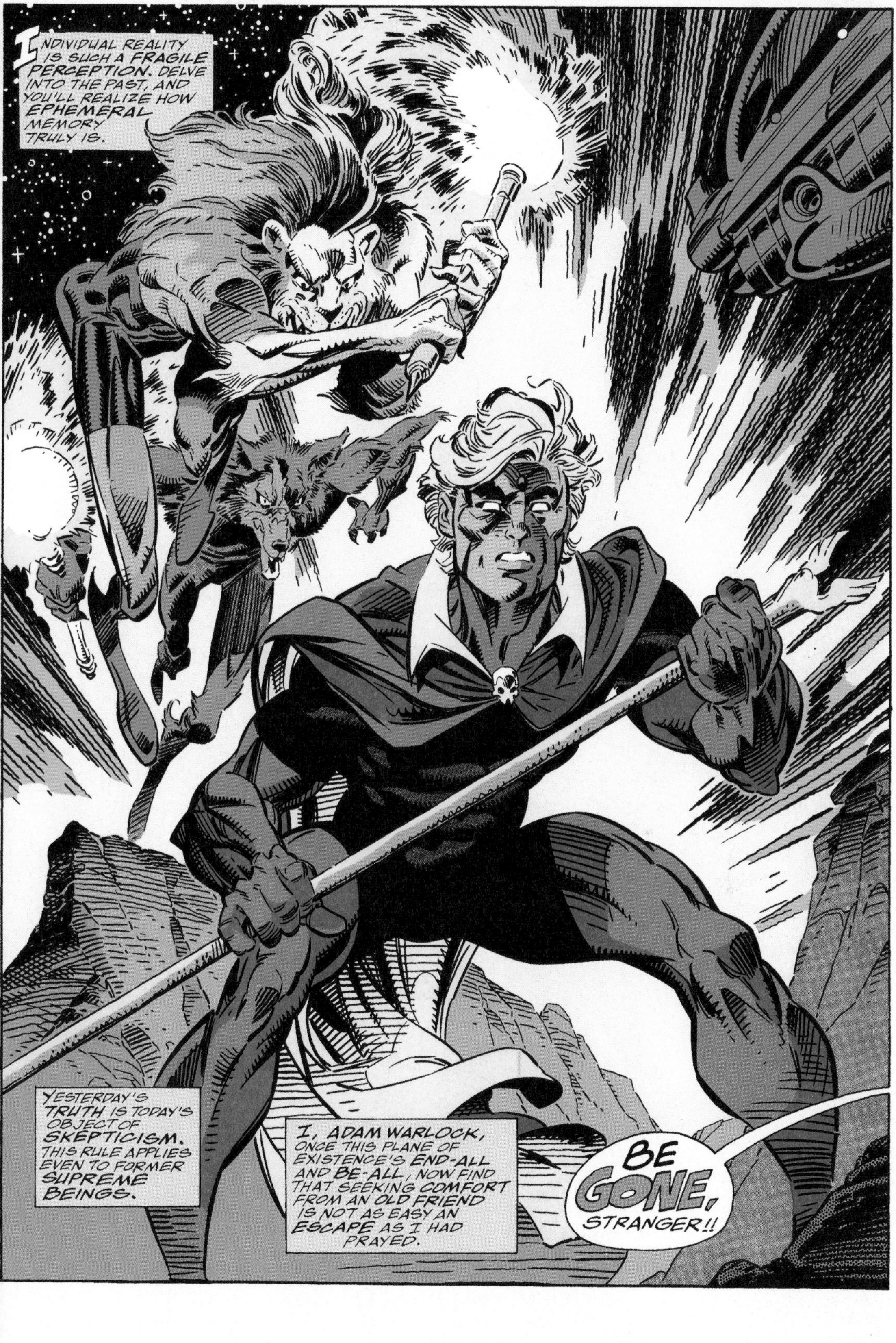
INDIVIDUAL REALITY IS SUCH A FRAGILE PERCEPTION. DELVE INTO THE PAST, AND YOU'LL REALIZE HOW EPHEMERAL MEMORY TRULY IS.
YESTERDAY'S TRUTH IS TODAY'S OBJECT OF SKEPTICISM. THIS RULE APPLIES EVEN TO FORMER SUPREME BEINGS.
I, ADAM WARLOCK, ONCE THIS PLANE OF EXISTENCE'S END-ALL AND BE-ALL, NOW FIND THAT SEEKING COMFORT FROM AN OLD FRIEND IS NOT AS EASY AN ESCAPE AS I HAD PRAYED.
BE GONE, STRANGER!!

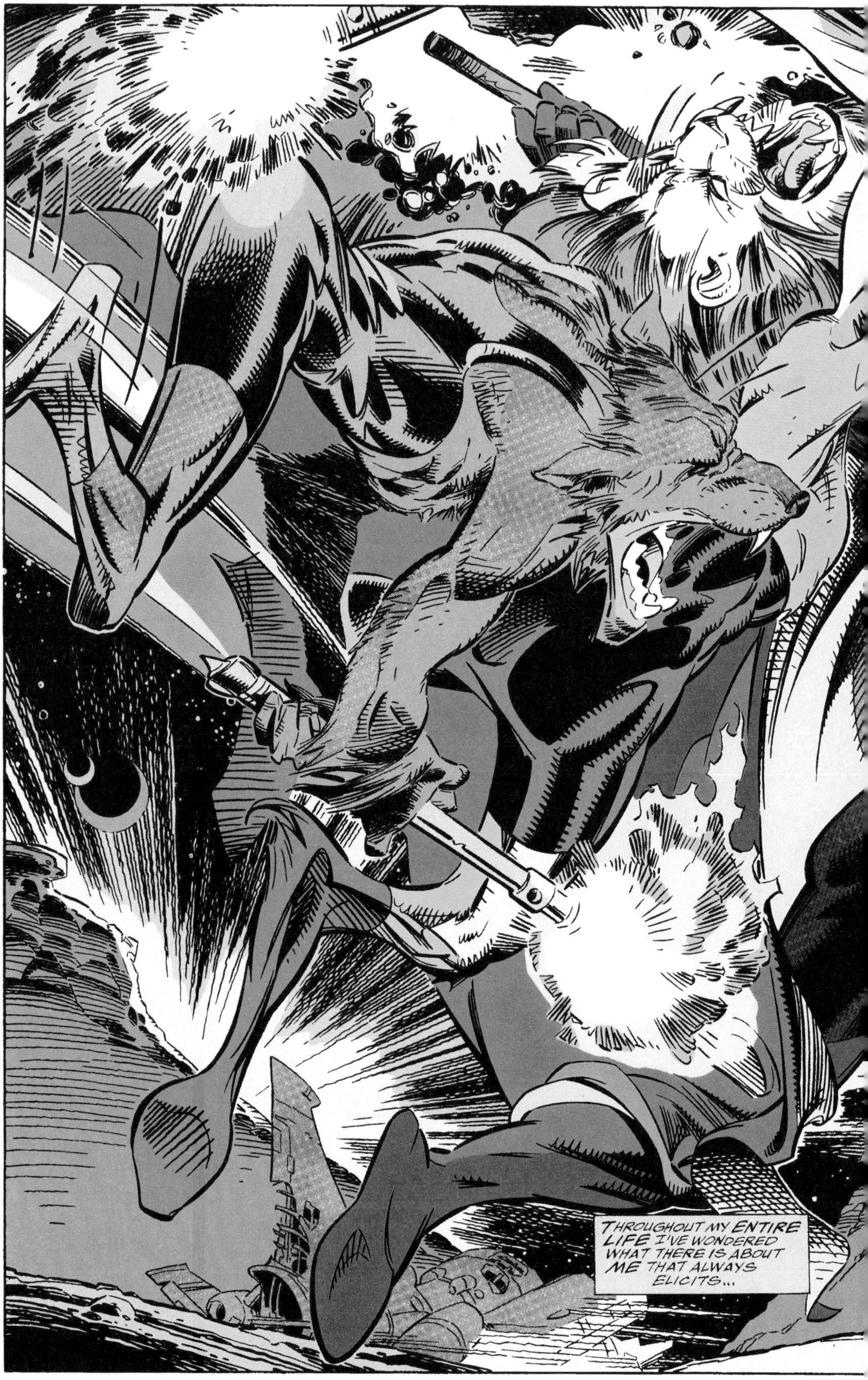
THROUGHOUT MY ENTIRE LIFE I'VE WONDERED WHAT THERE IS ABOUT ME THAT ALWAYS ELICITS...

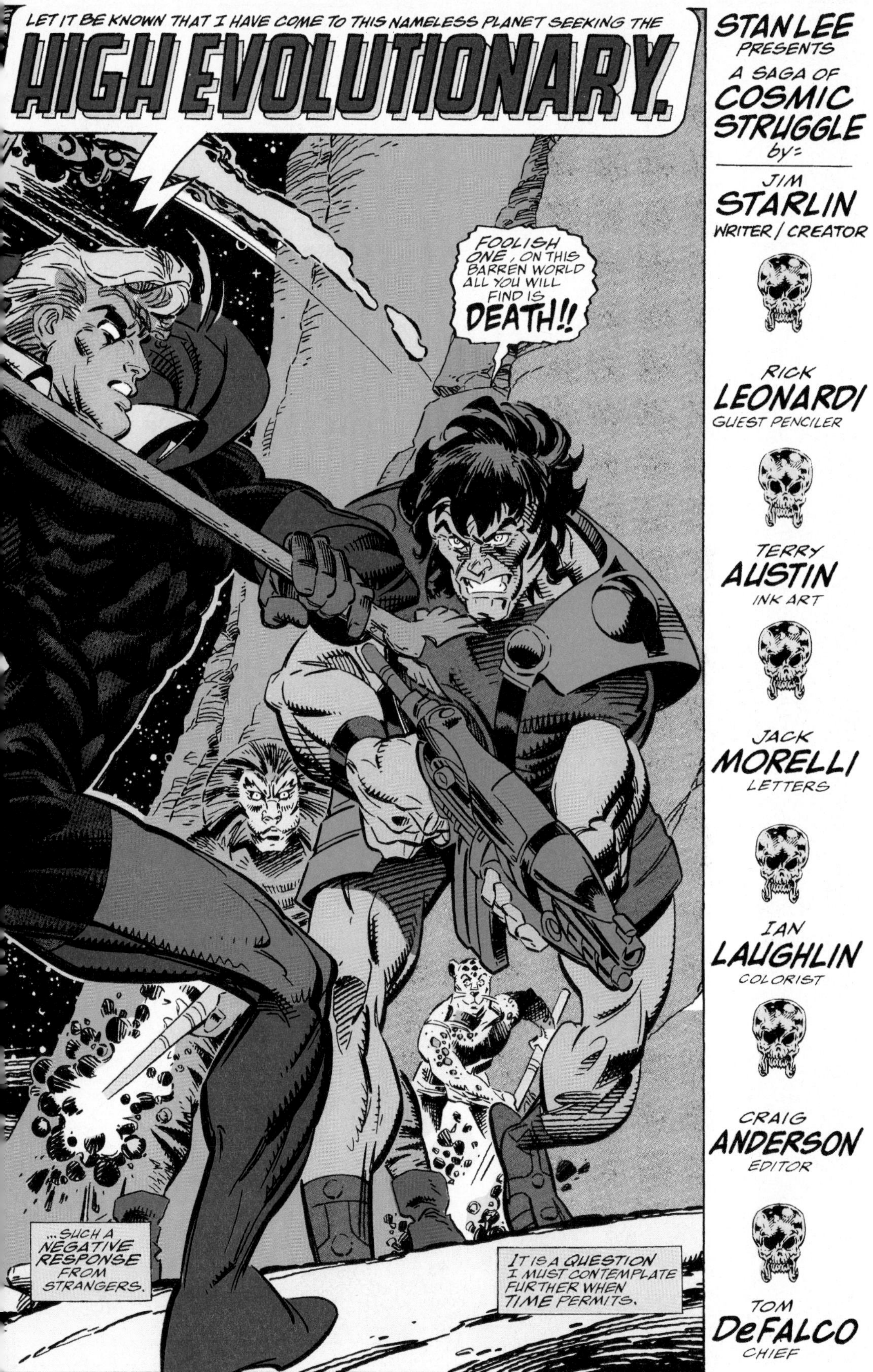
LET IT BE KNOWN THAT I HAVE COME TO THIS NAMELESS PLANET SEEKING THE
HIGH EVOLUTIONARY.
FOOLISH ONE, ON THIS BARREN WORLD ALL YOU WILL FIND IS DEATH!!
...SUCH A NEGATIVE RESPONSE FROM STRANGERS.
IT IS A QUESTION I MUST CONTEMPLATE FURTHER WHEN TIME PERMITS.
STAN LEE PRESENTS A SAGA OF COSMIC STRUGGLE by:
JIM STARLIN WRITER / CREATOR
RICK LEONARDI GUEST PENCILER
TERRY AUSTIN INK ART
JACK MORELLI LETTERS
IAN LAUGHLIN COLORIST
CRAIG ANDERSON EDITOR
TOM DeFALCO CHIEF

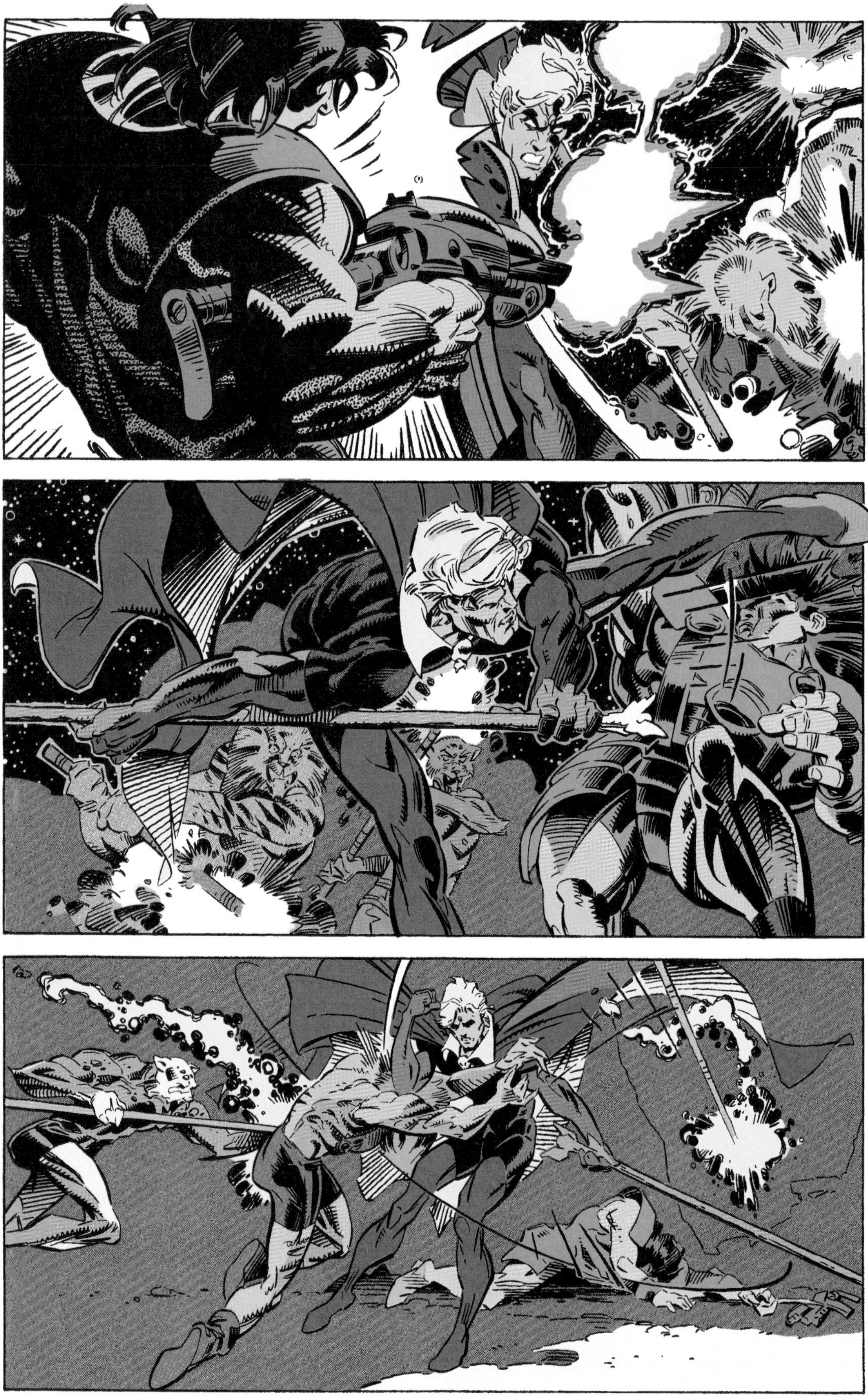

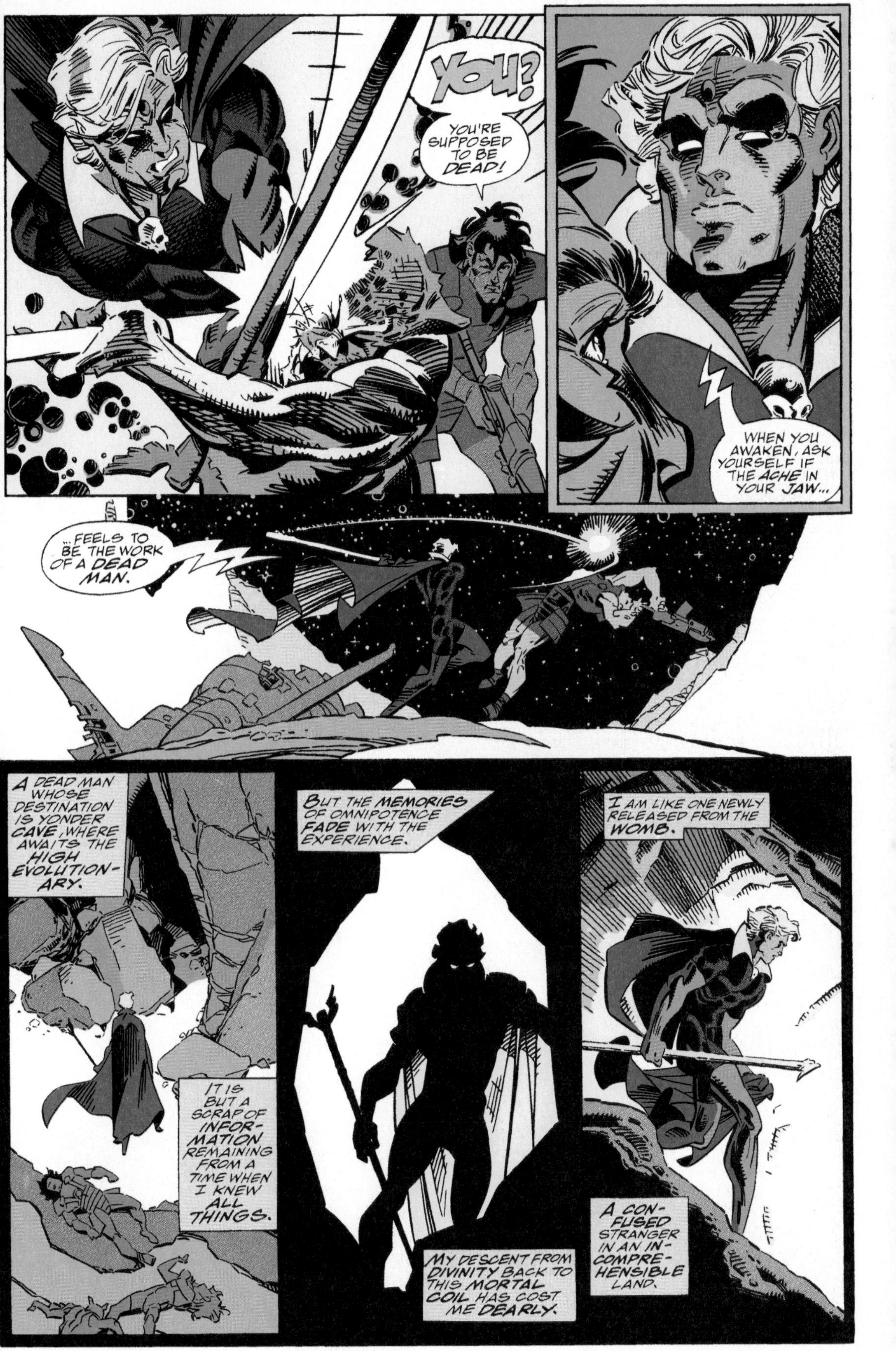
YOU?
YOU'RE SUPPOSED TO BE DEAD!
WHEN YOU AWAKEN, ASK YOURSELF IF THE ACHE IN YOUR JAW...
...FEELS TO BE THE WORK OF A DEAD MAN.
A DEAD MAN WHOSE DESTINATION IS YONDER CAVE, WHERE AWAITS THE HIGH EVOLUTIONARY.
IT IS BUT A SCRAP OF INFORMATION REMAINING FROM A TIME WHEN I KNEW ALL THINGS.
BUT THE MEMORIES OF OMNIPOTENCE FADE WITH THE EXPERIENCE.
MY DESCENT FROM DIVINITY BACK TO THIS MORTAL COIL HAS COST ME DEARLY.
I AM LIKE ONE NEWLY RELEASED FROM THE WOMB.
A CONFUSED STRANGER IN AN INCOMPREHENSIBLE LAND.

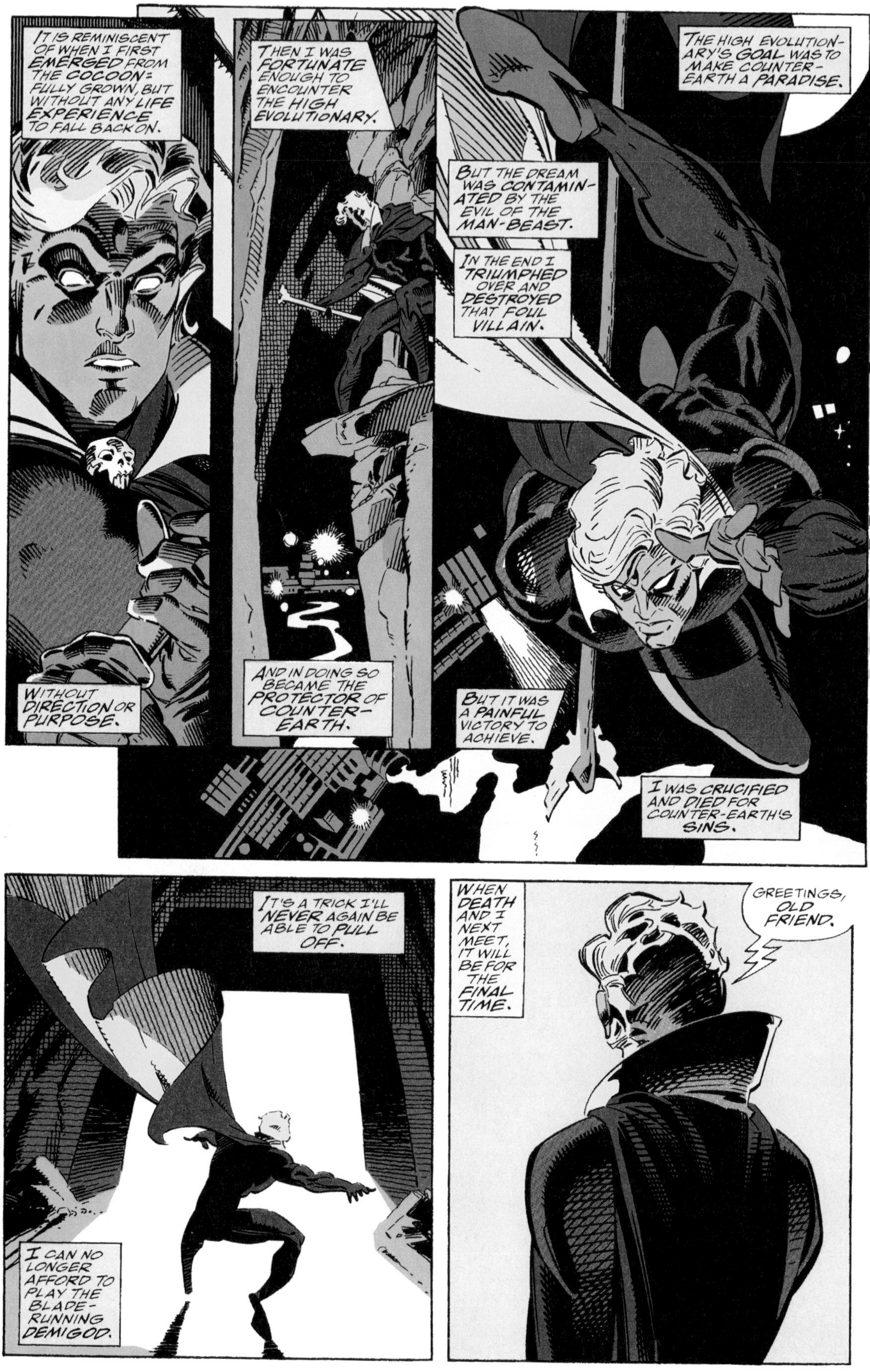

IT IS REMINISCENT OF WHEN I FIRST EMERGED FROM THE COCOON: FULLY GROWN, BUT WITHOUT ANY LIFE EXPERIENCE TO FALL BACK ON.
WITHOUT DIRECTION OR PURPOSE.
THEN I WAS FORTUNATE ENOUGH TO ENCOUNTER THE HIGH EVOLUTIONARY.
AND IN DOING SO BECAME THE PROTECTOR OF COUNTER-EARTH.
THE HIGH EVOLUTIONARY'S GOAL WAS TO MAKE COUNTER-EARTH A PARADISE.
BUT THE DREAM WAS CONTAMINATED BY THE EVIL OF THE MAN-BEAST.
IN THE END I TRIUMPHED OVER AND DESTROYED THAT FOUL VILLAIN.
BUT IT WAS A PAINFUL VICTORY TO ACHIEVE.
I WAS CRUCIFIED AND DIED FOR COUNTER-EARTH'S SINS.
IT'S A TRICK I'LL NEVER AGAIN BE ABLE TO PULL OFF.
I CAN NO LONGER AFFORD TO PLAY THE BLADE-RUNNING DEMIGOD.
WHEN DEATH AND I NEXT MEET, IT WILL BE FOR THE FINAL TIME.
GREETINGS, OLD FRIEND.

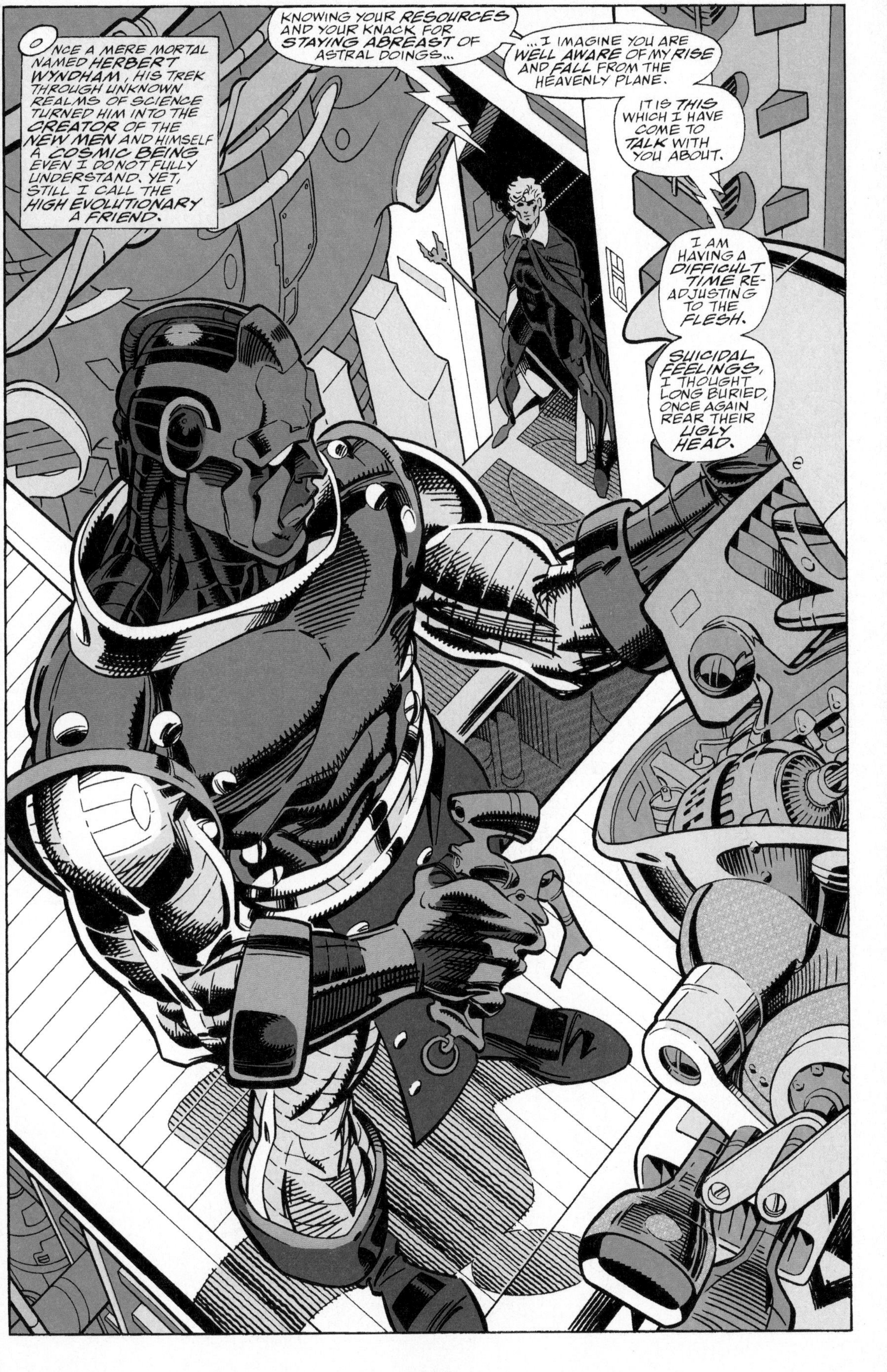
ONCE A MERE MORTAL NAMED HERBERT WYNDHAM, HIS TREK THROUGH UNKNOWN REALMS OF SCIENCE TURNED HIM INTO THE CREATOR OF THE NEW MEN AND HIMSELF A COSMIC BEING EVEN I DO NOT FULLY UNDERSTAND. YET, STILL I CALL THE HIGH EVOLUTIONARY A FRIEND.
KNOWING YOUR RESOURCES AND YOUR KNACK FOR STAYING ABREAST OF ASTRAL DOINGS...
...I IMAGINE YOU ARE WELL AWARE OF MY RISE AND FALL FROM THE HEAVENLY PLANE.
IT IS THIS WHICH I HAVE COME TO TALK WITH YOU ABOUT.
I AM HAVING A DIFFICULT TIME READJUSTING TO THE FLESH.
SUICIDAL FEELINGS, I THOUGHT LONG BURIED, ONCE AGAIN REAR THEIR UGLY HEAD.

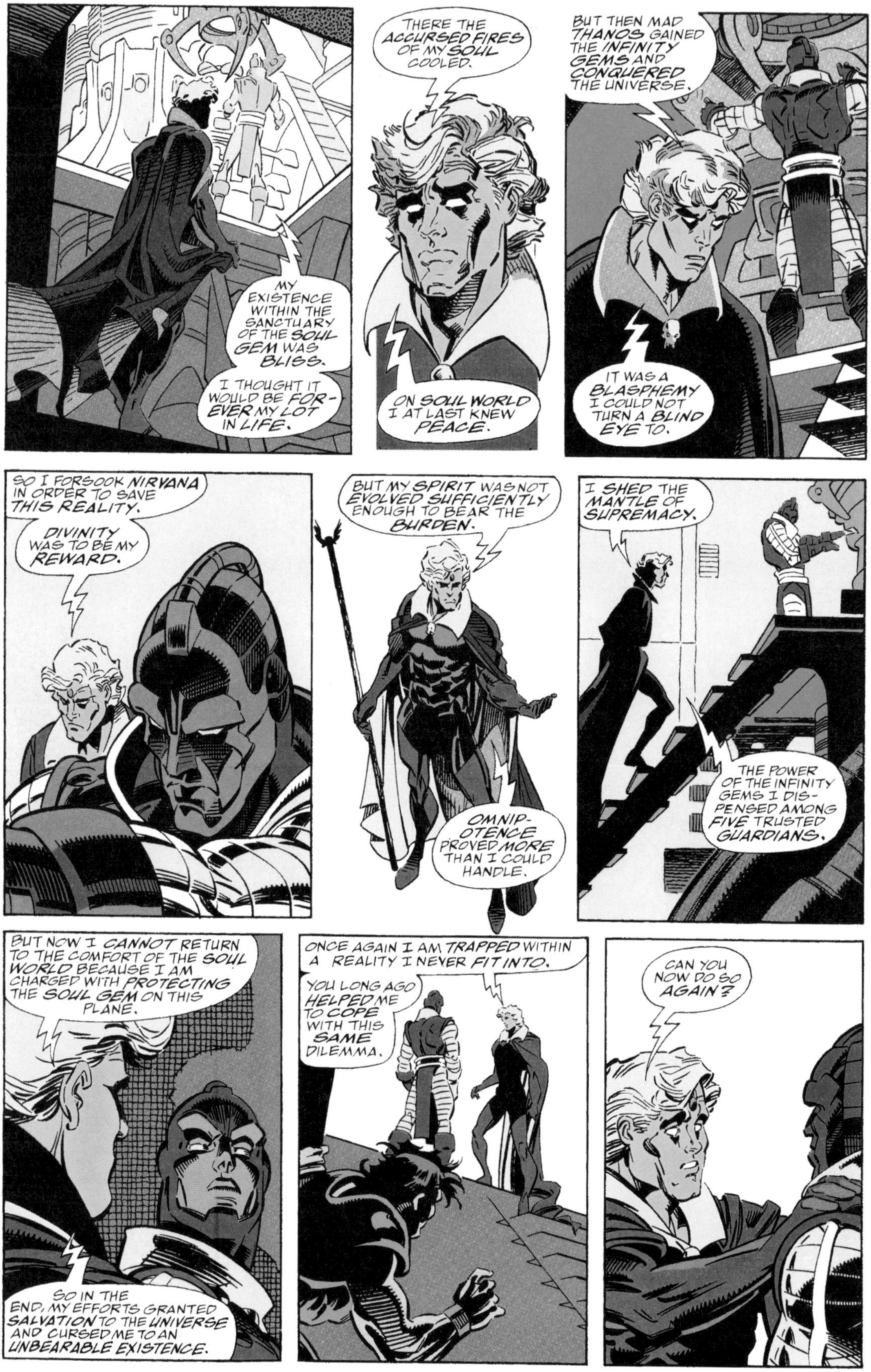
MY EXISTENCE WITHIN THE SANCTUARY OF THE SOUL GEM WAS BLISS.
I THOUGHT IT WOULD BE FOREVER MY LOT IN LIFE.
THERE THE ACCURSED FIRES OF MY SOUL COOLED.
ON SOUL WORLD I AT LAST KNEW PEACE.
BUT THEN MAD THANOS GAINED THE INFINITY GEMS AND CONQUERED THE UNIVERSE.
IT WAS A BLASPHEMY I COULD NOT TURN A BLIND EYE TO.
SO I FORSOOK NIRVANA IN ORDER TO SAVE THIS REALITY.
DIVINITY WAS TO BE MY REWARD.
BUT MY SPIRIT WAS NOT EVOLVED SUFFICIENTLY ENOUGH TO BEAR THE BURDEN.
OMNIPOTENCE PROVED MORE THAN I COULD HANDLE.
I SHED THE MANTLE OF SUPREMACY.
THE POWER OF THE INFINITY GEMS I DISPENSED AMONG FIVE TRUSTED GUARDIANS.
BUT NOW I CANNOT RETURN TO THE COMFORT OF THE SOUL WORLD BECAUSE I AM CHARGED WITH PROTECTING THE SOUL GEM ON THIS PLANE.
SO IN THE END, MY EFFORTS GRANTED SALVATION TO THE UNIVERSE AND CURSED ME TO AN UNBEARABLE EXISTENCE.
ONCE AGAIN I AM TRAPPED WITHIN A REALITY I NEVER FIT INTO.
YOU LONG AGO HELPED ME TO COPE WITH THIS SAME DILEMMA.
CAN YOU NOW DO SO AGAIN?

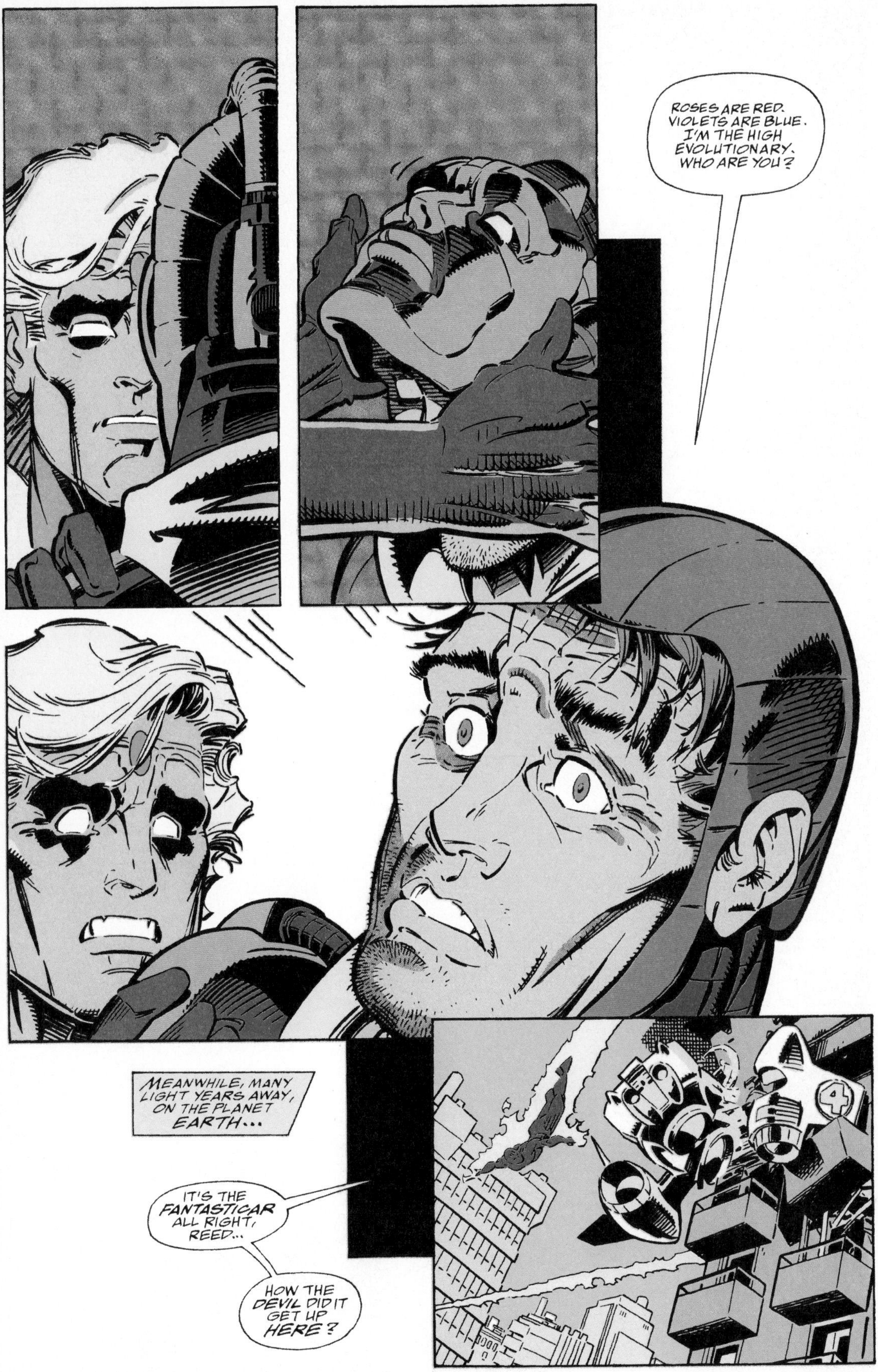
ROSES ARE RED. VIOLETS ARE BLUE. I'M THE HIGH EVOLUTIONARY. WHO ARE YOU?
MEANWHILE, MANY LIGHT YEARS AWAY, ON THE PLANET EARTH...
IT'S THE FANTASTICAR ALL RIGHT, REED...
HOW THE DEVIL DID IT GET UP HERE?

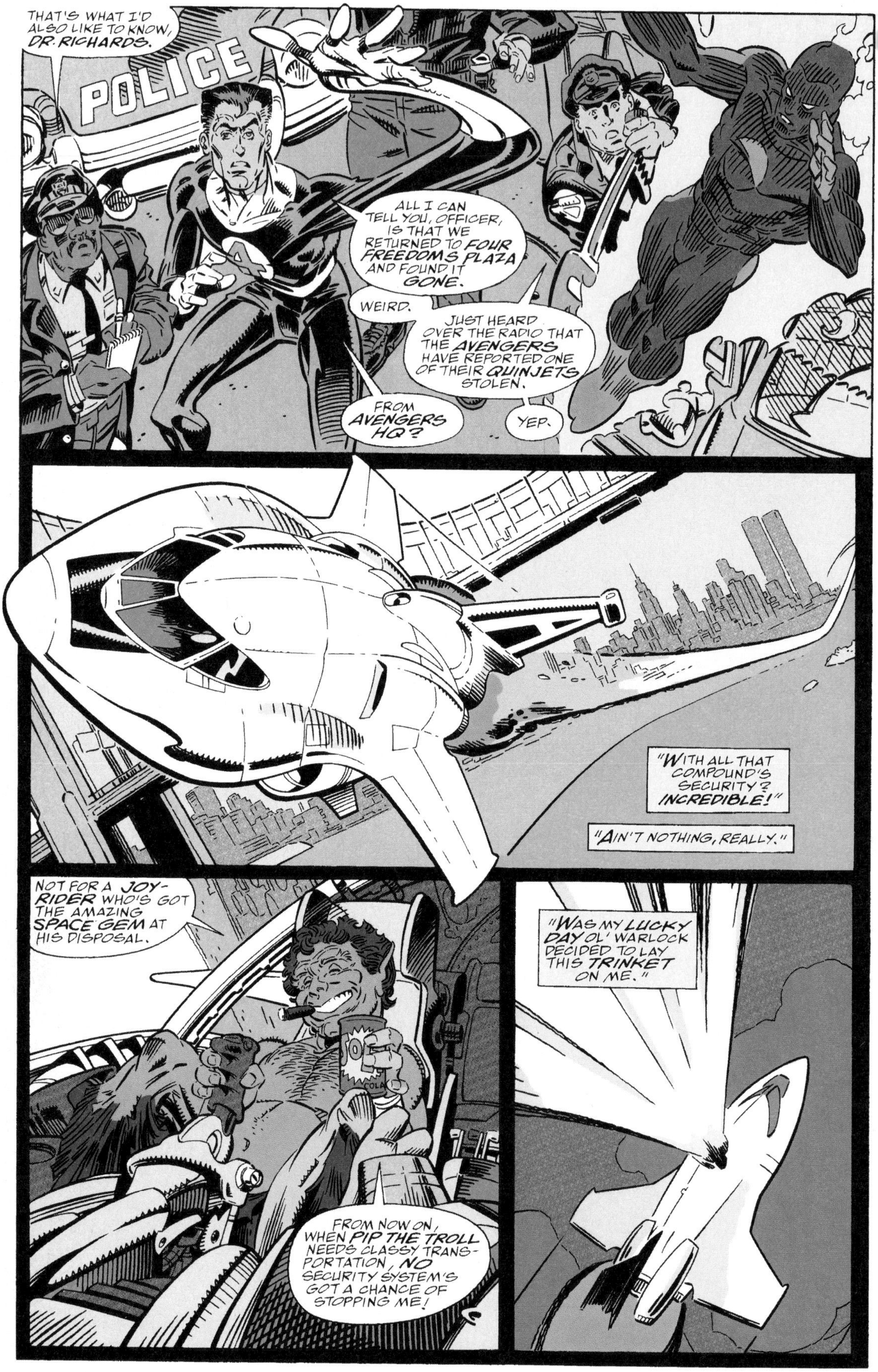
THAT'S WHAT I'D ALSO LIKE TO KNOW, DR. RICHARDS.
POLICE
ALL I CAN TELL YOU, OFFICER, IS THAT WE RETURNED TO FOUR FREEDOMS PLAZA AND FOUND IT GONE.
WEIRD.
JUST HEARD OVER THE RADIO THAT THE AVENGERS HAVE REPORTED ONE OF THEIR QUINJETS STOLEN.
FROM AVENGERS HQ?
YEP.
"WITH ALL THAT COMPOUND'S SECURITY? INCREDIBLE!"
"AIN'T NOTHING, REALLY."
NOT FOR A JOY-RIDER WHO'S GOT THE AMAZING SPACE GEM AT HIS DISPOSAL.
FROM NOW ON, WHEN PIP THE TROLL NEEDS CLASSY TRANS-PORTATION, NO SECURITY SYSTEM'S GOT A CHANCE OF STOPPING ME!
"WAS MY LUCKY DAY OL' WARLOCK DECIDED TO LAY THIS TRINKET ON ME."

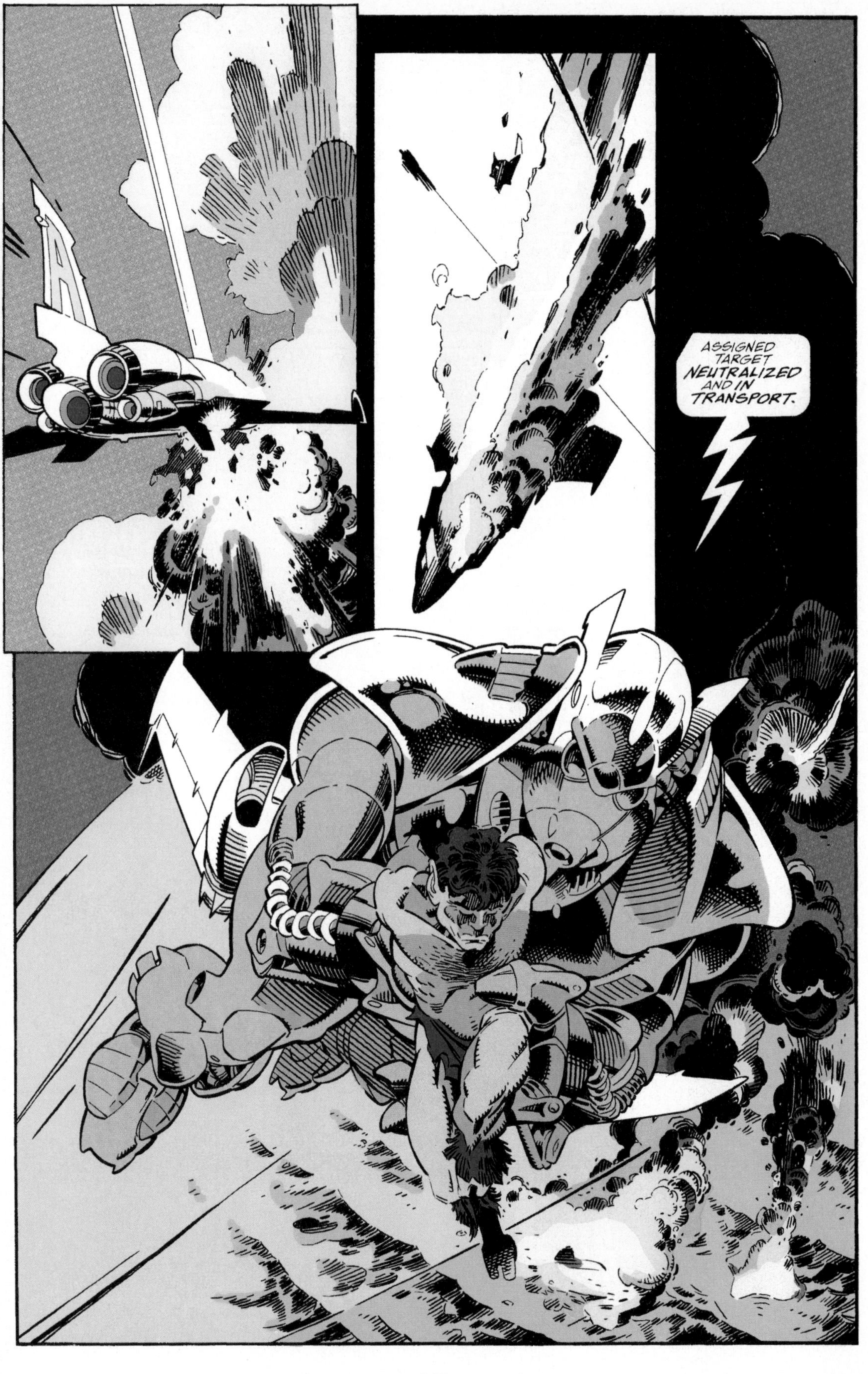
ASSIGNED TARGET NEUTRALIZED AND IN TRANSPORT.

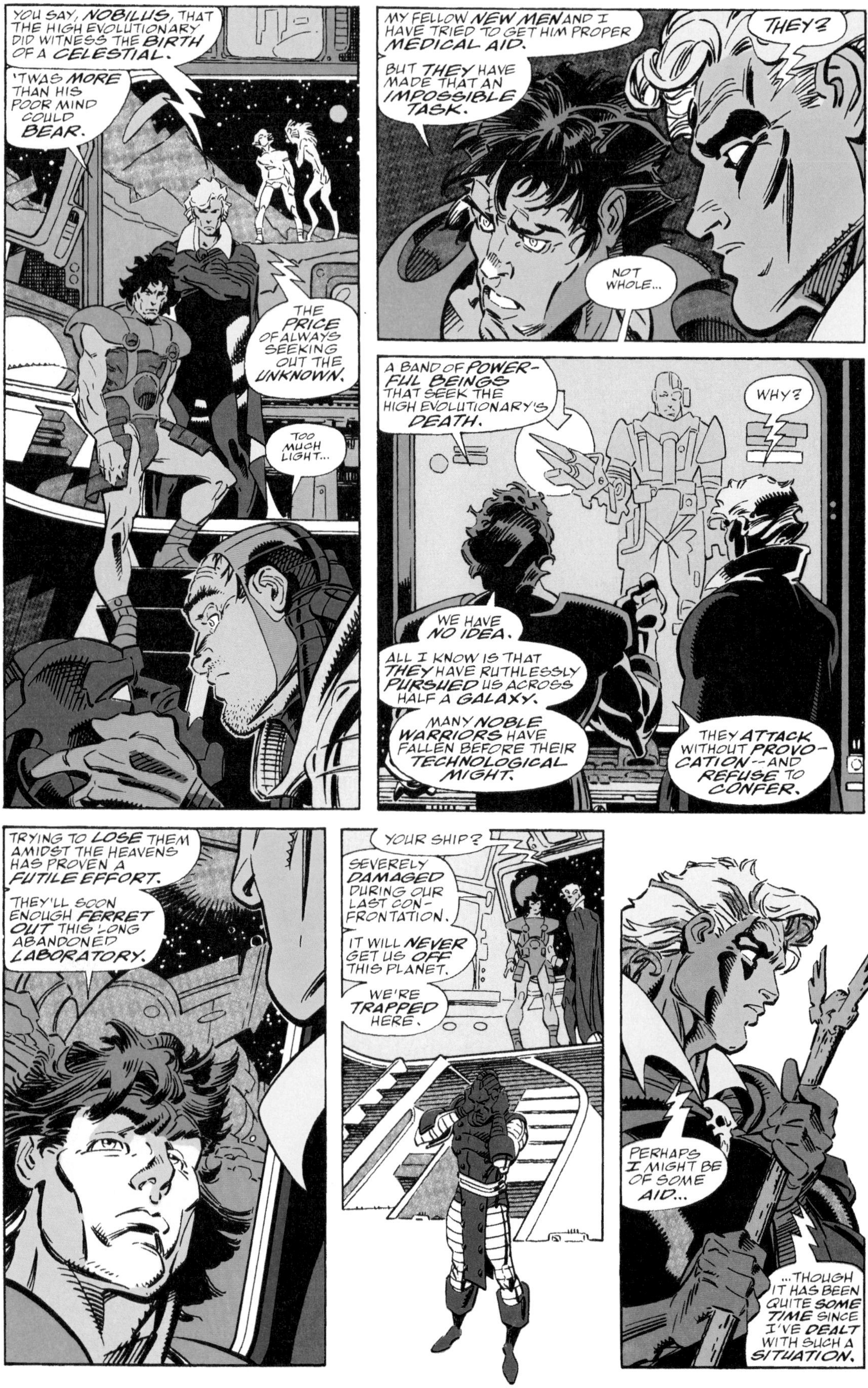

YOU SAY, NOBILUS, THAT THE HIGH EVOLUTIONARY DID WITNESS THE BIRTH OF A CELESTIAL.
'TWAS MORE THAN HIS POOR MIND COULD BEAR.
THE PRICE OF ALWAYS SEEKING OUT THE UNKNOWN.
TOO MUCH LIGHT...
MY FELLOW NEW MEN AND I HAVE TRIED TO GET HIM PROPER MEDICAL AID.
BUT THEY HAVE MADE THAT AN IMPOSSIBLE TASK.
THEY?
NOT WHOLE...
A BAND OF POWER-FUL BEINGS THAT SEEK THE HIGH EVOLUTIONARY'S DEATH.
WHY?
WE HAVE NO IDEA.
ALL I KNOW IS THAT THEY HAVE RUTHLESSLY PURSUED US ACROSS HALF A GALAXY.
MANY NOBLE WARRIORS HAVE FALLEN BEFORE THEIR TECHNOLOGICAL MIGHT.
THEY ATTACK WITHOUT PROVO-CATION--AND REFUSE TO CONFER.
TRYING TO LOSE THEM AMIDST THE HEAVENS HAS PROVEN A FUTILE EFFORT.
THEY'LL SOON ENOUGH FERRET OUT THIS LONG ABANDONED LABORATORY.
YOUR SHIP?
SEVERELY DAMAGED DURING OUR LAST CON-FRONTATION.
IT WILL NEVER GET US OFF THIS PLANET.
WE'RE TRAPPED HERE.
PERHAPS I MIGHT BE OF SOME AID...
...THOUGH IT HAS BEEN QUITE SOME TIME SINCE I'VE DEALT WITH SUCH A SITUATION.

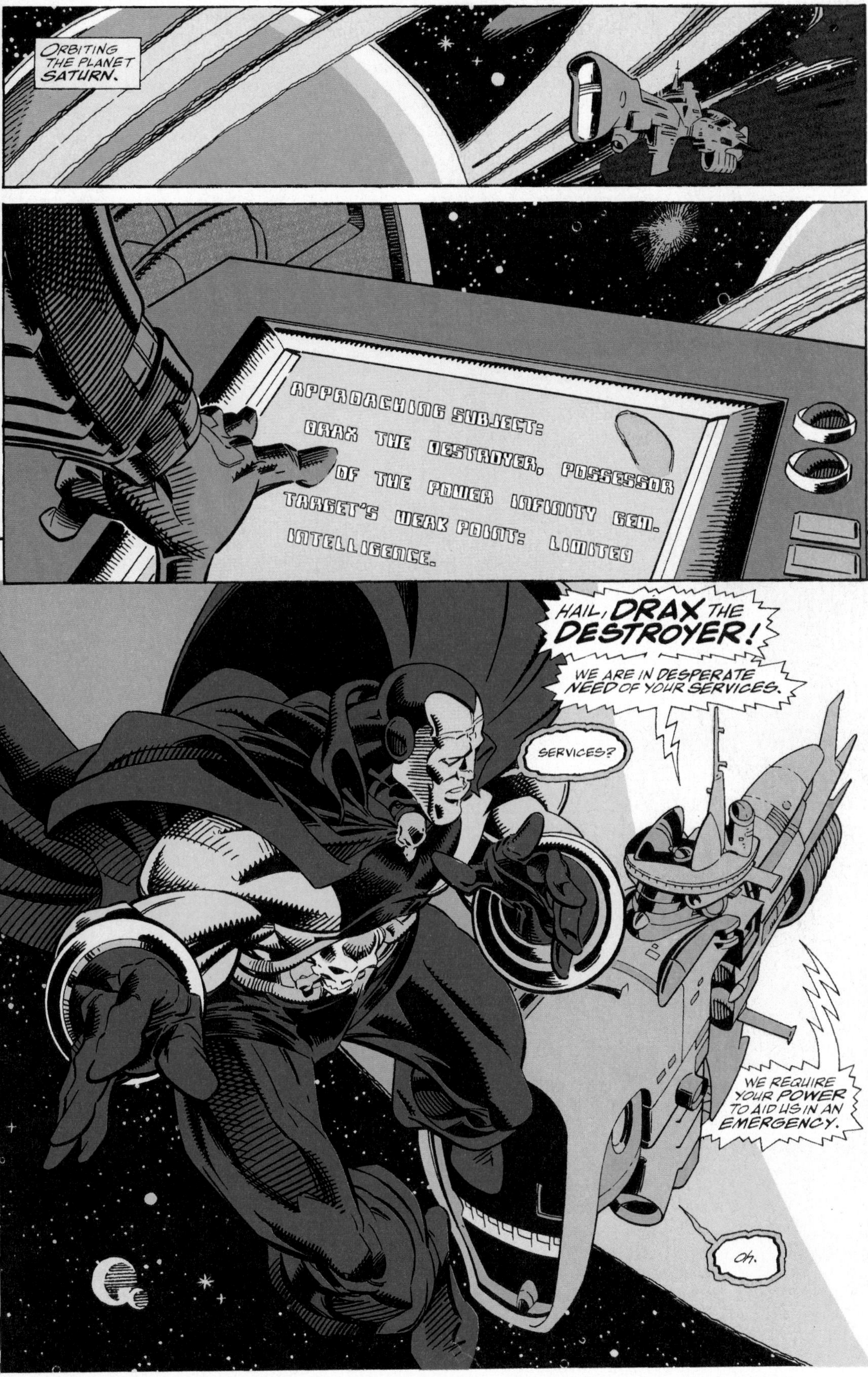
ORBITING THE PLANET SATURN.
APPROACHING SUBJECT:
DRAX THE DESTROYER, POSSESSOR OF THE POWER INFINITY GEM.
TARGET'S WEAK POINT: LIMITED INTELLIGENCE.
HAIL, DRAX THE DESTROYER!
WE ARE IN DESPERATE NEED OF YOUR SERVICES.
SERVICES?
WE REQUIRE YOUR POWER TO AID US IN AN EMERGENCY.
Oh.

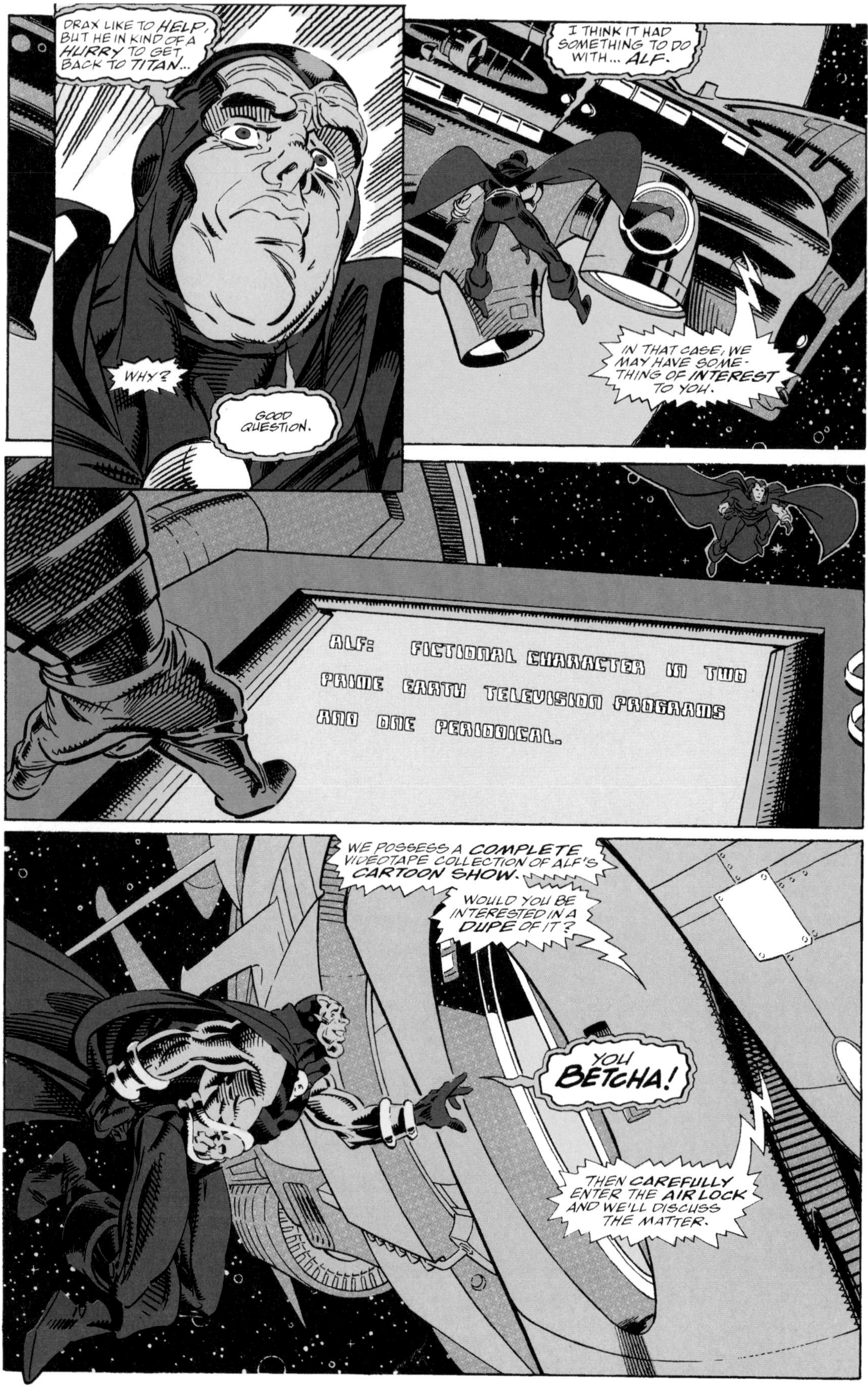
DRAX LIKE TO HELP, BUT HE IN KIND OF A HURRY TO GET BACK TO TITAN...
WHY?
GOOD QUESTION.
I THINK IT HAD SOMETHING TO DO WITH... ALF.
IN THAT CASE, WE MAY HAVE SOME-THING OF INTEREST TO YOU.
ALF: FICTIONAL CHARACTER IN TWO PRIME EARTH TELEVISION PROGRAMS AND ONE PERIODICAL.
WE POSSESS A COMPLETE VIDEOTAPE COLLECTION OF ALF'S CARTOON SHOW.
WOULD YOU BE INTERESTED IN A DUPE OF IT?
YOU BETCHA!
THEN CAREFULLY ENTER THE AIR LOCK AND WE'LL DISCUSS THE MATTER.

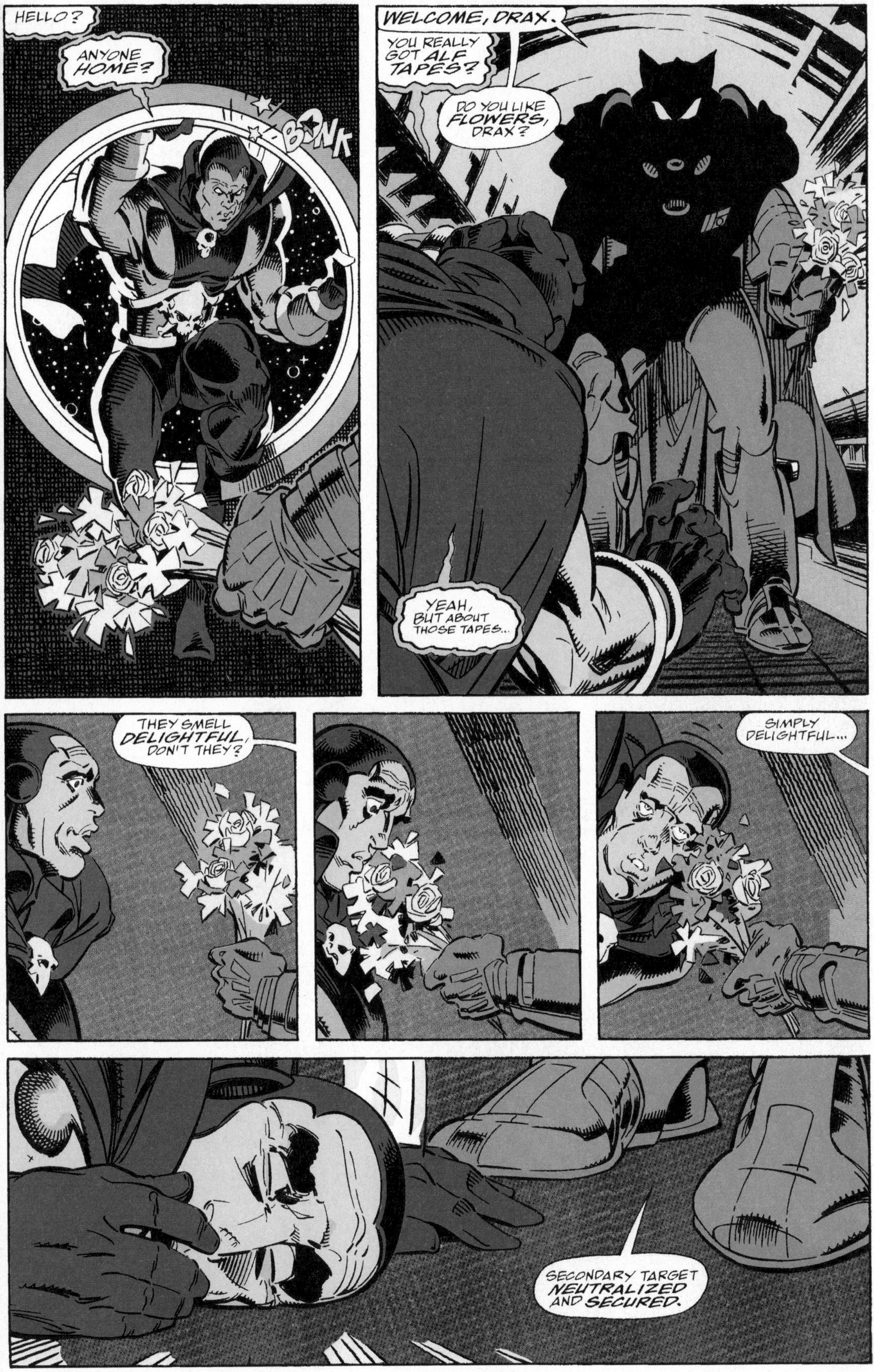
HELLO?
ANYONE HOME?
BONK
WELCOME, DRAX.
YOU REALLY GOT ALF TAPES?
DO YOU LIKE FLOWERS, DRAX?
YEAH, BUT ABOUT THOSE TAPES...
THEY SMELL DELIGHTFUL, DON'T THEY?
SIMPLY DELIGHTFUL...
SECONDARY TARGET NEUTRALIZED AND SECURED.

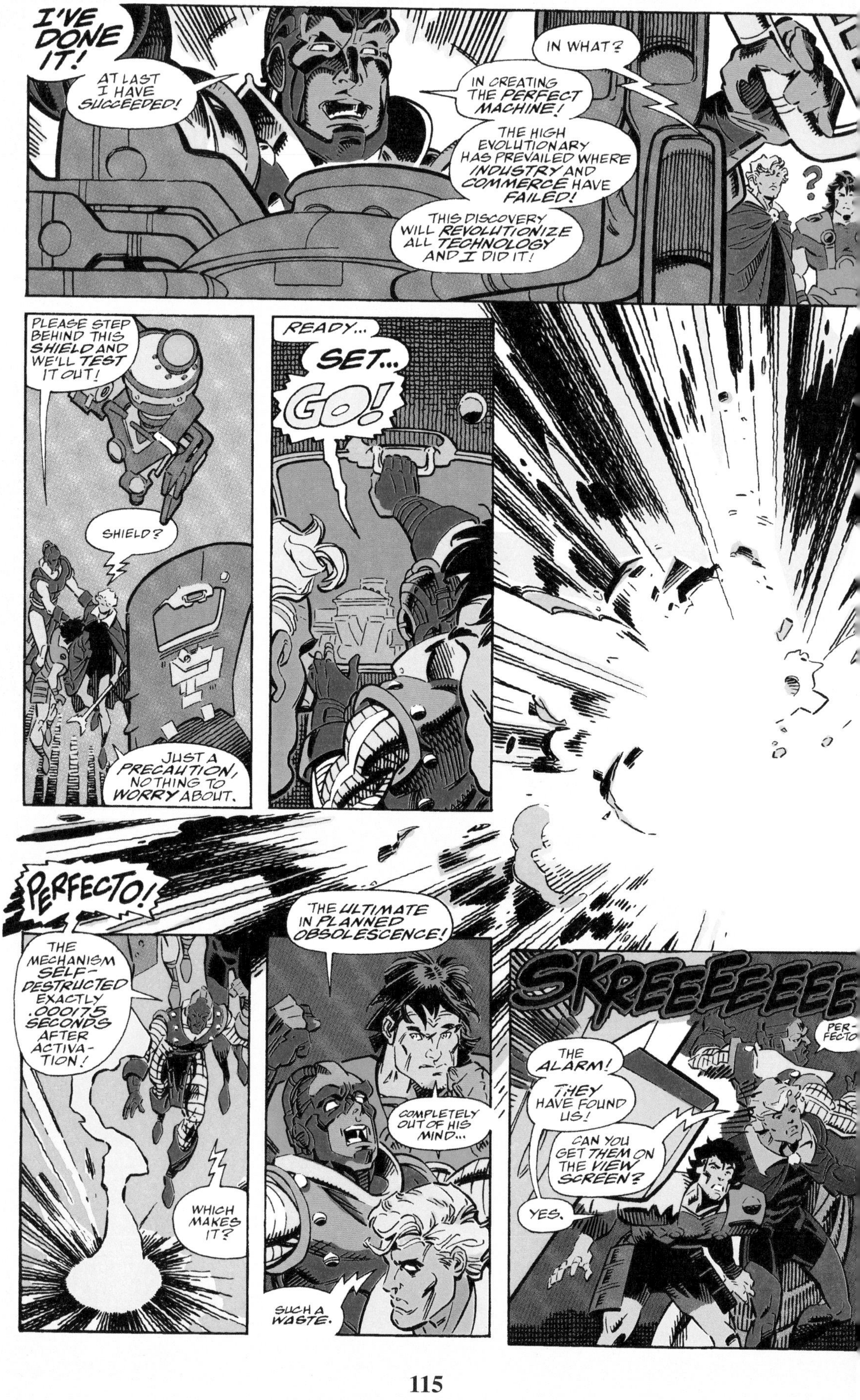
I'VE DONE IT!
AT LAST I HAVE SUCCEEDED!
IN WHAT?
IN CREATING THE PERFECT MACHINE!
THE HIGH EVOLUTIONARY HAS PREVAILED WHERE INDUSTRY AND COMMERCE HAVE FAILED!
THIS DISCOVERY WILL REVOLUTIONIZE ALL TECHNOLOGY AND I DID IT!
?
PLEASE STEP BEHIND THIS SHIELD AND WE'LL TEST IT OUT!
SHIELD?
JUST A PRECAUTION, NOTHING TO WORRY ABOUT.
READY...
SET...
GO!
PERFECTO!
THE MECHANISM SELF-DESTRUCTED EXACTLY .000175 SECONDS AFTER ACTIVATION!
WHICH MAKES IT?
THE ULTIMATE IN PLANNED OBSOLESCENCE!
COMPLETELY OUT OF HIS MIND...
SUCH A WASTE.
SKREEEEEEEE
PERFECTO
THE ALARM!
THEY HAVE FOUND US!
CAN YOU GET THEM ON THE VIEW SCREEN?
YES.

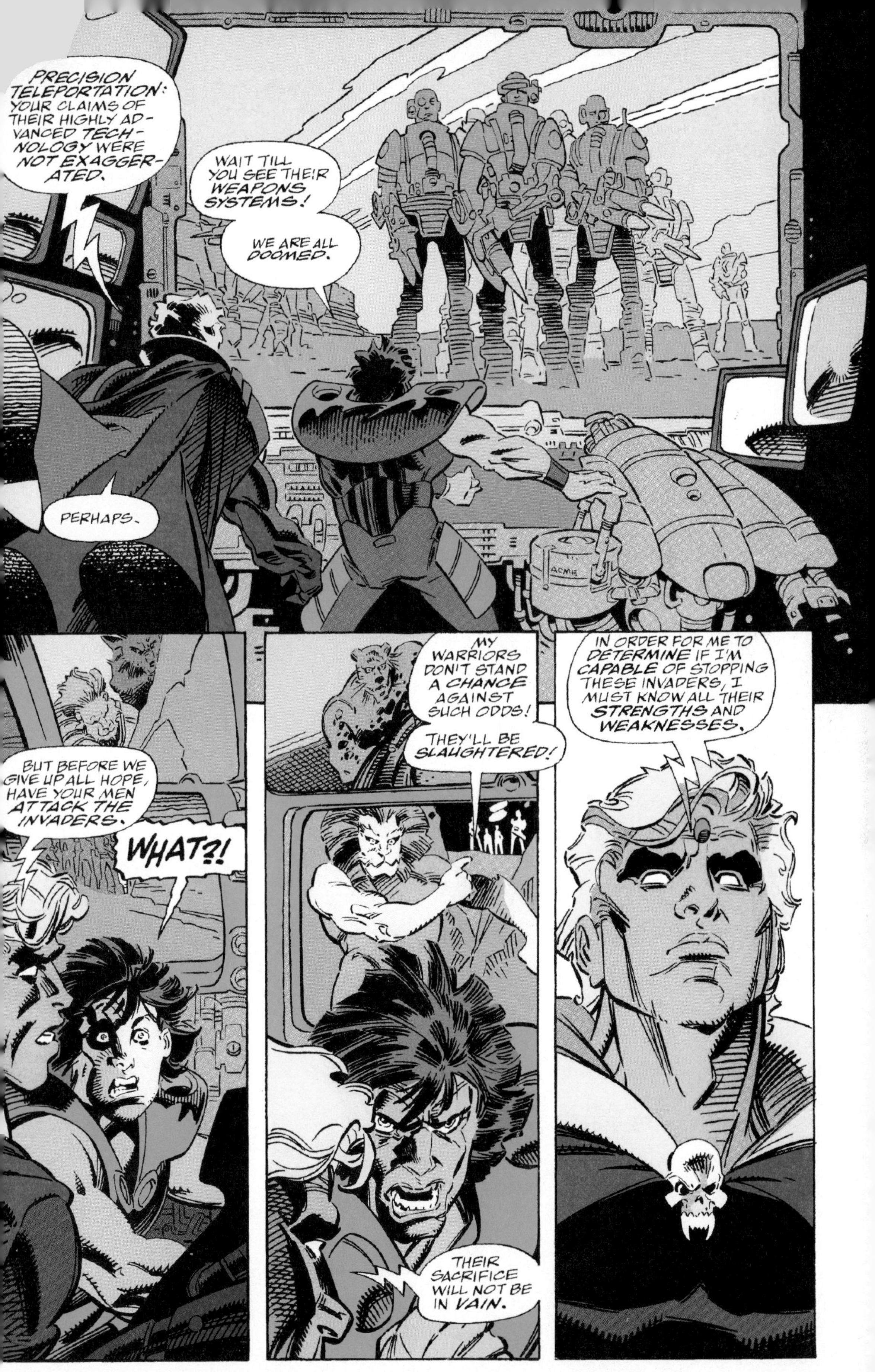
PRECISION TELEPORTATION: YOUR CLAIMS OF THEIR HIGHLY ADVANCED TECHNOLOGY WERE NOT EXAGGERATED.
WAIT TILL YOU SEE THEIR WEAPONS SYSTEMS!
WE ARE ALL DOOMED.
PERHAPS.
BUT BEFORE WE GIVE UP ALL HOPE, HAVE YOUR MEN ATTACK THE INVADERS.
WHAT?!
MY WARRIORS DON'T STAND A CHANCE AGAINST SUCH ODDS!
THEY'LL BE SLAUGHTERED!
THEIR SACRIFICE WILL NOT BE IN VAIN.
IN ORDER FOR ME TO DETERMINE IF I'M CAPABLE OF STOPPING THESE INVADERS, I MUST KNOW ALL THEIR STRENGTHS AND WEAKNESSES.

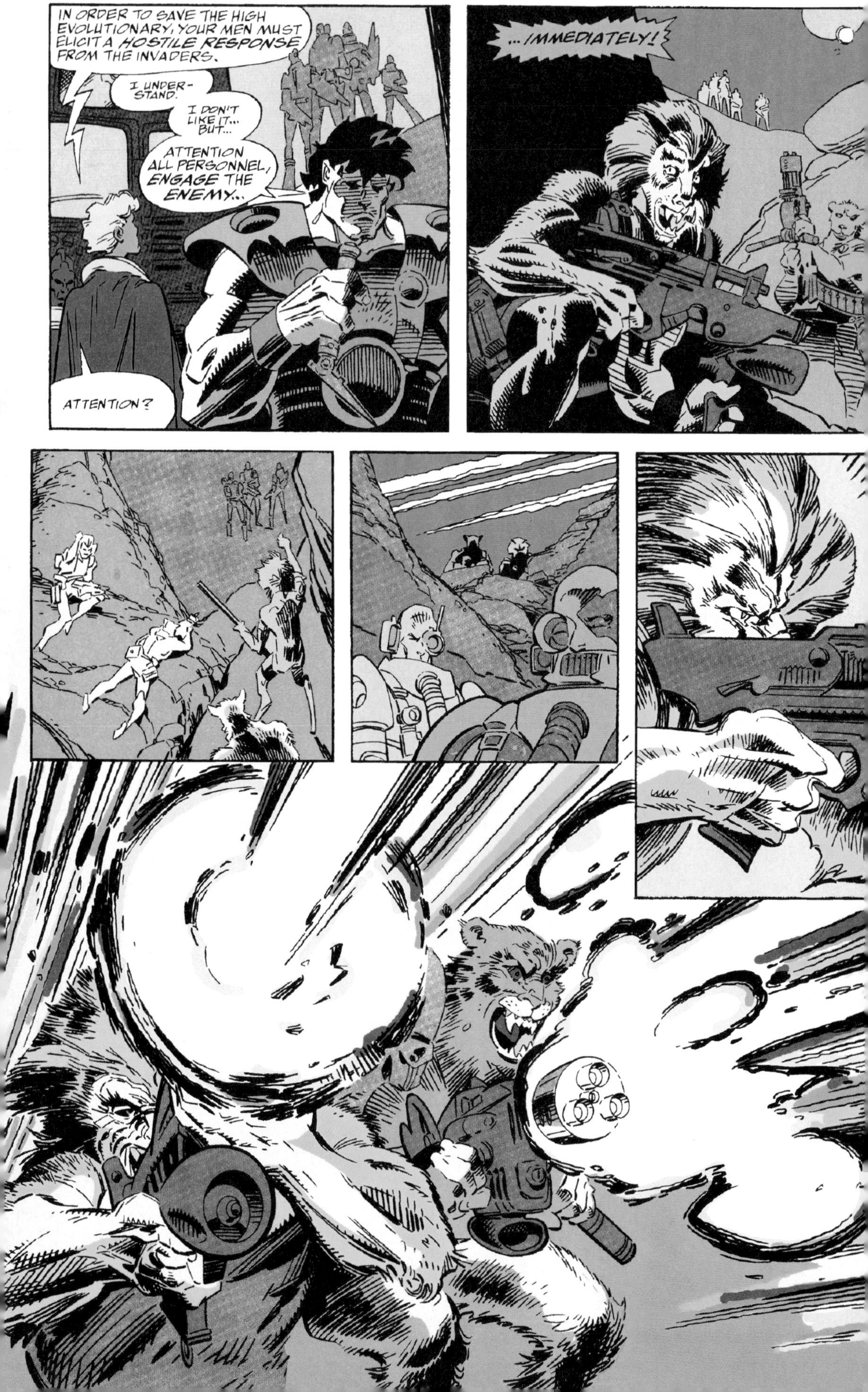
IN ORDER TO SAVE THE HIGH EVOLUTIONARY, YOUR MEN MUST ELICIT A HOSTILE RESPONSE FROM THE INVADERS.
I UNDERSTAND.
I DON'T LIKE IT... BUT...
ATTENTION ALL PERSONNEL, ENGAGE THE ENEMY...
ATTENTION?
...IMMEDIATELY!

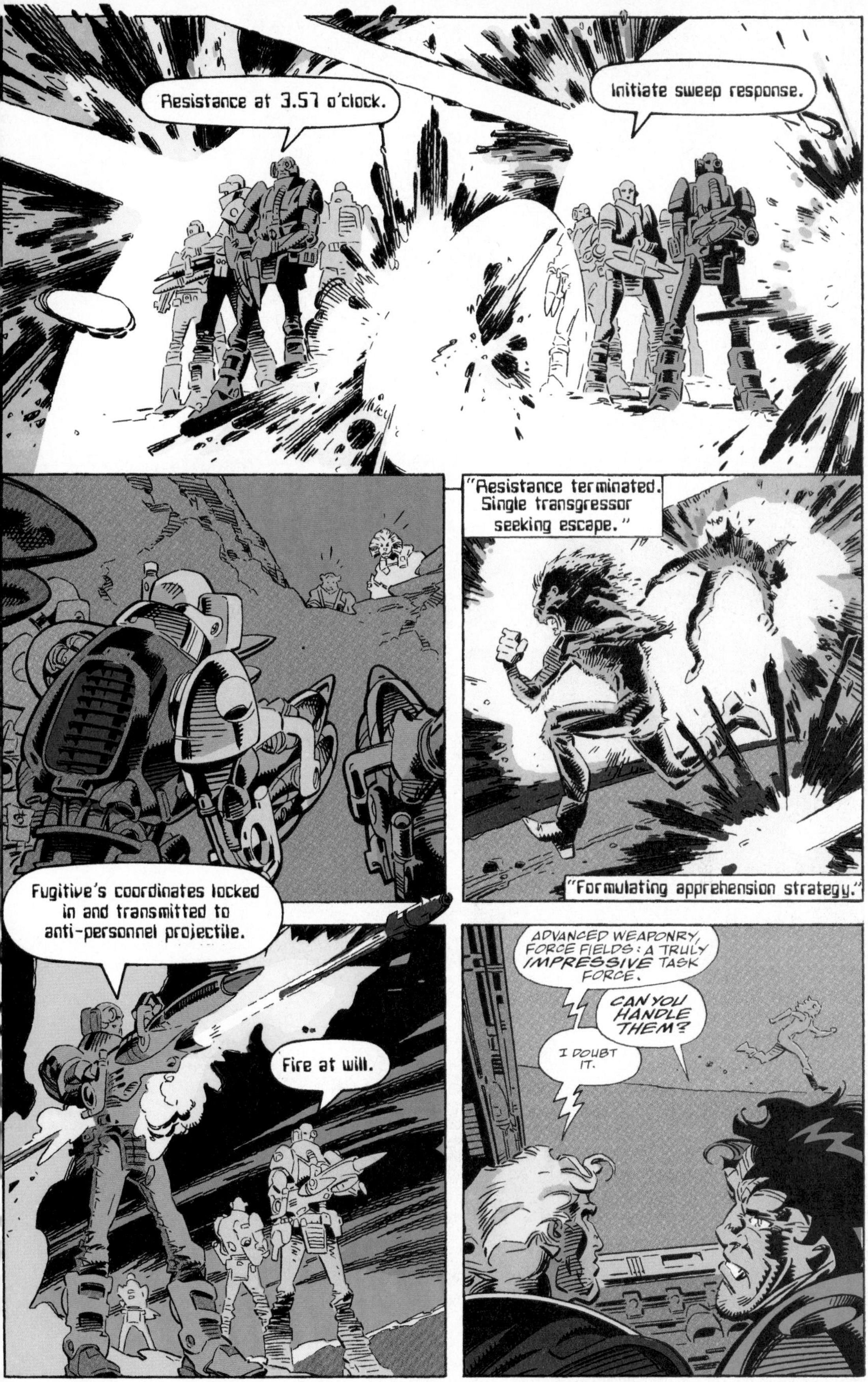
Resistance at 3.57 o'clock.
Initiate sweep response.
"Resistance terminated. Single transgressor seeking escape."
"Formulating apprehension strategy."
Fugitive's coordinates locked in and transmitted to anti-personnel projectile.
Fire at will.
ADVANCED WEAPONRY, FORCE FIELDS: A TRULY IMPRESSIVE TASK FORCE.
CAN YOU HANDLE THEM?
I DOUBT IT.

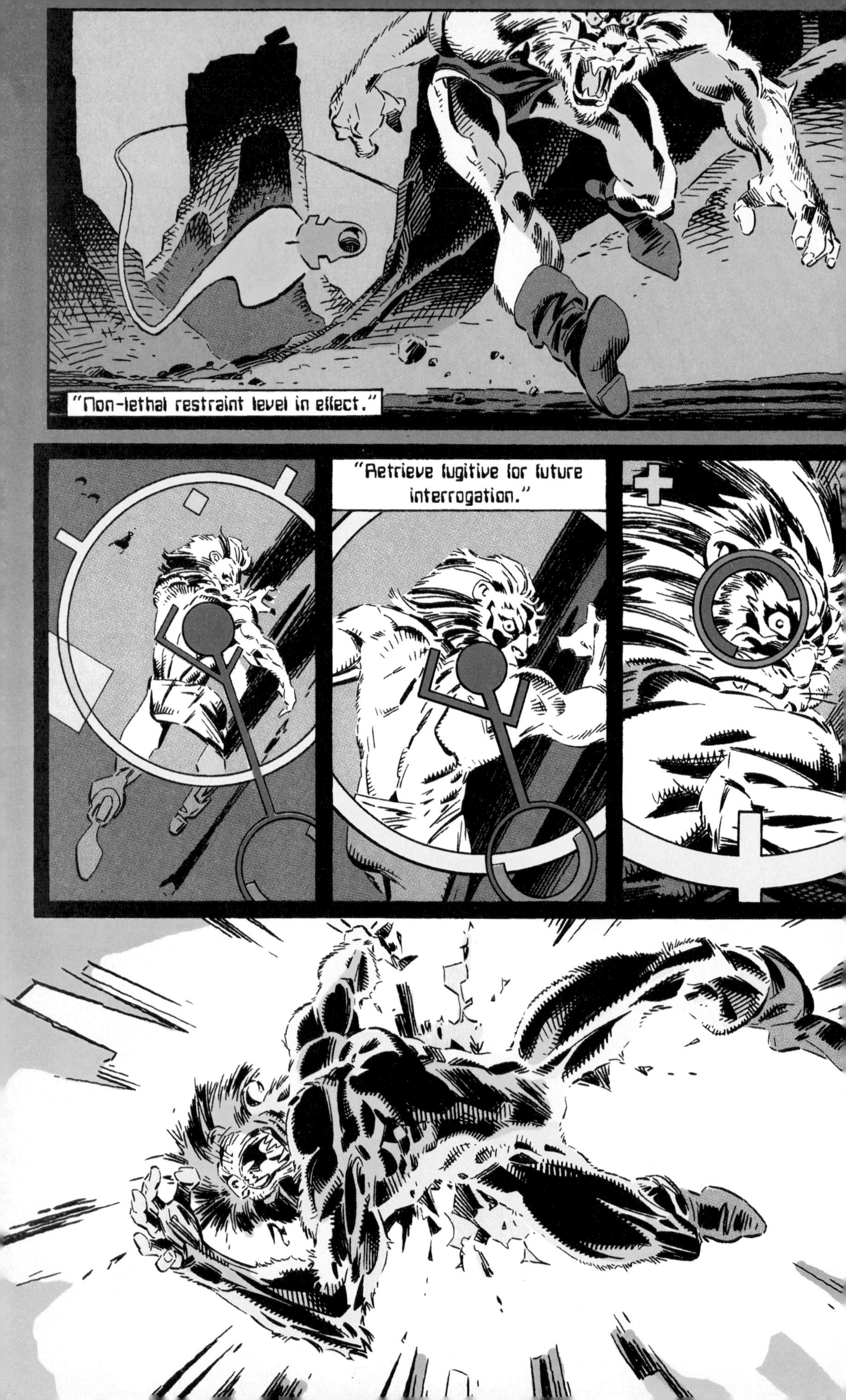
"Non-lethal restraint level in effect."
"Retrieve fugitive for future interrogation."

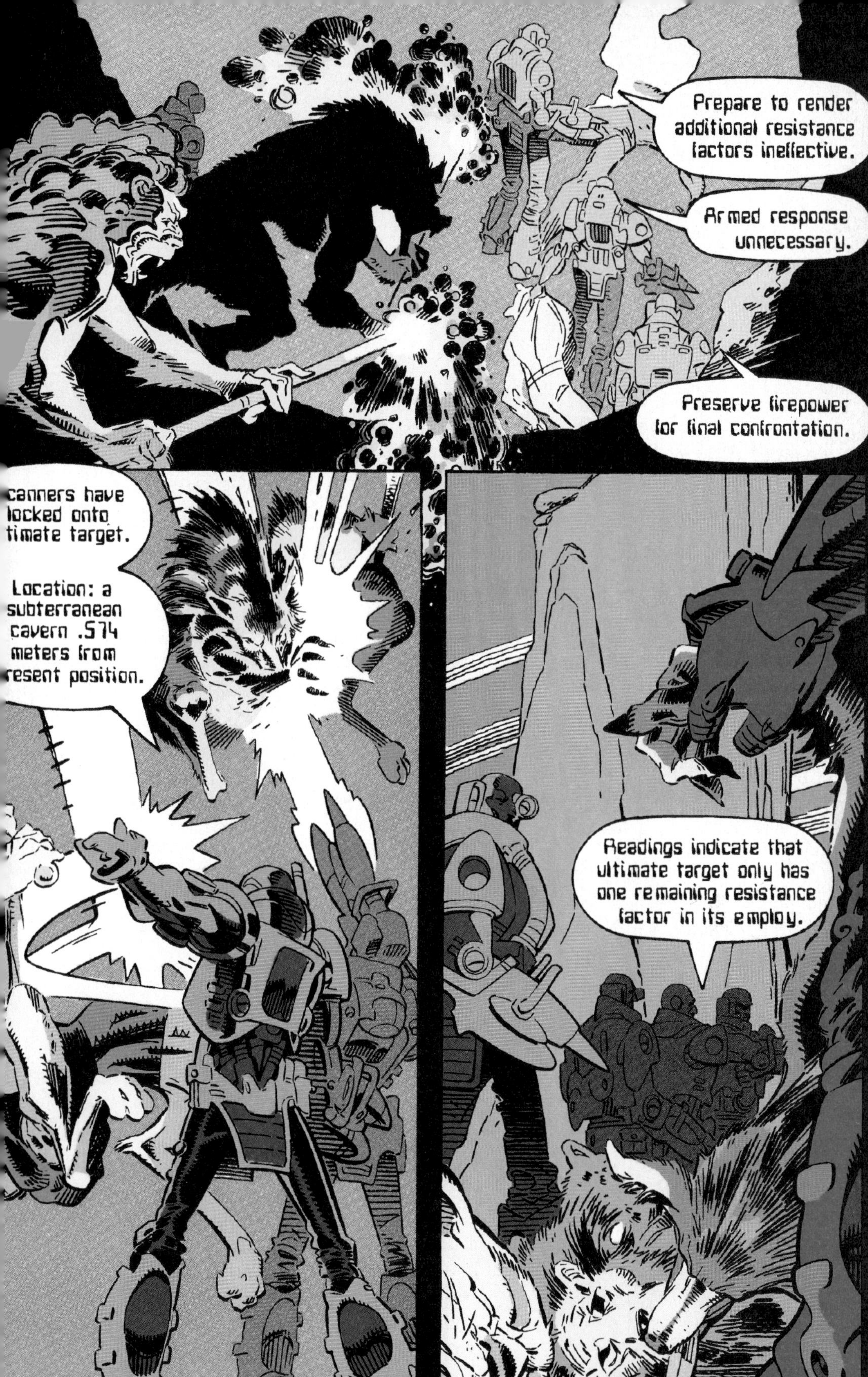
Prepare to render additional resistance factors ineffective.
Armed response unnecessary.
Preserve firepower for final confrontation.
canners have locked onto timate target.
Location: a subterranean cavern .574 meters from resent position.
Readings indicate that ultimate target only has one remaining resistance factor in its employ.

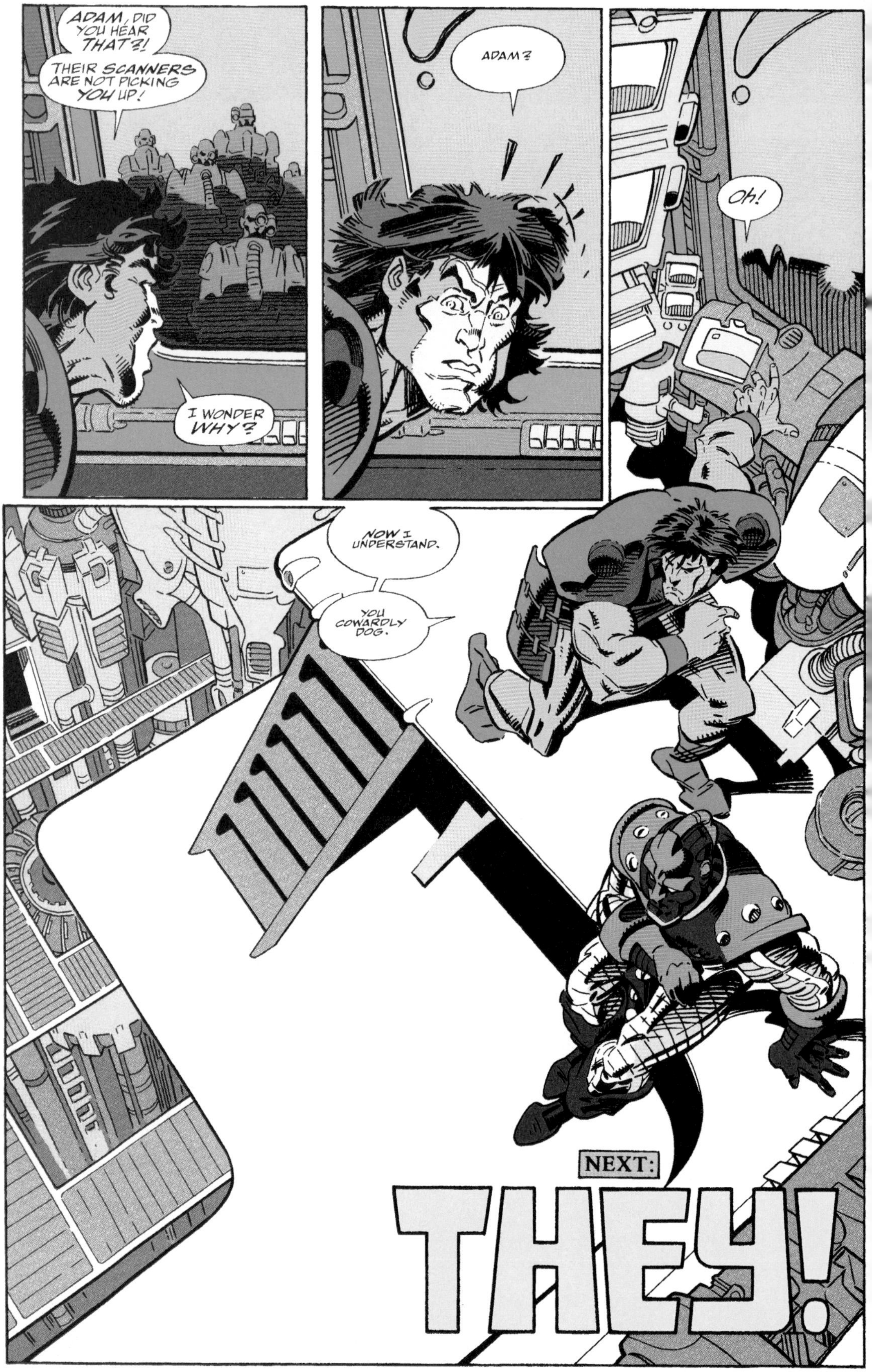
ADAM, DID YOU HEAR THAT?!
THEIR SCANNERS ARE NOT PICKING YOU UP!
I WONDER WHY?
ADAM?
Oh!
NOW I UNDERSTAND.
YOU COWARDLY DOG.
NEXT:
THEY!

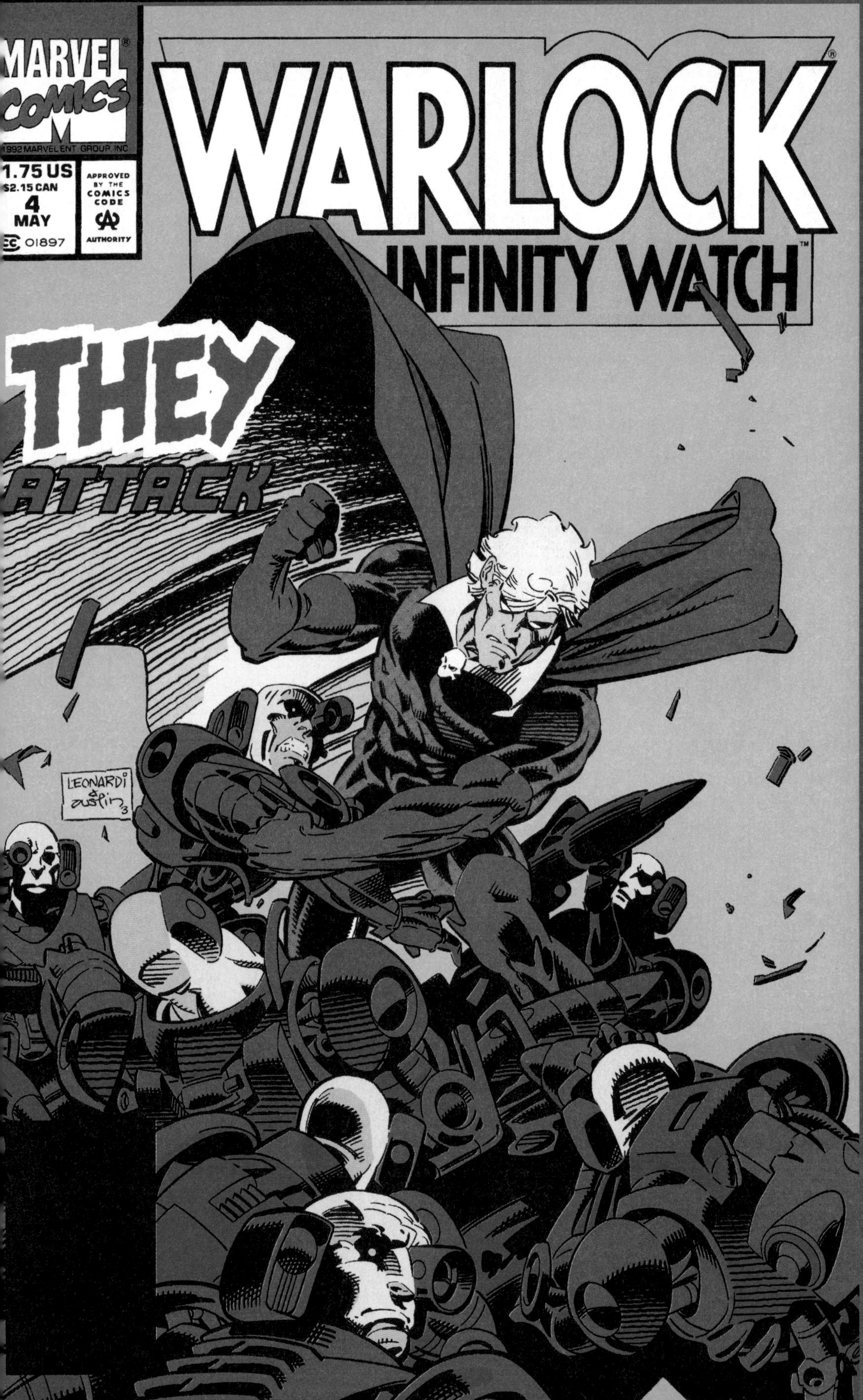
MARVEL COMICS
©1992 MARVEL ENT. GROUP, INC.
1.75 US
$2.15 CAN
4
MAY
APPROVED BY THE COMICS CODE AUTHORITY
01897
WARLOCK
INFINITY WATCH
THEY ATTACK
LEONARDI & AUSTIN

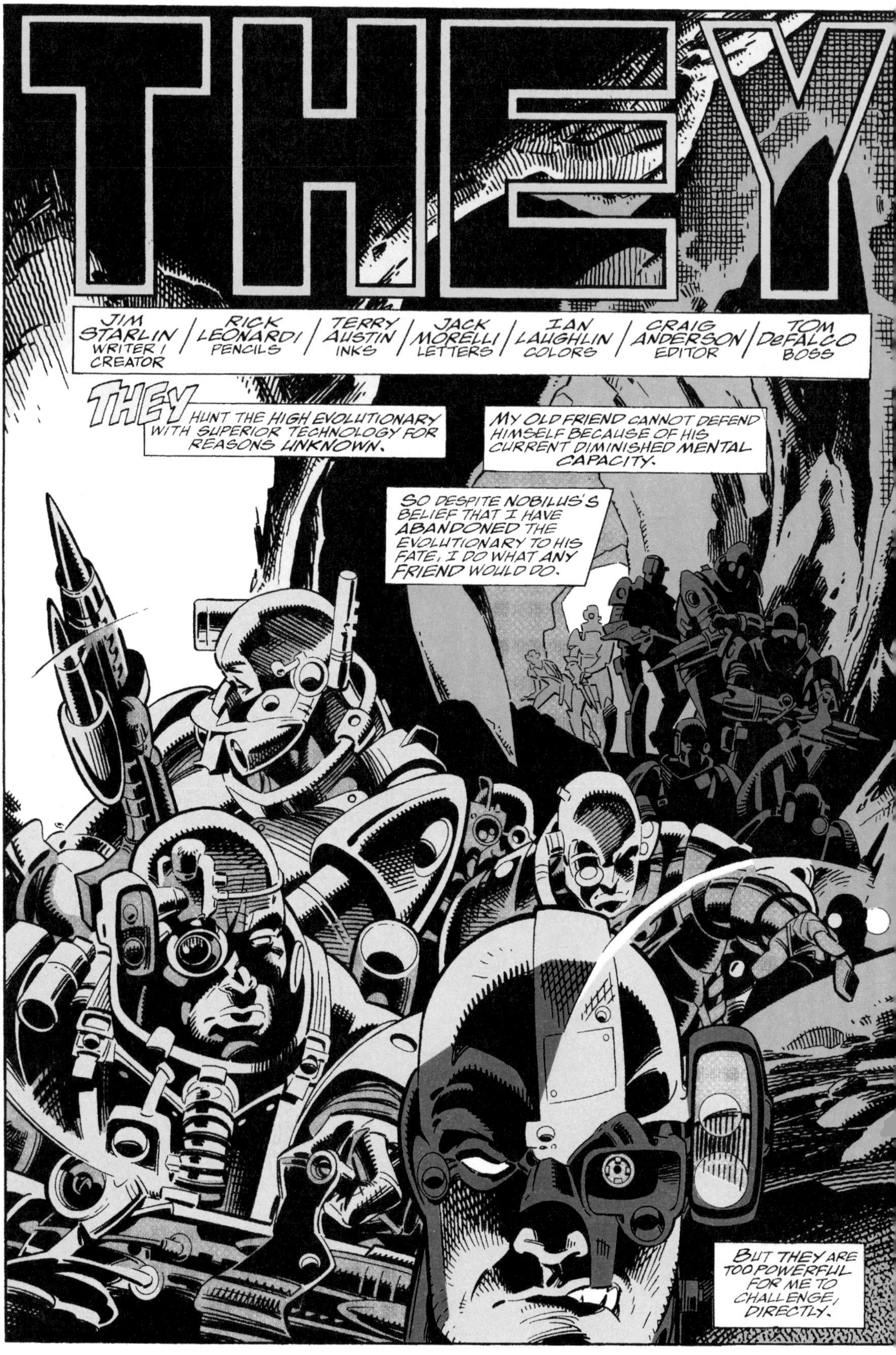
THEY
JIM STARLIN WRITER / CREATOR
RICK LEONARDI PENCILS
TERRY AUSTIN INKS
JACK MORELLI LETTERS
IAN LAUGHLIN COLORS
CRAIG ANDERSON EDITOR
TOM DeFALCO BOSS
THEY HUNT THE HIGH EVOLUTIONARY WITH SUPERIOR TECHNOLOGY FOR REASONS UNKNOWN.
MY OLD FRIEND CANNOT DEFEND HIMSELF BECAUSE OF HIS CURRENT DIMINISHED MENTAL CAPACITY.
SO DESPITE NOBILUS'S BELIEF THAT I HAVE ABANDONED THE EVOLUTIONARY TO HIS FATE, I DO WHAT ANY FRIEND WOULD DO.
BUT THEY ARE TOO POWERFUL FOR ME TO CHALLENGE, DIRECTLY.

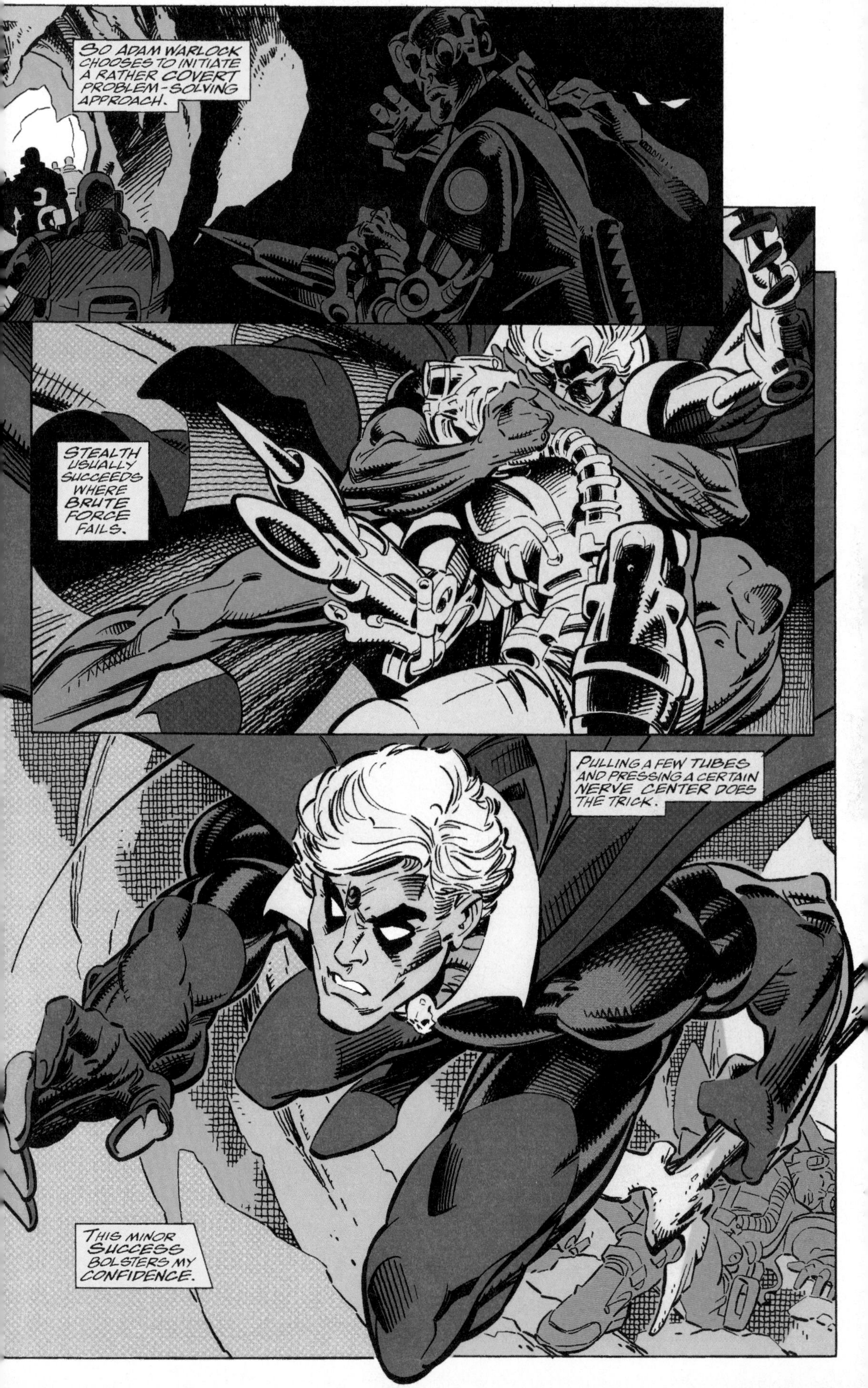
SO ADAM WARLOCK CHOOSES TO INITIATE A RATHER COVERT PROBLEM-SOLVING APPROACH.
STEALTH USUALLY SUCCEEDS WHERE BRUTE FORCE FAILS.
PULLING A FEW TUBES AND PRESSING A CERTAIN NERVE CENTER DOES THE TRICK.
THIS MINOR SUCCESS BOLSTERS MY CONFIDENCE.

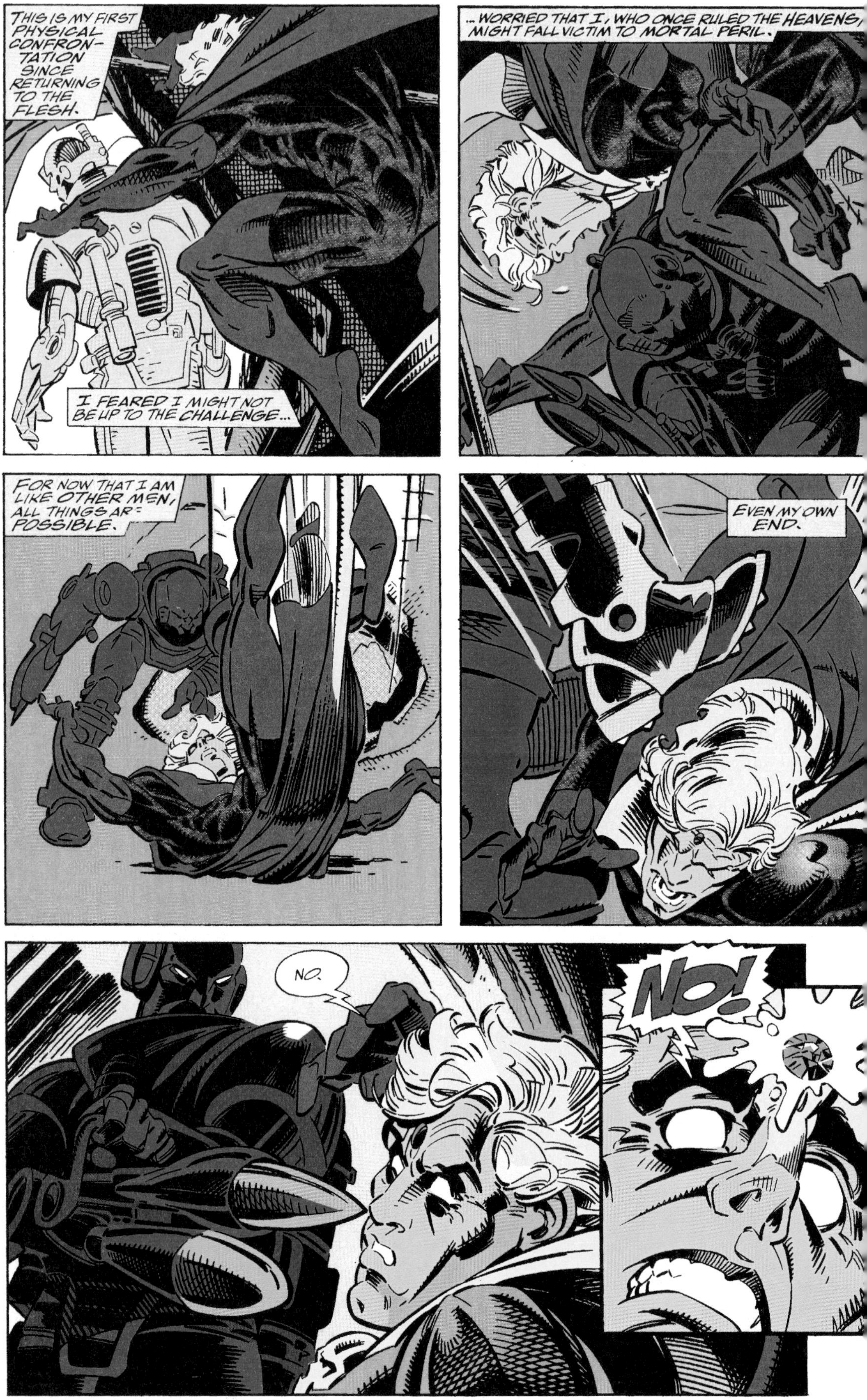
THIS IS MY FIRST PHYSICAL CONFRONTATION SINCE RETURNING TO THE FLESH.
I FEARED I MIGHT NOT BE UP TO THE CHALLENGE...
...WORRIED THAT I, WHO ONCE RULED THE HEAVENS, MIGHT FALL VICTIM TO MORTAL PERIL.
FOR NOW THAT I AM LIKE OTHER MEN, ALL THINGS ARE POSSIBLE.
EVEN MY OWN END.
NO.
NO!

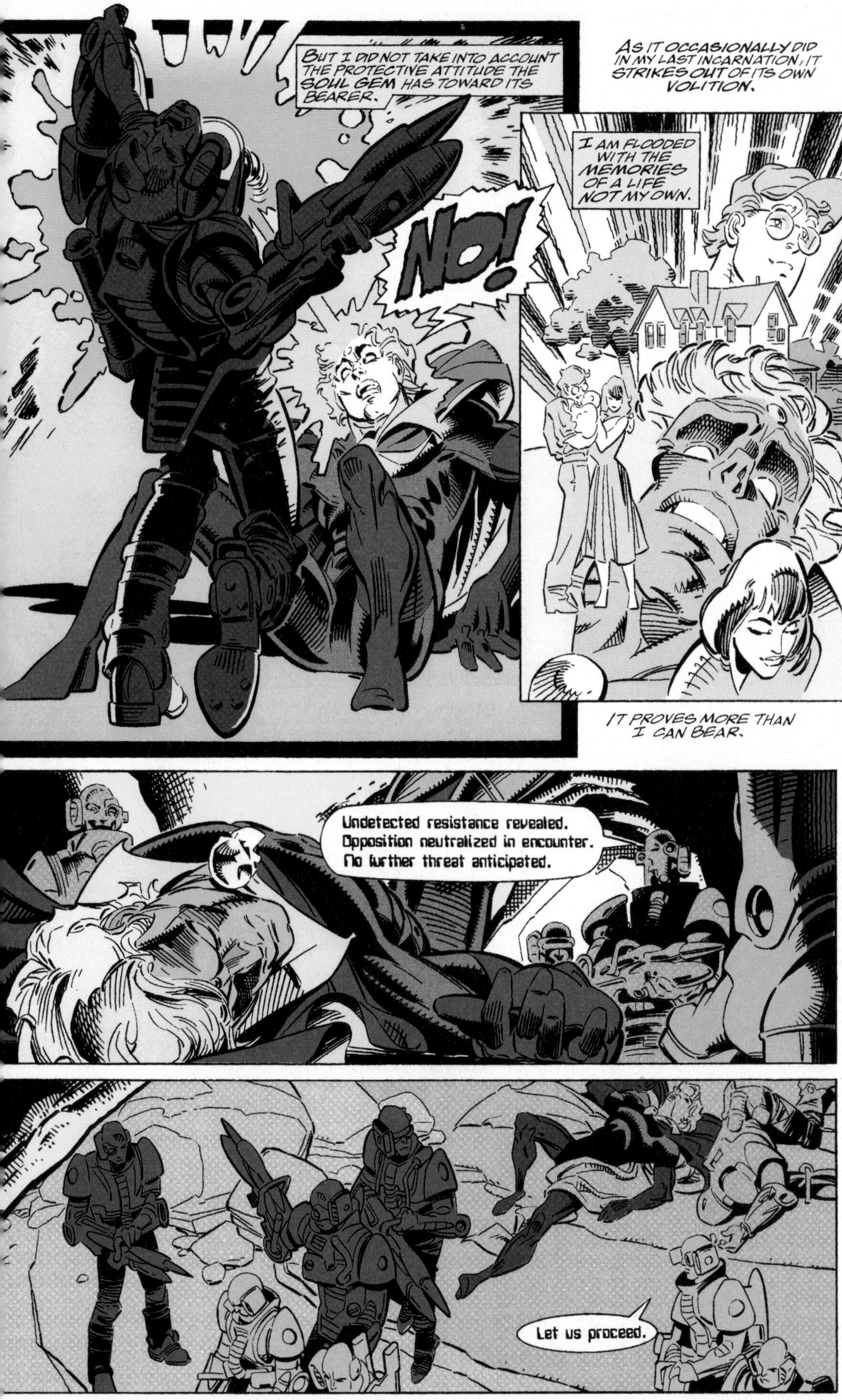
BUT I DID NOT TAKE INTO ACCOUNT THE PROTECTIVE ATTITUDE THE SOUL GEM HAS TOWARD ITS BEARER.
NO!
AS IT OCCASIONALLY DID IN MY LAST INCARNATION, IT STRIKES OUT OF ITS OWN VOLITION.
I AM FLOODED WITH THE MEMORIES OF A LIFE NOT MY OWN.
IT PROVES MORE THAN I CAN BEAR.
Undetected resistance revealed. Opposition neutralized in encounter. No further threat anticipated.
Let us proceed.

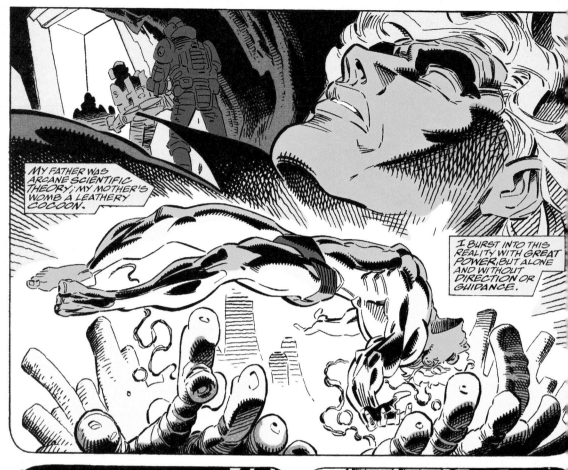

MY FATHER WAS ARCANE SCIENTIFIC THEORY; MY MOTHER'S WOMB A LEATHERY COCOON.

I BURST INTO THIS REALITY WITH GREAT POWER, BUT ALONE AND WITHOUT DIRECTION OR GUIDANCE.

FOR YEARS I WANDERED THE ETHER, LOST AND LIVING ONLY FOR THE MOMENT.

I SOON REALIZED I'D NOT LAST LONG ON MY PRESENT COURSE.

BUT AS GOOD FORTUNE WOULD HAVE IT, I EVENTUALLY ENCOUNTERED THE HIGH EVOLUTIONARY.

HE RECOGNIZED MY NEED FOR A HOLY GRAIL, AND PROVIDED IT.

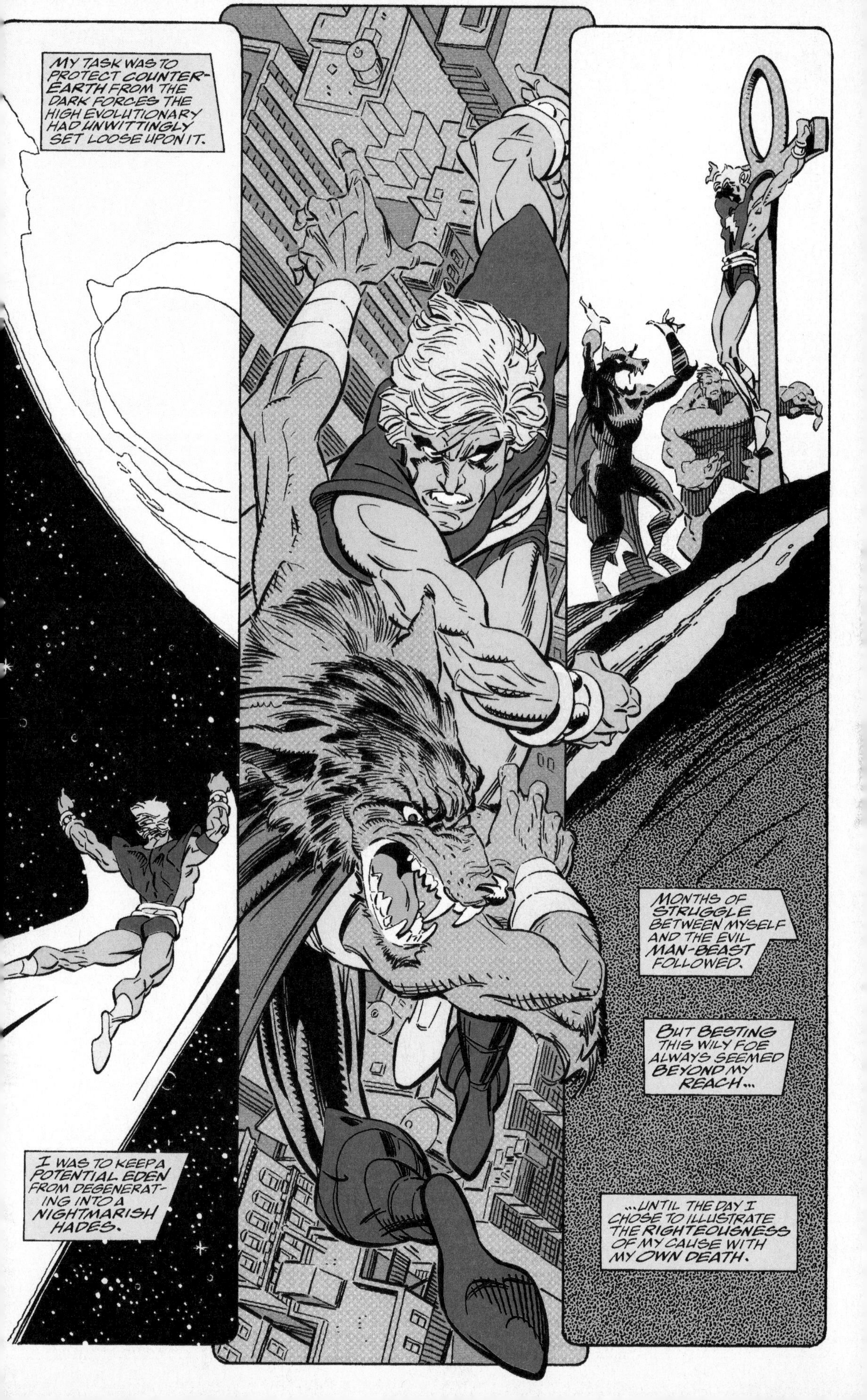
MY TASK WAS TO PROTECT COUNTER-EARTH FROM THE DARK FORCES THE HIGH EVOLUTIONARY HAD UNWITTINGLY SET LOOSE UPON IT.
I WAS TO KEEP A POTENTIAL EDEN FROM DEGENERATING INTO A NIGHTMARISH HADES.
MONTHS OF STRUGGLE BETWEEN MYSELF AND THE EVIL MAN-BEAST FOLLOWED.
BUT BESTING THIS WILY FOE ALWAYS SEEMED BEYOND MY REACH...
...UNTIL THE DAY I CHOSE TO ILLUSTRATE THE RIGHTEOUSNESS OF MY CAUSE WITH MY OWN DEATH.

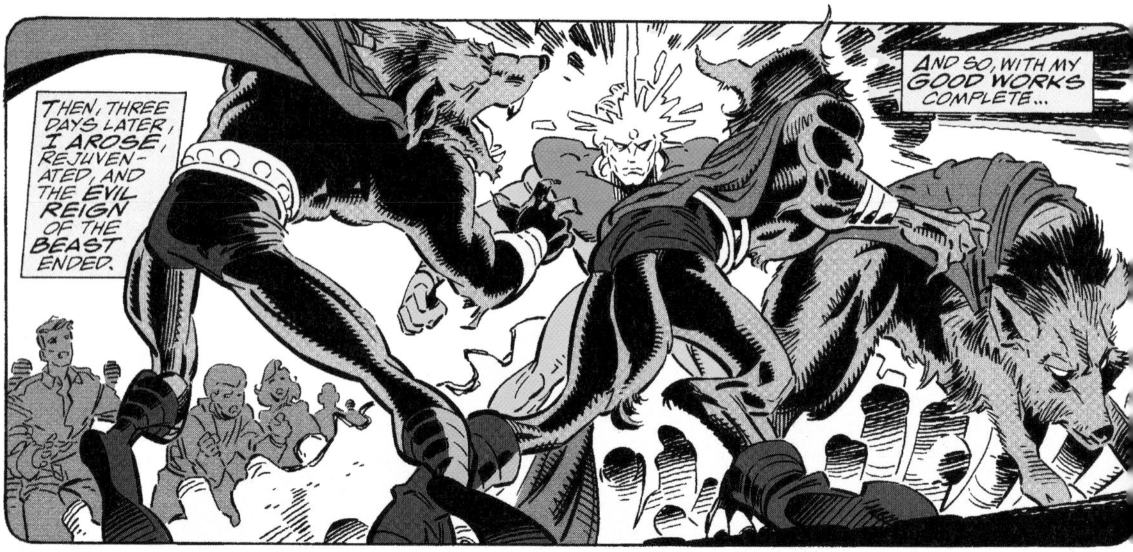
THEN, THREE DAYS LATER, I AROSE, REJUVENATED, AND THE EVIL REIGN OF THE BEAST ENDED.
AND SO, WITH MY GOOD WORKS COMPLETE...

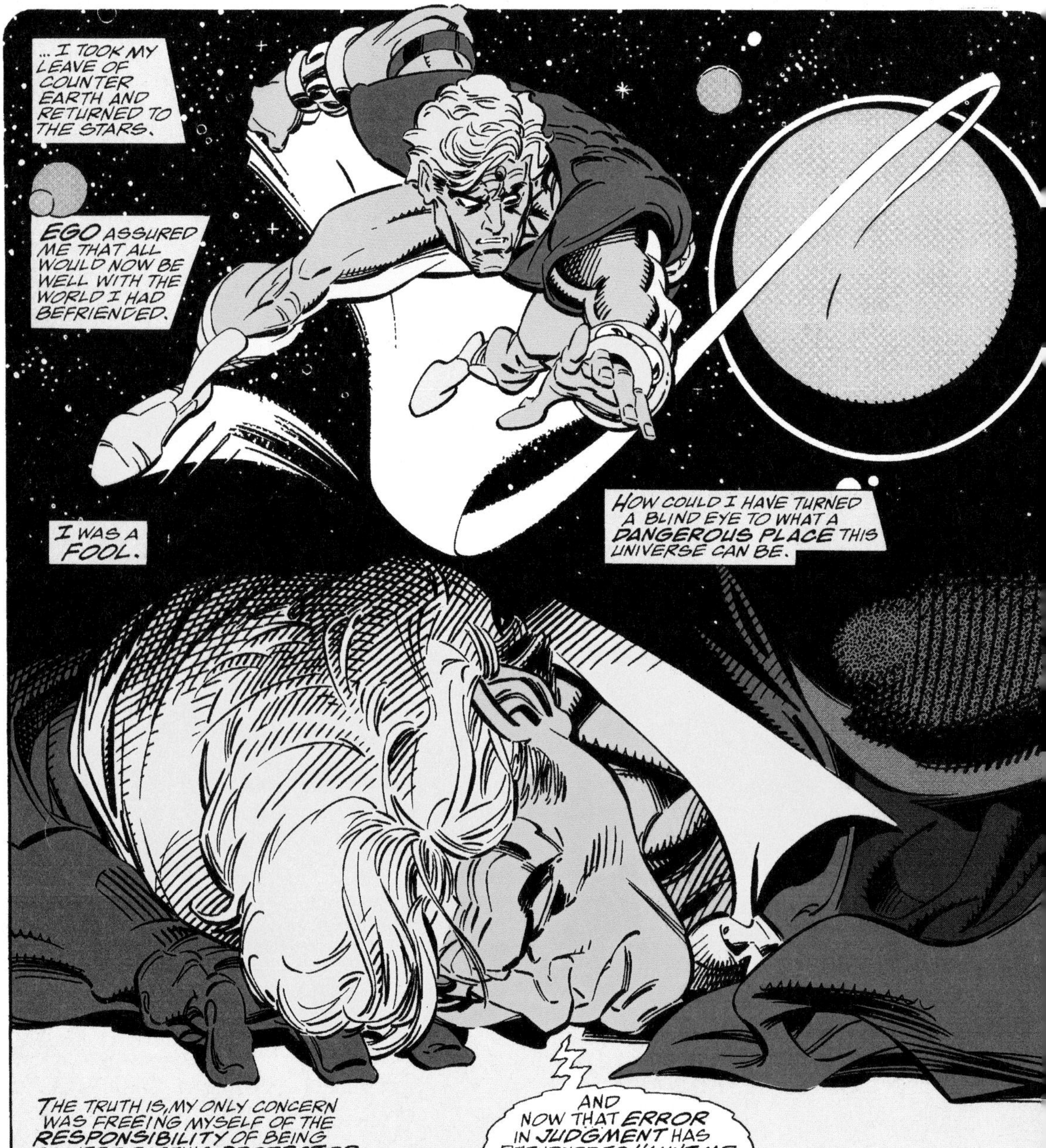
...I TOOK MY LEAVE OF COUNTER EARTH AND RETURNED TO THE STARS.
EGO ASSURED ME THAT ALL WOULD NOW BE WELL WITH THE WORLD I HAD BEFRIENDED.
I WAS A FOOL.
HOW COULD I HAVE TURNED A BLIND EYE TO WHAT A DANGEROUS PLACE THIS UNIVERSE CAN BE.
THE TRUTH IS, MY ONLY CONCERN WAS FREEING MYSELF OF THE RESPONSIBILITY OF BEING COUNTER-EARTH'S PROTECTOR.
AND NOW THAT ERROR IN JUDGMENT HAS RETURNED TO HAUNT ME.

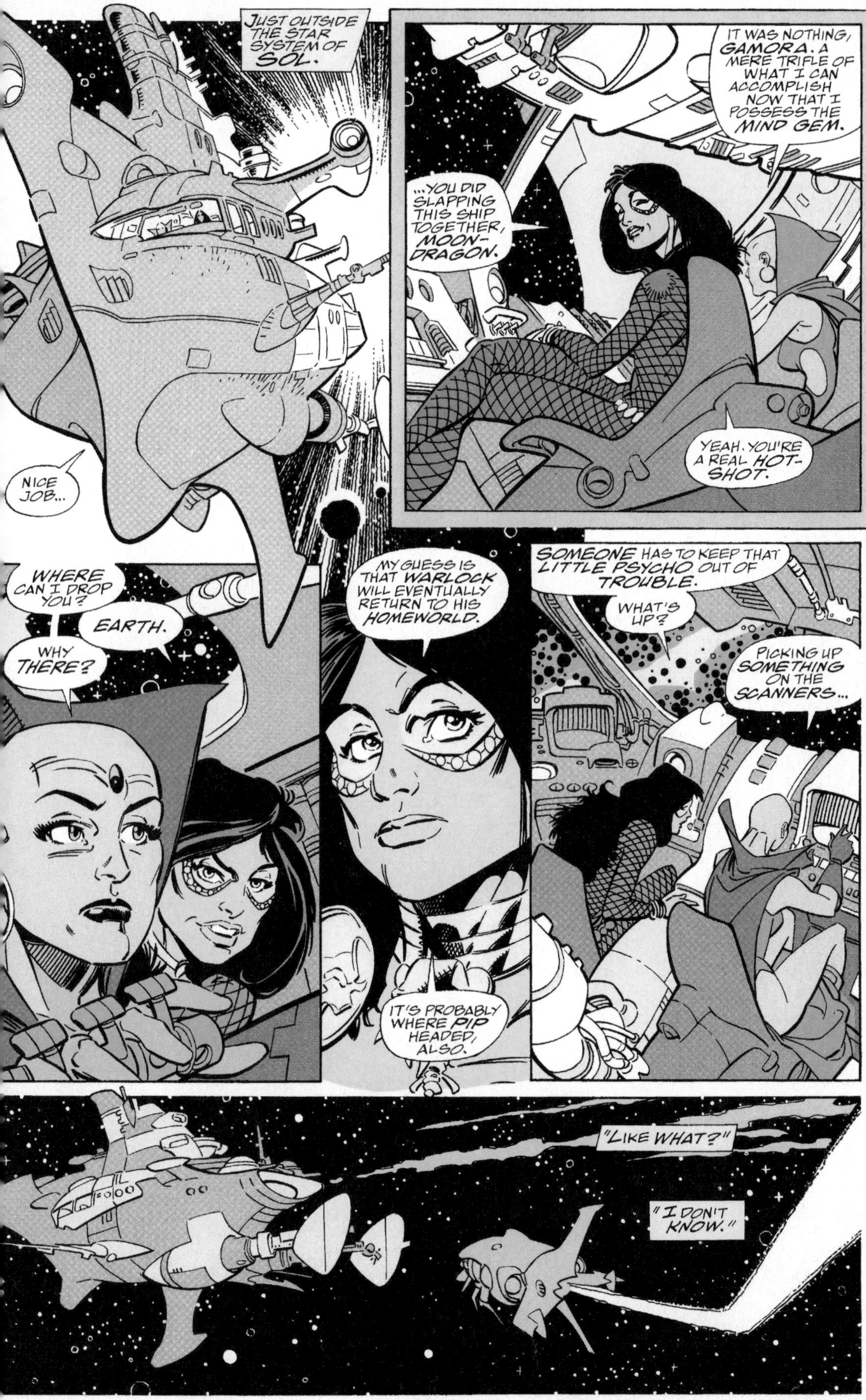
JUST OUTSIDE THE STAR SYSTEM OF SOL.
NICE JOB...
...YOU DID SLAPPING THIS SHIP TOGETHER, MOON-DRAGON.
IT WAS NOTHING, GAMORA. A MERE TRIFLE OF WHAT I CAN ACCOMPLISH NOW THAT I POSSESS THE MIND GEM.
YEAH. YOU'RE A REAL HOT-SHOT.
WHERE CAN I DROP YOU?
EARTH.
WHY THERE?
MY GUESS IS THAT WARLOCK WILL EVENTUALLY RETURN TO HIS HOMEWORLD.
IT'S PROBABLY WHERE PIP HEADED, ALSO.
SOMEONE HAS TO KEEP THAT LITTLE PSYCHO OUT OF TROUBLE.
WHAT'S UP?
PICKING UP SOMETHING ON THE SCANNERS...
"LIKE WHAT?"
"I DON'T KNOW."

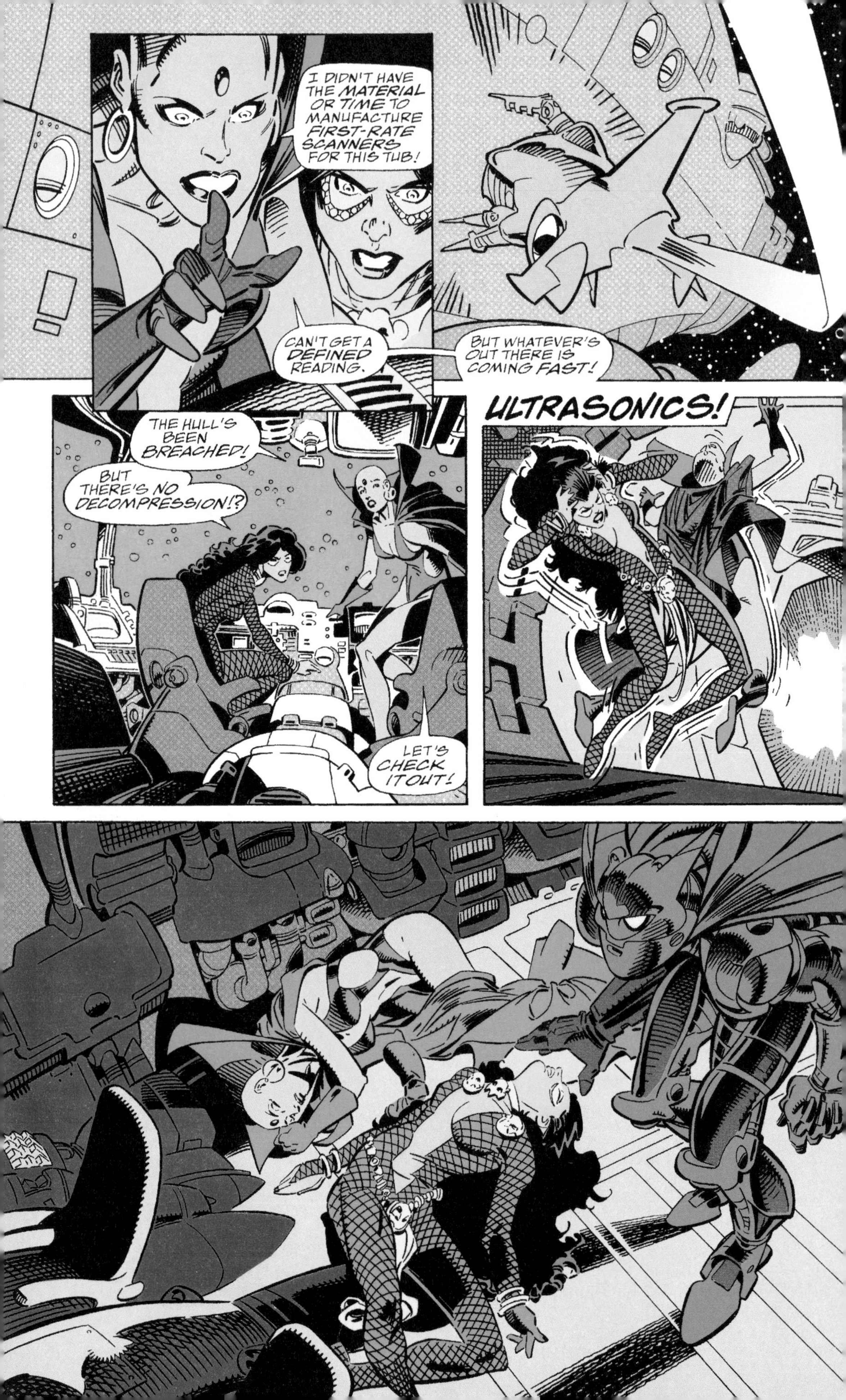
I DIDN'T HAVE THE MATERIAL OR TIME TO MANUFACTURE FIRST-RATE SCANNERS FOR THIS TUB!
CAN'T GET A DEFINED READING.
BUT WHATEVER'S OUT THERE IS COMING FAST!
THE HULL'S BEEN BREACHED!
BUT THERE'S NO DECOMPRESSION!?
LET'S CHECK IT OUT!
ULTRASONICS!

I CAN HEAR THEM COMING.

BUT FEAR NOT, MY LORD HIGH EVOLUTIONARY. NOBILUS SHALL NOT ABANDON YOU AS OTHERS HAVE.

THEY SHALL ONLY GET YOU OVER MY DEAD BODY!

NOBILUS IS A GOOD BOY. SUCH A GOOD BOY.

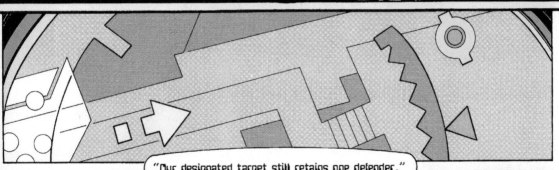

"Our designated target still retains one defender."

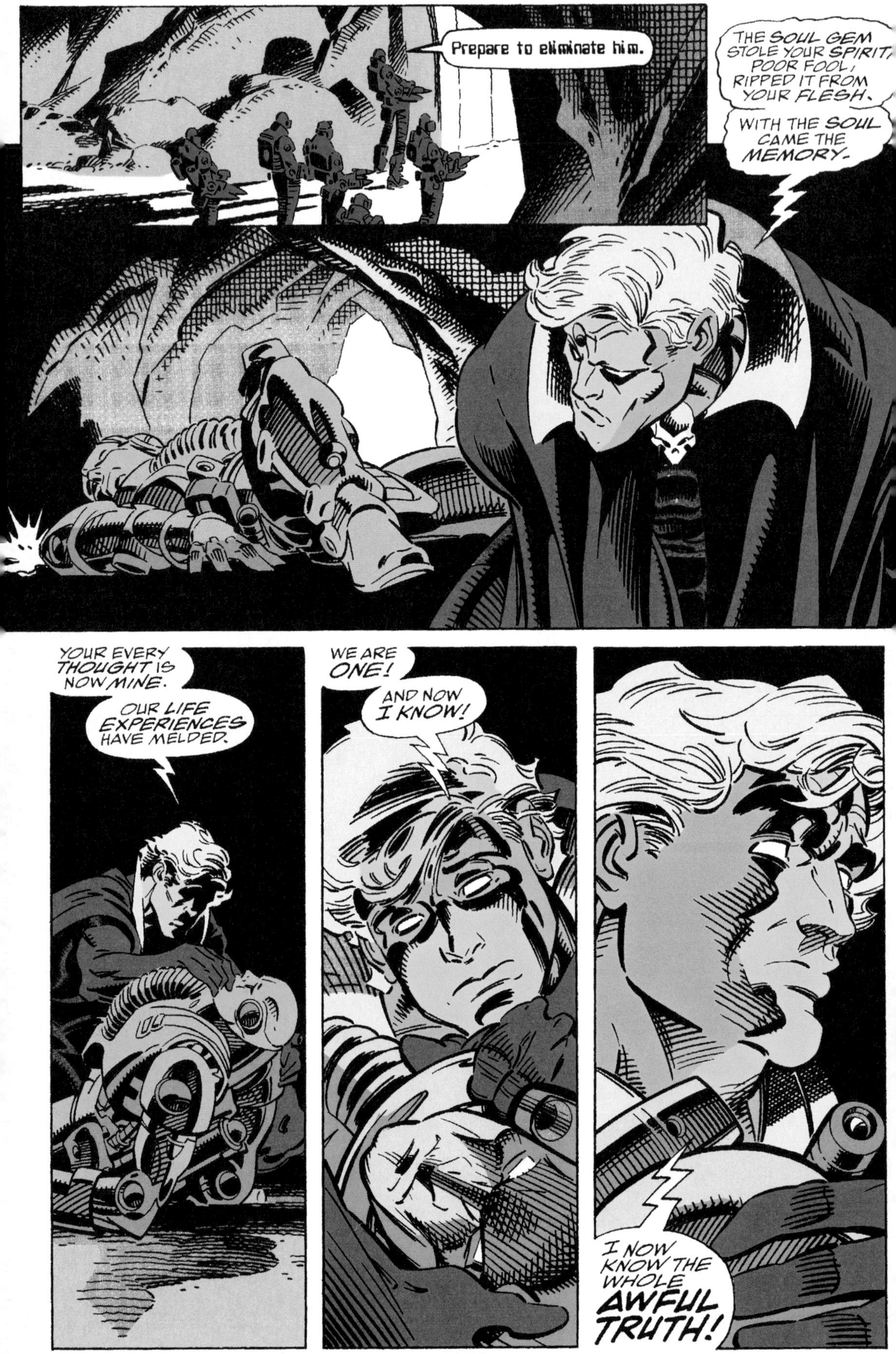

Prepare to eliminate him.
THE SOUL GEM STOLE YOUR SPIRIT, POOR FOOL; RIPPED IT FROM YOUR FLESH.
WITH THE SOUL CAME THE MEMORY.
YOUR EVERY THOUGHT IS NOW MINE.
OUR LIFE EXPERIENCES HAVE MELDED.
WE ARE ONE!
AND NOW I KNOW!
I NOW KNOW THE WHOLE AWFUL TRUTH!

"Institute assault."

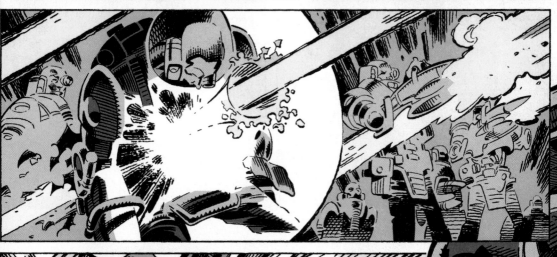

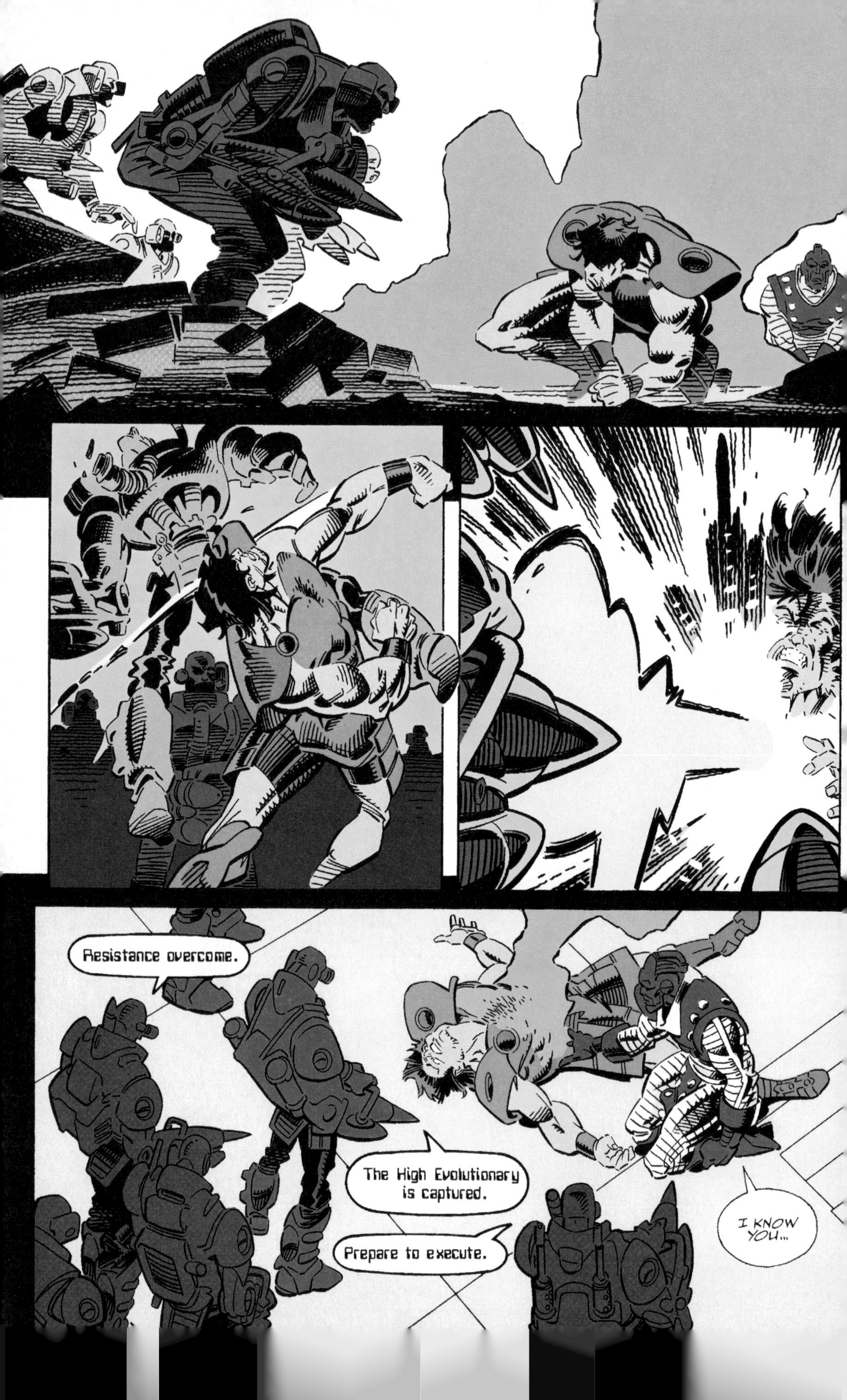
Resistance overcome.
The High Evolutionary is captured.
Prepare to execute.
I KNOW YOU...

COUNTER-EARTH FELL UNDER THE COVETOUS EYE OF ONE SPHINXOR, OF THE PEGASUSIAN MOVING COMPANY.

AND DESPITE THE BEST EFFORTS OF THE HIGH EVOLUTIONARY, THE THING, HIS COMPANION ALICIA MASTERS, AND THE MYSTERIOUS STARHAWK, THE PLANET WAS RIPPED FROM ITS ORBIT AND STOLEN.

APPARENTLY SPHINXOR SOLD MY ONE-TIME HOME, AS A CURIOSITY, TO AN INCREDIBLE RACE OF SUPER-BEINGS CALLED THE BEYONDERS.

RESCUING COUNTER-EARTH WAS A TASK BEYOND THE POWER OF EVEN THE HIGH EVOLUTIONARY.

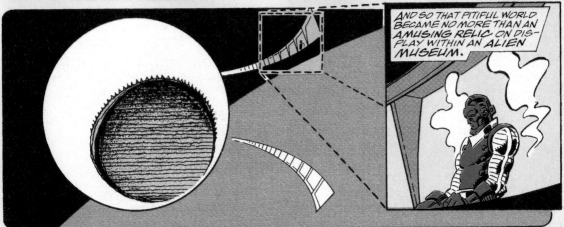

AND SO THAT PITIFUL WORLD BECAME NO MORE THAN AN AMUSING RELIC ON DISPLAY WITHIN AN ALIEN MUSEUM.

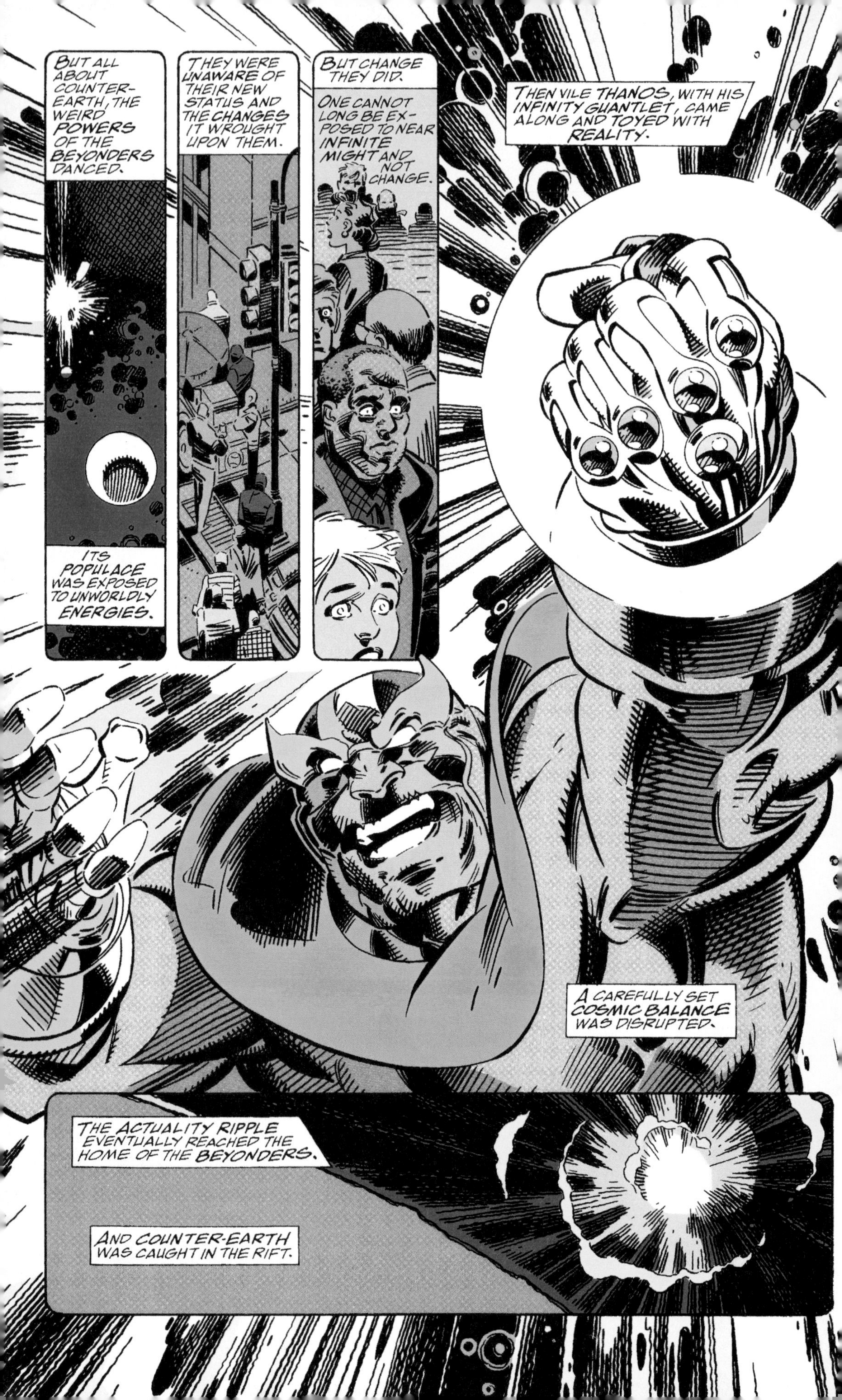
BUT ALL ABOUT COUNTER-EARTH, THE WEIRD POWERS OF THE BEYONDERS DANCED.
ITS POPULACE WAS EXPOSED TO UNWORLDLY ENERGIES.
THEY WERE UNAWARE OF THEIR NEW STATUS AND THE CHANGES IT WROUGHT UPON THEM.
BUT CHANGE THEY DID.
ONE CANNOT LONG BE EXPOSED TO NEAR INFINITE MIGHT AND NOT CHANGE.
THEN VILE THANOS, WITH HIS INFINITY GUANTLET, CAME ALONG AND TOYED WITH REALITY.
A CAREFULLY SET COSMIC BALANCE WAS DISRUPTED.
THE ACTUALITY RIPPLE EVENTUALLY REACHED THE HOME OF THE BEYONDERS.
AND COUNTER-EARTH WAS CAUGHT IN THE RIFT.

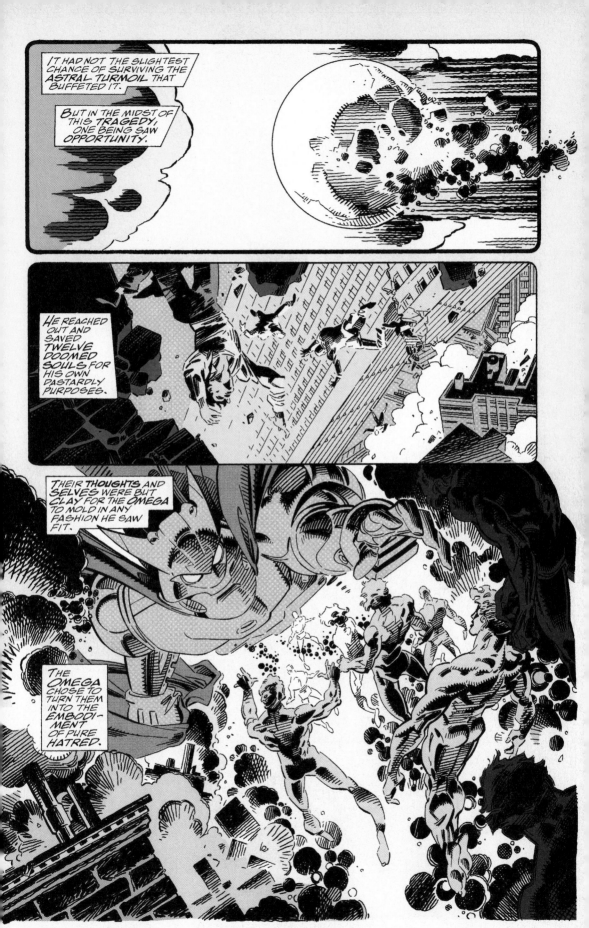

IT HAD NOT THE SLIGHTEST CHANCE OF SURVIVING THE *ASTRAL TURMOIL* THAT BUFFETED IT.

BUT IN THE MIDST OF THIS *TRAGEDY*, ONE BEING SAW *OPPORTUNITY*.

HE REACHED OUT AND SAVED *TWELVE DOOMED SOULS* FOR HIS OWN DASTARDLY PURPOSES.

THEIR *THOUGHTS* AND *SELVES* WERE BUT *CLAY* FOR THE *OMEGA* TO MOLD IN ANY FASHION HE SAW FIT.

THE *OMEGA* CHOSE TO TURN THEM INTO THE EMBODIMENT OF PURE *HATRED*.

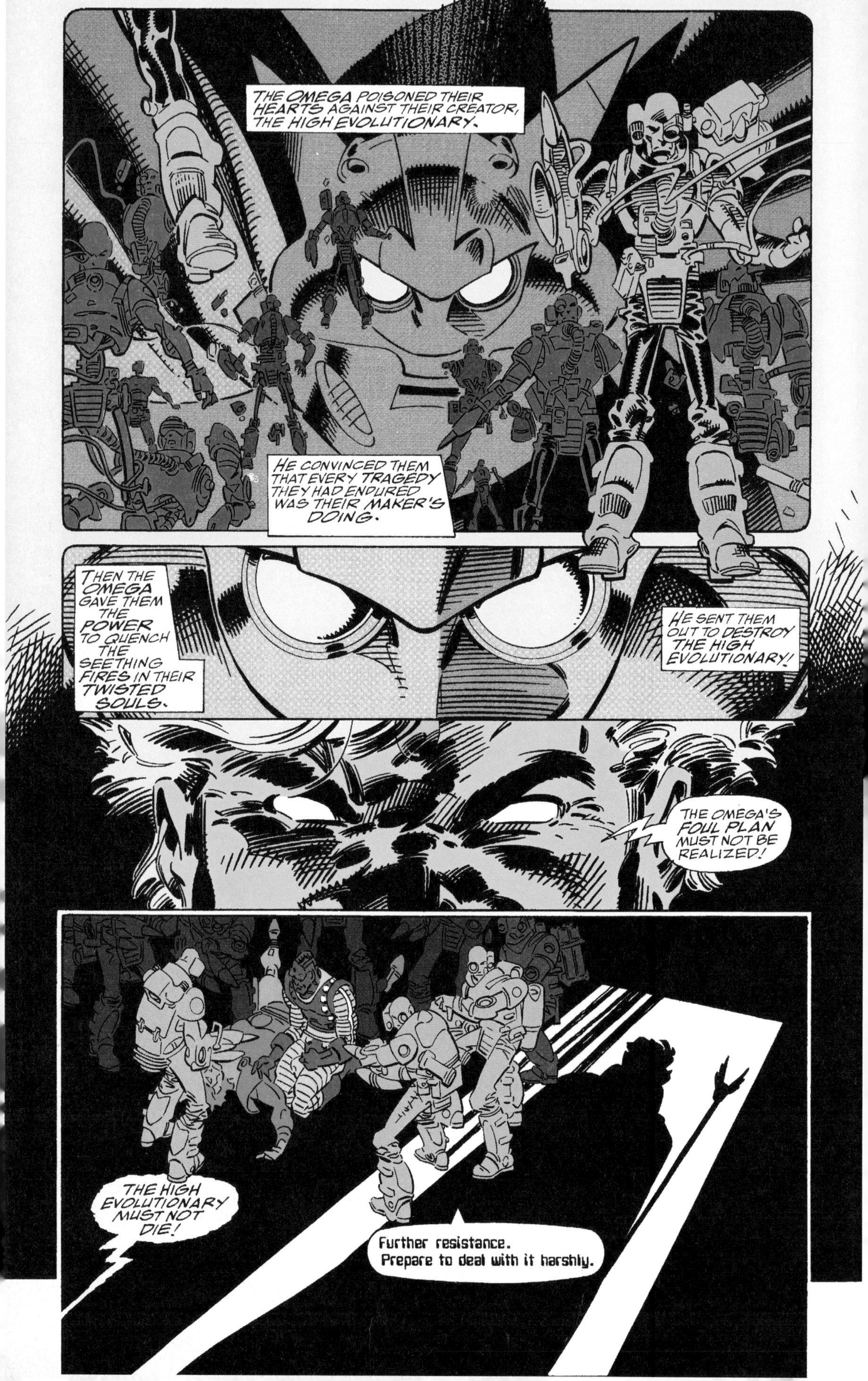

THE OMEGA POISONED THEIR HEARTS AGAINST THEIR CREATOR, THE HIGH EVOLUTIONARY.
HE CONVINCED THEM THAT EVERY TRAGEDY THEY HAD ENDURED WAS THEIR MAKER'S DOING.
THEN THE OMEGA GAVE THEM THE POWER TO QUENCH THE SEETHING FIRES IN THEIR TWISTED SOULS.
HE SENT THEM OUT TO DESTROY THE HIGH EVOLUTIONARY!
THE OMEGA'S FOUL PLAN MUST NOT BE REALIZED!
THE HIGH EVOLUTIONARY MUST NOT DIE!
Further resistance.
Prepare to deal with it harshly.

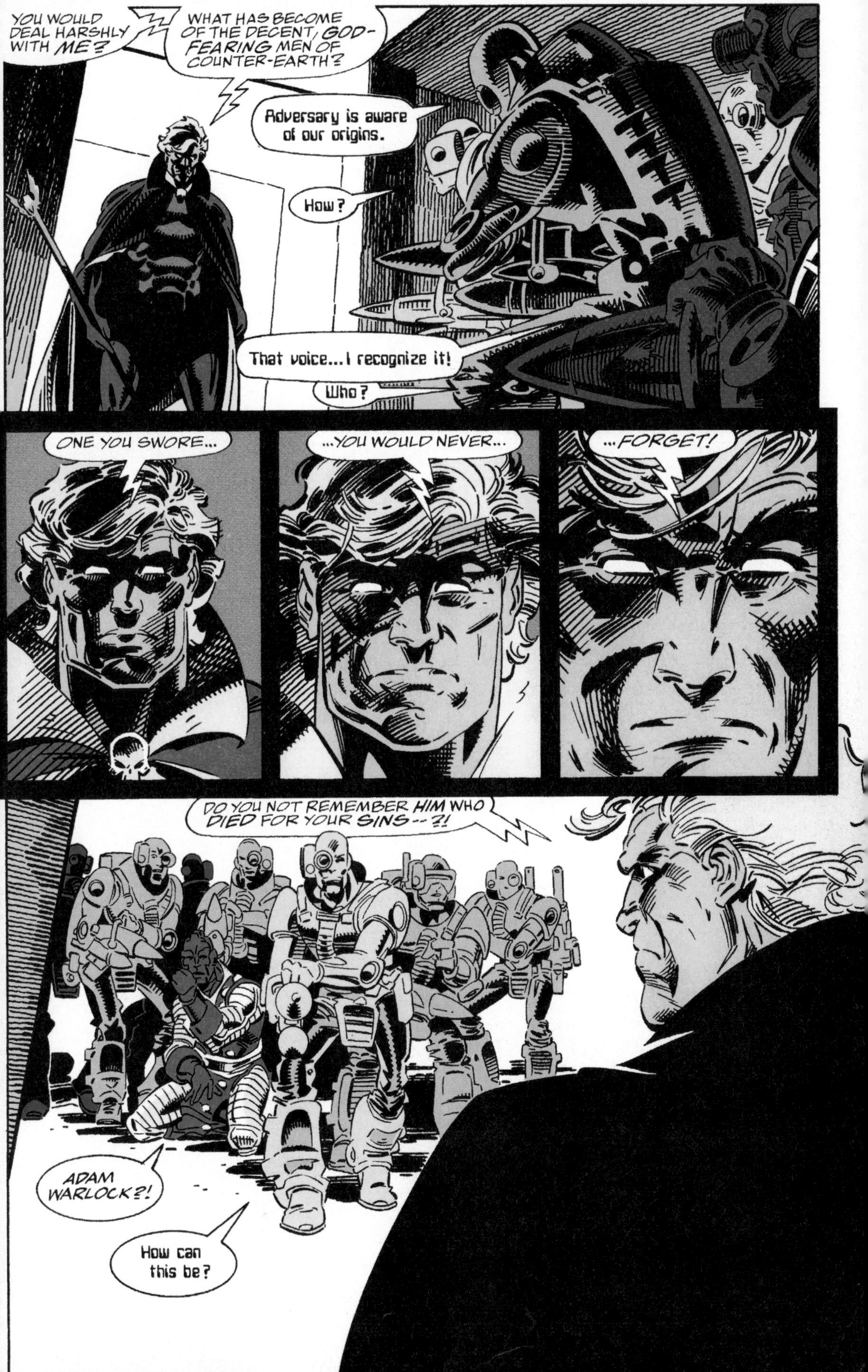
YOU WOULD DEAL HARSHLY WITH ME?
WHAT HAS BECOME OF THE DECENT, GOD-FEARING MEN OF COUNTER-EARTH?
Adversary is aware of our origins.
How?
That voice...I recognize it!
Who?
ONE YOU SWORE...
...YOU WOULD NEVER...
...FORGET!
DO YOU NOT REMEMBER HIM WHO DIED FOR YOUR SINS--?!
ADAM WARLOCK?!
How can this be?

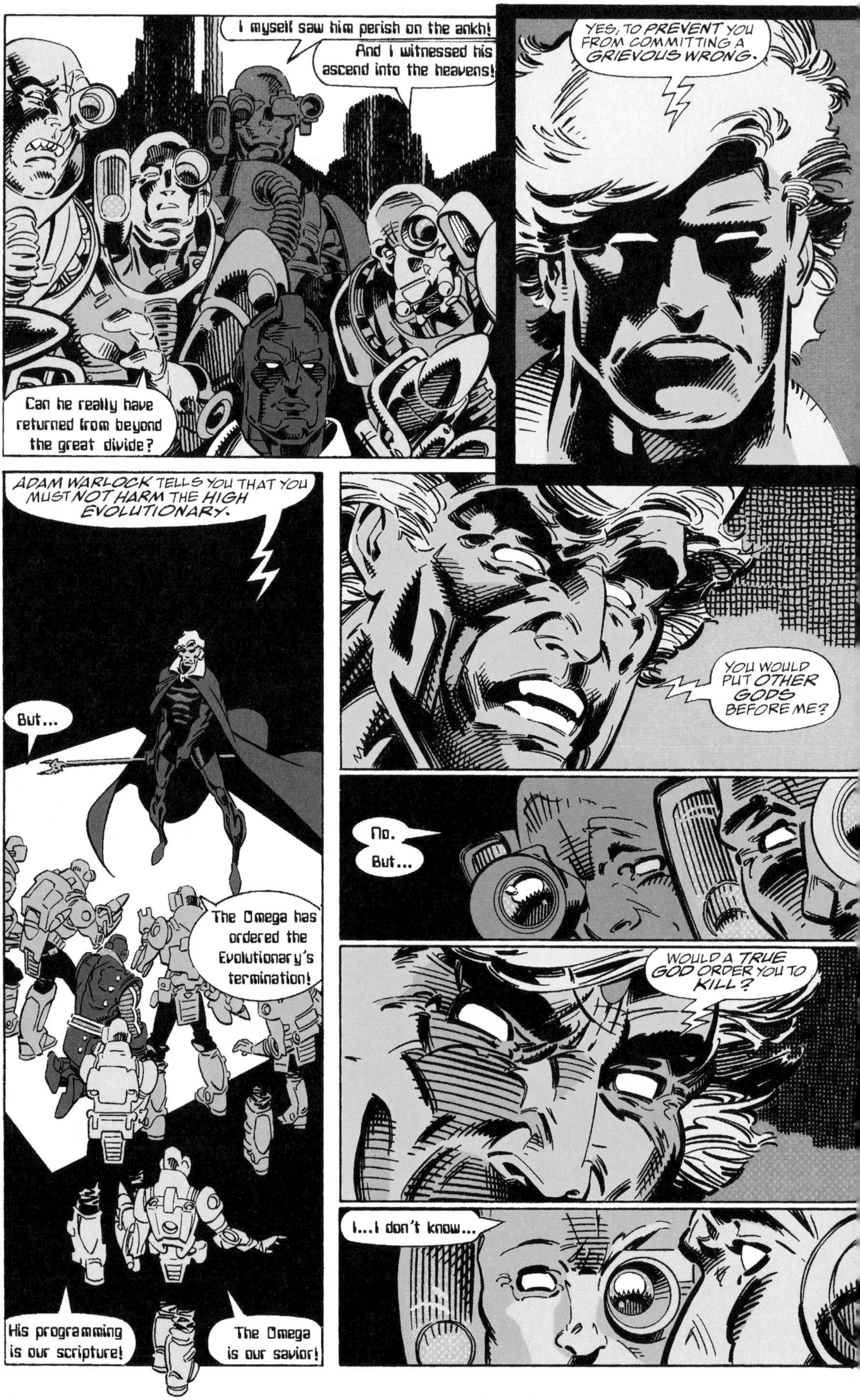
I myself saw him perish on the ankh!
And I witnessed his ascend into the heavens!
Can he really have returned from beyond the great divide?
YES, TO PREVENT YOU FROM COMMITTING A GRIEVOUS WRONG.
ADAM WARLOCK TELLS YOU THAT YOU MUST NOT HARM THE HIGH EVOLUTIONARY.
But...
The Omega has ordered the Evolutionary's termination!
His programming is our scripture!
The Omega is our savior!
YOU WOULD PUT OTHER GODS BEFORE ME?
No.
But...
WOULD A TRUE GOD ORDER YOU TO KILL?
I...I don't know...

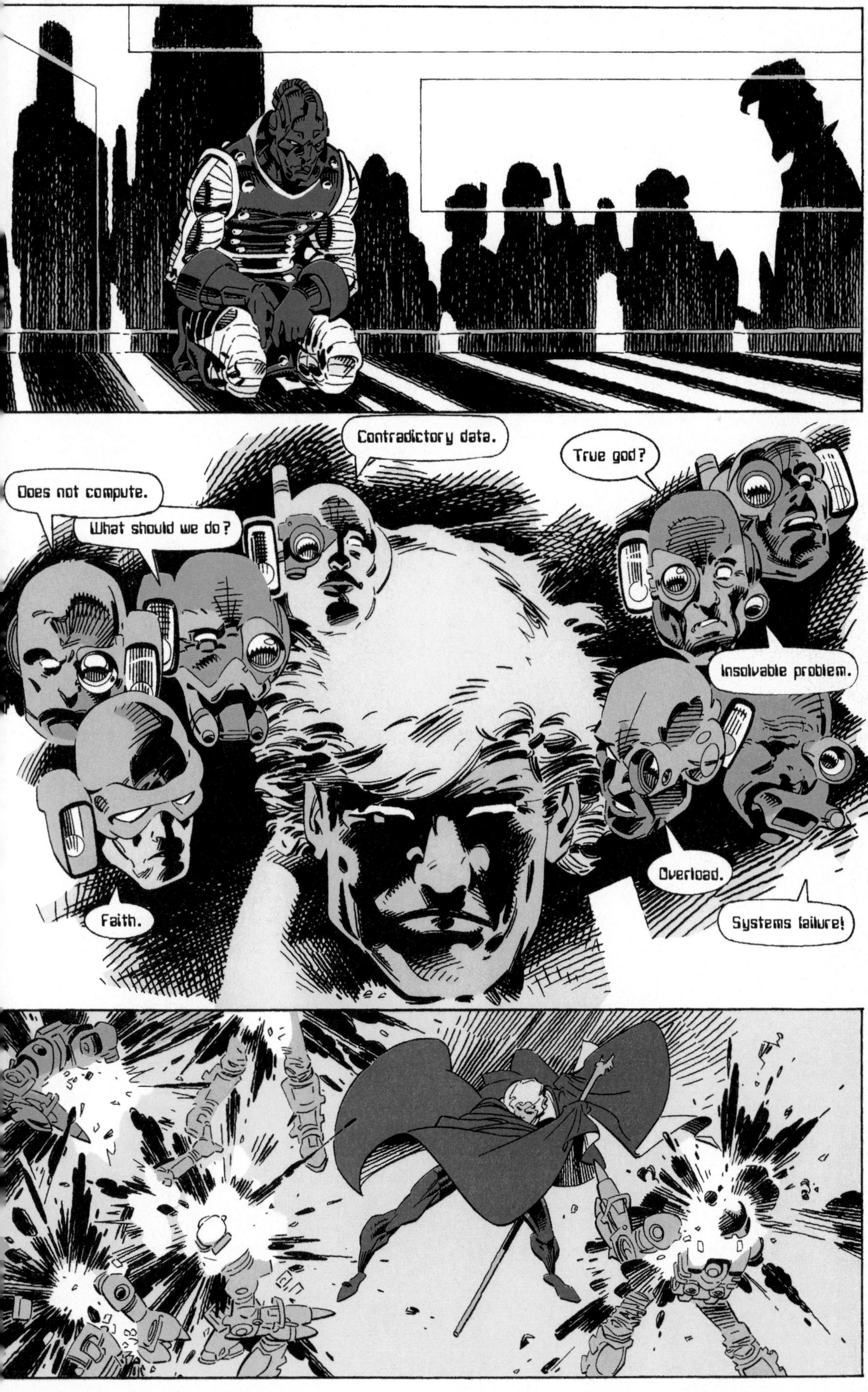
Does not compute.
What should we do?
Contradictory data.
True god?
Insolvable problem.
Faith.
Overload.
Systems failure!

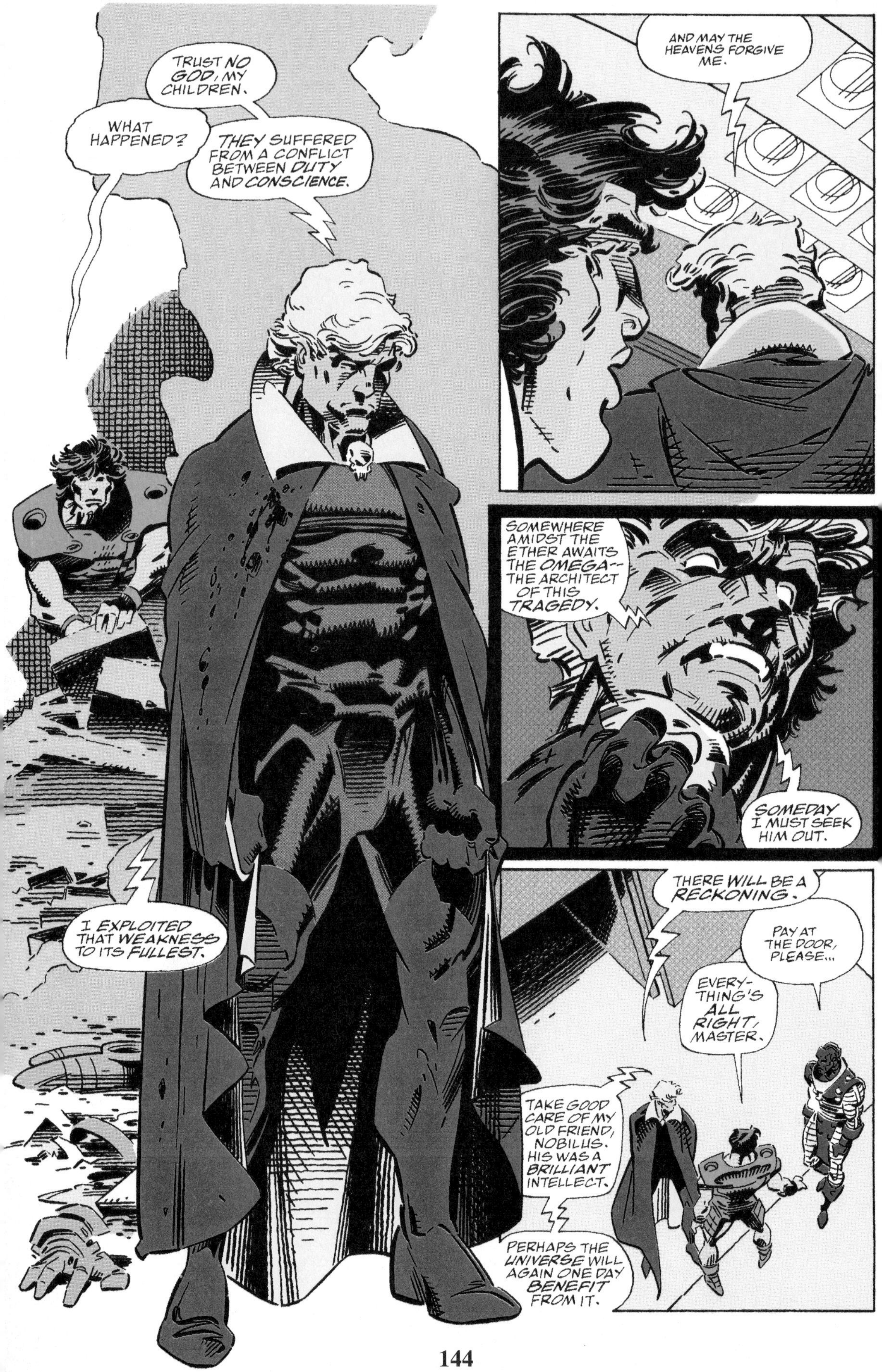
WHAT HAPPENED?
TRUST NO GOD, MY CHILDREN.
THEY SUFFERED FROM A CONFLICT BETWEEN DUTY AND CONSCIENCE.
I EXPLOITED THAT WEAKNESS TO ITS FULLEST.
AND MAY THE HEAVENS FORGIVE ME.
SOMEWHERE AMIDST THE ETHER AWAITS THE OMEGA-- THE ARCHITECT OF THIS TRAGEDY.
SOMEDAY I MUST SEEK HIM OUT.
THERE WILL BE A RECKONING.
PAY AT THE DOOR, PLEASE...
EVERY-THING'S ALL RIGHT, MASTER.
TAKE GOOD CARE OF MY OLD FRIEND, NOBILUS. HIS WAS A BRILLIANT INTELLECT.
PERHAPS THE UNIVERSE WILL AGAIN ONE DAY BENEFIT FROM IT.

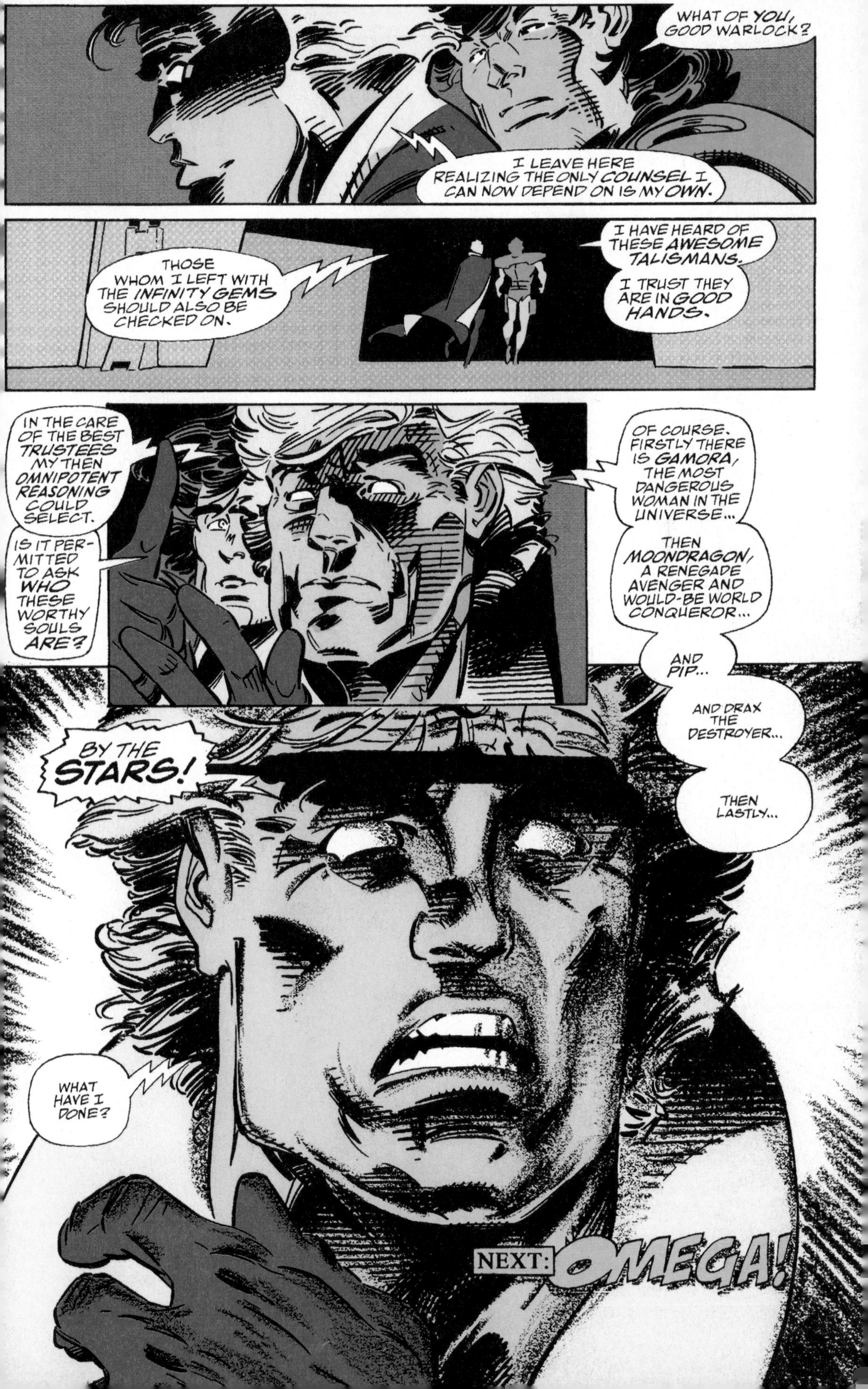
WHAT OF YOU, GOOD WARLOCK?
I LEAVE HERE REALIZING THE ONLY COUNSEL I CAN NOW DEPEND ON IS MY OWN.
THOSE WHOM I LEFT WITH THE INFINITY GEMS SHOULD ALSO BE CHECKED ON.
I HAVE HEARD OF THESE AWESOME TALISMANS.
I TRUST THEY ARE IN GOOD HANDS.
IN THE CARE OF THE BEST TRUSTEES MY THEN OMNIPOTENT REASONING COULD SELECT.
IS IT PERMITTED TO ASK WHO THESE WORTHY SOULS ARE?
OF COURSE. FIRSTLY THERE IS GAMORA, THE MOST DANGEROUS WOMAN IN THE UNIVERSE...
THEN MOONDRAGON, A RENEGADE AVENGER AND WOULD-BE WORLD CONQUEROR...
AND PIP...
AND DRAX THE DESTROYER...
THEN LASTLY...
BY THE STARS!
WHAT HAVE I DONE?
NEXT: OMEGA!

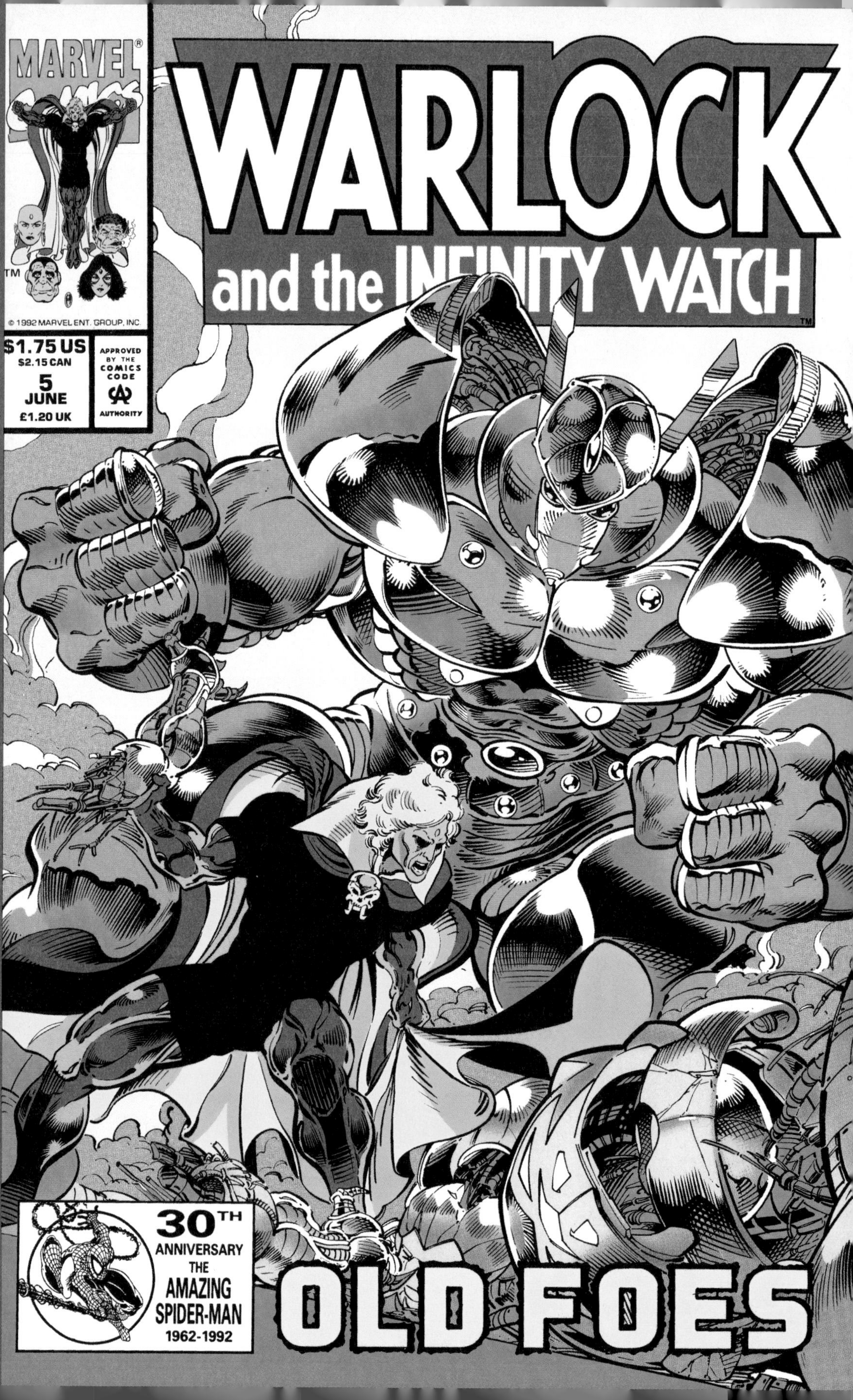
MARVEL COMICS
WARLOCK
and the INFINITY WATCH
© 1992 MARVEL ENT. GROUP, INC.
$1.75 US
$2.15 CAN
5
JUNE
£1.20 UK
APPROVED BY THE COMICS CODE AUTHORITY
30TH ANNIVERSARY THE AMAZING SPIDER-MAN 1962-1992
OLD FOES

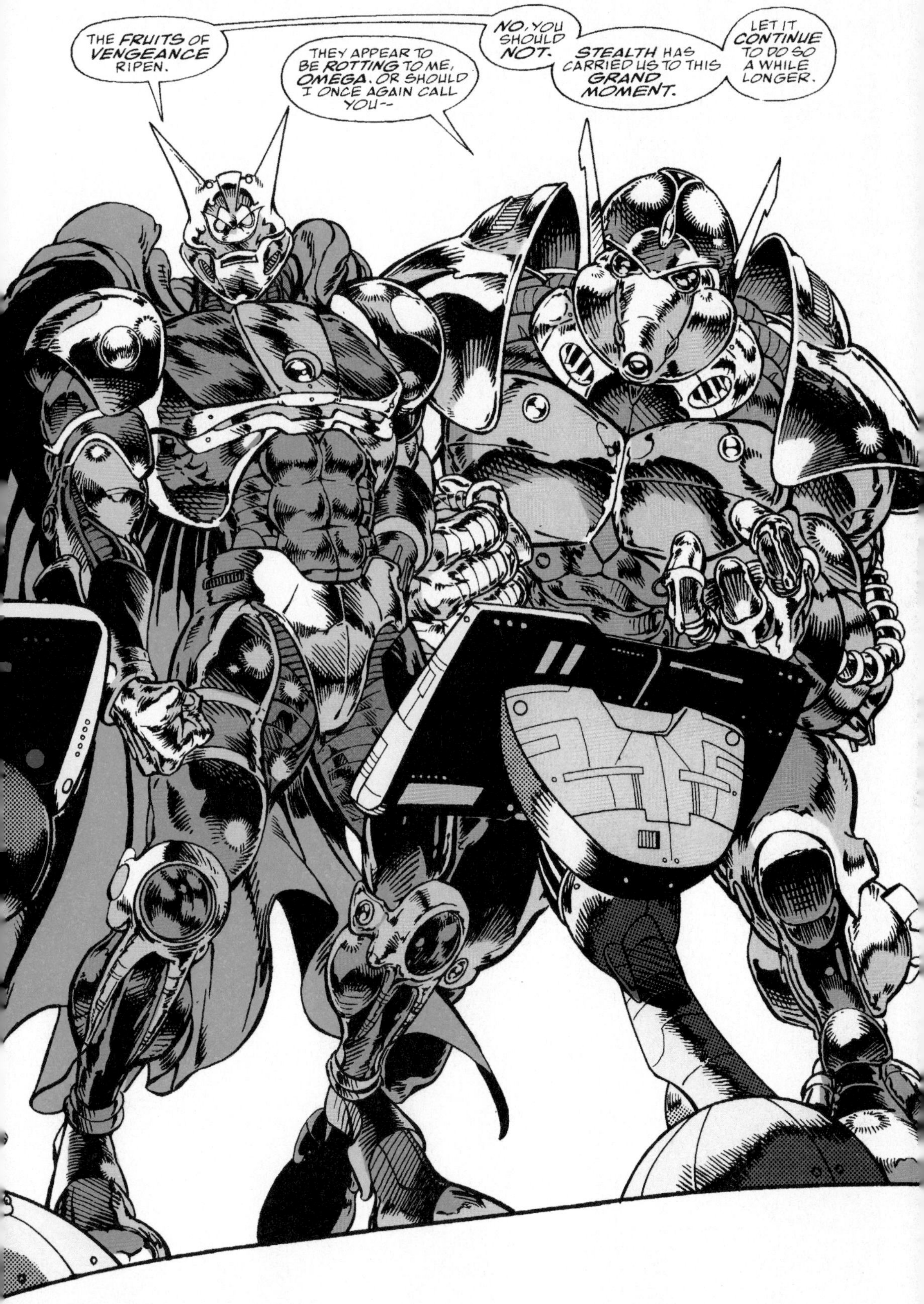
THE FRUITS OF VENGEANCE RIPEN.
THEY APPEAR TO BE ROTTING TO ME, OMEGA. OR SHOULD I ONCE AGAIN CALL YOU--
NO, YOU SHOULD NOT.
STEALTH HAS CARRIED US TO THIS GRAND MOMENT.
LET IT CONTINUE TO DO SO A WHILE LONGER.

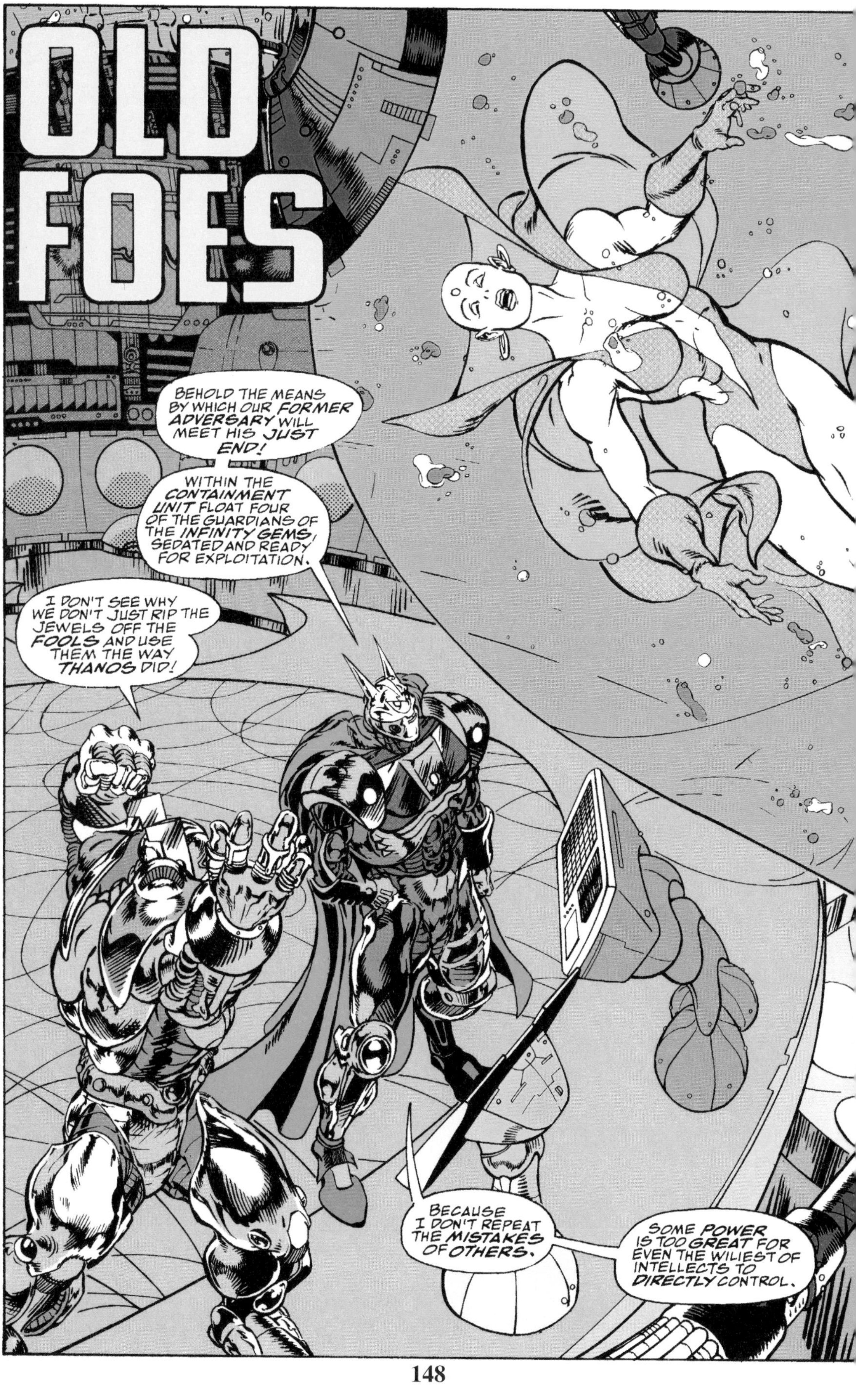
OLD FOES
BEHOLD THE MEANS BY WHICH OUR FORMER ADVERSARY WILL MEET HIS JUST END!
WITHIN THE CONTAINMENT UNIT FLOAT FOUR OF THE GUARDIANS OF THE INFINITY GEMS, SEDATED AND READY FOR EXPLOITATION.
I DON'T SEE WHY WE DON'T JUST RIP THE JEWELS OFF THE FOOLS AND USE THEM THE WAY THANOS DID!
BECAUSE I DON'T REPEAT THE MISTAKES OF OTHERS.
SOME POWER IS TOO GREAT FOR EVEN THE WILIEST OF INTELLECTS TO DIRECTLY CONTROL.

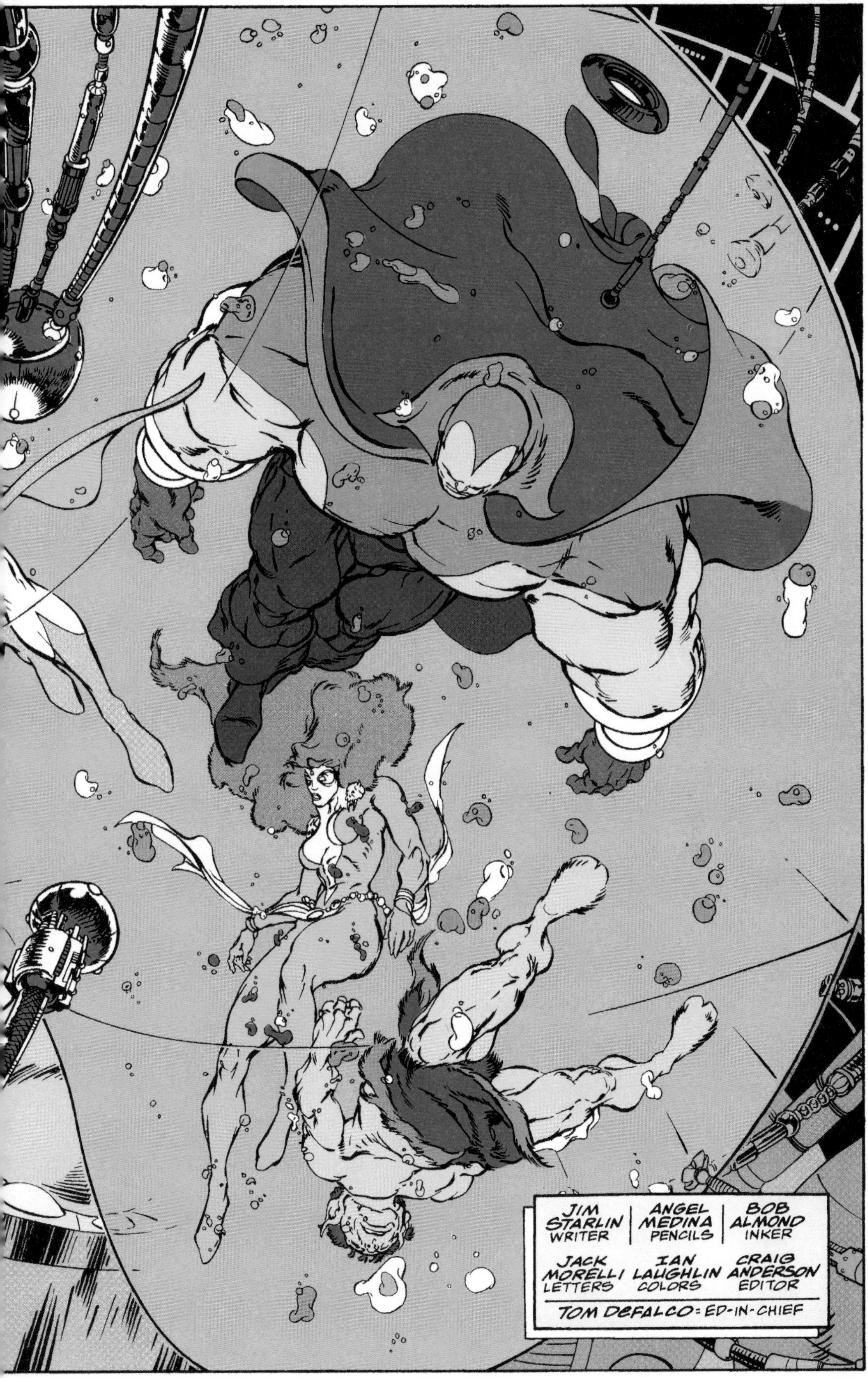
JIM STARLIN WRITER
ANGEL MEDINA PENCILS
BOB ALMOND INKER
JACK MORELLI LETTERS
IAN LAUGHLIN COLORS
CRAIG ANDERSON EDITOR
TOM DEFALCO: ED-IN-CHIEF

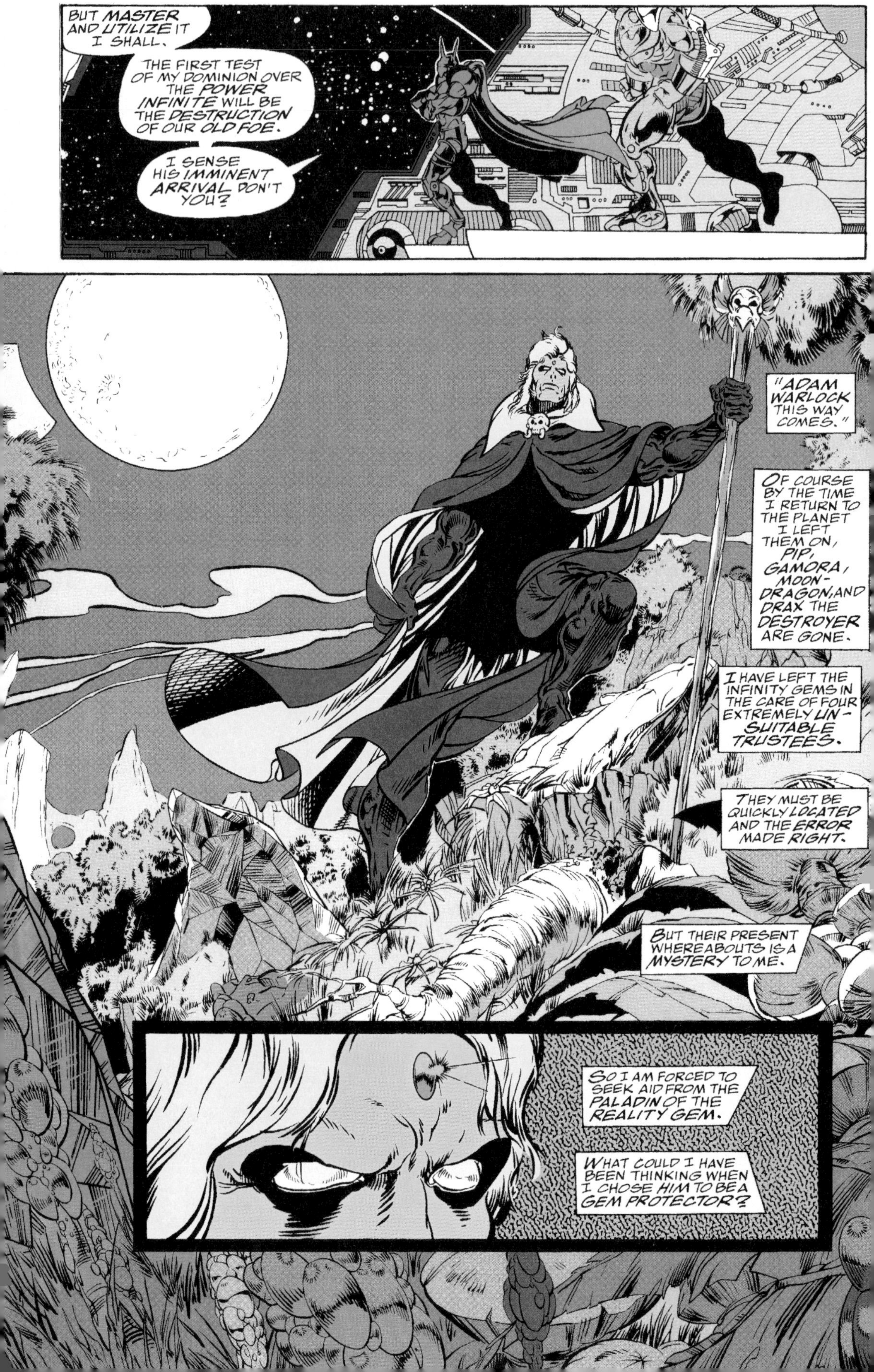
BUT MASTER AND UTILIZE IT I SHALL.
THE FIRST TEST OF MY DOMINION OVER THE POWER INFINITE WILL BE THE DESTRUCTION OF OUR OLD FOE.
I SENSE HIS IMMINENT ARRIVAL. DON'T YOU?
"ADAM WARLOCK THIS WAY COMES."
OF COURSE BY THE TIME I RETURN TO THE PLANET I LEFT THEM ON, PIP, GAMORA, MOON-DRAGON, AND DRAX THE DESTROYER ARE GONE.
I HAVE LEFT THE INFINITY GEMS IN THE CARE OF FOUR EXTREMELY UN-SUITABLE TRUSTEES.
THEY MUST BE QUICKLY LOCATED AND THE ERROR MADE RIGHT.
BUT THEIR PRESENT WHEREABOUTS IS A MYSTERY TO ME.
SO I AM FORCED TO SEEK AID FROM THE PALADIN OF THE REALITY GEM.
WHAT COULD I HAVE BEEN THINKING WHEN I CHOSE HIM TO BE A GEM PROTECTOR?

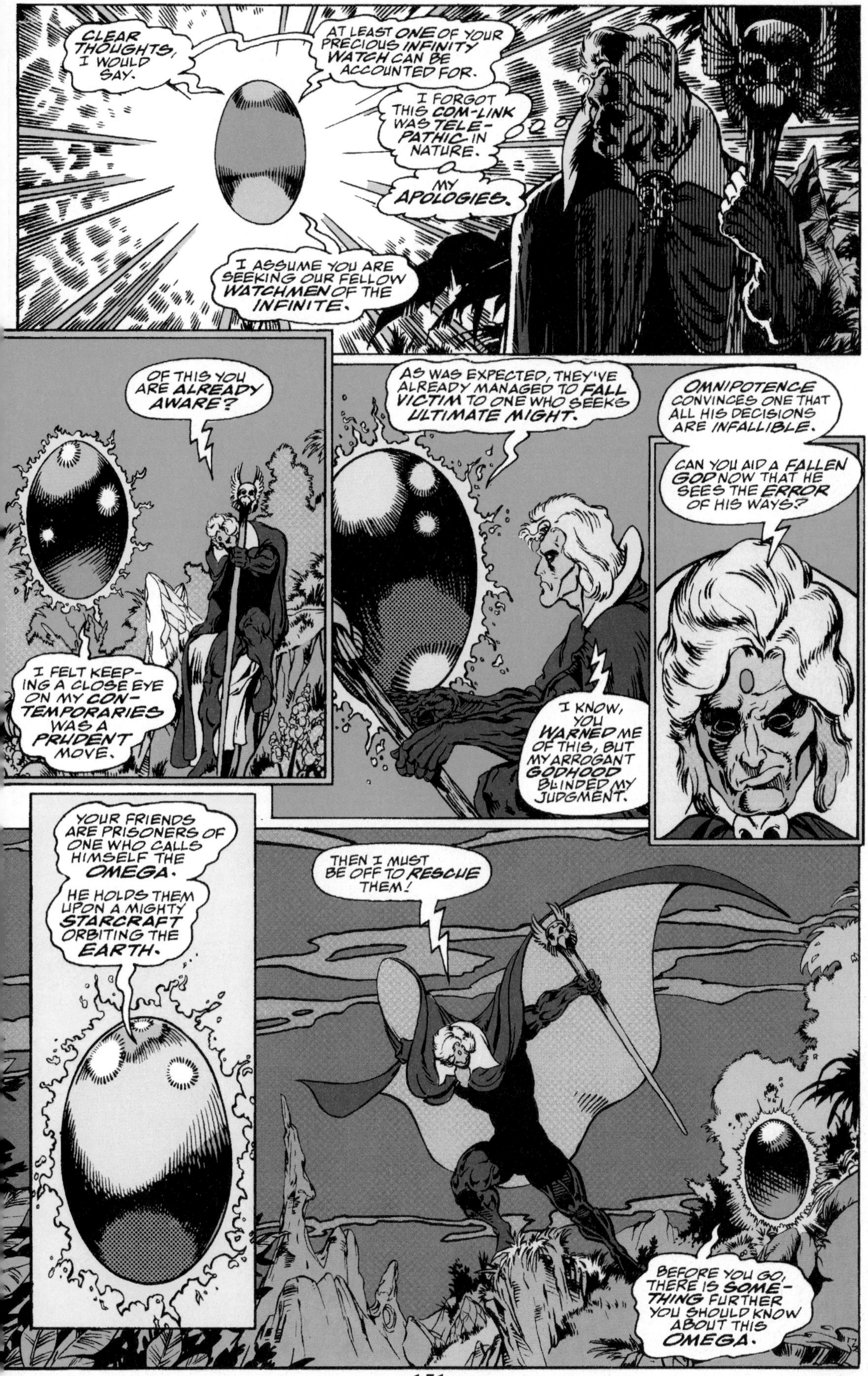
CLEAR THOUGHTS, I WOULD SAY.
AT LEAST ONE OF YOUR PRECIOUS INFINITY WATCH CAN BE ACCOUNTED FOR.
I FORGOT THIS COM-LINK WAS TELEPATHIC IN NATURE.
MY APOLOGIES.
I ASSUME YOU ARE SEEKING OUR FELLOW WATCHMEN OF THE INFINITE.
OF THIS YOU ARE ALREADY AWARE?
I FELT KEEPING A CLOSE EYE ON MY CONTEMPORARIES WAS A PRUDENT MOVE.
AS WAS EXPECTED, THEY'VE ALREADY MANAGED TO FALL VICTIM TO ONE WHO SEEKS ULTIMATE MIGHT.
I KNOW, YOU WARNED ME OF THIS, BUT MY ARROGANT GODHOOD BLINDED MY JUDGMENT.
OMNIPOTENCE CONVINCES ONE THAT ALL HIS DECISIONS ARE INFALLIBLE.
CAN YOU AID A FALLEN GOD NOW THAT HE SEES THE ERROR OF HIS WAYS?
YOUR FRIENDS ARE PRISONERS OF ONE WHO CALLS HIMSELF THE OMEGA.
HE HOLDS THEM UPON A MIGHTY STARCRAFT ORBITING THE EARTH.
THEN I MUST BE OFF TO RESCUE THEM!
BEFORE YOU GO, THERE IS SOMETHING FURTHER YOU SHOULD KNOW ABOUT THIS OMEGA.

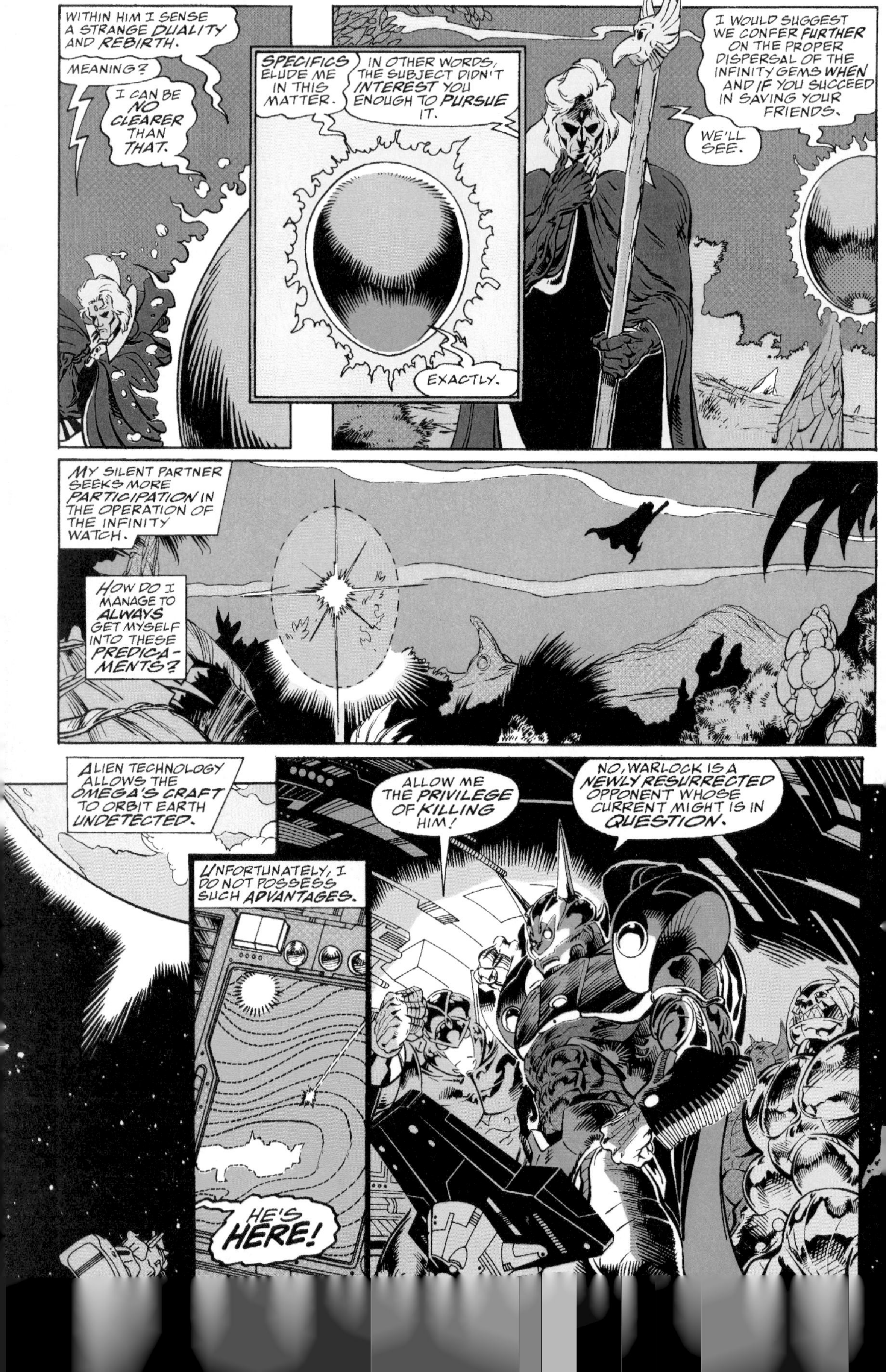
WITHIN HIM I SENSE A STRANGE DUALITY AND REBIRTH.
MEANING?
I CAN BE NO CLEARER THAN THAT.
SPECIFICS ELUDE ME IN THIS MATTER.
IN OTHER WORDS, THE SUBJECT DIDN'T INTEREST YOU ENOUGH TO PURSUE IT.
EXACTLY.
I WOULD SUGGEST WE CONFER FURTHER ON THE PROPER DISPERSAL OF THE INFINITY GEMS WHEN AND IF YOU SUCCEED IN SAVING YOUR FRIENDS.
WE'LL SEE.
MY SILENT PARTNER SEEKS MORE PARTICIPATION IN THE OPERATION OF THE INFINITY WATCH.
HOW DO I MANAGE TO ALWAYS GET MYSELF INTO THESE PREDICA-MENTS?
ALIEN TECHNOLOGY ALLOWS THE OMEGA'S CRAFT TO ORBIT EARTH UNDETECTED.
UNFORTUNATELY, I DO NOT POSSESS SUCH ADVANTAGES.
HE'S HERE!
ALLOW ME THE PRIVILEGE OF KILLING HIM!
NO, WARLOCK IS A NEWLY RESURRECTED OPPONENT WHOSE CURRENT MIGHT IS IN QUESTION.

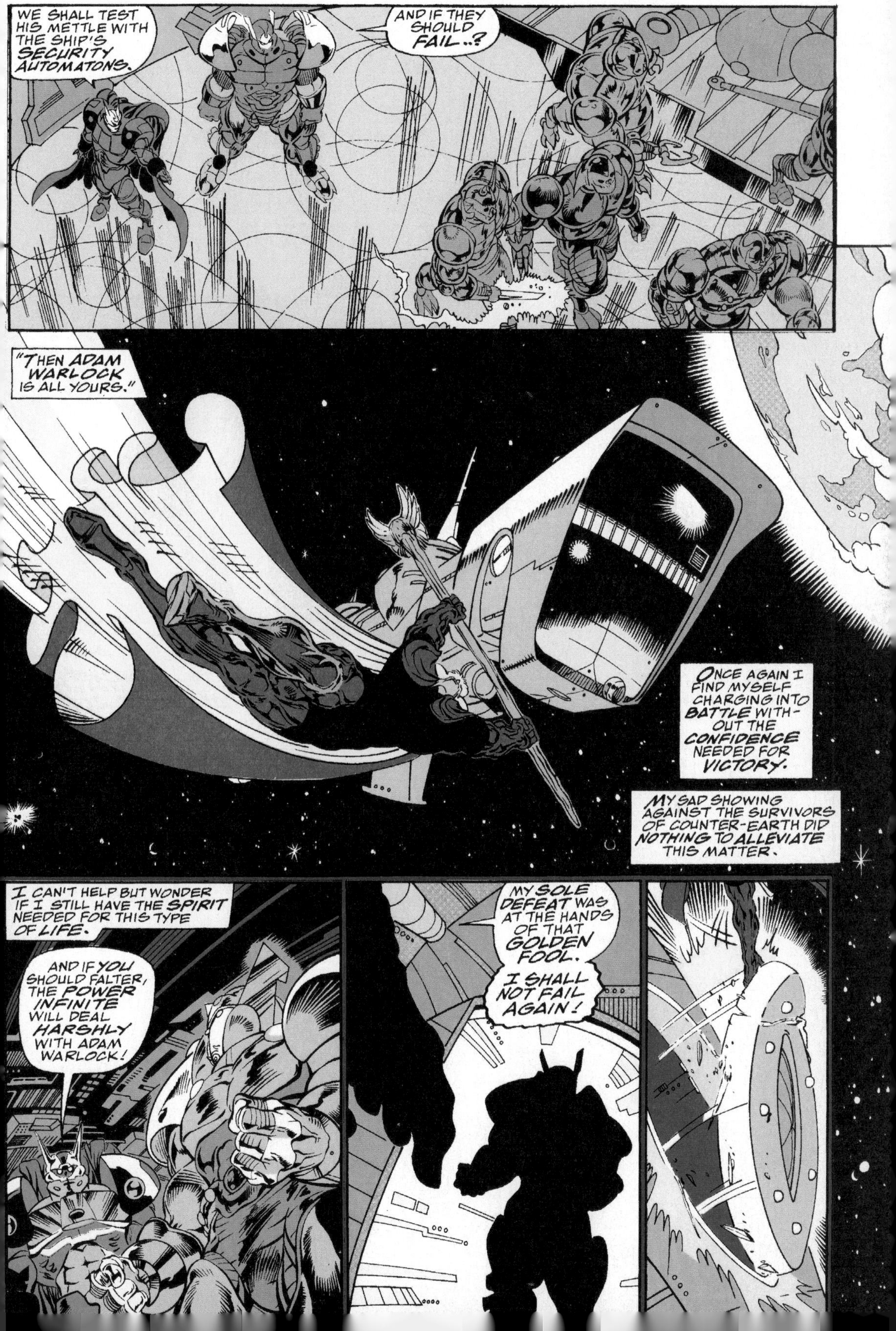
WE SHALL TEST HIS METTLE WITH THE SHIP'S SECURITY AUTOMATONS.
AND IF THEY SHOULD FAIL..?
"THEN ADAM WARLOCK IS ALL YOURS."
ONCE AGAIN I FIND MYSELF CHARGING INTO BATTLE WITH-OUT THE CONFIDENCE NEEDED FOR VICTORY.
MY SAD SHOWING AGAINST THE SURVIVORS OF COUNTER-EARTH DID NOTHING TO ALLEVIATE THIS MATTER.
I CAN'T HELP BUT WONDER IF I STILL HAVE THE SPIRIT NEEDED FOR THIS TYPE OF LIFE.
AND IF YOU SHOULD FALTER, THE POWER INFINITE WILL DEAL HARSHLY WITH ADAM WARLOCK!
MY SOLE DEFEAT WAS AT THE HANDS OF THAT GOLDEN FOOL.
I SHALL NOT FAIL AGAIN!

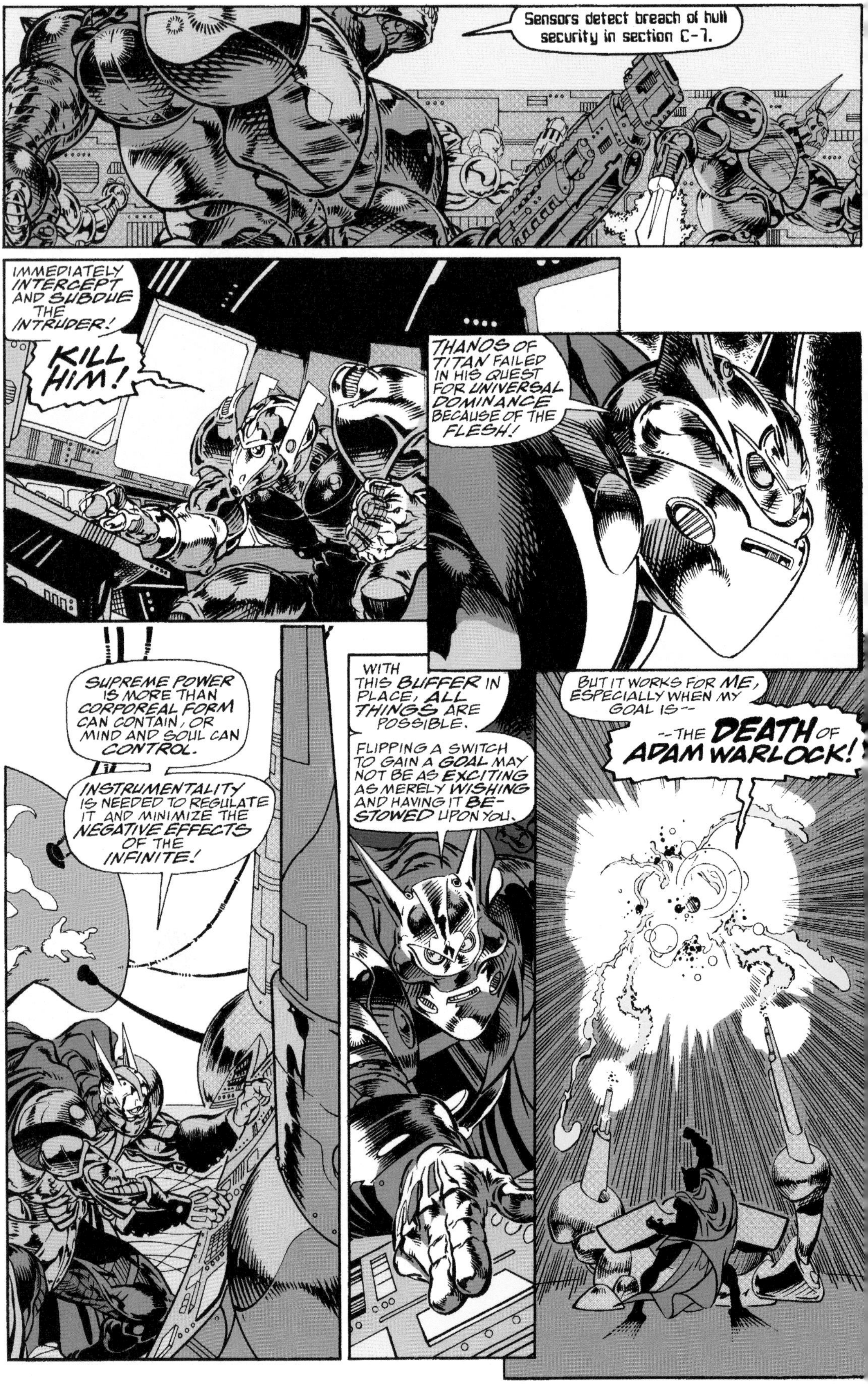
Sensors detect breach of hull security in section C-7.
IMMEDIATELY INTERCEPT AND SUBDUE THE INTRUDER!
KILL HIM!
THANOS OF TITAN FAILED IN HIS QUEST FOR UNIVERSAL DOMINANCE BECAUSE OF THE FLESH!
SUPREME POWER IS MORE THAN CORPOREAL FORM CAN CONTAIN, OR MIND AND SOUL CAN CONTROL.
INSTRUMENTALITY IS NEEDED TO REGULATE IT AND MINIMIZE THE NEGATIVE EFFECTS OF THE INFINITE!
WITH THIS BUFFER IN PLACE, ALL THINGS ARE POSSIBLE.
FLIPPING A SWITCH TO GAIN A GOAL MAY NOT BE AS EXCITING AS MERELY WISHING AND HAVING IT BESTOWED UPON YOU.
BUT IT WORKS FOR ME, ESPECIALLY WHEN MY GOAL IS--
--THE DEATH OF ADAM WARLOCK!

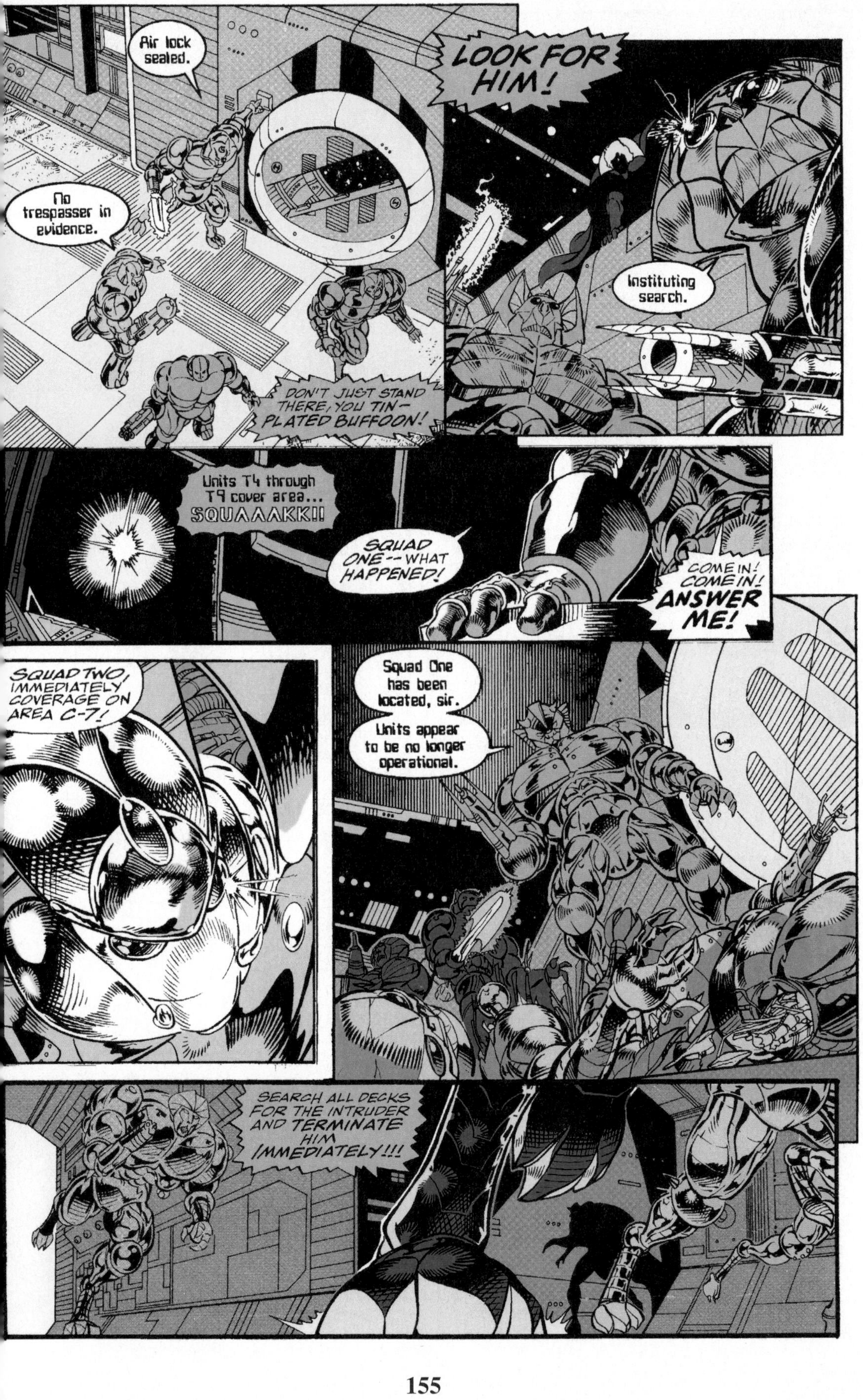
Air lock sealed.
No trespasser in evidence.
LOOK FOR HIM!
DON'T JUST STAND THERE, YOU TIN-PLATED BUFFOON!
Instituting search.
Units T4 through T9 cover area... SQUAAAKK!!
SQUAD ONE--WHAT HAPPENED!
COME IN! COME IN! ANSWER ME!
SQUAD TWO, IMMEDIATELY COVERAGE ON AREA C-7!
Squad One has been located, sir.
Units appear to be no longer operational.
SEARCH ALL DECKS FOR THE INTRUDER AND TERMINATE HIM IMMEDIATELY!!!

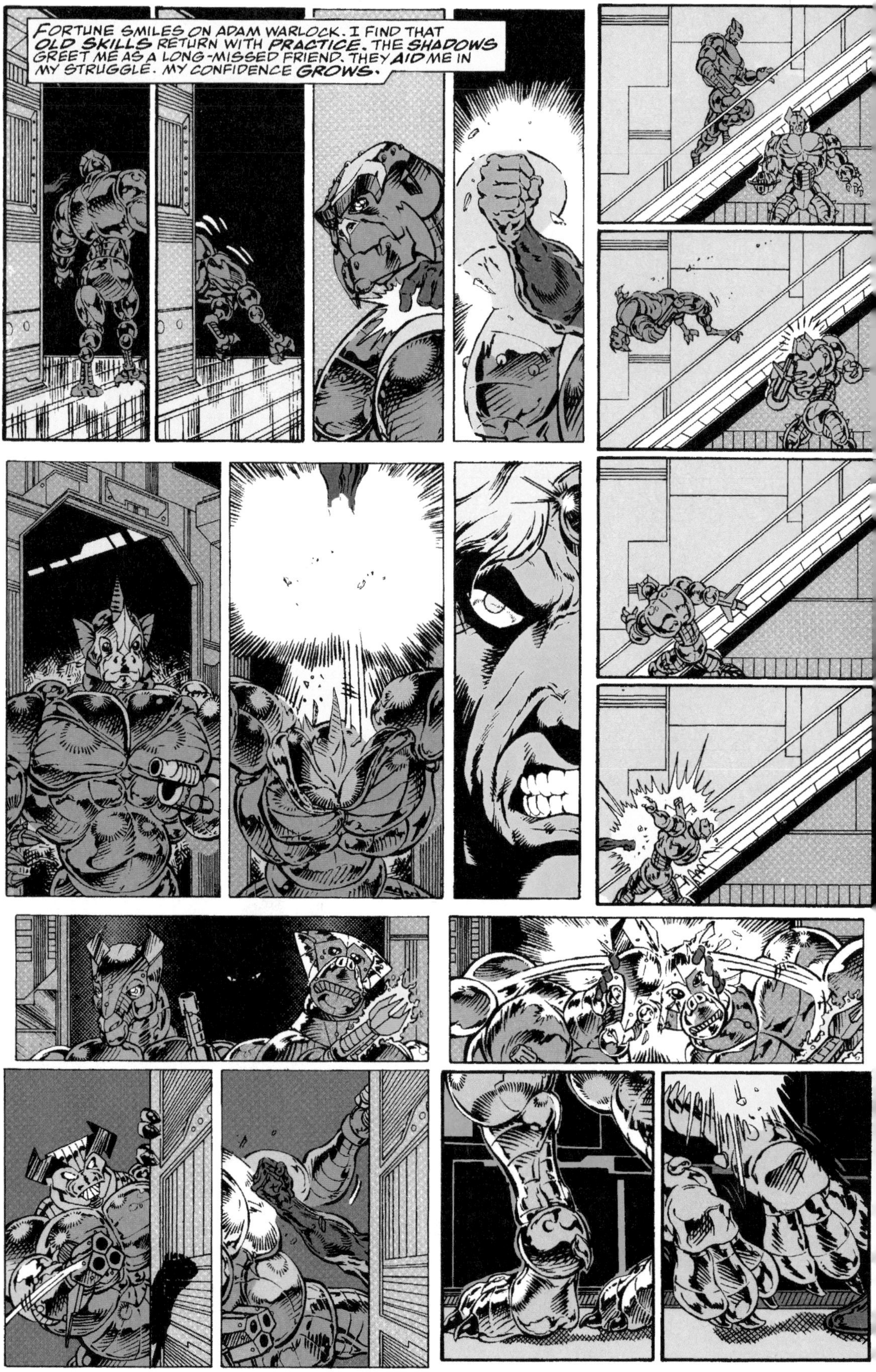
FORTUNE SMILES ON ADAM WARLOCK. I FIND THAT OLD SKILLS RETURN WITH PRACTICE. THE SHADOWS GREET ME AS A LONG-MISSED FRIEND. THEY AID ME IN MY STRUGGLE. MY CONFIDENCE GROWS.

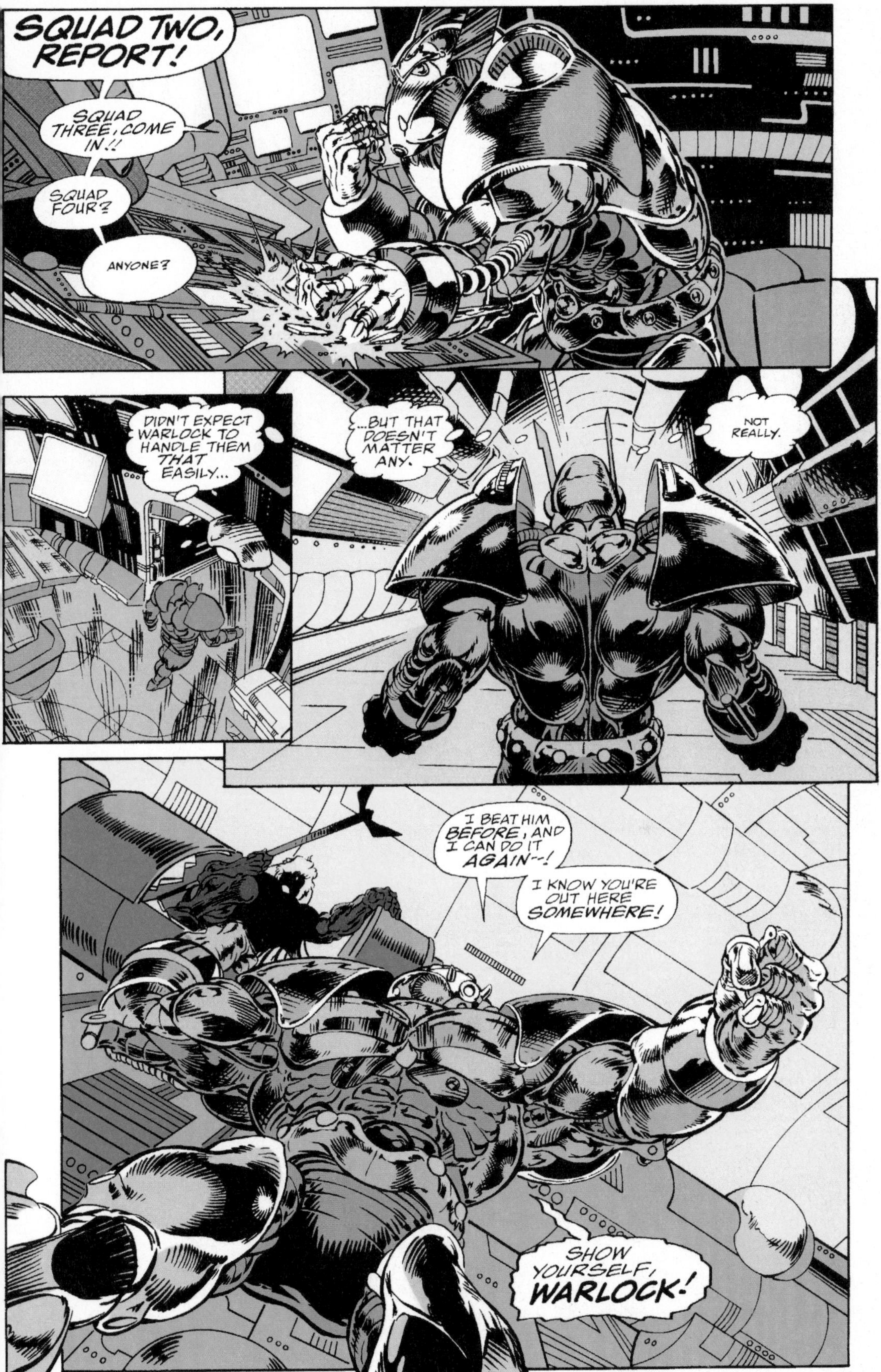
SQUAD TWO, REPORT!
SQUAD THREE, COME IN!!
SQUAD FOUR?
ANYONE?
DIDN'T EXPECT WARLOCK TO HANDLE THEM THAT EASILY...
...BUT THAT DOESN'T MATTER ANY.
NOT REALLY.
I BEAT HIM BEFORE, AND I CAN DO IT AGAIN--!
I KNOW YOU'RE OUT HERE SOMEWHERE!
SHOW YOURSELF, WARLOCK!

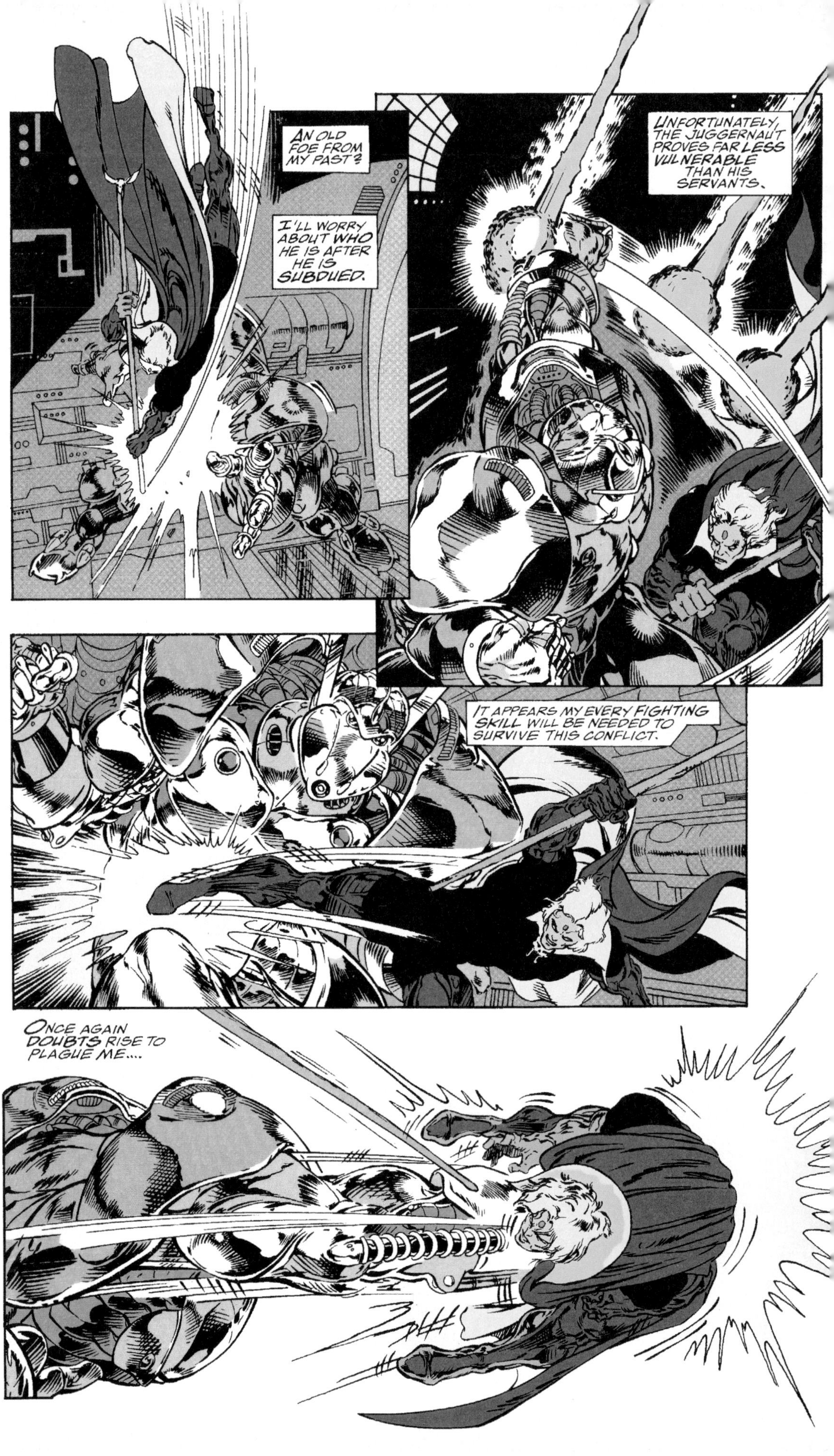

AN OLD FOE FROM MY PAST?
I'LL WORRY ABOUT WHO HE IS AFTER HE IS SUBDUED.
UNFORTUNATELY, THE JUGGERNAUT PROVES FAR LESS VULNERABLE THAN HIS SERVANTS.
IT APPEARS MY EVERY FIGHTING SKILL WILL BE NEEDED TO SURVIVE THIS CONFLICT.
ONCE AGAIN DOUBTS RISE TO PLAGUE ME....

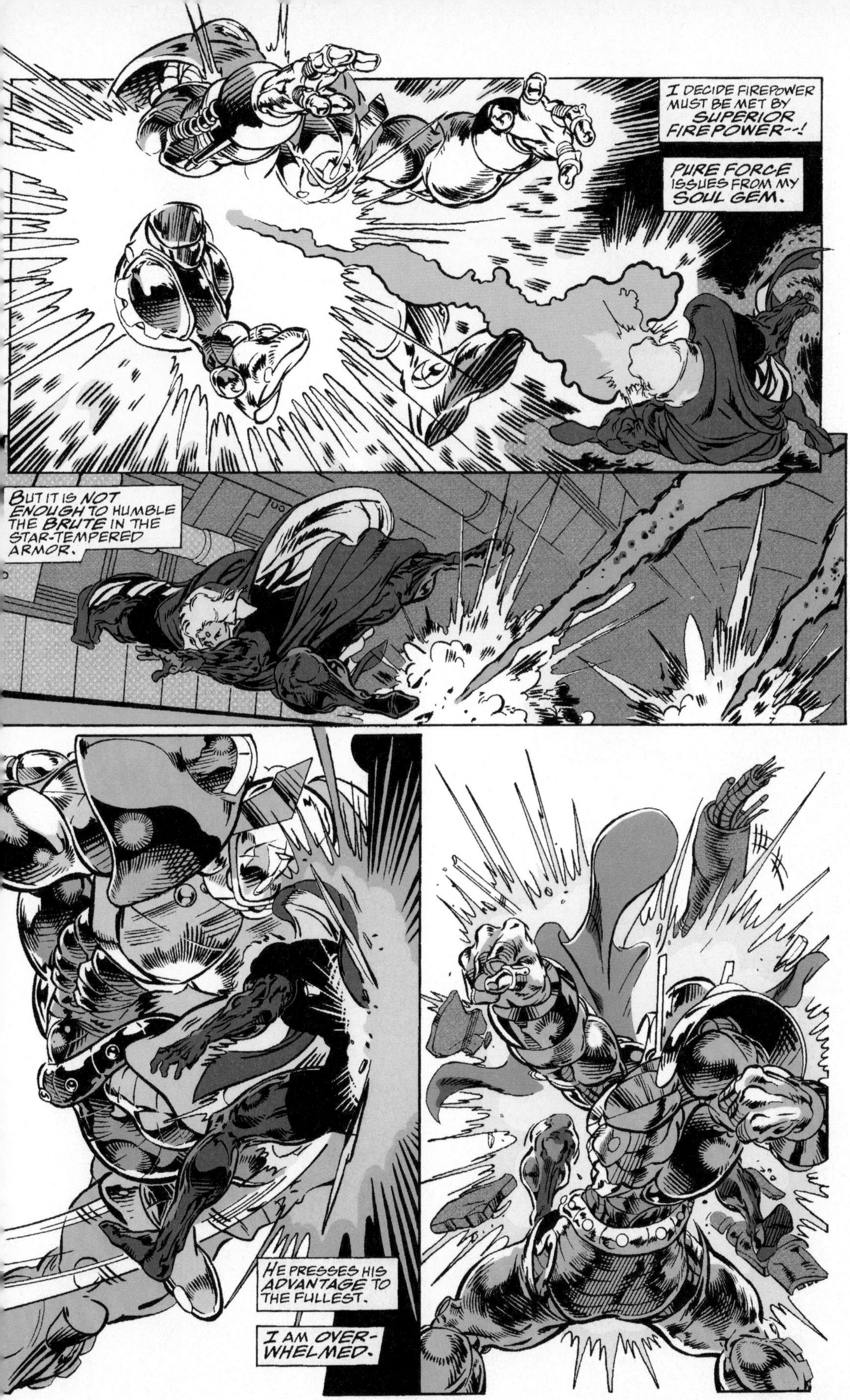
I DECIDE FIREPOWER MUST BE MET BY SUPERIOR FIREPOWER--!
PURE FORCE ISSUES FROM MY SOUL GEM.
BUT IT IS NOT ENOUGH TO HUMBLE THE BRUTE IN THE STAR-TEMPERED ARMOR.
HE PRESSES HIS ADVANTAGE TO THE FULLEST.
I AM OVER-WHELMED.

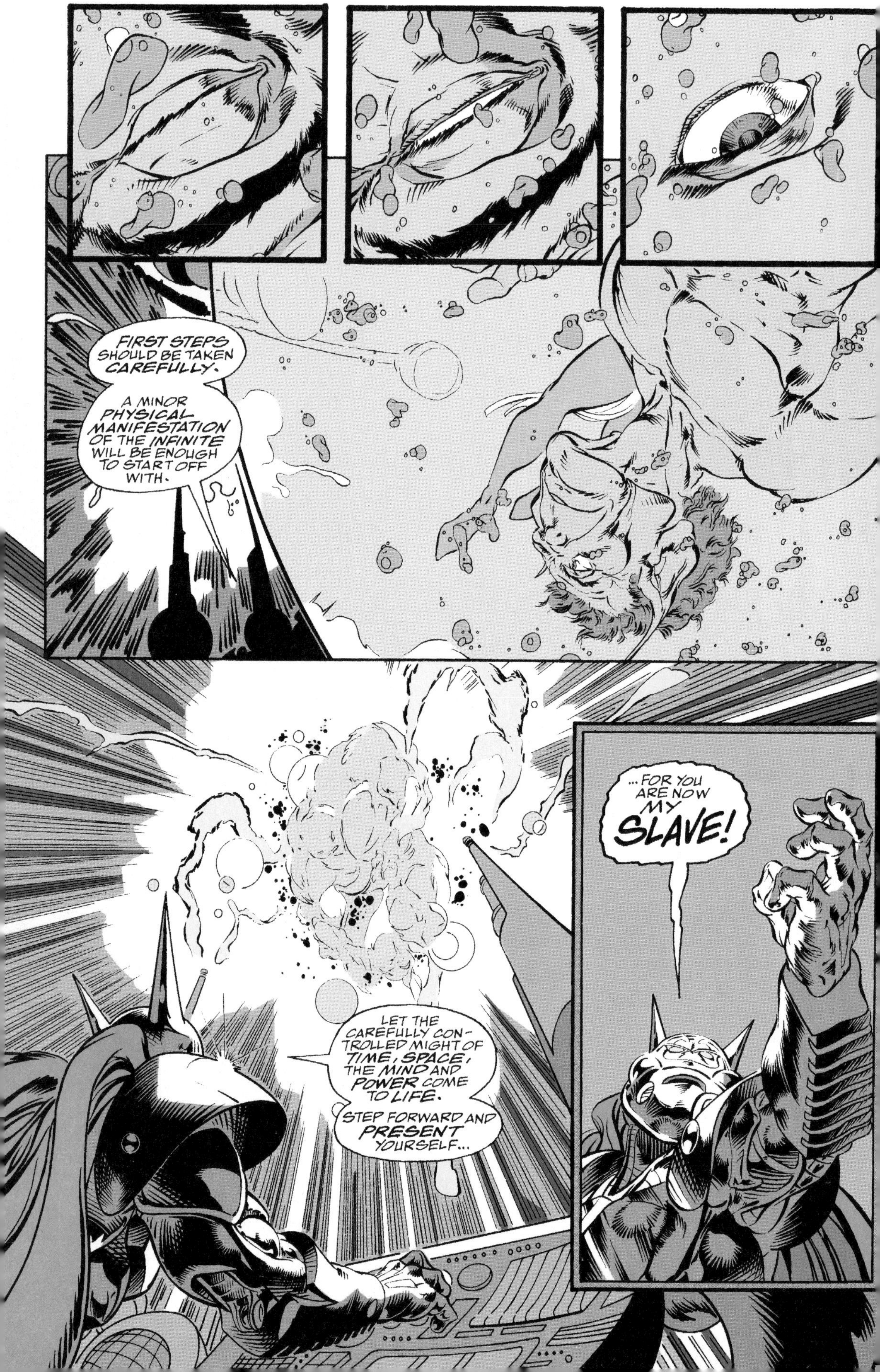
FIRST STEPS SHOULD BE TAKEN CAREFULLY.
A MINOR PHYSICAL MANIFESTATION OF THE INFINITE WILL BE ENOUGH TO START OFF WITH.
LET THE CAREFULLY CONTROLLED MIGHT OF TIME, SPACE, THE MIND AND POWER COME TO LIFE.
STEP FORWARD AND PRESENT YOURSELF...
...FOR YOU ARE NOW MY SLAVE!

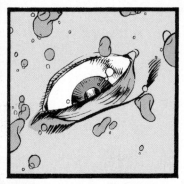

THE DISADVANTAGES OF RETURNING TO THIS PHYSICAL PLANE OF EXISTENCE ARE BECOMING PAINFULLY OBVIOUS!

TOO LONG DID I SPEND ON PEACEFUL SOUL WORLD.

HOW DEARLY I WISH TO RETURN THERE.

BUT IF I EVER HOPE TO ONCE AGAIN SEE THAT EMERALD PARADISE, I MUST ACT QUICKLY...

...AND WITHOUT MERCY!

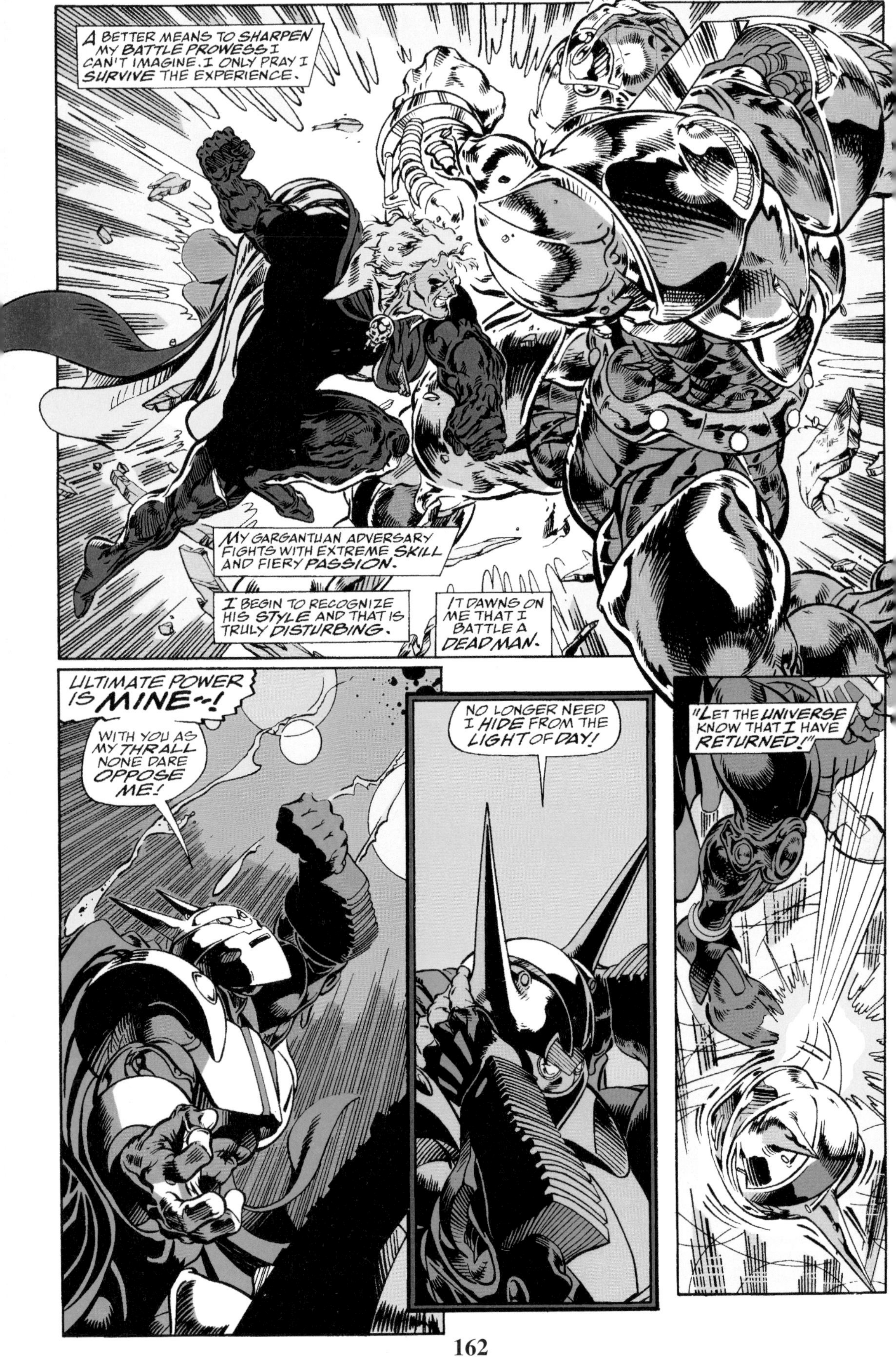
A BETTER MEANS TO SHARPEN MY BATTLE PROWESS I CAN'T IMAGINE. I ONLY PRAY I SURVIVE THE EXPERIENCE.
MY GARGANTUAN ADVERSARY FIGHTS WITH EXTREME SKILL AND FIERY PASSION.
I BEGIN TO RECOGNIZE HIS STYLE AND THAT IS TRULY DISTURBING.
IT DAWNS ON ME THAT I BATTLE A DEAD MAN.
ULTIMATE POWER IS MINE--!
WITH YOU AS MY THRALL NONE DARE OPPOSE ME!
NO LONGER NEED I HIDE FROM THE LIGHT OF DAY!
"LET THE UNIVERSE KNOW THAT I HAVE RETURNED!"

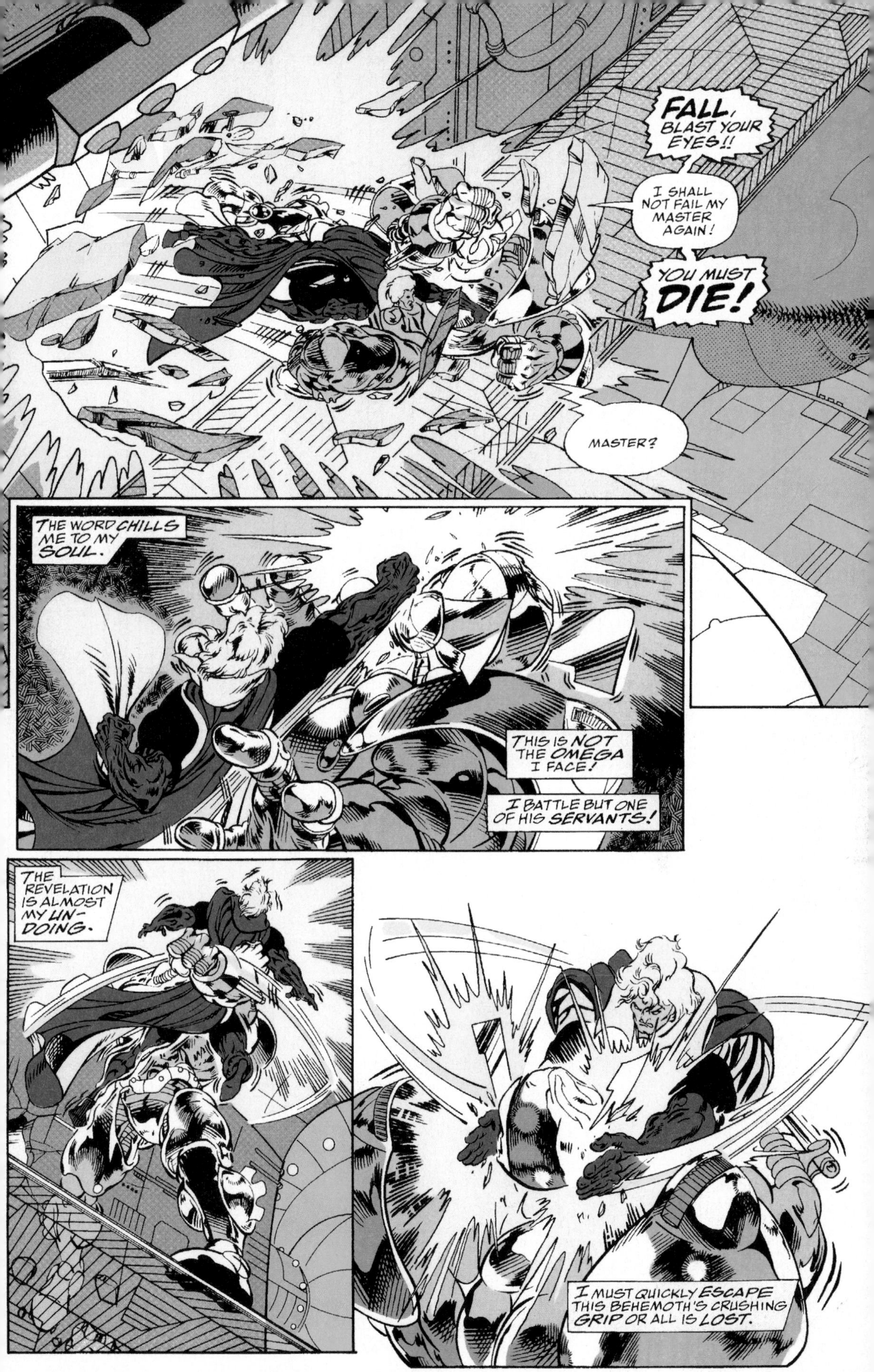
FALL, BLAST YOUR EYES!!
I SHALL NOT FAIL MY MASTER AGAIN!
YOU MUST DIE!
MASTER?
THE WORD CHILLS ME TO MY SOUL.
THIS IS NOT THE OMEGA I FACE!
I BATTLE BUT ONE OF HIS SERVANTS!
THE REVELATION IS ALMOST MY UN-DOING.
I MUST QUICKLY ESCAPE THIS BEHEMOTH'S CRUSHING GRIP OR ALL IS LOST.

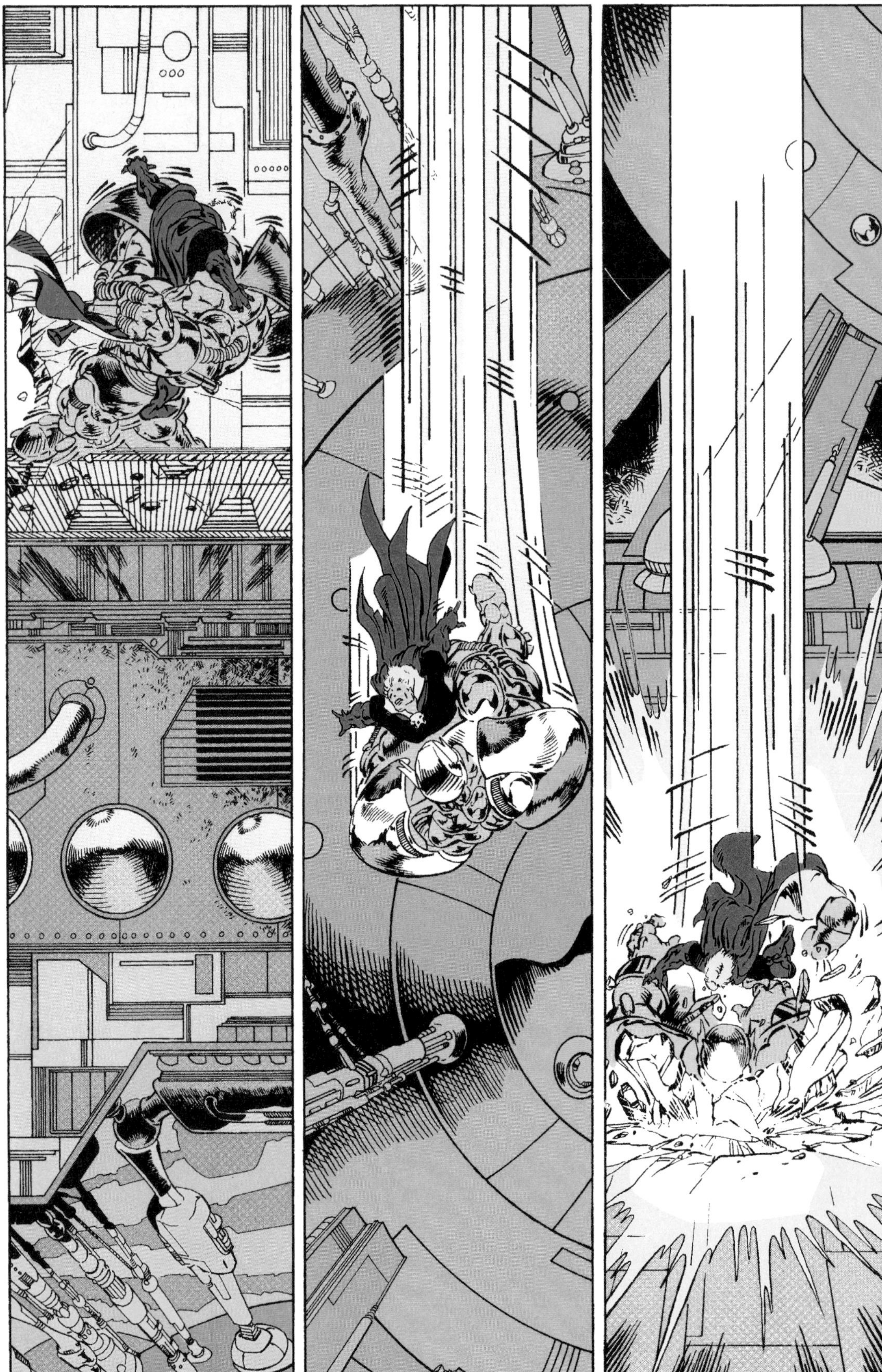

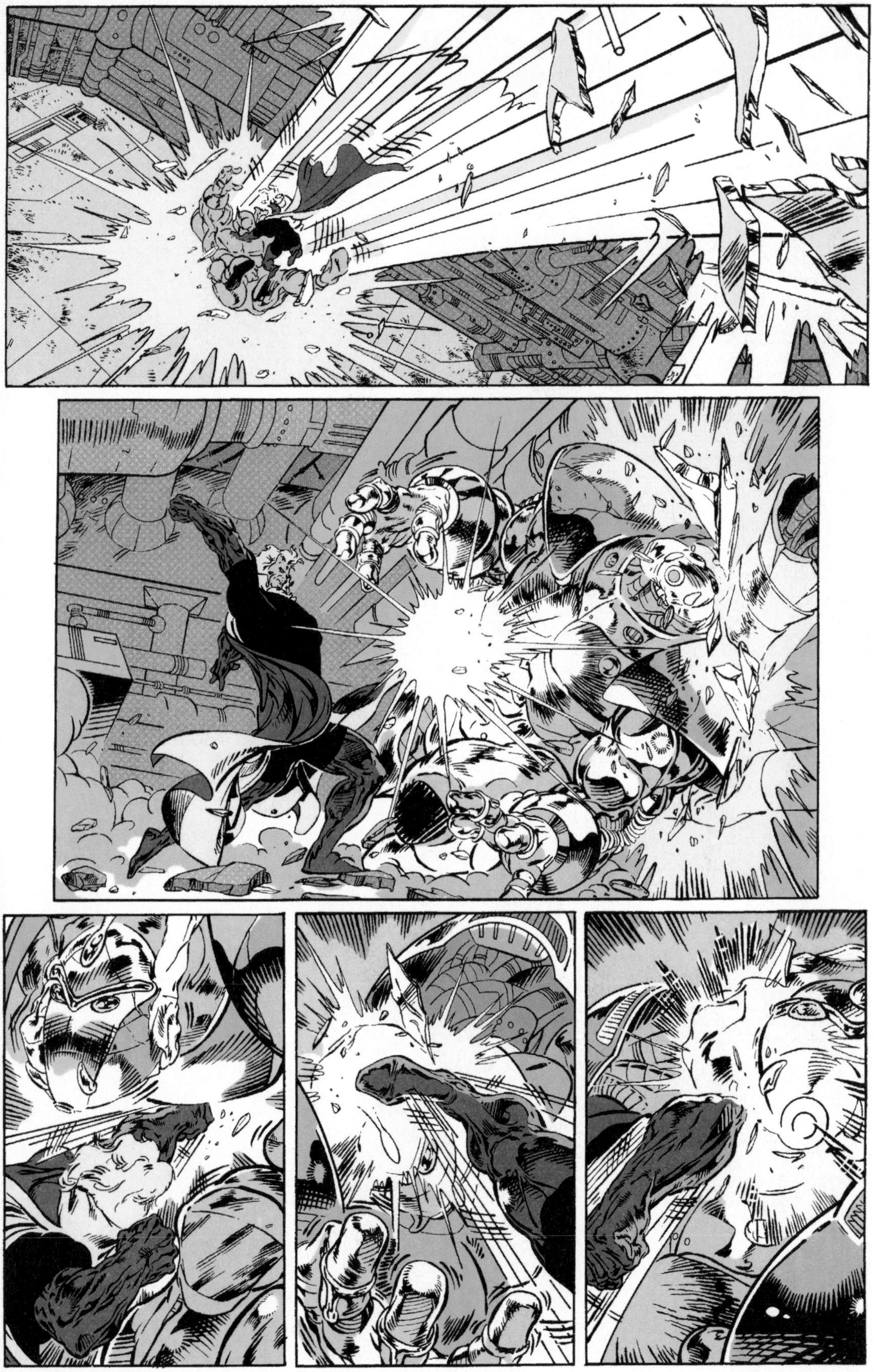

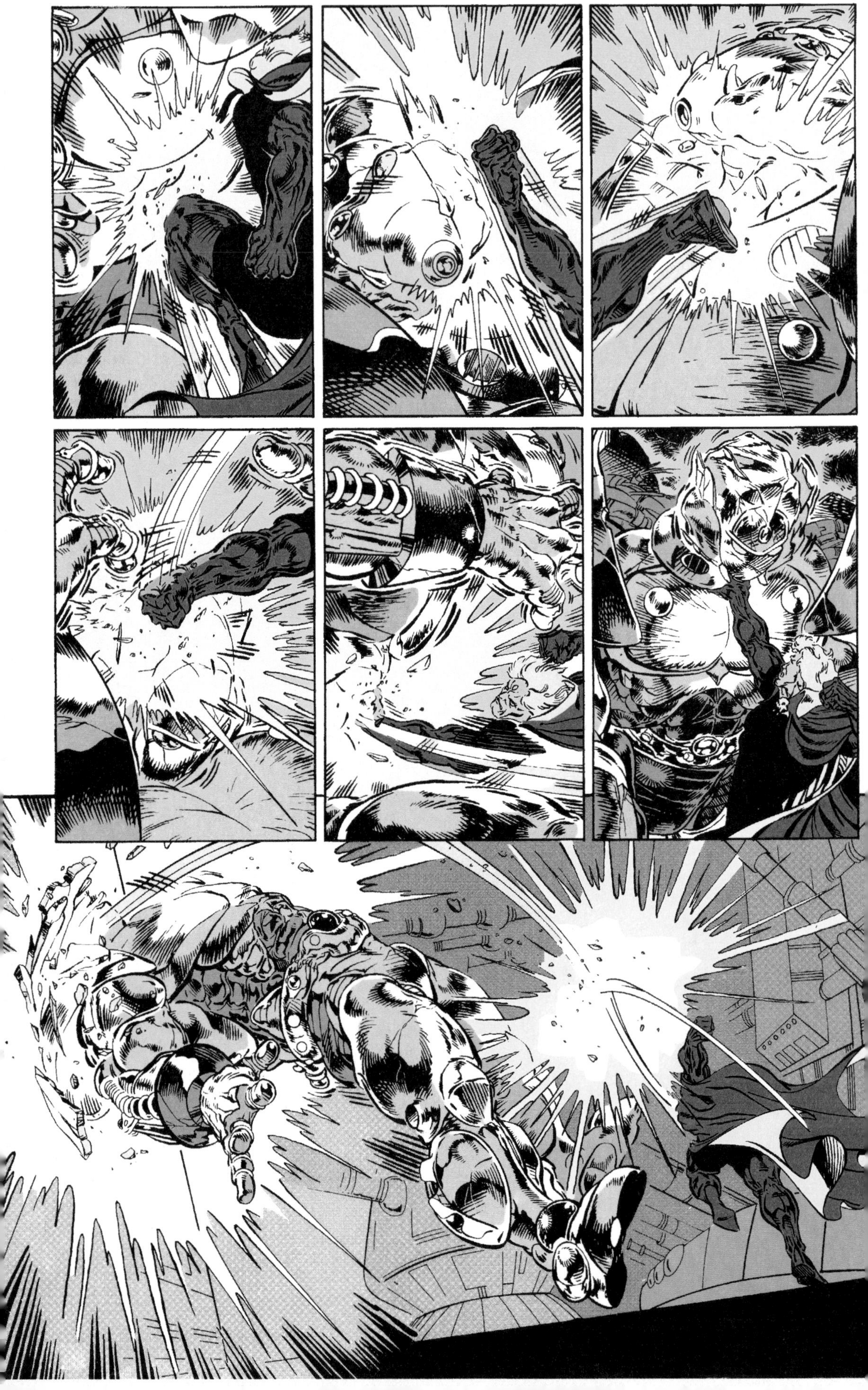

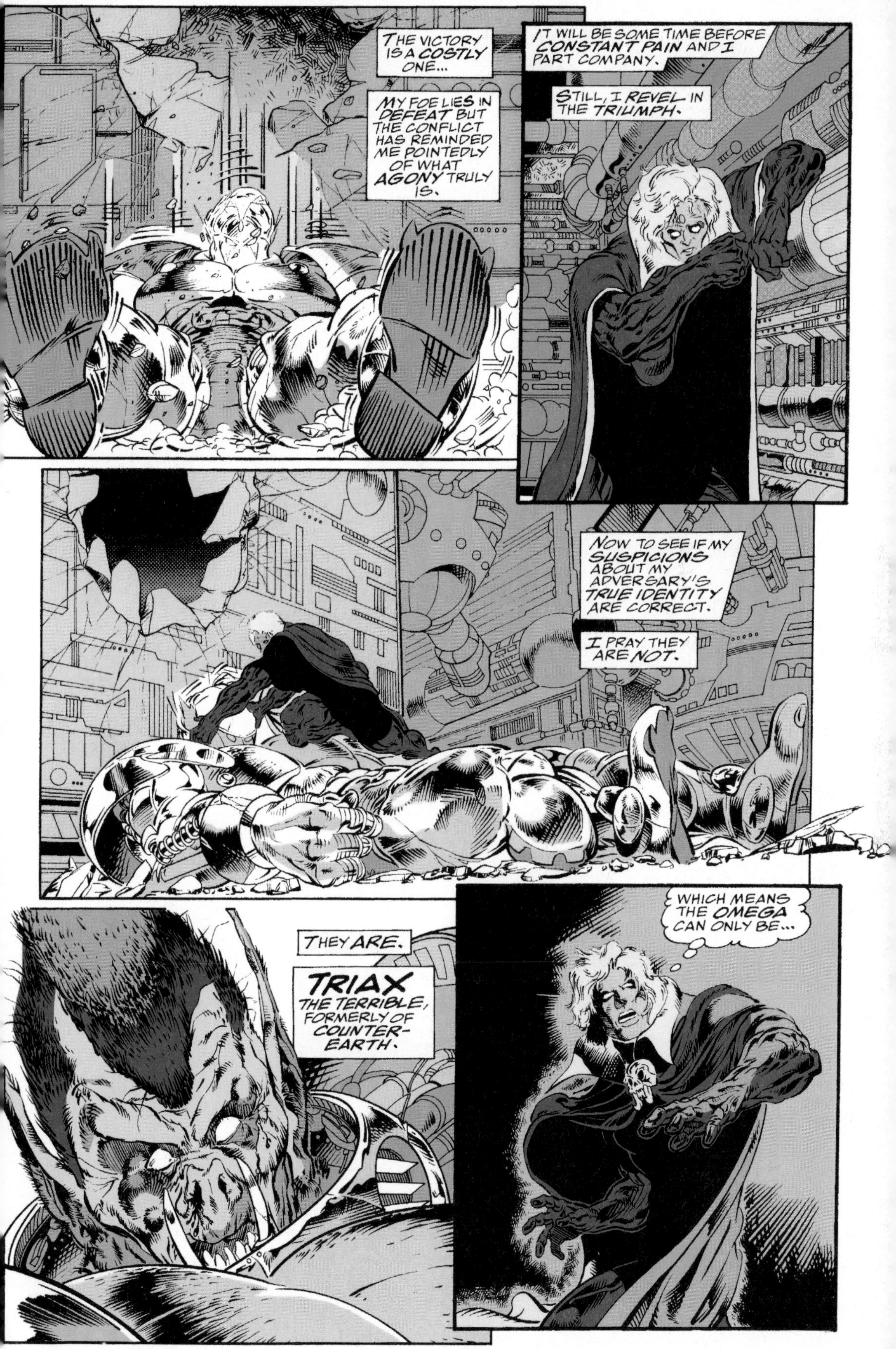
THE VICTORY IS A COSTLY ONE...
MY FOE LIES IN DEFEAT BUT THE CONFLICT HAS REMINDED ME POINTEDLY OF WHAT AGONY TRULY IS.
IT WILL BE SOME TIME BEFORE CONSTANT PAIN AND I PART COMPANY.
STILL, I REVEL IN THE TRIUMPH.
NOW TO SEE IF MY SUSPICIONS ABOUT MY ADVERSARY'S TRUE IDENTITY ARE CORRECT.
I PRAY THEY ARE NOT.
THEY ARE.
TRIAX THE TERRIBLE, FORMERLY OF COUNTER-EARTH.
WHICH MEANS THE OMEGA CAN ONLY BE...

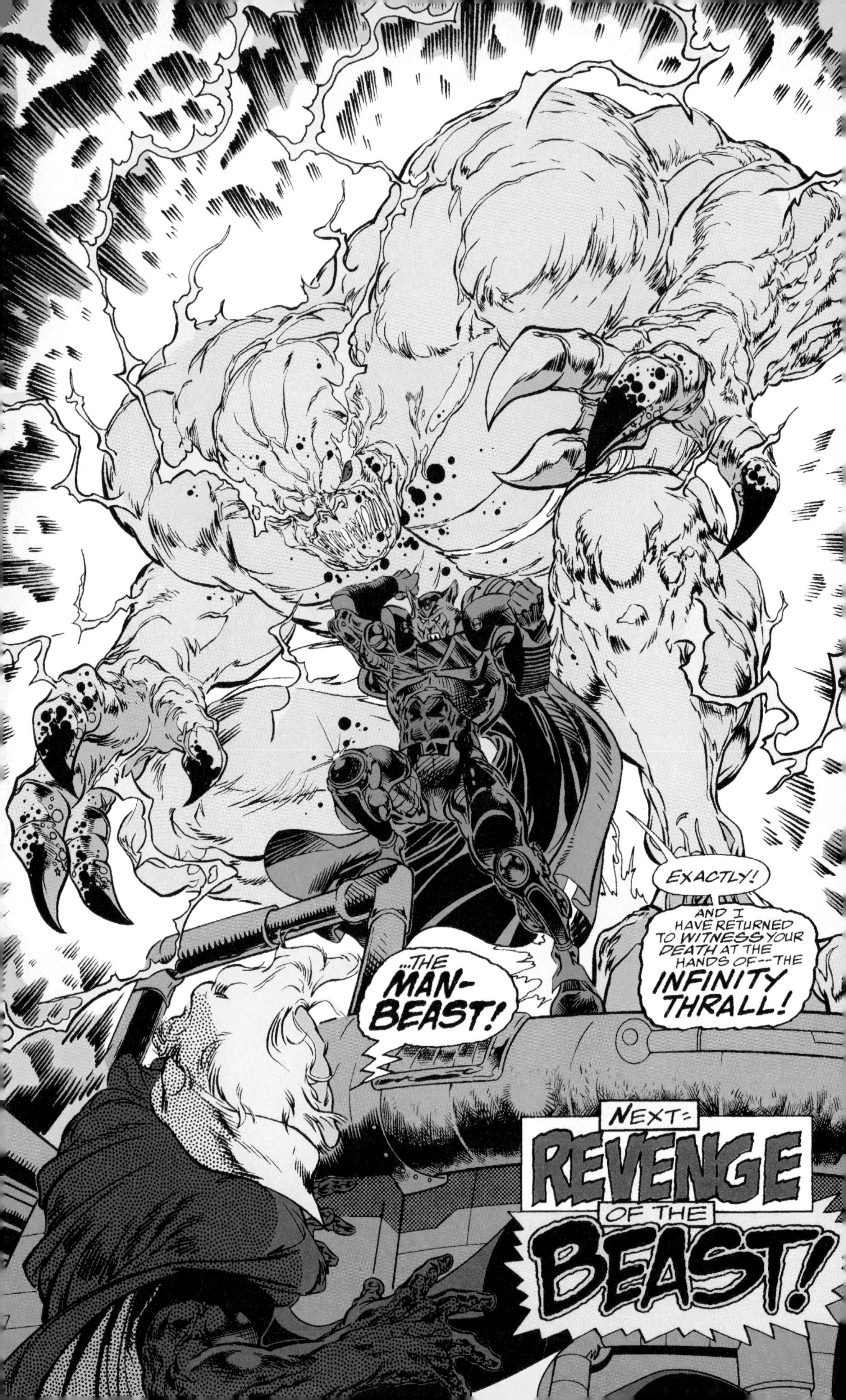
...THE MAN-BEAST!
EXACTLY!
AND I HAVE RETURNED TO WITNESS YOUR DEATH AT THE HANDS OF--THE INFINITY THRALL!
NEXT:
REVENGE OF THE BEAST!

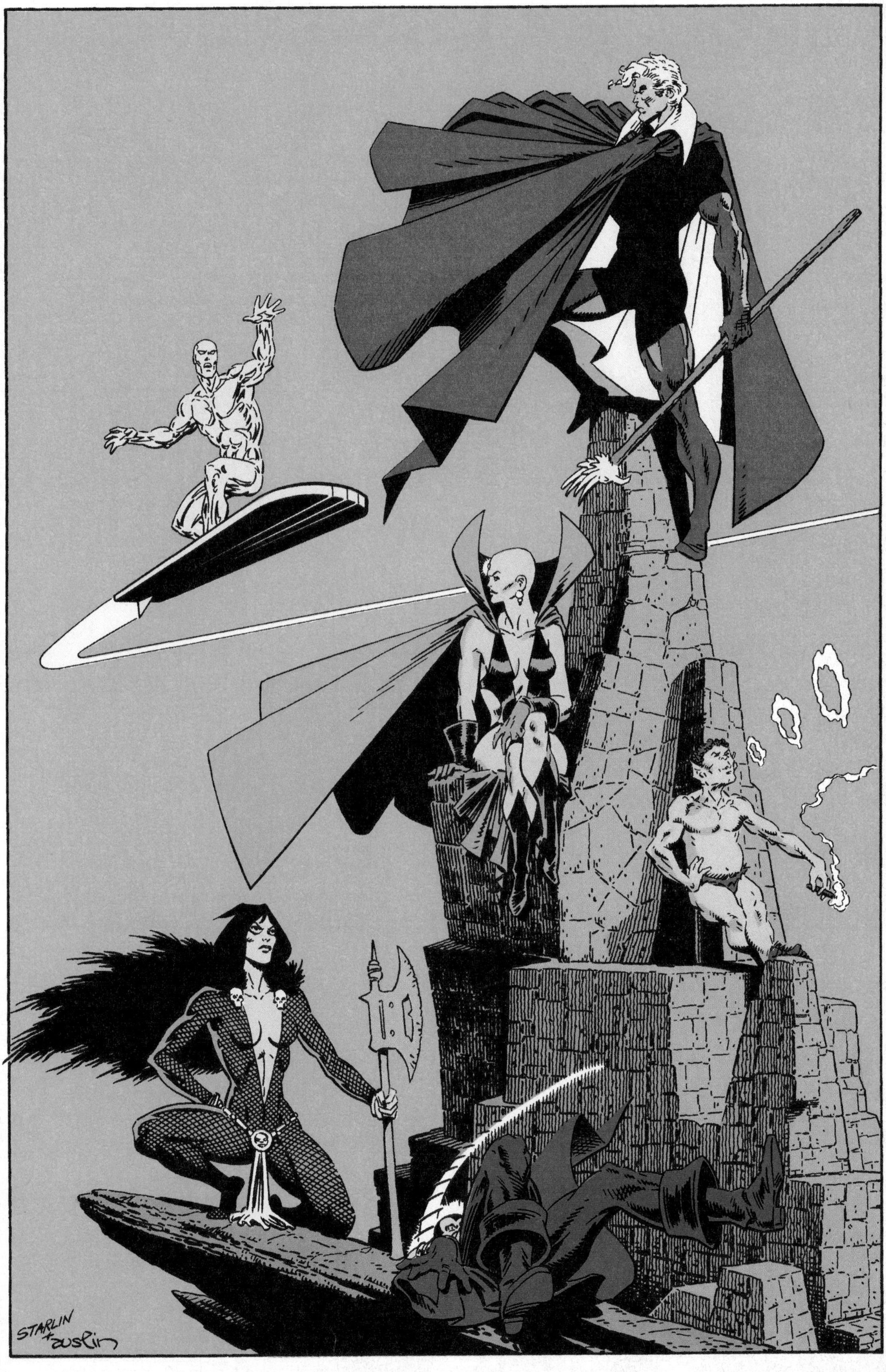
STARLIN
+ austin

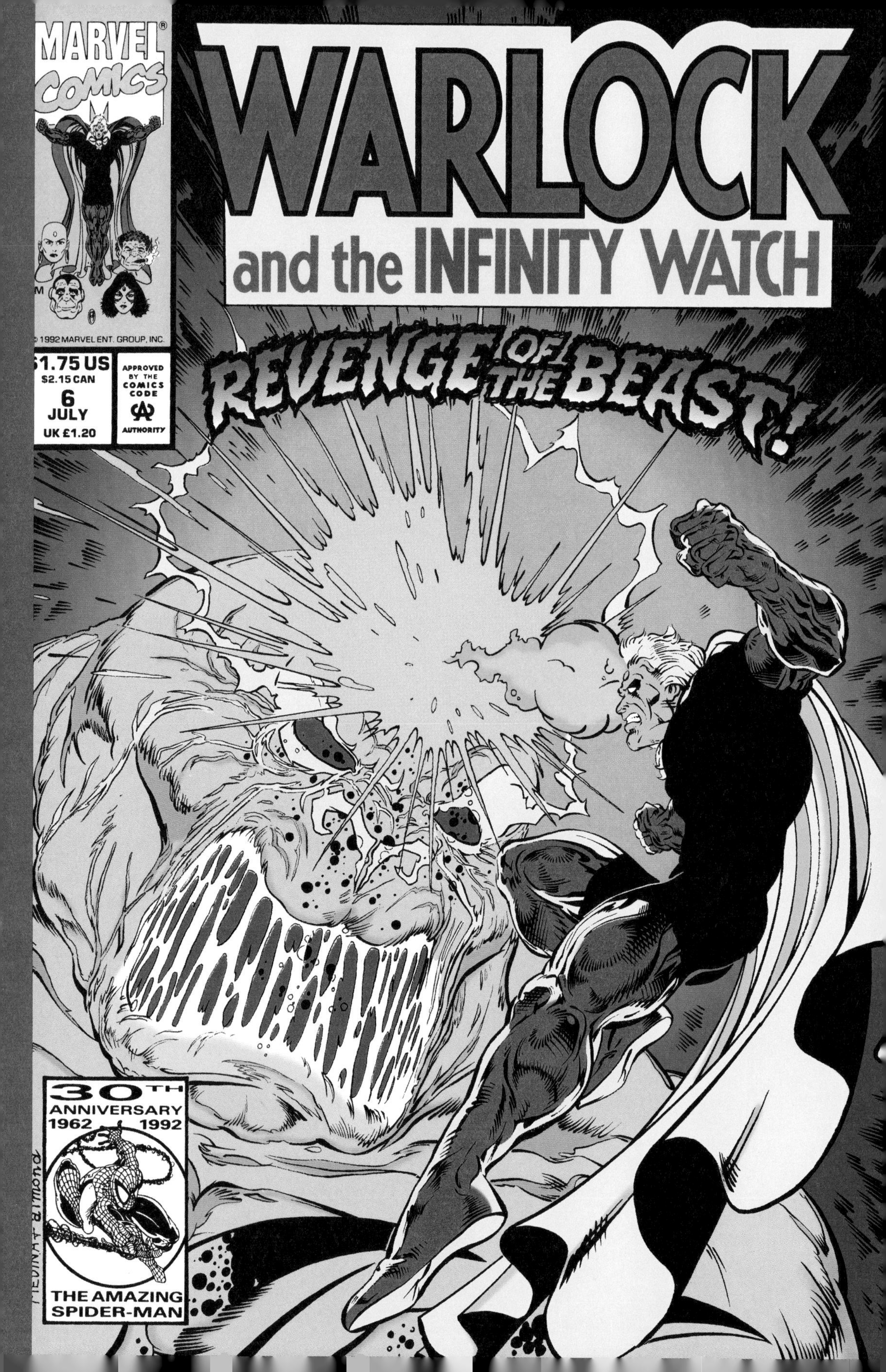
MARVEL COMICS
WARLOCK
and the INFINITY WATCH
© 1992 MARVEL ENT. GROUP, INC.
$1.75 US
$2.15 CAN
6
JULY
UK £1.20
APPROVED BY THE COMICS CODE AUTHORITY
REVENGE OF THE BEAST!
30TH ANNIVERSARY
1962 1992
THE AMAZING SPIDER-MAN

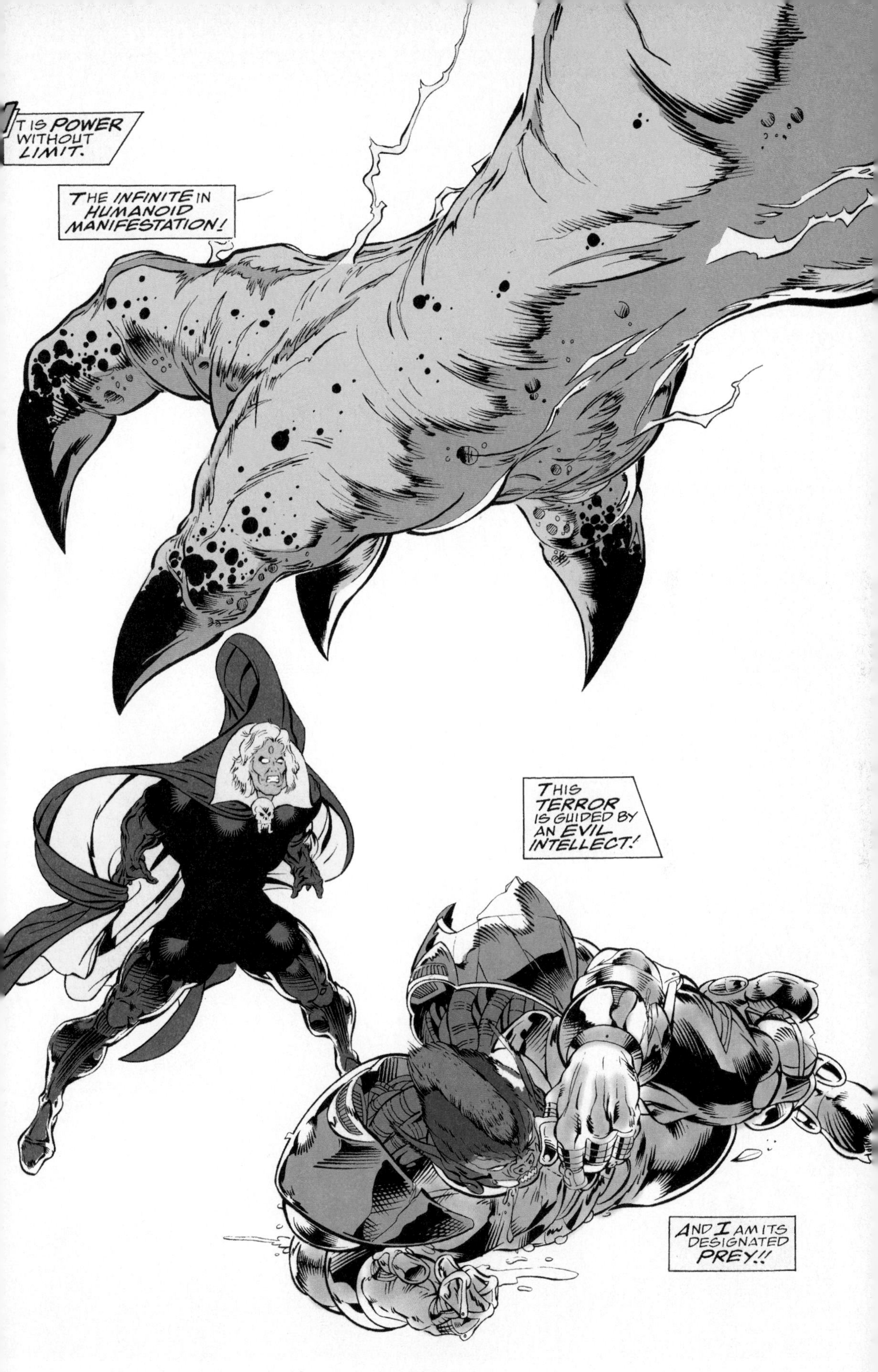
IT IS POWER WITHOUT LIMIT.
THE INFINITE IN HUMANOID MANIFESTATION!
THIS TERROR IS GUIDED BY AN EVIL INTELLECT!
AND I AM ITS DESIGNATED PREY!!

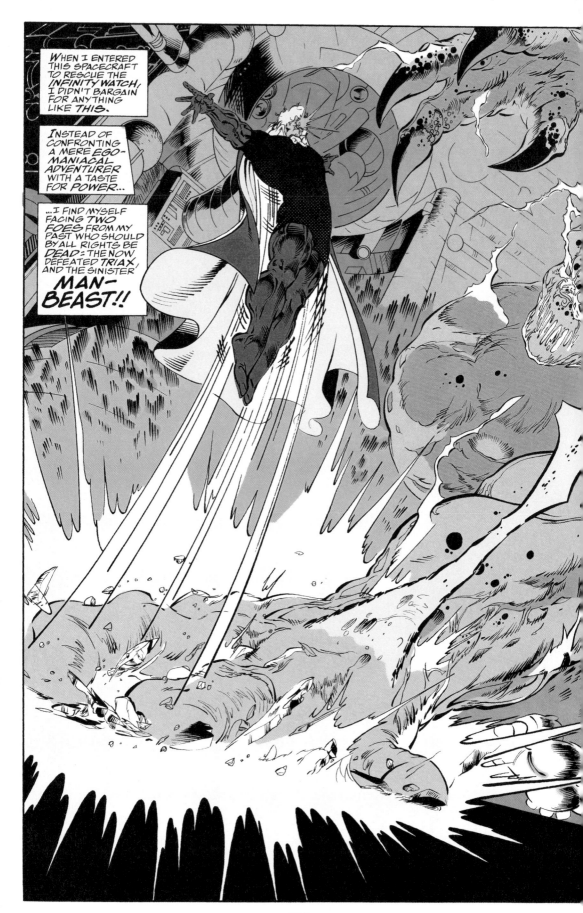

WHEN I ENTERED THIS SPACECRAFT TO RESCUE THE *INFINITY WATCH,* I DIDN'T BARGAIN FOR ANYTHING LIKE *THIS.*

INSTEAD OF CONFRONTING A MERE *EGO-MANIACAL ADVENTURER* WITH A TASTE FOR *POWER*...

...I FIND MYSELF FACING *TWO FOES* FROM MY PAST WHO SHOULD BY ALL RIGHTS BE *DEAD* – THE NOW DEFEATED *TRIAX,* AND THE SINISTER *MAN-BEAST!!*

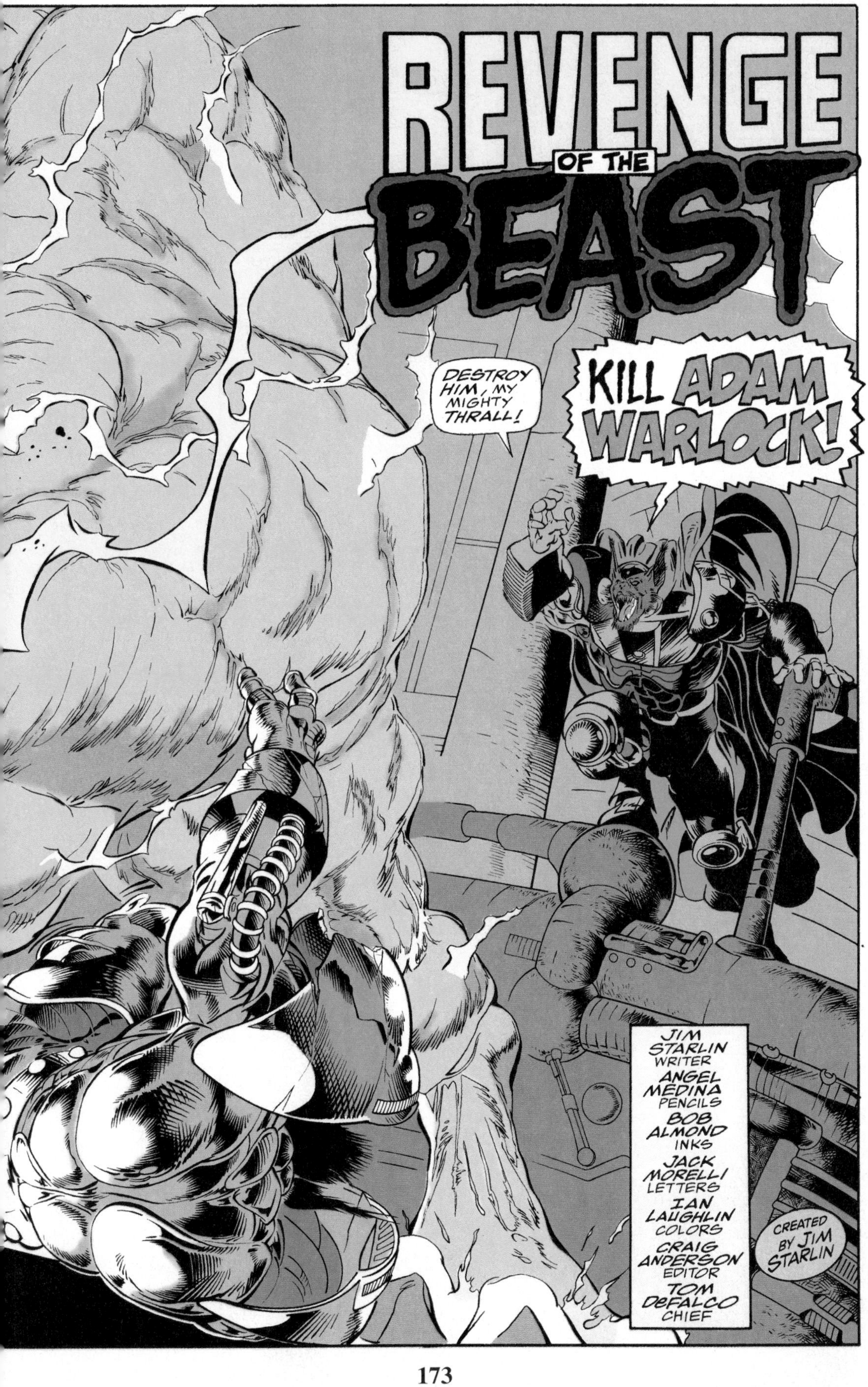
REVENGE OF THE BEAST
DESTROY HIM, MY MIGHTY THRALL!
KILL ADAM WARLOCK!
JIM STARLIN WRITER
ANGEL MEDINA PENCILS
BOB ALMOND INKS
JACK MORELLI LETTERS
IAN LAUGHLIN COLORS
CRAIG ANDERSON EDITOR
TOM DeFALCO CHIEF
CREATED BY JIM STARLIN

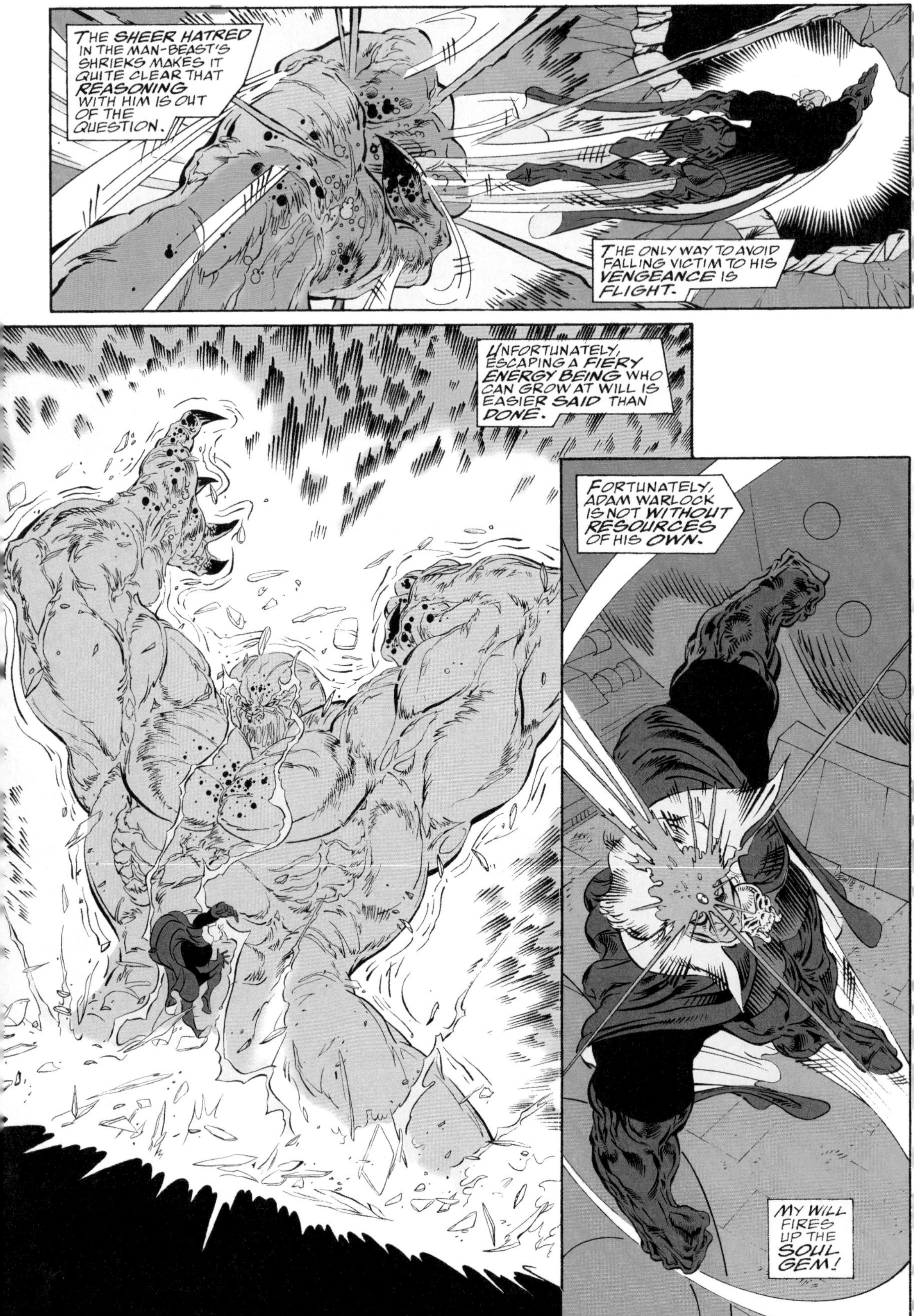
THE SHEER HATRED IN THE MAN-BEAST'S SHRIEKS MAKES IT QUITE CLEAR THAT REASONING WITH HIM IS OUT OF THE QUESTION.
THE ONLY WAY TO AVOID FALLING VICTIM TO HIS VENGEANCE IS FLIGHT.
UNFORTUNATELY, ESCAPING A FIERY ENERGY BEING WHO CAN GROW AT WILL IS EASIER SAID THAN DONE.
FORTUNATELY, ADAM WARLOCK IS NOT WITHOUT RESOURCES OF HIS OWN.
MY WILL FIRES UP THE SOUL GEM!

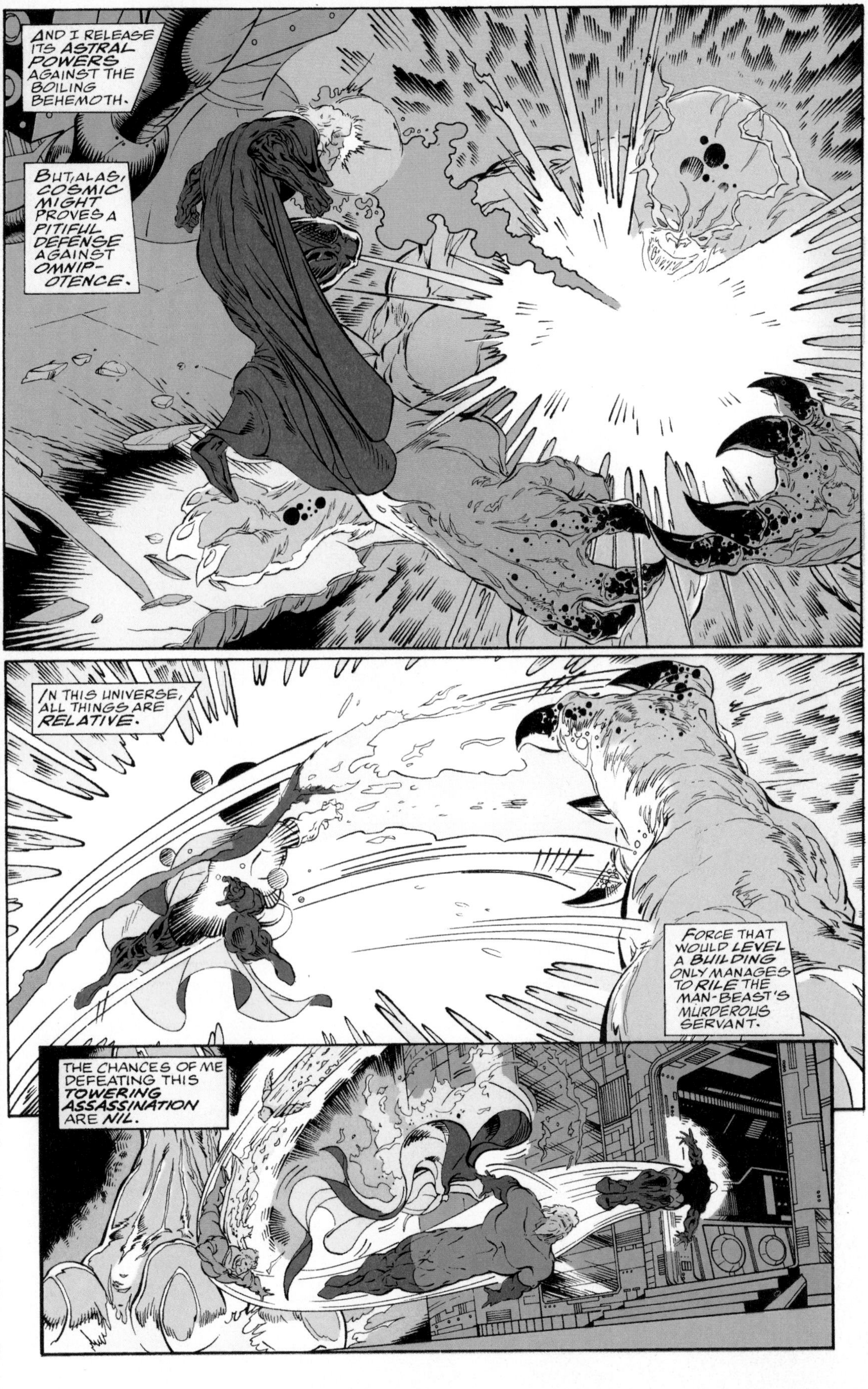
AND I RELEASE ITS ASTRAL POWERS AGAINST THE BOILING BEHEMOTH.
BUT, ALAS, COSMIC MIGHT PROVES A PITIFUL DEFENSE AGAINST OMNIPOTENCE.
IN THIS UNIVERSE, ALL THINGS ARE RELATIVE.
FORCE THAT WOULD LEVEL A BUILDING ONLY MANAGES TO RILE THE MAN-BEAST'S MURDEROUS SERVANT.
THE CHANCES OF ME DEFEATING THIS TOWERING ASSASSINATION ARE NIL.

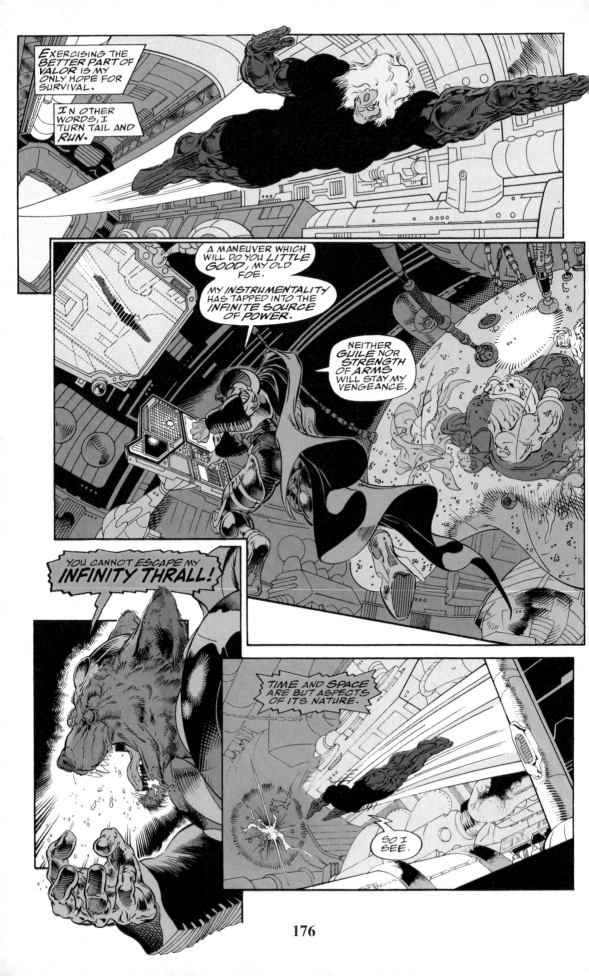

EXERCISING THE BETTER PART OF VALOR IS MY ONLY HOPE FOR SURVIVAL.

IN OTHER WORDS, I TURN TAIL AND RUN.

A MANEUVER WHICH WILL DO YOU LITTLE GOOD, MY OLD FOE.

MY INSTRUMENTALITY HAS TAPPED INTO THE INFINITE SOURCE OF POWER.

NEITHER GUILE NOR STRENGTH OF ARMS WILL STAY MY VENGEANCE.

YOU CANNOT ESCAPE MY INFINITY THRALL!

TIME AND SPACE ARE BUT ASPECTS OF ITS NATURE.

SO I SEE.

176

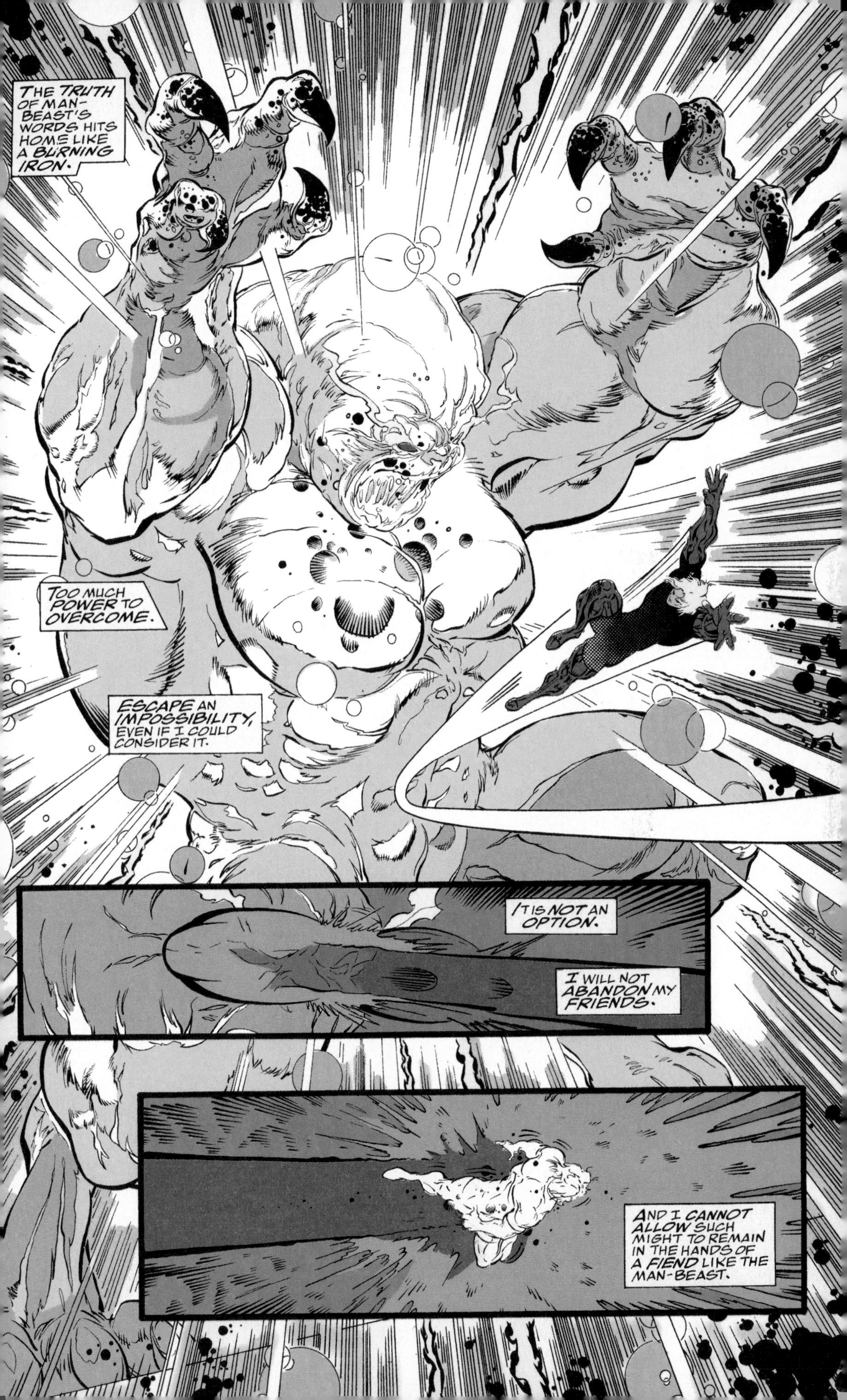
THE TRUTH OF MAN-BEAST'S WORDS HITS HOME LIKE A BURNING IRON.
TOO MUCH POWER TO OVERCOME.
ESCAPE AN IMPOSSIBILITY, EVEN IF I COULD CONSIDER IT.
IT IS NOT AN OPTION.
I WILL NOT ABANDON MY FRIENDS.
AND I CANNOT ALLOW SUCH MIGHT TO REMAIN IN THE HANDS OF A FIEND LIKE THE MAN-BEAST.

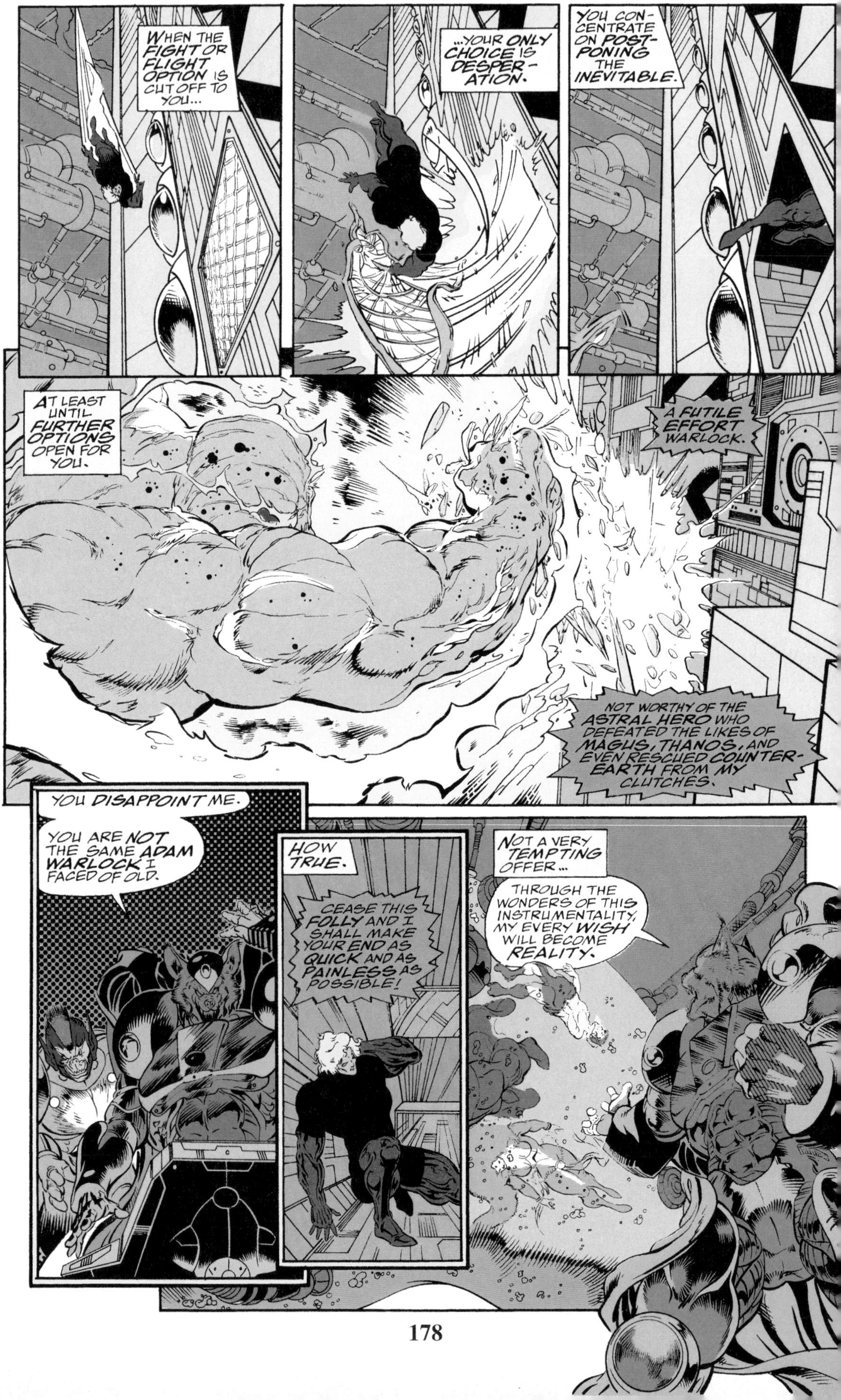

WHEN THE FIGHT OR FLIGHT OPTION IS CUT OFF TO YOU...
...YOUR ONLY CHOICE IS DESPERATION.
YOU CONCENTRATE ON POSTPONING THE INEVITABLE.
AT LEAST UNTIL FURTHER OPTIONS OPEN FOR YOU.
A FUTILE EFFORT WARLOCK.
NOT WORTHY OF THE ASTRAL HERO WHO DEFEATED THE LIKES OF MAGUS, THANOS, AND EVEN RESCUED COUNTER-EARTH FROM MY CLUTCHES.
YOU DISAPPOINT ME.
YOU ARE NOT THE SAME ADAM WARLOCK I FACED OF OLD.
HOW TRUE.
CEASE THIS FOLLY AND I SHALL MAKE YOUR END AS QUICK AND AS PAINLESS AS POSSIBLE!
NOT A VERY TEMPTING OFFER...
THROUGH THE WONDERS OF THIS INSTRUMENTALITY, MY EVERY WISH WILL BECOME REALITY.

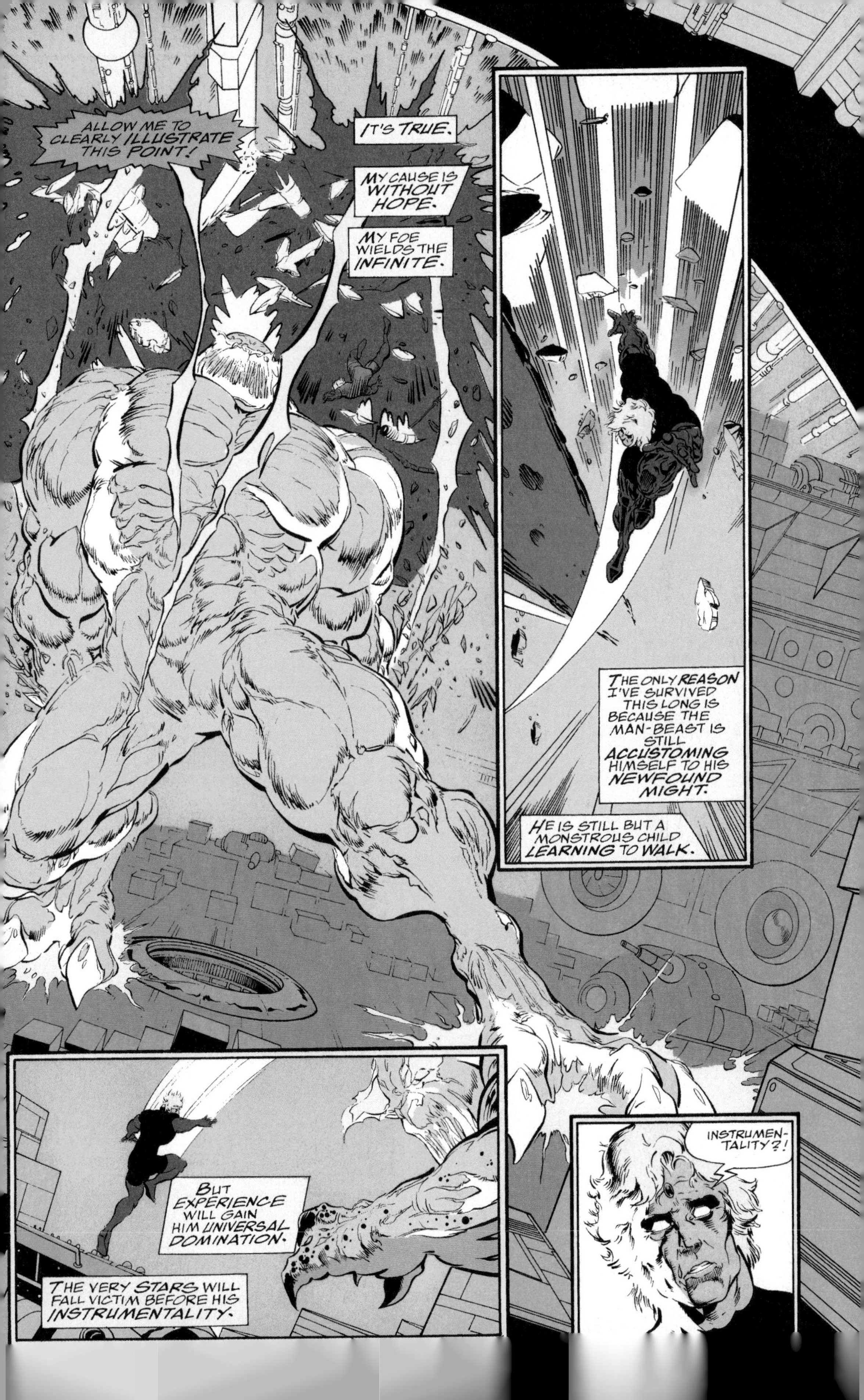
ALLOW ME TO CLEARLY ILLUSTRATE THIS POINT!
IT'S TRUE.
MY CAUSE IS WITHOUT HOPE.
MY FOE WIELDS THE INFINITE.
THE ONLY REASON I'VE SURVIVED THIS LONG IS BECAUSE THE MAN-BEAST IS STILL ACCUSTOMING HIMSELF TO HIS NEWFOUND MIGHT.
HE IS STILL BUT A MONSTROUS CHILD LEARNING TO WALK.
BUT EXPERIENCE WILL GAIN HIM UNIVERSAL DOMINATION.
THE VERY STARS WILL FALL VICTIM BEFORE HIS INSTRUMENTALITY.
INSTRUMENTALITY?!

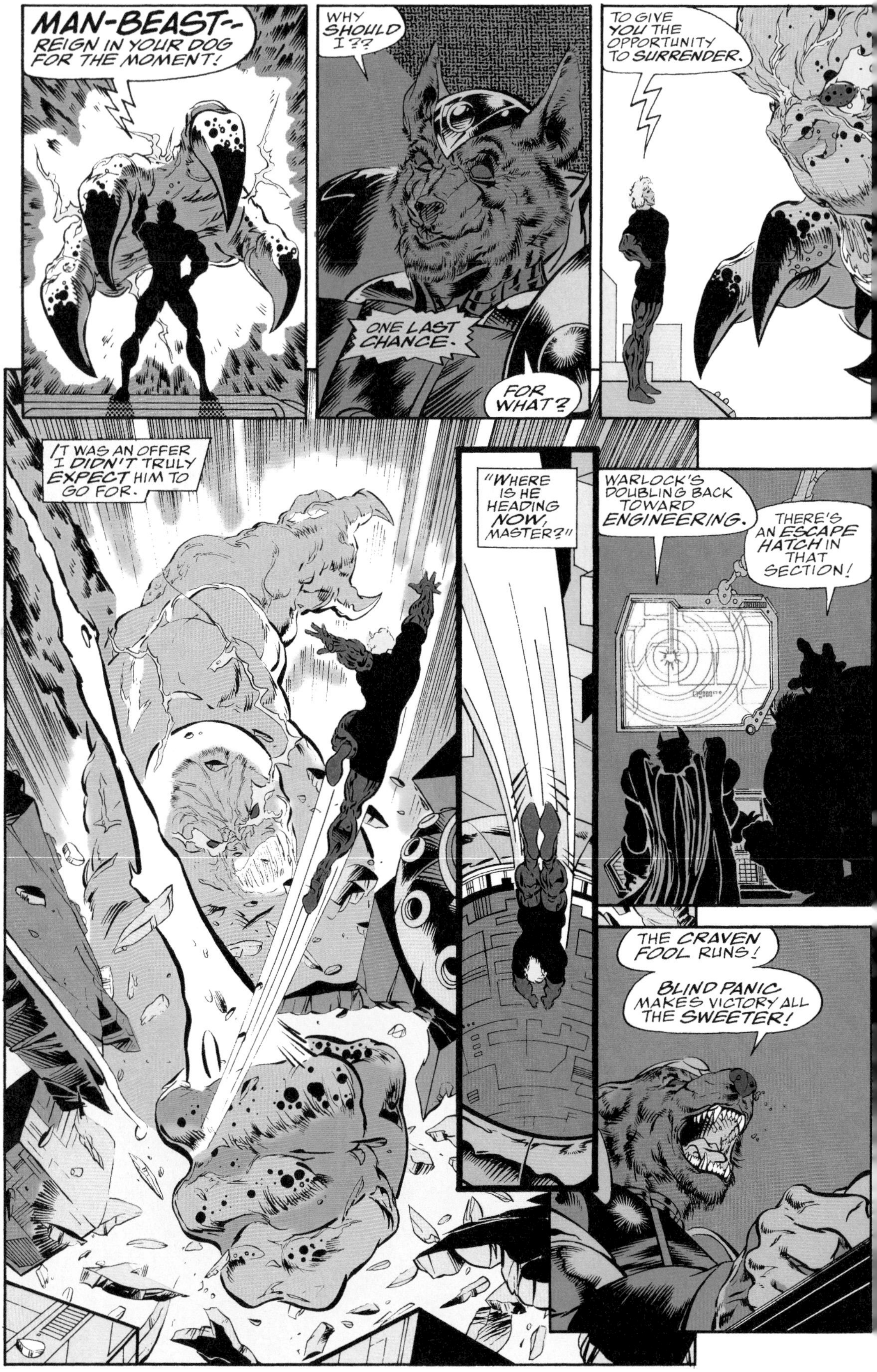
MAN-BEAST-- REIGN IN YOUR DOG FOR THE MOMENT!
WHY SHOULD I??
ONE LAST CHANCE.
FOR WHAT?
TO GIVE YOU THE OPPORTUNITY TO SURRENDER.
IT WAS AN OFFER I DIDN'T TRULY EXPECT HIM TO GO FOR.
"WHERE IS HE HEADING NOW, MASTER?"
WARLOCK'S DOUBLING BACK TOWARD ENGINEERING.
THERE'S AN ESCAPE HATCH IN THAT SECTION!
THE CRAVEN FOOL RUNS!
BLIND PANIC MAKES VICTORY ALL THE SWEETER!

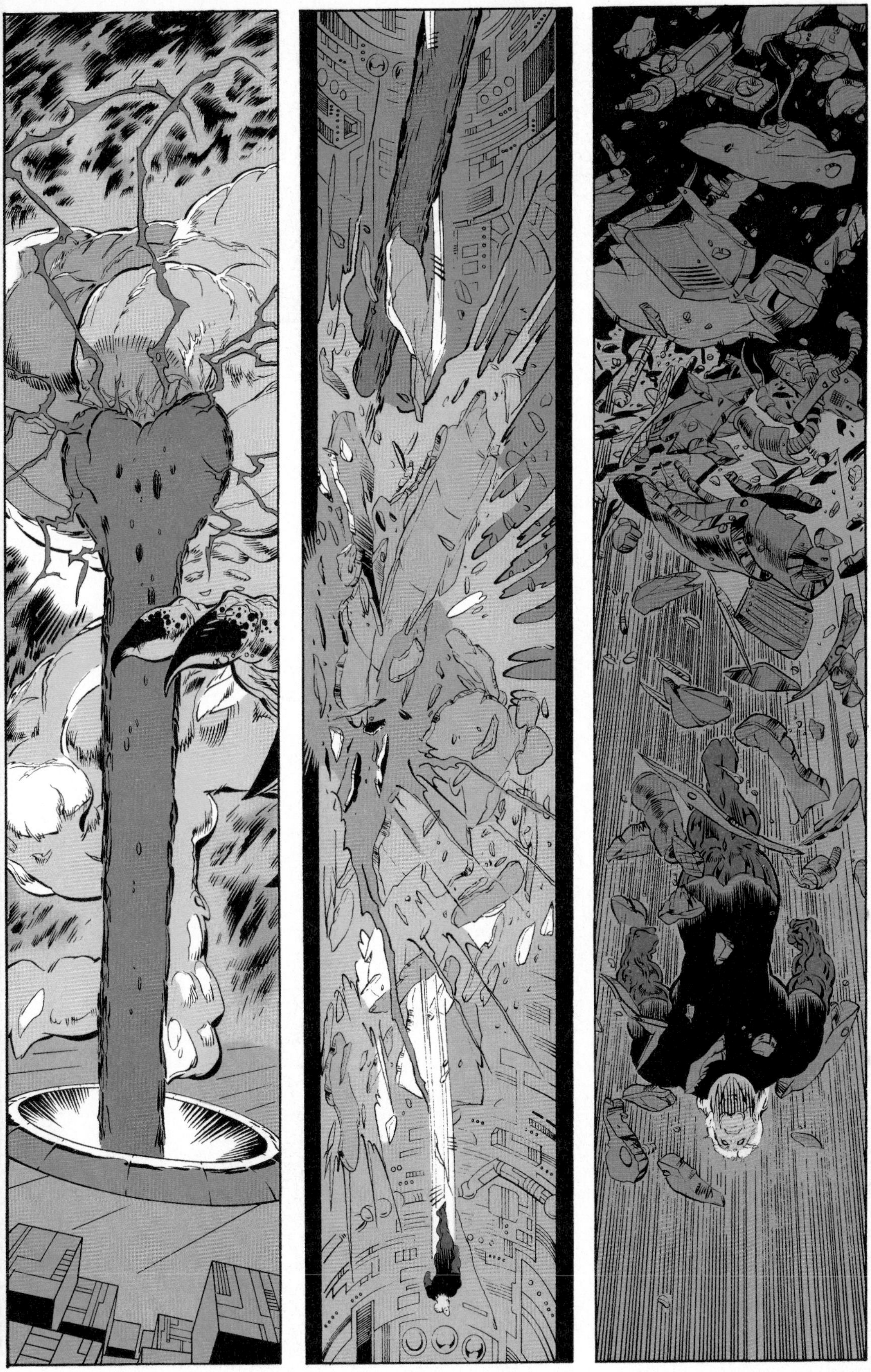

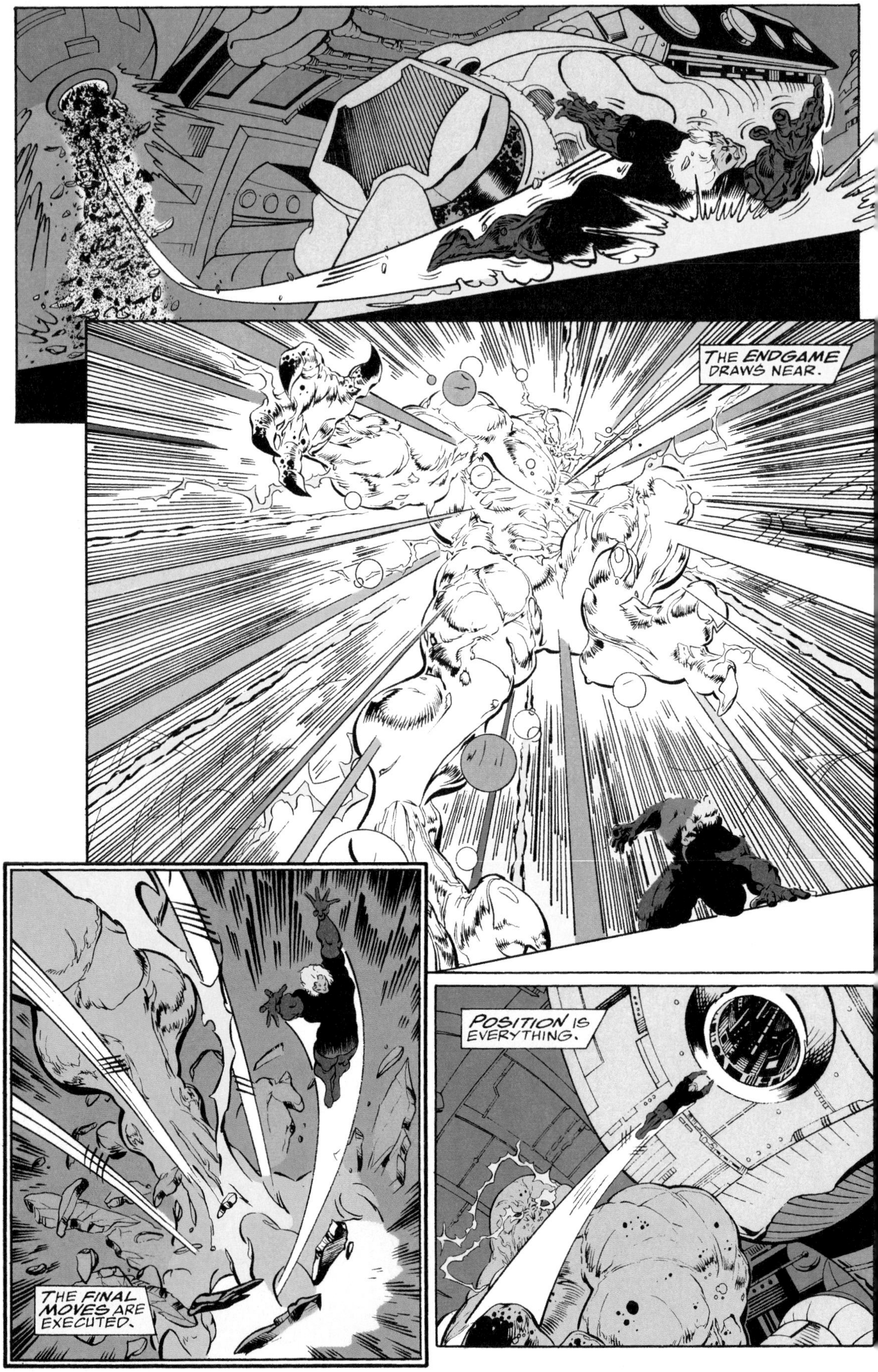
THE ENDGAME DRAWS NEAR.
THE FINAL MOVES ARE EXECUTED.
POSITION IS EVERYTHING.

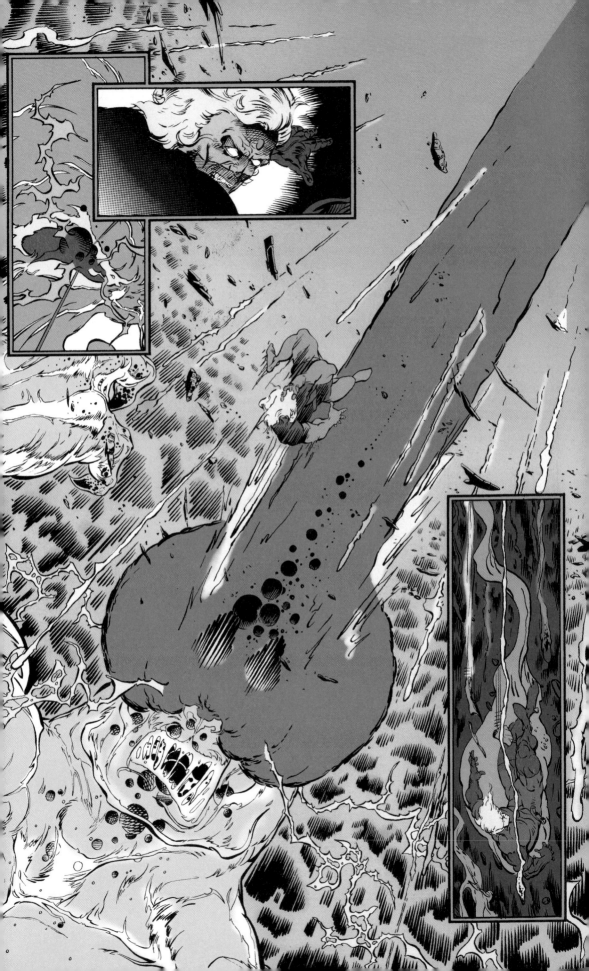

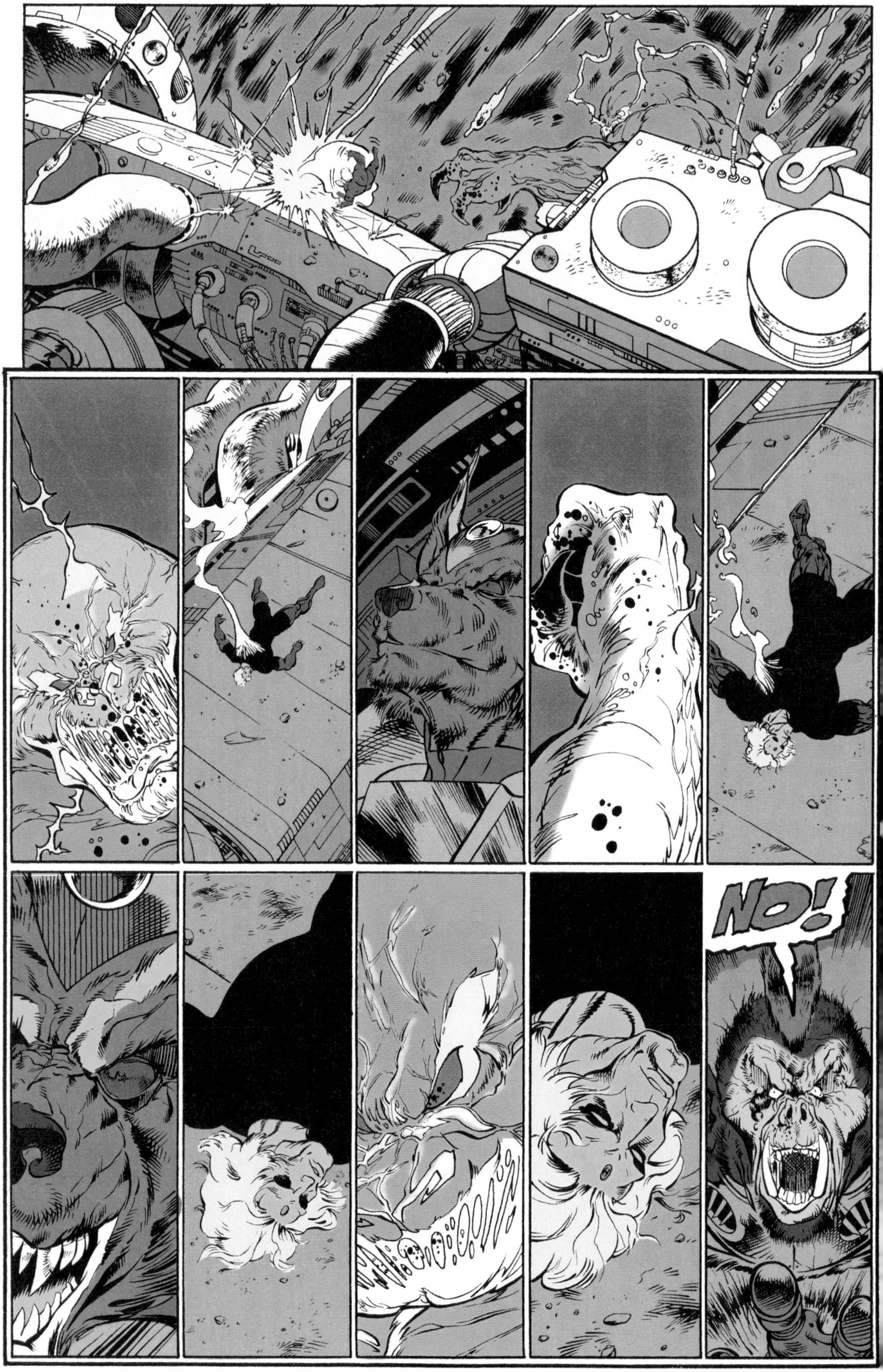
NO!

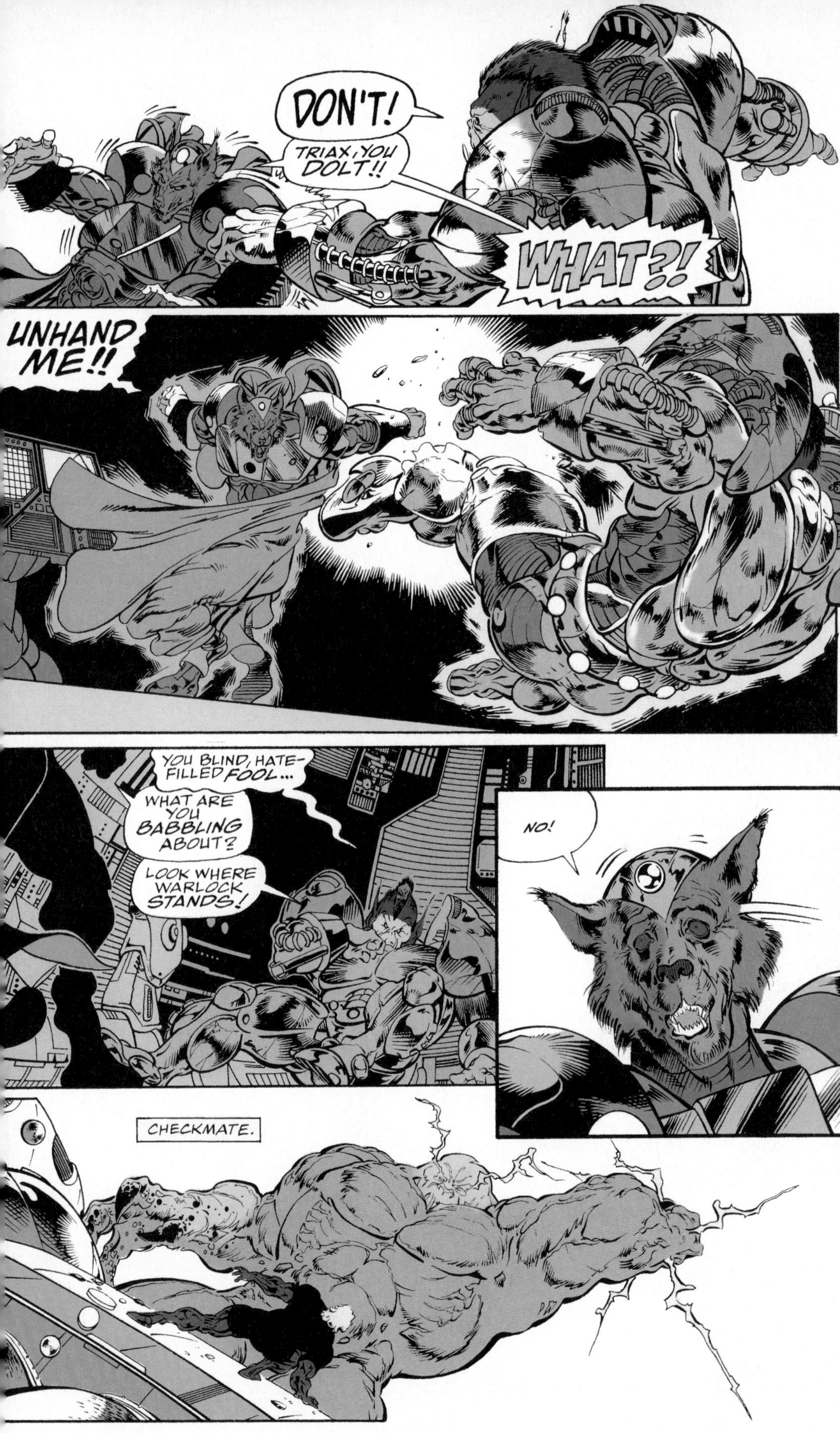
DON'T!
TRIAX, YOU DOLT!!
WHAT?!
UNHAND ME!!
YOU BLIND, HATE-FILLED FOOL...
WHAT ARE YOU BABBLING ABOUT?
LOOK WHERE WARLOCK STANDS!
NO!
CHECKMATE.

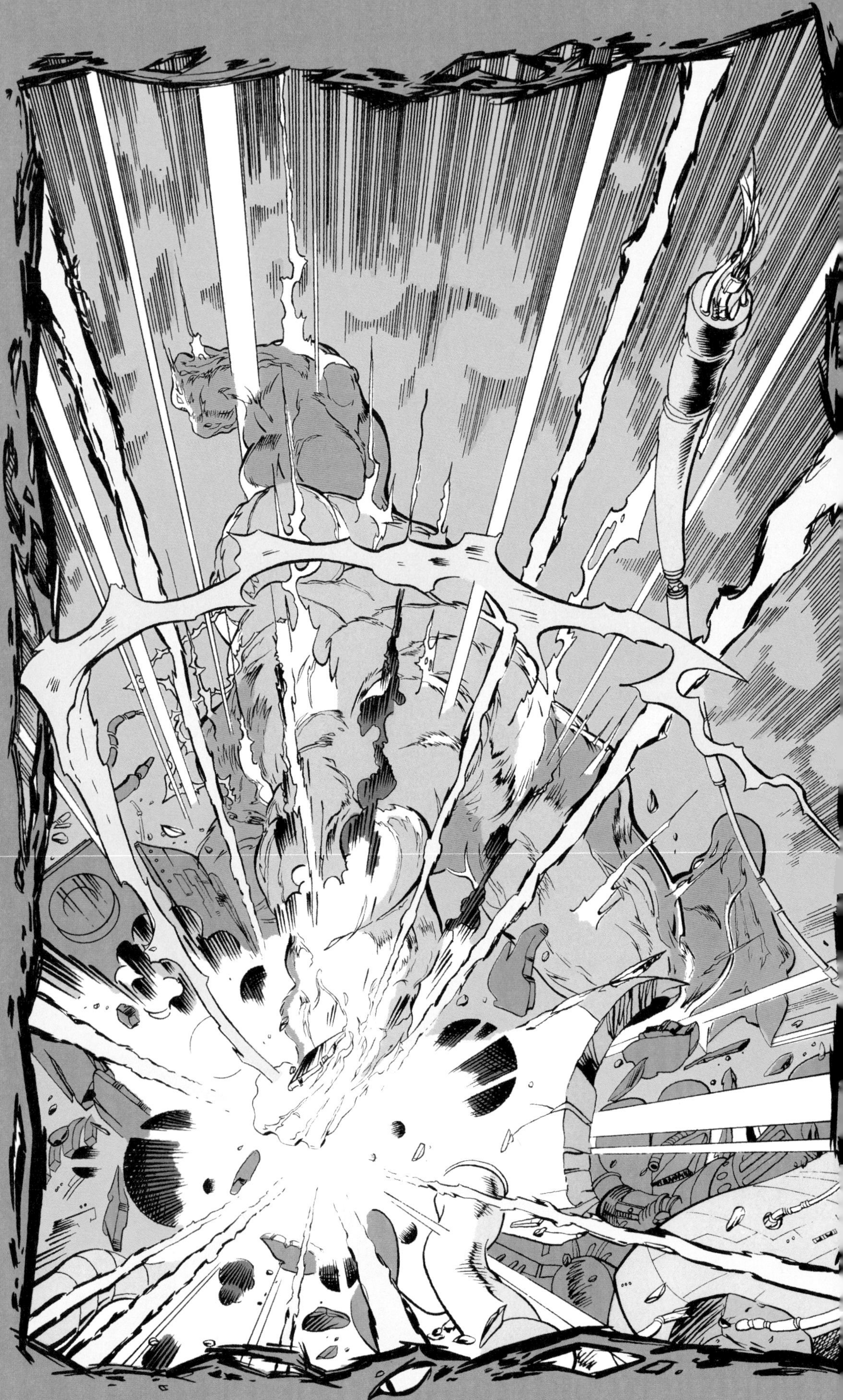

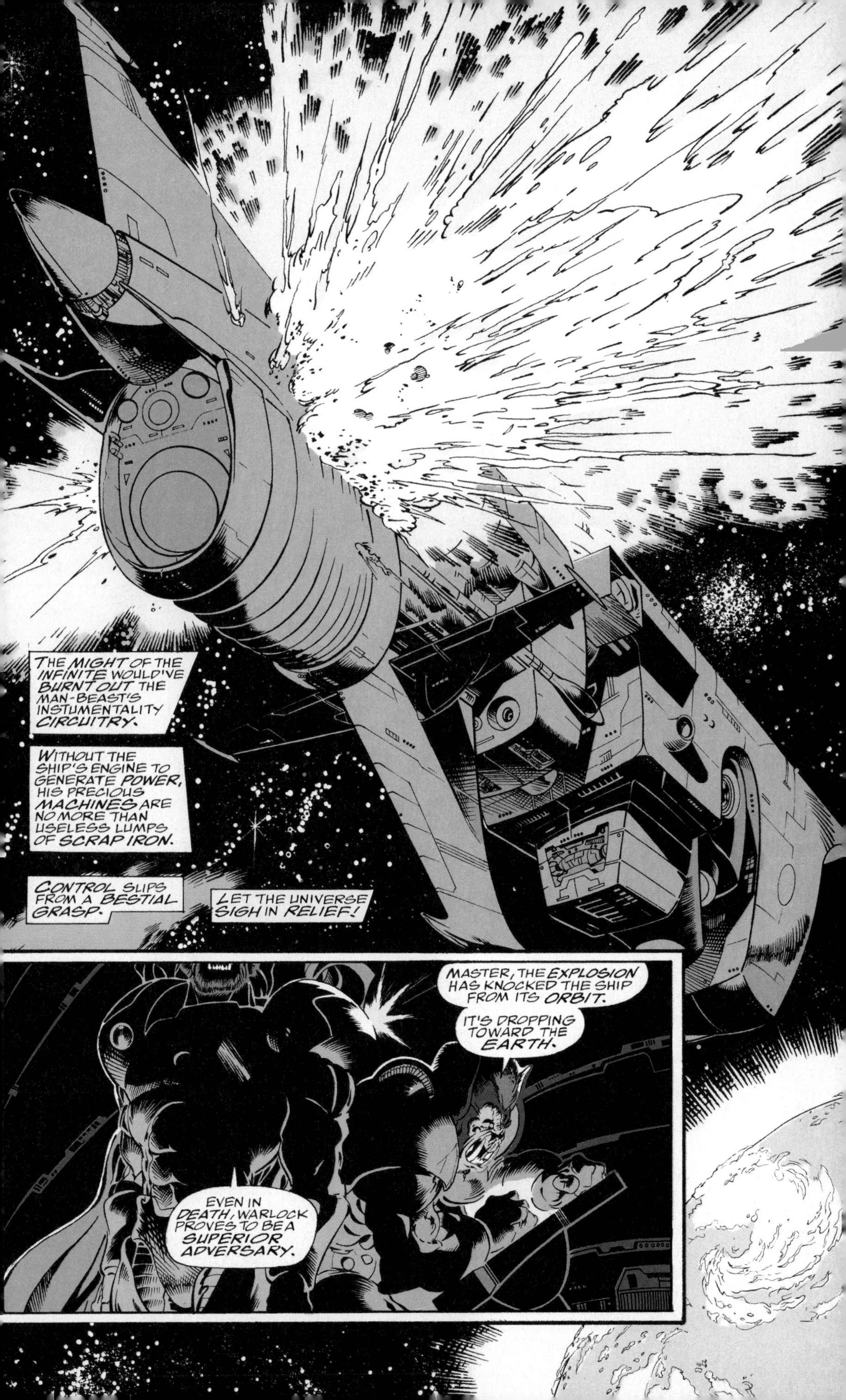
THE MIGHT OF THE INFINITE WOULD'VE BURNT OUT THE MAN-BEAST'S INSTUMENTALITY CIRCUITRY.
WITHOUT THE SHIP'S ENGINE TO GENERATE POWER, HIS PRECIOUS MACHINES ARE NO MORE THAN USELESS LUMPS OF SCRAP IRON.
CONTROL SLIPS FROM A BESTIAL GRASP.
LET THE UNIVERSE SIGH IN RELIEF!
MASTER, THE EXPLOSION HAS KNOCKED THE SHIP FROM ITS ORBIT.
IT'S DROPPING TOWARD THE EARTH.
EVEN IN DEATH, WARLOCK PROVES TO BE A SUPERIOR ADVERSARY.

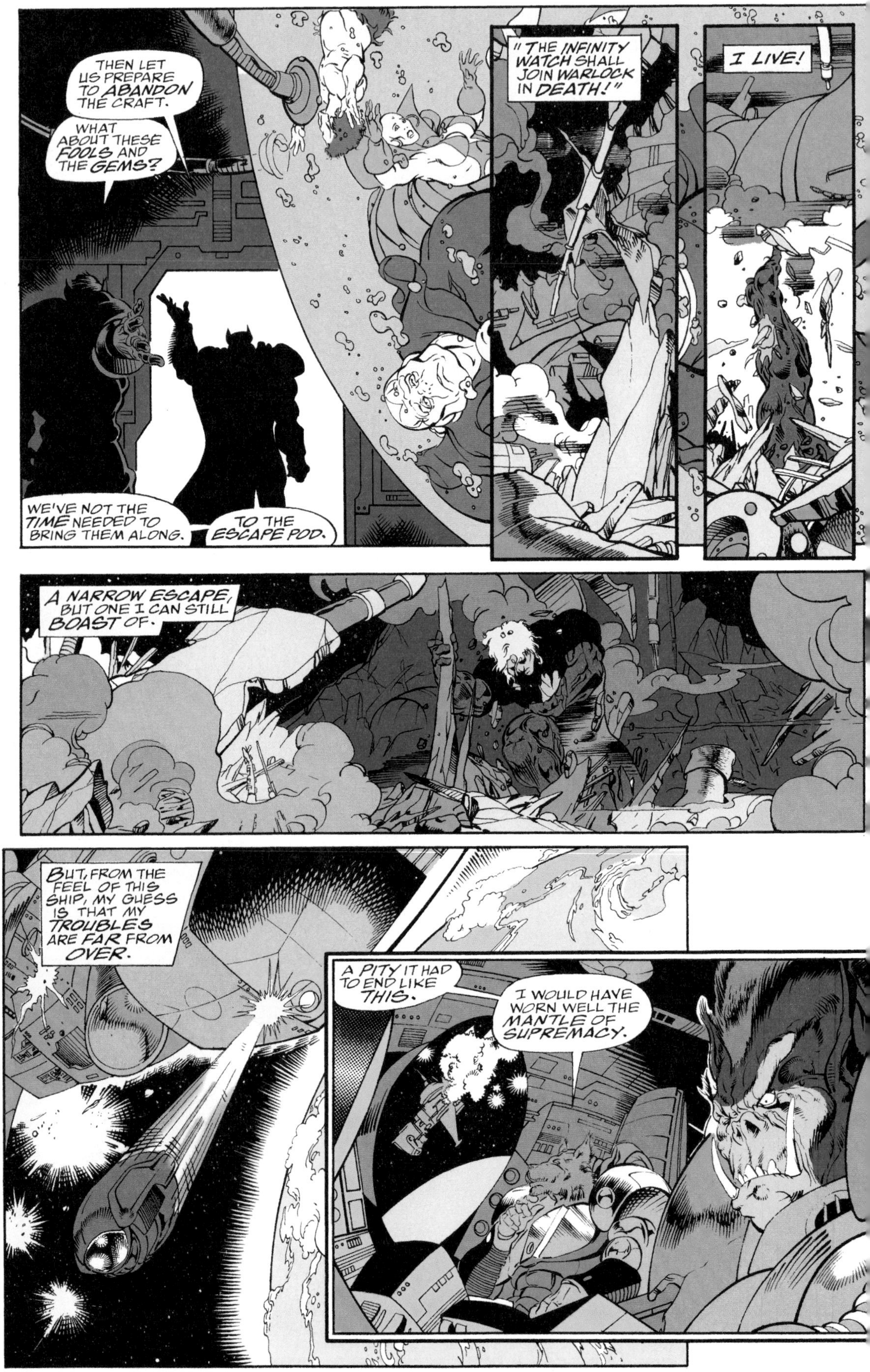
THEN LET US PREPARE TO ABANDON THE CRAFT.
WHAT ABOUT THESE FOOLS AND THE GEMS?
WE'VE NOT THE TIME NEEDED TO BRING THEM ALONG.
TO THE ESCAPE POD.
"THE INFINITY WATCH SHALL JOIN WARLOCK IN DEATH!"
I LIVE!
A NARROW ESCAPE, BUT ONE I CAN STILL BOAST OF.
BUT, FROM THE FEEL OF THIS SHIP, MY GUESS IS THAT MY TROUBLES ARE FAR FROM OVER.
A PITY IT HAD TO END LIKE THIS.
I WOULD HAVE WORN WELL THE MANTLE OF SUPREMACY.

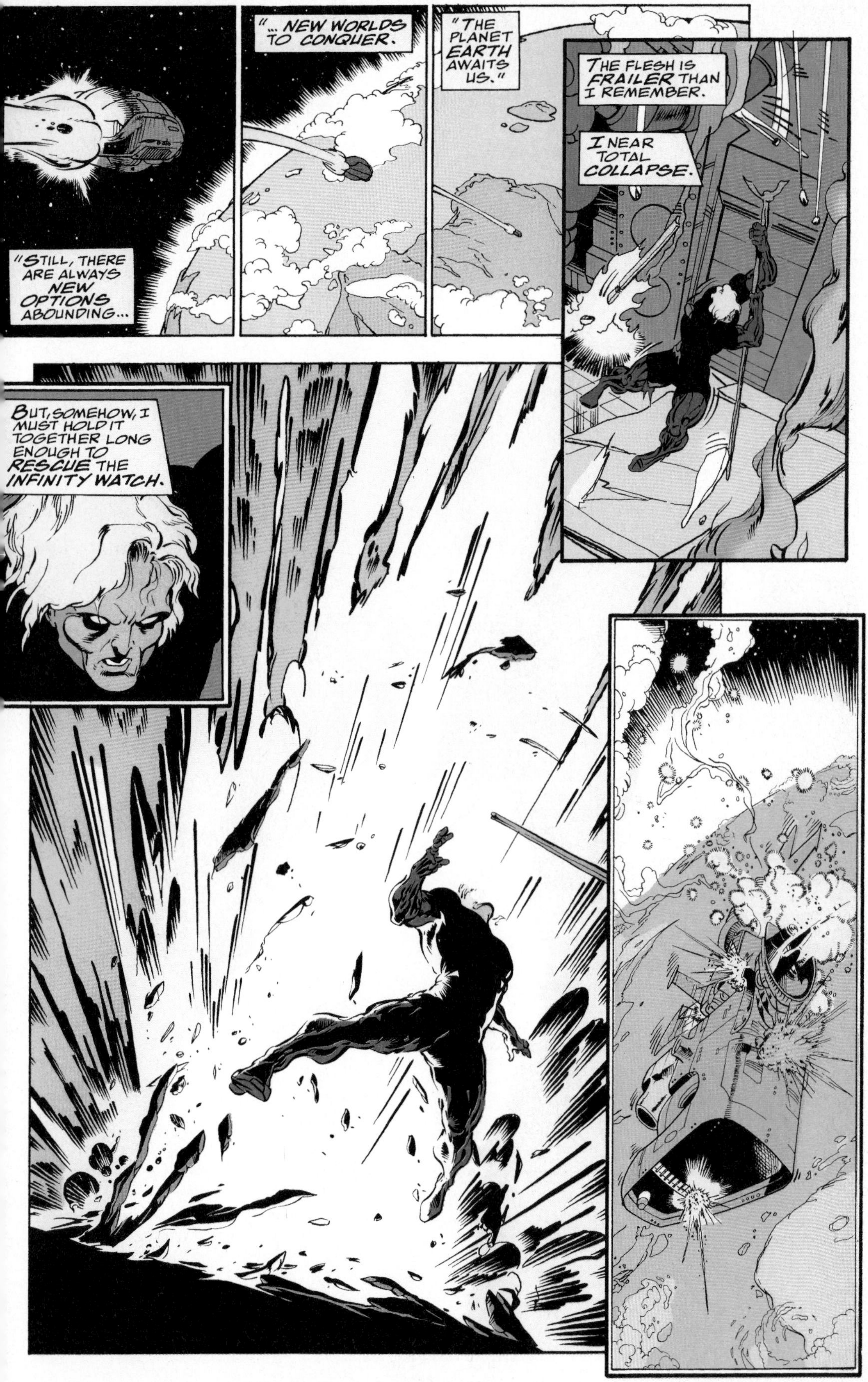
"STILL, THERE ARE ALWAYS NEW OPTIONS ABOUNDING...
"... NEW WORLDS TO CONQUER.
"THE PLANET EARTH AWAITS US."
THE FLESH IS FRAILER THAN I REMEMBER.
I NEAR TOTAL COLLAPSE.
BUT, SOMEHOW, I MUST HOLD IT TOGETHER LONG ENOUGH TO RESCUE THE INFINITY WATCH.

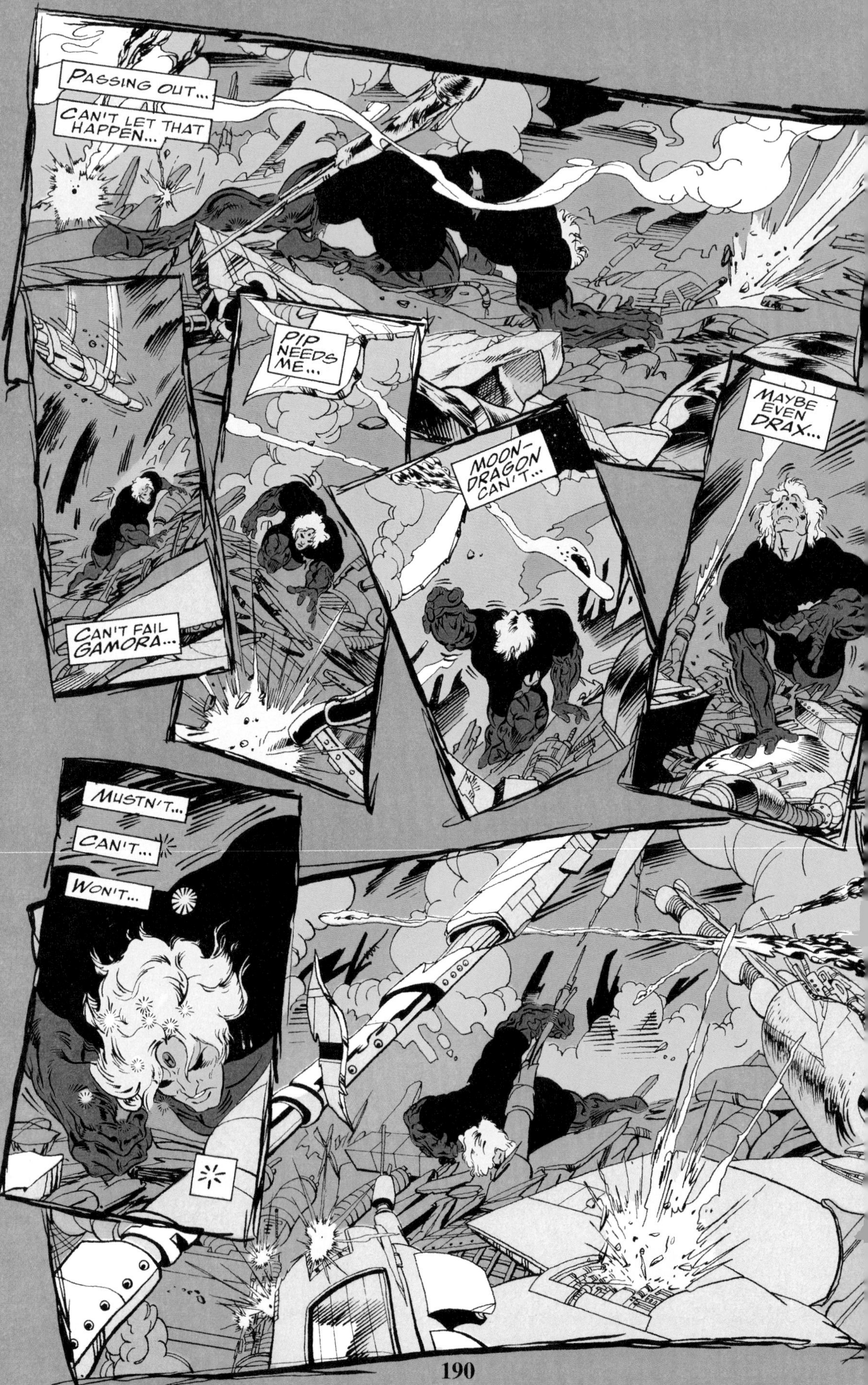
PASSING OUT...
CAN'T LET THAT HAPPEN...
CAN'T FAIL GAMORA...
PIP NEEDS ME...
MOON-DRAGON CAN'T...
MAYBE EVEN DRAX...
MUSTN'T...
CAN'T...
WON'T...

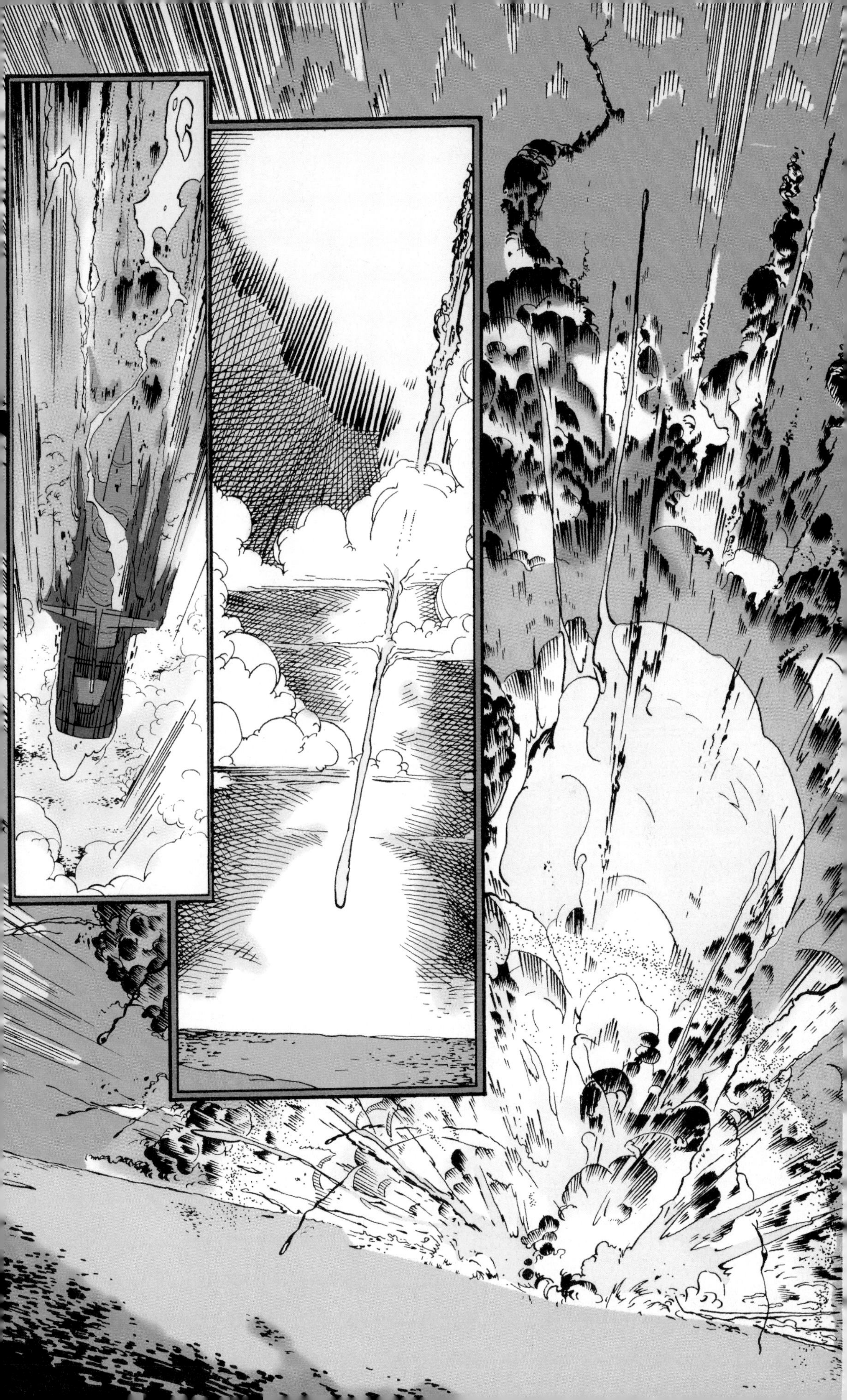

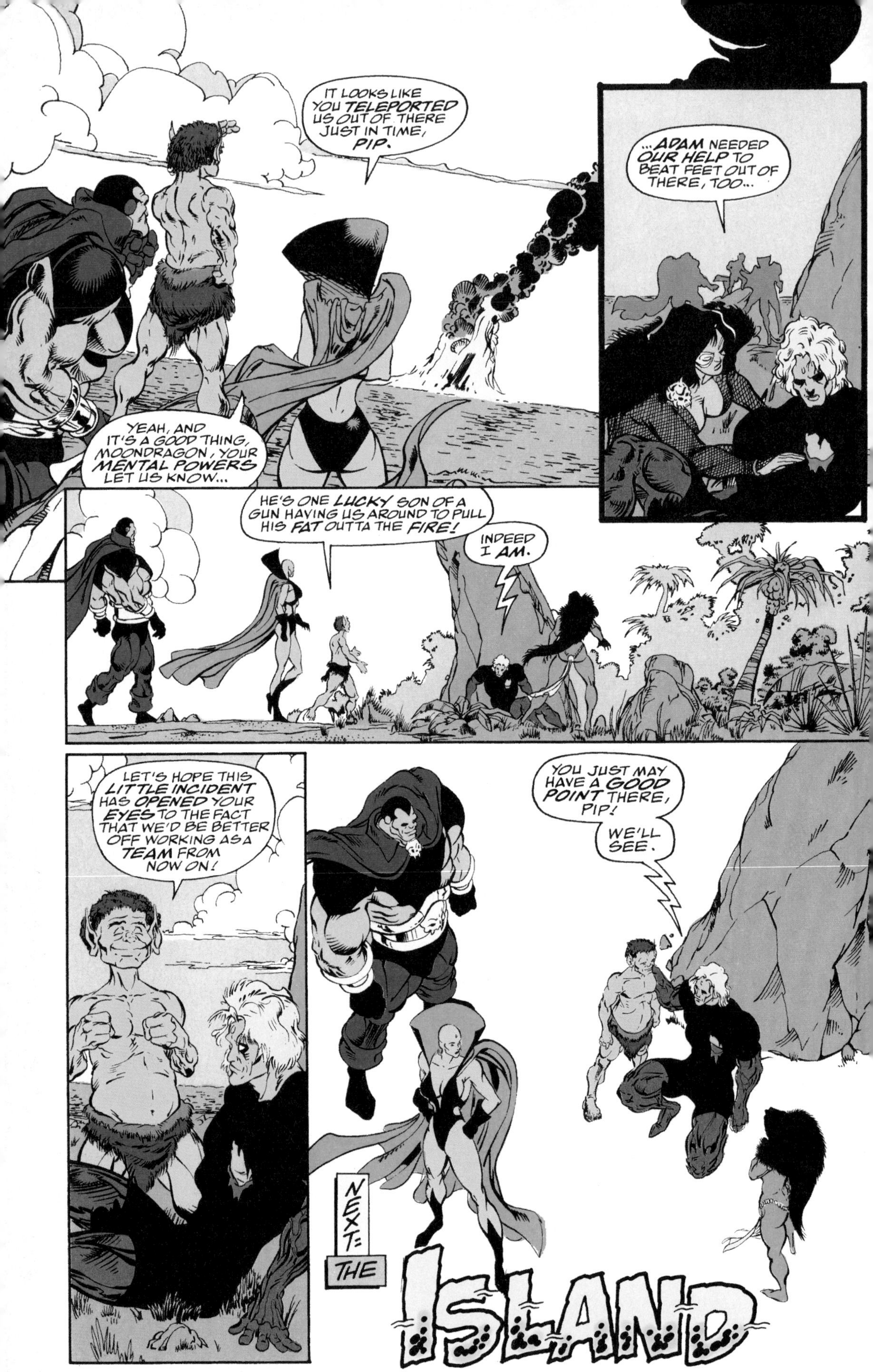
IT LOOKS LIKE YOU TELEPORTED US OUT OF THERE JUST IN TIME, PIP.
YEAH, AND IT'S A GOOD THING, MOONDRAGON, YOUR MENTAL POWERS LET US KNOW...
...ADAM NEEDED OUR HELP TO BEAT FEET OUT OF THERE, TOO...
HE'S ONE LUCKY SON OF A GUN HAVING US AROUND TO PULL HIS FAT OUTTA THE FIRE!
INDEED I AM.
LET'S HOPE THIS LITTLE INCIDENT HAS OPENED YOUR EYES TO THE FACT THAT WE'D BE BETTER OFF WORKING AS A TEAM FROM NOW ON!
YOU JUST MAY HAVE A GOOD POINT THERE, PIP!
WE'LL SEE.
NEXT: THE ISLAND

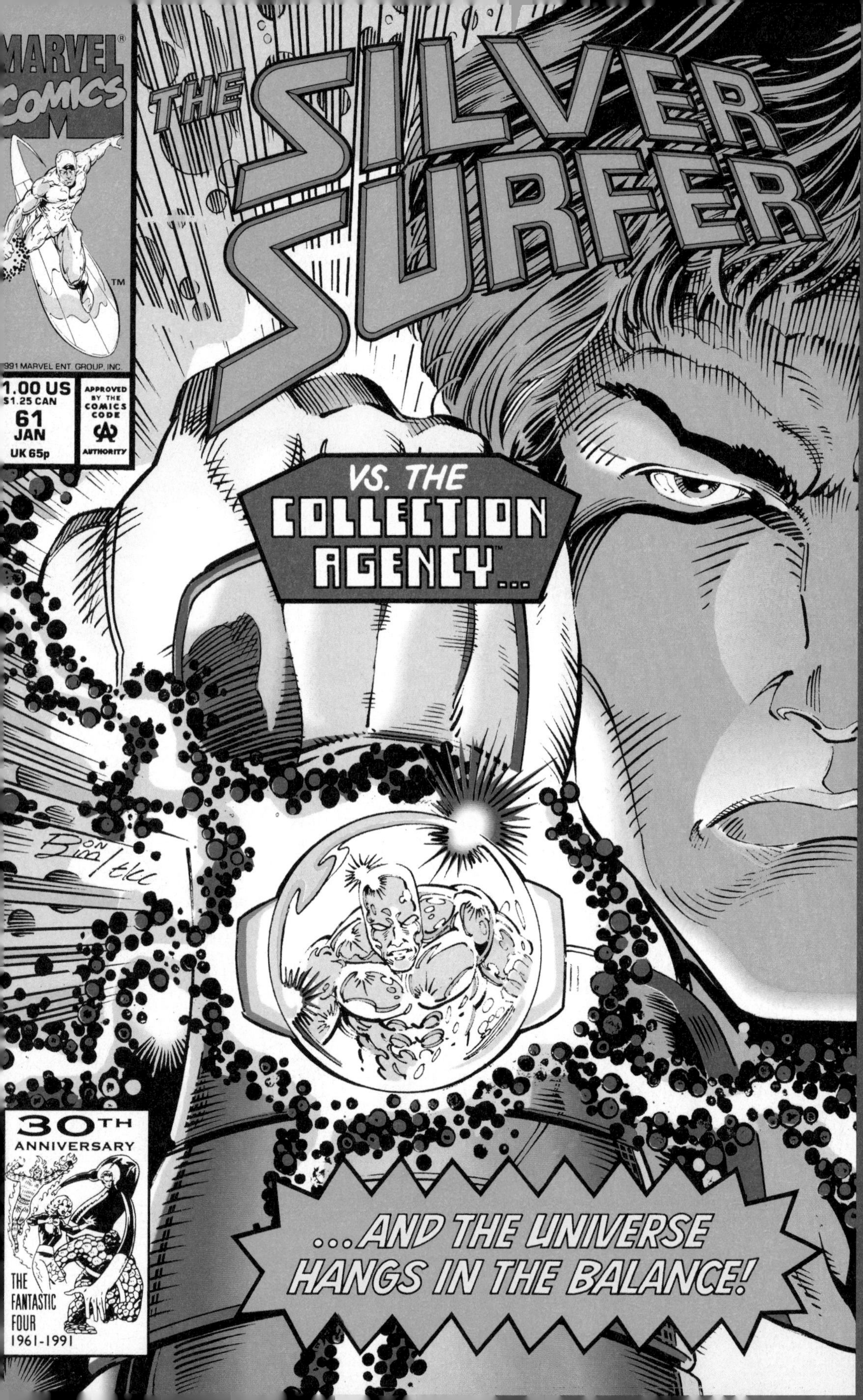
MARVEL COMICS
THE SILVER SURFER
991 MARVEL ENT. GROUP, INC.
1.00 US
$1.25 CAN
61
JAN
UK 65p
APPROVED BY THE COMICS CODE AUTHORITY
VS. THE
COLLECTION AGENCY...
30TH ANNIVERSARY
THE FANTASTIC FOUR
1961-1991
...AND THE UNIVERSE HANGS IN THE BALANCE!

TO SAVE HIS PLANET, NORRIN RADD SURRENDERED HIS FREEDOM TO BECOME HERALD TO THE WORLD-DEVOURING GALACTUS. COATED WITH GALACTIC GLAZE, GIVEN A SURFBOARD OBEYING HIS MENTAL COMMANDS, AND GRANTED THE POWER COSMIC, HE NOW SOARS THE UNIVERSE A SHINING SENTINEL OF THE SPACEWAYS! STAN LEE PRESENTS . . . THE SILVER SURFER!

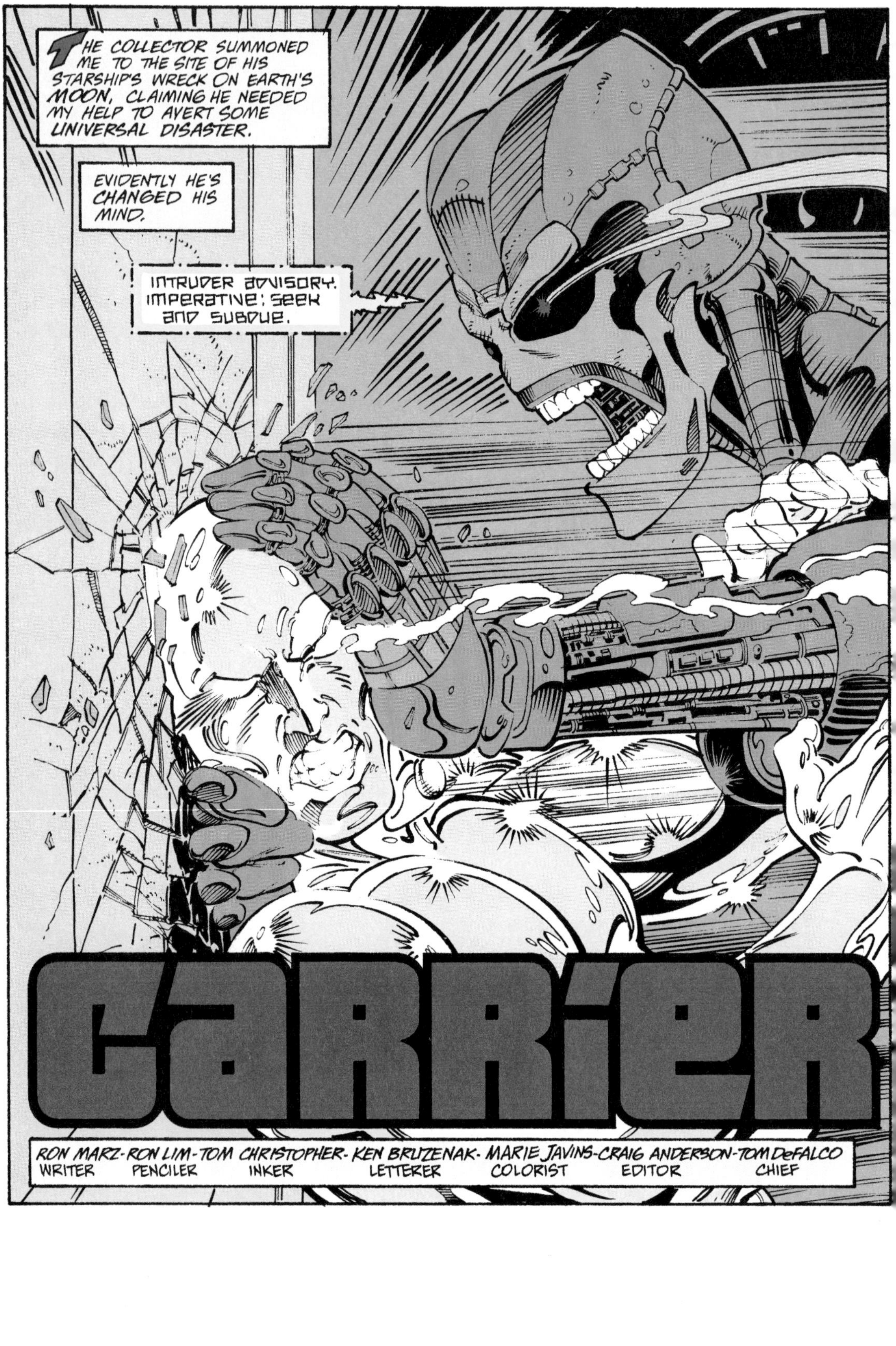
THE COLLECTOR SUMMONED ME TO THE SITE OF HIS STARSHIP'S WRECK ON EARTH'S MOON, CLAIMING HE NEEDED MY HELP TO AVERT SOME UNIVERSAL DISASTER.
EVIDENTLY HE'S CHANGED HIS MIND.
INTRUDER ADVISORY. IMPERATIVE: SEEK AND SUBDUE.
CARRIER
RON MARZ-RON LIM-TOM CHRISTOPHER-KEN BRUZENAK-MARIE JAVINS-CRAIG ANDERSON-TOM DeFALCO
WRITER PENCILER INKER LETTERER COLORIST EDITOR CHIEF

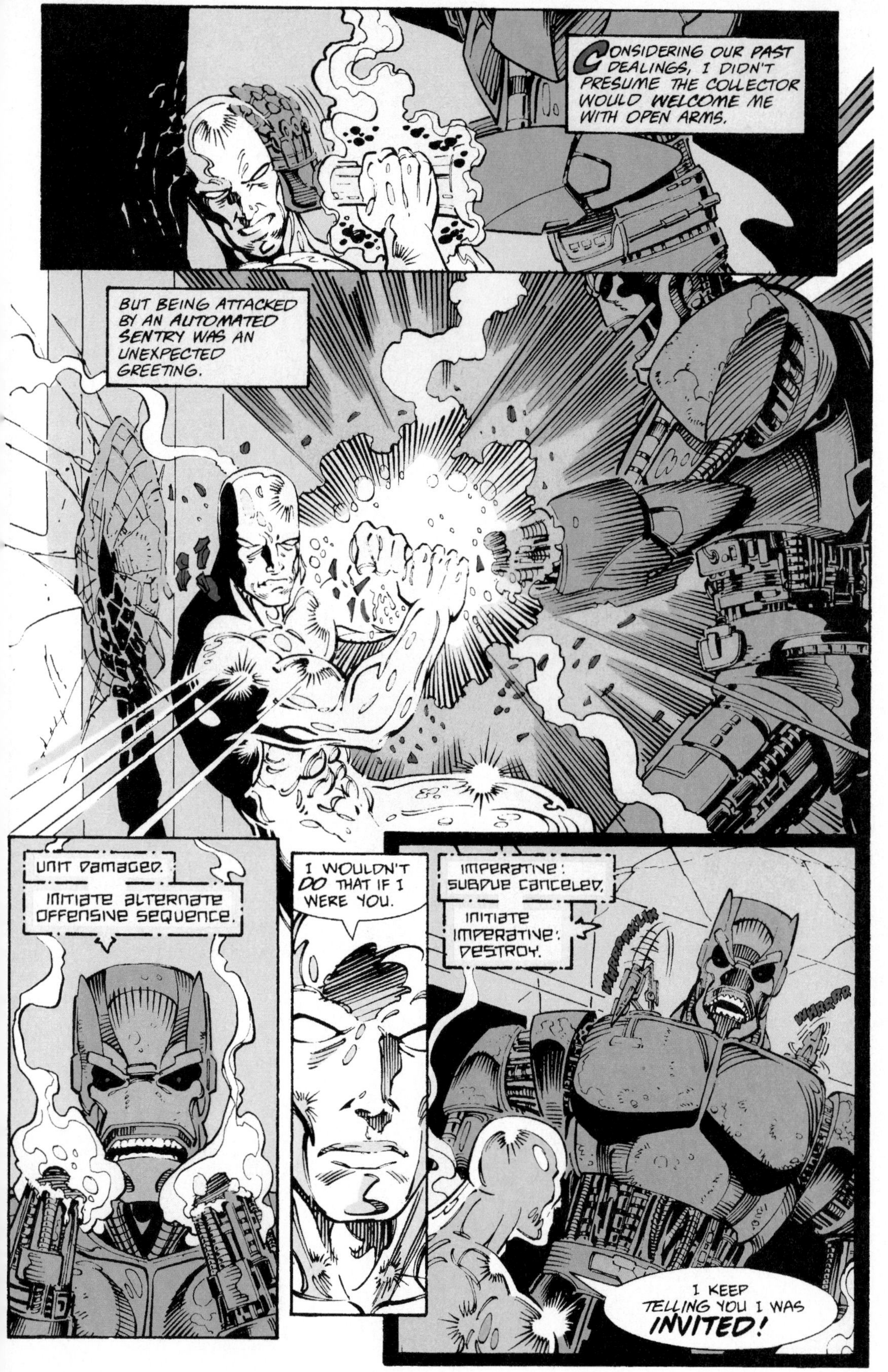
CONSIDERING OUR PAST DEALINGS, I DIDN'T PRESUME THE COLLECTOR WOULD WELCOME ME WITH OPEN ARMS.
BUT BEING ATTACKED BY AN AUTOMATED SENTRY WAS AN UNEXPECTED GREETING.
UNIT DAMAGED.
INITIATE ALTERNATE OFFENSIVE SEQUENCE.
I WOULDN'T DO THAT IF I WERE YOU.
IMPERATIVE: SUBDUE CANCELED.
INITIATE IMPERATIVE: DESTROY.
WHRRRR
I KEEP TELLING YOU I WAS INVITED!

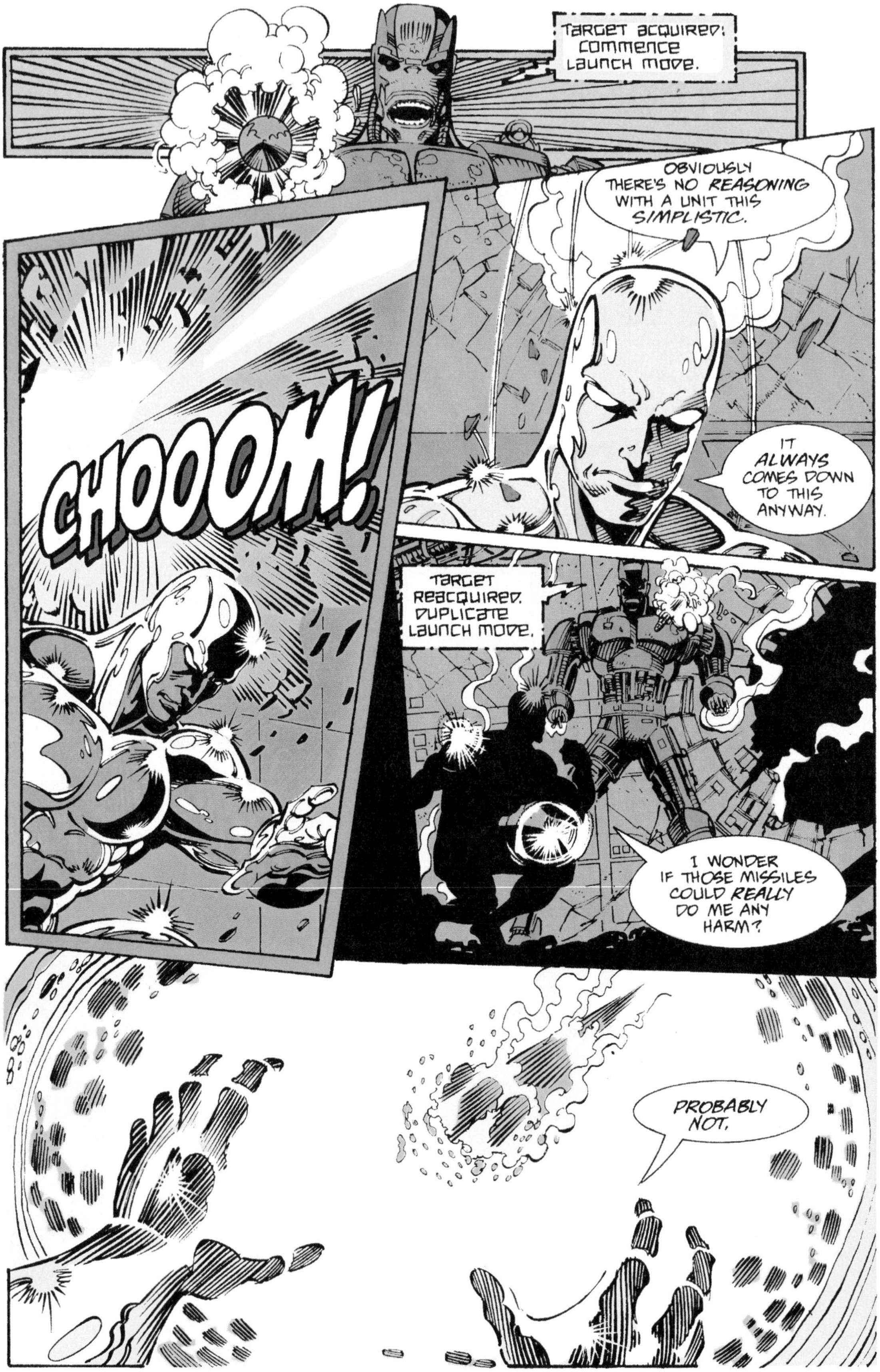
Target acquired: Commence Launch mode.
OBVIOUSLY THERE'S NO REASONING WITH A UNIT THIS SIMPLISTIC.
CHOOOM!
IT ALWAYS COMES DOWN TO THIS ANYWAY.
Target Reacquired. Duplicate Launch mode.
I WONDER IF THOSE MISSILES COULD REALLY DO ME ANY HARM?
PROBABLY NOT.

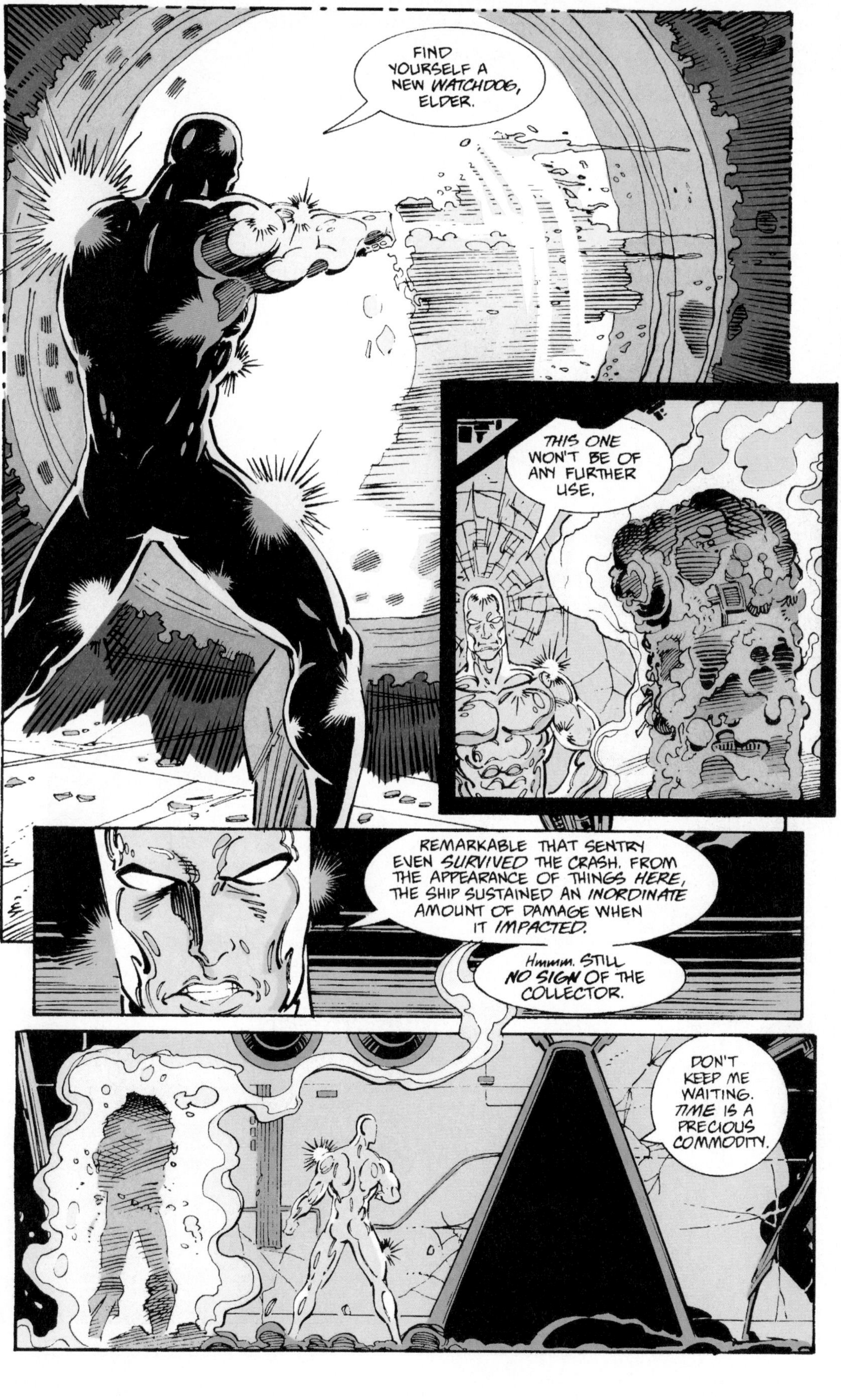

FIND YOURSELF A NEW WATCHDOG, ELDER.
THIS ONE WON'T BE OF ANY FURTHER USE.
REMARKABLE THAT SENTRY EVEN SURVIVED THE CRASH. FROM THE APPEARANCE OF THINGS HERE, THE SHIP SUSTAINED AN INORDINATE AMOUNT OF DAMAGE WHEN IT IMPACTED.
Hmmm. STILL NO SIGN OF THE COLLECTOR.
DON'T KEEP ME WAITING. TIME IS A PRECIOUS COMMODITY.

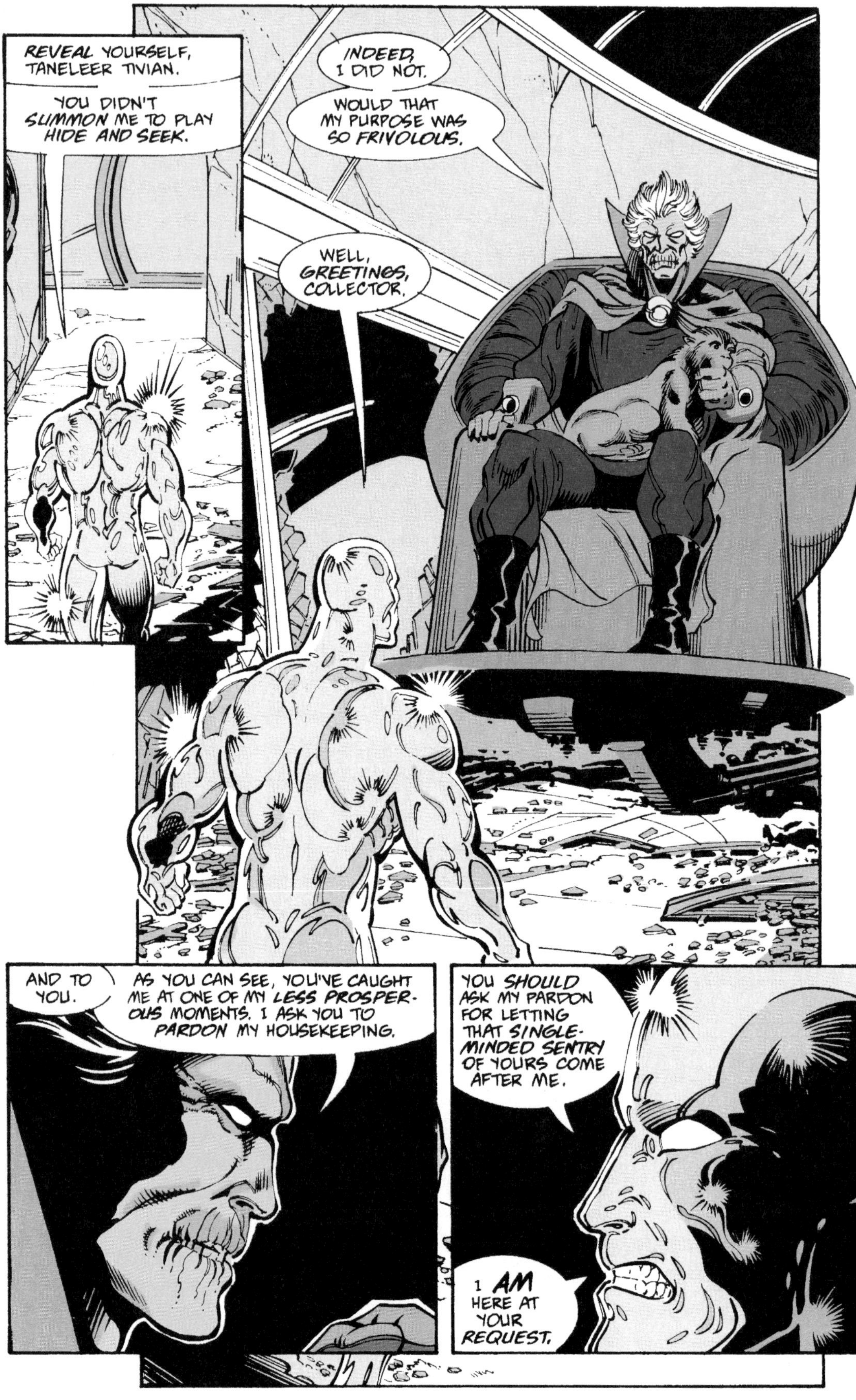
REVEAL YOURSELF, TANELEER TIVIAN.
YOU DIDN'T SUMMON ME TO PLAY HIDE AND SEEK.
INDEED, I DID NOT.
WOULD THAT MY PURPOSE WAS SO FRIVOLOUS.
WELL, GREETINGS, COLLECTOR.
AND TO YOU.
AS YOU CAN SEE, YOU'VE CAUGHT ME AT ONE OF MY LESS PROSPER-OUS MOMENTS. I ASK YOU TO PARDON MY HOUSEKEEPING.
YOU SHOULD ASK MY PARDON FOR LETTING THAT SINGLE-MINDED SENTRY OF YOURS COME AFTER ME.
I AM HERE AT YOUR REQUEST.

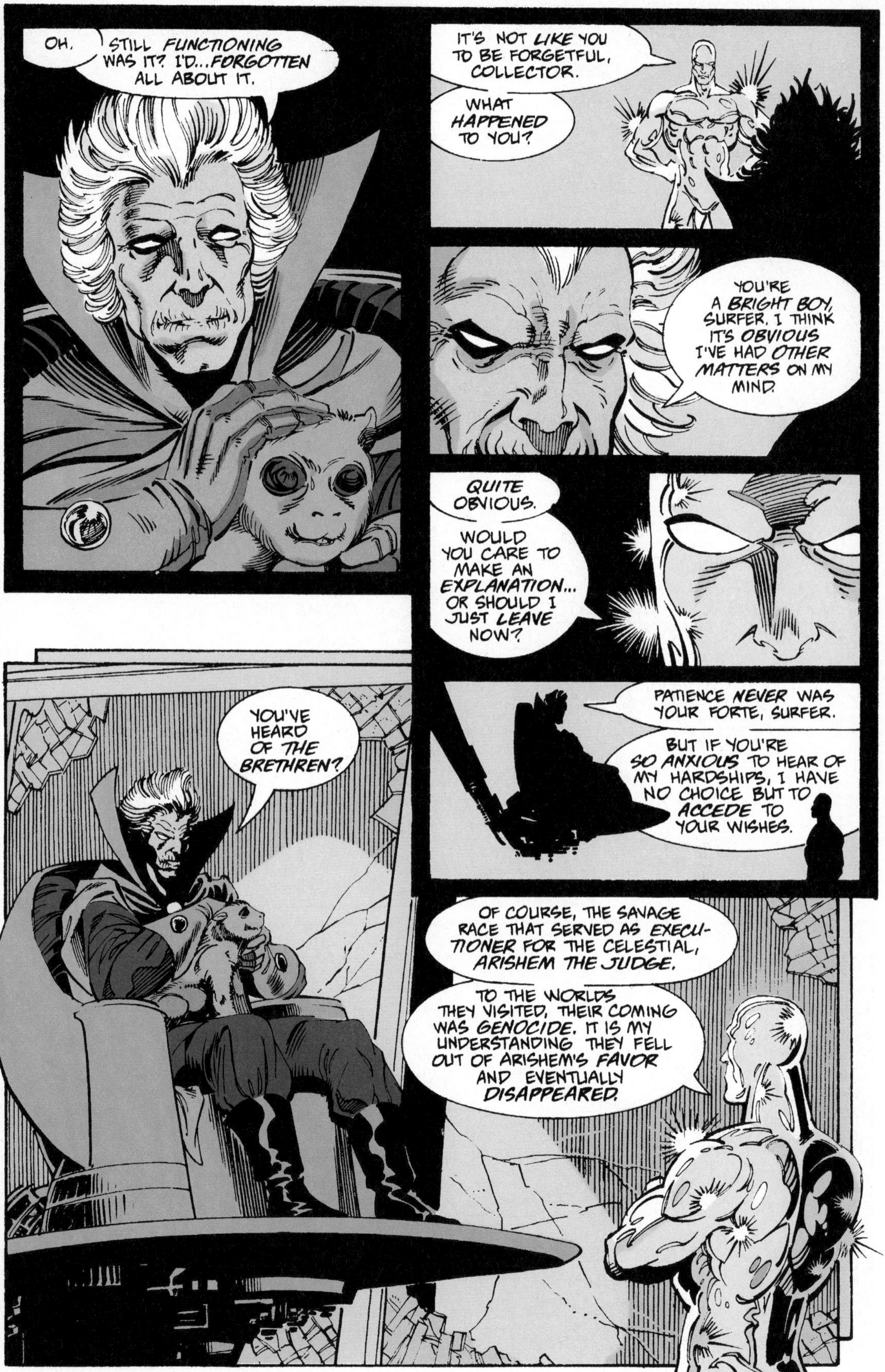
OH. STILL FUNCTIONING WAS IT? I'D...FORGOTTEN ALL ABOUT IT.
IT'S NOT LIKE YOU TO BE FORGETFUL, COLLECTOR.
WHAT HAPPENED TO YOU?
YOU'RE A BRIGHT BOY, SURFER. I THINK IT'S OBVIOUS I'VE HAD OTHER MATTERS ON MY MIND.
QUITE OBVIOUS.
WOULD YOU CARE TO MAKE AN EXPLANATION... OR SHOULD I JUST LEAVE NOW?
PATIENCE NEVER WAS YOUR FORTE, SURFER.
BUT IF YOU'RE SO ANXIOUS TO HEAR OF MY HARDSHIPS, I HAVE NO CHOICE BUT TO ACCEDE TO YOUR WISHES.
YOU'VE HEARD OF THE BRETHREN?
OF COURSE, THE SAVAGE RACE THAT SERVED AS EXECU-TIONER FOR THE CELESTIAL, ARISHEM THE JUDGE.
TO THE WORLDS THEY VISITED, THEIR COMING WAS GENOCIDE. IT IS MY UNDERSTANDING THEY FELL OUT OF ARISHEM'S FAVOR AND EVENTUALLY DISAPPEARED.

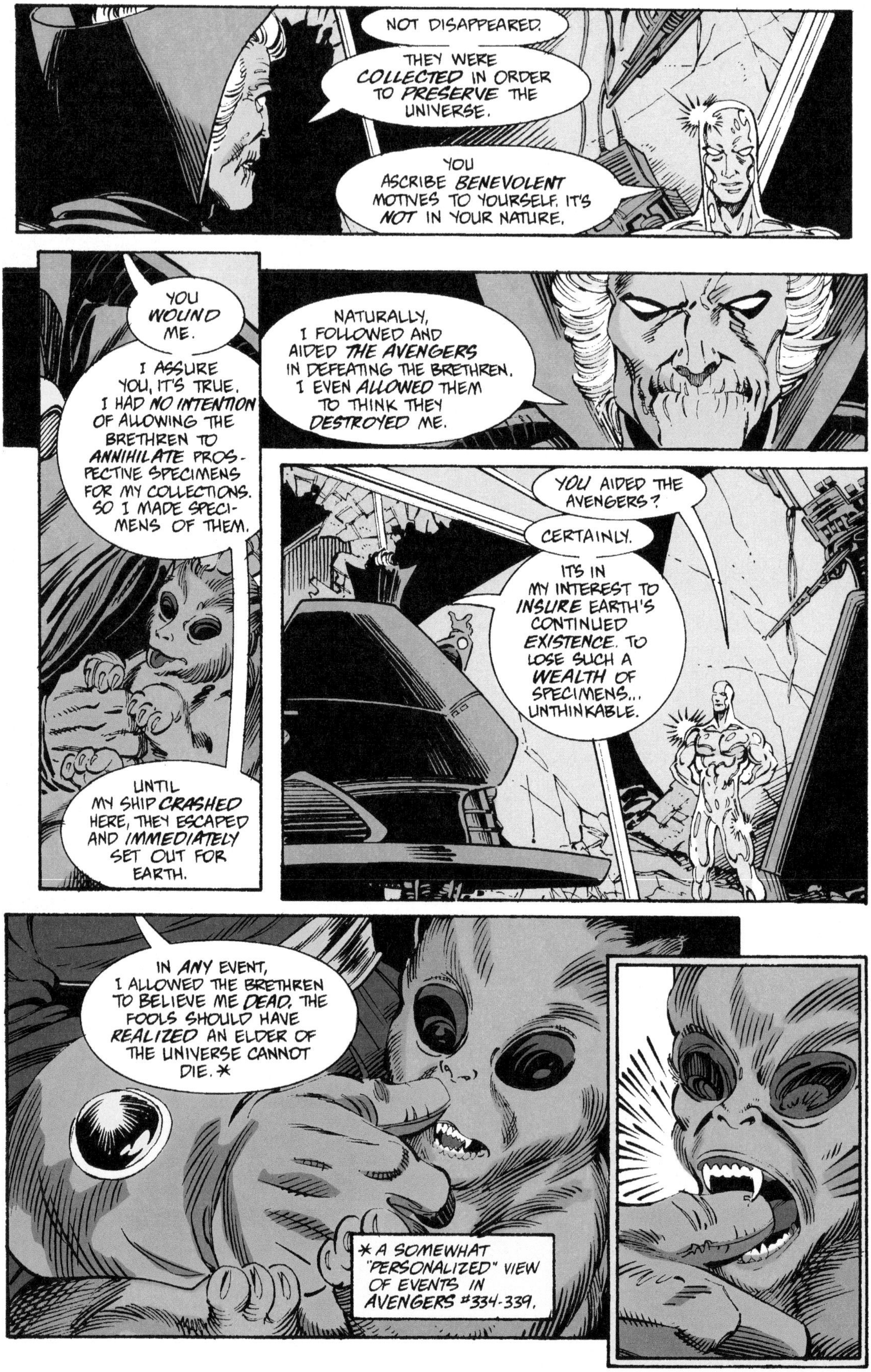
NOT DISAPPEARED.
THEY WERE COLLECTED IN ORDER TO PRESERVE THE UNIVERSE.
YOU ASCRIBE BENEVOLENT MOTIVES TO YOURSELF. IT'S NOT IN YOUR NATURE.
YOU WOUND ME.
I ASSURE YOU, IT'S TRUE. I HAD NO INTENTION OF ALLOWING THE BRETHREN TO ANNIHILATE PROSPECTIVE SPECIMENS FOR MY COLLECTIONS. SO I MADE SPECIMENS OF THEM.
UNTIL MY SHIP CRASHED HERE, THEY ESCAPED AND IMMEDIATELY SET OUT FOR EARTH.
NATURALLY, I FOLLOWED AND AIDED THE AVENGERS IN DEFEATING THE BRETHREN. I EVEN ALLOWED THEM TO THINK THEY DESTROYED ME.
YOU AIDED THE AVENGERS?
CERTAINLY.
IT'S IN MY INTEREST TO INSURE EARTH'S CONTINUED EXISTENCE. TO LOSE SUCH A WEALTH OF SPECIMENS... UNTHINKABLE.
IN ANY EVENT, I ALLOWED THE BRETHREN TO BELIEVE ME DEAD. THE FOOLS SHOULD HAVE REALIZED AN ELDER OF THE UNIVERSE CANNOT DIE. *
* A SOMEWHAT "PERSONALIZED" VIEW OF EVENTS IN AVENGERS #334-339.

OW!

WRETCHED ANIMAL.

PETS.

I SIMULATED MY DEATH AND TRANSPORTED BACK HERE TO BEGIN REPAIRS SO I COULD LEAVE THIS BACKWATER QUADRANT.

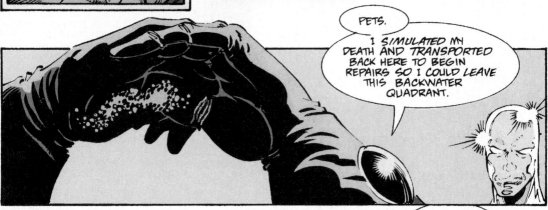

BUT WHEN THE BRETHREN FLED EARTH, THEY PASSED THIS WAY.

IN ORDER TO MAINTAIN THE ILLUSION OF MY DEATH, I HID FROM THEM. I ALLOWED THEM TO TAKE THEIR REVENGE ON MY SHIP.

AND SO YOU FIND ME...LIKE THIS.

YOU WISH ME TO COLLECT THE BRETHREN FOR YOU.

YOU'RE SORELY MISTAKEN. YOU ANGERED THEM, YOU FIND THEM.

I'D WELCOME SUCH A FACILE TASK. OURS, HOWEVER, IS OF FAR GREATER COMPLEXITY.

FOLLOW ME.

WHEN THE VINDICTIVE LITTLE *PESTS* RAVAGED MY SHIP, THEY *FREED* MUCH OF MY COLLECTION.

MOST OF IT I CAN RETRIEVE OR REPLACE...

...BUT WHAT WAS HOUSED *HERE*, EVEN *I* DARE NOT ATTEMPT RECAPTURING.

THIS CONTAINED A *MADNESS-INDUCING VIRUS*. ACTUALLY, A *CHILD* OF THE *MONDANI* RACE, CARRYING THE VIRUS.

I'VE NEVER BEEN ABLE TO ASCERTAIN ITS *EXACT* NATURE, BUT I'M CERTAIN OF ITS *SYMPTOMS*--DEMENTIA, PARANOIA, SCHIZOPHRENIA, HALLUCINATIONS.

THE END RESULT IS ALWAYS *DEATH*.

EVERY KNOWN RACE IS SUSCEPTIBLE, THOUGH IT INCUBATES IN SOME LONGER THAN OTHERS. THE MONDANI ARE *UNUSUALLY* RESISTANT, BUT THEY, TOO, EVENTUALLY SUFFER THE SAME FATE.

THE VIRUS *LIVES* TO REPRODUCE--IT SEEMS TO HAVE *NO* OTHER PURPOSE.

THE *PARENT* VIRUS REMAINS ATTACHED TO A STABLE HOST WHILE IT SPAWNS "OFFSPRING" AND RELEASES THEM INTO THE AIR. THESE PROGENY *TARGET* ANY HIGHER ORGANISM WITHIN RANGE AND *INFECT* IT.

ONCE *INFECTED*, THE ORGANISM'S CENTRAL NERVOUS SYSTEM SUFFERS A *COMPLETE BREAKDOWN*, LEADING TO DEATH.

LUCKILY, THE SECOND-GENERATION VIRAL FORMS *DIE* WHEN THEIR HOST ORGANISMS DO. THE PARENT-VIRUS *SURVIVES*, THOUGH, CHANGING HOSTS WHEN A MORE *VIABLE* ONE PRESENTS ITSELF.

THAT'S WHY *YOU'RE* HERE.

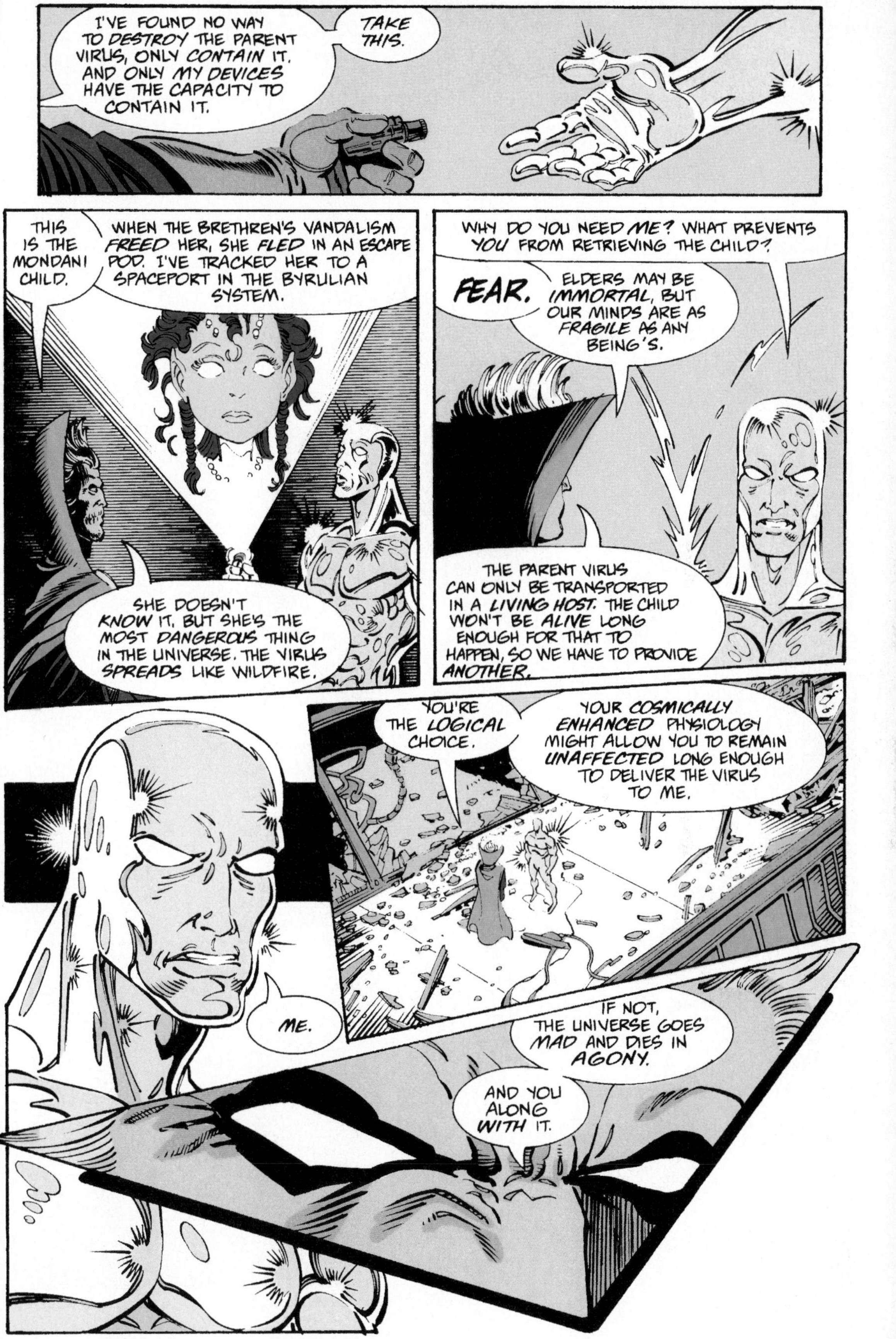
I'VE FOUND NO WAY TO DESTROY THE PARENT VIRUS, ONLY CONTAIN IT. AND ONLY MY DEVICES HAVE THE CAPACITY TO CONTAIN IT.
TAKE THIS.
THIS IS THE MONDANI CHILD.
WHEN THE BRETHREN'S VANDALISM FREED HER, SHE FLED IN AN ESCAPE POD. I'VE TRACKED HER TO A SPACEPORT IN THE BYRULIAN SYSTEM.
SHE DOESN'T KNOW IT, BUT SHE'S THE MOST DANGEROUS THING IN THE UNIVERSE. THE VIRUS SPREADS LIKE WILDFIRE.
WHY DO YOU NEED ME? WHAT PREVENTS YOU FROM RETRIEVING THE CHILD?
FEAR.
ELDERS MAY BE IMMORTAL, BUT OUR MINDS ARE AS FRAGILE AS ANY BEING'S.
THE PARENT VIRUS CAN ONLY BE TRANSPORTED IN A LIVING HOST. THE CHILD WON'T BE ALIVE LONG ENOUGH FOR THAT TO HAPPEN, SO WE HAVE TO PROVIDE ANOTHER.
YOU'RE THE LOGICAL CHOICE.
YOUR COSMICALLY ENHANCED PHYSIOLOGY MIGHT ALLOW YOU TO REMAIN UNAFFECTED LONG ENOUGH TO DELIVER THE VIRUS TO ME.
ME.
IF NOT, THE UNIVERSE GOES MAD AND DIES IN AGONY.
AND YOU ALONG WITH IT.

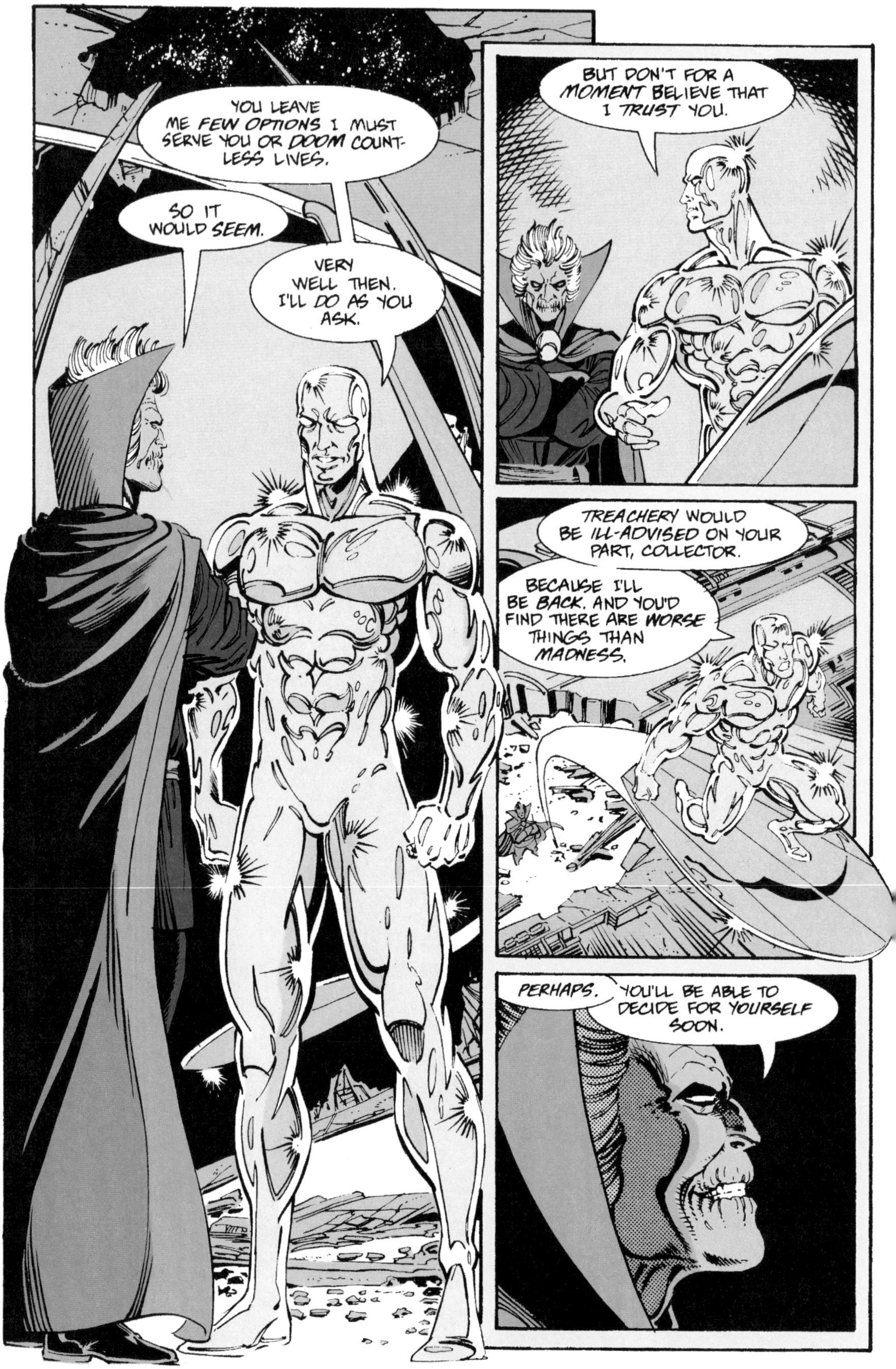
YOU LEAVE ME FEW OPTIONS I MUST SERVE YOU OR DOOM COUNT-LESS LIVES.
SO IT WOULD SEEM.
VERY WELL THEN. I'LL DO AS YOU ASK.
BUT DON'T FOR A MOMENT BELIEVE THAT I TRUST YOU.
TREACHERY WOULD BE ILL-ADVISED ON YOUR PART, COLLECTOR.
BECAUSE I'LL BE BACK. AND YOU'D FIND THERE ARE WORSE THINGS THAN MADNESS.
PERHAPS.
YOU'LL BE ABLE TO DECIDE FOR YOURSELF SOON.

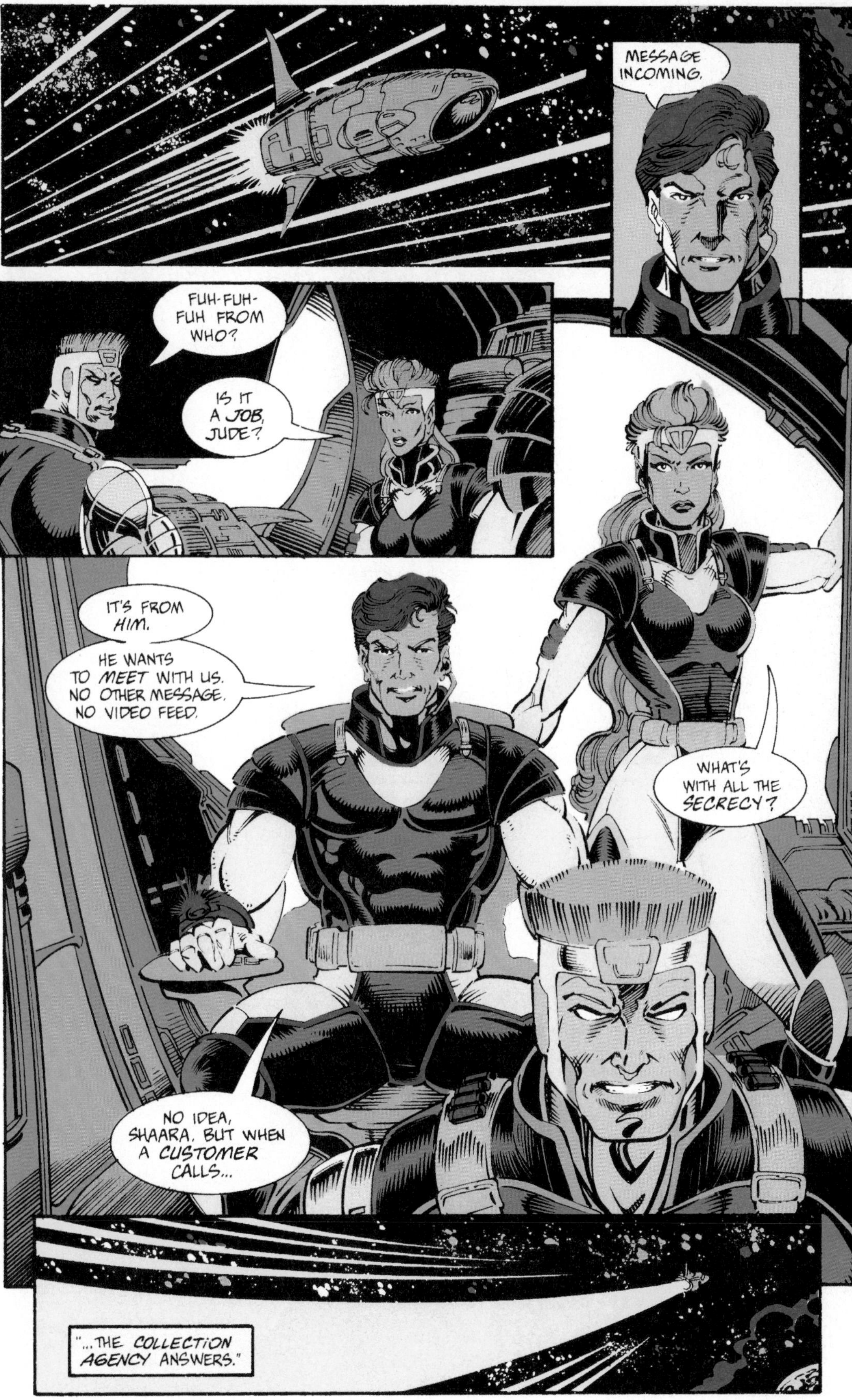
MESSAGE INCOMING.
FUH-FUH-FUH FROM WHO?
IS IT A JOB, JUDE?
IT'S FROM HIM.
HE WANTS TO MEET WITH US. NO OTHER MESSAGE. NO VIDEO FEED.
WHAT'S WITH ALL THE SECRECY?
NO IDEA, SHAARA. BUT WHEN A CUSTOMER CALLS...
"...THE COLLECTION AGENCY ANSWERS."

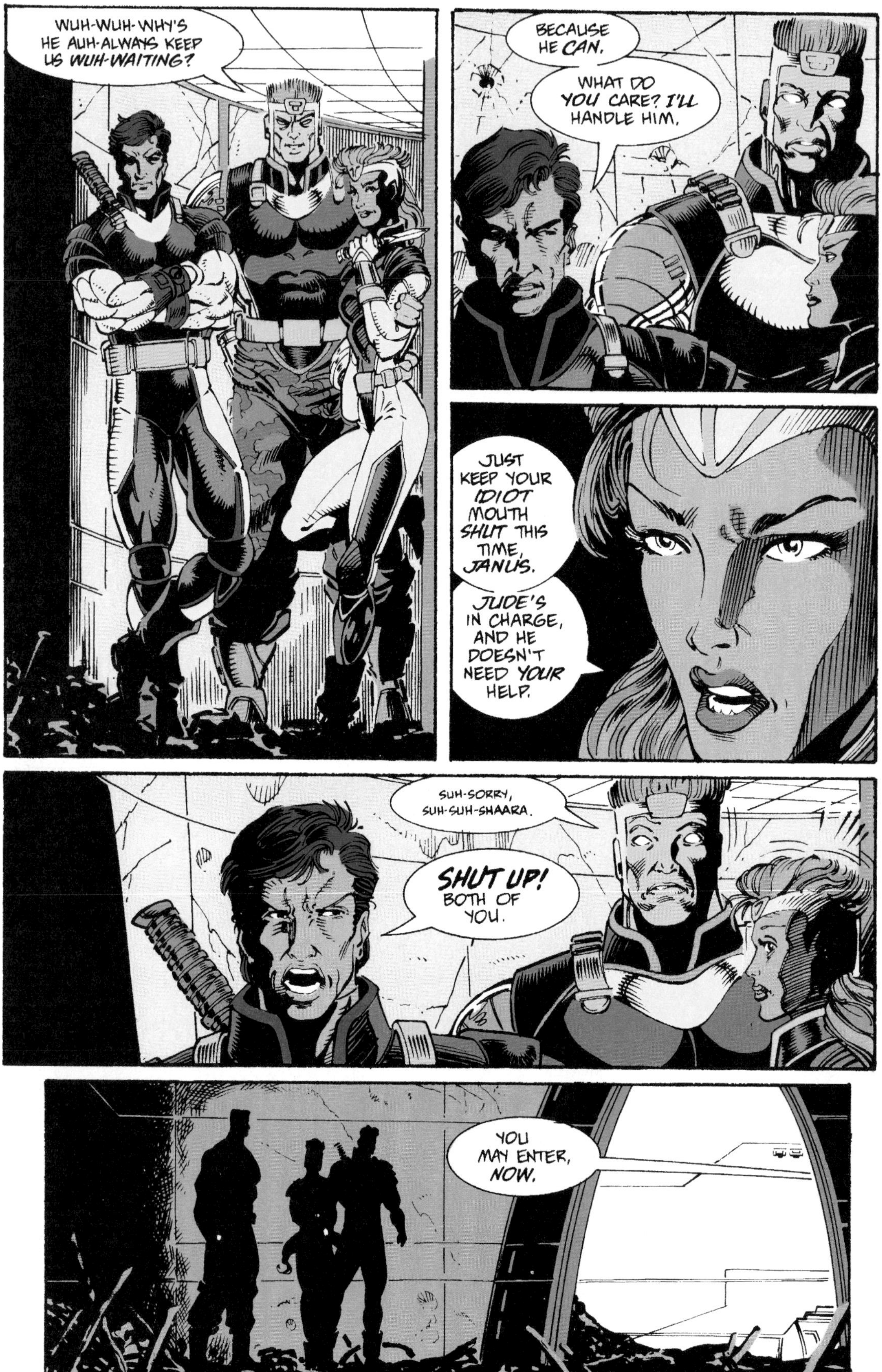
WUH-WUH-WHY'S HE AUH-ALWAYS KEEP US WUH-WAITING?
BECAUSE HE CAN.
WHAT DO YOU CARE? I'LL HANDLE HIM.
JUST KEEP YOUR IDIOT MOUTH SHUT THIS TIME, JANUS.
JUDE'S IN CHARGE, AND HE DOESN'T NEED YOUR HELP.
SUH-SORRY, SUH-SUH-SHAARA.
SHUT UP! BOTH OF YOU.
YOU MAY ENTER, NOW.

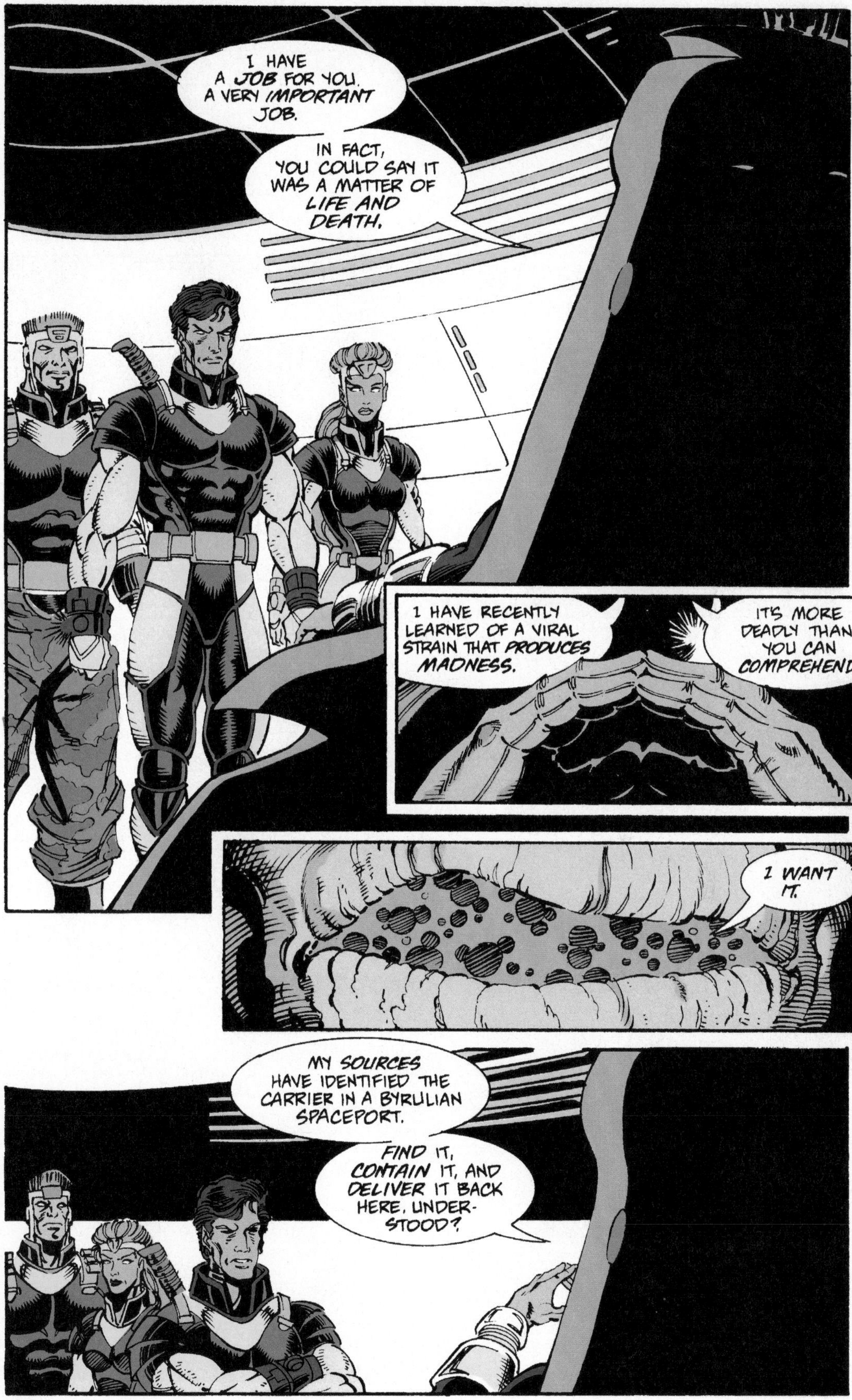
I HAVE A JOB FOR YOU. A VERY IMPORTANT JOB.
IN FACT, YOU COULD SAY IT WAS A MATTER OF LIFE AND DEATH.
I HAVE RECENTLY LEARNED OF A VIRAL STRAIN THAT PRODUCES MADNESS.
IT'S MORE DEADLY THAN YOU CAN COMPREHEND.
I WANT IT.
MY SOURCES HAVE IDENTIFIED THE CARRIER IN A BYRULIAN SPACEPORT.
FIND IT, CONTAIN IT, AND DELIVER IT BACK HERE, UNDER-STOOD?

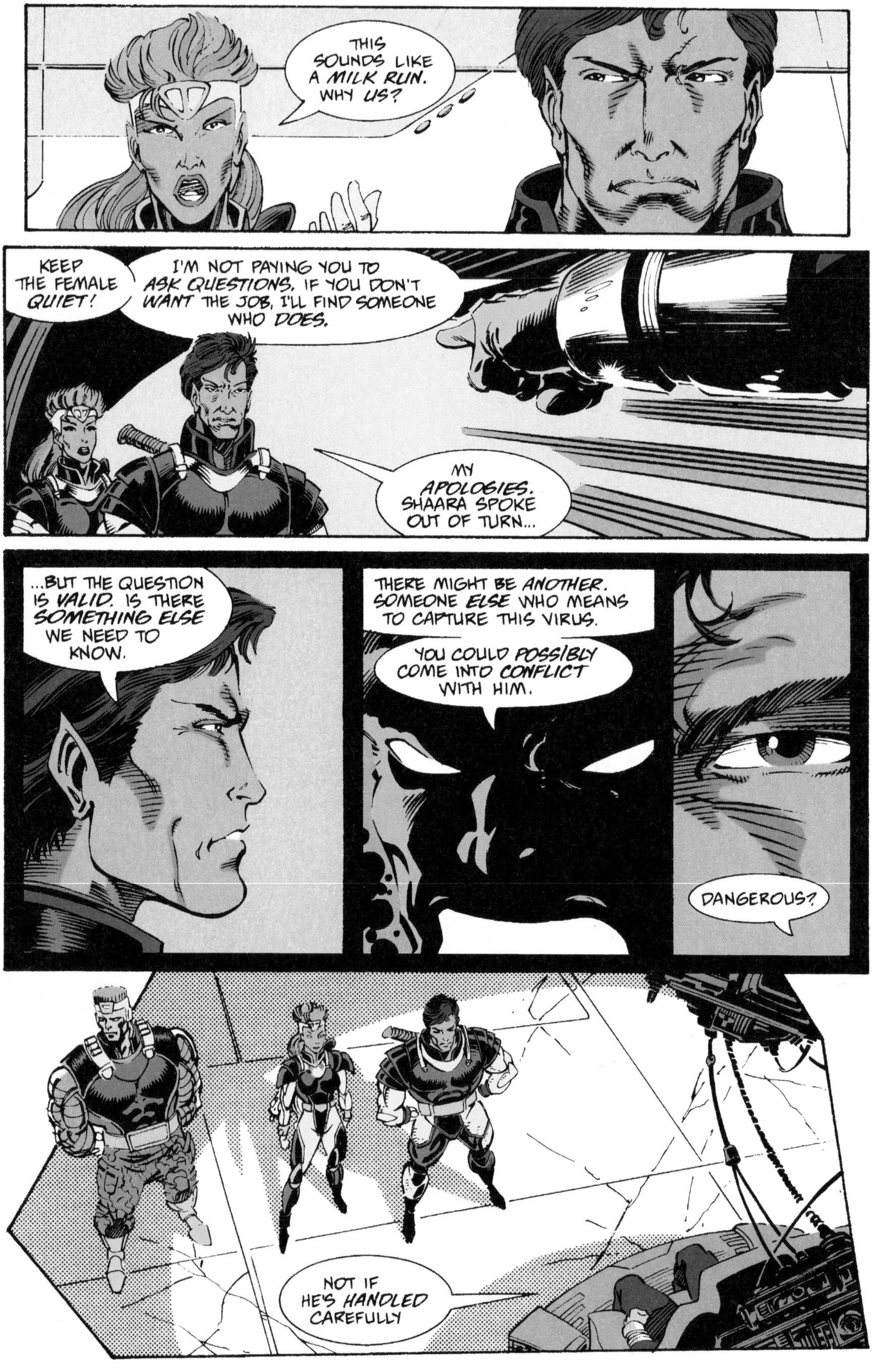
THIS SOUNDS LIKE A MILK RUN. WHY US?
KEEP THE FEMALE QUIET!
I'M NOT PAYING YOU TO ASK QUESTIONS. IF YOU DON'T WANT THE JOB, I'LL FIND SOMEONE WHO DOES.
MY APOLOGIES. SHAARA SPOKE OUT OF TURN...
...BUT THE QUESTION IS VALID. IS THERE SOMETHING ELSE WE NEED TO KNOW.
THERE MIGHT BE ANOTHER. SOMEONE ELSE WHO MEANS TO CAPTURE THIS VIRUS.
YOU COULD POSSIBLY COME INTO CONFLICT WITH HIM.
DANGEROUS?
NOT IF HE'S HANDLED CAREFULLY

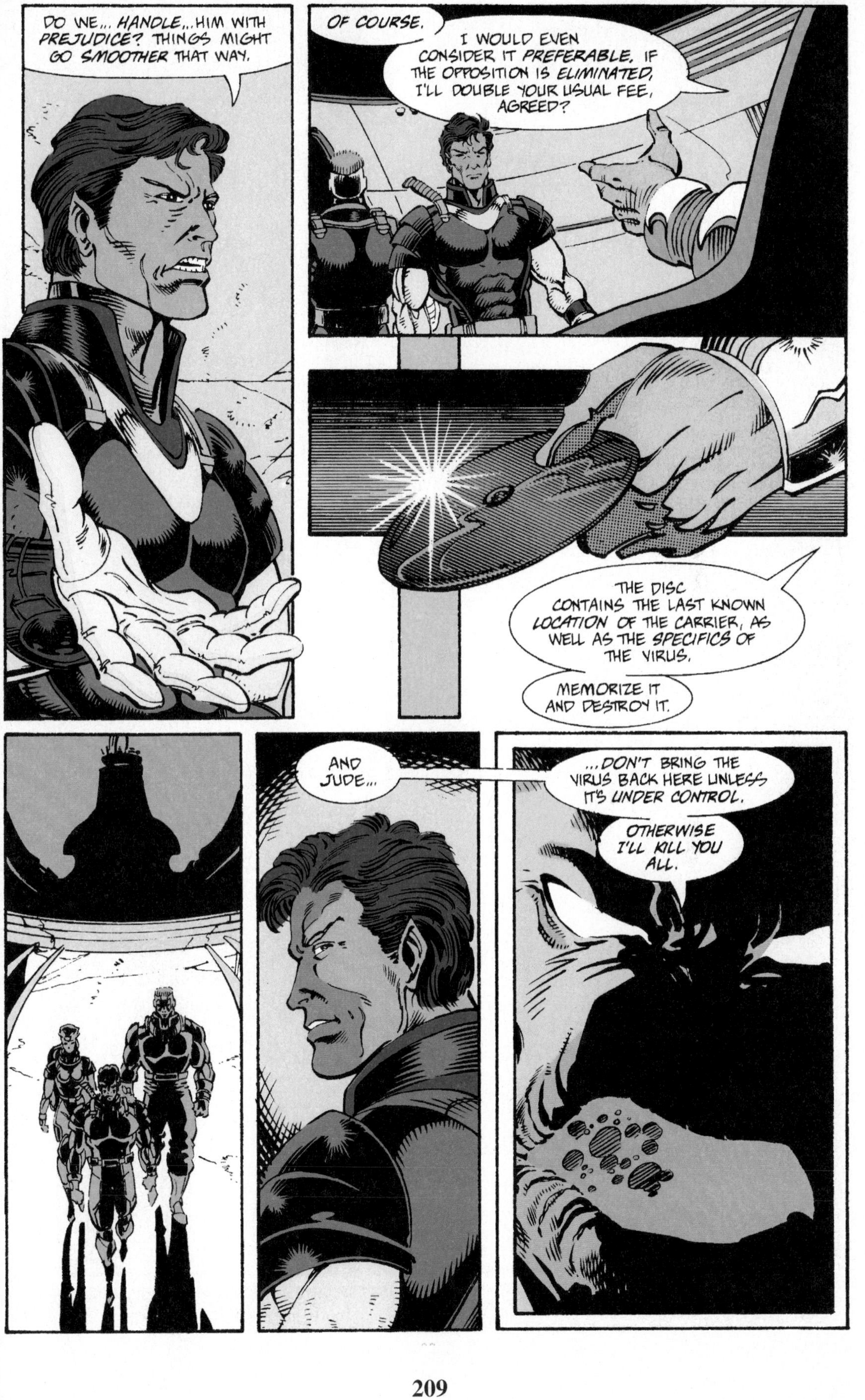
DO WE... HANDLE... HIM WITH PREJUDICE? THINGS MIGHT GO SMOOTHER THAT WAY.
OF COURSE.
I WOULD EVEN CONSIDER IT PREFERABLE. IF THE OPPOSITION IS ELIMINATED, I'LL DOUBLE YOUR USUAL FEE. AGREED?
THE DISC CONTAINS THE LAST KNOWN LOCATION OF THE CARRIER, AS WELL AS THE SPECIFICS OF THE VIRUS.
MEMORIZE IT AND DESTROY IT.
AND JUDE...
...DON'T BRING THE VIRUS BACK HERE UNLESS IT'S UNDER CONTROL.
OTHERWISE I'LL KILL YOU ALL.

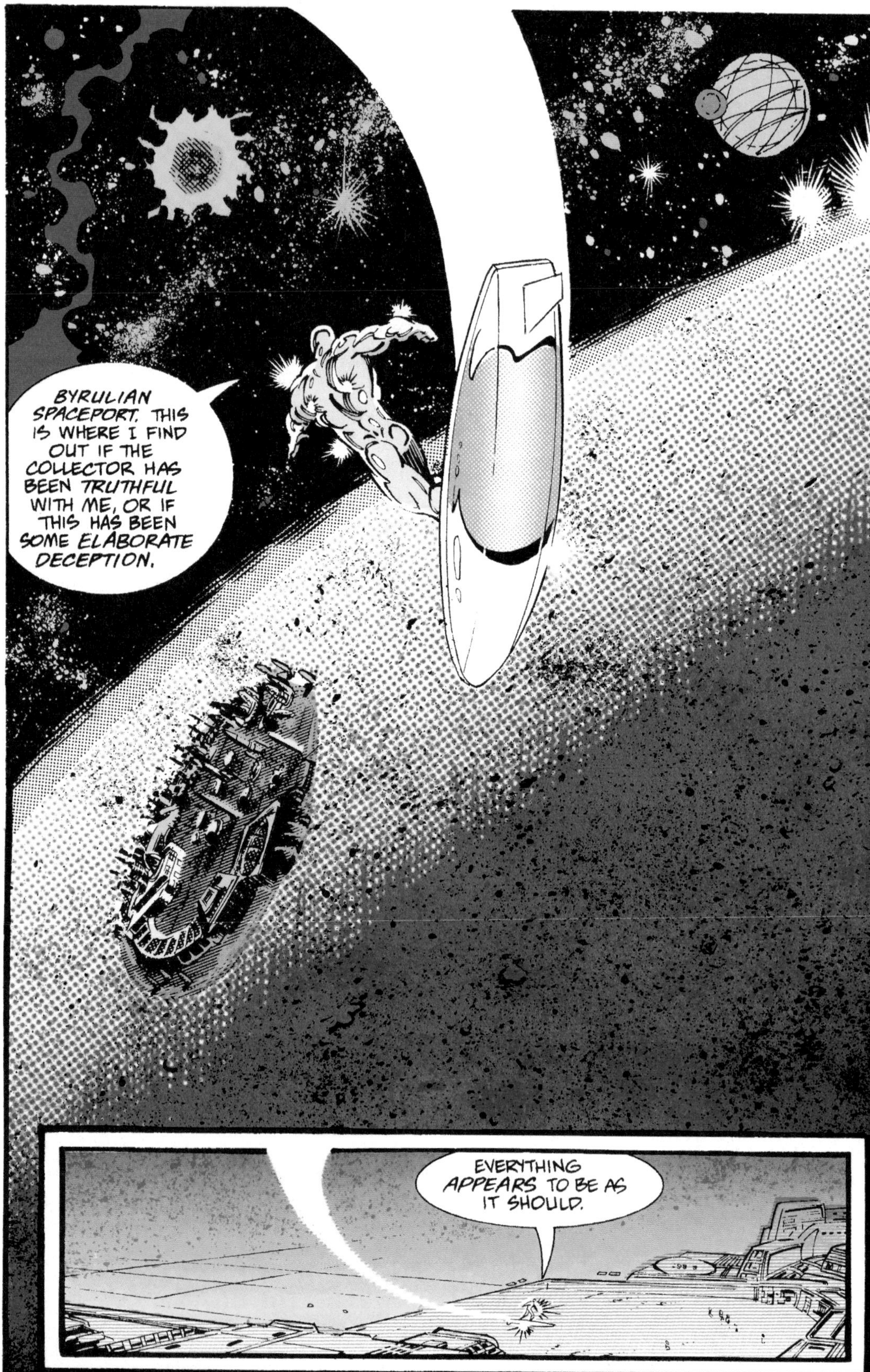
BYRULIAN SPACEPORT. THIS IS WHERE I FIND OUT IF THE COLLECTOR HAS BEEN TRUTHFUL WITH ME, OR IF THIS HAS BEEN SOME ELABORATE DECEPTION.
EVERYTHING APPEARS TO BE AS IT SHOULD.

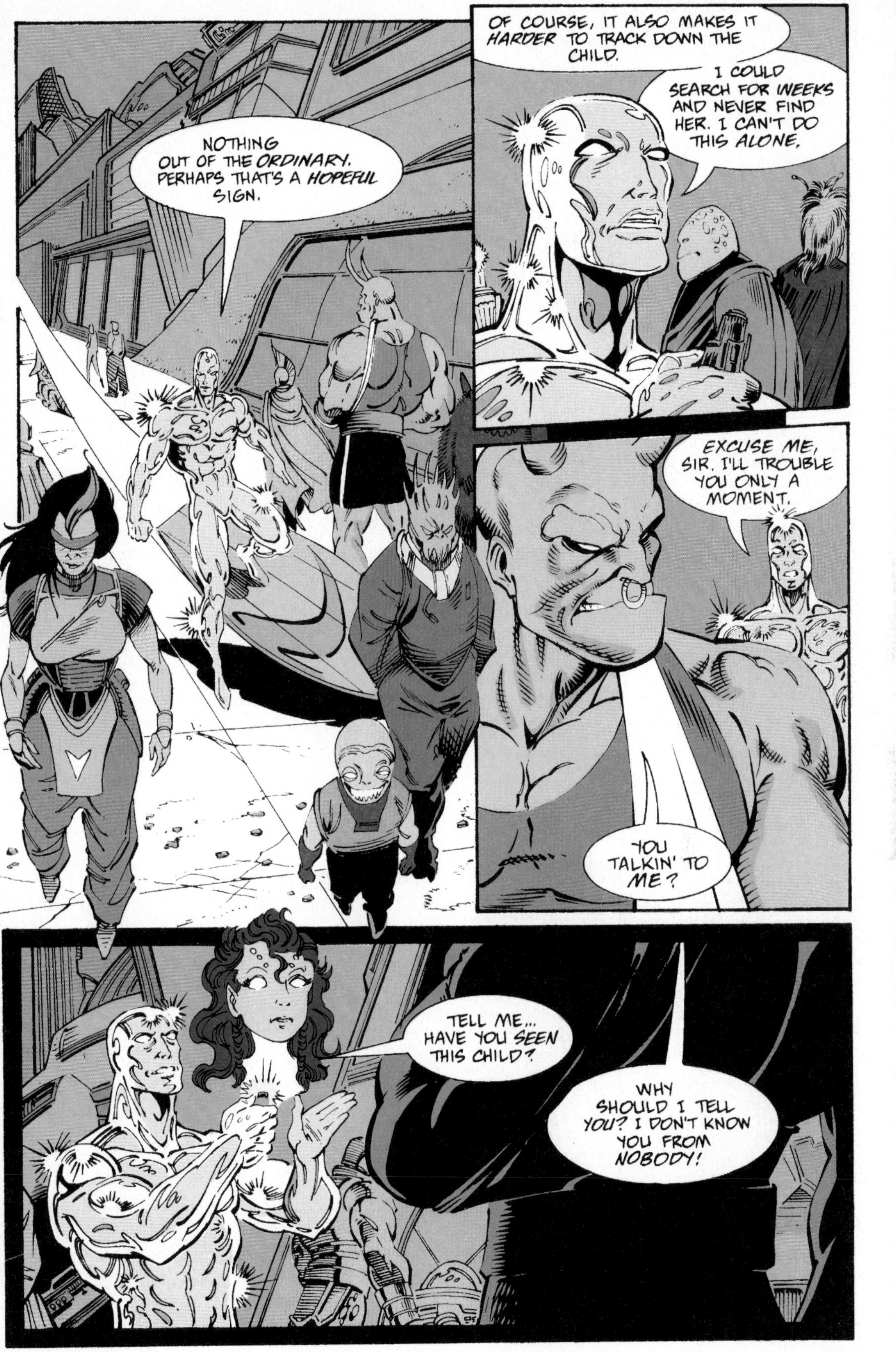

NOTHING OUT OF THE ORDINARY. PERHAPS THAT'S A HOPEFUL SIGN.
OF COURSE, IT ALSO MAKES IT HARDER TO TRACK DOWN THE CHILD.
I COULD SEARCH FOR WEEKS AND NEVER FIND HER. I CAN'T DO THIS ALONE.
EXCUSE ME, SIR. I'LL TROUBLE YOU ONLY A MOMENT.
YOU TALKIN' TO ME?
TELL ME... HAVE YOU SEEN THIS CHILD?
WHY SHOULD I TELL YOU? I DON'T KNOW YOU FROM NOBODY!

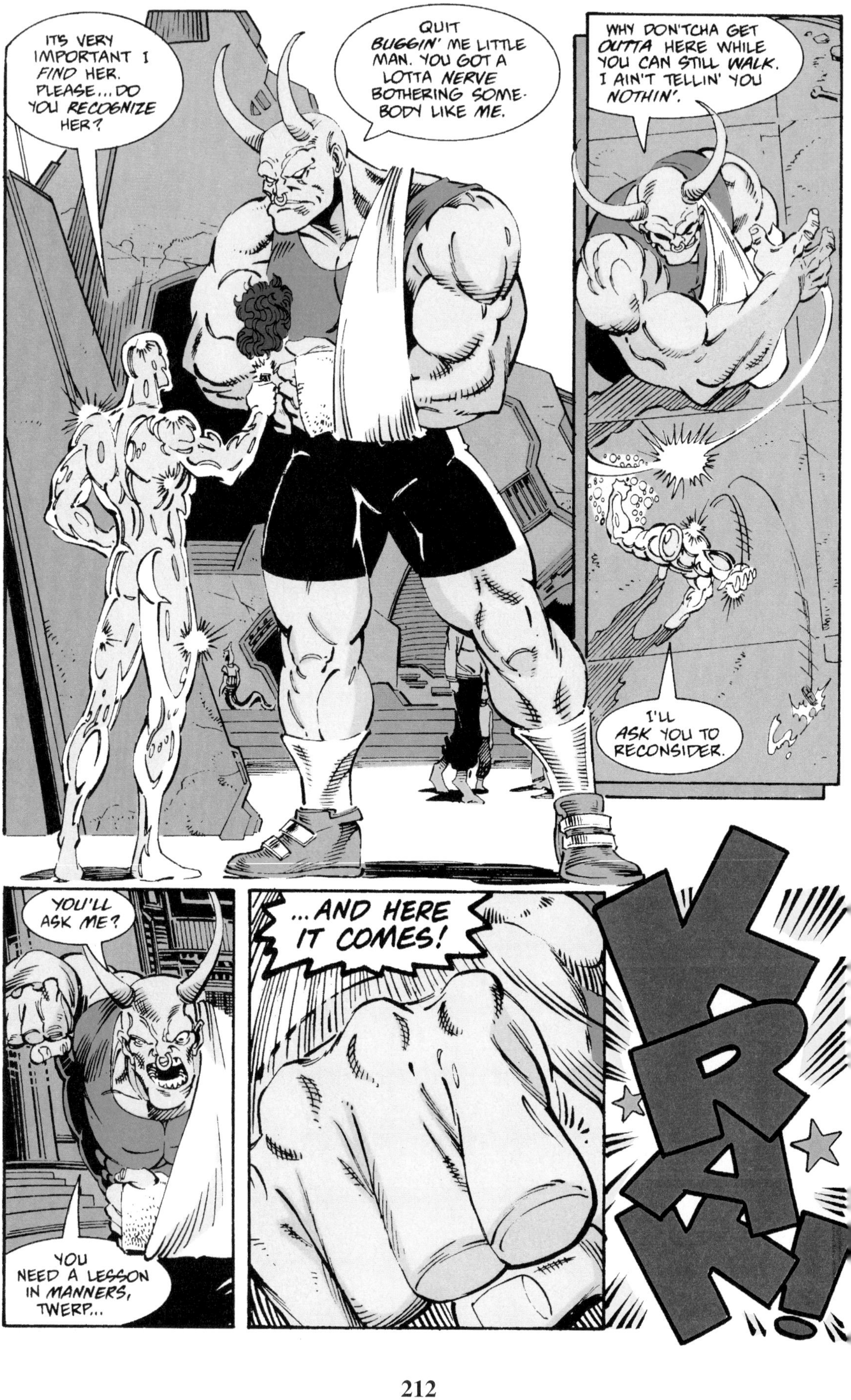
IT'S VERY IMPORTANT I FIND HER. PLEASE... DO YOU RECOGNIZE HER?
QUIT BUGGIN' ME LITTLE MAN. YOU GOT A LOTTA NERVE BOTHERING SOME-BODY LIKE ME.
WHY DON'TCHA GET OUTTA HERE WHILE YOU CAN STILL WALK. I AIN'T TELLIN' YOU NOTHIN'.
I'LL ASK YOU TO RECONSIDER.
YOU'LL ASK ME?
YOU NEED A LESSON IN MANNERS, TWERP...
...AND HERE IT COMES!
KRAK!

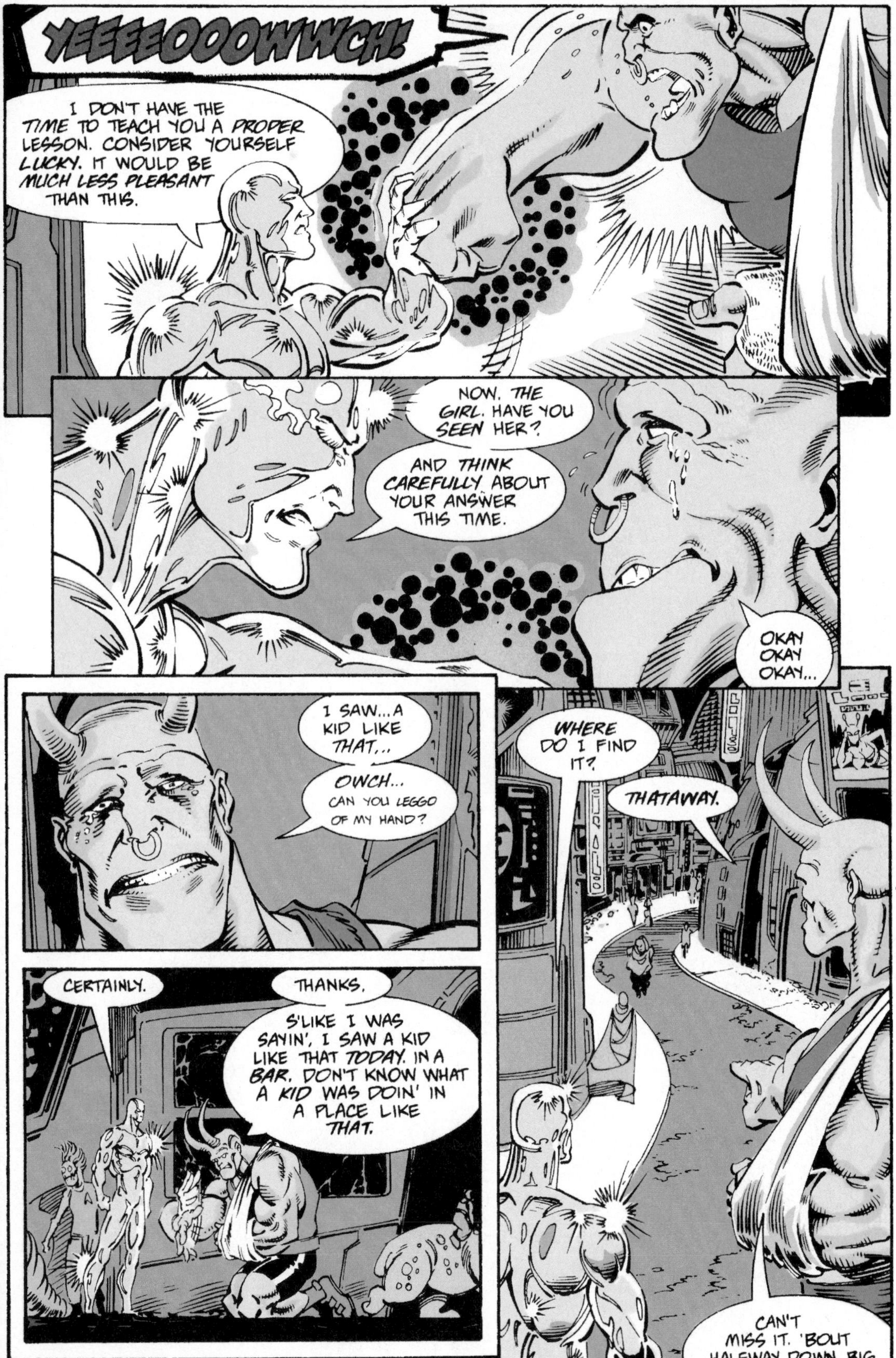
YEEEEOOOWWCH!
I DON'T HAVE THE TIME TO TEACH YOU A PROPER LESSON. CONSIDER YOURSELF LUCKY. IT WOULD BE MUCH LESS PLEASANT THAN THIS.
NOW. THE GIRL. HAVE YOU SEEN HER?
AND THINK CAREFULLY ABOUT YOUR ANSWER THIS TIME.
OKAY OKAY OKAY...
I SAW... A KID LIKE THAT...
OWCH... CAN YOU LEGGO OF MY HAND?
CERTAINLY.
THANKS.
S'LIKE I WAS SAYIN', I SAW A KID LIKE THAT TODAY. IN A BAR. DON'T KNOW WHAT A KID WAS DOIN' IN A PLACE LIKE THAT.
WHERE DO I FIND IT?
THATAWAY.
CAN'T MISS IT. 'BOUT HALFWAY DOWN. BIG WINDOW IN FRONT.

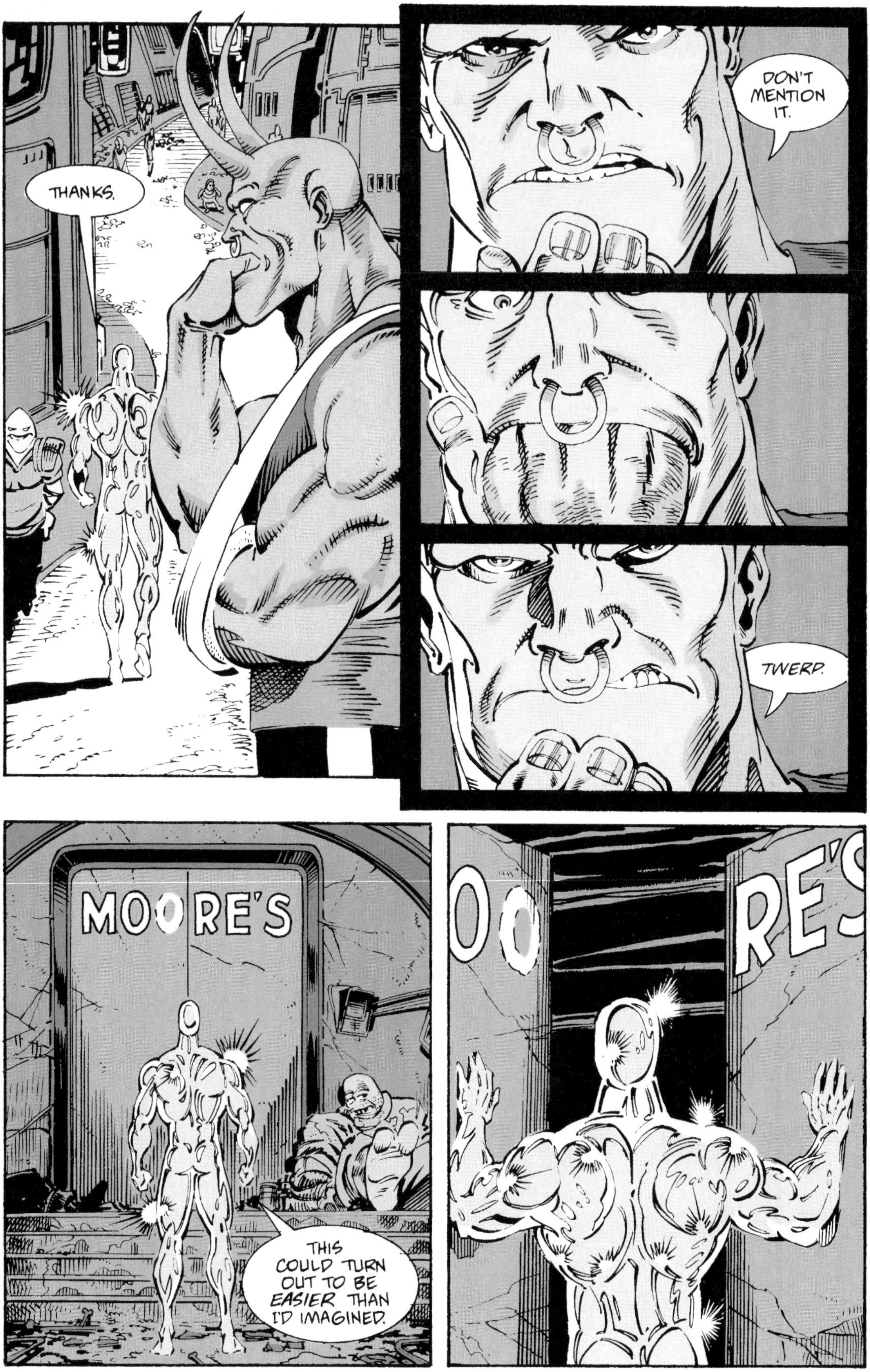
THANKS.
DON'T MENTION IT.
TWERP.
MOORE'S
OO RE'S
THIS COULD TURN OUT TO BE EASIER THAN I'D IMAGINED.

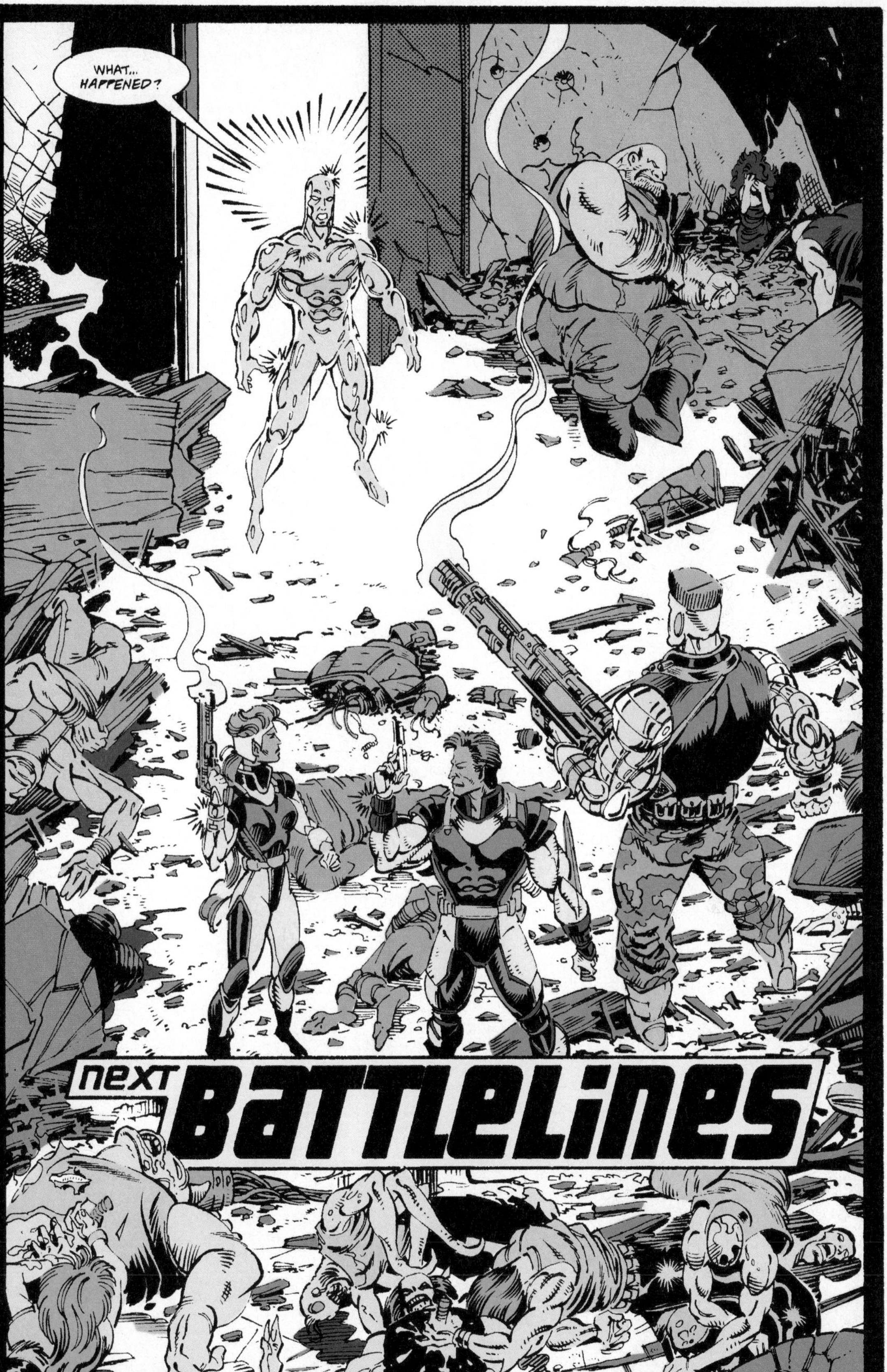
WHAT... HAPPENED?
NEXT
BATTLELINES

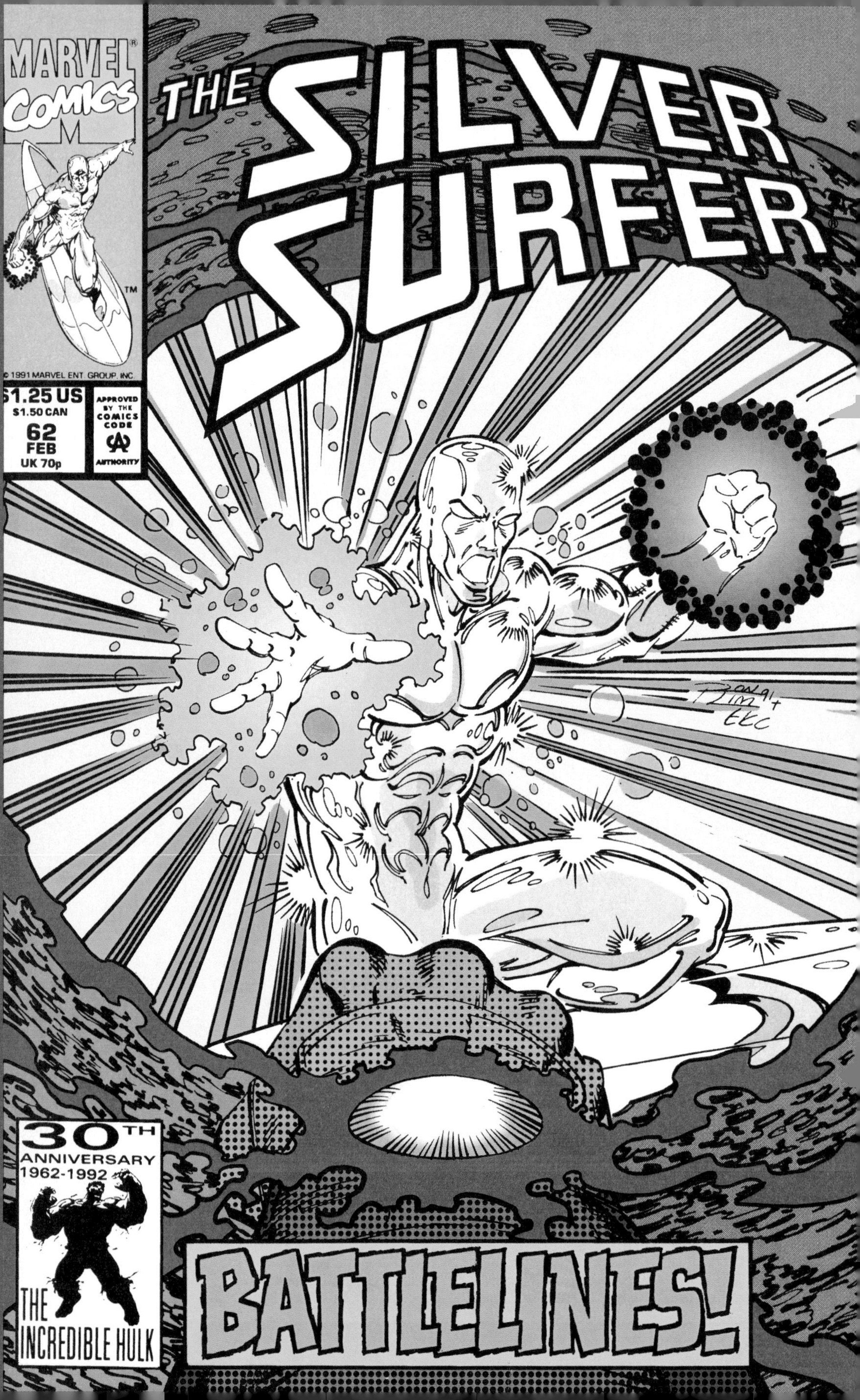
MARVEL COMICS
THE SILVER SURFER
© 1991 MARVEL ENT. GROUP, INC.
$1.25 US
$1.50 CAN
62
FEB
UK 70p
APPROVED BY THE COMICS CODE AUTHORITY
30TH ANNIVERSARY 1962-1992
THE INCREDIBLE HULK
BATTLELINES!

TO SAVE HIS PLANET, NORRIN RADD SURRENDERED HIS FREEDOM TO BECOME HERALD TO THE WORLD-DEVOURING GALACTUS. COATED WITH GALACTIC GLAZE, GIVEN A SURFBOARD OBEYING HIS MENTAL COMMANDS, AND GRANTED THE POWER COSMIC, HE NOW SOARS THE UNIVERSE A SHINING SENTINEL OF THE SPACEWAYS! STAN LEE PRESENTS . . . THE SILVER SURFER!

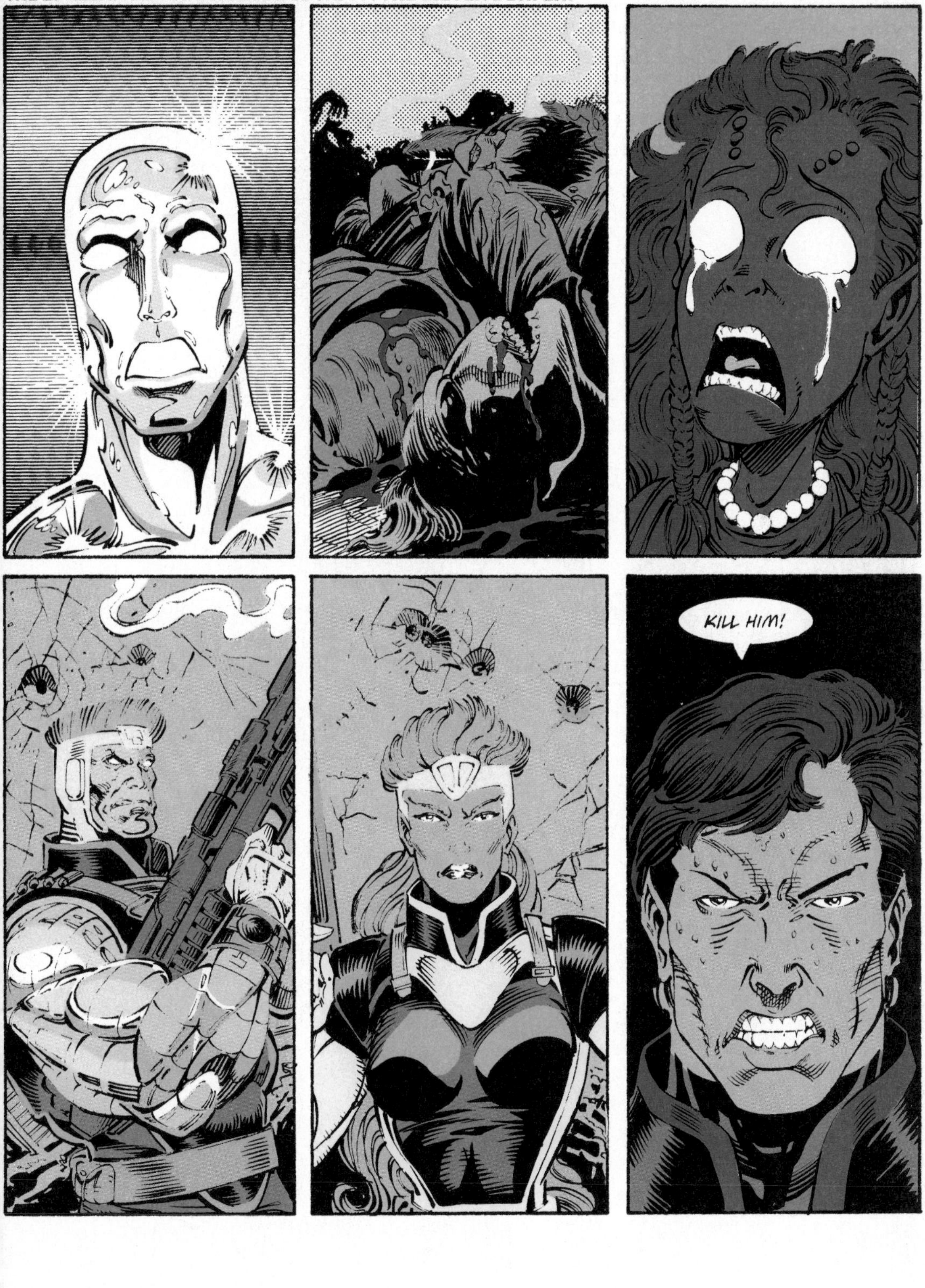
KILL HIM!

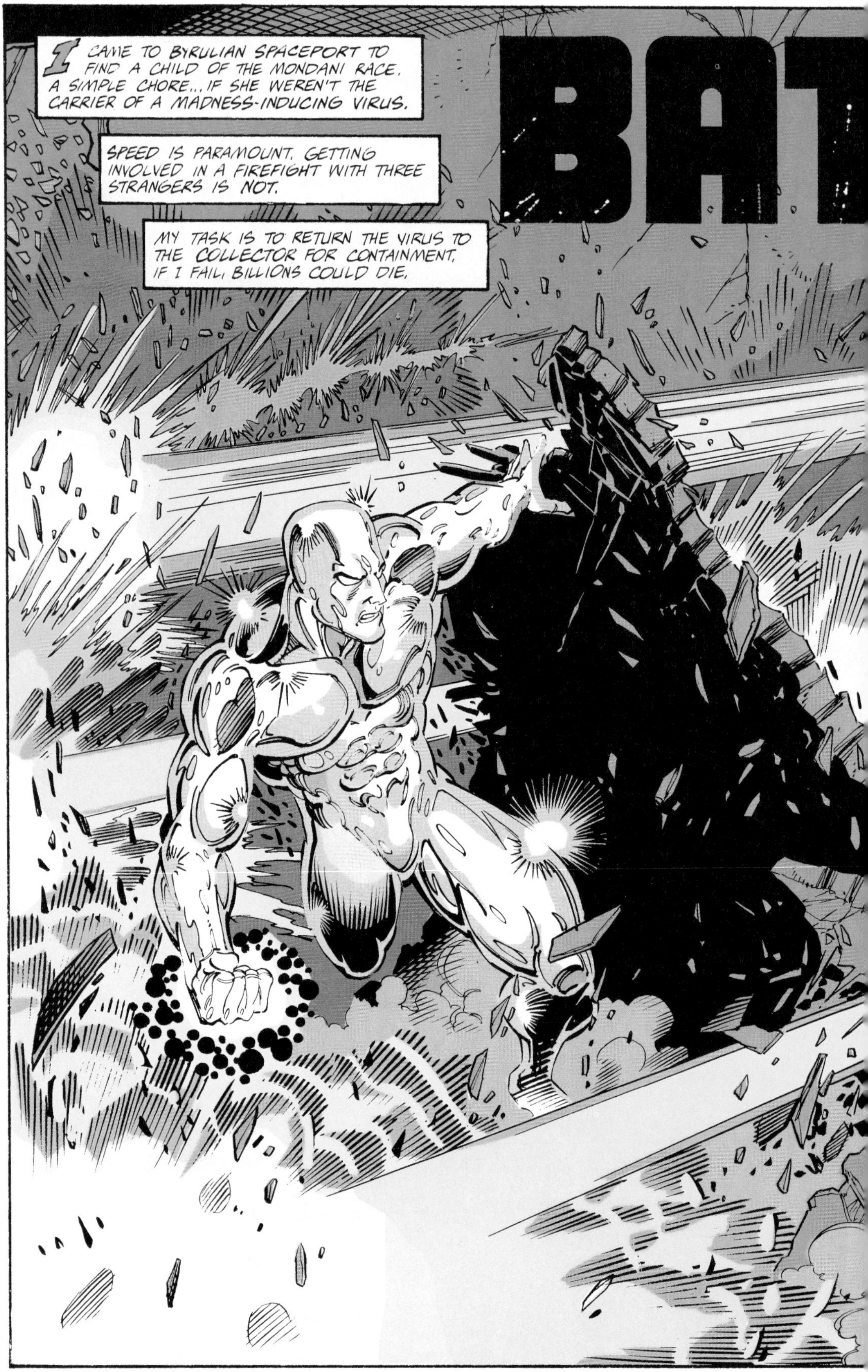
I CAME TO BYRULIAN SPACEPORT TO FIND A CHILD OF THE MONDANI RACE. A SIMPLE CHORE... IF SHE WEREN'T THE CARRIER OF A MADNESS-INDUCING VIRUS.
SPEED IS PARAMOUNT. GETTING INVOLVED IN A FIREFIGHT WITH THREE STRANGERS IS NOT.
MY TASK IS TO RETURN THE VIRUS TO THE COLLECTOR FOR CONTAINMENT. IF I FAIL, BILLIONS COULD DIE.
BAT

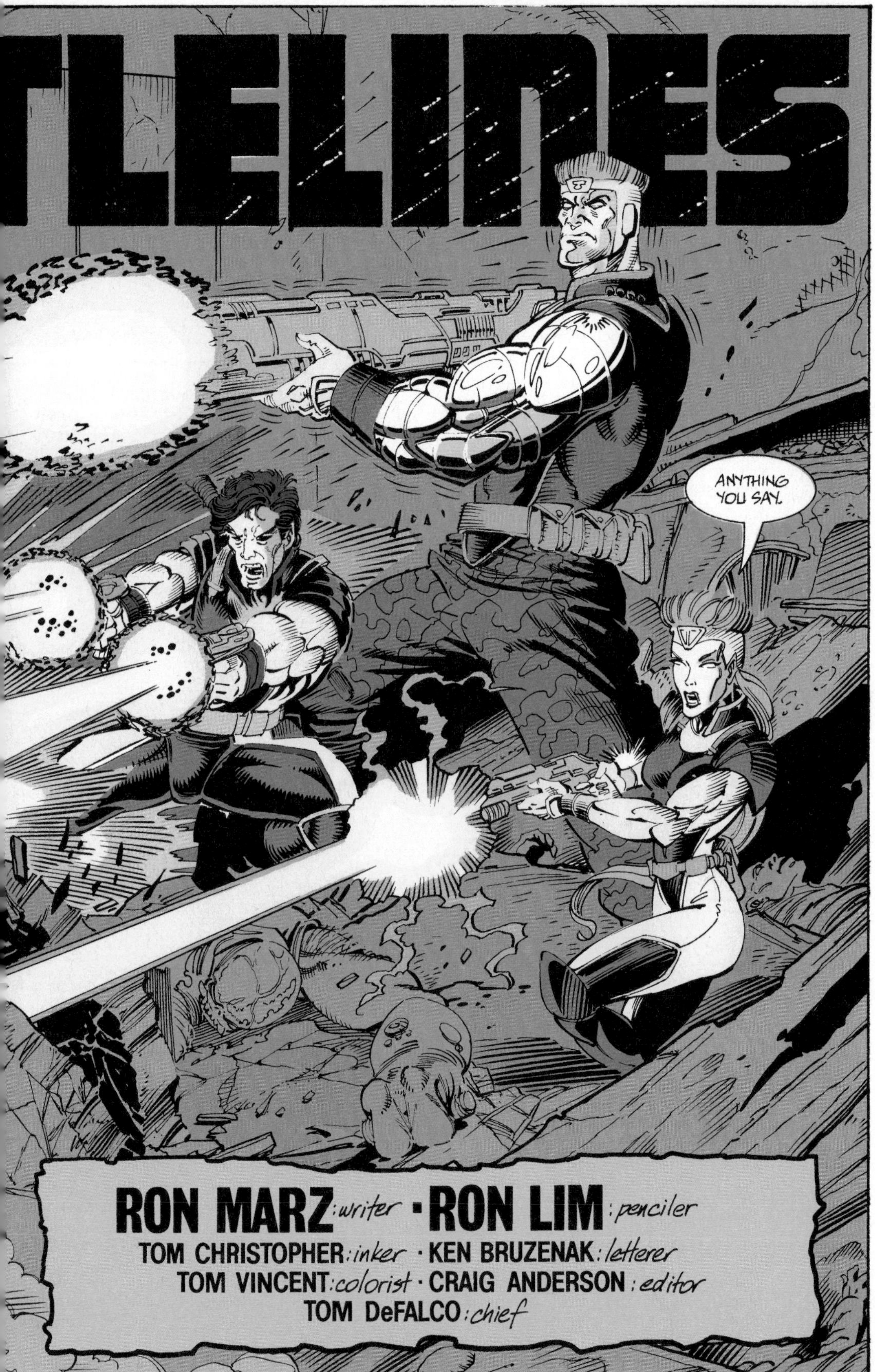
TLELINES
ANYTHING YOU SAY.
RON MARZ:writer · RON LIM:penciler
TOM CHRISTOPHER:inker · KEN BRUZENAK:letterer
TOM VINCENT:colorist · CRAIG ANDERSON:editor
TOM DeFALCO:chief

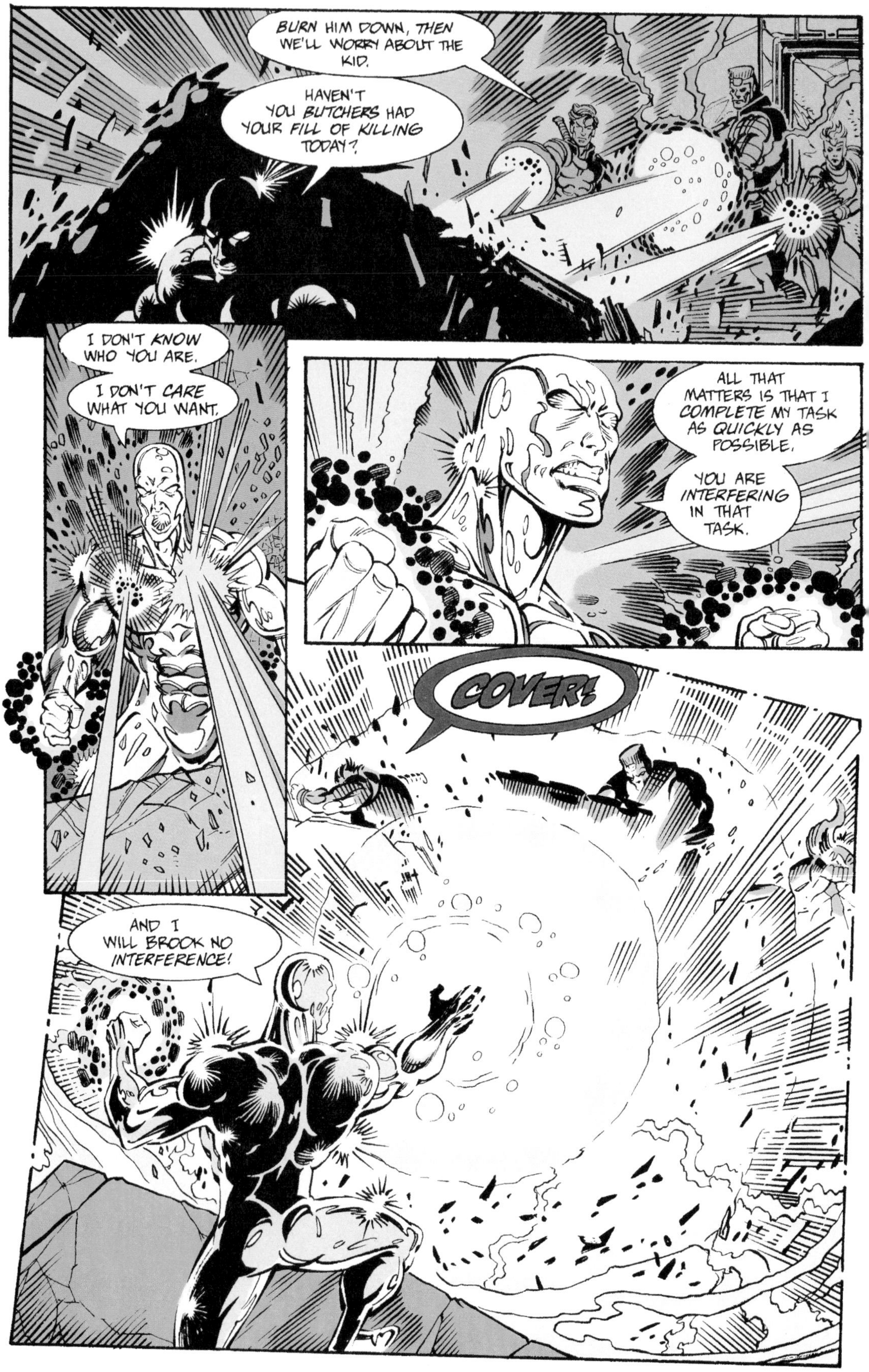
BURN HIM DOWN, THEN WE'LL WORRY ABOUT THE KID.
HAVEN'T YOU BUTCHERS HAD YOUR FILL OF KILLING TODAY?
I DON'T KNOW WHO YOU ARE.
I DON'T CARE WHAT YOU WANT.
ALL THAT MATTERS IS THAT I COMPLETE MY TASK AS QUICKLY AS POSSIBLE.
YOU ARE INTERFERING IN THAT TASK.
COVER!
AND I WILL BROOK NO INTERFERENCE!

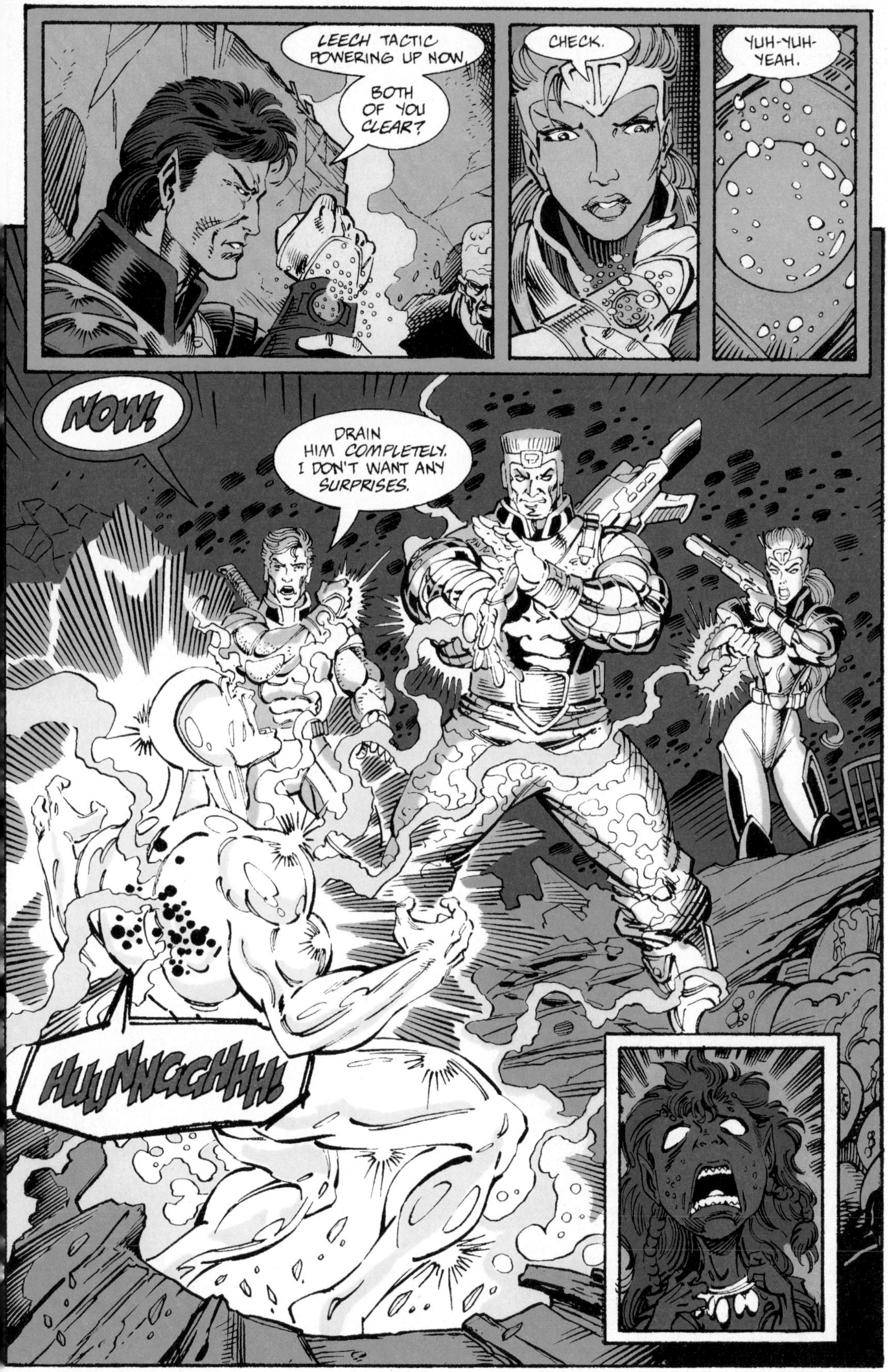
LEECH TACTIC POWERING UP NOW.
BOTH OF YOU CLEAR?
CHECK.
YUH-YUH-YEAH.
NOW!
DRAIN HIM COMPLETELY. I DON'T WANT ANY SURPRISES.
HUUNNGGHHH!

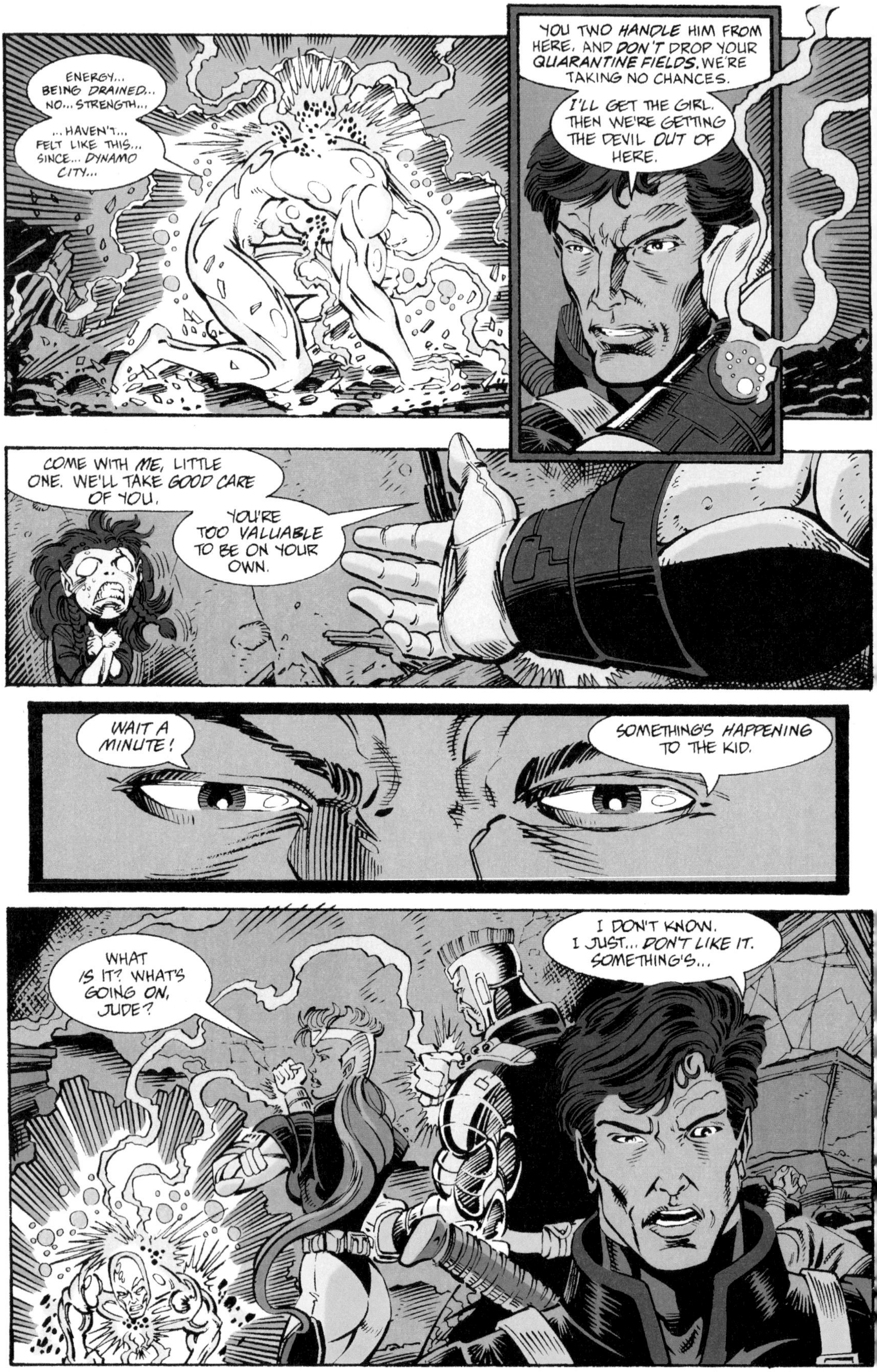
ENERGY... BEING DRAINED... NO... STRENGTH...
...HAVEN'T... FELT LIKE THIS... SINCE... DYNAMO CITY...
YOU TWO HANDLE HIM FROM HERE. AND DON'T DROP YOUR QUARANTINE FIELDS. WE'RE TAKING NO CHANCES.
I'LL GET THE GIRL. THEN WE'RE GETTING THE DEVIL OUT OF HERE.
COME WITH ME, LITTLE ONE. WE'LL TAKE GOOD CARE OF YOU.
YOU'RE TOO VALUABLE TO BE ON YOUR OWN.
WAIT A MINUTE!
SOMETHING'S HAPPENING TO THE KID.
WHAT IS IT? WHAT'S GOING ON, JUDE?
I DON'T KNOW. I JUST... DON'T LIKE IT. SOMETHING'S...

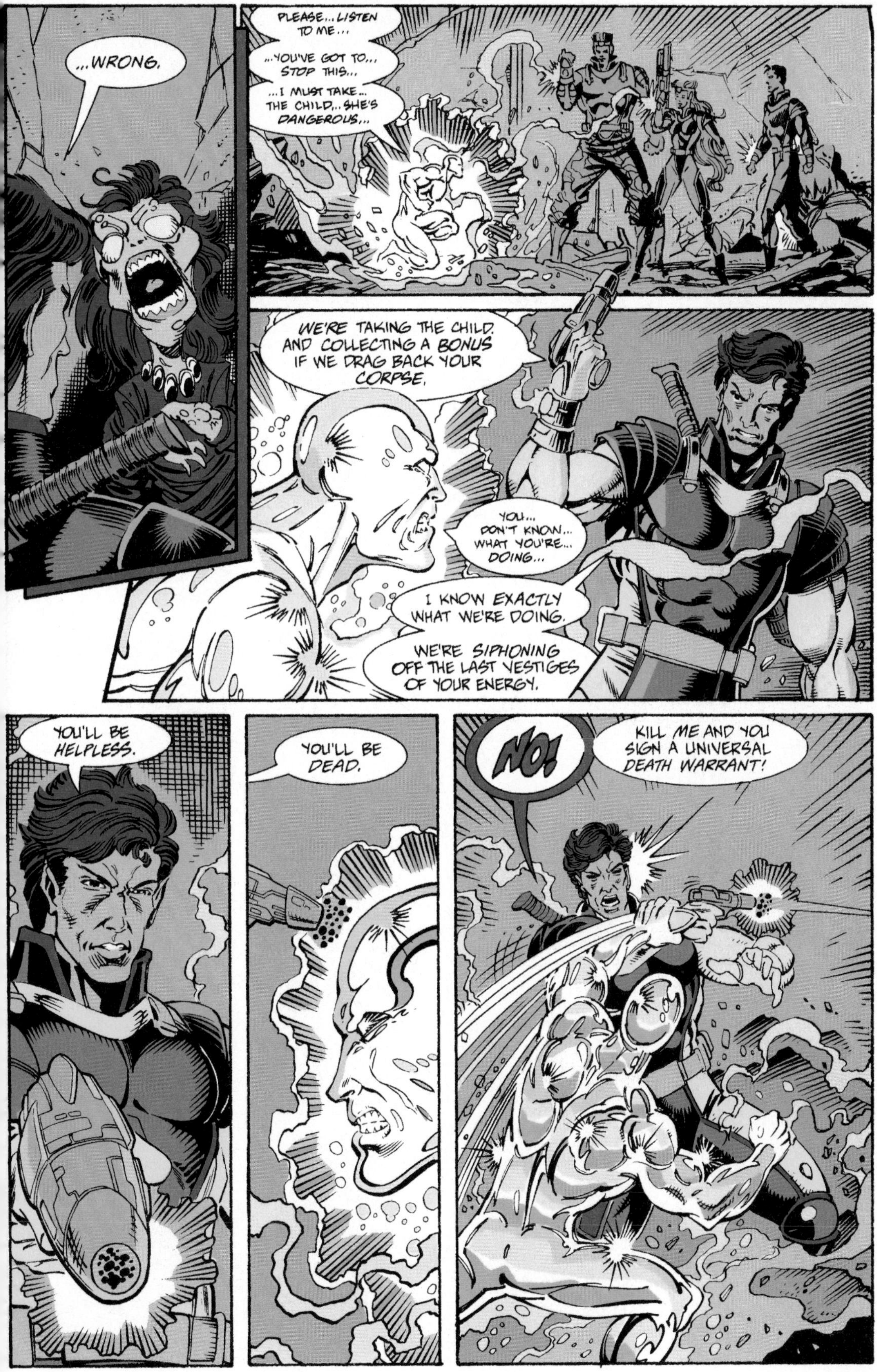
...WRONG.
PLEASE... LISTEN TO ME...
...YOU'VE GOT TO... STOP THIS...
...I MUST TAKE... THE CHILD... SHE'S DANGEROUS...
WE'RE TAKING THE CHILD. AND COLLECTING A BONUS IF WE DRAG BACK YOUR CORPSE.
YOU... DON'T KNOW... WHAT YOU'RE... DOING...
I KNOW EXACTLY WHAT WE'RE DOING.
WE'RE SIPHONING OFF THE LAST VESTIGES OF YOUR ENERGY.
YOU'LL BE HELPLESS.
YOU'LL BE DEAD.
NO!
KILL ME AND YOU SIGN A UNIVERSAL DEATH WARRANT!

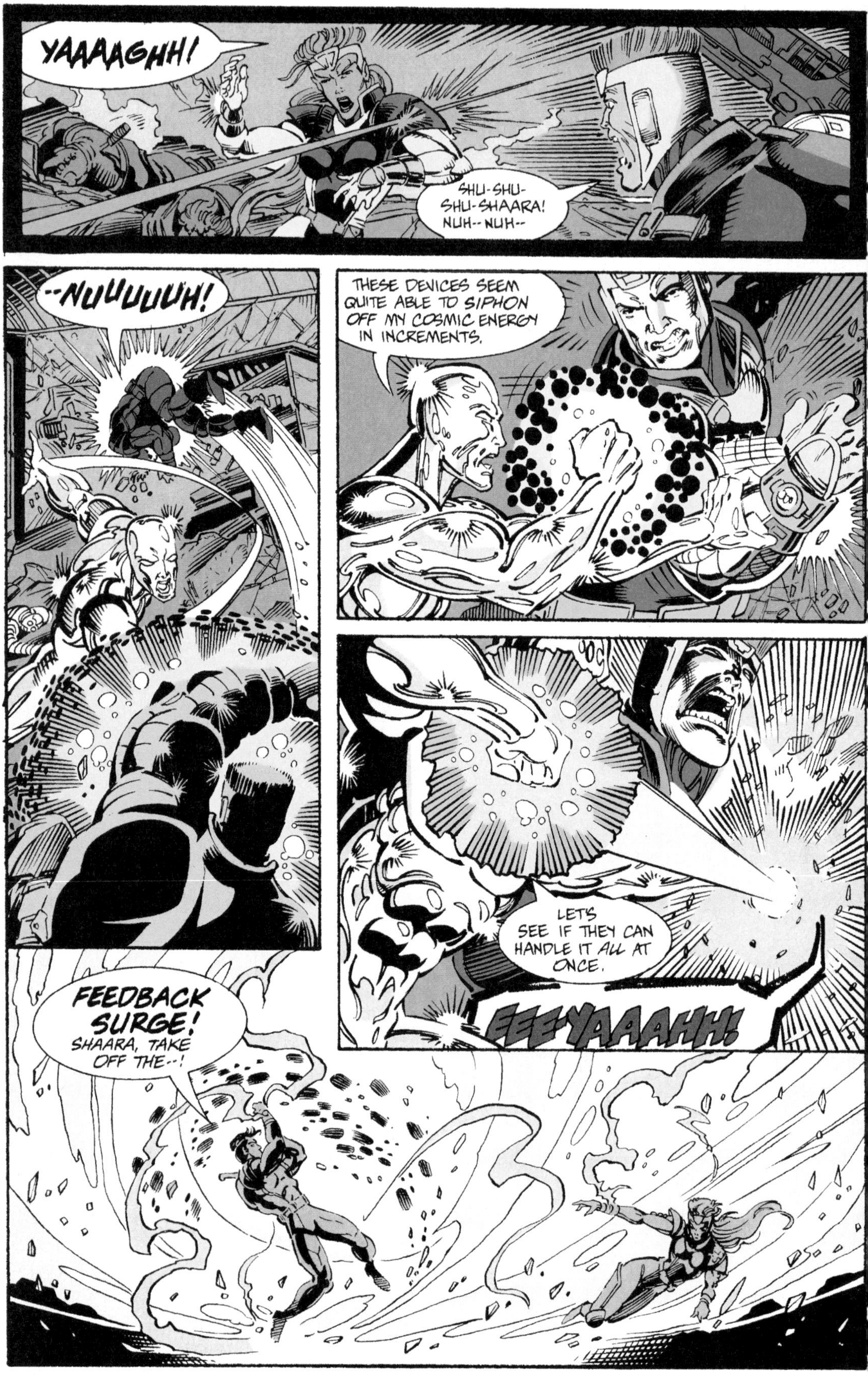
YAAAAGHH!
SHU-SHU-SHU-SHAARA! NUH-- NUH--
--NUUUUUH!
THESE DEVICES SEEM QUITE ABLE TO SIPHON OFF MY COSMIC ENERGY IN INCREMENTS.
LET'S SEE IF THEY CAN HANDLE IT ALL AT ONCE.
EEEYAAAHH!
FEEDBACK SURGE! SHAARA, TAKE OFF THE--!

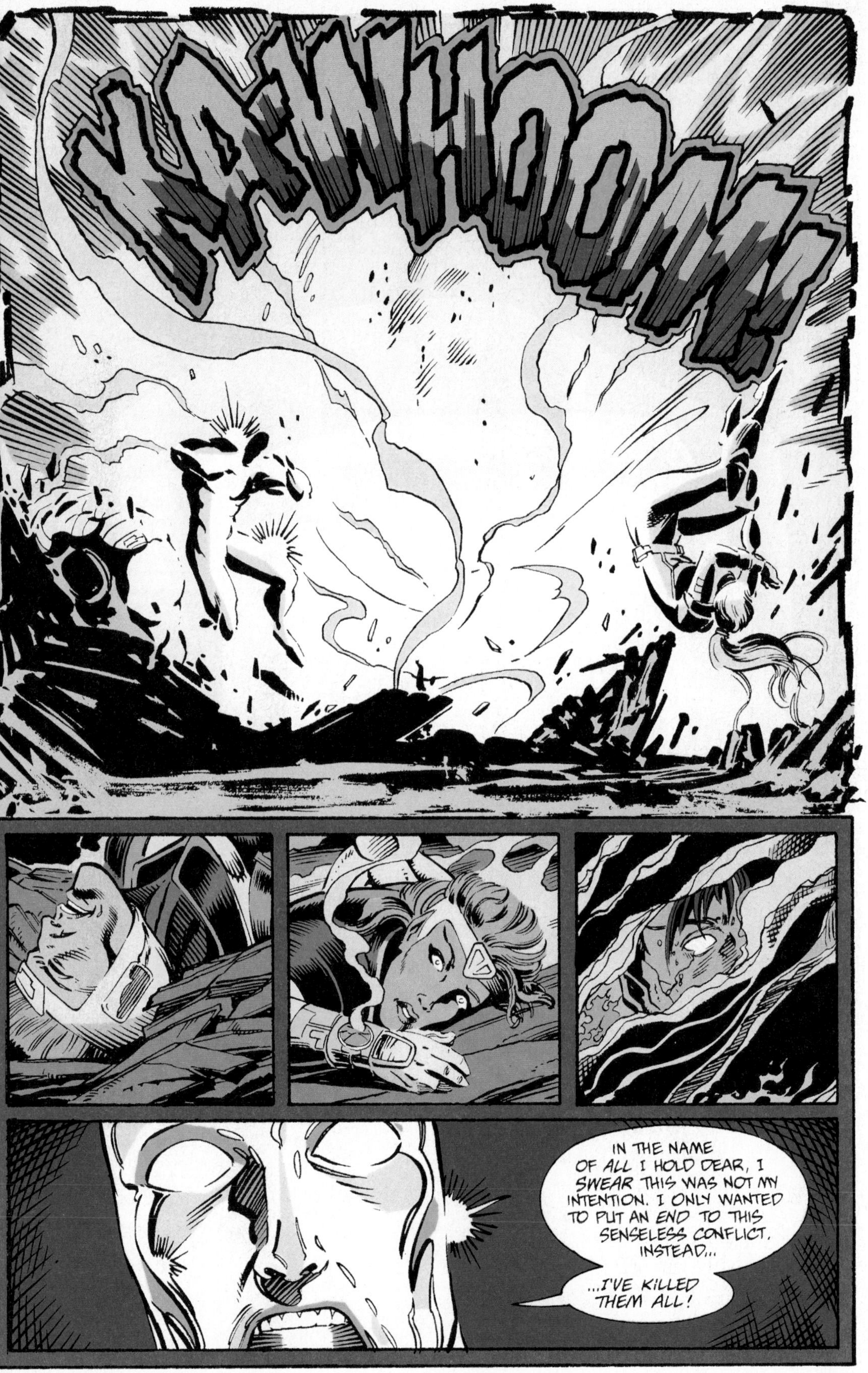
KA-WHOOM!
IN THE NAME OF ALL I HOLD DEAR, I SWEAR THIS WAS NOT MY INTENTION. I ONLY WANTED TO PUT AN END TO THIS SENSELESS CONFLICT. INSTEAD...
...I'VE KILLED THEM ALL!

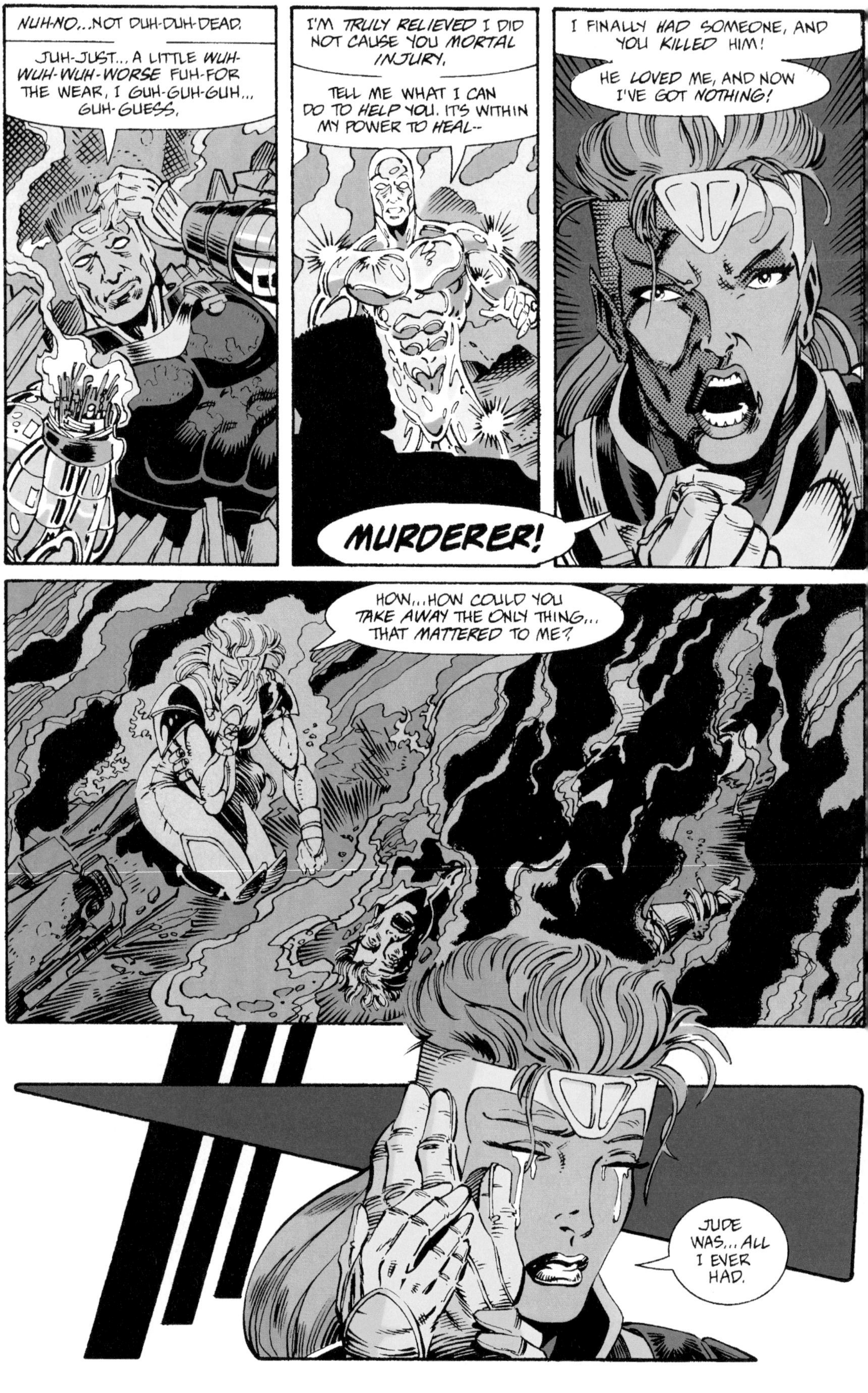
NUH-NO... NOT DUH-DUH-DEAD.
JUH-JUST... A LITTLE WUH-WUH-WUH-WORSE FUH-FOR THE WEAR, I GUH-GUH-GUH... GUH-GUESS.
I'M TRULY RELIEVED I DID NOT CAUSE YOU MORTAL INJURY.
TELL ME WHAT I CAN DO TO HELP YOU. IT'S WITHIN MY POWER TO HEAL--
I FINALLY HAD SOMEONE, AND YOU KILLED HIM!
HE LOVED ME, AND NOW I'VE GOT NOTHING!
MURDERER!
HOW... HOW COULD YOU TAKE AWAY THE ONLY THING... THAT MATTERED TO ME?
JUDE WAS... ALL I EVER HAD.

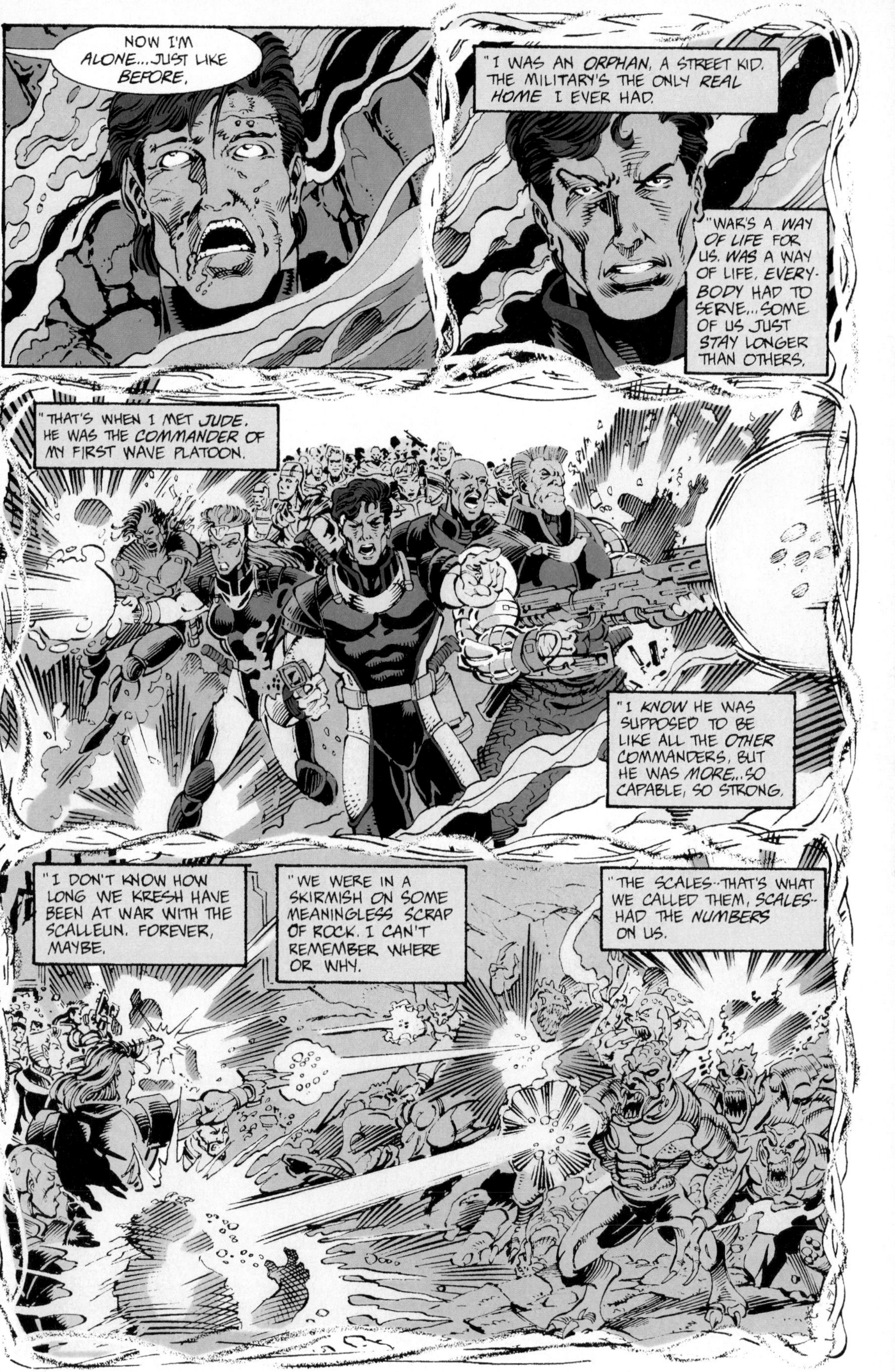
NOW I'M ALONE... JUST LIKE BEFORE.
"I WAS AN ORPHAN, A STREET KID. THE MILITARY'S THE ONLY REAL HOME I EVER HAD.
"WAR'S A WAY OF LIFE FOR US. WAS A WAY OF LIFE. EVERYBODY HAD TO SERVE... SOME OF US JUST STAY LONGER THAN OTHERS.
"THAT'S WHEN I MET JUDE. HE WAS THE COMMANDER OF MY FIRST WAVE PLATOON.
"I KNOW HE WAS SUPPOSED TO BE LIKE ALL THE OTHER COMMANDERS, BUT HE WAS MORE... SO CAPABLE, SO STRONG.
"I DON'T KNOW HOW LONG WE KRESH HAVE BEEN AT WAR WITH THE SCALLEUN. FOREVER, MAYBE.
"WE WERE IN A SKIRMISH ON SOME MEANINGLESS SCRAP OF ROCK. I CAN'T REMEMBER WHERE OR WHY.
"THE SCALES--THAT'S WHAT WE CALLED THEM, SCALES--HAD THE NUMBERS ON US.

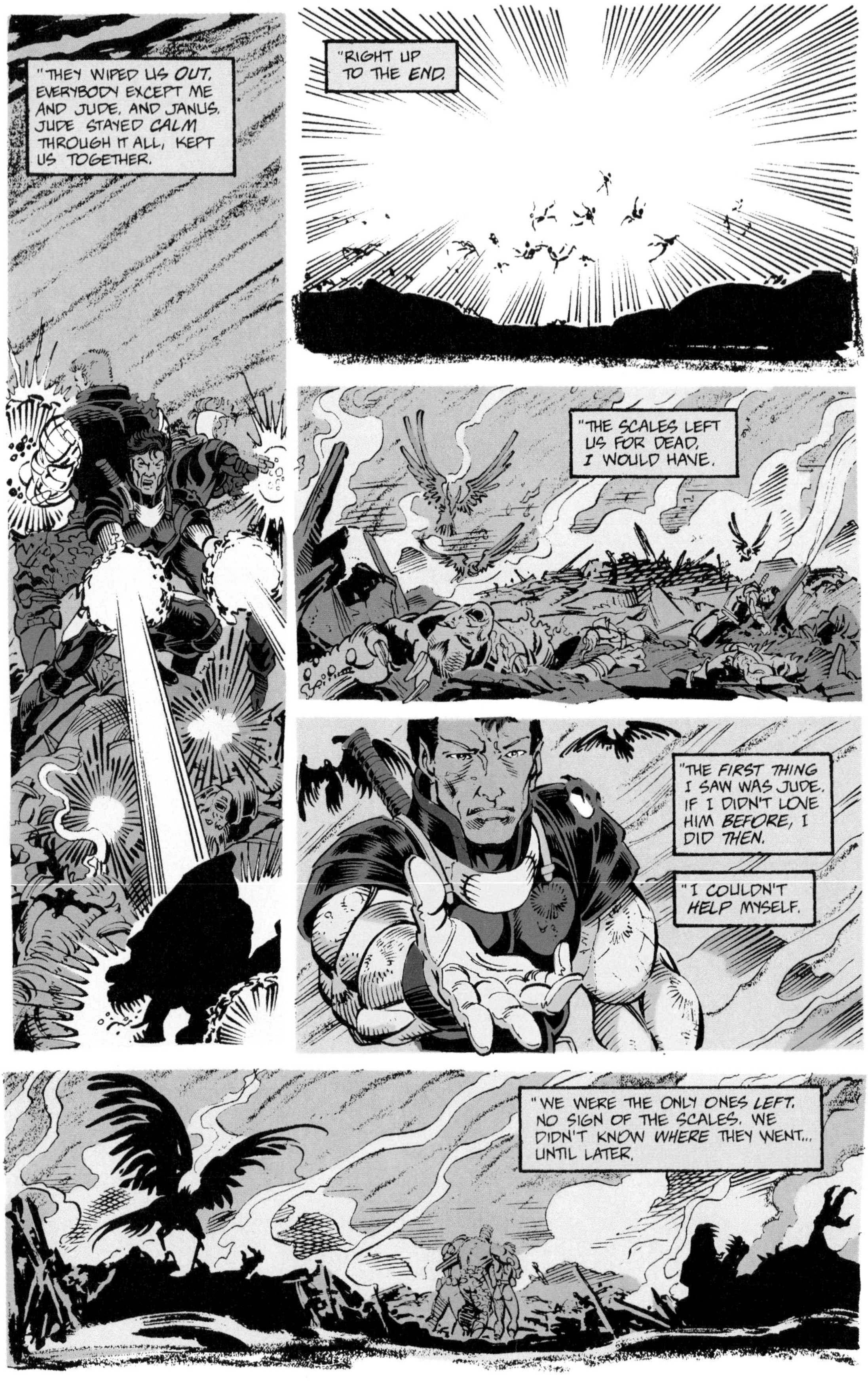
"THEY WIPED US OUT. EVERYBODY EXCEPT ME AND JUDE. AND JANUS. JUDE STAYED CALM THROUGH IT ALL, KEPT US TOGETHER.
"RIGHT UP TO THE END.
"THE SCALES LEFT US FOR DEAD. I WOULD HAVE.
"THE FIRST THING I SAW WAS JUDE. IF I DIDN'T LOVE HIM BEFORE, I DID THEN.
"I COULDN'T HELP MYSELF.
"WE WERE THE ONLY ONES LEFT. NO SIGN OF THE SCALES. WE DIDN'T KNOW WHERE THEY WENT... UNTIL LATER.

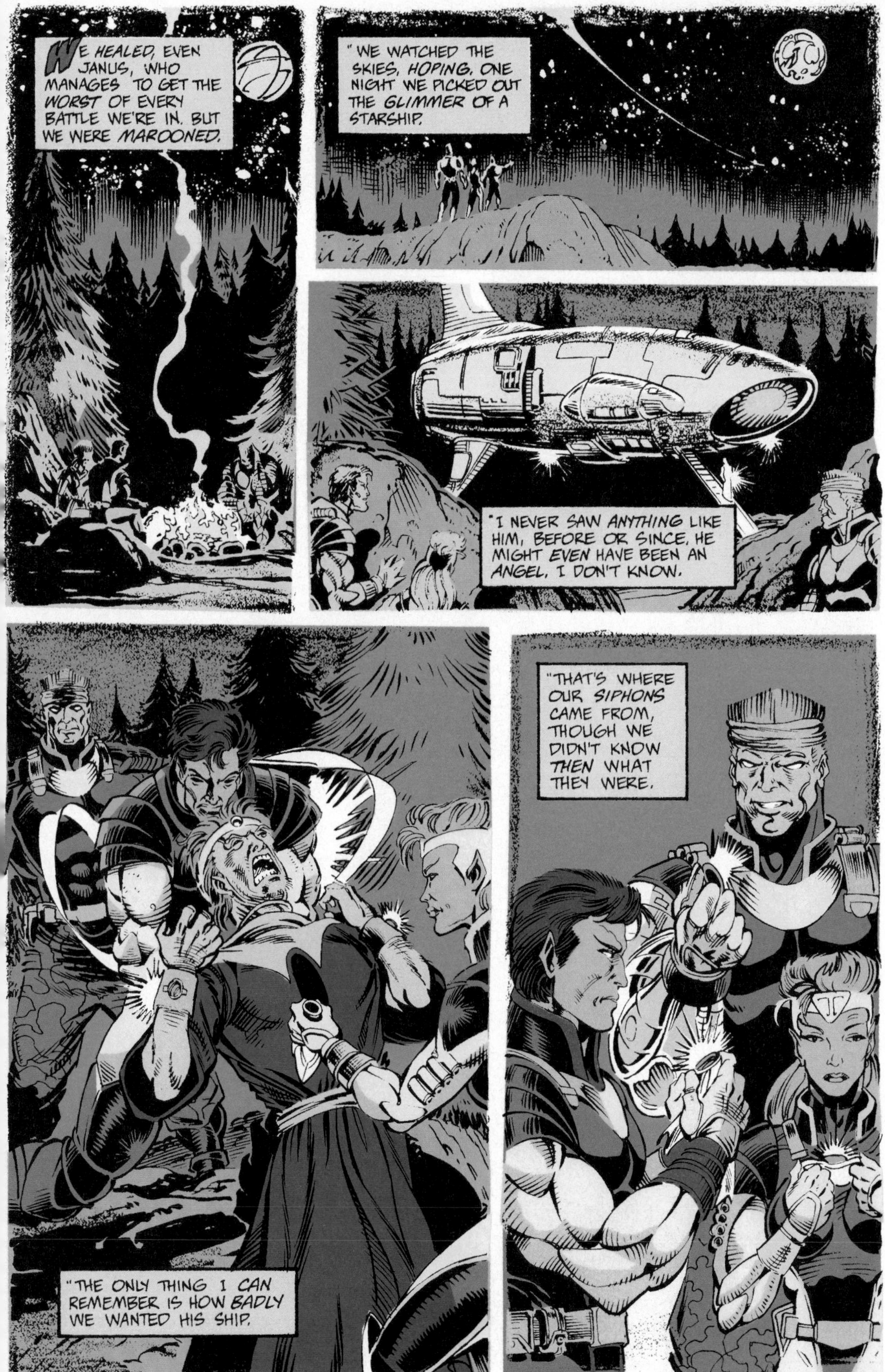
WE HEALED, EVEN JANUS, WHO MANAGES TO GET THE WORST OF EVERY BATTLE WE'RE IN. BUT WE WERE MAROONED.
"WE WATCHED THE SKIES, HOPING. ONE NIGHT WE PICKED OUT THE GLIMMER OF A STARSHIP.
"I NEVER SAW ANYTHING LIKE HIM, BEFORE OR SINCE. HE MIGHT EVEN HAVE BEEN AN ANGEL, I DON'T KNOW.
"THE ONLY THING I CAN REMEMBER IS HOW BADLY WE WANTED HIS SHIP.
"THAT'S WHERE OUR SIPHONS CAME FROM, THOUGH WE DIDN'T KNOW THEN WHAT THEY WERE.

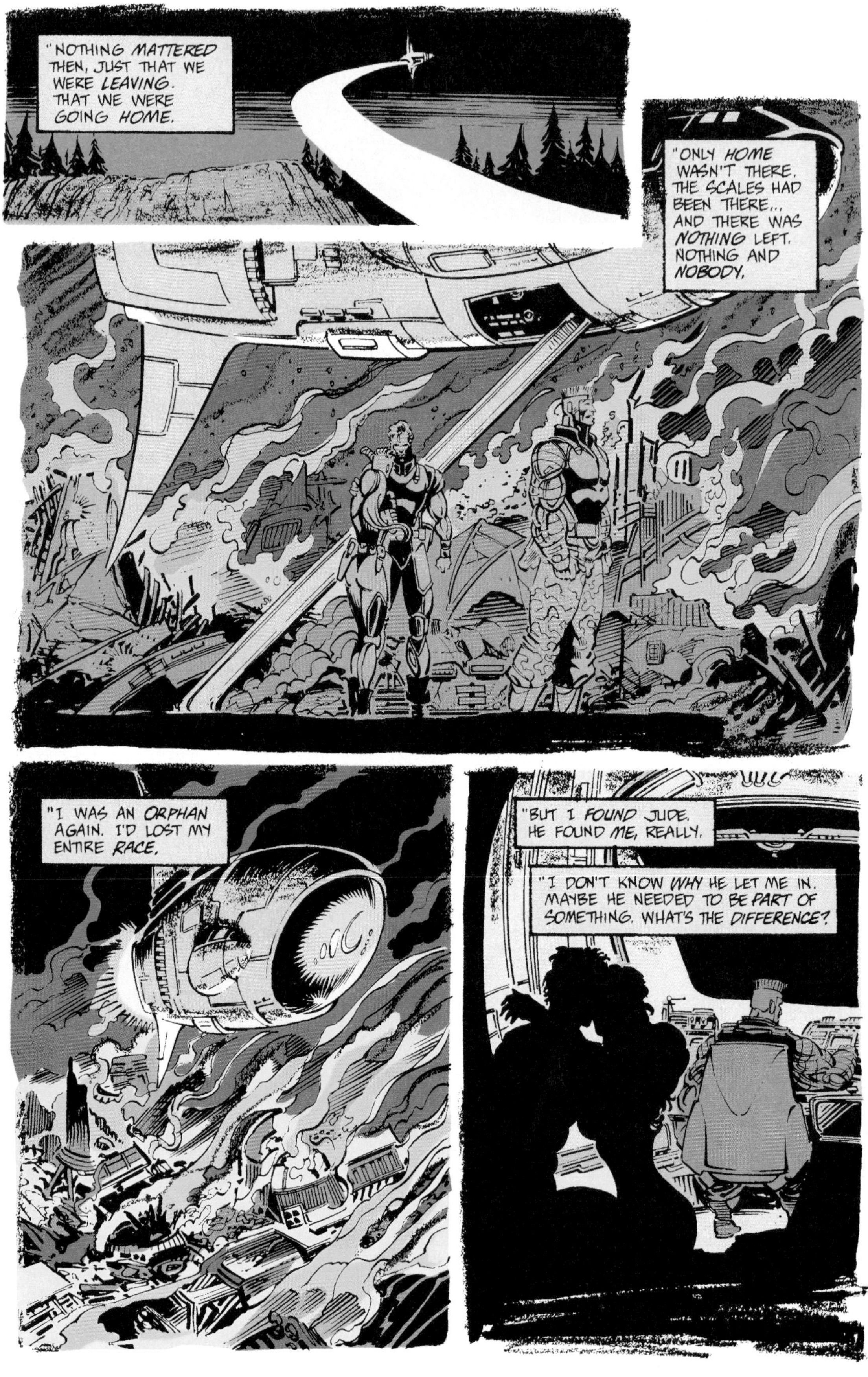
"NOTHING MATTERED THEN, JUST THAT WE WERE LEAVING. THAT WE WERE GOING HOME.
"ONLY HOME WASN'T THERE. THE SCALES HAD BEEN THERE... AND THERE WAS NOTHING LEFT. NOTHING AND NOBODY.
"I WAS AN ORPHAN AGAIN. I'D LOST MY ENTIRE RACE.
"BUT I FOUND JUDE. HE FOUND ME, REALLY.
"I DON'T KNOW WHY HE LET ME IN. MAYBE HE NEEDED TO BE PART OF SOMETHING. WHAT'S THE DIFFERENCE?

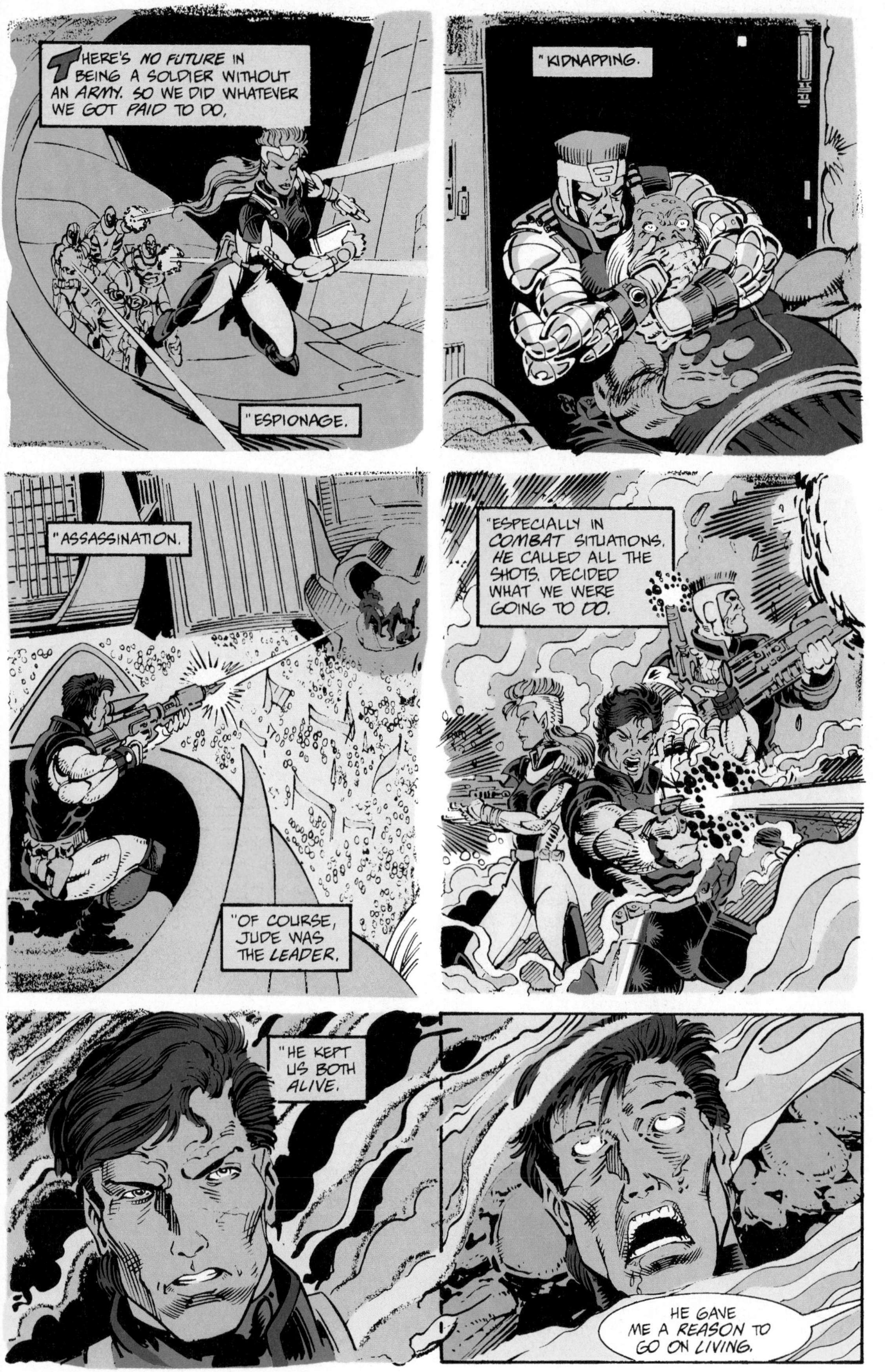
THERE'S NO FUTURE IN BEING A SOLDIER WITHOUT AN ARMY. SO WE DID WHATEVER WE GOT PAID TO DO,
"ESPIONAGE.
"KIDNAPPING.
"ASSASSINATION.
"OF COURSE, JUDE WAS THE LEADER.
"ESPECIALLY IN COMBAT SITUATIONS. HE CALLED ALL THE SHOTS. DECIDED WHAT WE WERE GOING TO DO.
"HE KEPT US BOTH ALIVE.
HE GAVE ME A REASON TO GO ON LIVING.

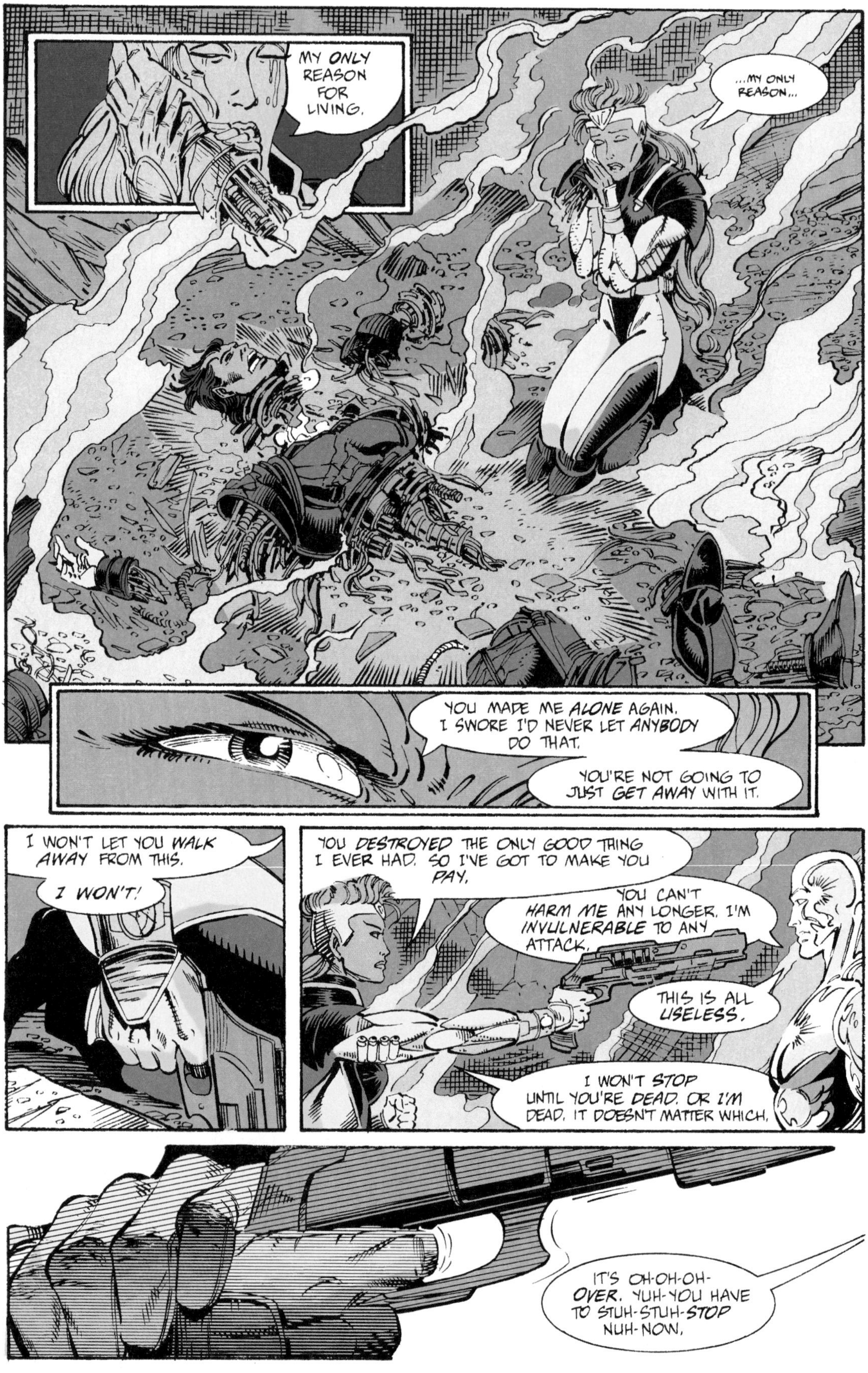
MY ONLY REASON FOR LIVING.
...MY ONLY REASON...
YOU MADE ME ALONE AGAIN. I SWORE I'D NEVER LET ANYBODY DO THAT.
YOU'RE NOT GOING TO JUST GET AWAY WITH IT.
I WON'T LET YOU WALK AWAY FROM THIS.
I WON'T!
YOU DESTROYED THE ONLY GOOD THING I EVER HAD. SO I'VE GOT TO MAKE YOU PAY.
YOU CAN'T HARM ME ANY LONGER. I'M INVULNERABLE TO ANY ATTACK.
THIS IS ALL USELESS.
I WON'T STOP UNTIL YOU'RE DEAD. OR I'M DEAD. IT DOESN'T MATTER WHICH.
IT'S OH-OH-OH-OVER. YUH-YOU HAVE TO STUH-STUH-STOP NUH-NOW.

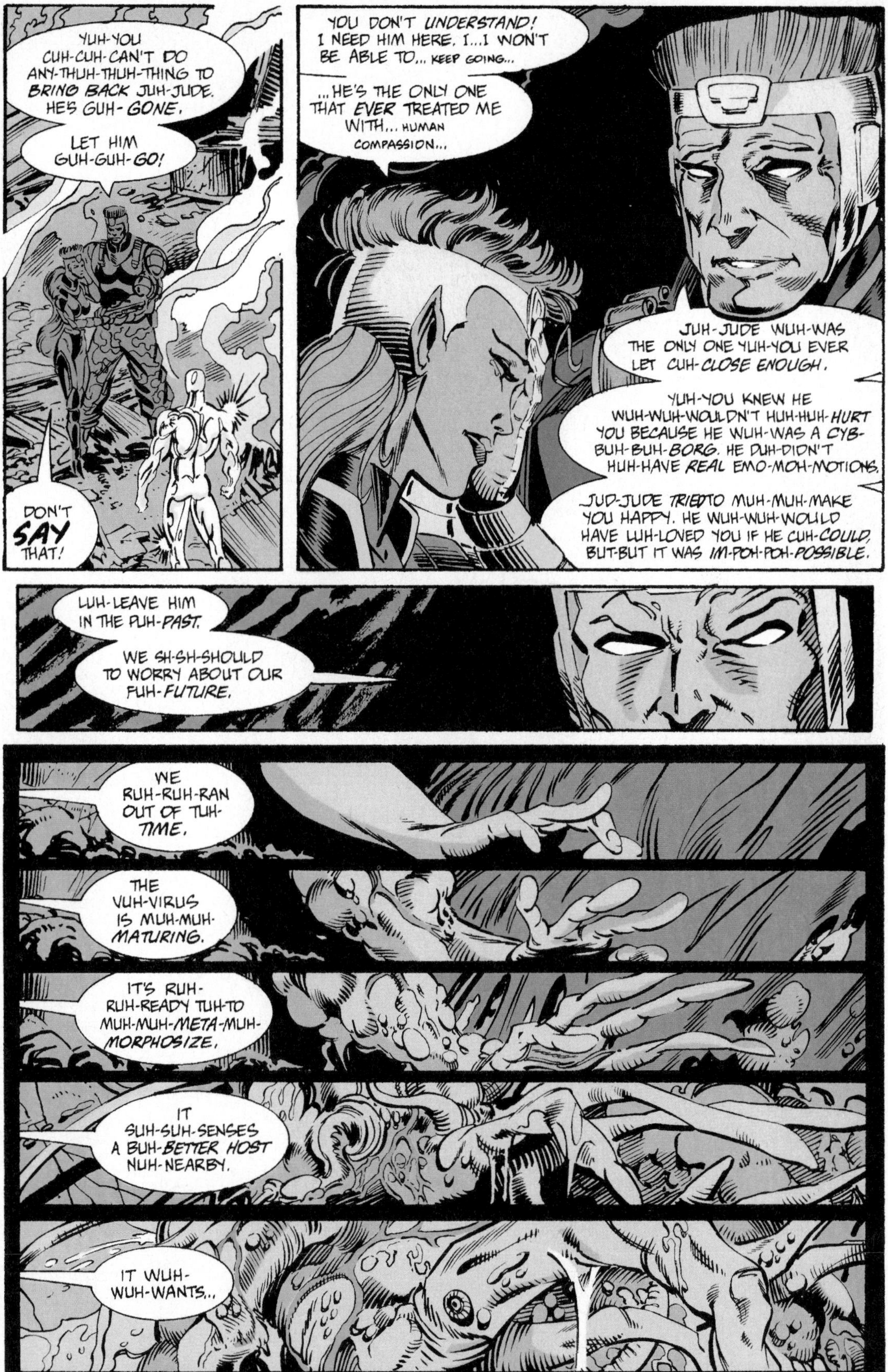

YUH-YOU CUH-CUH-CAN'T DO ANY-THUH-THUH-THING TO BRING BACK JUH-JUDE. HE'S GUH-GONE.
LET HIM GUH-GUH-GO!
DON'T SAY THAT!
YOU DON'T UNDERSTAND! I NEED HIM HERE. I...I WON'T BE ABLE TO... KEEP GOING...
...HE'S THE ONLY ONE THAT EVER TREATED ME WITH... HUMAN COMPASSION...
JUH-JUDE WUH-WAS THE ONLY ONE YUH-YOU EVER LET CUH-CLOSE ENOUGH.
YUH-YOU KNEW HE WUH-WUH-WOULDN'T HUH-HUH-HURT YOU BECAUSE HE WUH-WAS A CYB-BUH-BUH-BORG. HE DUH-DIDN'T HUH-HAVE REAL EMO-MOH-MOTIONS.
JUD-JUDE TRIED TO MUH-MUH-MAKE YOU HAPPY. HE WUH-WUH-WOULD HAVE LUH-LOVED YOU IF HE CUH-COULD, BUT-BUT IT WAS IM-POH-POH-POSSIBLE.
LUH-LEAVE HIM IN THE PUH-PAST.
WE SH-SH-SHOULD TO WORRY ABOUT OUR FUH-FUTURE.
WE RUH-RUH-RAN OUT OF TUH-TIME.
THE VUH-VIRUS IS MUH-MUH-MATURING.
IT'S RUH-RUH-READY TUH-TO MUH-MUH-META-MUH-MORPHOSIZE.
IT SUH-SUH-SENSES A BUH-BETTER HOST NUH-NEARBY.
IT WUH-WUH-WANTS...

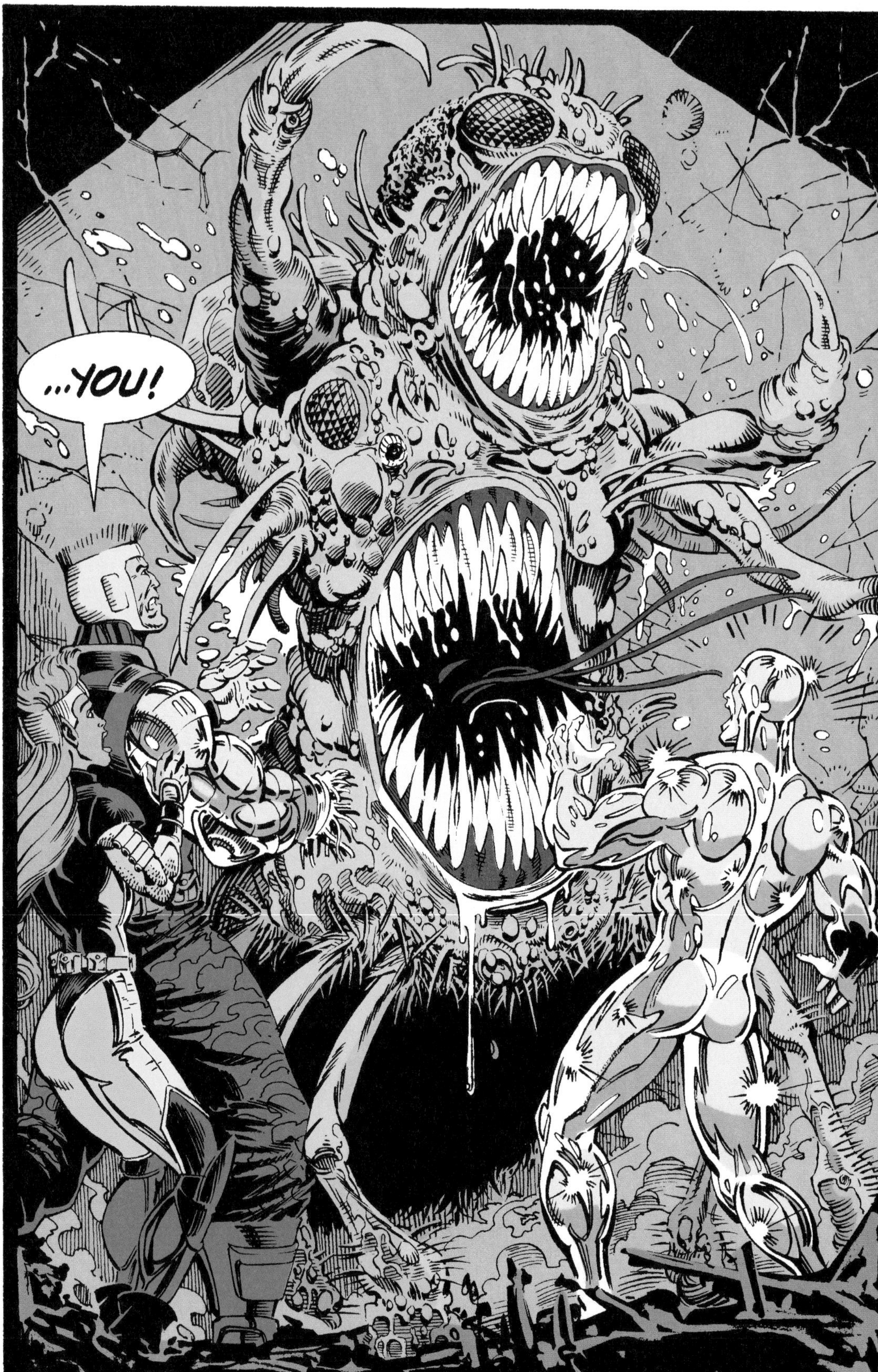
...YOU!

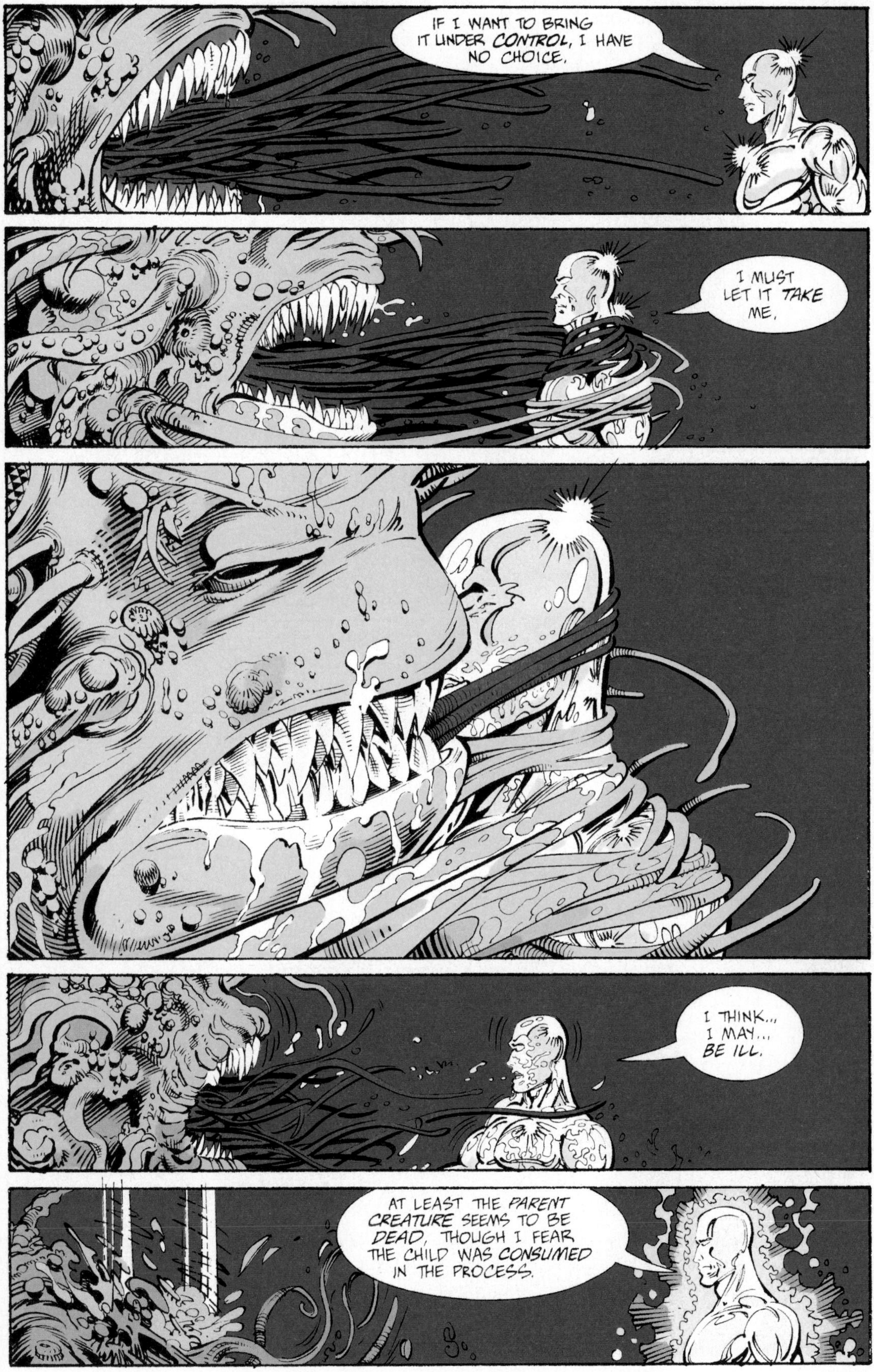
IF I WANT TO BRING IT UNDER CONTROL, I HAVE NO CHOICE.
I MUST LET IT TAKE ME.
I THINK... I MAY... BE ILL.
AT LEAST THE PARENT CREATURE SEEMS TO BE DEAD, THOUGH I FEAR THE CHILD WAS CONSUMED IN THE PROCESS.

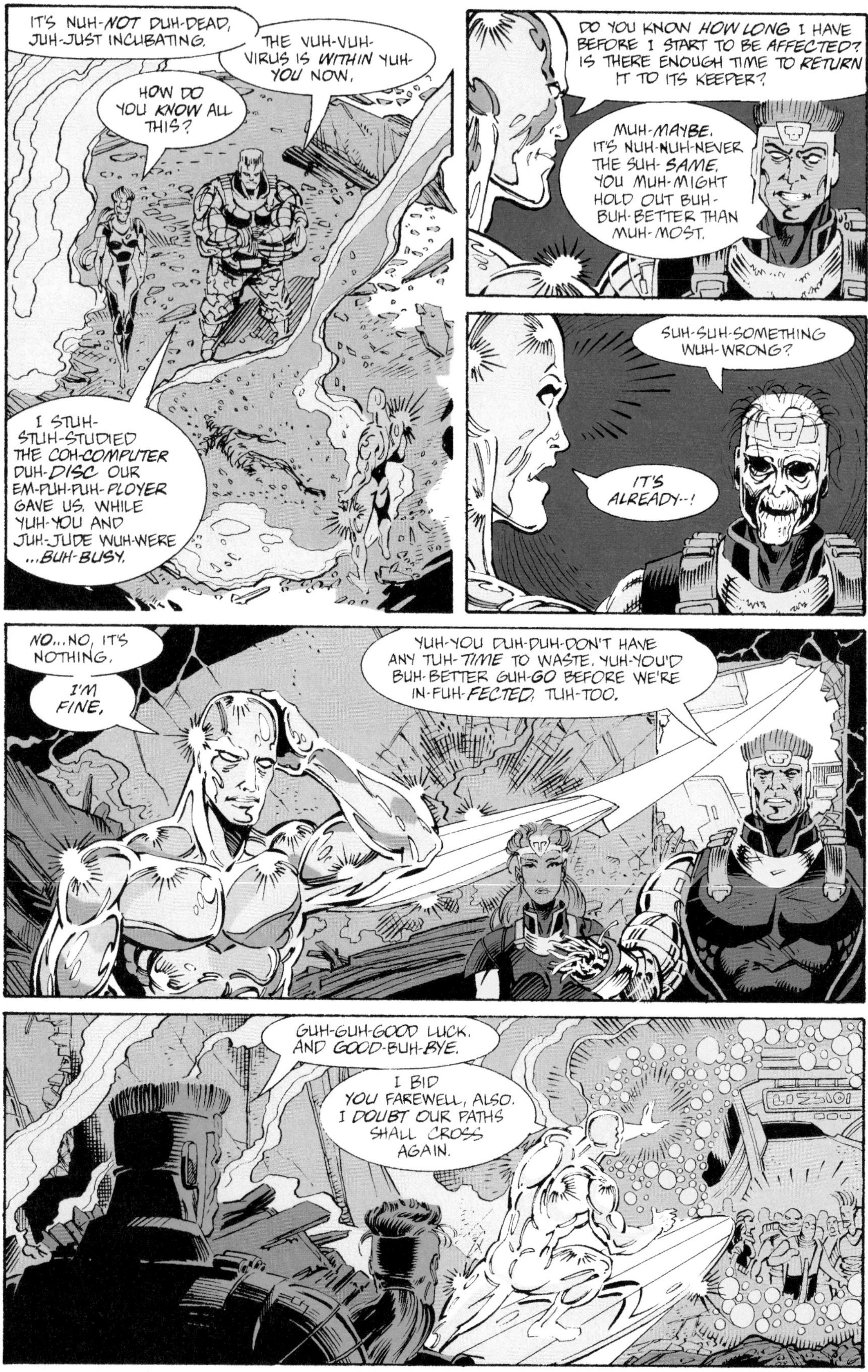

IT'S NUH-NOT DUH-DEAD, JUH-JUST INCUBATING.
THE VUH-VUH-VIRUS IS WITHIN YUH-YOU NOW.
HOW DO YOU KNOW ALL THIS?
I STUH-STUH-STUDIED THE COH-COMPUTER DUH-DISC OUR EM-PUH-PUH-PLOYER GAVE US. WHILE YUH-YOU AND JUH-JUDE WUH-WERE ...BUH-BUSY.
DO YOU KNOW HOW LONG I HAVE BEFORE I START TO BE AFFECTED? IS THERE ENOUGH TIME TO RETURN IT TO ITS KEEPER?
MUH-MAYBE. IT'S NUH-NUH-NEVER THE SUH-SAME. YOU MUH-MIGHT HOLD OUT BUH-BUH-BETTER THAN MUH-MOST.
SUH-SUH-SOMETHING WUH-WRONG?
IT'S ALREADY--!
NO...NO, IT'S NOTHING.
I'M FINE.
YUH-YOU DUH-DUH-DON'T HAVE ANY TUH-TIME TO WASTE. YUH-YOU'D BUH-BETTER GUH-GO BEFORE WE'RE IN-FUH-FECTED, TUH-TOO.
GUH-GUH-GOOD LUCK. AND GOOD-BUH-BYE.
I BID YOU FAREWELL, ALSO. I DOUBT OUR PATHS SHALL CROSS AGAIN.

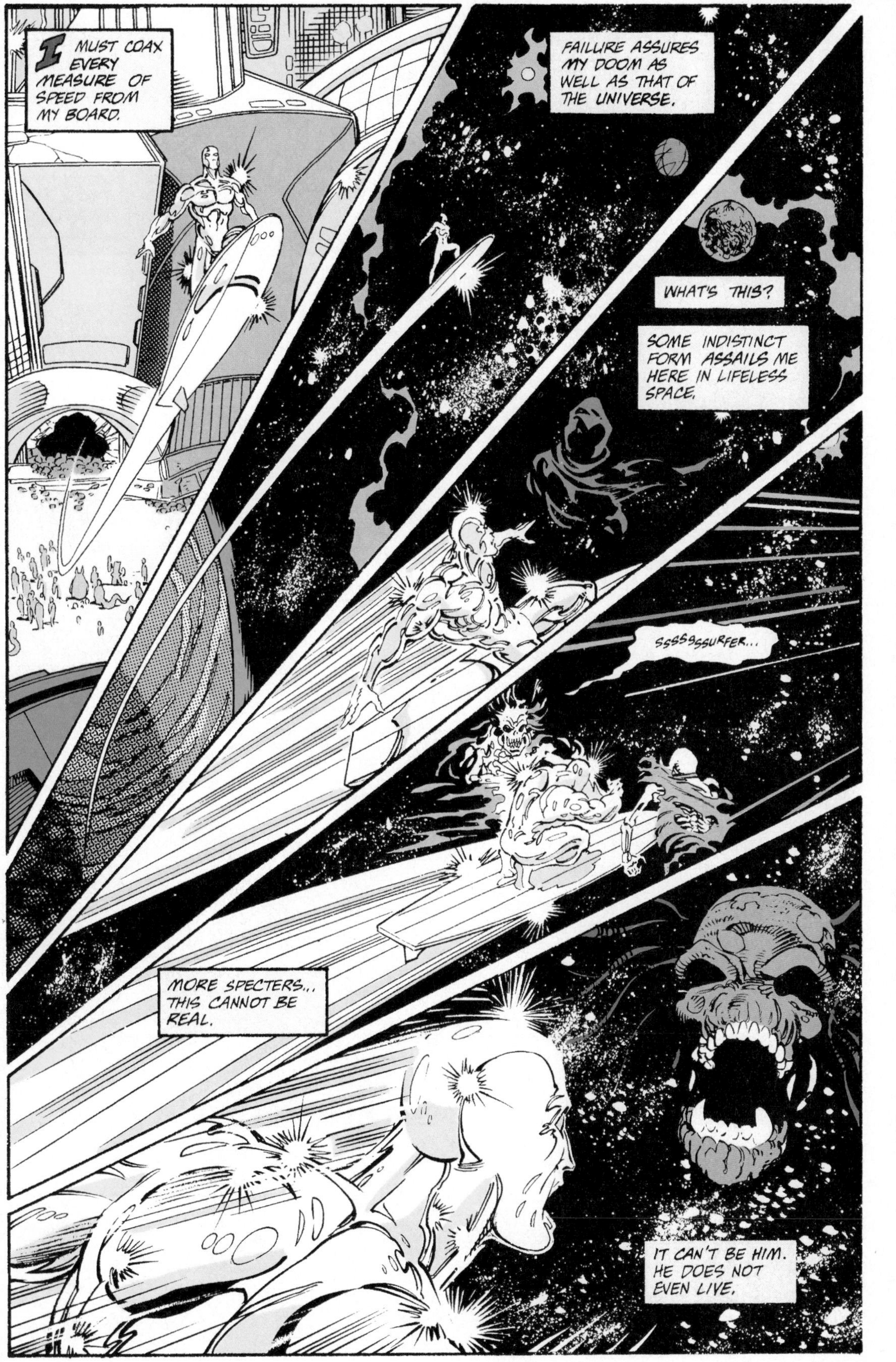

I MUST COAX EVERY MEASURE OF SPEED FROM MY BOARD.
FAILURE ASSURES MY DOOM AS WELL AS THAT OF THE UNIVERSE.
WHAT'S THIS?
SOME INDISTINCT FORM ASSAILS ME HERE IN LIFELESS SPACE.
SSSSSSSURFER...
MORE SPECTERS... THIS CANNOT BE REAL.
IT CAN'T BE HIM. HE DOES NOT EVEN LIVE.

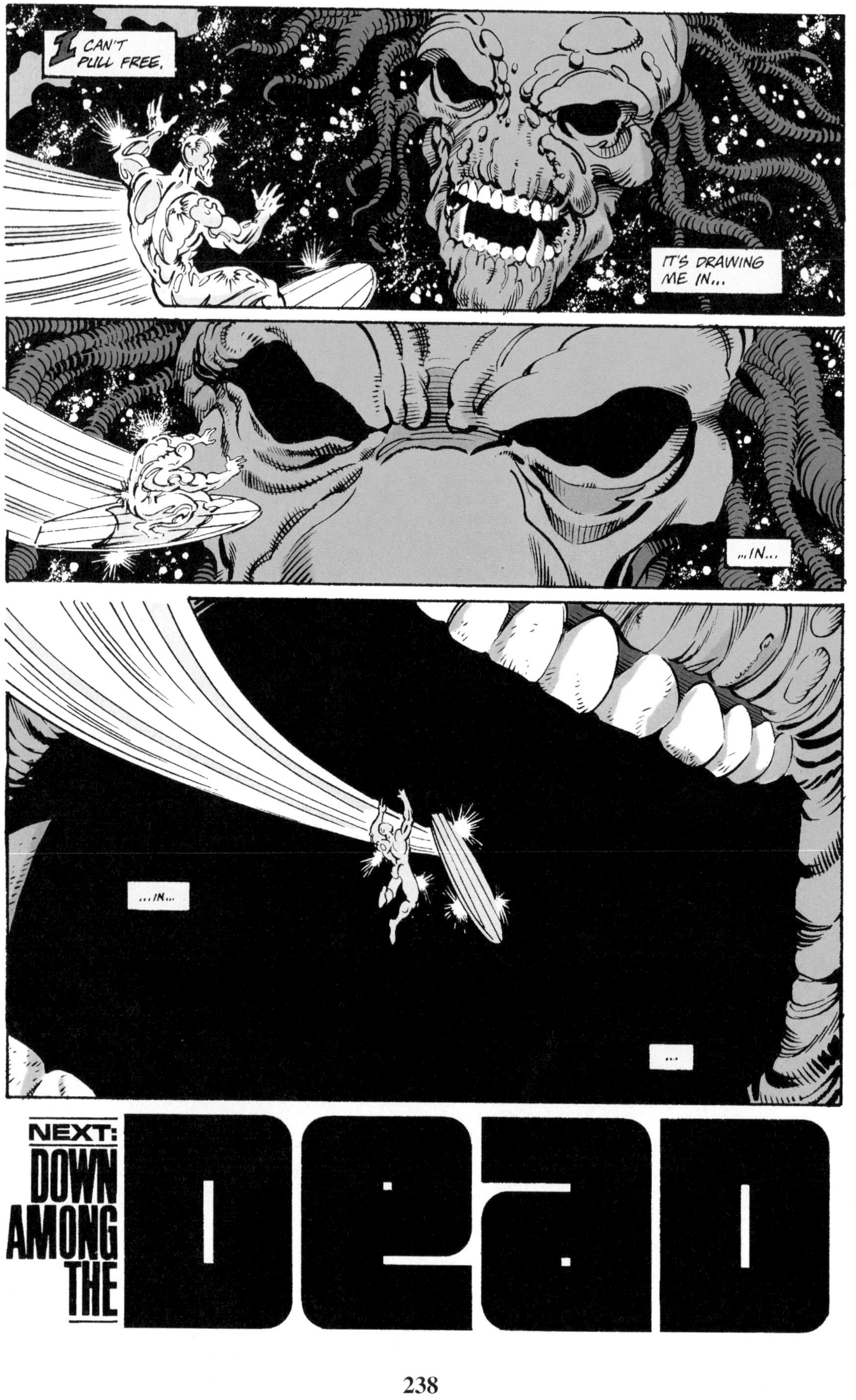
I CAN'T PULL FREE.
IT'S DRAWING ME IN...
...IN...
...IN...
...

NEXT: DOWN AMONG THE DEAD

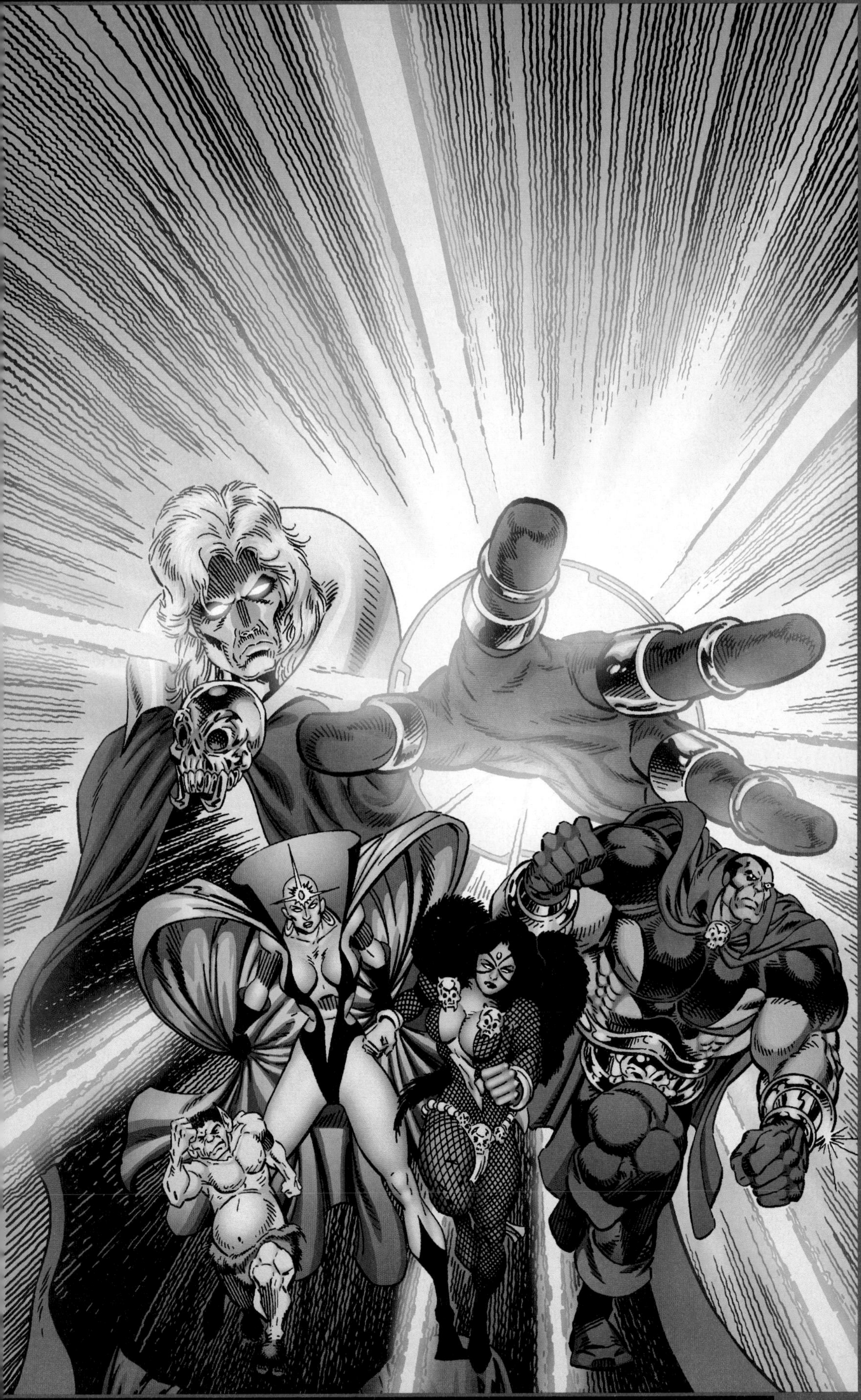

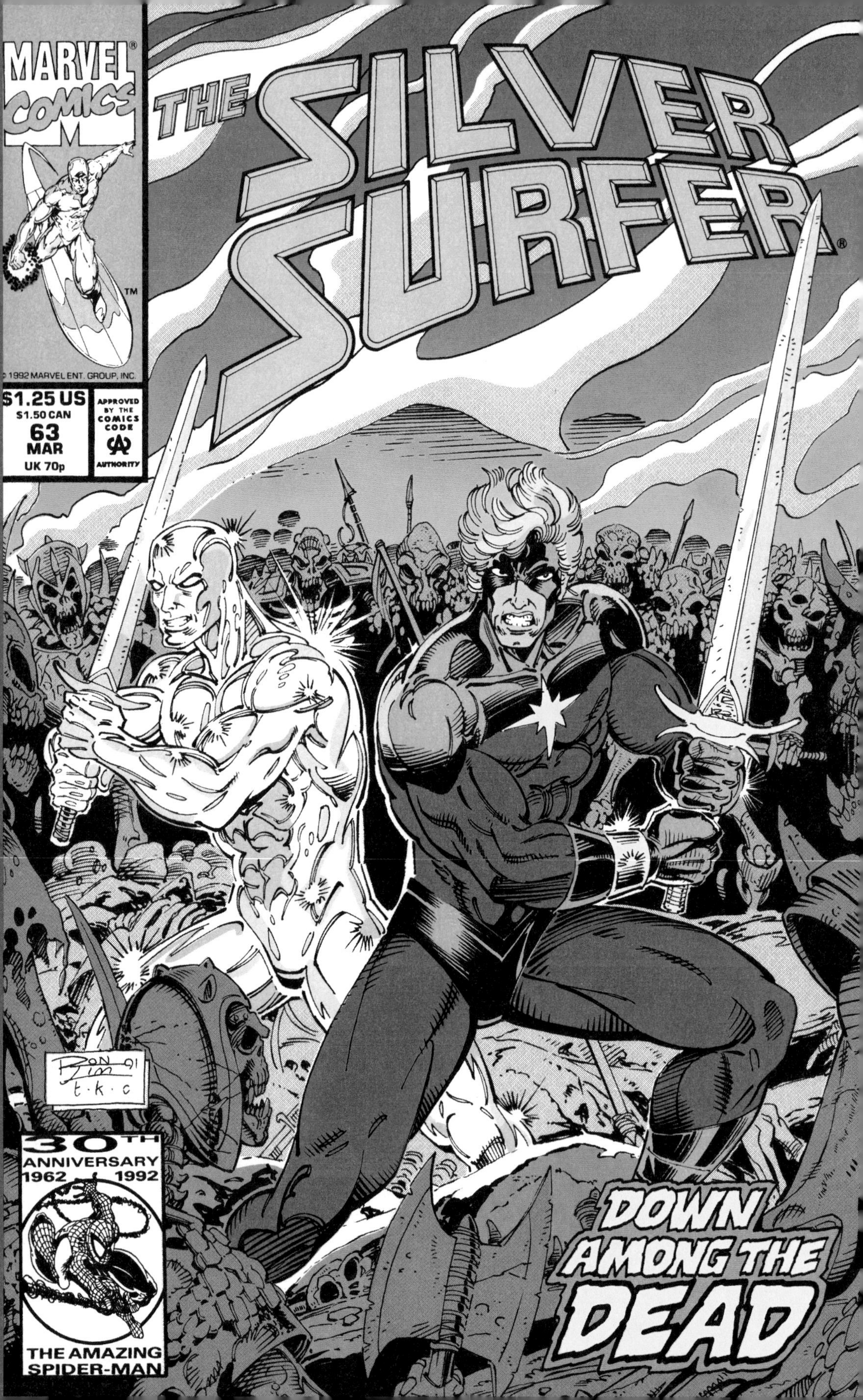
MARVEL COMICS
THE SILVER SURFER
© 1992 MARVEL ENT. GROUP, INC.
$1.25 US
$1.50 CAN
63
MAR
UK 70p
APPROVED BY THE COMICS CODE AUTHORITY
30TH ANNIVERSARY 1962 1992
THE AMAZING SPIDER-MAN
DOWN AMONG THE DEAD

TO SAVE HIS PLANET, **NORRIN RADD** SURRENDERED HIS FREEDOM TO BECOME HERALD TO THE WORLD-DEVOURING **GALACTUS**. COATED WITH GALACTIC GLAZE, GIVEN A SURFBOARD OBEYING HIS MENTAL COMMANDS, AND GRANTED THE POWER COSMIC, HE NOW SOARS THE UNIVERSE, A SHINING SENTINEL OF THE SPACEWAYS! STAN LEE PRESENTS . . . ***THE SILVER SURFER!***

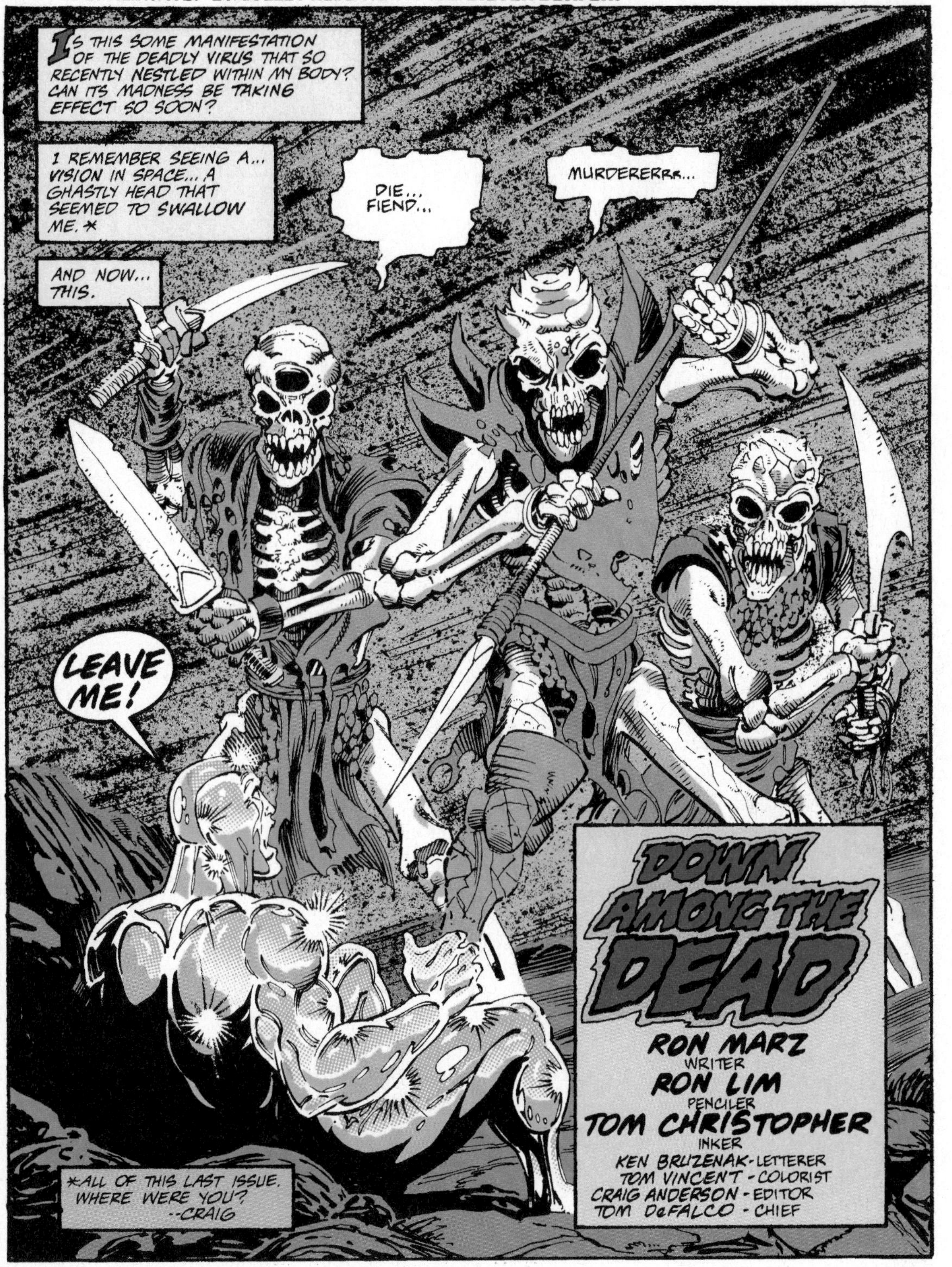

IS THIS SOME MANIFESTATION OF THE DEADLY VIRUS THAT SO RECENTLY NESTLED WITHIN MY BODY? CAN ITS MADNESS BE TAKING EFFECT SO SOON?
I REMEMBER SEEING A... VISION IN SPACE... A GHASTLY HEAD THAT SEEMED TO SWALLOW ME. *
AND NOW... THIS.
DIE... FIEND...
MURDERERRR...
LEAVE ME!
DOWN AMONG THE DEAD
RON MARZ WRITER
RON LIM PENCILER
TOM CHRISTOPHER INKER
KEN BRUZENAK - LETTERER
TOM VINCENT - COLORIST
CRAIG ANDERSON - EDITOR
TOM DeFALCO - CHIEF
*ALL OF THIS LAST ISSUE. WHERE WERE YOU? --CRAIG

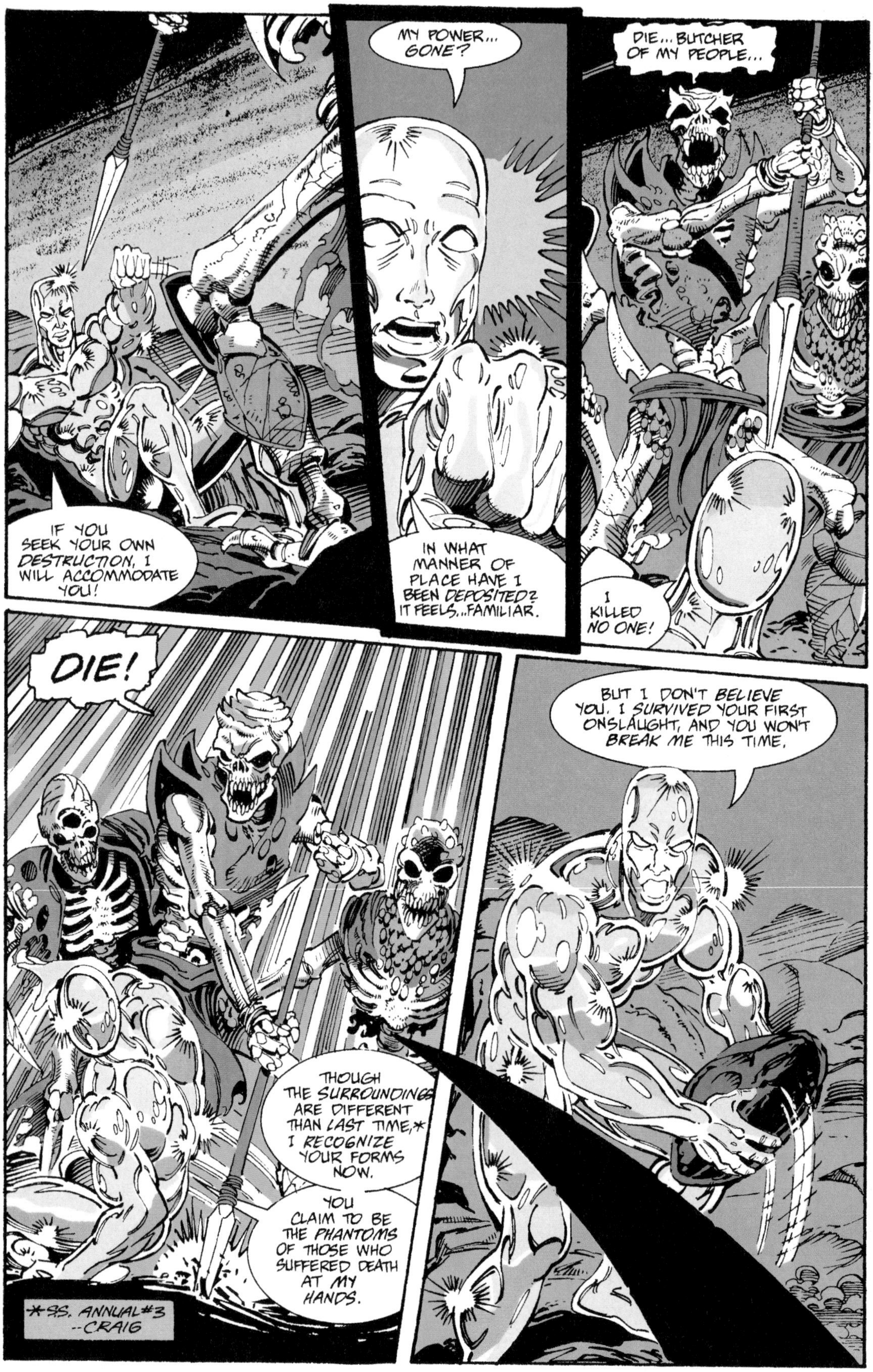

MY POWER... GONE?
DIE... BUTCHER OF MY PEOPLE...
IF YOU SEEK YOUR OWN DESTRUCTION, I WILL ACCOMMODATE YOU!
IN WHAT MANNER OF PLACE HAVE I BEEN DEPOSITED? IT FEELS...FAMILIAR.
I KILLED NO ONE!
DIE!
THOUGH THE SURROUNDINGS ARE DIFFERENT THAN LAST TIME,* I RECOGNIZE YOUR FORMS NOW.
YOU CLAIM TO BE THE PHANTOMS OF THOSE WHO SUFFERED DEATH AT MY HANDS.
*S.S. ANNUAL #3 --CRAIG
BUT I DON'T BELIEVE YOU. I SURVIVED YOUR FIRST ONSLAUGHT, AND YOU WON'T BREAK ME THIS TIME.

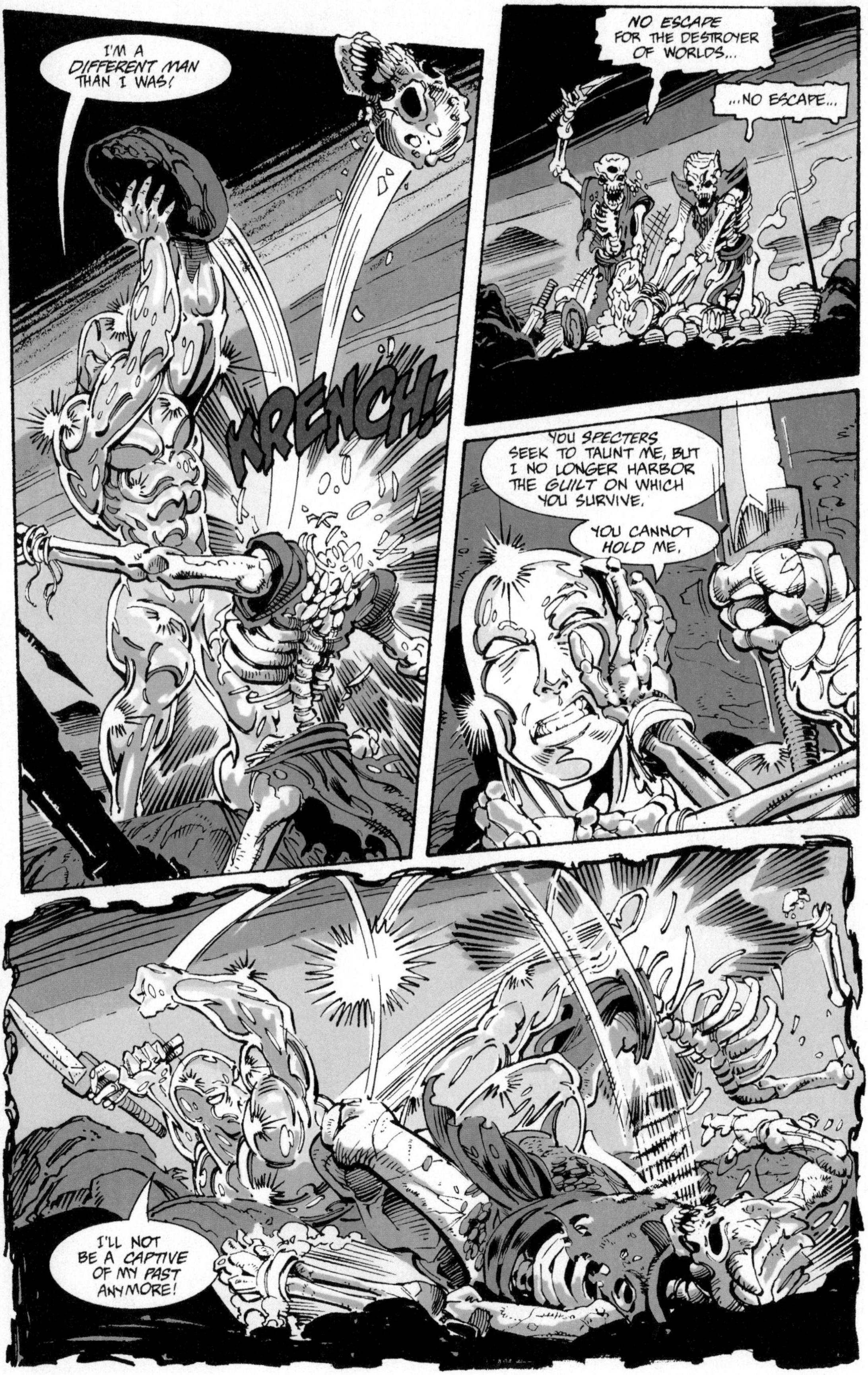
I'M A DIFFERENT MAN THAN I WAS!
KRENCH!
NO ESCAPE FOR THE DESTROYER OF WORLDS...
...NO ESCAPE...
YOU SPECTERS SEEK TO TAUNT ME, BUT I NO LONGER HARBOR THE GUILT ON WHICH YOU SURVIVE.
YOU CANNOT HOLD ME.
I'LL NOT BE A CAPTIVE OF MY PAST ANYMORE!

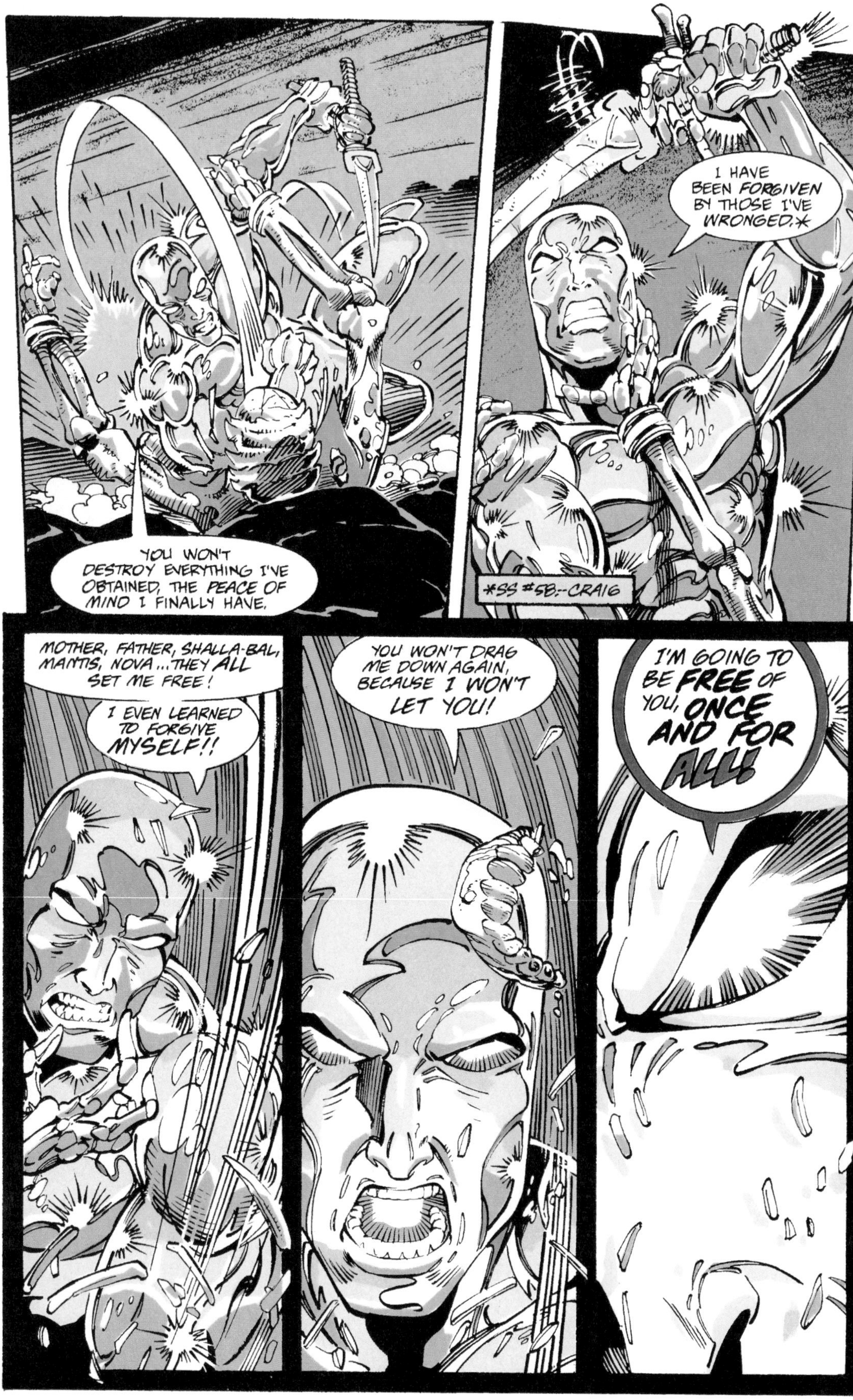
I HAVE BEEN FORGIVEN BY THOSE I'VE WRONGED.*
YOU WON'T DESTROY EVERYTHING I'VE OBTAINED, THE PEACE OF MIND I FINALLY HAVE.
*SS #58.-CRAIG
MOTHER, FATHER, SHALLA-BAL, MANTIS, NOVA... THEY ALL SET ME FREE!
I EVEN LEARNED TO FORGIVE MYSELF!!
YOU WON'T DRAG ME DOWN AGAIN, BECAUSE I WON'T LET YOU!
I'M GOING TO BE FREE OF YOU, ONCE AND FOR ALL!

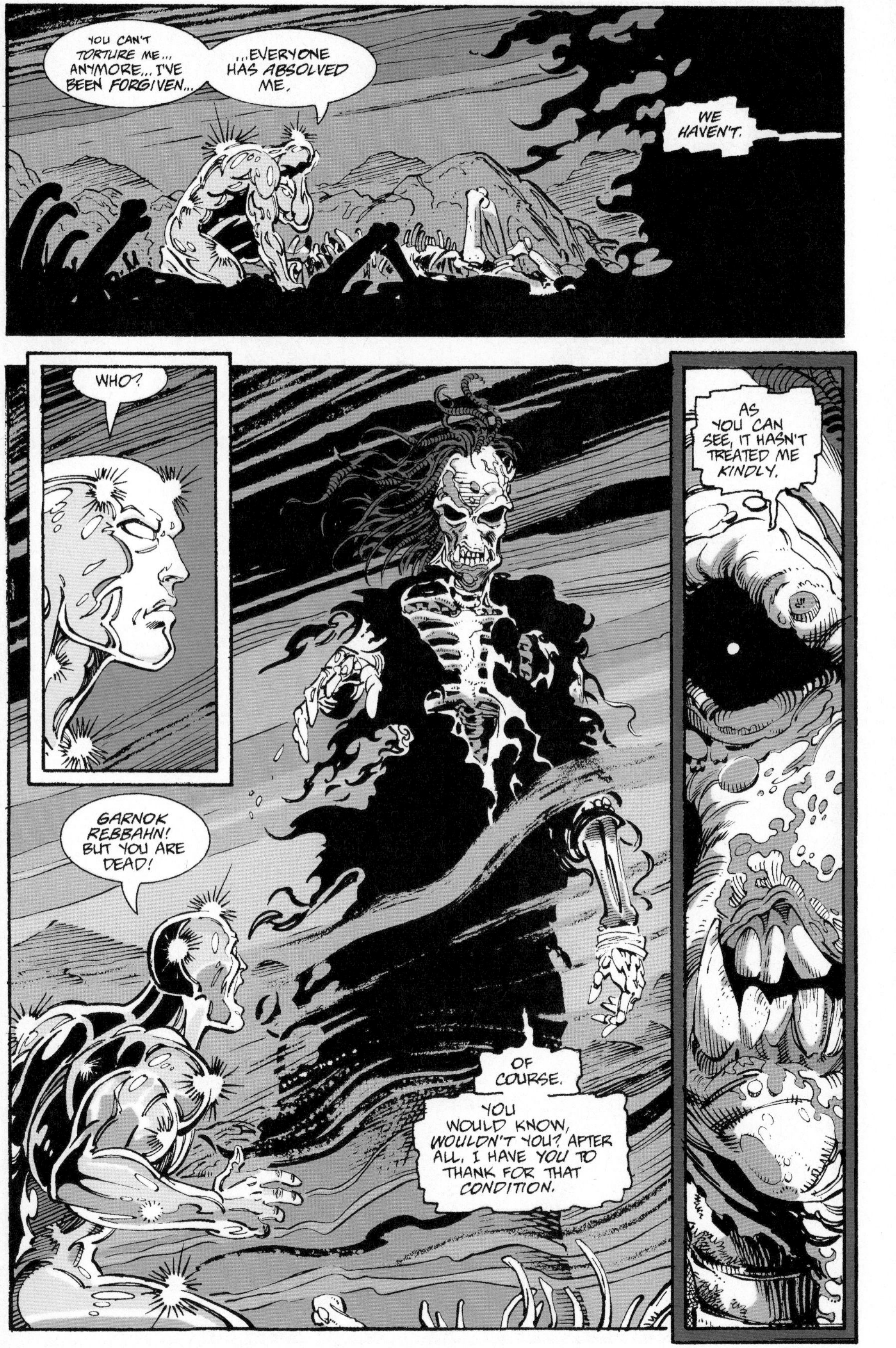
YOU CAN'T TORTURE ME... ANYMORE... I'VE BEEN FORGIVEN...
...EVERYONE HAS ABSOLVED ME.
WE HAVEN'T.
WHO?
AS YOU CAN SEE, IT HASN'T TREATED ME KINDLY.
GARNOK REBBAHN! BUT YOU ARE DEAD!
OF COURSE.
YOU WOULD KNOW, WOULDN'T YOU? AFTER ALL, I HAVE YOU TO THANK FOR THAT CONDITION.

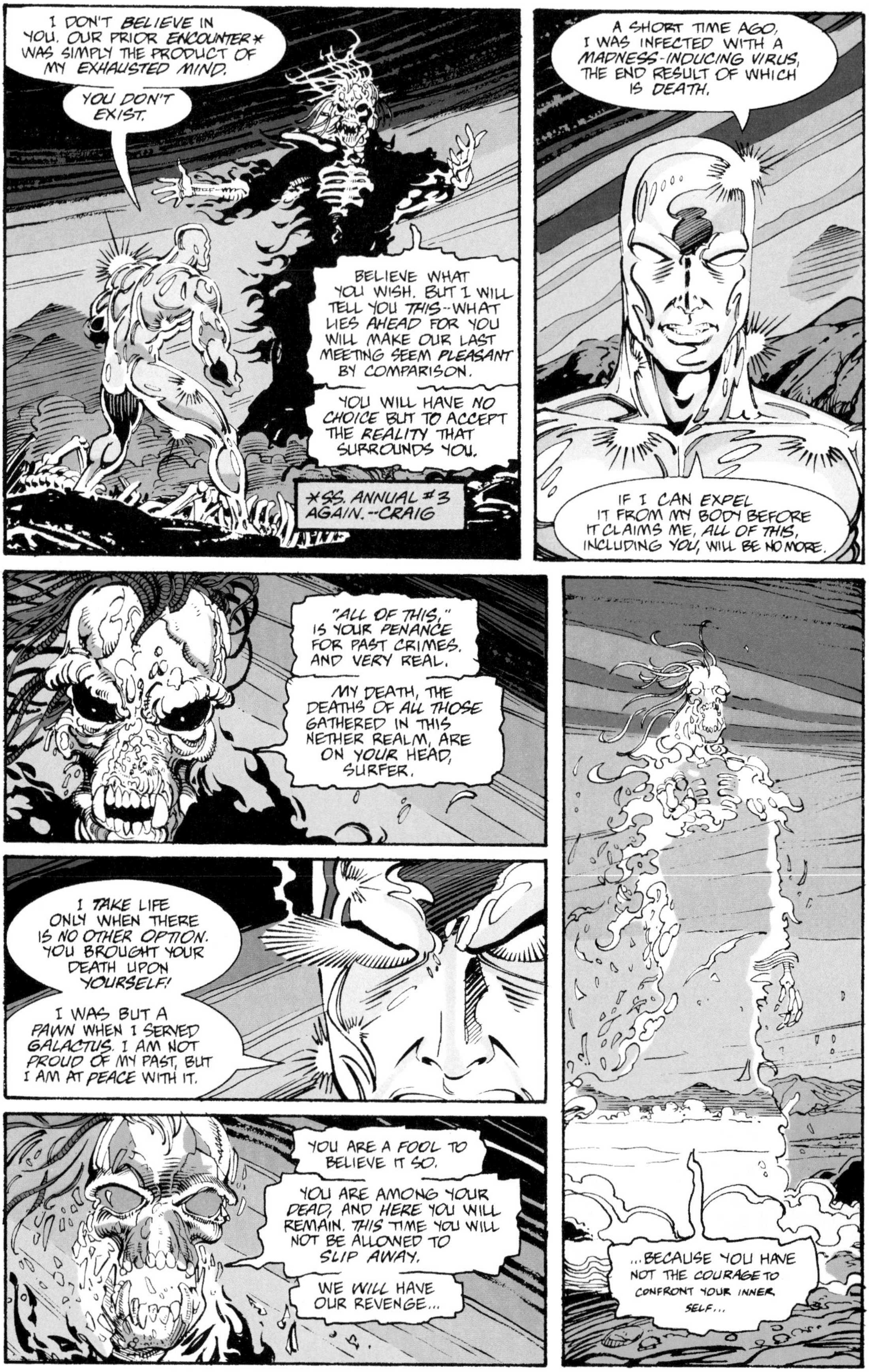

I DON'T BELIEVE IN YOU. OUR PRIOR ENCOUNTER* WAS SIMPLY THE PRODUCT OF MY EXHAUSTED MIND.
YOU DON'T EXIST.
BELIEVE WHAT YOU WISH. BUT I WILL TELL YOU THIS--WHAT LIES AHEAD FOR YOU WILL MAKE OUR LAST MEETING SEEM PLEASANT BY COMPARISON.
YOU WILL HAVE NO CHOICE BUT TO ACCEPT THE REALITY THAT SURROUNDS YOU.
*S.S. ANNUAL #3 AGAIN.--CRAIG
A SHORT TIME AGO, I WAS INFECTED WITH A MADNESS-INDUCING VIRUS, THE END RESULT OF WHICH IS DEATH.
IF I CAN EXPEL IT FROM MY BODY BEFORE IT CLAIMS ME, ALL OF THIS, INCLUDING YOU, WILL BE NO MORE.
"ALL OF THIS," IS YOUR PENANCE FOR PAST CRIMES, AND VERY REAL.
MY DEATH, THE DEATHS OF ALL THOSE GATHERED IN THIS NETHER REALM, ARE ON YOUR HEAD, SURFER.
I TAKE LIFE ONLY WHEN THERE IS NO OTHER OPTION. YOU BROUGHT YOUR DEATH UPON YOURSELF!
I WAS BUT A PAWN WHEN I SERVED GALACTUS. I AM NOT PROUD OF MY PAST, BUT I AM AT PEACE WITH IT.
YOU ARE A FOOL TO BELIEVE IT SO.
YOU ARE AMONG YOUR DEAD, AND HERE YOU WILL REMAIN. THIS TIME YOU WILL NOT BE ALLOWED TO SLIP AWAY.
WE WILL HAVE OUR REVENGE...
...BECAUSE YOU HAVE NOT THE COURAGE TO CONFRONT YOUR INNER SELF...

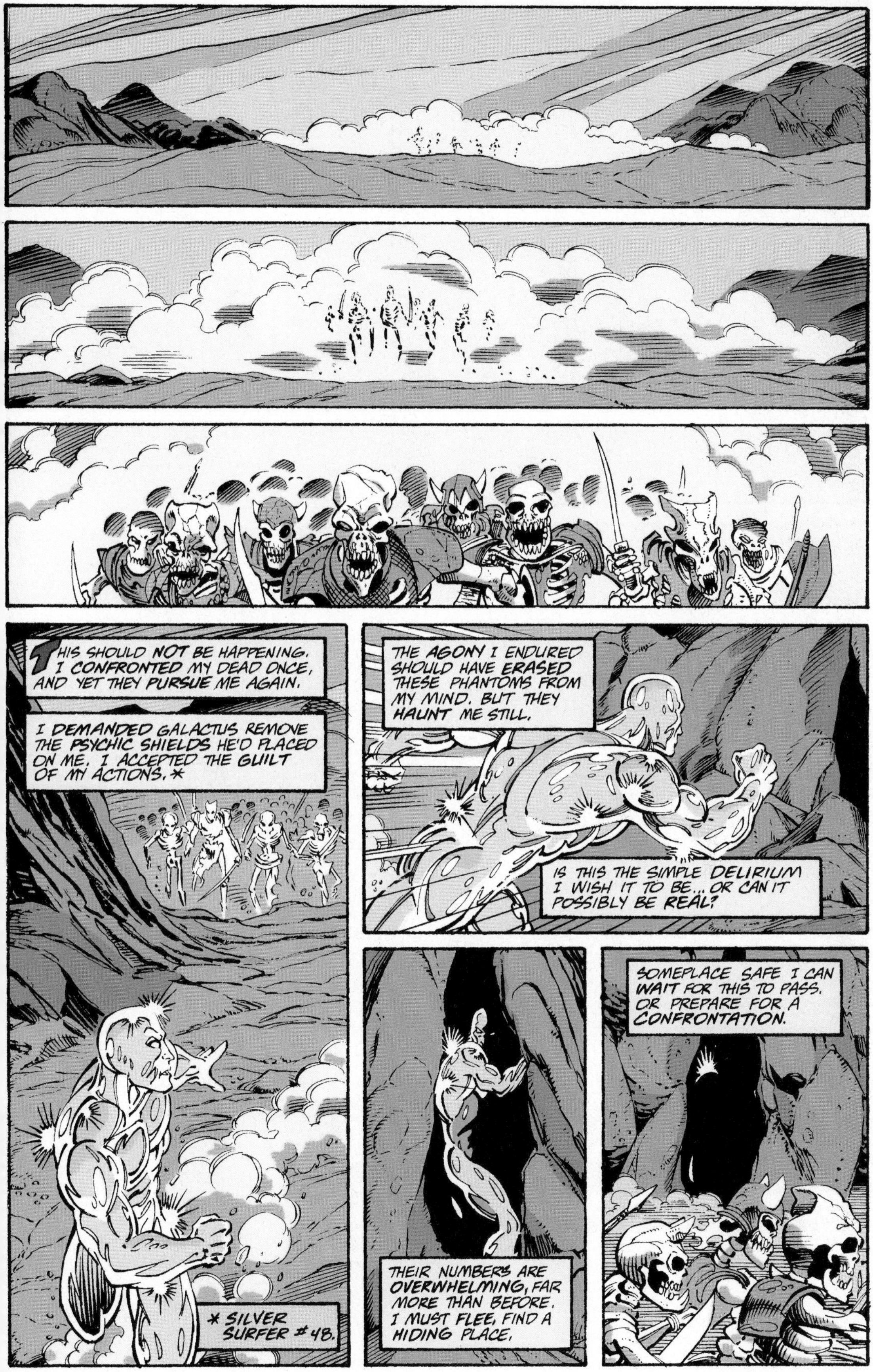
THIS SHOULD NOT BE HAPPENING. I CONFRONTED MY DEAD ONCE, AND YET THEY PURSUE ME AGAIN.
I DEMANDED GALACTUS REMOVE THE PSYCHIC SHIELDS HE'D PLACED ON ME. I ACCEPTED THE GUILT OF MY ACTIONS.*
* SILVER SURFER #48.
THE AGONY I ENDURED SHOULD HAVE ERASED THESE PHANTOMS FROM MY MIND. BUT THEY HAUNT ME STILL.
IS THIS THE SIMPLE DELIRIUM I WISH IT TO BE... OR CAN IT POSSIBLY BE REAL?
THEIR NUMBERS ARE OVERWHELMING, FAR MORE THAN BEFORE. I MUST FLEE, FIND A HIDING PLACE.
SOMEPLACE SAFE I CAN WAIT FOR THIS TO PASS. OR PREPARE FOR A CONFRONTATION.

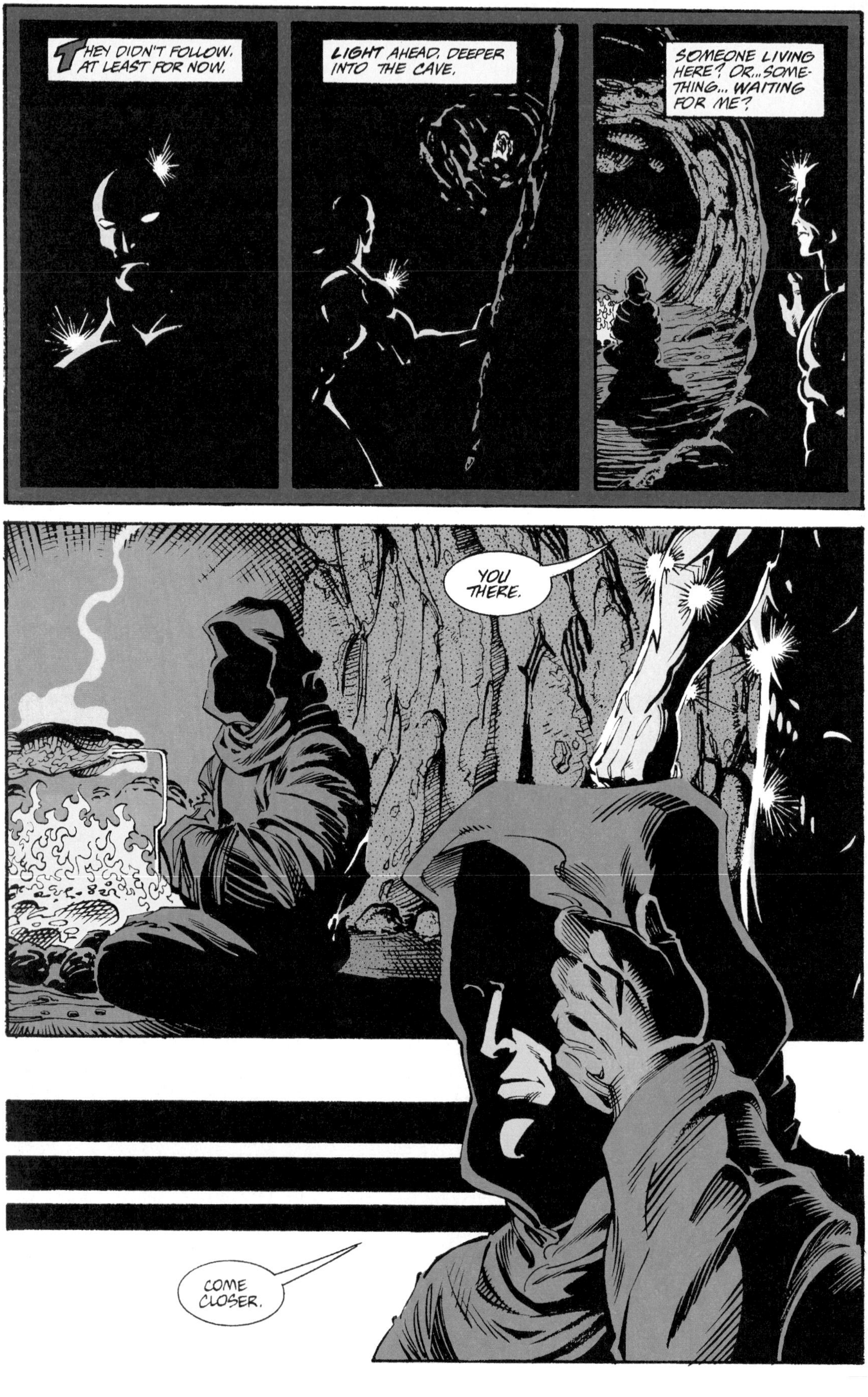
THEY DIDN'T FOLLOW. AT LEAST FOR NOW.
LIGHT AHEAD. DEEPER INTO THE CAVE.
SOMEONE LIVING HERE? OR... SOMETHING... WAITING FOR ME?
YOU THERE.
COME CLOSER.

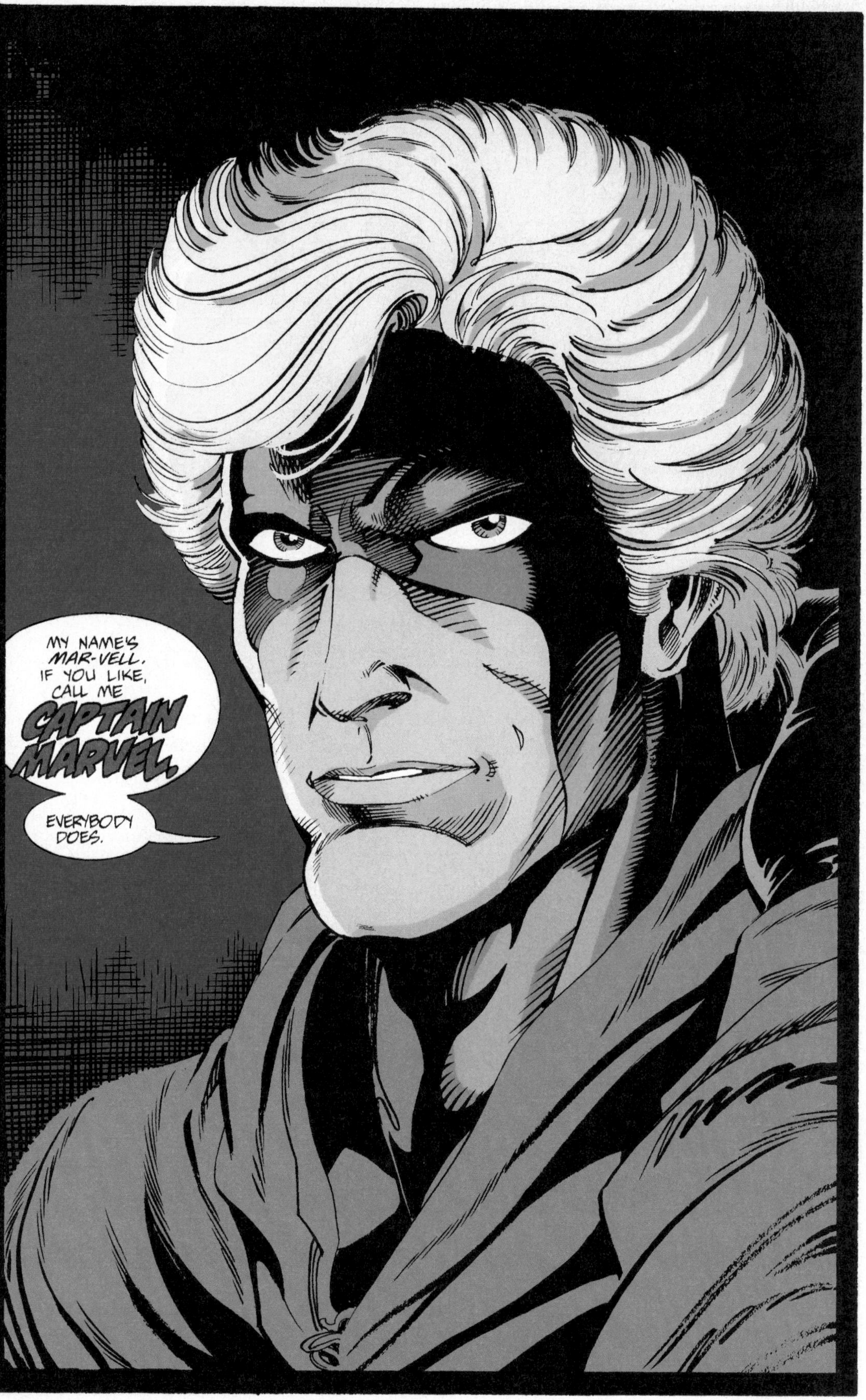
MY NAME'S MAR-VELL. IF YOU LIKE, CALL ME CAPTAIN MARVEL.
EVERYBODY DOES.

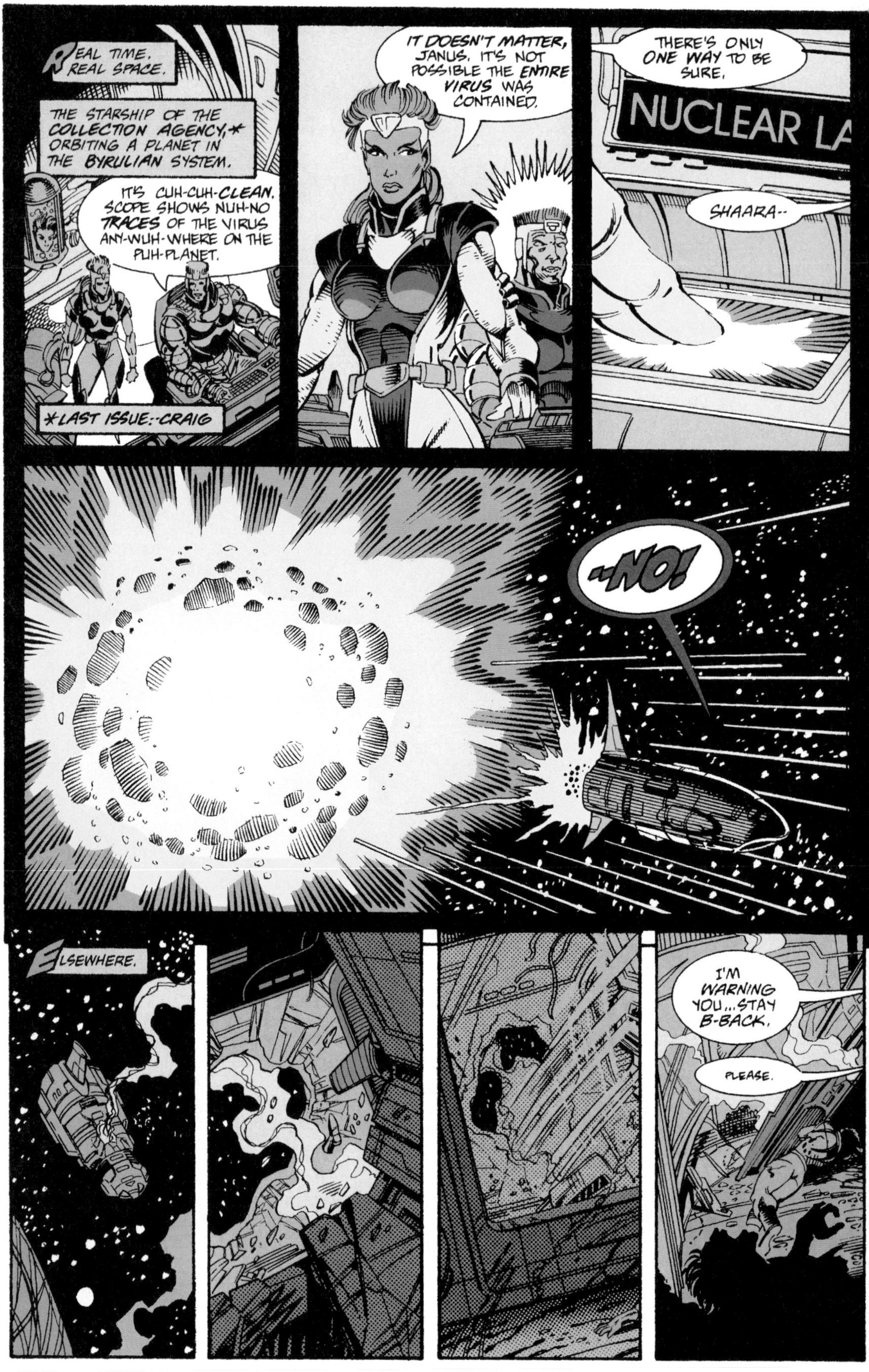
REAL TIME. REAL SPACE.
THE STARSHIP OF THE COLLECTION AGENCY,* ORBITING A PLANET IN THE BYRULIAN SYSTEM.
IT'S CUH-CUH-CLEAN. SCOPE SHOWS NUH-NO TRACES OF THE VIRUS ANY-WUH-WHERE ON THE PUH-PLANET.
*LAST ISSUE:-CRAIG
IT DOESN'T MATTER, JANUS. IT'S NOT POSSIBLE THE ENTIRE VIRUS WAS CONTAINED.
THERE'S ONLY ONE WAY TO BE SURE.
NUCLEAR LA
SHAARA--
--NO!
ELSEWHERE.
I'M WARNING YOU...STAY B-BACK.
PLEASE.

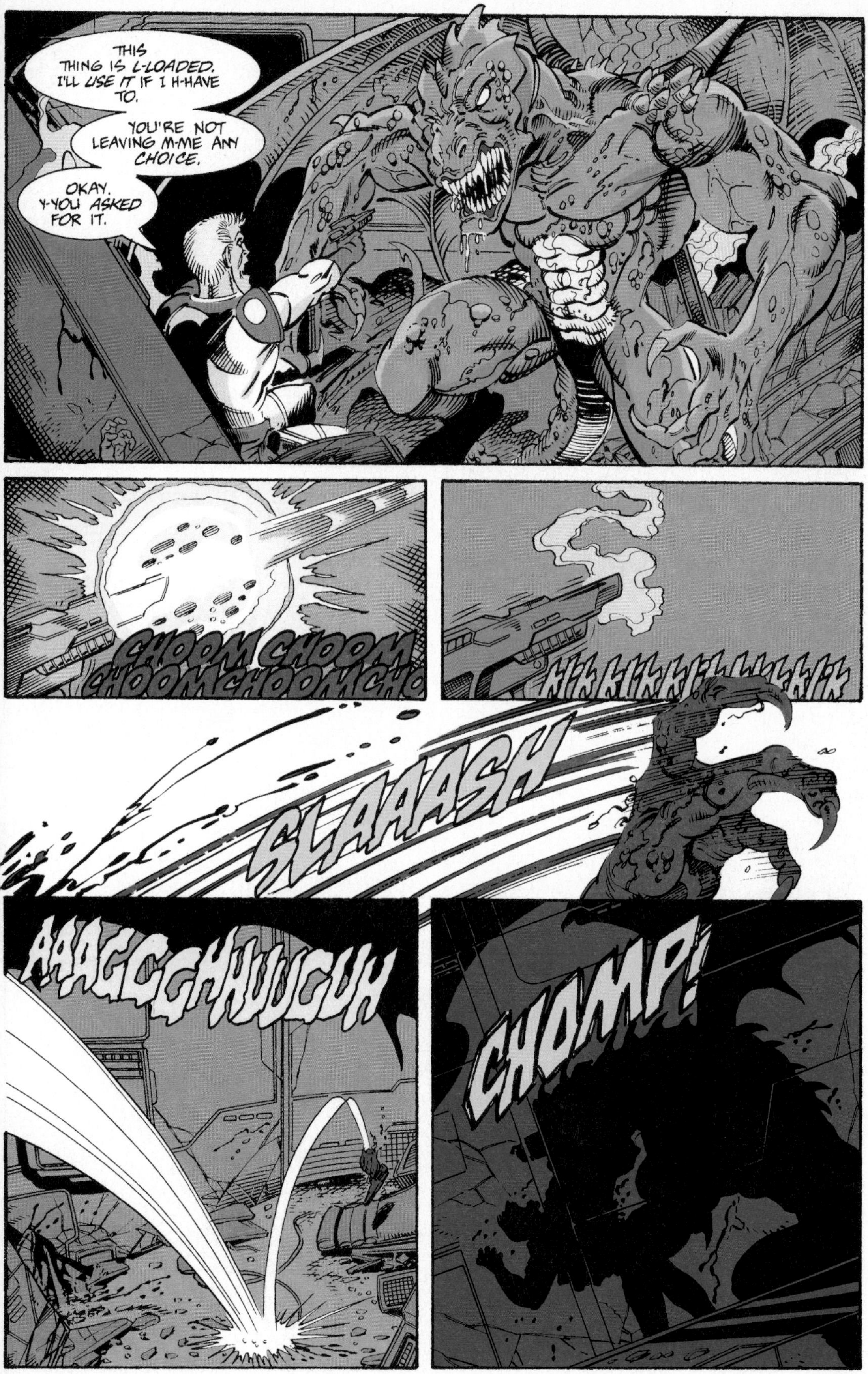
THIS THING IS L-LOADED. I'LL USE IT IF I H-HAVE TO.
YOU'RE NOT LEAVING M-ME ANY CHOICE.
OKAY. Y-YOU ASKED FOR IT.
CHOOM CHOOM CHOOMCHOOMCHO
SLAAAASH
AAAGGGHHUUGUH
CHOMP!

...HASN'T BEEN *NECESSARY* FOR ME TO *EAT* IN SO LONG, I'D FORGOTTEN WHAT A PLEASURE IT IS.

I PROBABLY DON'T *NEED* TO EITHER, JUST ONE OF THOSE *HABITS* I CAN'T BREAK. LIKE BREATHING.

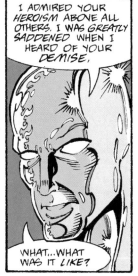

YOU... BELIEVE YOU'RE *DEAD*, TOO?

I *GUESS* SO, WHY ELSE WOULD I BE *HERE*?

I MEAN, I REMEMBER *DYING.*

I ADMIRED YOUR *HEROISM* ABOVE ALL OTHERS. I WAS GREATLY *SADDENED* WHEN I HEARD OF YOUR *DEMISE.*

WHAT...WHAT WAS IT *LIKE*?

IT WAS...*EASY.* I *REMEMBER* THAT.

ONCE I LEARNED HOW TO *LET GO,* IT WAS EASY.

BUT THAT'S *ALL* I REMEMBER--I *DIED,* NOW I'M *HERE,* NOTHING IN BETWEEN.

EATING AGAIN...THIS IS *WONDERFUL.*

IT'S *HALF-COOKED.* I JUST WONDER WHERE THE *GAME* COMES FROM. EVERYTHING ELSE HERE IS DEAD.

I HAVEN'T EATEN IN *AGES.* I DON'T *NEED* TO. WHY *NOW*?

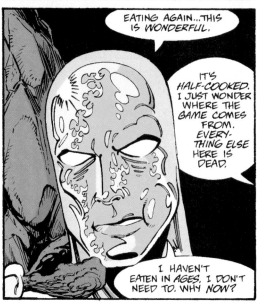

THINGS DON'T WORK THE SAME HERE, MY POWERS ARE *GONE*? YOURS, *TOO*?

THEY ARE. IT SEEMS TO BE HAPPENING A *LOT* LATELY.

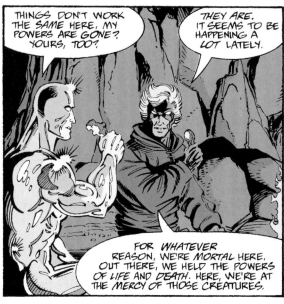

FOR *WHATEVER* REASON, WE'RE *MORTAL* HERE. OUT THERE, WE HELD THE POWERS OF *LIFE* AND *DEATH.* HERE, WE'RE AT THE *MERCY* OF THOSE CREATURES.

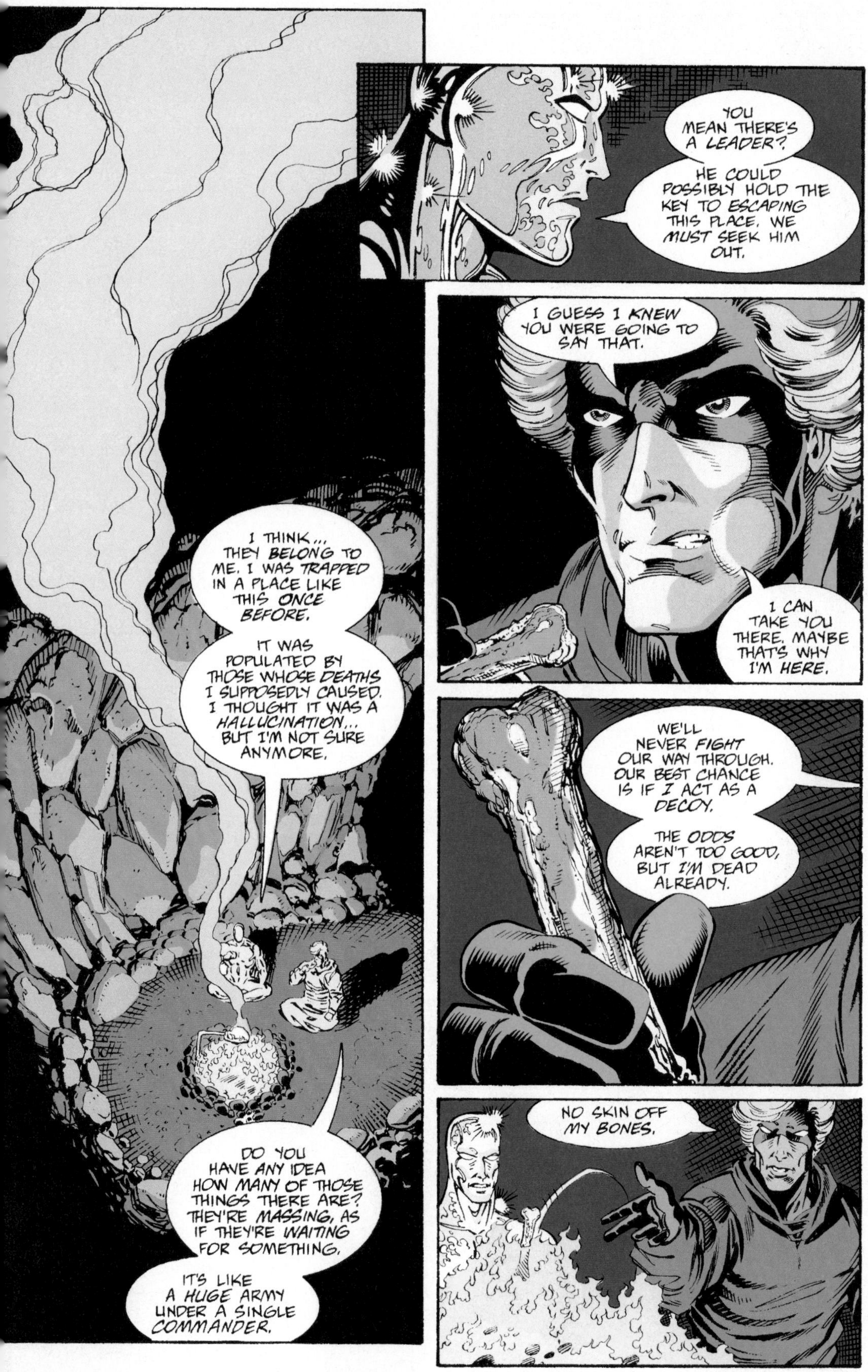
YOU MEAN THERE'S A LEADER?
HE COULD POSSIBLY HOLD THE KEY TO ESCAPING THIS PLACE. WE MUST SEEK HIM OUT.
I GUESS I KNEW YOU WERE GOING TO SAY THAT.
I CAN TAKE YOU THERE. MAYBE THAT'S WHY I'M HERE.
WE'LL NEVER FIGHT OUR WAY THROUGH. OUR BEST CHANCE IS IF I ACT AS A DECOY.
THE ODDS AREN'T TOO GOOD, BUT I'M DEAD ALREADY.
NO SKIN OFF MY BONES.
I THINK... THEY BELONG TO ME. I WAS TRAPPED IN A PLACE LIKE THIS ONCE BEFORE.
IT WAS POPULATED BY THOSE WHOSE DEATHS I SUPPOSEDLY CAUSED. I THOUGHT IT WAS A HALLUCINATION... BUT I'M NOT SURE ANYMORE.
DO YOU HAVE ANY IDEA HOW MANY OF THOSE THINGS THERE ARE? THEY'RE MASSING, AS IF THEY'RE WAITING FOR SOMETHING.
IT'S LIKE A HUGE ARMY UNDER A SINGLE COMMANDER.

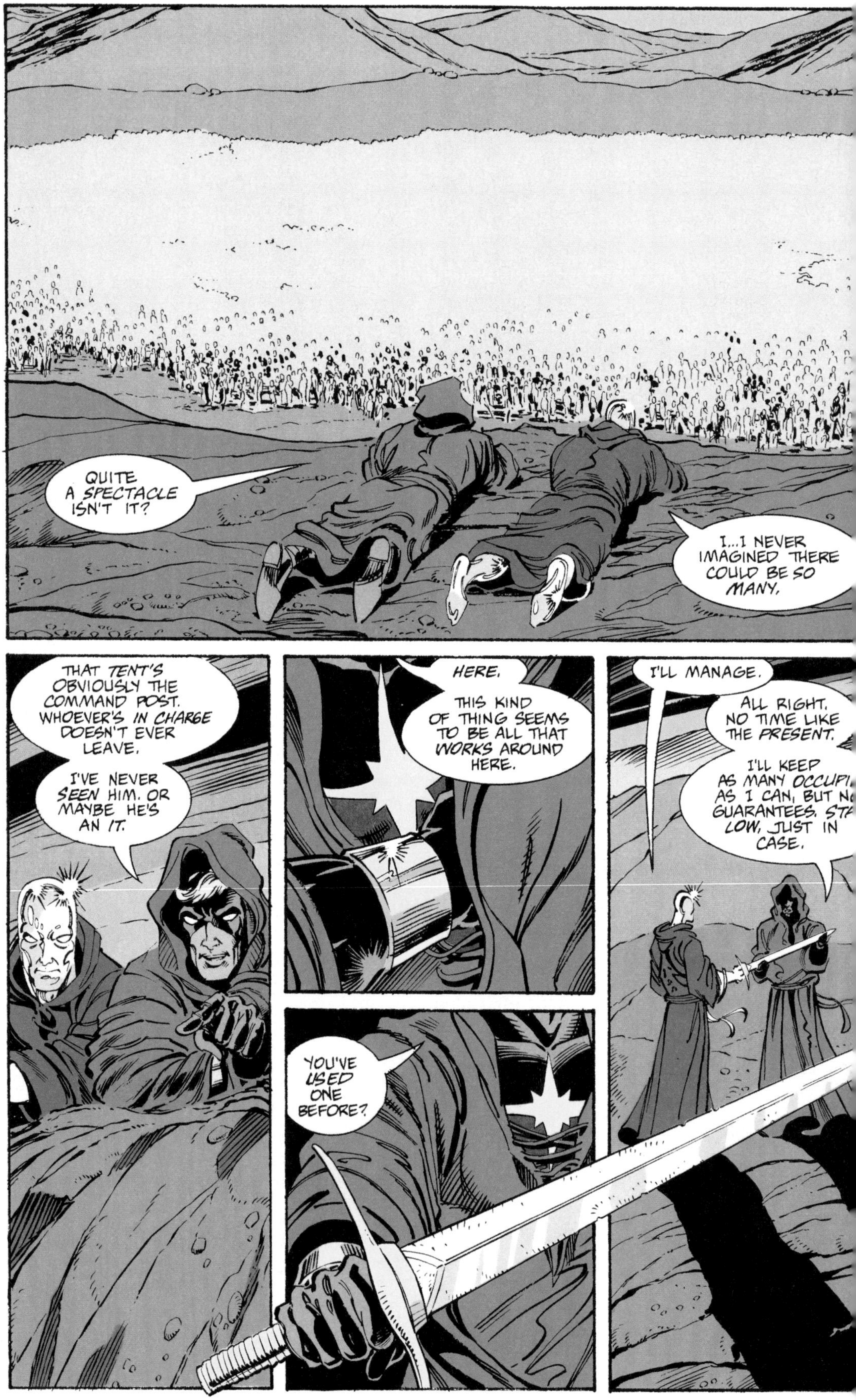
QUITE A SPECTACLE ISN'T IT?
I...I NEVER IMAGINED THERE COULD BE SO MANY.
THAT TENT'S OBVIOUSLY THE COMMAND POST. WHOEVER'S IN CHARGE DOESN'T EVER LEAVE.
I'VE NEVER SEEN HIM. OR MAYBE HE'S AN IT.
HERE.
THIS KIND OF THING SEEMS TO BE ALL THAT WORKS AROUND HERE.
YOU'VE USED ONE BEFORE?
I'LL MANAGE.
ALL RIGHT. NO TIME LIKE THE PRESENT.
I'LL KEEP AS MANY OCCUPI AS I CAN, BUT N GUARANTEES. ST LOW, JUST IN CASE.

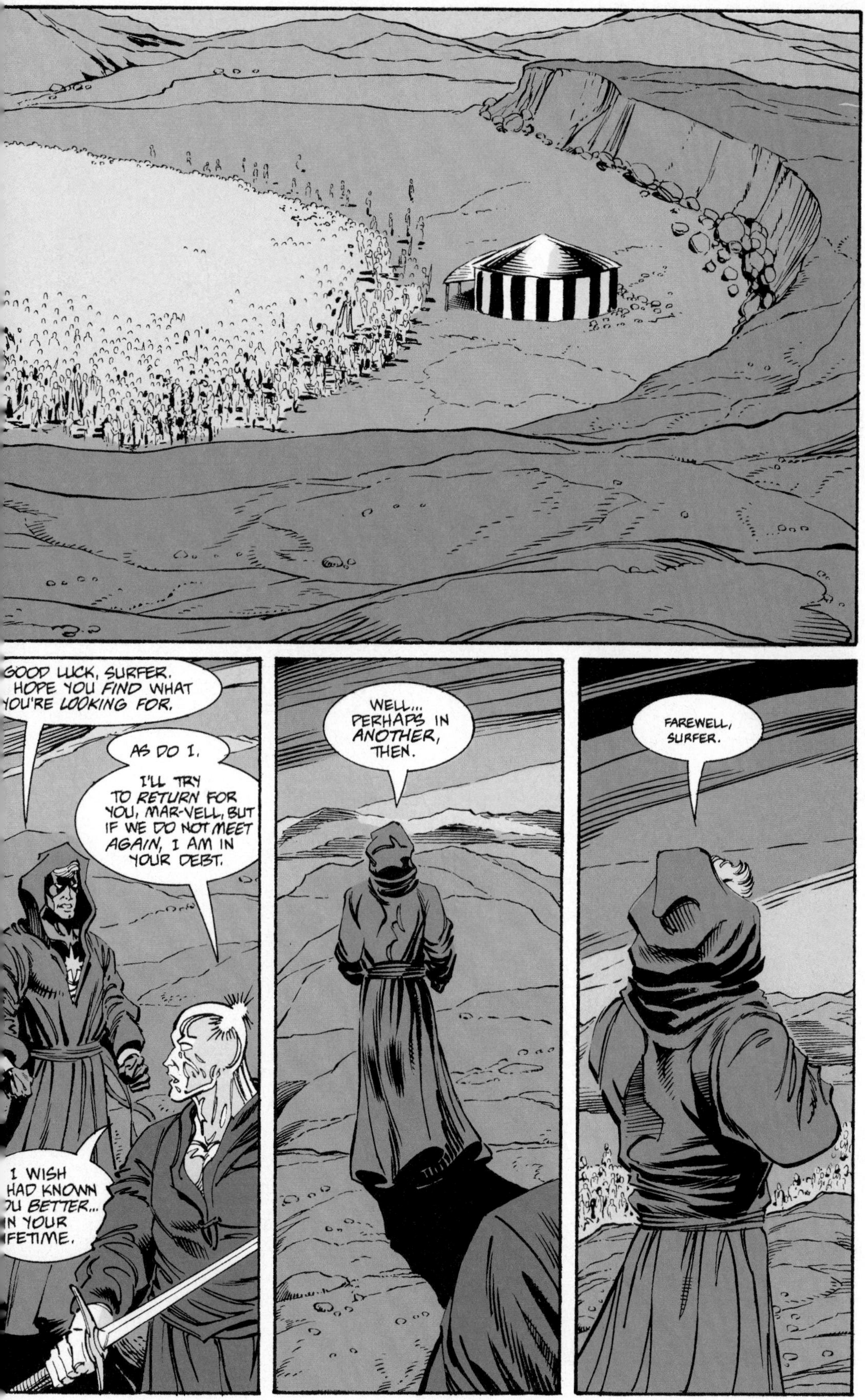
GOOD LUCK, SURFER. HOPE YOU FIND WHAT YOU'RE LOOKING FOR.
AS DO I.
I'LL TRY TO RETURN FOR YOU, MAR-VELL, BUT IF WE DO NOT MEET AGAIN, I AM IN YOUR DEBT.
I WISH HAD KNOWN OU BETTER... N YOUR IFETIME.
WELL... PERHAPS IN ANOTHER, THEN.
FAREWELL, SURFER.

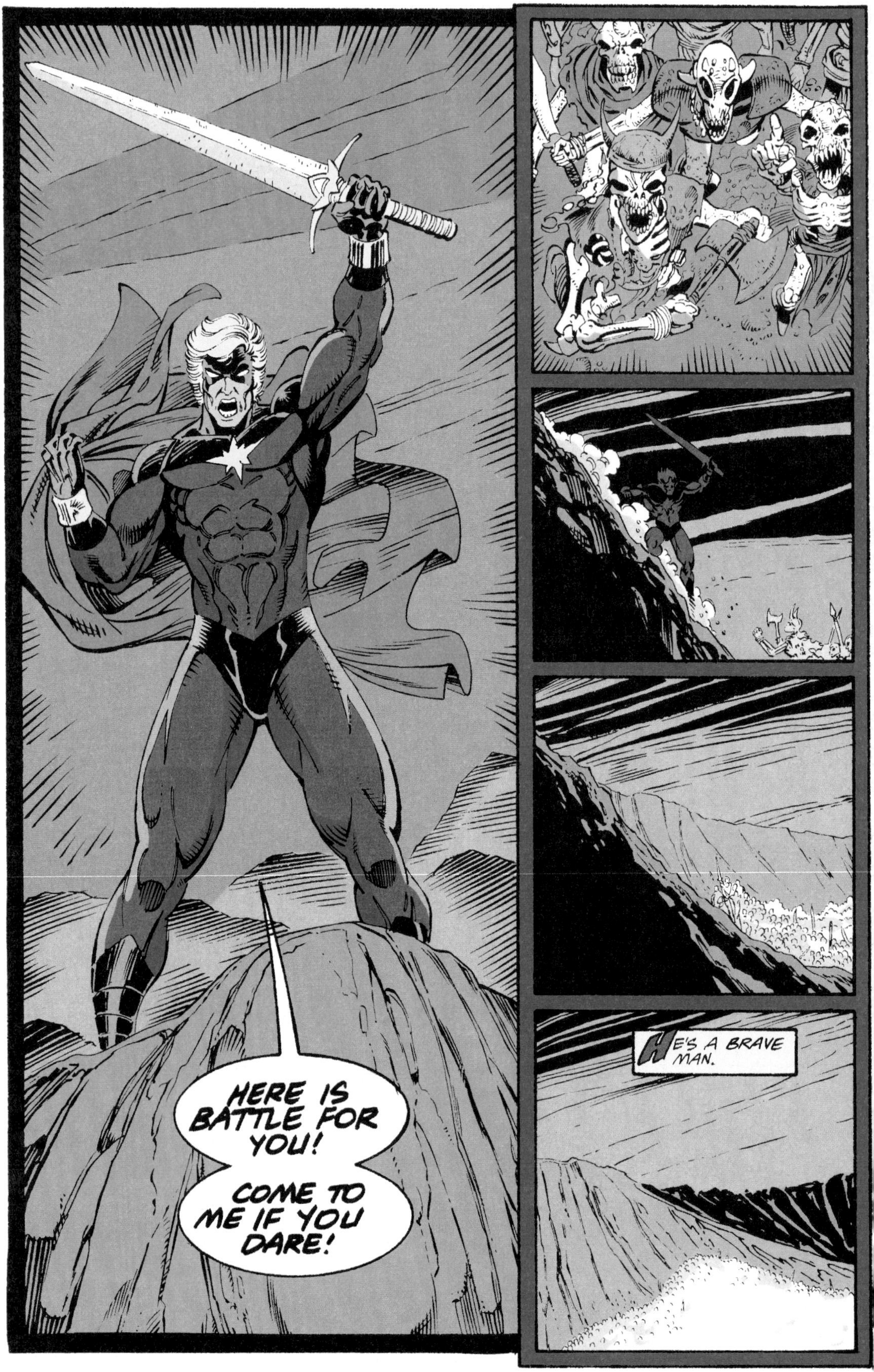
HERE IS BATTLE FOR YOU!
COME TO ME IF YOU DARE!
HE'S A BRAVE MAN.

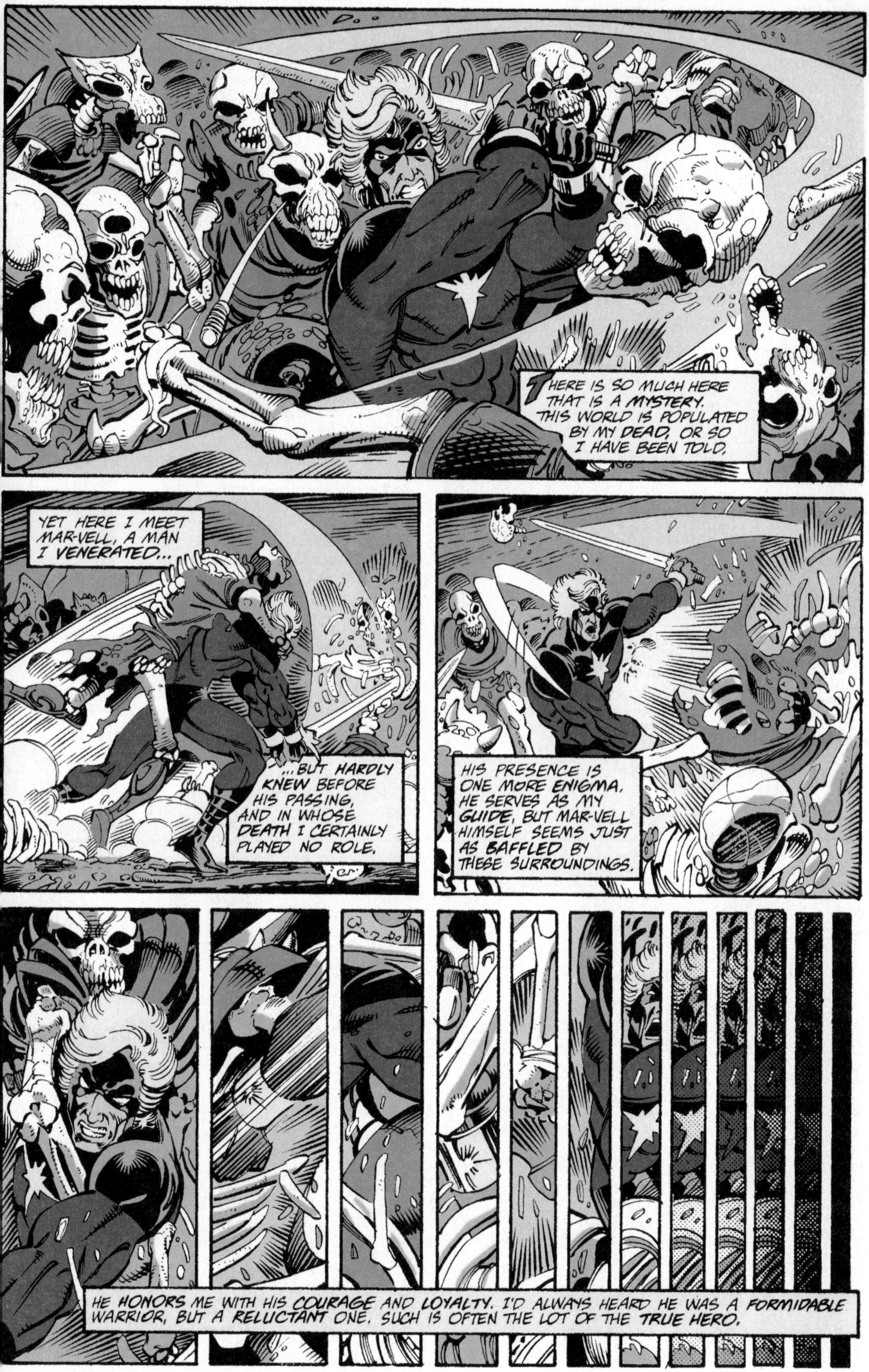
THERE IS SO MUCH HERE THAT IS A MYSTERY. THIS WORLD IS POPULATED BY MY DEAD, OR SO I HAVE BEEN TOLD.
YET HERE I MEET MAR-VELL, A MAN I VENERATED...
...BUT HARDLY KNEW BEFORE HIS PASSING, AND IN WHOSE DEATH I CERTAINLY PLAYED NO ROLE.
HIS PRESENCE IS ONE MORE ENIGMA. HE SERVES AS MY GUIDE, BUT MAR-VELL HIMSELF SEEMS JUST AS BAFFLED BY THESE SURROUNDINGS.
HE HONORS ME WITH HIS COURAGE AND LOYALTY. I'D ALWAYS HEARD HE WAS A FORMIDABLE WARRIOR, BUT A RELUCTANT ONE. SUCH IS OFTEN THE LOT OF THE TRUE HERO.

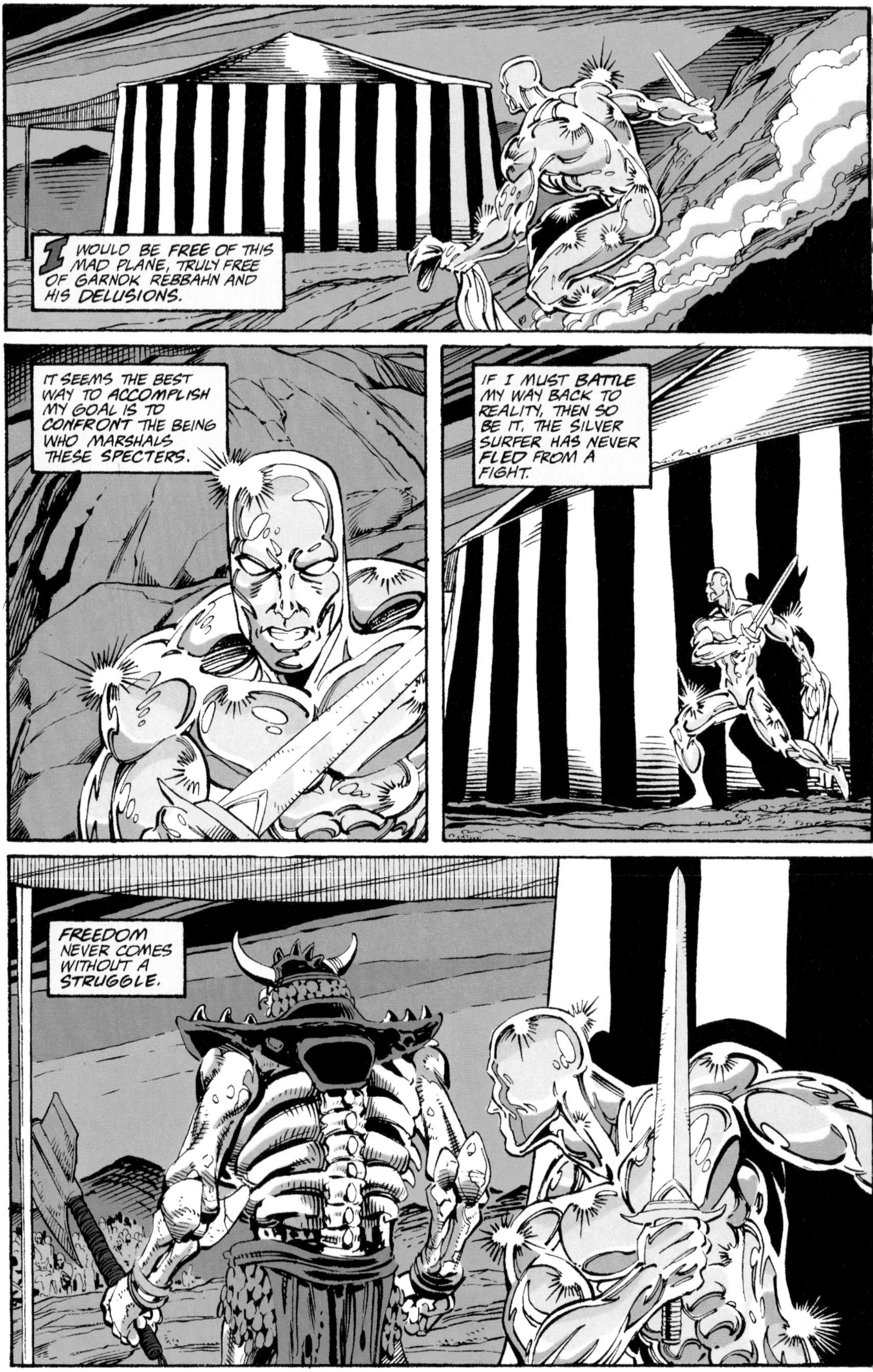
I WOULD BE FREE OF THIS MAD PLANE, TRULY FREE OF GARNOK REBBAHN AND HIS DELUSIONS.
IT SEEMS THE BEST WAY TO ACCOMPLISH MY GOAL IS TO CONFRONT THE BEING WHO MARSHALS THESE SPECTERS.
IF I MUST BATTLE MY WAY BACK TO REALITY, THEN SO BE IT. THE SILVER SURFER HAS NEVER FLED FROM A FIGHT.
FREEDOM NEVER COMES WITHOUT A STRUGGLE.

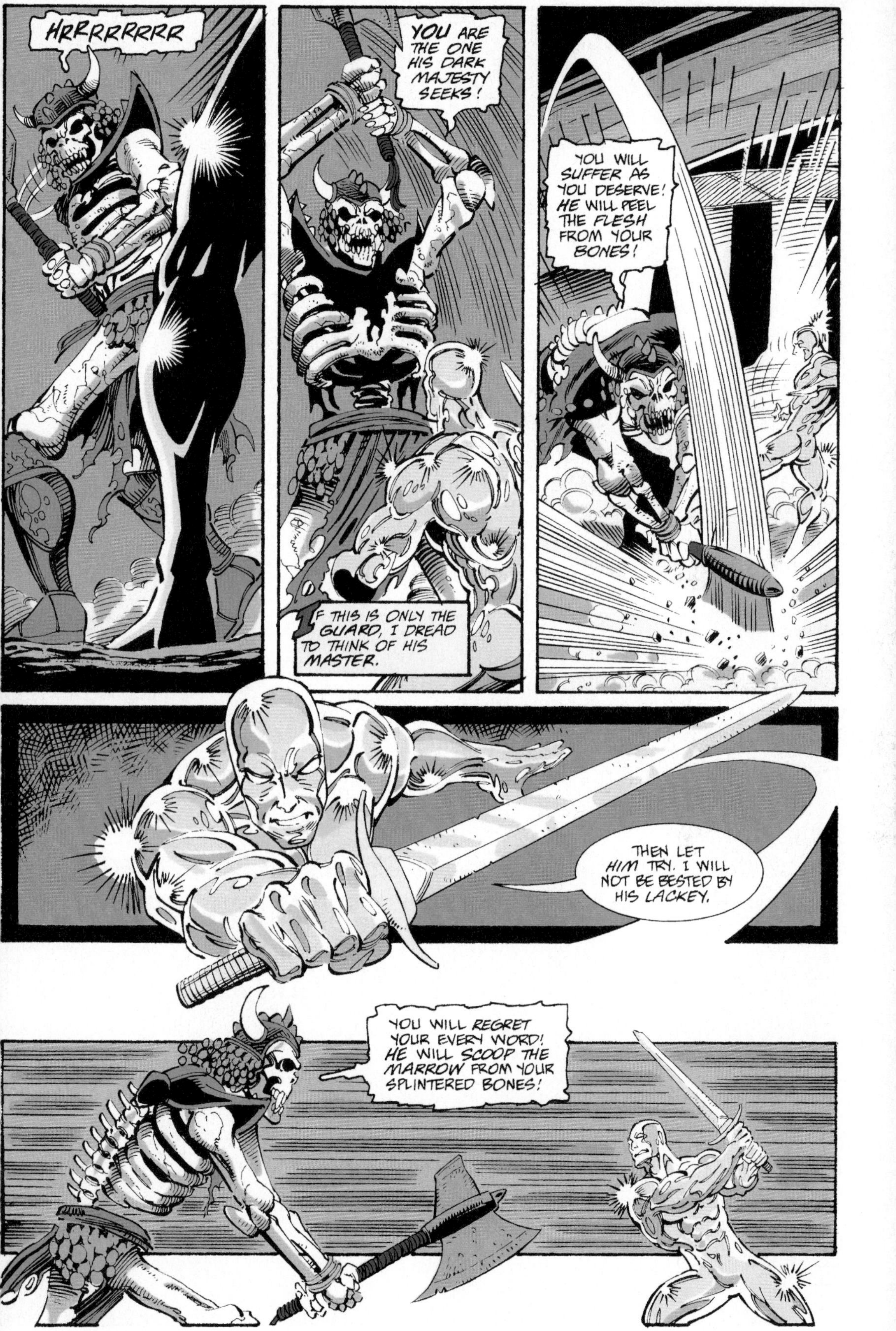
HRRRRRRRR
YOU ARE THE ONE HIS DARK MAJESTY SEEKS!
IF THIS IS ONLY THE GUARD, I DREAD TO THINK OF HIS MASTER.
YOU WILL SUFFER AS YOU DESERVE! HE WILL PEEL THE FLESH FROM YOUR BONES!
THEN LET HIM TRY. I WILL NOT BE BESTED BY HIS LACKEY.
YOU WILL REGRET YOUR EVERY WORD! HE WILL SCOOP THE MARROW FROM YOUR SPLINTERED BONES!

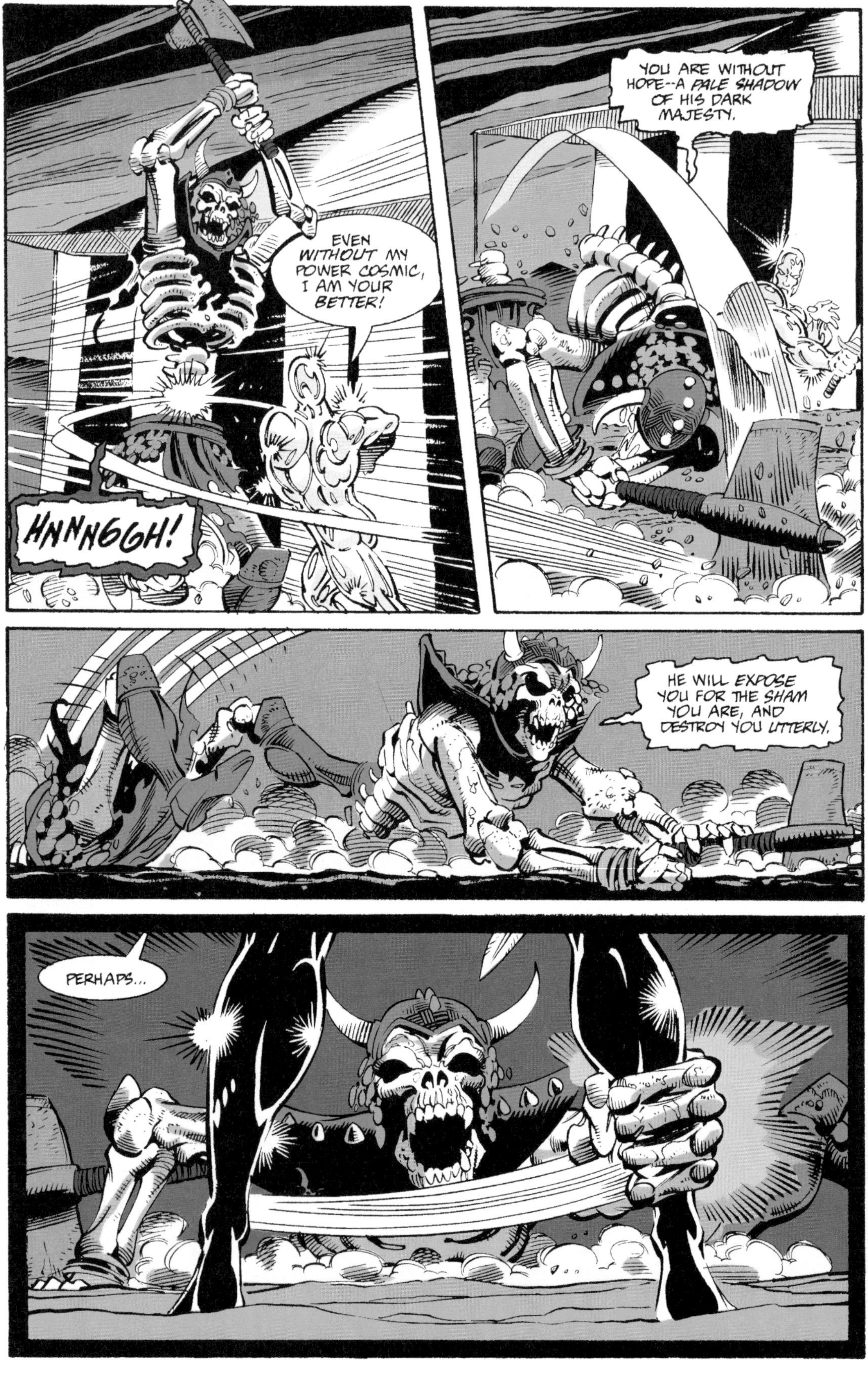
EVEN WITHOUT MY POWER COSMIC, I AM YOUR BETTER!
HNNNGGH!
YOU ARE WITHOUT HOPE--A PALE SHADOW OF HIS DARK MAJESTY.
HE WILL EXPOSE YOU FOR THE SHAM YOU ARE, AND DESTROY YOU UTTERLY.
PERHAPS...

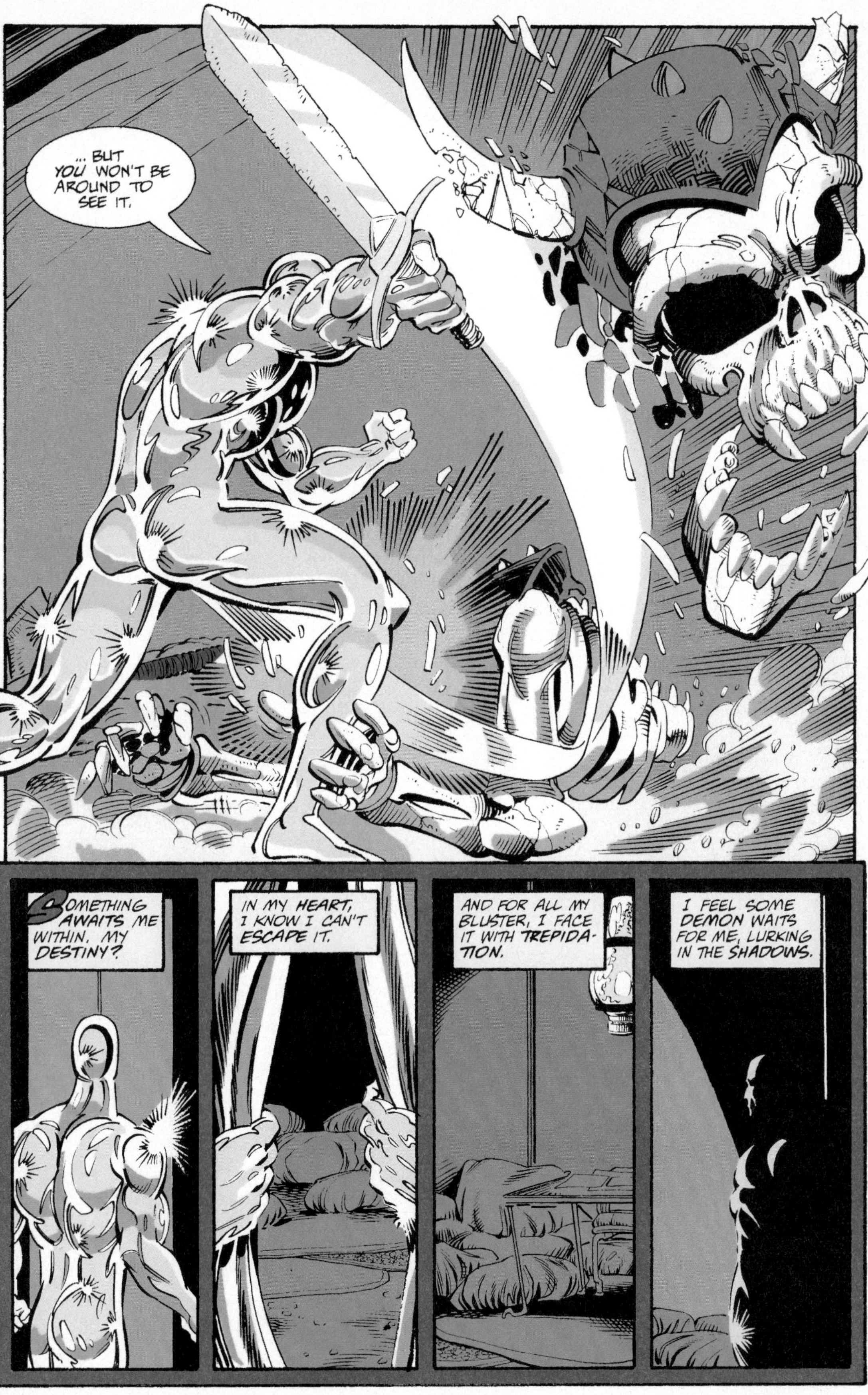
... BUT YOU WON'T BE AROUND TO SEE IT.
SOMETHING AWAITS ME WITHIN. MY DESTINY?
IN MY HEART, I KNOW I CAN'T ESCAPE IT.
AND FOR ALL MY BLUSTER, I FACE IT WITH TREPIDA-TION.
I FEEL SOME DEMON WAITS FOR ME, LURKING IN THE SHADOWS.

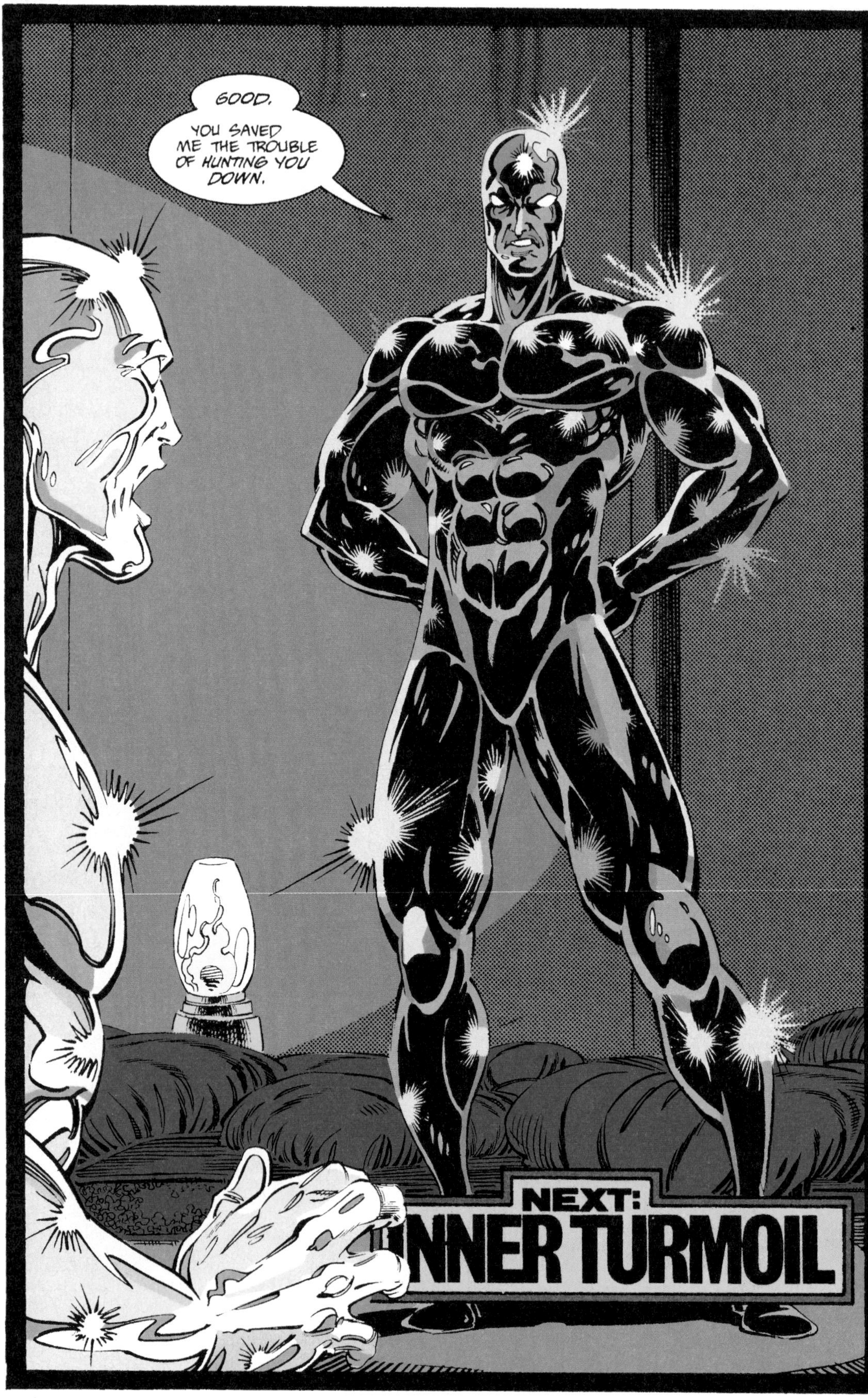
GOOD.
YOU SAVED ME THE TROUBLE OF HUNTING YOU DOWN.
NEXT:
INNER TURMOIL

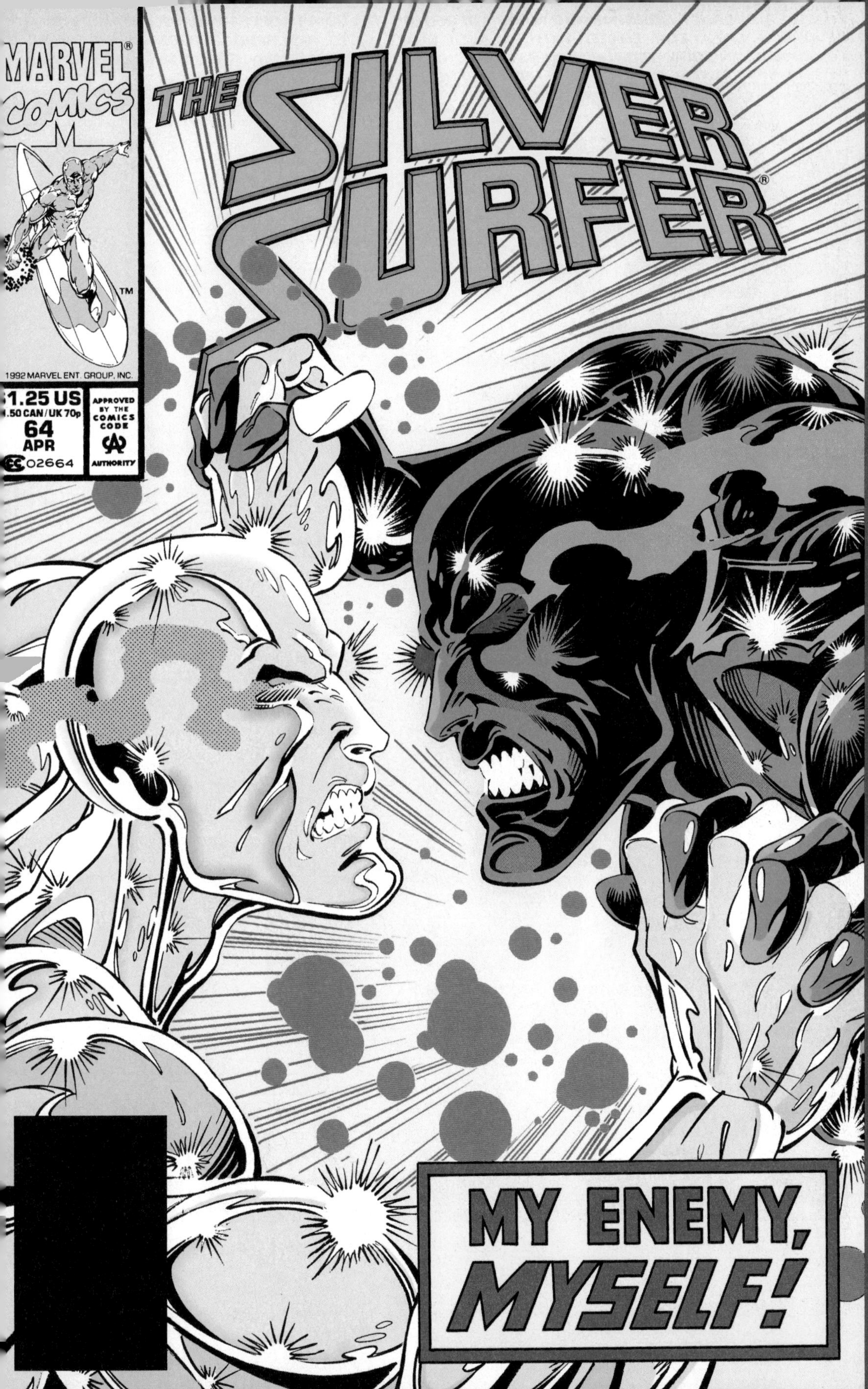
MARVEL COMICS
THE SILVER SURFER
TM
1992 MARVEL ENT. GROUP, INC.
$1.25 US
$1.50 CAN / UK 70p
64
APR
02664
APPROVED BY THE COMICS CODE AUTHORITY
MY ENEMY, MYSELF!

TO SAVE HIS PLANET, **NORRIN RADD** SURRENDERED HIS FREEDOM TO BECOME HERALD TO THE WORLD-DEVOURING **GALACTUS**. COATED WITH GALACTIC GLAZE, GIVEN A SURFBOARD OBEYING HIS MENTAL COMMANDS, AND GRANTED THE POWER COSMIC, HE NOW SOARS THE UNIVERSE, A SHINING SENTINEL OF THE SPACEWAYS! STAN LEE PRESENTS ... **THE SILVER SURFER!**

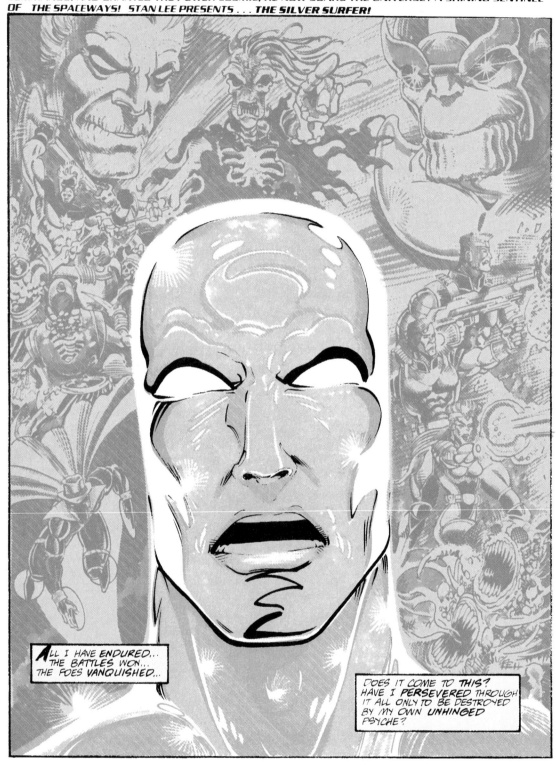

ALL I HAVE ENDURED... THE BATTLES WON... THE FOES VANQUISHED...

DOES IT COME TO **THIS**? HAVE I **PERSEVERED** THROUGH IT ALL ONLY TO BE DESTROYED BY MY OWN **UNHINGED** PSYCHE?

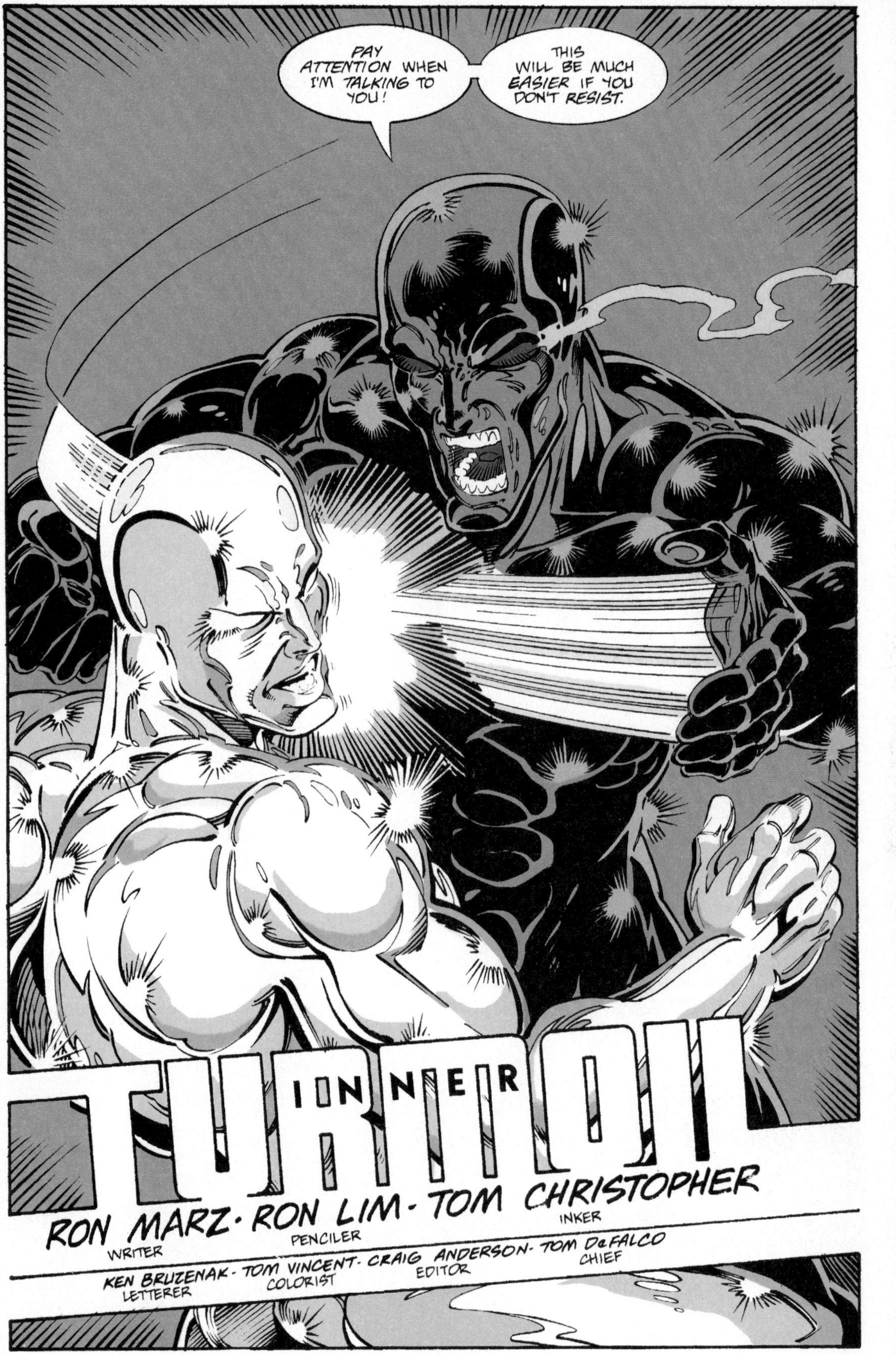
PAY ATTENTION WHEN I'M TALKING TO YOU!
THIS WILL BE MUCH EASIER IF YOU DON'T RESIST.
INNER TURMOIL
RON MARZ · RON LIM · TOM CHRISTOPHER
WRITER PENCILER INKER
KEN BRUZENAK · TOM VINCENT · CRAIG ANDERSON · TOM DeFALCO
LETTERER COLORIST EDITOR CHIEF

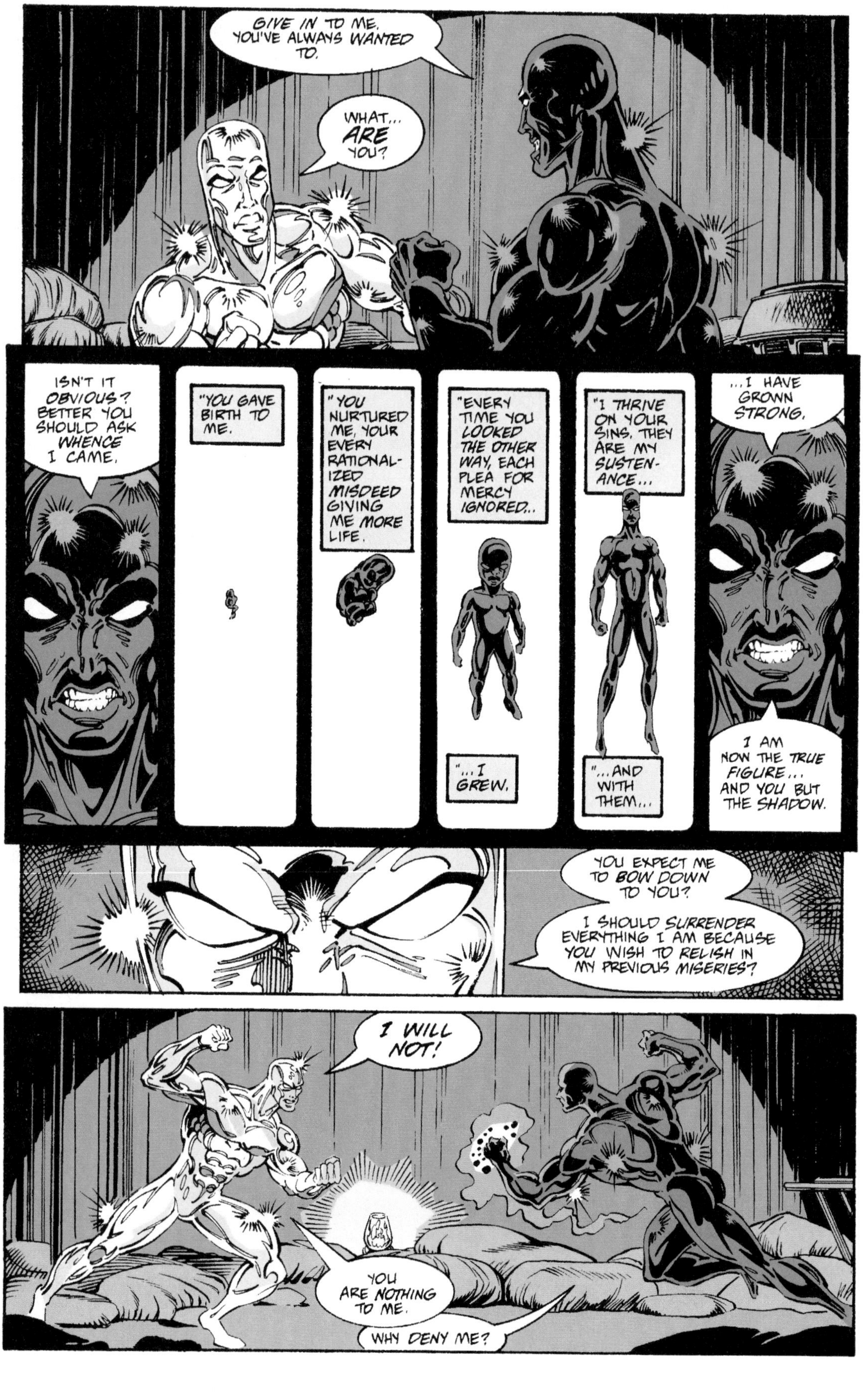

GIVE IN TO ME. YOU'VE ALWAYS WANTED TO.
WHAT... ARE YOU?
ISN'T IT OBVIOUS? BETTER YOU SHOULD ASK WHENCE I CAME.
"YOU GAVE BIRTH TO ME.
"YOU NURTURED ME, YOUR EVERY RATIONALIZED MISDEED GIVING ME MORE LIFE.
"EVERY TIME YOU LOOKED THE OTHER WAY, EACH PLEA FOR MERCY IGNORED...
"...I GREW.
"I THRIVE ON YOUR SINS. THEY ARE MY SUSTENANCE...
"...AND WITH THEM...
...I HAVE GROWN STRONG.
I AM NOW THE TRUE FIGURE... AND YOU BUT THE SHADOW.
YOU EXPECT ME TO BOW DOWN TO YOU?
I SHOULD SURRENDER EVERYTHING I AM BECAUSE YOU WISH TO RELISH IN MY PREVIOUS MISERIES?
I WILL NOT!
YOU ARE NOTHING TO ME.
WHY DENY ME?

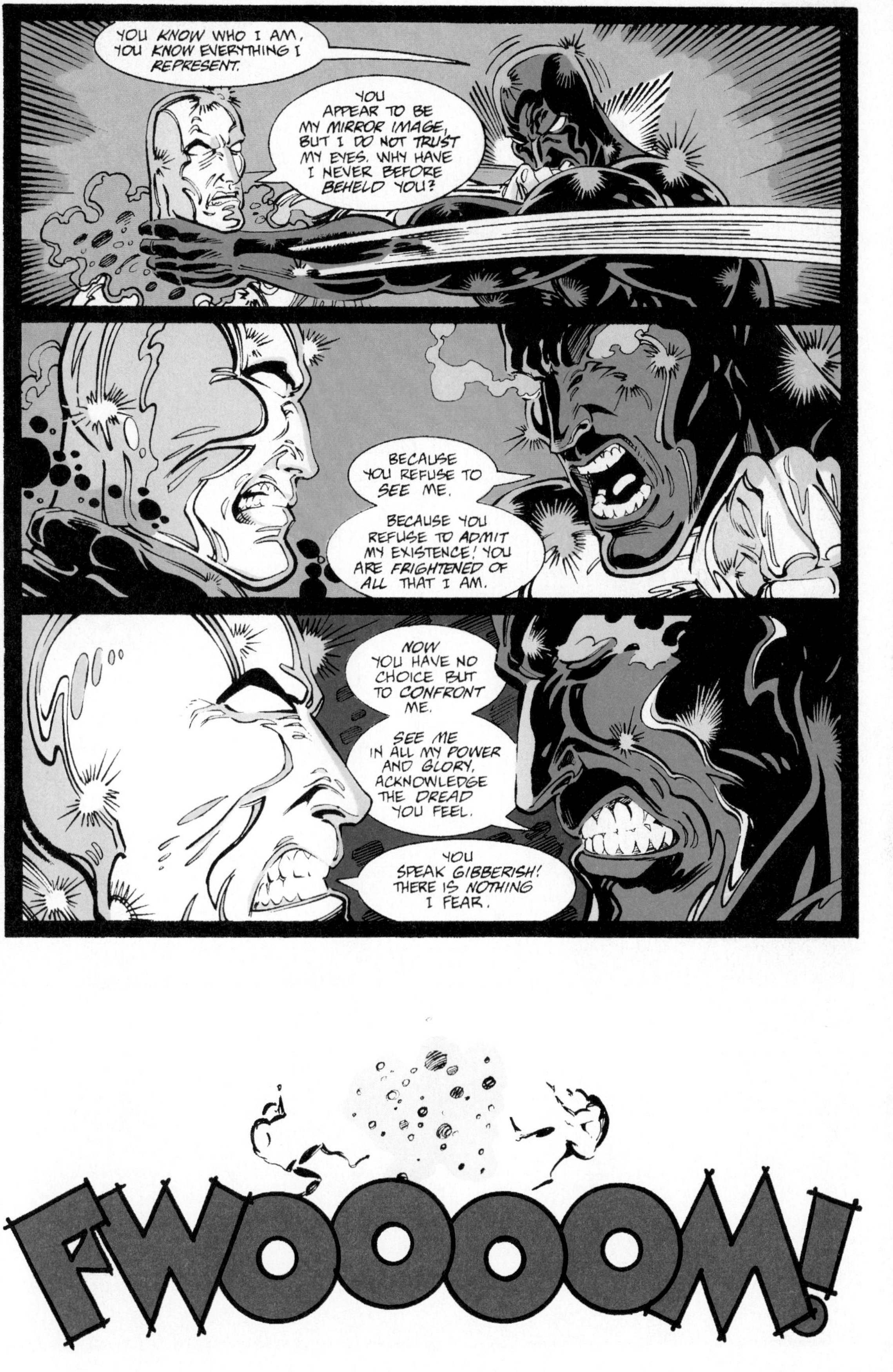
YOU KNOW WHO I AM, YOU KNOW EVERYTHING I REPRESENT.
YOU APPEAR TO BE MY MIRROR IMAGE, BUT I DO NOT TRUST MY EYES. WHY HAVE I NEVER BEFORE BEHELD YOU?
BECAUSE YOU REFUSE TO SEE ME.
BECAUSE YOU REFUSE TO ADMIT MY EXISTENCE! YOU ARE FRIGHTENED OF ALL THAT I AM.
NOW YOU HAVE NO CHOICE BUT TO CONFRONT ME.
SEE ME IN ALL MY POWER AND GLORY. ACKNOWLEDGE THE DREAD YOU FEEL.
YOU SPEAK GIBBERISH! THERE IS NOTHING I FEAR.
FWOOOOM!

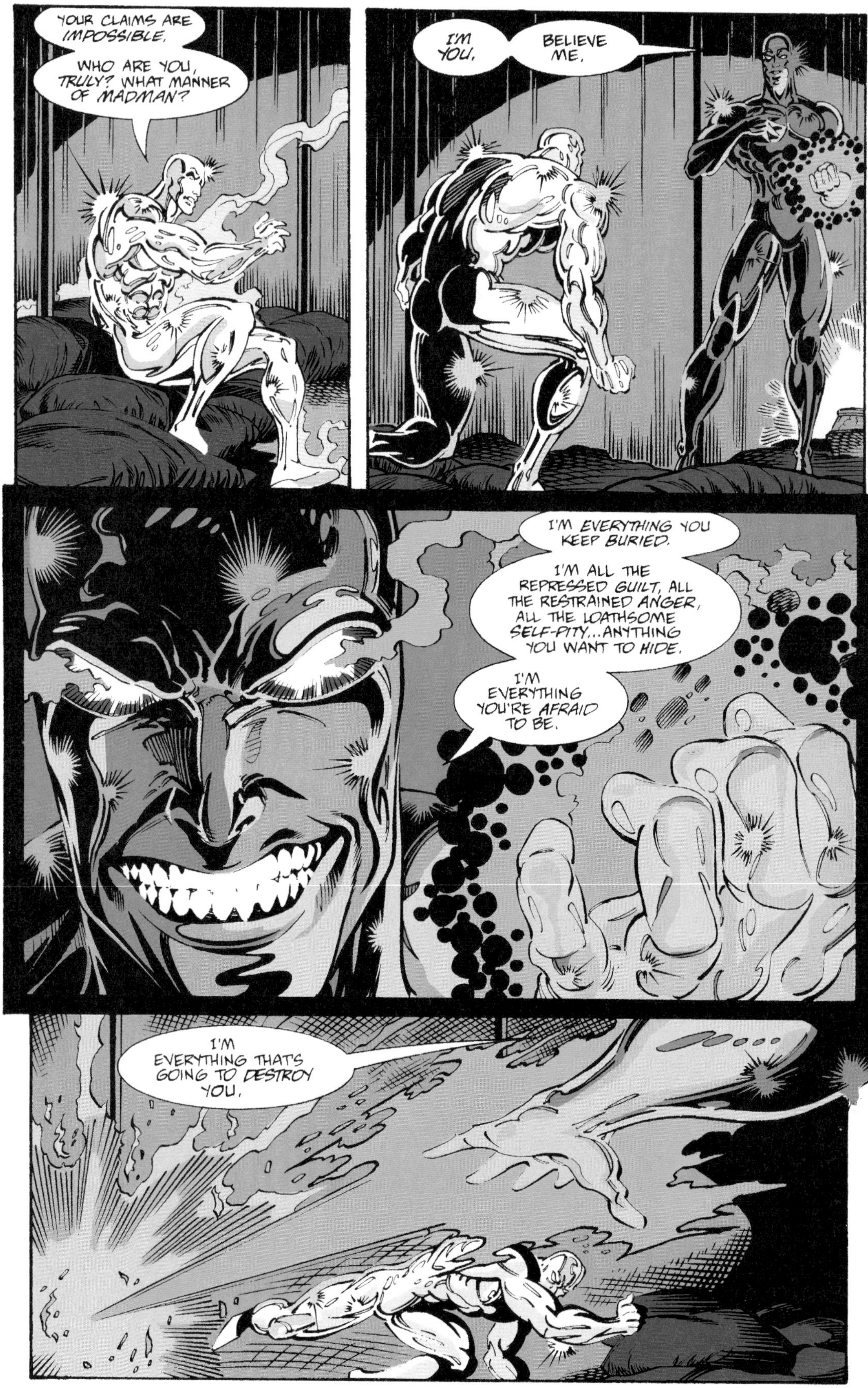
YOUR CLAIMS ARE IMPOSSIBLE.
WHO ARE YOU, TRULY? WHAT MANNER OF MADMAN?
I'M YOU.
BELIEVE ME.
I'M EVERYTHING YOU KEEP BURIED.
I'M ALL THE REPRESSED GUILT, ALL THE RESTRAINED ANGER, ALL THE LOATHSOME SELF-PITY...ANYTHING YOU WANT TO HIDE.
I'M EVERYTHING YOU'RE AFRAID TO BE.
I'M EVERYTHING THAT'S GOING TO DESTROY YOU.

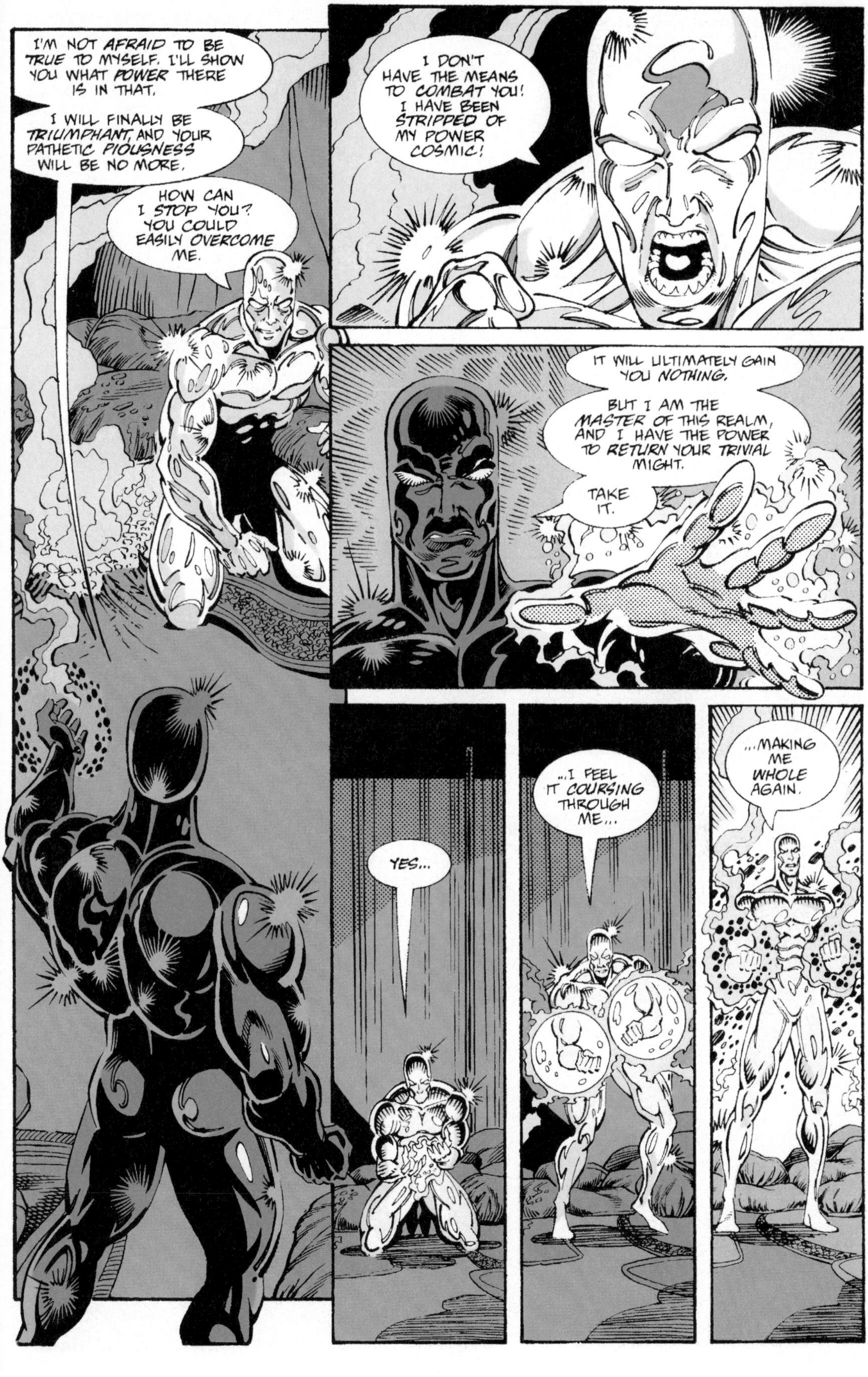

I'M NOT AFRAID TO BE TRUE TO MYSELF. I'LL SHOW YOU WHAT POWER THERE IS IN THAT.
I WILL FINALLY BE TRIUMPHANT, AND YOUR PATHETIC PIOUSNESS WILL BE NO MORE.
HOW CAN I STOP YOU? YOU COULD EASILY OVERCOME ME.
I DON'T HAVE THE MEANS TO COMBAT YOU! I HAVE BEEN STRIPPED OF MY POWER COSMIC!
IT WILL ULTIMATELY GAIN YOU NOTHING.
BUT I AM THE MASTER OF THIS REALM, AND I HAVE THE POWER TO RETURN YOUR TRIVIAL MIGHT.
TAKE IT.
YES...
...I FEEL IT COURSING THROUGH ME...
...MAKING ME WHOLE AGAIN.

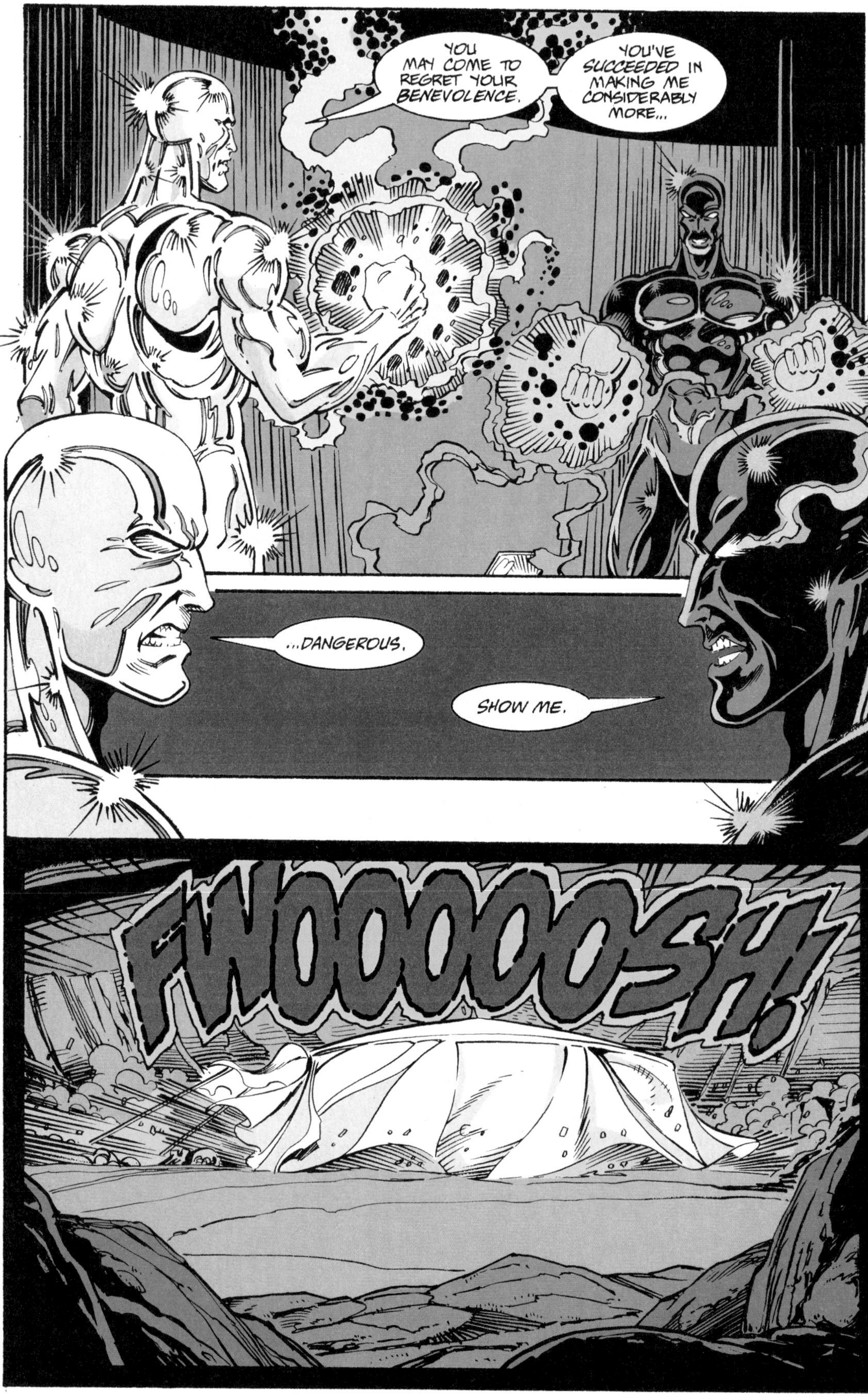
YOU MAY COME TO REGRET YOUR BENEVOLENCE.
YOU'VE SUCCEEDED IN MAKING ME CONSIDERABLY MORE...
...DANGEROUS.
SHOW ME.
FWOOOOOSH!

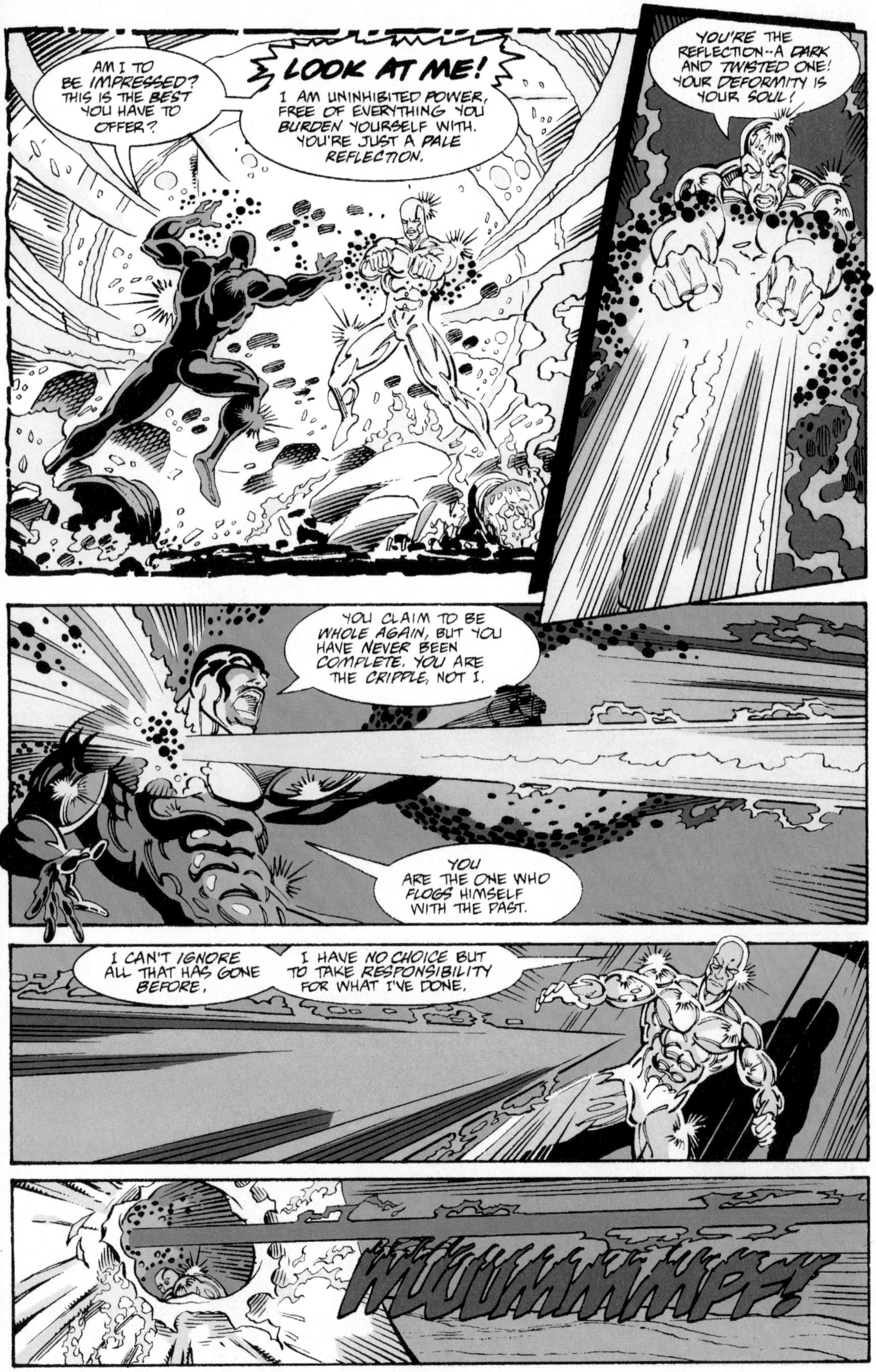
AM I TO BE IMPRESSED? THIS IS THE BEST YOU HAVE TO OFFER?
LOOK AT ME!
I AM UNINHIBITED POWER, FREE OF EVERYTHING YOU BURDEN YOURSELF WITH. YOU'RE JUST A PALE REFLECTION.
YOU'RE THE REFLECTION--A DARK AND TWISTED ONE! YOUR DEFORMITY IS YOUR SOUL!
YOU CLAIM TO BE WHOLE AGAIN, BUT YOU HAVE NEVER BEEN COMPLETE. YOU ARE THE CRIPPLE, NOT I.
YOU ARE THE ONE WHO FLOGS HIMSELF WITH THE PAST.
I CAN'T IGNORE ALL THAT HAS GONE BEFORE.
I HAVE NO CHOICE BUT TO TAKE RESPONSIBILITY FOR WHAT I'VE DONE.
WUUUMMMMPF!

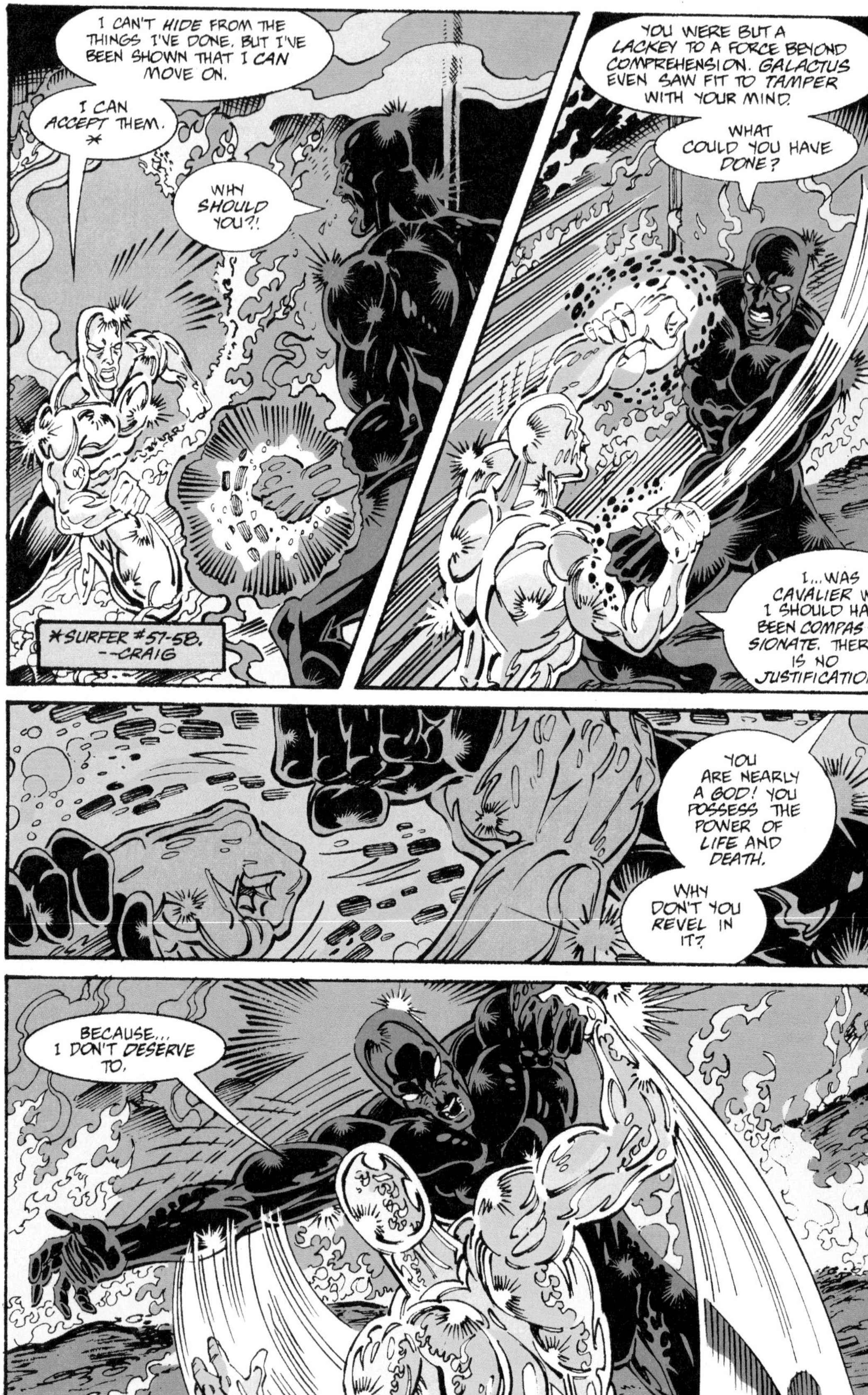
I CAN'T HIDE FROM THE THINGS I'VE DONE. BUT I'VE BEEN SHOWN THAT I CAN MOVE ON.
I CAN ACCEPT THEM. *
WHY SHOULD YOU?!
*SURFER #57-58. --CRAIG
YOU WERE BUT A LACKEY TO A FORCE BEYOND COMPREHENSION. GALACTUS EVEN SAW FIT TO TAMPER WITH YOUR MIND.
WHAT COULD YOU HAVE DONE?
I... WAS CAVALIER WHEN I SHOULD HAVE BEEN COMPASSIONATE. THERE IS NO JUSTIFICATION.
YOU ARE NEARLY A GOD! YOU POSSESS THE POWER OF LIFE AND DEATH.
WHY DON'T YOU REVEL IN IT?
BECAUSE... I DON'T DESERVE TO.

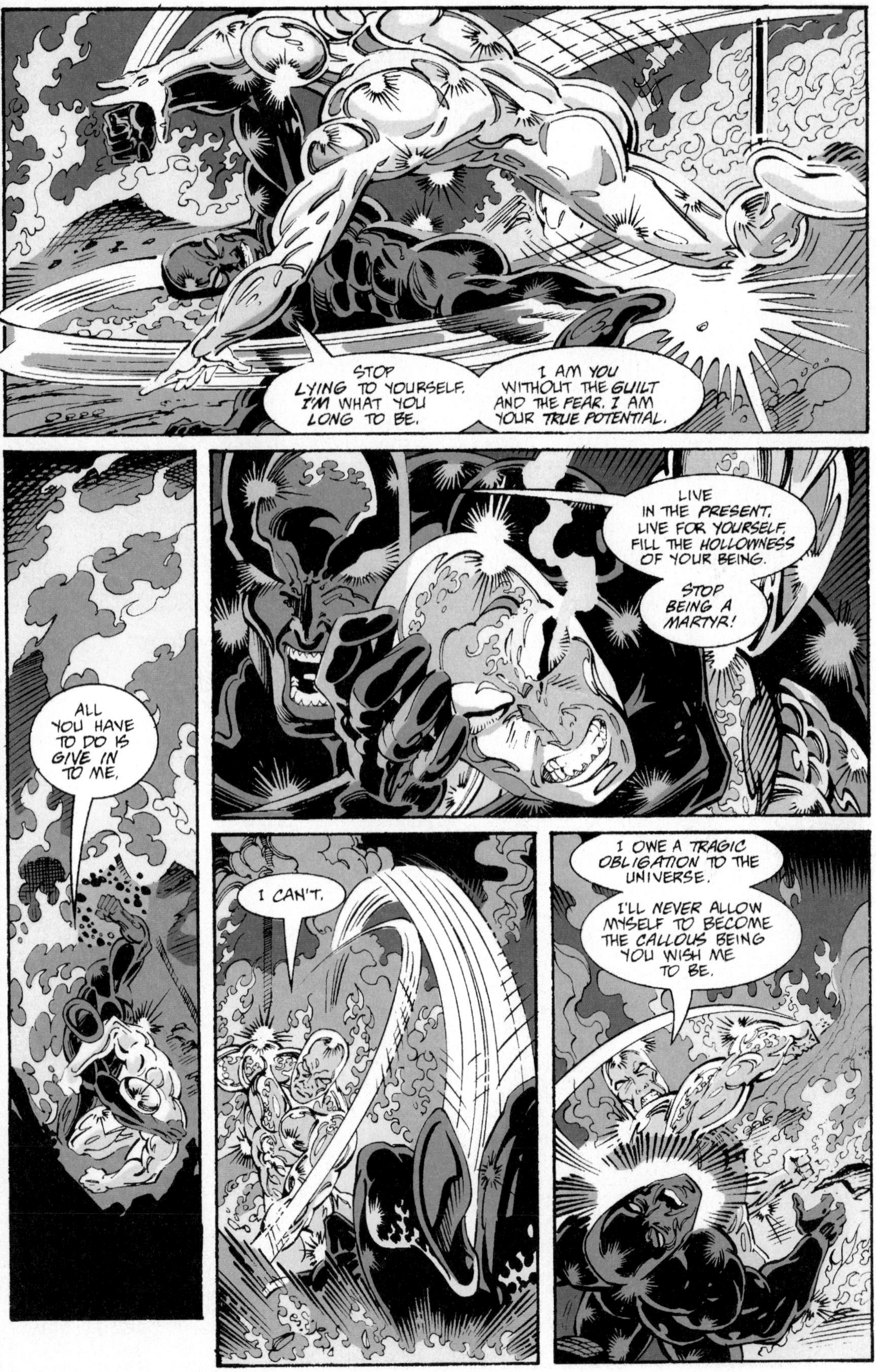

STOP LYING TO YOURSELF. I'M WHAT YOU LONG TO BE.
I AM YOU WITHOUT THE GUILT AND THE FEAR. I AM YOUR TRUE POTENTIAL.
ALL YOU HAVE TO DO IS GIVE IN TO ME.
LIVE IN THE PRESENT. LIVE FOR YOURSELF. FILL THE HOLLOWNESS OF YOUR BEING.
STOP BEING A MARTYR!
I CAN'T.
I OWE A TRAGIC OBLIGATION TO THE UNIVERSE.
I'LL NEVER ALLOW MYSELF TO BECOME THE CALLOUS BEING YOU WISH ME TO BE.

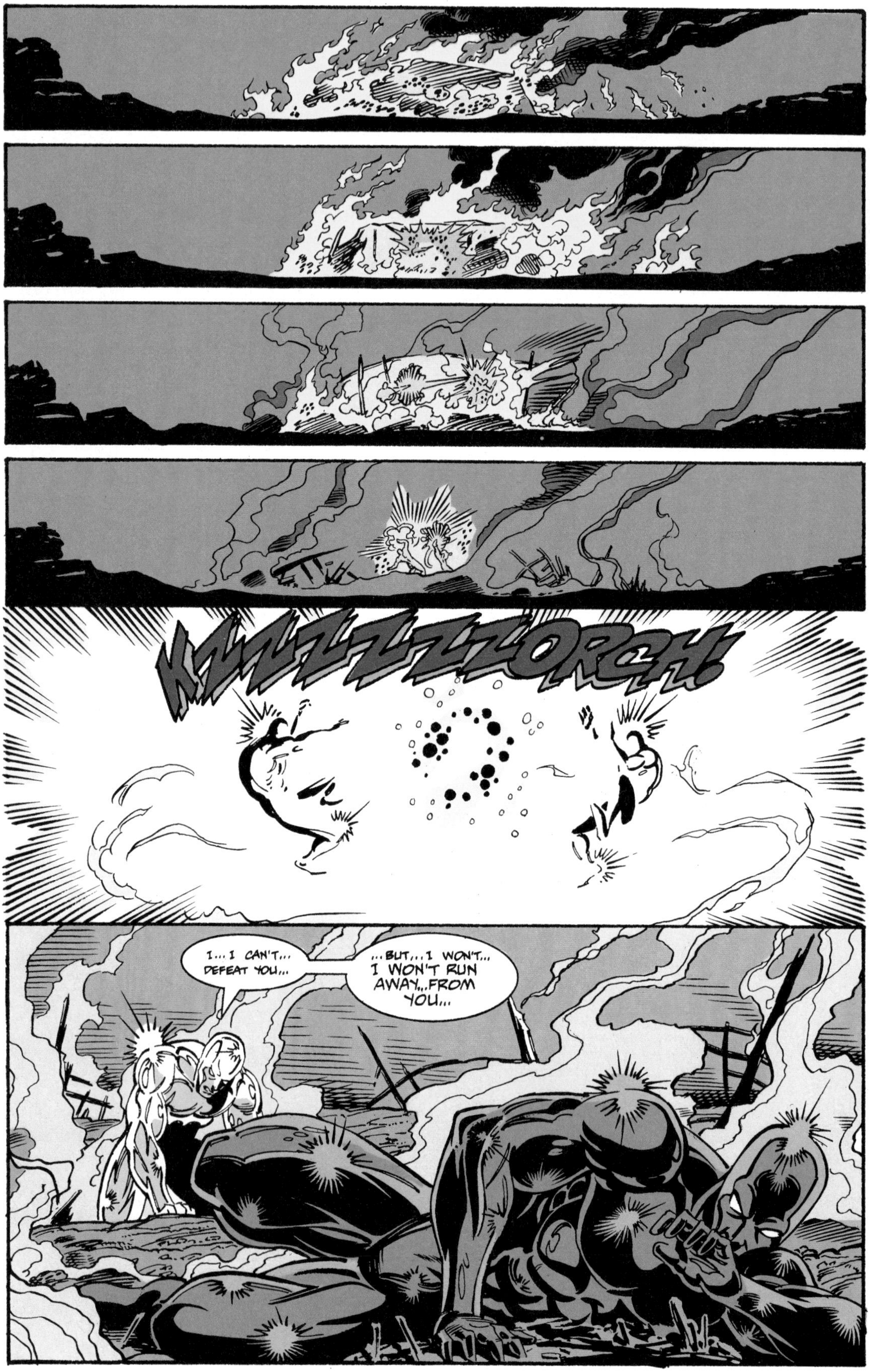
KZZZZZZORCH!
I... I CAN'T... DEFEAT YOU...
...BUT... I WON'T... I WON'T RUN AWAY... FROM YOU...

THERE NEVER WILL BE A VICTOR, WILL THERE? YOU AND I ARE TOO EVENLY MATCHED, TWO SIDES OF THE SAME COIN.

HOW CAN I EXPECT TO DEFEAT MYSELF?

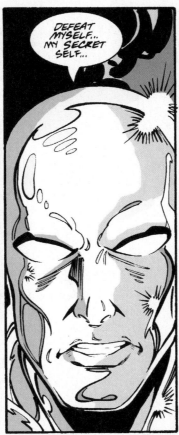

DEFEAT MYSELF... MY SECRET SELF...

YOU'RE BABBLING.

GET UP. WE'RE NOT FINISHED.

YES, WE ARE.

YOU KNOW, DON'T YOU? YOU KNEW ALL ALONG. BUT YOU DON'T WANT IT TO BE LIKE THAT.

YOU DON'T WANT TO GIVE UP WHAT YOU ARE.

YOU WANTED IT TO BE YOUR WAY, JUST LIKE I INSISTED ON MY WAY. BUT NEITHER WORKS. NEITHER'S RIGHT.

YOU CAN'T... I DON'T KNOW WHAT YOU'RE TALKING ABOUT.

I'M GOING TO BEAT YOU. I'M... I'M GOING TO WIN.

NO. THERE CAN'T BE A WINNER.

EVER.

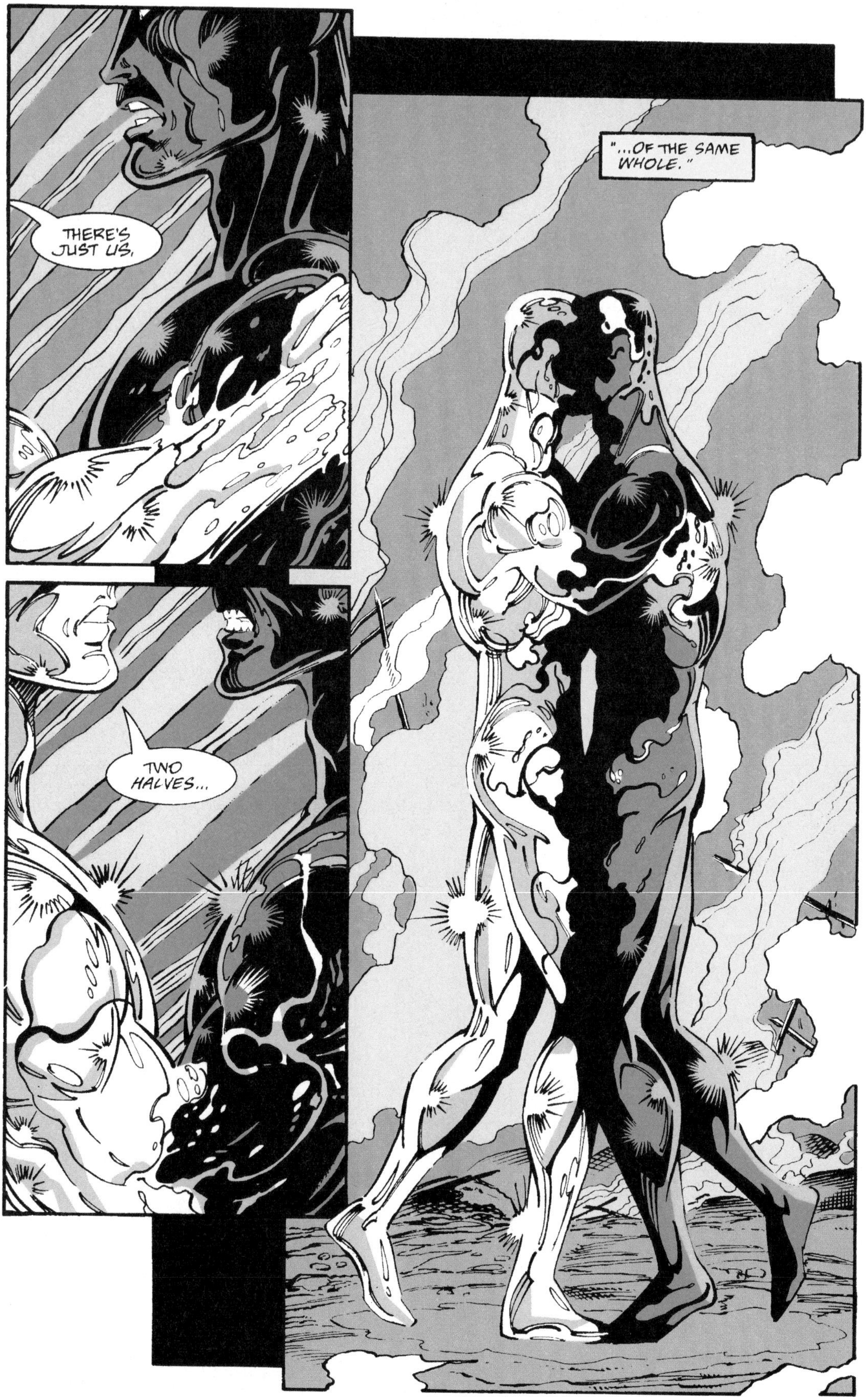
THERE'S JUST US,
TWO HALVES...
"...OF THE SAME WHOLE."

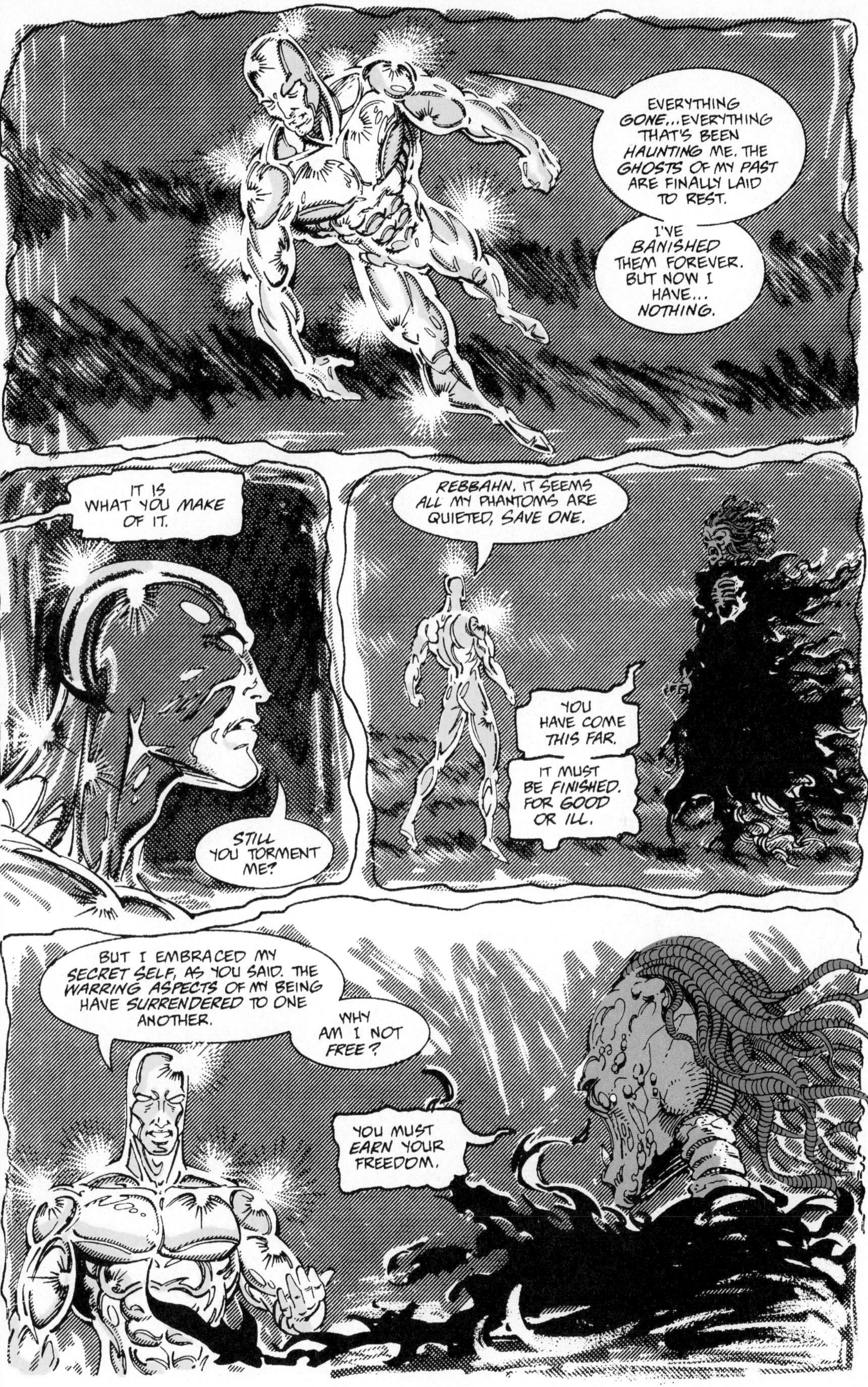
EVERYTHING GONE...EVERYTHING THAT'S BEEN HAUNTING ME. THE GHOSTS OF MY PAST ARE FINALLY LAID TO REST.
I'VE BANISHED THEM FOREVER. BUT NOW I HAVE... NOTHING.
IT IS WHAT YOU MAKE OF IT.
STILL YOU TORMENT ME?
REBBAHN. IT SEEMS ALL MY PHANTOMS ARE QUIETED, SAVE ONE.
YOU HAVE COME THIS FAR.
IT MUST BE FINISHED. FOR GOOD OR ILL.
BUT I EMBRACED MY SECRET SELF, AS YOU SAID. THE WARRING ASPECTS OF MY BEING HAVE SURRENDERED TO ONE ANOTHER.
WHY AM I NOT FREE?
YOU MUST EARN YOUR FREEDOM.

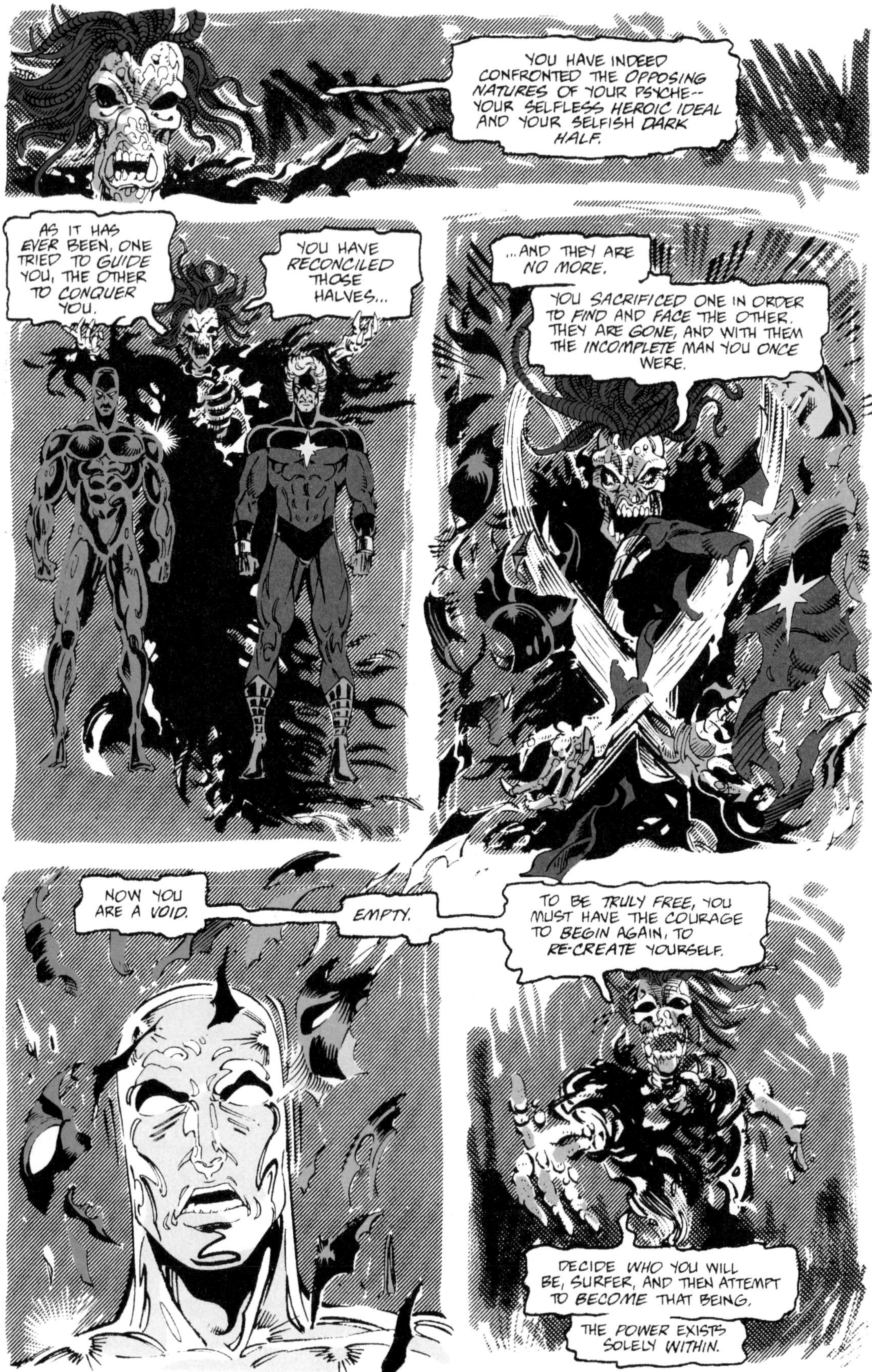
YOU HAVE INDEED CONFRONTED THE OPPOSING NATURES OF YOUR PSYCHE-- YOUR SELFLESS HEROIC IDEAL AND YOUR SELFISH DARK HALF.
AS IT HAS EVER BEEN, ONE TRIED TO GUIDE YOU, THE OTHER TO CONQUER YOU.
YOU HAVE RECONCILED THOSE HALVES...
...AND THEY ARE NO MORE.
YOU SACRIFICED ONE IN ORDER TO FIND AND FACE THE OTHER. THEY ARE GONE, AND WITH THEM THE INCOMPLETE MAN YOU ONCE WERE.
NOW YOU ARE A VOID.
EMPTY.
TO BE TRULY FREE, YOU MUST HAVE THE COURAGE TO BEGIN AGAIN, TO RE-CREATE YOURSELF.
DECIDE WHO YOU WILL BE, SURFER, AND THEN ATTEMPT TO BECOME THAT BEING.
THE POWER EXISTS SOLELY WITHIN.

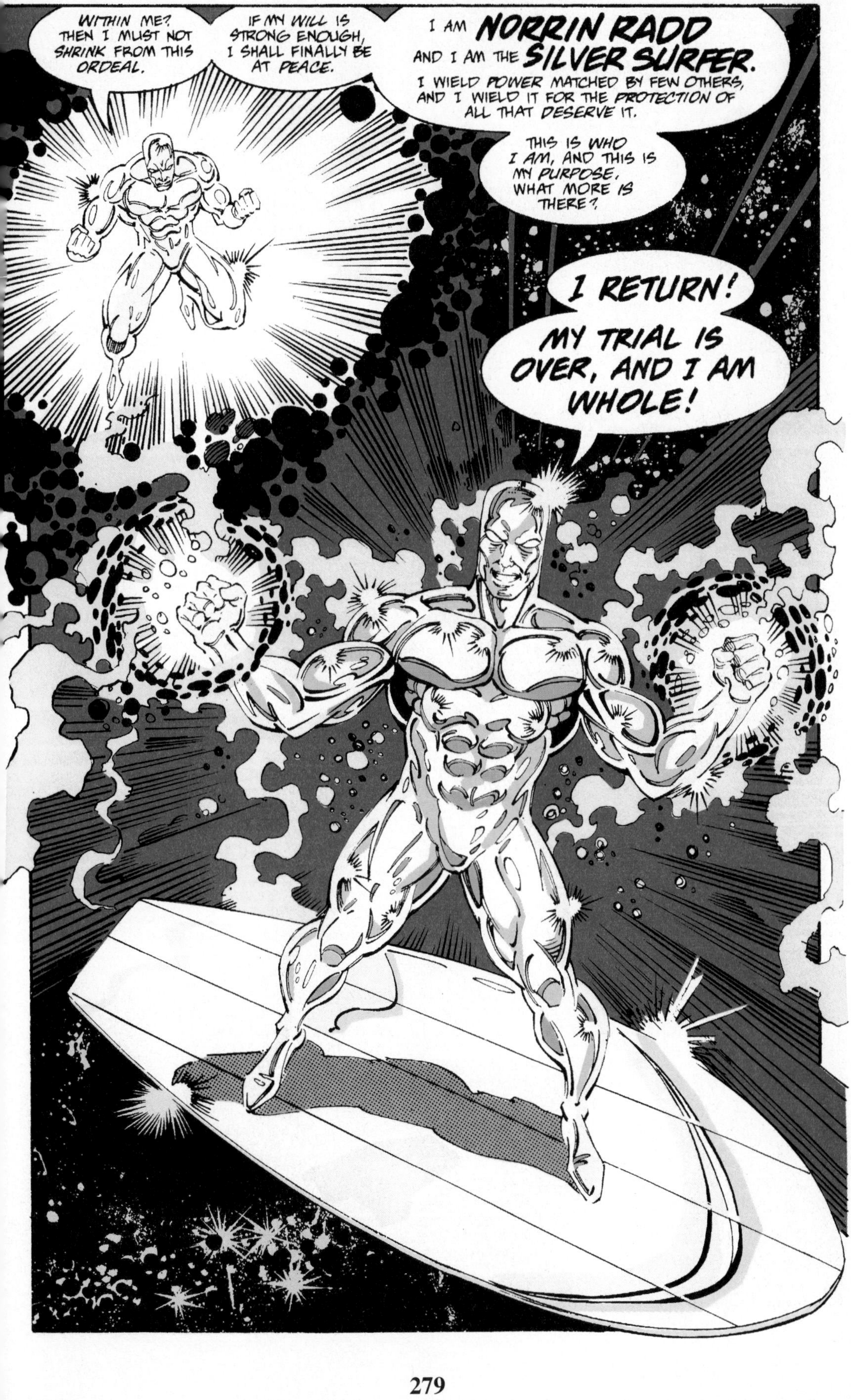
WITHIN ME? THEN I MUST NOT SHRINK FROM THIS ORDEAL.
IF MY WILL IS STRONG ENOUGH, I SHALL FINALLY BE AT PEACE.
I AM NORRIN RADD AND I AM THE SILVER SURFER.
I WIELD POWER MATCHED BY FEW OTHERS, AND I WIELD IT FOR THE PROTECTION OF ALL THAT DESERVE IT.
THIS IS WHO I AM, AND THIS IS MY PURPOSE. WHAT MORE IS THERE?
I RETURN!
MY TRIAL IS OVER, AND I AM WHOLE!

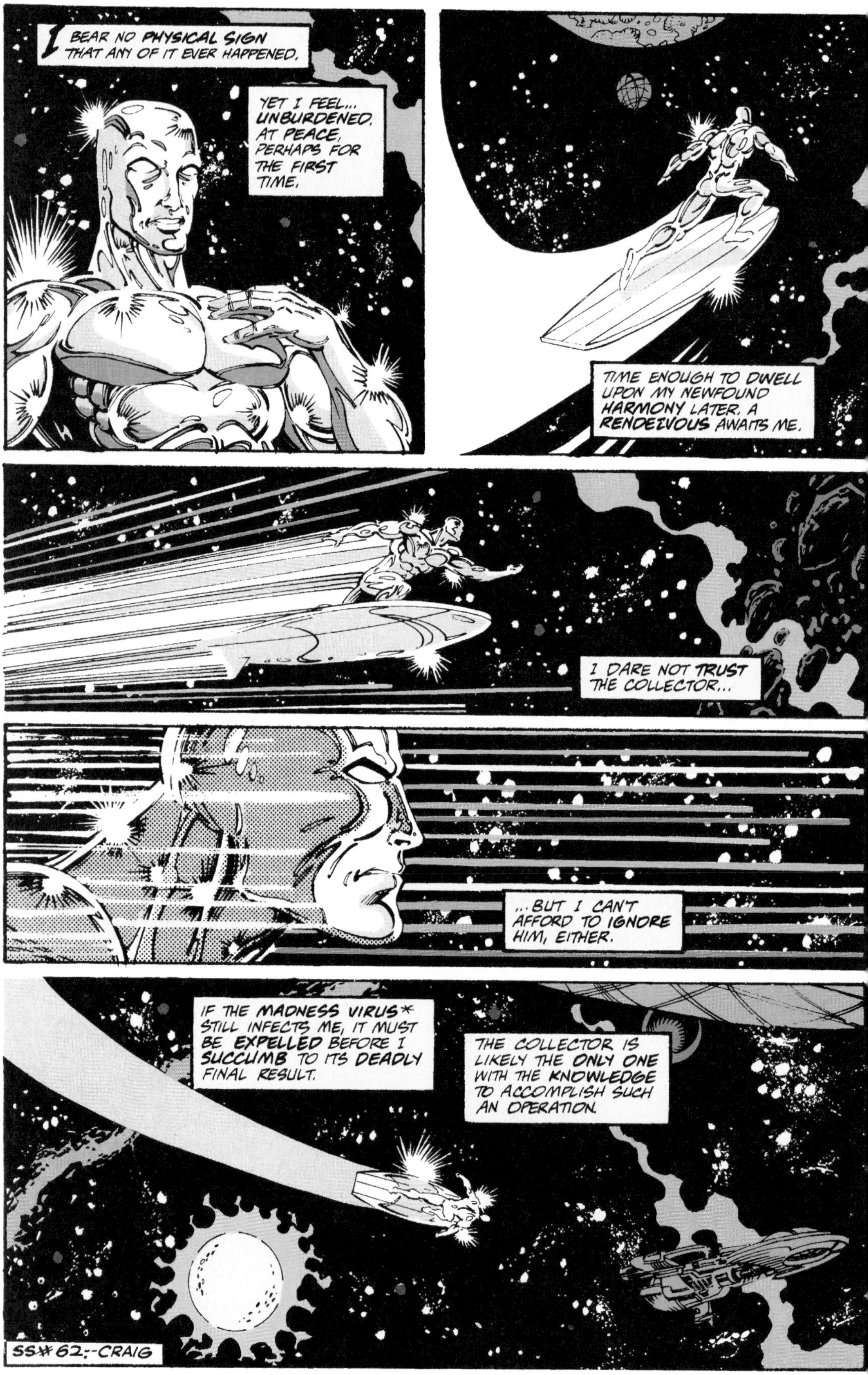
I BEAR NO PHYSICAL SIGN THAT ANY OF IT EVER HAPPENED.
YET I FEEL... UNBURDENED. AT PEACE. PERHAPS FOR THE FIRST TIME.
TIME ENOUGH TO DWELL UPON MY NEWFOUND HARMONY LATER. A RENDEZVOUS AWAITS ME.
I DARE NOT TRUST THE COLLECTOR...
...BUT I CAN'T AFFORD TO IGNORE HIM, EITHER.
IF THE MADNESS VIRUS* STILL INFECTS ME, IT MUST BE EXPELLED BEFORE I SUCCUMB TO ITS DEADLY FINAL RESULT.
THE COLLECTOR IS LIKELY THE ONLY ONE WITH THE KNOWLEDGE TO ACCOMPLISH SUCH AN OPERATION.
SS#62.--CRAIG

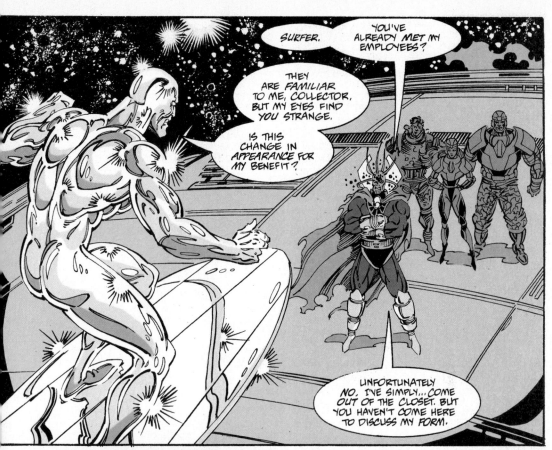

SURFER.

YOU'VE ALREADY *MET* MY *EMPLOYEES*?

THEY ARE *FAMILIAR* TO ME, COLLECTOR, BUT MY EYES FIND YOU STRANGE.

IS THIS CHANGE IN APPEARANCE FOR MY BENEFIT?

UNFORTUNATELY NO, I'VE SIMPLY...COME OUT OF THE CLOSET. BUT YOU HAVEN'T COME HERE TO DISCUSS MY *FORM*.

I'M GLAD TO SEE YOU. I BEGAN TO FEAR FOR YOUR SAFETY WHEN YOU DISAPPEARED FROM MY SENSORS BRIEFLY.

I SHOULD HAVE KNOWN *NOTHING* BARS THE PATH OF THE *SILVER SURFER*.

NOW, I BELIEVE YOU'RE IN POSSESSION OF SOME *PROPERTY* OF MINE. IF YOU WOULD--

--*WHAT*?! THERE ARE *NO* TRACES OF THE VIRUS WITHIN YOU! WHERE IS IT?

GONE FOR GOOD, AS YOU'VE JUST CONFIRMED.

I HAD CERTAIN...*EXPERIENCES*...WHILE THE VIRUS AFFECTED MY MIND. THEY ALLOWED ME TO *EXORCISE* THE DEMONS THAT WERE MY TORMENTORS FOR SO LONG.

I ASSUME WHEN MY PSYCHE WAS *CLEANSED*, THE VIRUS HAD NO *WEAKNESSES* TO FEED UPON, LEAVING IT *VULNERABLE* TO MY COSMIC IMMUNITY.

YOU *DESTROYED* IT BECAUSE YOU'RE *WELL-ADJUSTED* ALL THE SUDDEN!?

YOU DIDN'T HAVE THE *RIGHT*! IT WAS *MINE*!

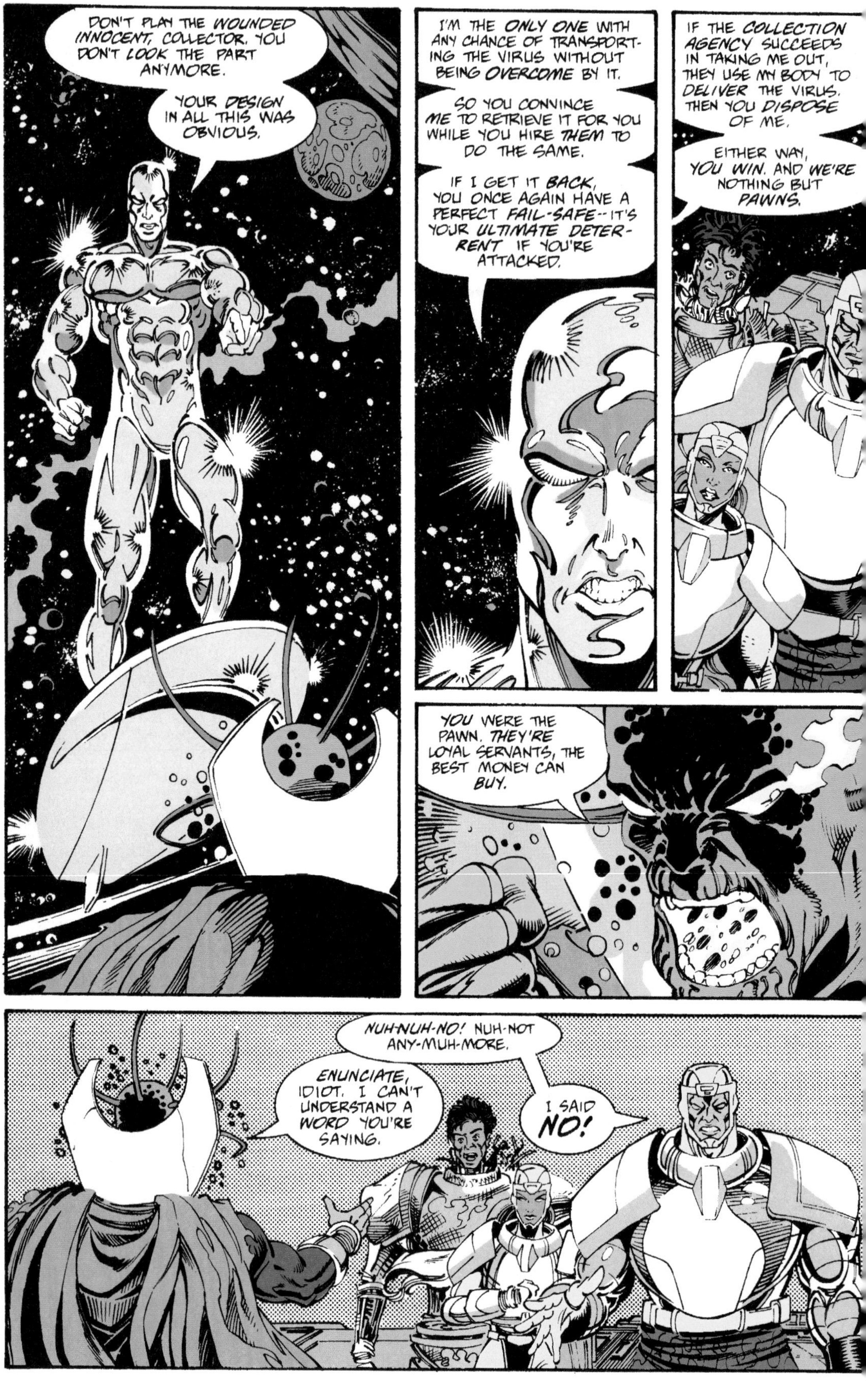
DON'T PLAY THE WOUNDED INNOCENT, COLLECTOR. YOU DON'T LOOK THE PART ANYMORE.
YOUR DESIGN IN ALL THIS WAS OBVIOUS.
I'M THE ONLY ONE WITH ANY CHANCE OF TRANSPORTING THE VIRUS WITHOUT BEING OVERCOME BY IT.
SO YOU CONVINCE ME TO RETRIEVE IT FOR YOU WHILE YOU HIRE THEM TO DO THE SAME.
IF I GET IT BACK, YOU ONCE AGAIN HAVE A PERFECT FAIL-SAFE-- IT'S YOUR ULTIMATE DETERRENT IF YOU'RE ATTACKED.
IF THE COLLECTION AGENCY SUCCEEDS IN TAKING ME OUT, THEY USE MY BODY TO DELIVER THE VIRUS. THEN YOU DISPOSE OF ME.
EITHER WAY, YOU WIN. AND WE'RE NOTHING BUT PAWNS.
YOU WERE THE PAWN. THEY'RE LOYAL SERVANTS, THE BEST MONEY CAN BUY.
NUH-NUH-NO! NUH-NOT ANY-MUH-MORE.
ENUNCIATE, IDIOT. I CAN'T UNDERSTAND A WORD YOU'RE SAYING.
I SAID NO!

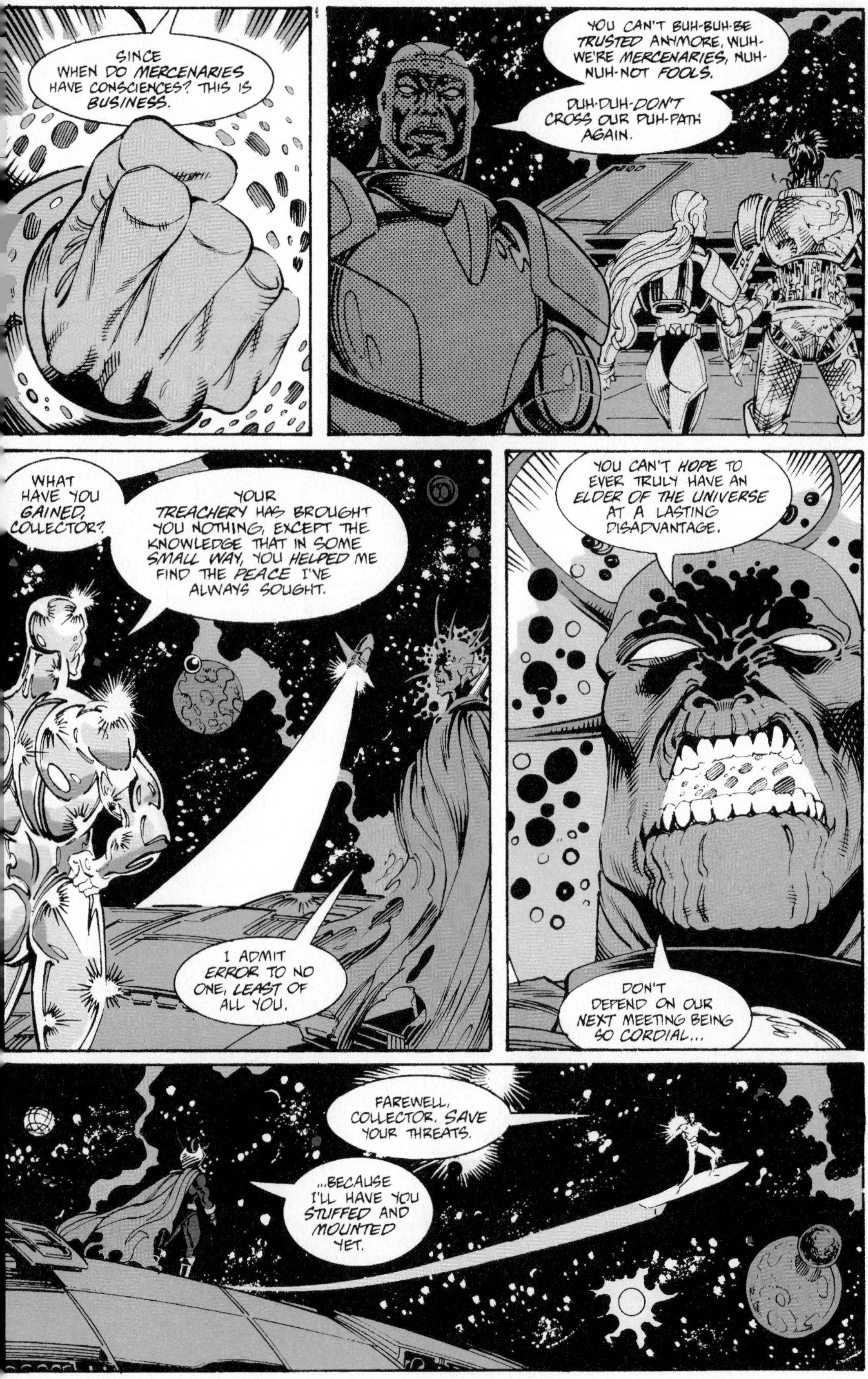
SINCE WHEN DO MERCENARIES HAVE CONSCIENCES? THIS IS BUSINESS.
YOU CAN'T BUH-BUH-BE TRUSTED ANYMORE, NUH-WE'RE MERCENARIES, NUH-NUH-NOT FOOLS.
DUH-DUH-DON'T CROSS OUR PUH-PATH AGAIN.
WHAT HAVE YOU GAINED, COLLECTOR?
YOUR TREACHERY HAS BROUGHT YOU NOTHING, EXCEPT THE KNOWLEDGE THAT IN SOME SMALL WAY, YOU HELPED ME FIND THE PEACE I'VE ALWAYS SOUGHT.
I ADMIT ERROR TO NO ONE, LEAST OF ALL YOU.
YOU CAN'T HOPE TO EVER TRULY HAVE AN ELDER OF THE UNIVERSE AT A LASTING DISADVANTAGE.
DON'T DEPEND ON OUR NEXT MEETING BEING SO CORDIAL...
FAREWELL, COLLECTOR. SAVE YOUR THREATS.
...BECAUSE I'LL HAVE YOU STUFFED AND MOUNTED YET.

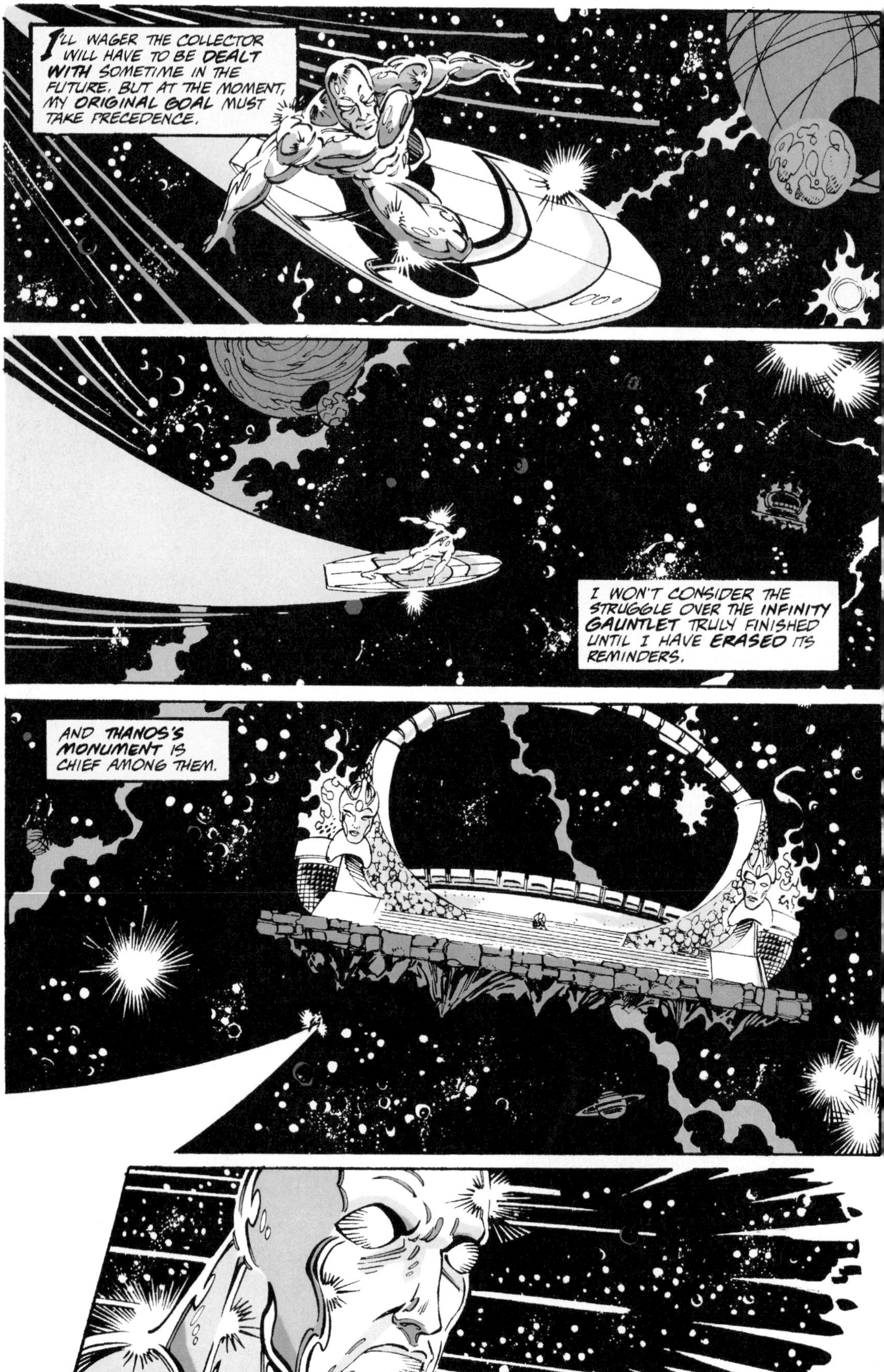
I'LL WAGER THE COLLECTOR WILL HAVE TO BE DEALT WITH SOMETIME IN THE FUTURE. BUT AT THE MOMENT, MY ORIGINAL GOAL MUST TAKE PRECEDENCE.
I WON'T CONSIDER THE STRUGGLE OVER THE INFINITY GAUNTLET TRULY FINISHED UNTIL I HAVE ERASED ITS REMINDERS.
AND THANOS'S MONUMENT IS CHIEF AMONG THEM.

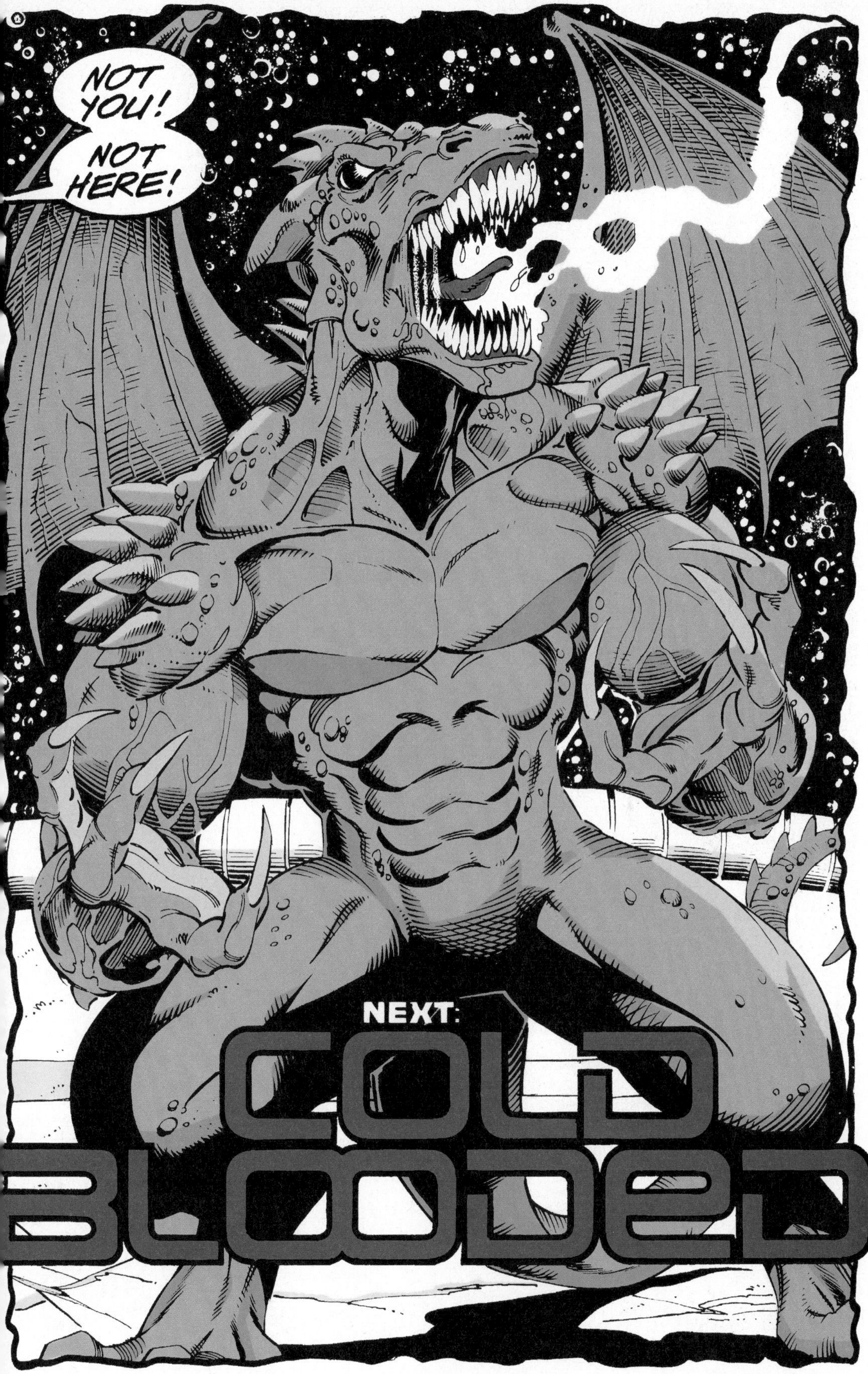
NOT YOU!
NOT HERE!
NEXT:
COLD BLOODED

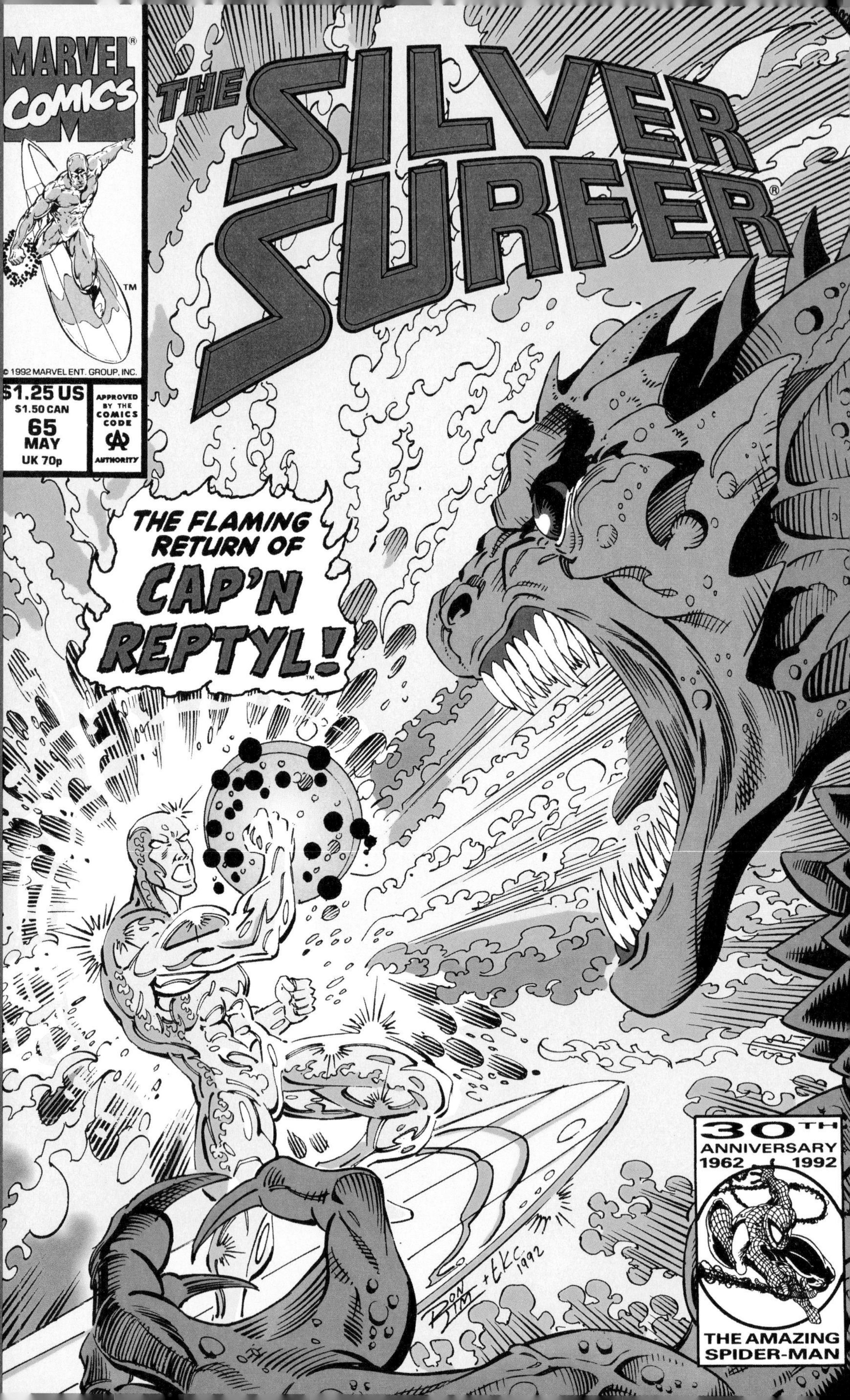
MARVEL® COMICS
THE SILVER SURFER®
TM
© 1992 MARVEL ENT. GROUP, INC.
$1.25 US
$1.50 CAN
65
MAY
UK 70p
APPROVED BY THE COMICS CODE AUTHORITY
THE FLAMING RETURN OF CAP'N REPTYL!
30TH ANNIVERSARY 1962 1992
THE AMAZING SPIDER-MAN

TO SAVE HIS PLANET, **NORRIN RADD** SURRENDERED HIS FREEDOM TO BECOME HERALD TO THE WORLD-DEVOURING **GALACTUS**. COATED WITH GALACTIC GLAZE, GIVEN A SURFBOARD OBEYING HIS MENTAL COMMANDS, AND GRANTED THE POWER COSMIC, HE NOW SOARS THE UNIVERSE, A SHINING SENTINEL OF THE SPACEWAYS! STAN LEE PRESENTS . . . **THE SILVER SURFER!**

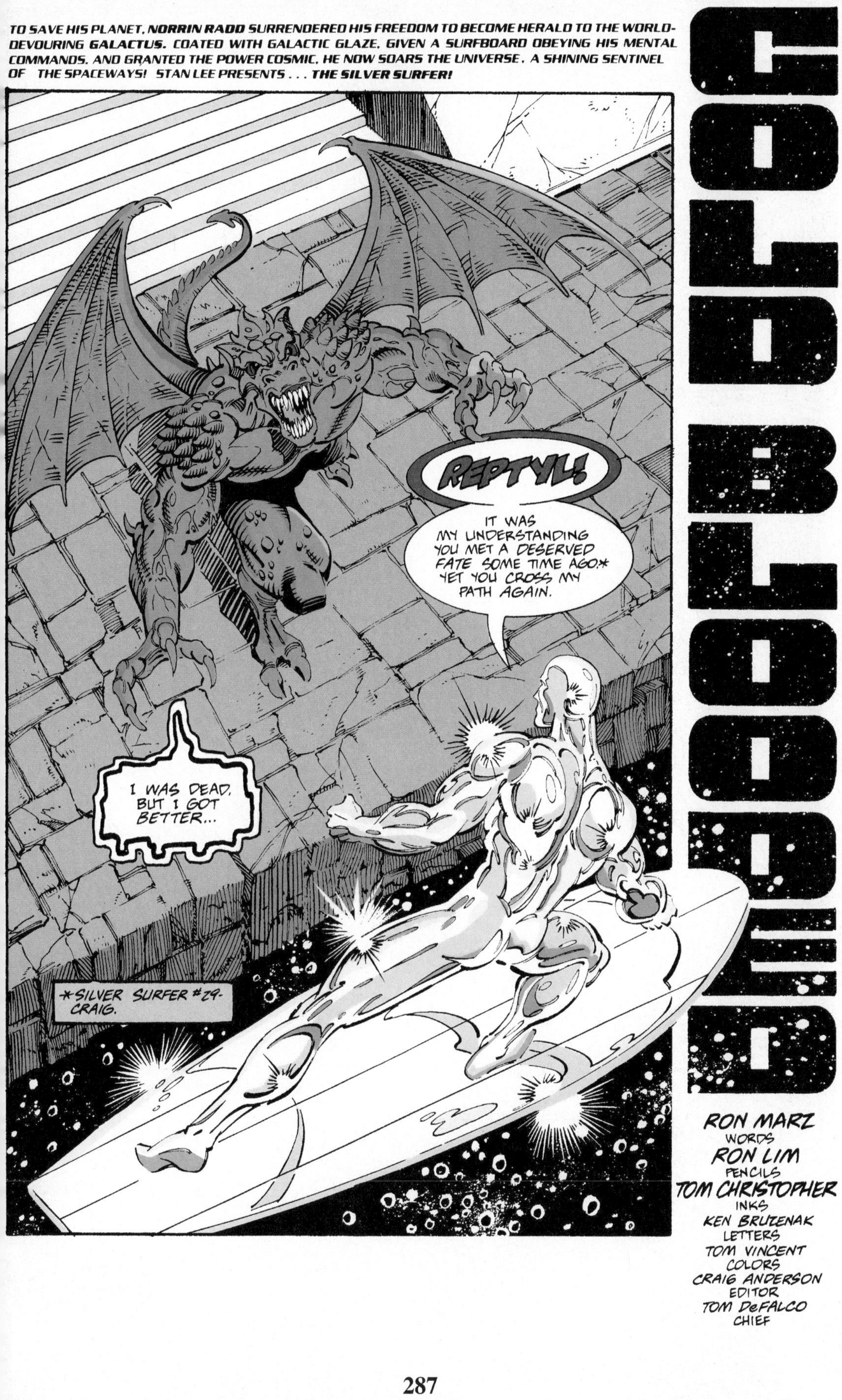

REPTYL!
IT WAS MY UNDERSTANDING YOU MET A DESERVED FATE SOME TIME AGO.* YET YOU CROSS MY PATH AGAIN.
I WAS DEAD, BUT I GOT BETTER...
*SILVER SURFER #29-CRAIG.

COLD BLOODED

RON MARZ
WORDS
RON LIM
PENCILS
TOM CHRISTOPHER
INKS
KEN BRUZENAK
LETTERS
TOM VINCENT
COLORS
CRAIG ANDERSON
EDITOR
TOM DeFALCO
CHIEF

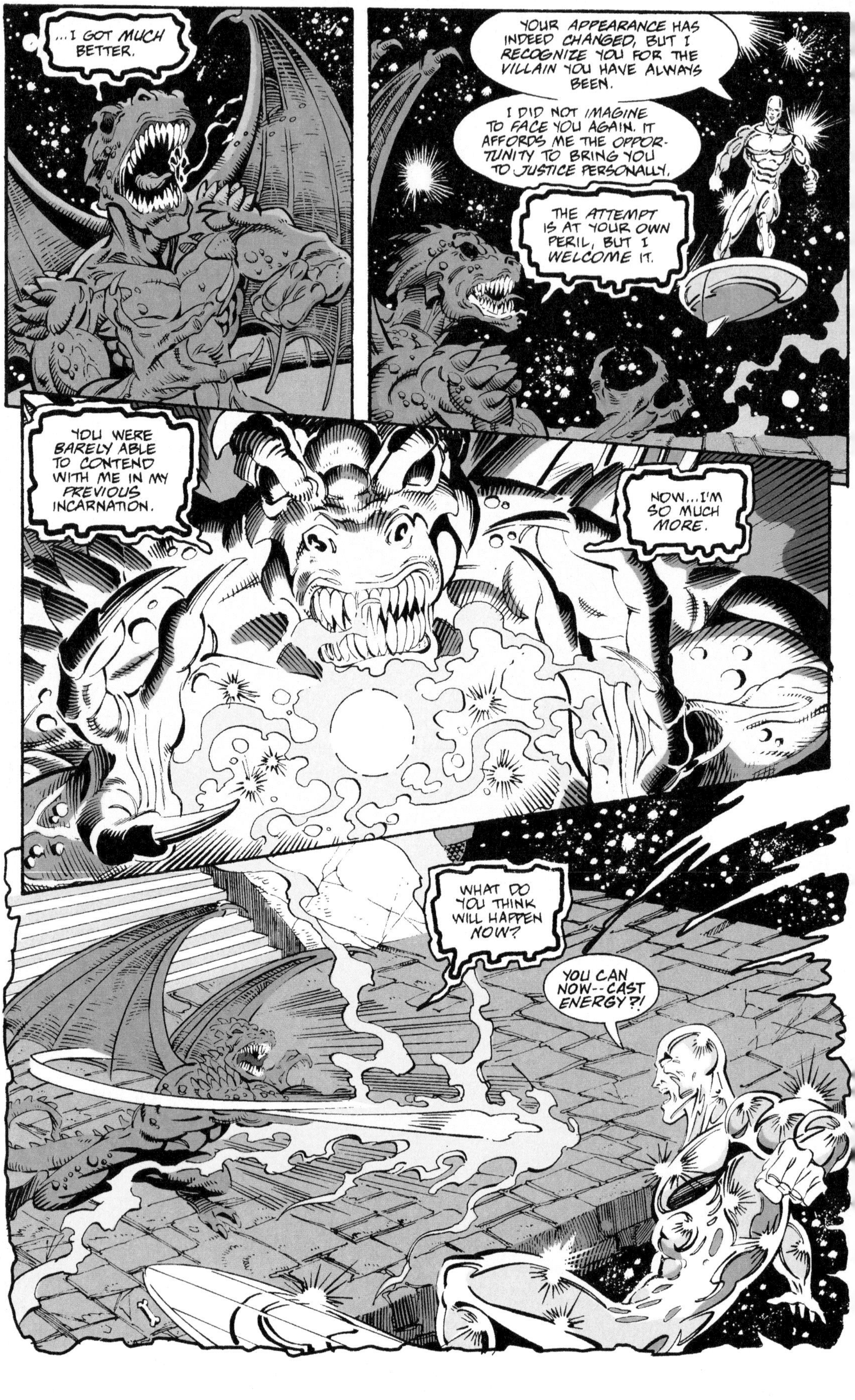
...I GOT MUCH BETTER.
YOUR APPEARANCE HAS INDEED CHANGED, BUT I RECOGNIZE YOU FOR THE VILLAIN YOU HAVE ALWAYS BEEN.
I DID NOT IMAGINE TO FACE YOU AGAIN. IT AFFORDS ME THE OPPORTUNITY TO BRING YOU TO JUSTICE PERSONALLY.
THE ATTEMPT IS AT YOUR OWN PERIL, BUT I WELCOME IT.
YOU WERE BARELY ABLE TO CONTEND WITH ME IN MY PREVIOUS INCARNATION.
NOW...I'M SO MUCH MORE.
WHAT DO YOU THINK WILL HAPPEN NOW?
YOU CAN NOW--CAST ENERGY?!

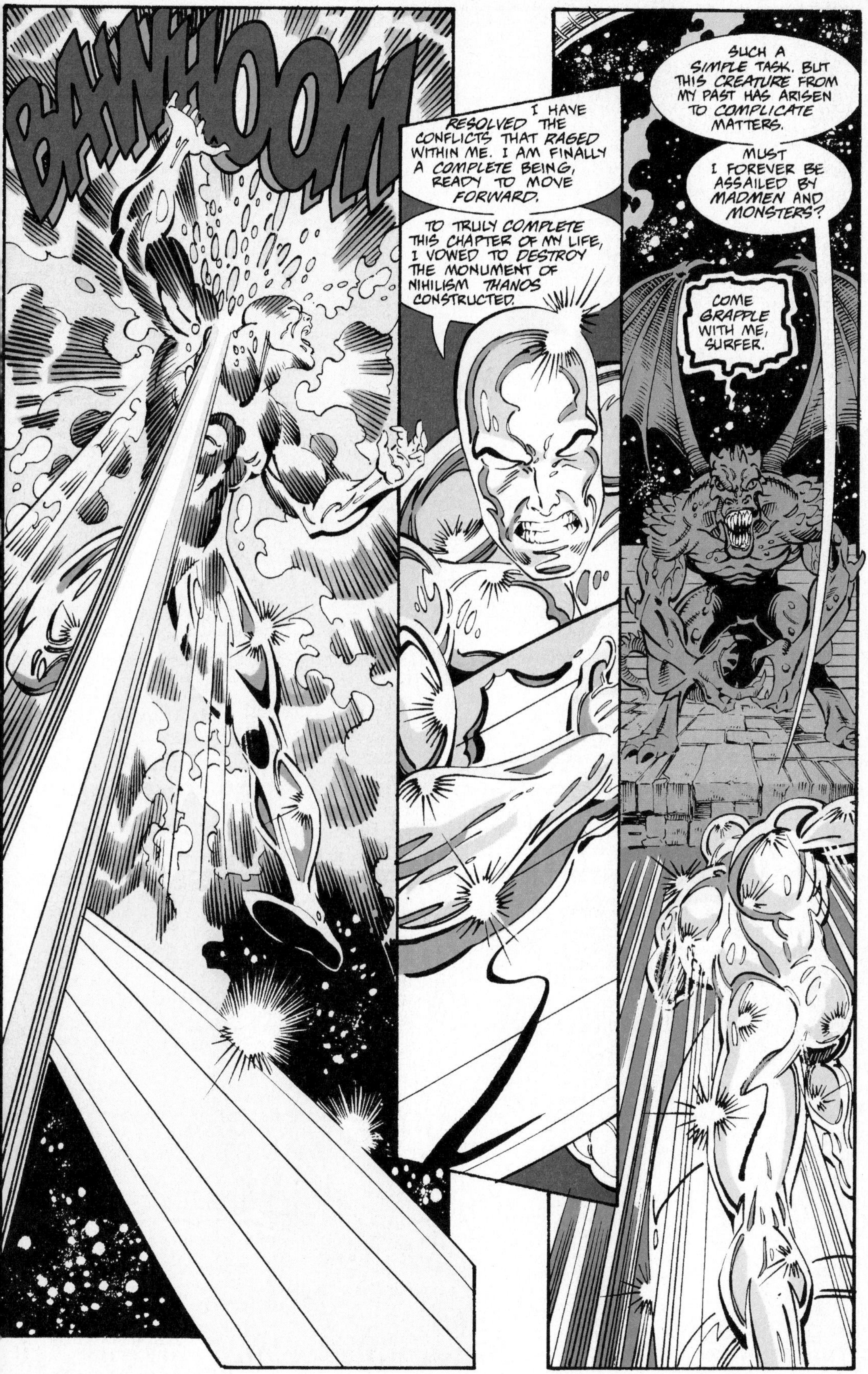
BAWHOOM
I HAVE RESOLVED THE CONFLICTS THAT RAGED WITHIN ME. I AM FINALLY A COMPLETE BEING, READY TO MOVE FORWARD.
TO TRULY COMPLETE THIS CHAPTER OF MY LIFE, I VOWED TO DESTROY THE MONUMENT OF NIHILISM THANOS CONSTRUCTED.
SUCH A SIMPLE TASK. BUT THIS CREATURE FROM MY PAST HAS ARISEN TO COMPLICATE MATTERS.
MUST I FOREVER BE ASSAILED BY MADMEN AND MONSTERS?
COME GRAPPLE WITH ME, SURFER.

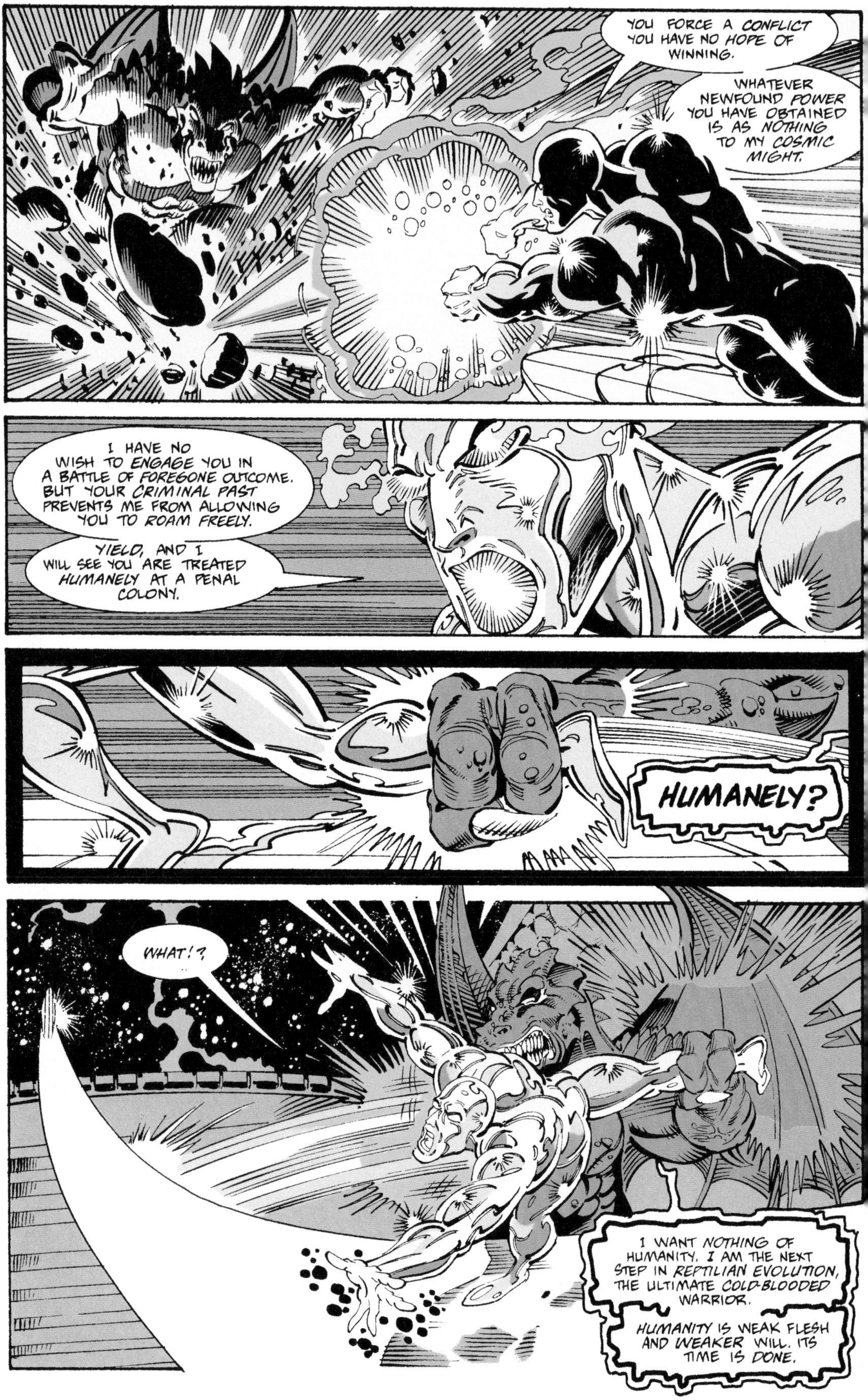
YOU FORCE A CONFLICT YOU HAVE NO HOPE OF WINNING.
WHATEVER NEWFOUND POWER YOU HAVE OBTAINED IS AS NOTHING TO MY COSMIC MIGHT.
I HAVE NO WISH TO ENGAGE YOU IN A BATTLE OF FOREGONE OUTCOME. BUT YOUR CRIMINAL PAST PREVENTS ME FROM ALLOWING YOU TO ROAM FREELY.
YIELD, AND I WILL SEE YOU ARE TREATED HUMANELY AT A PENAL COLONY.
HUMANELY?
WHAT!?
I WANT NOTHING OF HUMANITY. I AM THE NEXT STEP IN REPTILIAN EVOLUTION, THE ULTIMATE COLD-BLOODED WARRIOR.
HUMANITY IS WEAK FLESH AND WEAKER WILL. ITS TIME IS DONE.

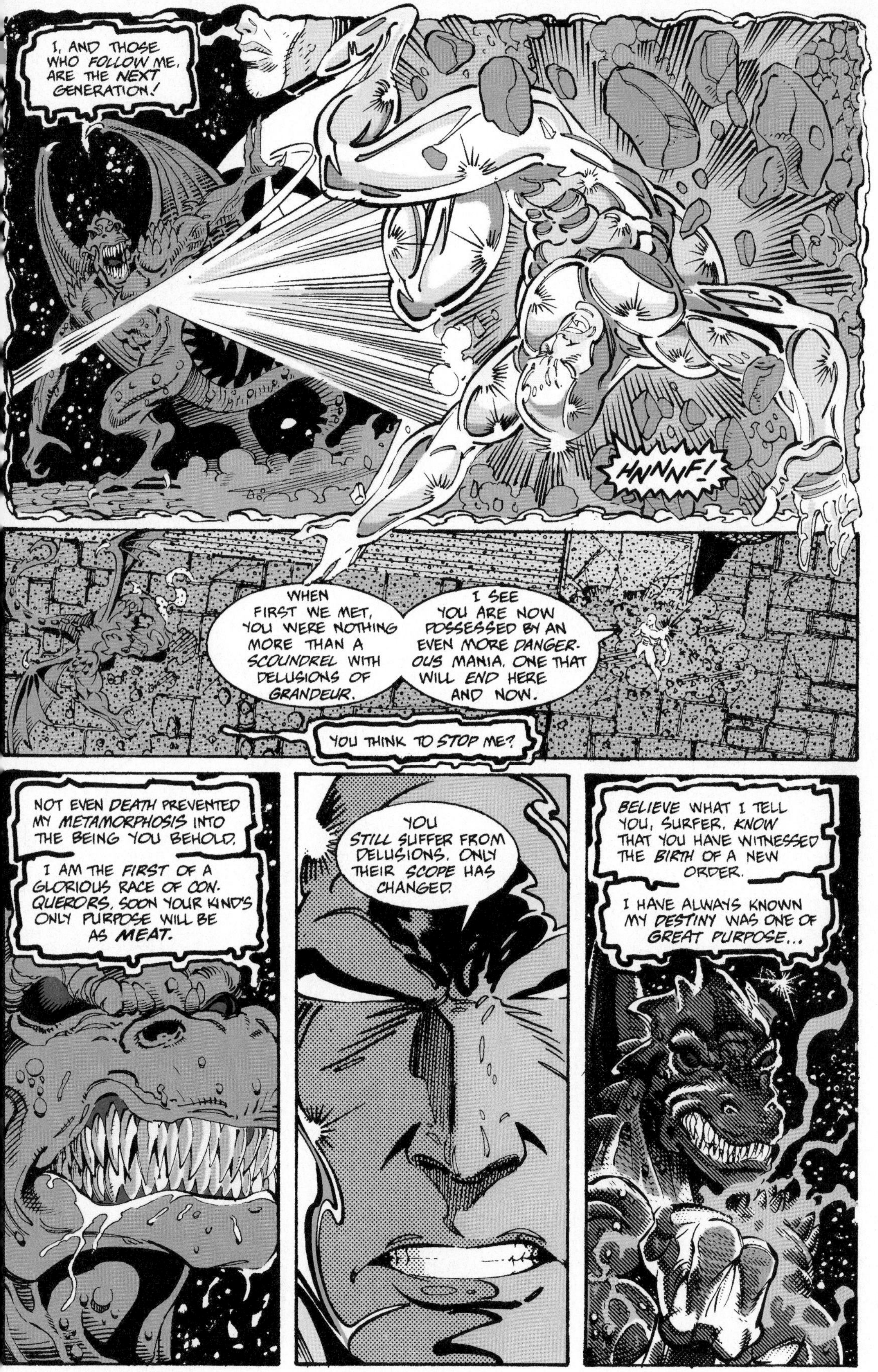
I, AND THOSE WHO FOLLOW ME, ARE THE NEXT GENERATION!
HNNNF!
WHEN FIRST WE MET, YOU WERE NOTHING MORE THAN A SCOUNDREL WITH DELUSIONS OF GRANDEUR.
I SEE YOU ARE NOW POSSESSED BY AN EVEN MORE DANGEROUS MANIA, ONE THAT WILL END HERE AND NOW.
YOU THINK TO STOP ME?
NOT EVEN DEATH PREVENTED MY METAMORPHOSIS INTO THE BEING YOU BEHOLD.
I AM THE FIRST OF A GLORIOUS RACE OF CONQUERORS, SOON YOUR KIND'S ONLY PURPOSE WILL BE AS MEAT.
YOU STILL SUFFER FROM DELUSIONS. ONLY THEIR SCOPE HAS CHANGED.
BELIEVE WHAT I TELL YOU, SURFER. KNOW THAT YOU HAVE WITNESSED THE BIRTH OF A NEW ORDER.
I HAVE ALWAYS KNOWN MY DESTINY WAS ONE OF GREAT PURPOSE...

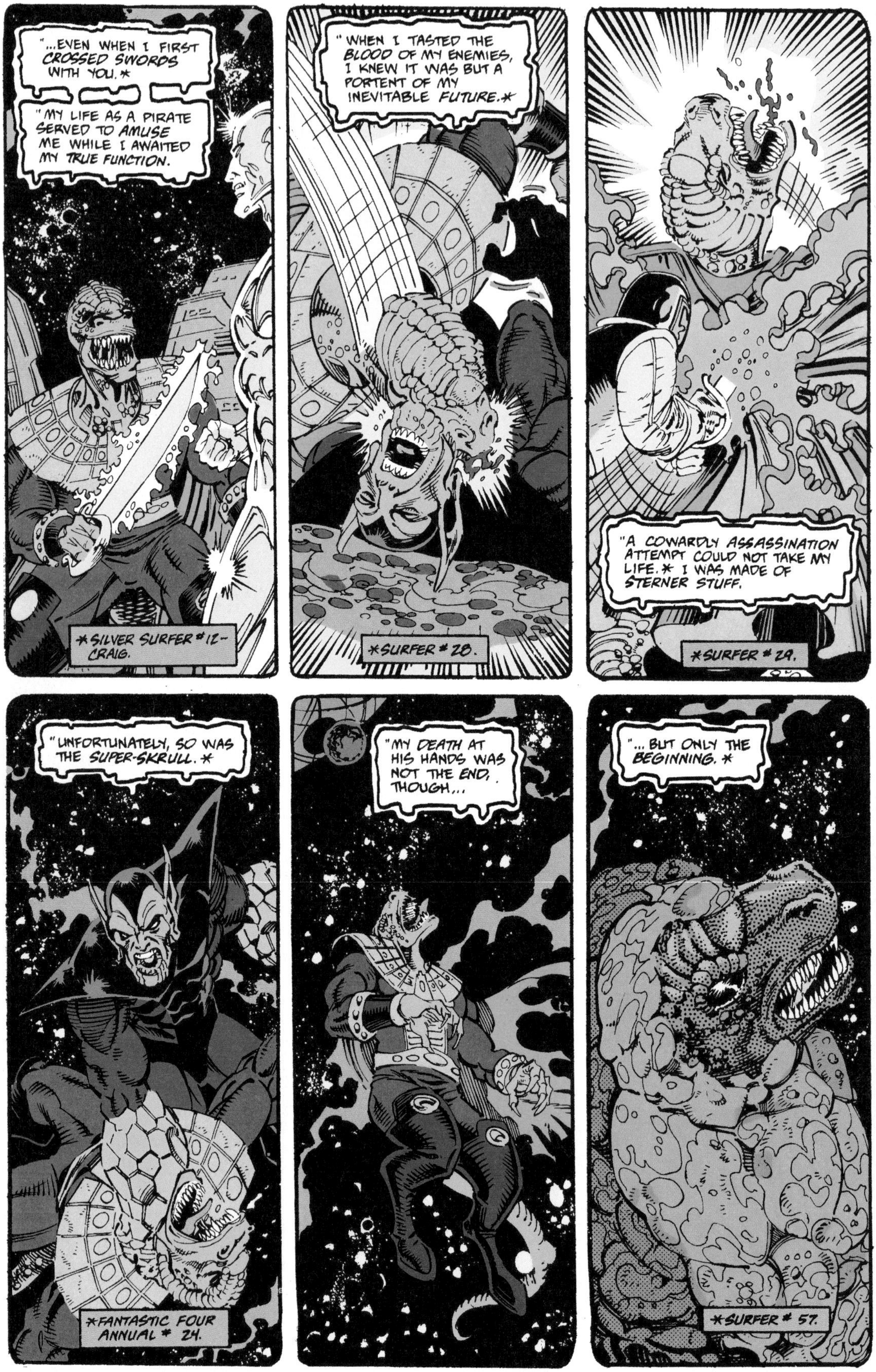
"...EVEN WHEN I FIRST CROSSED SWORDS WITH YOU.*
"MY LIFE AS A PIRATE SERVED TO AMUSE ME WHILE I AWAITED MY TRUE FUNCTION.
*SILVER SURFER #12 - CRAIG.
"WHEN I TASTED THE BLOOD OF MY ENEMIES, I KNEW IT WAS BUT A PORTENT OF MY INEVITABLE FUTURE.*
*SURFER #28.
"A COWARDLY ASSASSINATION ATTEMPT COULD NOT TAKE MY LIFE.* I WAS MADE OF STERNER STUFF.
*SURFER #29.
"UNFORTUNATELY, SO WAS THE SUPER-SKRULL.*
*FANTASTIC FOUR ANNUAL #24.
"MY DEATH AT HIS HANDS WAS NOT THE END, THOUGH...
"...BUT ONLY THE BEGINNING.*
*SURFER #57.

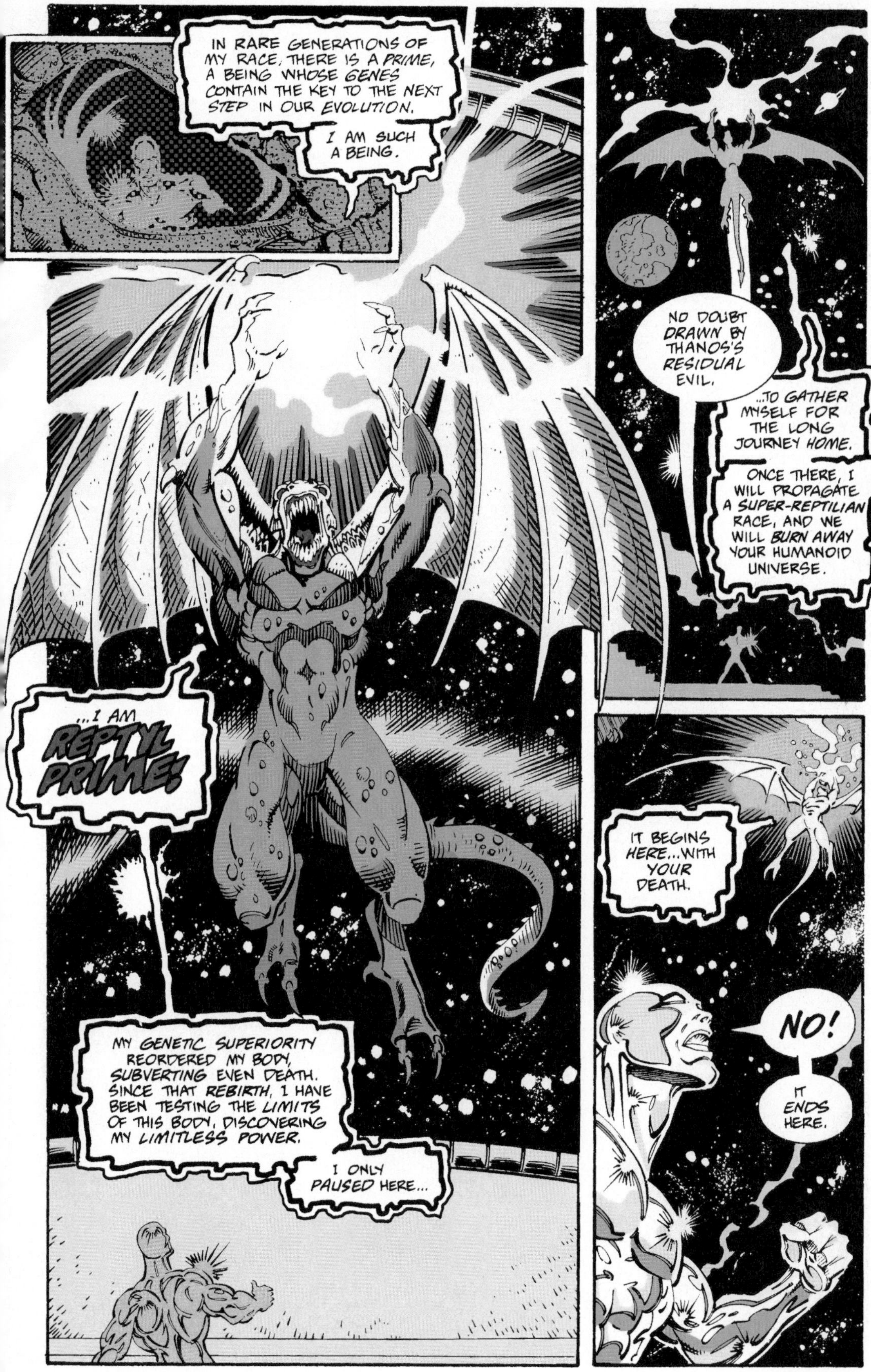
IN RARE GENERATIONS OF MY RACE, THERE IS A PRIME, A BEING WHOSE GENES CONTAIN THE KEY TO THE NEXT STEP IN OUR EVOLUTION.
I AM SUCH A BEING.
...I AM REPTYL PRIME!
MY GENETIC SUPERIORITY REORDERED MY BODY, SUBVERTING EVEN DEATH. SINCE THAT REBIRTH, I HAVE BEEN TESTING THE LIMITS OF THIS BODY, DISCOVERING MY LIMITLESS POWER.
I ONLY PAUSED HERE...
NO DOUBT DRAWN BY THANOS'S RESIDUAL EVIL.
...TO GATHER MYSELF FOR THE LONG JOURNEY HOME.
ONCE THERE, I WILL PROPAGATE A SUPER-REPTILIAN RACE, AND WE WILL BURN AWAY YOUR HUMANOID UNIVERSE.
IT BEGINS HERE...WITH YOUR DEATH.
NO!
IT ENDS HERE.

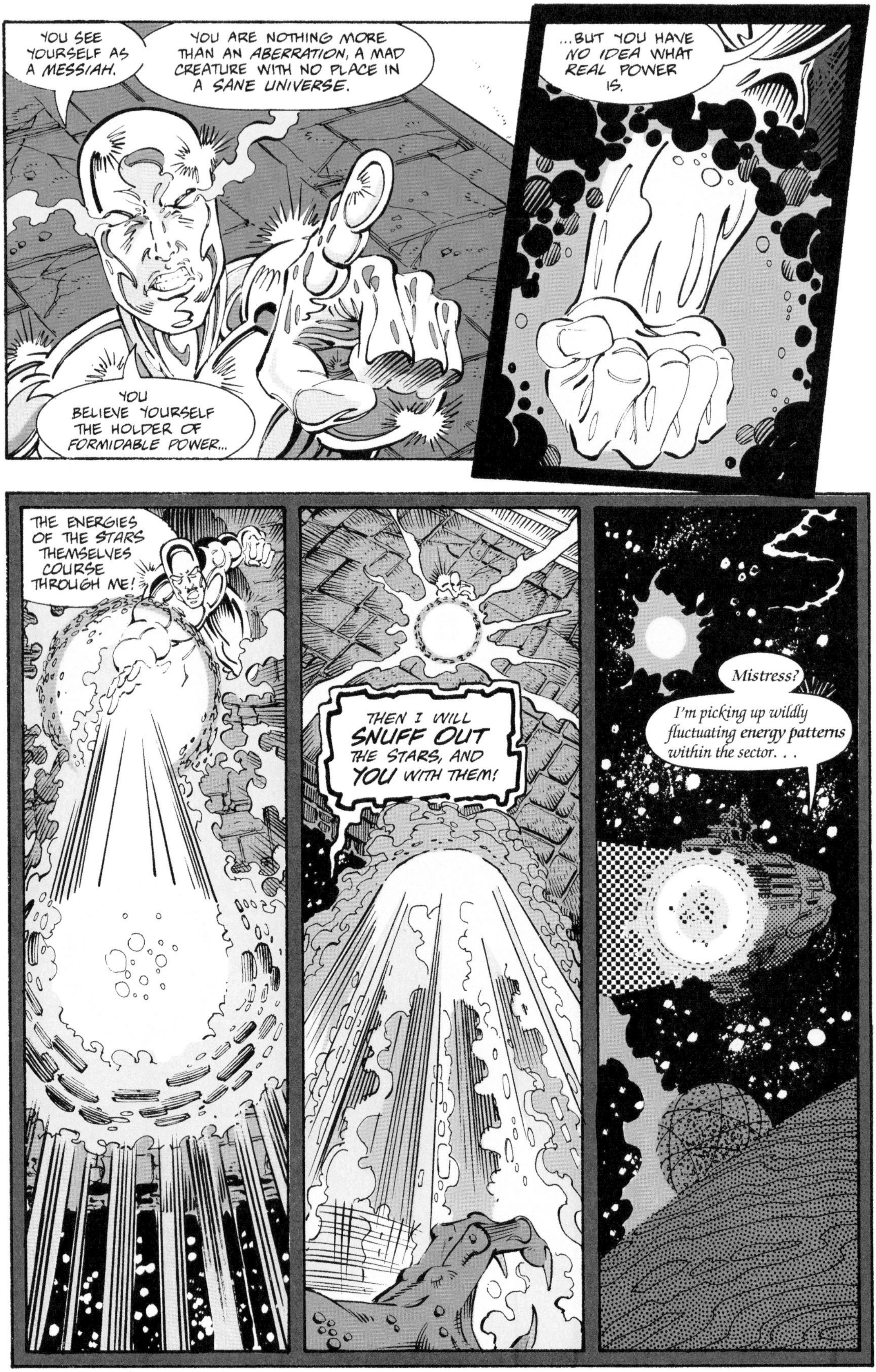
YOU SEE YOURSELF AS A MESSIAH.
YOU ARE NOTHING MORE THAN AN ABERRATION, A MAD CREATURE WITH NO PLACE IN A SANE UNIVERSE.
YOU BELIEVE YOURSELF THE HOLDER OF FORMIDABLE POWER...
...BUT YOU HAVE NO IDEA WHAT REAL POWER IS.
THE ENERGIES OF THE STARS THEMSELVES COURSE THROUGH ME!
THEN I WILL SNUFF OUT THE STARS, AND YOU WITH THEM!
Mistress?
I'm picking up wildly fluctuating energy patterns within the sector. . .

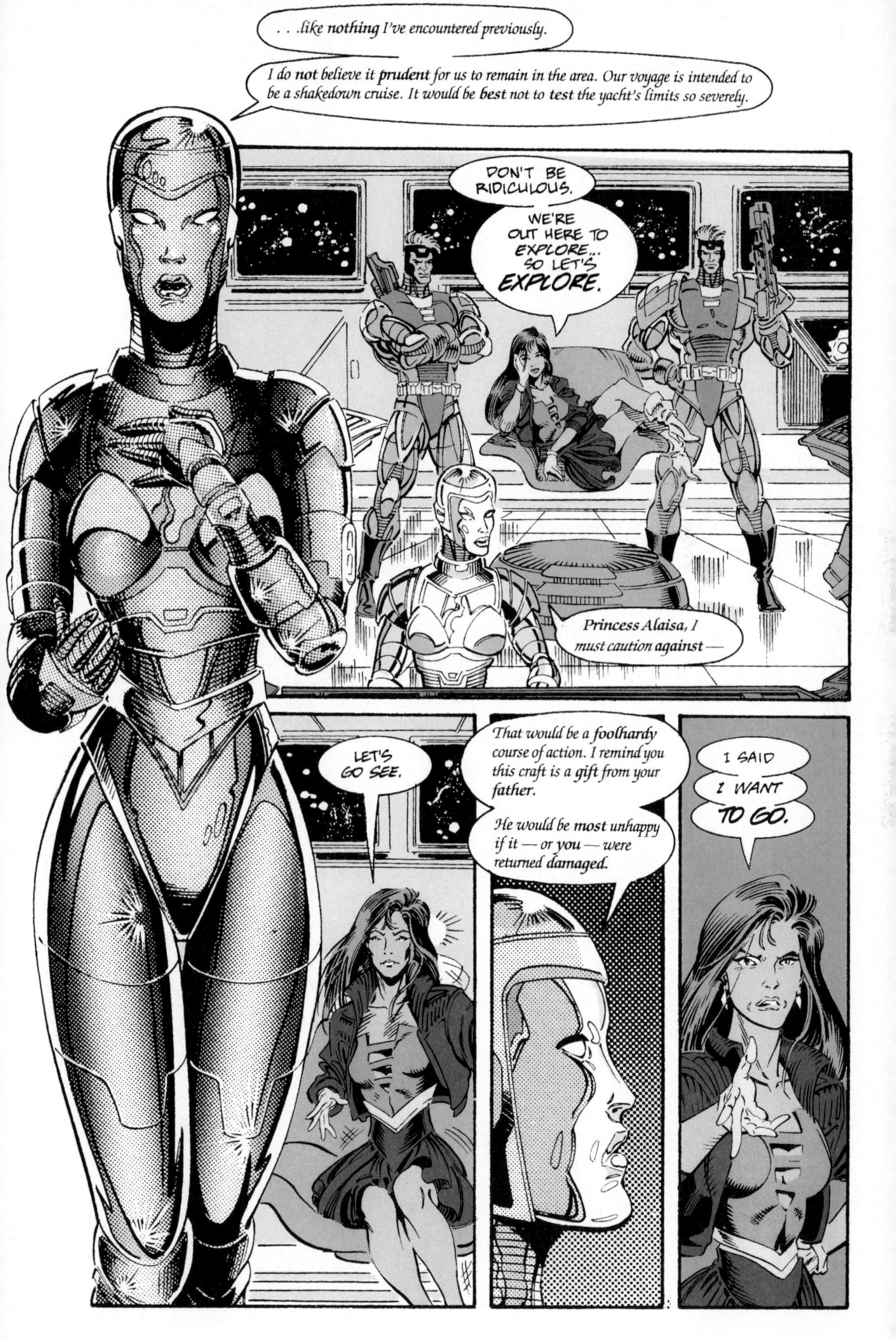
. . .like nothing I've encountered previously.
I do not believe it prudent for us to remain in the area. Our voyage is intended to be a shakedown cruise. It would be best not to test the yacht's limits so severely.
DON'T BE RIDICULOUS.
WE'RE OUT HERE TO EXPLORE... SO LET'S EXPLORE.
Princess Alaisa, I must caution against —
LET'S GO SEE.
That would be a foolhardy course of action. I remind you this craft is a gift from your father.
He would be most unhappy if it — or you — were returned damaged.
I SAID
I WANT
TO GO.

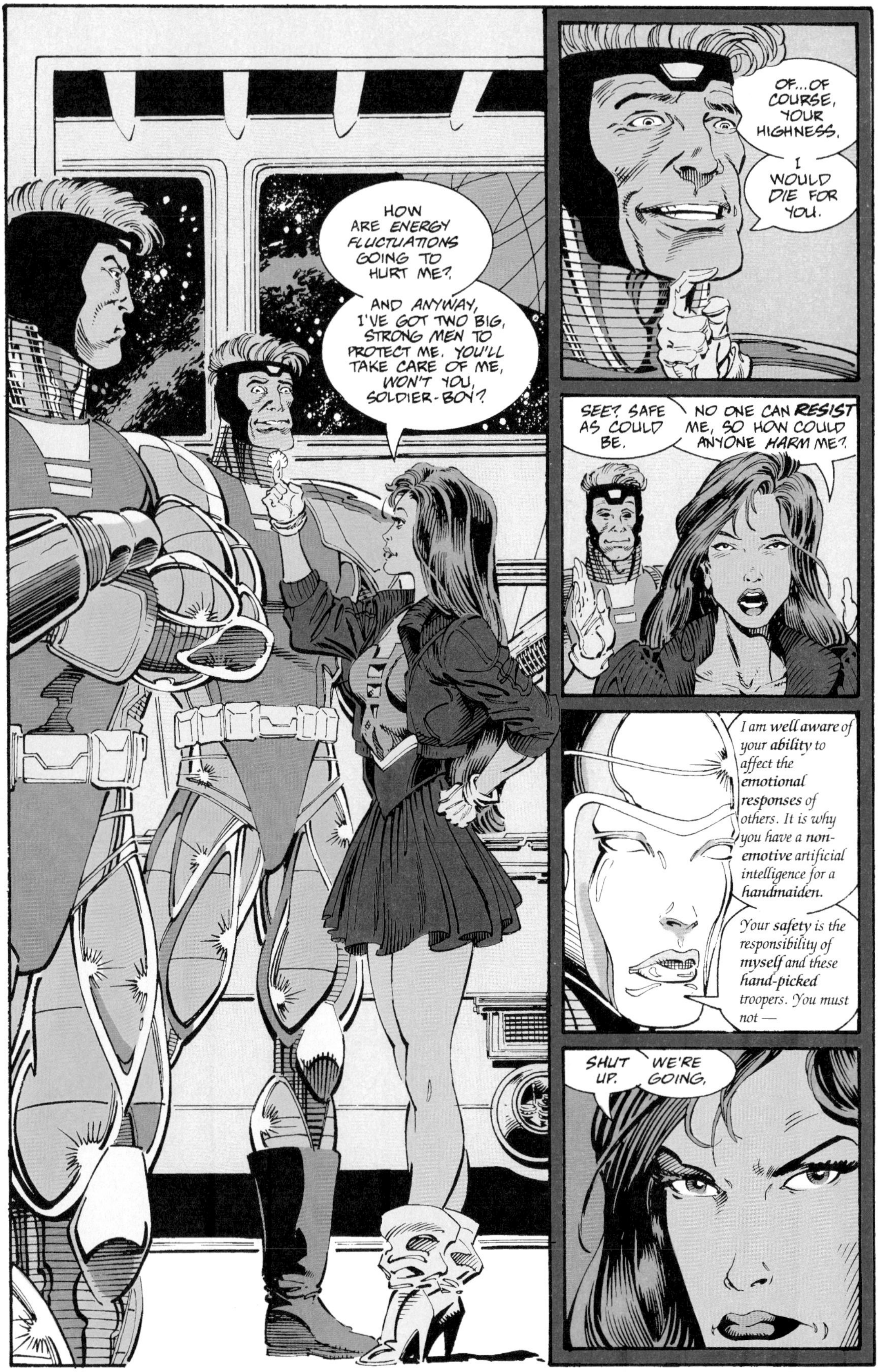
HOW ARE ENERGY FLUCTUATIONS GOING TO HURT ME?
AND ANYWAY, I'VE GOT TWO BIG, STRONG MEN TO PROTECT ME. YOU'LL TAKE CARE OF ME, WON'T YOU, SOLDIER-BOY?
OF...OF COURSE, YOUR HIGHNESS.
I WOULD DIE FOR YOU.
SEE? SAFE AS COULD BE.
NO ONE CAN RESIST ME, SO HOW COULD ANYONE HARM ME?
I am well aware of your ability to affect the emotional responses of others. It is why you have a non-emotive artificial intelligence for a handmaiden.
Your safety is the responsibility of myself and these hand-picked troopers. You must not —
SHUT UP.
WE'RE GOING.

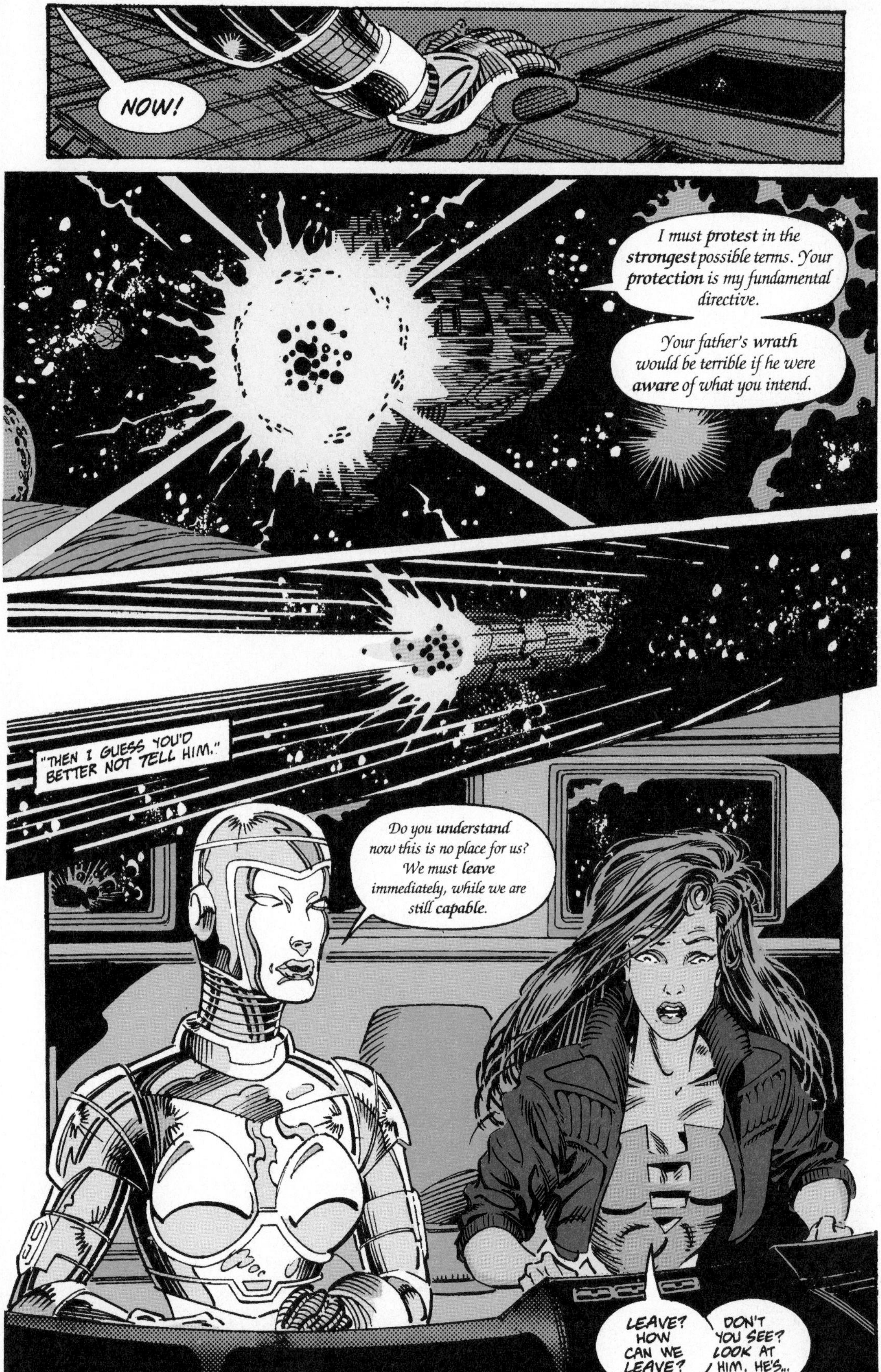
NOW!
I must protest in the strongest possible terms. Your protection is my fundamental directive.
Your father's wrath would be terrible if he were aware of what you intend.
"THEN I GUESS YOU'D BETTER NOT TELL HIM."
Do you understand now this is no place for us? We must leave immediately, while we are still capable.
LEAVE? HOW CAN WE LEAVE?
DON'T YOU SEE? LOOK AT HIM. HE'S...

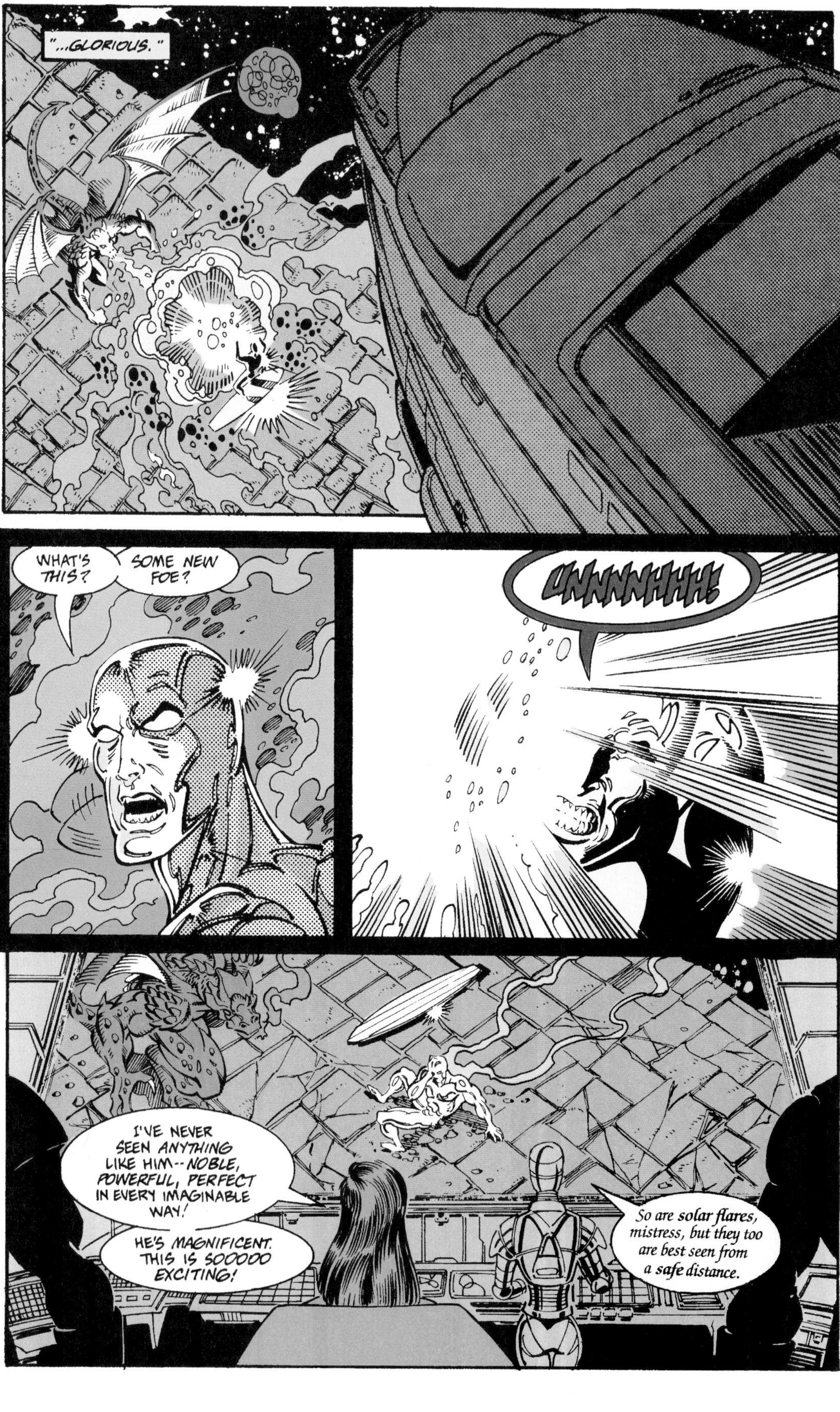
"...GLORIOUS."
WHAT'S THIS?
SOME NEW FOE?
UNNNNHHH!
I'VE NEVER SEEN ANYTHING LIKE HIM--NOBLE, POWERFUL, PERFECT IN EVERY IMAGINABLE WAY!
HE'S MAGNIFICENT. THIS IS SOOOOO EXCITING!
So are solar flares, mistress, but they too are best seen from a safe distance.

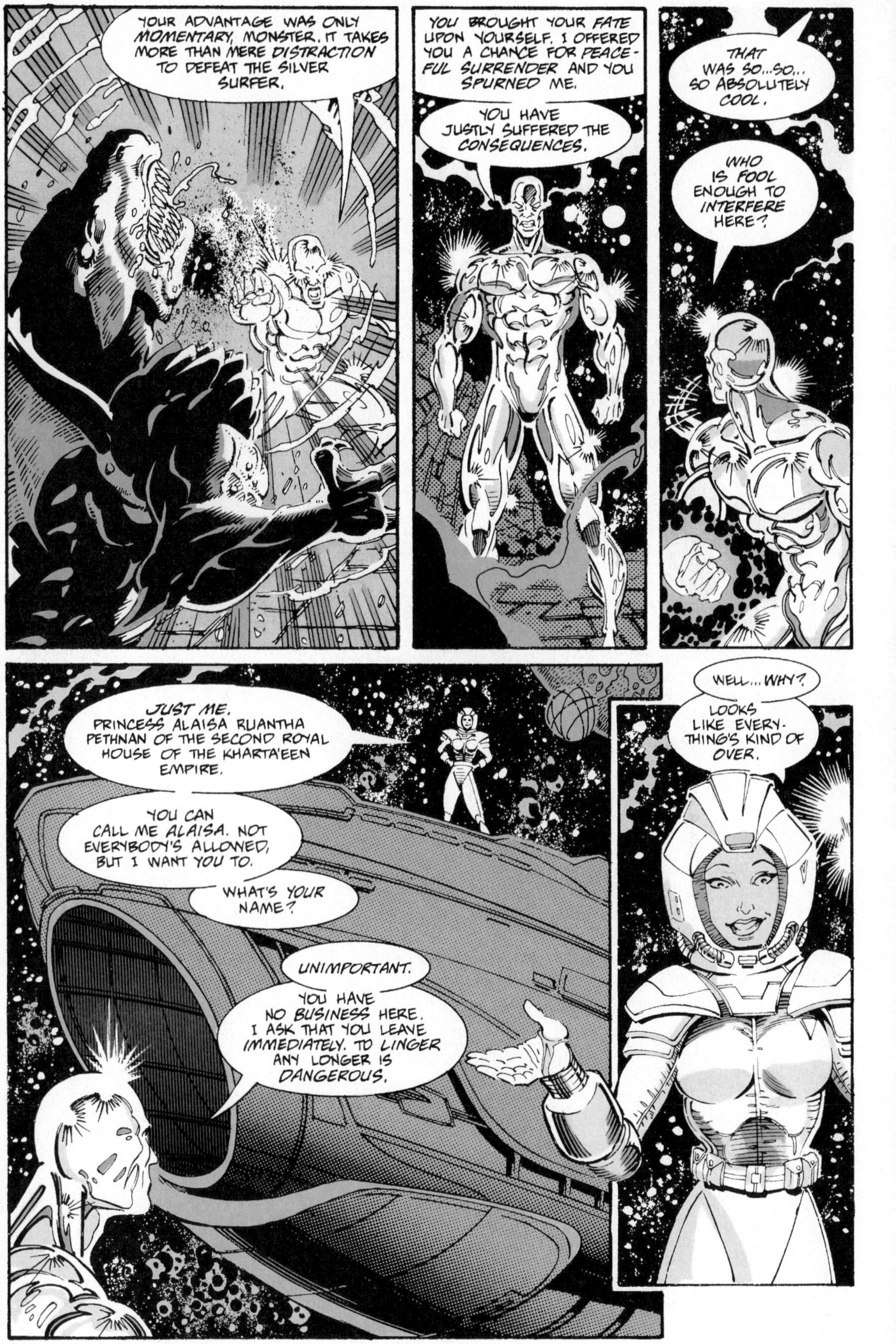
YOUR ADVANTAGE WAS ONLY MOMENTARY, MONSTER. IT TAKES MORE THAN MERE DISTRACTION TO DEFEAT THE SILVER SURFER.
YOU BROUGHT YOUR FATE UPON YOURSELF. I OFFERED YOU A CHANCE FOR PEACEFUL SURRENDER AND YOU SPURNED ME.
YOU HAVE JUSTLY SUFFERED THE CONSEQUENCES.
THAT WAS SO...SO... SO ABSOLUTELY COOL.
WHO IS FOOL ENOUGH TO INTERFERE HERE?
JUST ME. PRINCESS ALAISA RUANTHA PETHNAN OF THE SECOND ROYAL HOUSE OF THE KHARTA'EEN EMPIRE.
YOU CAN CALL ME ALAISA. NOT EVERYBODY'S ALLOWED, BUT I WANT YOU TO.
WHAT'S YOUR NAME?
UNIMPORTANT.
YOU HAVE NO BUSINESS HERE. I ASK THAT YOU LEAVE IMMEDIATELY. TO LINGER ANY LONGER IS DANGEROUS.
WELL... WHY?
LOOKS LIKE EVERYTHING'S KIND OF OVER.

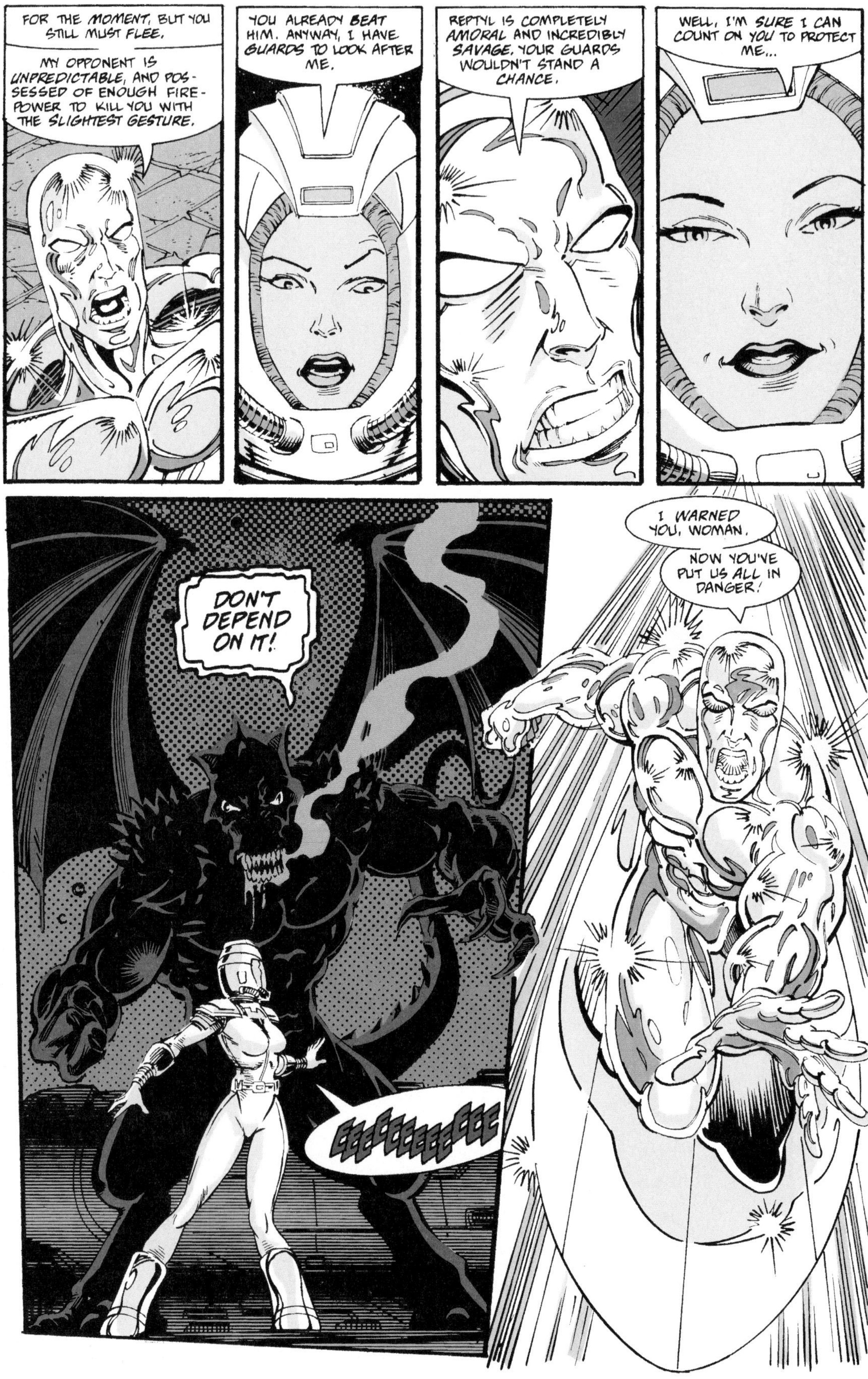
FOR THE MOMENT, BUT YOU STILL MUST FLEE.
MY OPPONENT IS UNPREDICTABLE, AND POSSESSED OF ENOUGH FIREPOWER TO KILL YOU WITH THE SLIGHTEST GESTURE.
YOU ALREADY BEAT HIM. ANYWAY, I HAVE GUARDS TO LOOK AFTER ME.
REPTYL IS COMPLETELY AMORAL AND INCREDIBLY SAVAGE. YOUR GUARDS WOULDN'T STAND A CHANCE.
WELL, I'M SURE I CAN COUNT ON YOU TO PROTECT ME...
DON'T DEPEND ON IT!
EEEEEEEEEEEEE
I WARNED YOU, WOMAN.
NOW YOU'VE PUT US ALL IN DANGER!

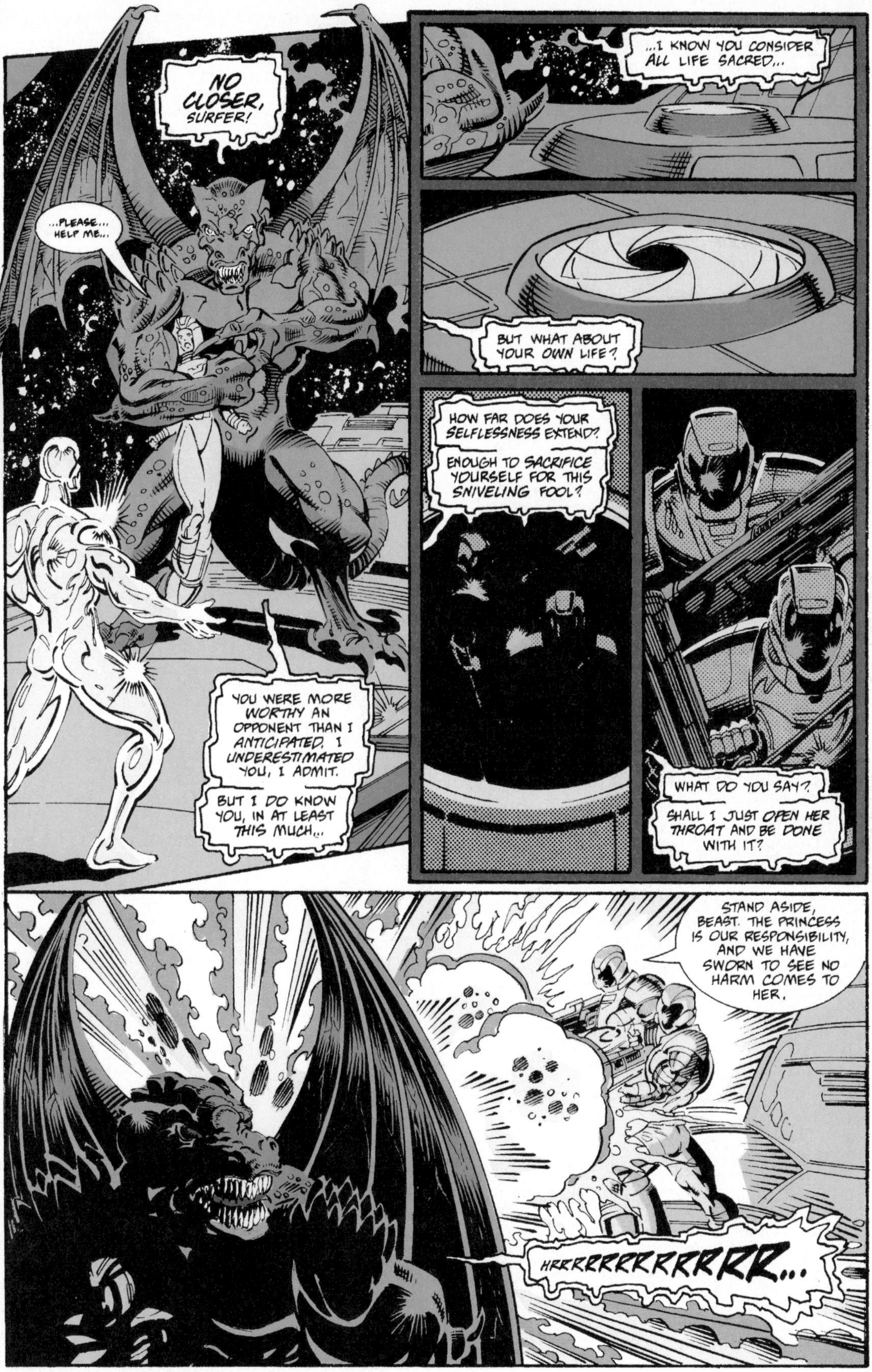
NO CLOSER, SURFER!
...PLEASE... HELP ME...
YOU WERE MORE WORTHY AN OPPONENT THAN I ANTICIPATED. I UNDERESTIMATED YOU, I ADMIT.
BUT I DO KNOW YOU, IN AT LEAST THIS MUCH...
...I KNOW YOU CONSIDER ALL LIFE SACRED...
BUT WHAT ABOUT YOUR OWN LIFE?
HOW FAR DOES YOUR SELFLESSNESS EXTEND?
ENOUGH TO SACRIFICE YOURSELF FOR THIS SNIVELING FOOL?
WHAT DO YOU SAY?
SHALL I JUST OPEN HER THROAT AND BE DONE WITH IT?
STAND ASIDE, BEAST. THE PRINCESS IS OUR RESPONSIBILITY, AND WE HAVE SWORN TO SEE NO HARM COMES TO HER.
HRRRRRRRRRRR...

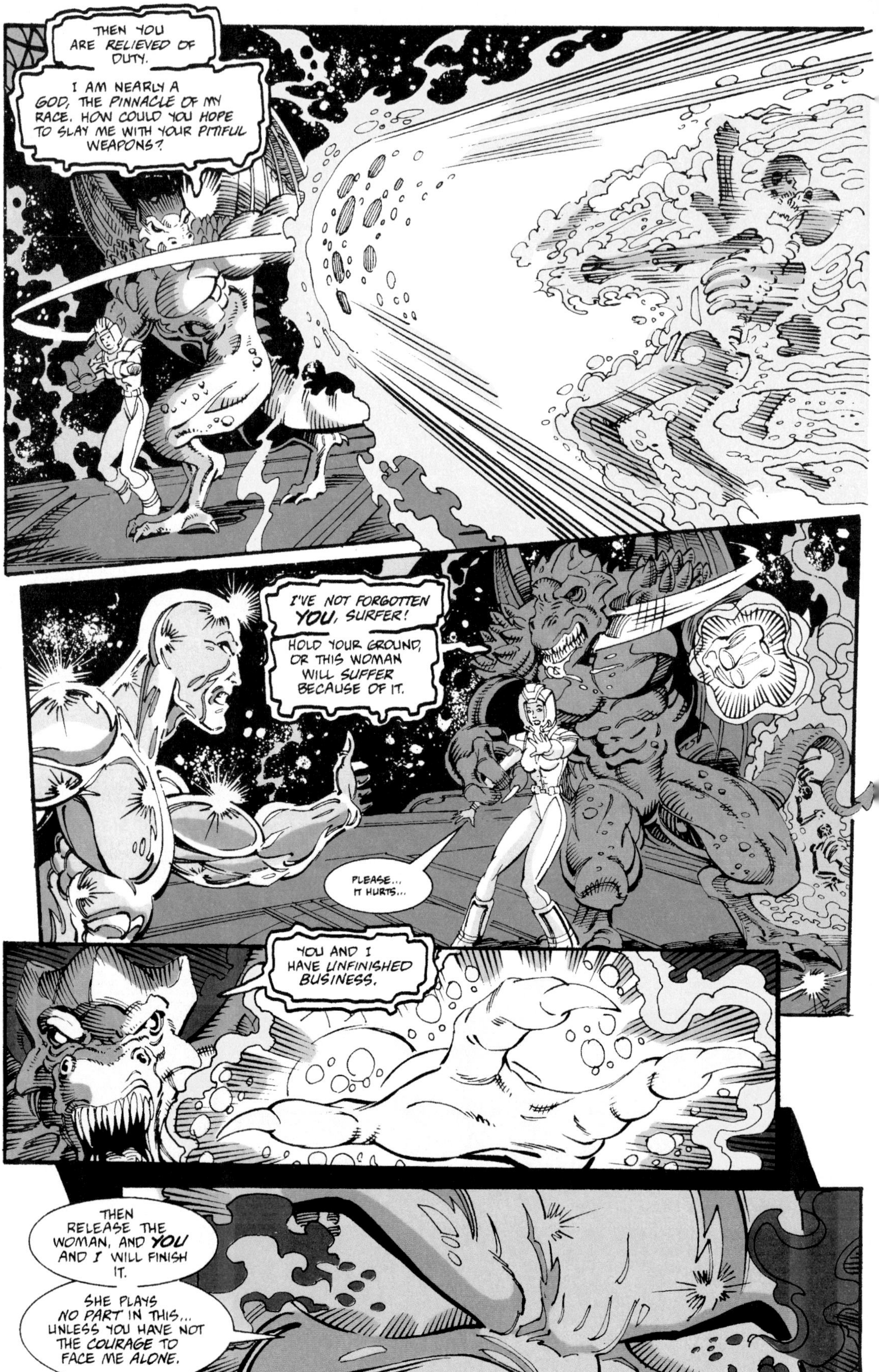
THEN YOU ARE RELIEVED OF DUTY.
I AM NEARLY A GOD, THE PINNACLE OF MY RACE. HOW COULD YOU HOPE TO SLAY ME WITH YOUR PITIFUL WEAPONS?
I'VE NOT FORGOTTEN YOU, SURFER!
HOLD YOUR GROUND, OR THIS WOMAN WILL SUFFER BECAUSE OF IT.
PLEASE... IT HURTS...
YOU AND I HAVE UNFINISHED BUSINESS.
THEN RELEASE THE WOMAN, AND YOU AND I WILL FINISH IT.
SHE PLAYS NO PART IN THIS... UNLESS YOU HAVE NOT THE COURAGE TO FACE ME ALONE.

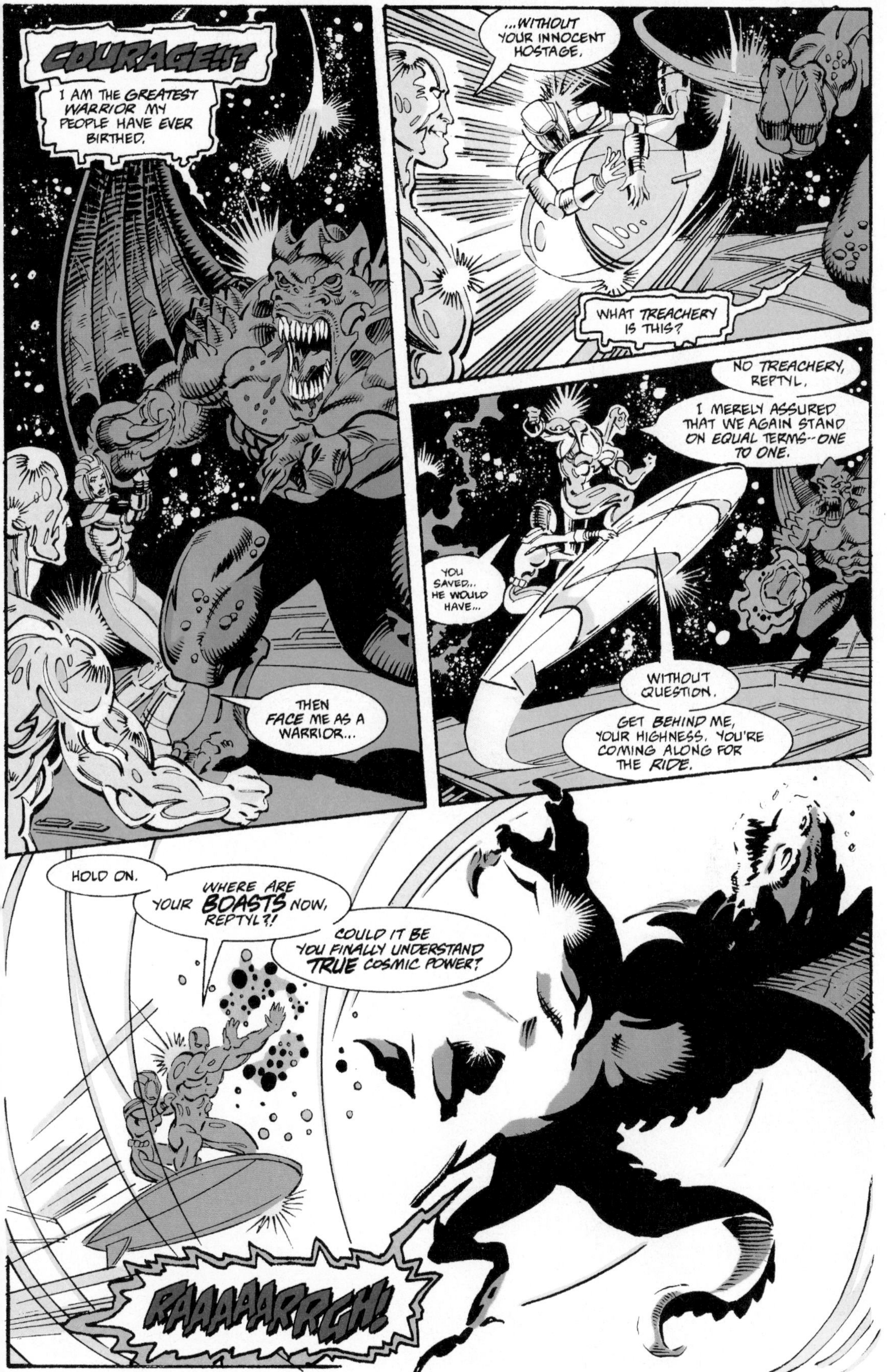
COURAGE!?
I AM THE GREATEST WARRIOR MY PEOPLE HAVE EVER BIRTHED.
THEN FACE ME AS A WARRIOR...
...WITHOUT YOUR INNOCENT HOSTAGE.
WHAT TREACHERY IS THIS?
NO TREACHERY, REPTYL.
I MERELY ASSURED THAT WE AGAIN STAND ON EQUAL TERMS--ONE TO ONE.
YOU SAVED... HE WOULD HAVE...
WITHOUT QUESTION.
GET BEHIND ME, YOUR HIGHNESS. YOU'RE COMING ALONG FOR THE RIDE.
HOLD ON.
WHERE ARE YOUR BOASTS NOW, REPTYL?!
COULD IT BE YOU FINALLY UNDERSTAND TRUE COSMIC POWER?
RAAAAARRGH!

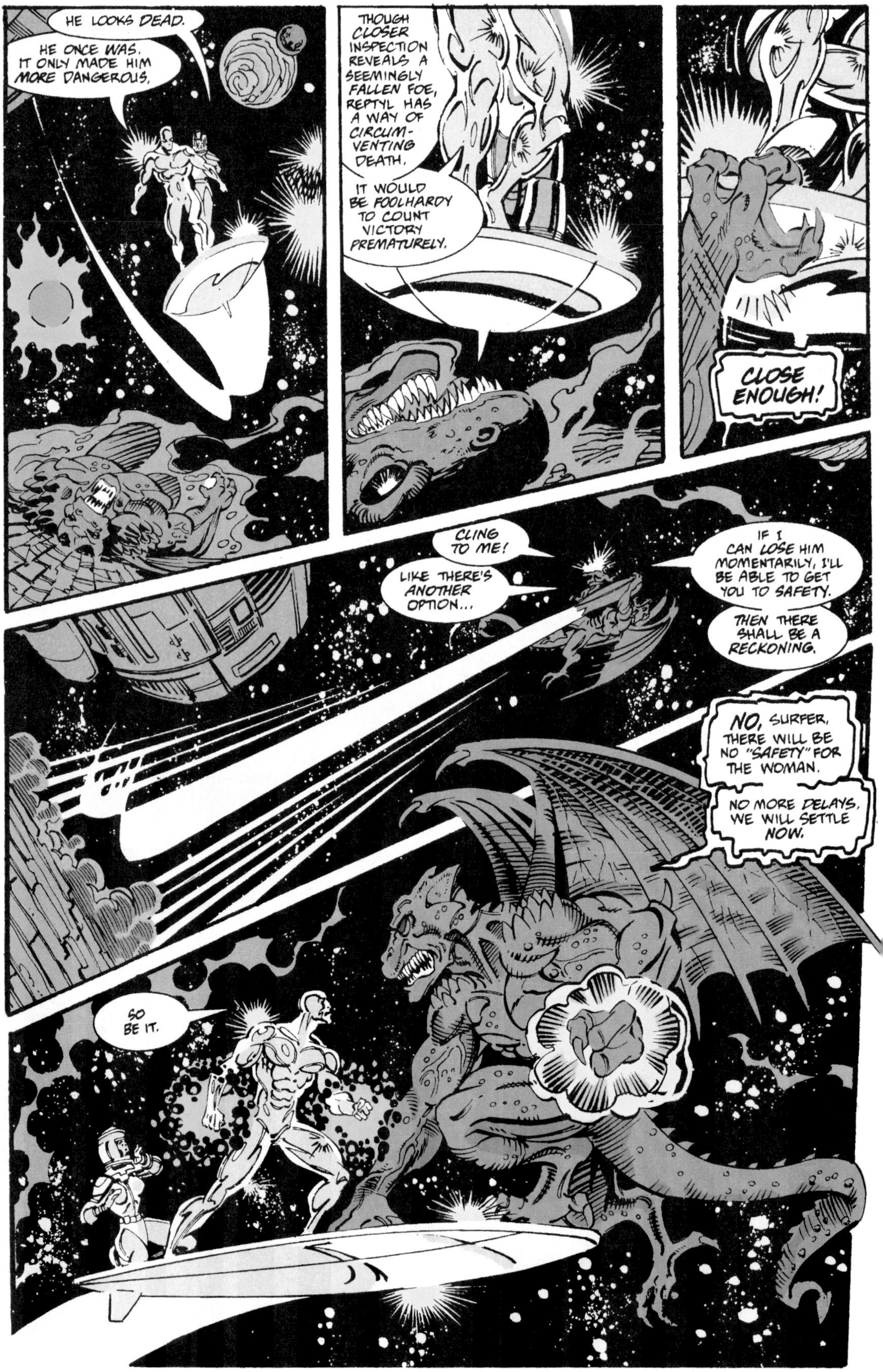
HE LOOKS DEAD.
HE ONCE WAS. IT ONLY MADE HIM MORE DANGEROUS.
THOUGH CLOSER INSPECTION REVEALS A SEEMINGLY FALLEN FOE, REPTYL HAS A WAY OF CIRCUM-VENTING DEATH.
IT WOULD BE FOOLHARDY TO COUNT VICTORY PREMATURELY.
CLOSE ENOUGH!
CLING TO ME!
LIKE THERE'S ANOTHER OPTION...
IF I CAN LOSE HIM MOMENTARILY, I'LL BE ABLE TO GET YOU TO SAFETY.
THEN THERE SHALL BE A RECKONING.
NO, SURFER, THERE WILL BE NO "SAFETY" FOR THE WOMAN.
NO MORE DELAYS. WE WILL SETTLE NOW.
SO BE IT.

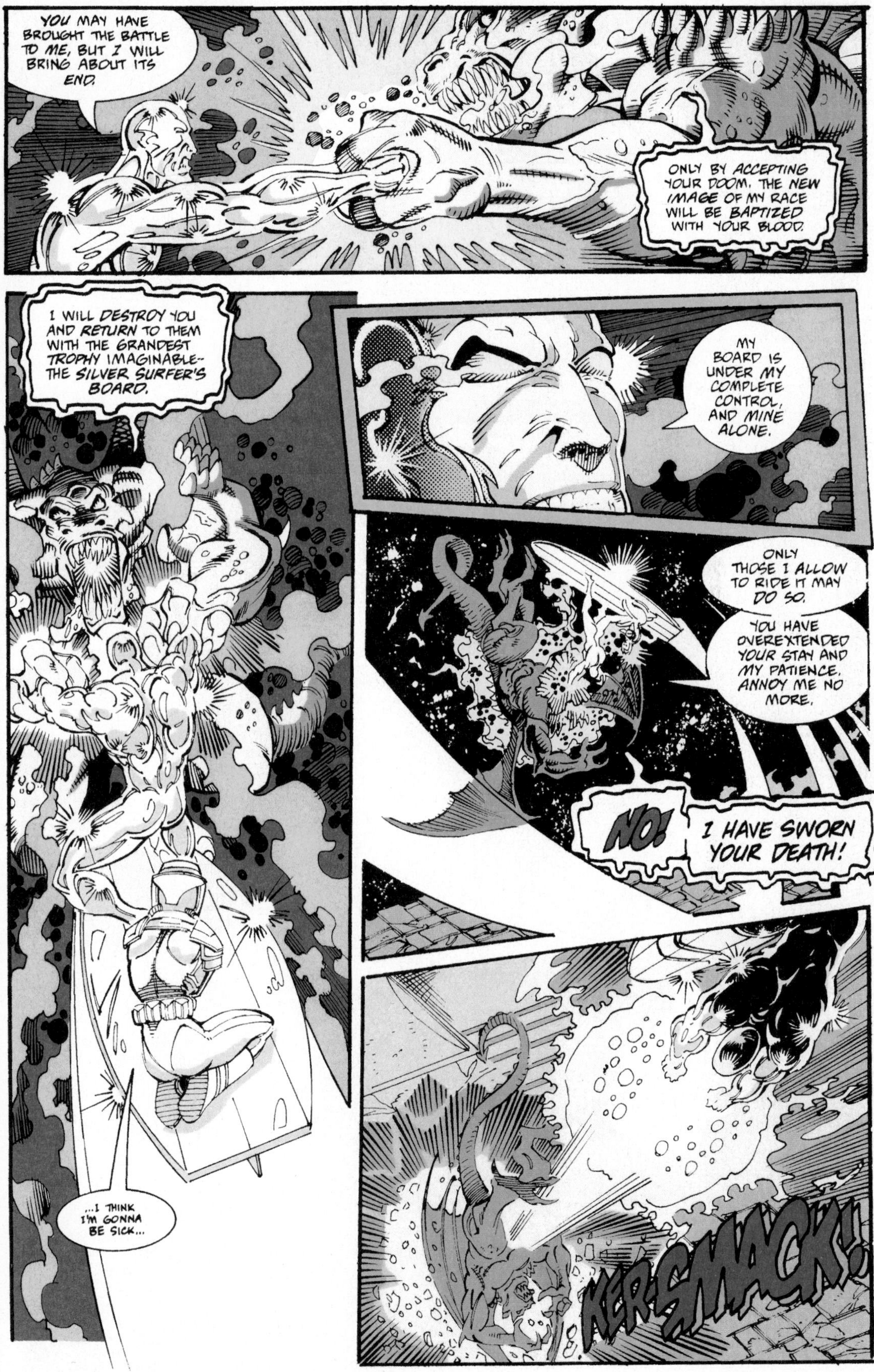
YOU MAY HAVE BROUGHT THE BATTLE TO ME, BUT I WILL BRING ABOUT ITS END.
ONLY BY ACCEPTING YOUR DOOM, THE NEW IMAGE OF MY RACE WILL BE BAPTIZED WITH YOUR BLOOD.
I WILL DESTROY YOU AND RETURN TO THEM WITH THE GRANDEST TROPHY IMAGINABLE-- THE SILVER SURFER'S BOARD.
MY BOARD IS UNDER MY COMPLETE CONTROL, AND MINE ALONE.
ONLY THOSE I ALLOW TO RIDE IT MAY DO SO.
YOU HAVE OVEREXTENDED YOUR STAY AND MY PATIENCE. ANNOY ME NO MORE.
NO!
I HAVE SWORN YOUR DEATH!
...I THINK I'M GONNA BE SICK...
KER-SMACK!!

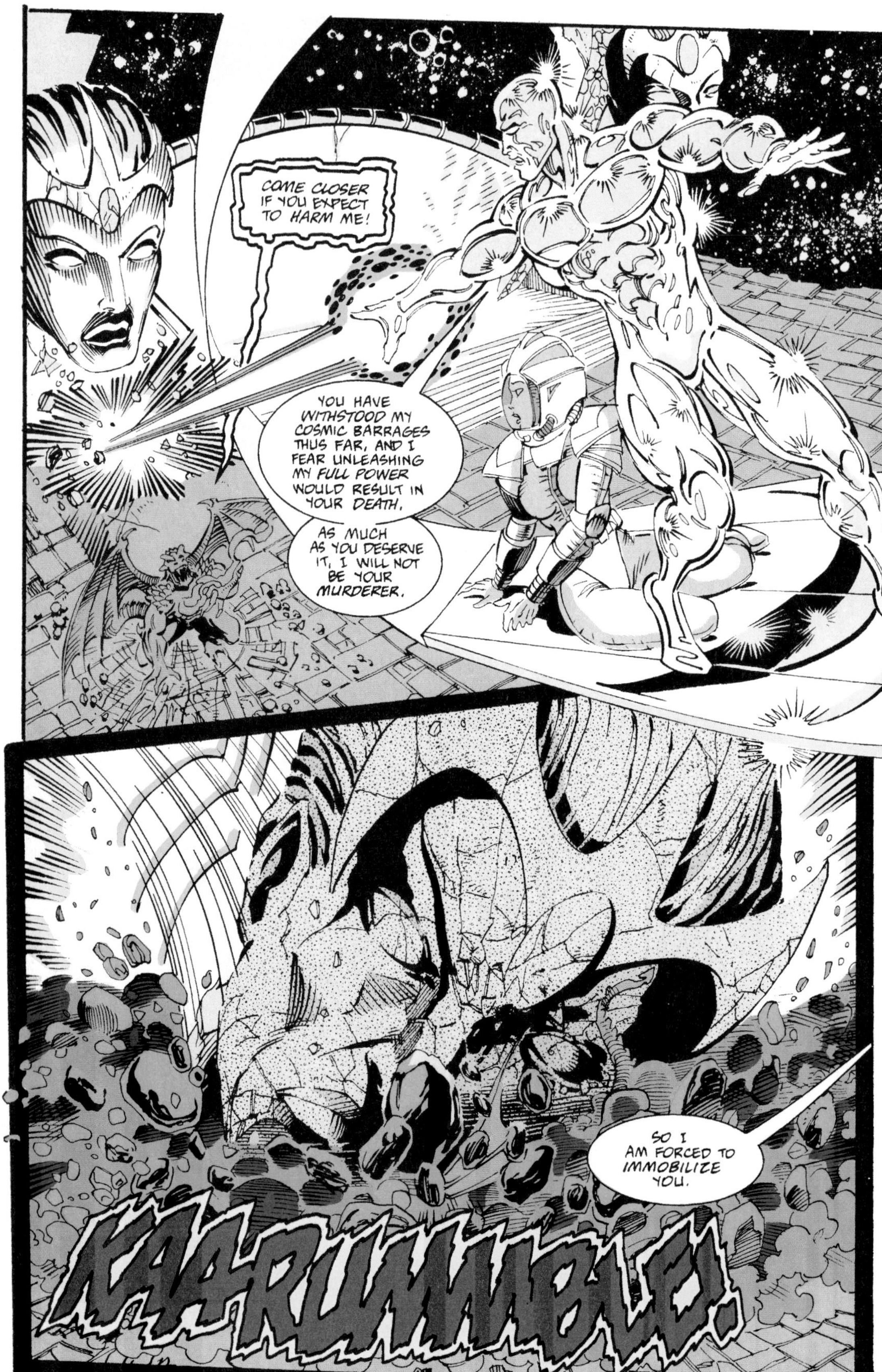
COME CLOSER IF YOU EXPECT TO HARM ME!
YOU HAVE WITHSTOOD MY COSMIC BARRAGES THUS FAR, AND I FEAR UNLEASHING MY *FULL POWER* WOULD RESULT IN YOUR *DEATH.*
AS MUCH AS YOU *DESERVE* IT, I WILL NOT BE YOUR *MURDERER.*
SO I AM *FORCED* TO *IMMOBILIZE* YOU.
KAARUMMBLE!

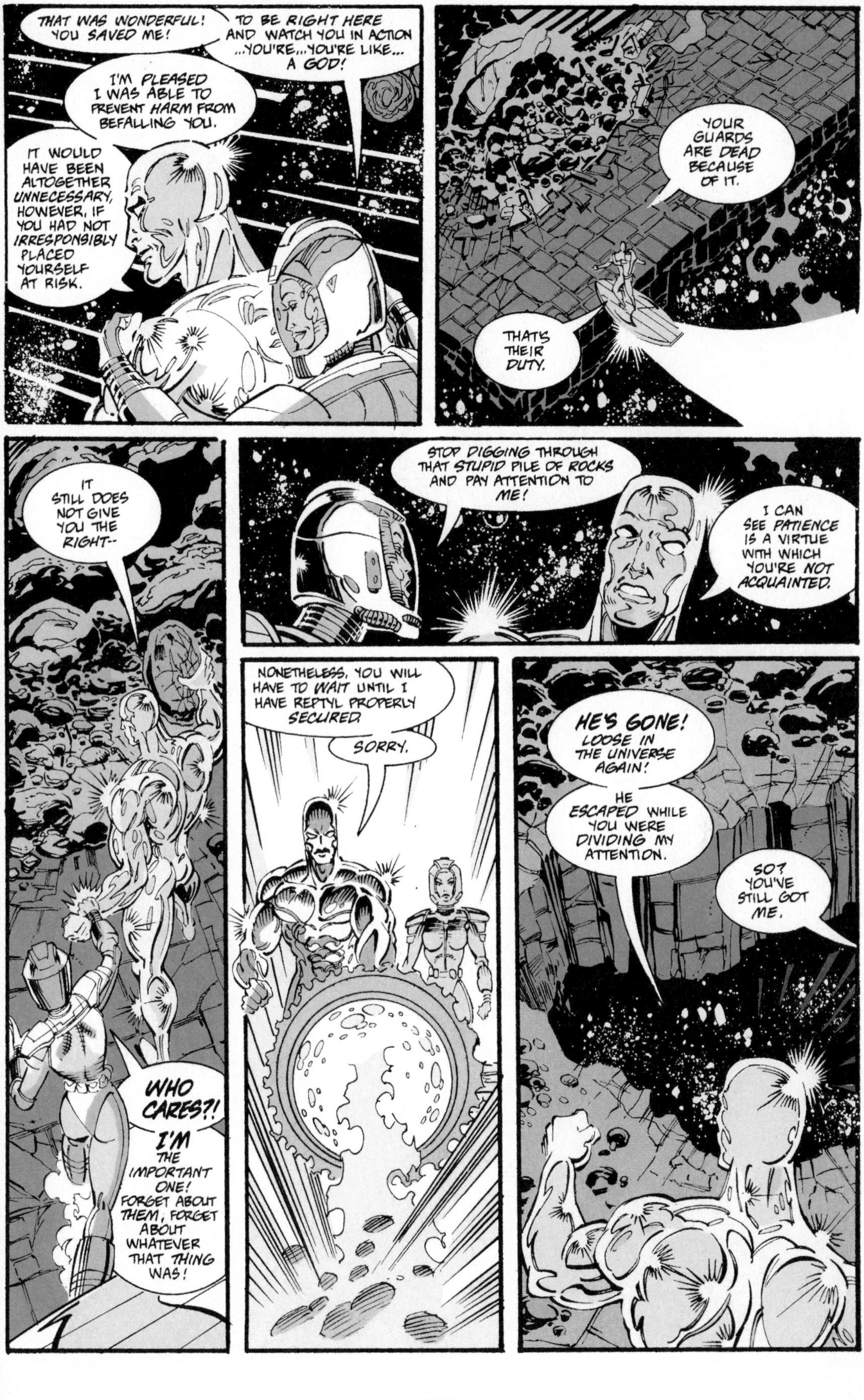
THAT WAS WONDERFUL! YOU SAVED ME!
TO BE RIGHT HERE AND WATCH YOU IN ACTION ...YOU'RE... YOU'RE LIKE... A GOD!
I'M PLEASED I WAS ABLE TO PREVENT HARM FROM BEFALLING YOU.
IT WOULD HAVE BEEN ALTOGETHER UNNECESSARY, HOWEVER, IF YOU HAD NOT IRRESPONSIBLY PLACED YOURSELF AT RISK.
YOUR GUARDS ARE DEAD BECAUSE OF IT.
THAT'S THEIR DUTY.
IT STILL DOES NOT GIVE YOU THE RIGHT--
WHO CARES?!
I'M THE IMPORTANT ONE! FORGET ABOUT THEM, FORGET ABOUT WHATEVER THAT THING WAS!
STOP DIGGING THROUGH THAT STUPID PILE OF ROCKS AND PAY ATTENTION TO ME!
I CAN SEE PATIENCE IS A VIRTUE WITH WHICH YOU'RE NOT ACQUAINTED.
NONETHELESS, YOU WILL HAVE TO WAIT UNTIL I HAVE REPTYL PROPERLY SECURED.
SORRY.
HE'S GONE! LOOSE IN THE UNIVERSE AGAIN!
HE ESCAPED WHILE YOU WERE DIVIDING MY ATTENTION.
SO? YOU'VE STILL GOT ME.

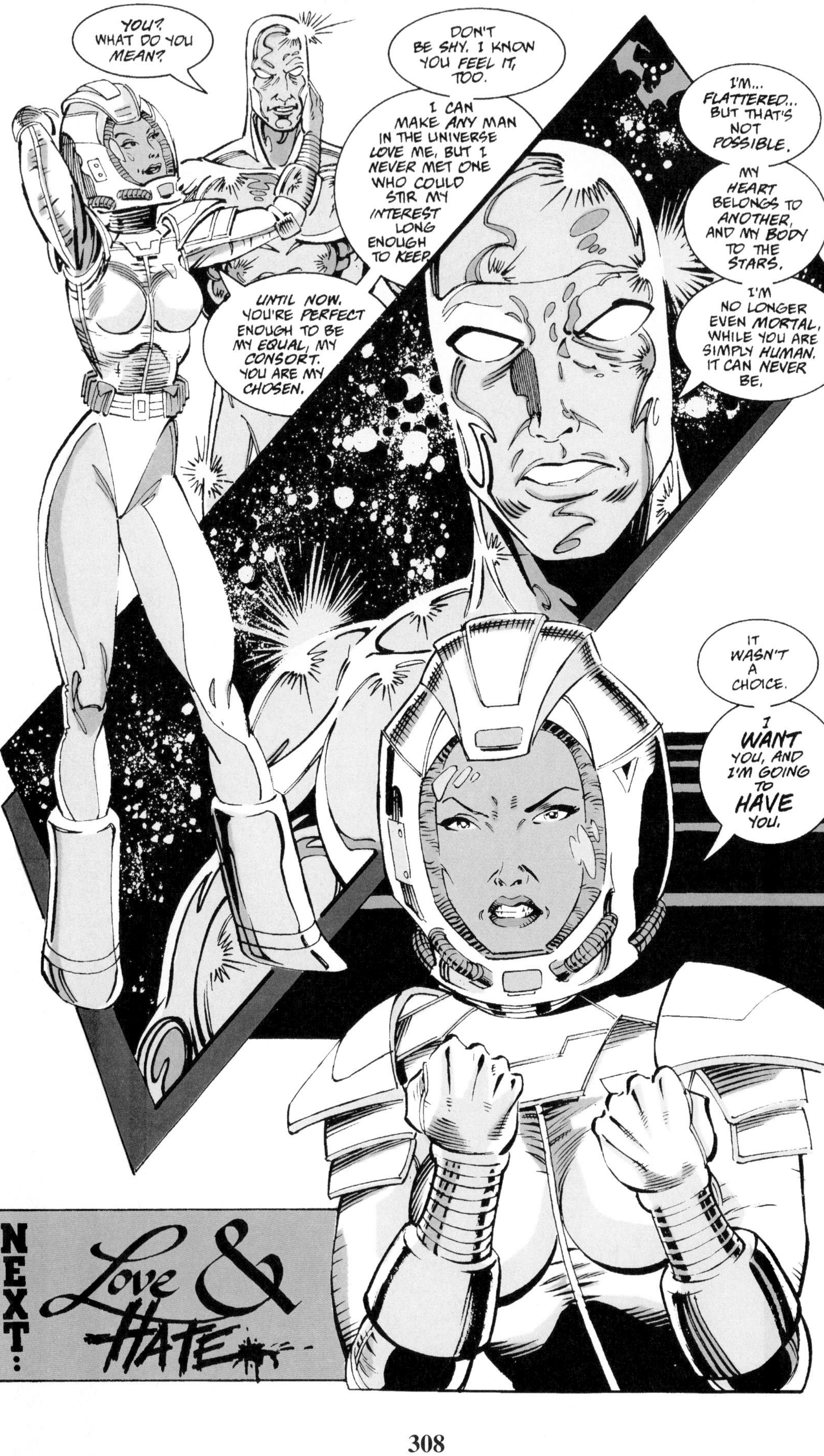
YOU? WHAT DO YOU MEAN?
DON'T BE SHY. I KNOW YOU FEEL IT, TOO.
I CAN MAKE ANY MAN IN THE UNIVERSE LOVE ME, BUT I NEVER MET ONE WHO COULD STIR MY INTEREST LONG ENOUGH TO KEEP.
UNTIL NOW. YOU'RE PERFECT ENOUGH TO BE MY EQUAL, MY CONSORT. YOU ARE MY CHOSEN.
I'M... FLATTERED... BUT THAT'S NOT POSSIBLE.
MY HEART BELONGS TO ANOTHER, AND MY BODY TO THE STARS.
I'M NO LONGER EVEN MORTAL, WHILE YOU ARE SIMPLY HUMAN. IT CAN NEVER BE.
IT WASN'T A CHOICE.
I WANT YOU, AND I'M GOING TO HAVE YOU.
NEXT: Love & HATE

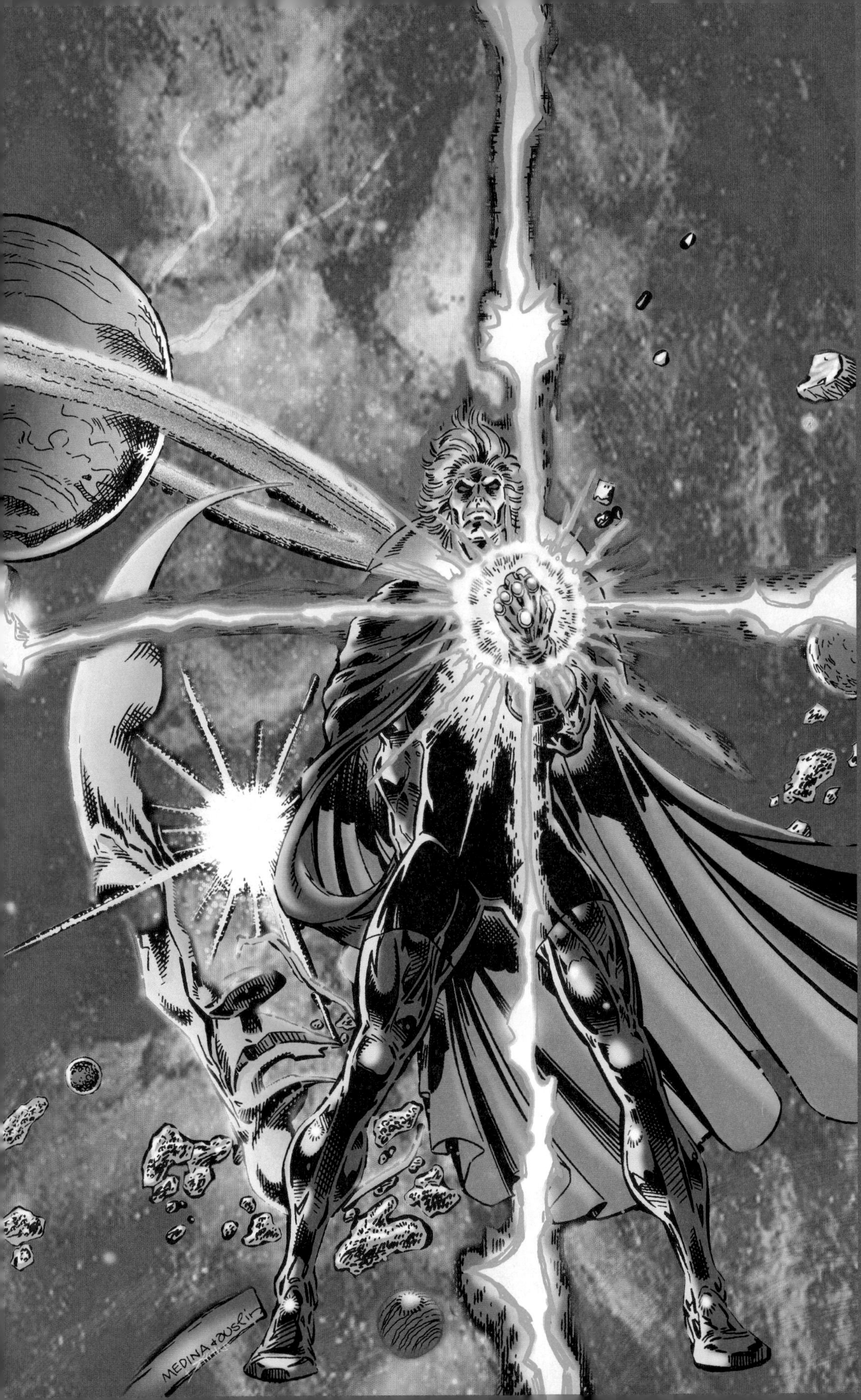
MEDINA

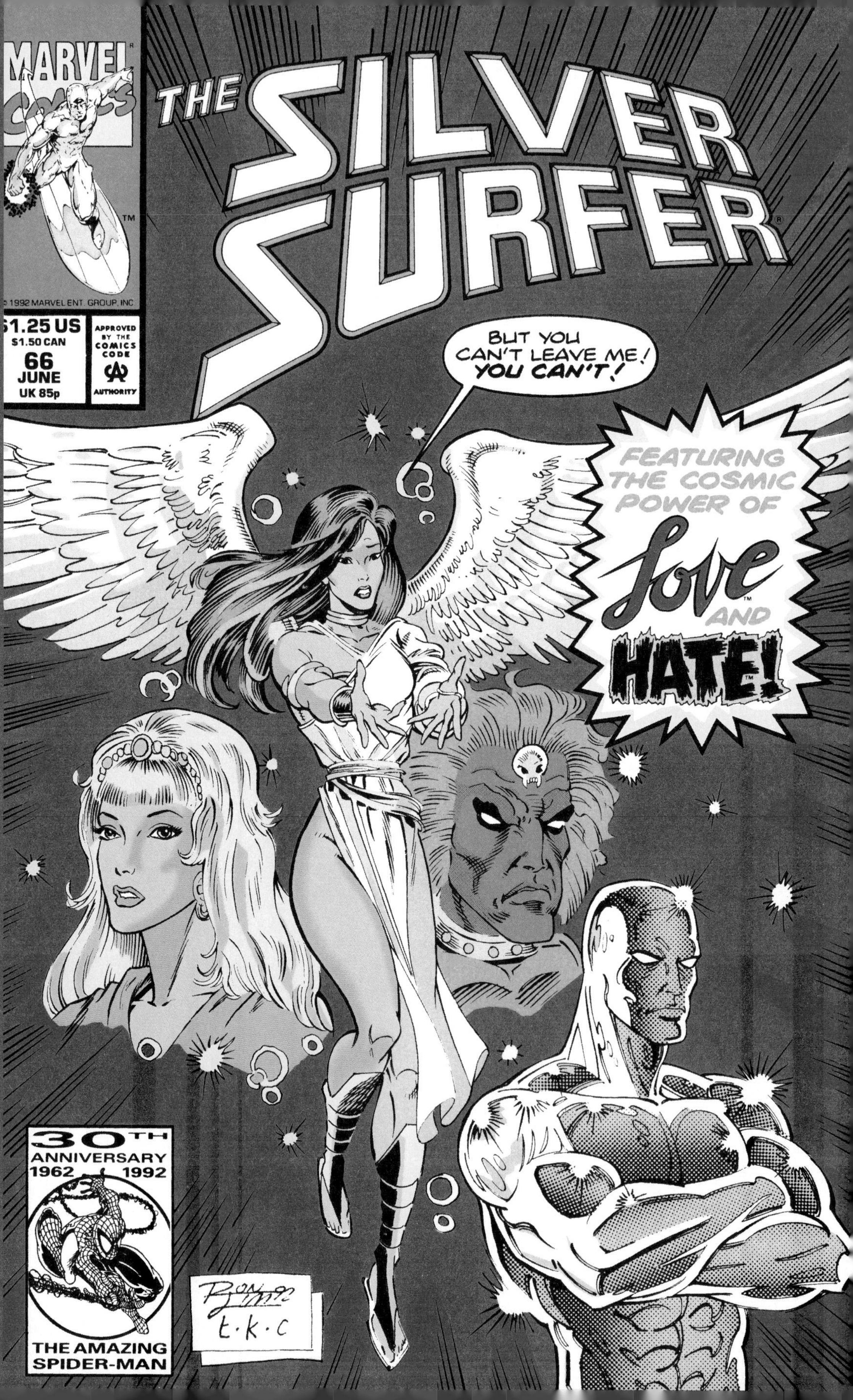
MARVEL COMICS
THE SILVER SURFER
© 1992 MARVEL ENT. GROUP, INC.
$1.25 US
$1.50 CAN
66
JUNE
UK 85p
APPROVED BY THE COMICS CODE AUTHORITY
BUT YOU CAN'T LEAVE ME! YOU CAN'T!
FEATURING THE COSMIC POWER OF
Love AND HATE!
30TH ANNIVERSARY 1962 1992
THE AMAZING SPIDER-MAN

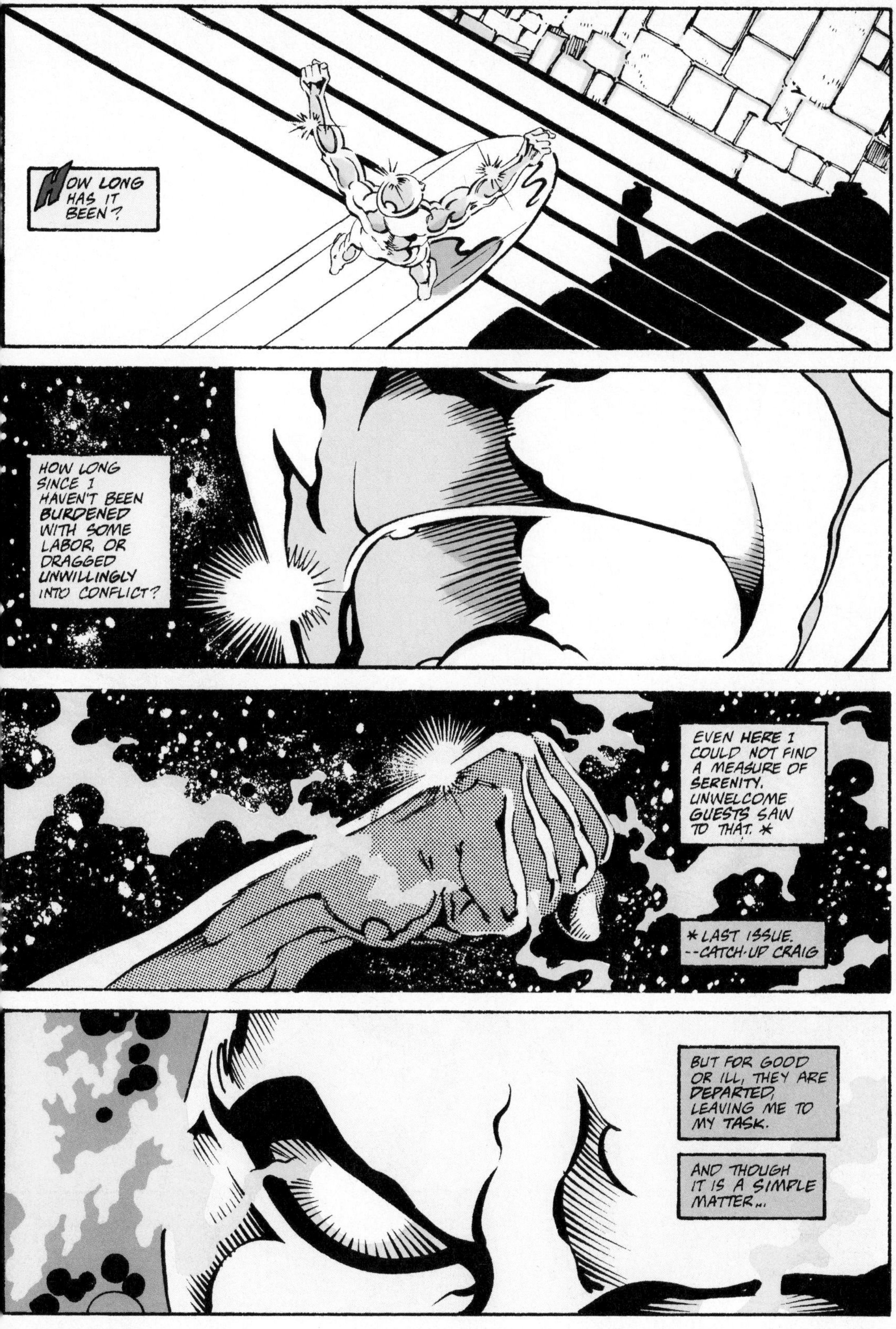
HOW LONG HAS IT BEEN?
HOW LONG SINCE I HAVEN'T BEEN BURDENED WITH SOME LABOR, OR DRAGGED UNWILLINGLY INTO CONFLICT?
EVEN HERE I COULD NOT FIND A MEASURE OF SERENITY. UNWELCOME GUESTS SAW TO THAT. *
*LAST ISSUE. --CATCH-UP CRAIG
BUT FOR GOOD OR ILL, THEY ARE DEPARTED, LEAVING ME TO MY TASK.
AND THOUGH IT IS A SIMPLE MATTER...

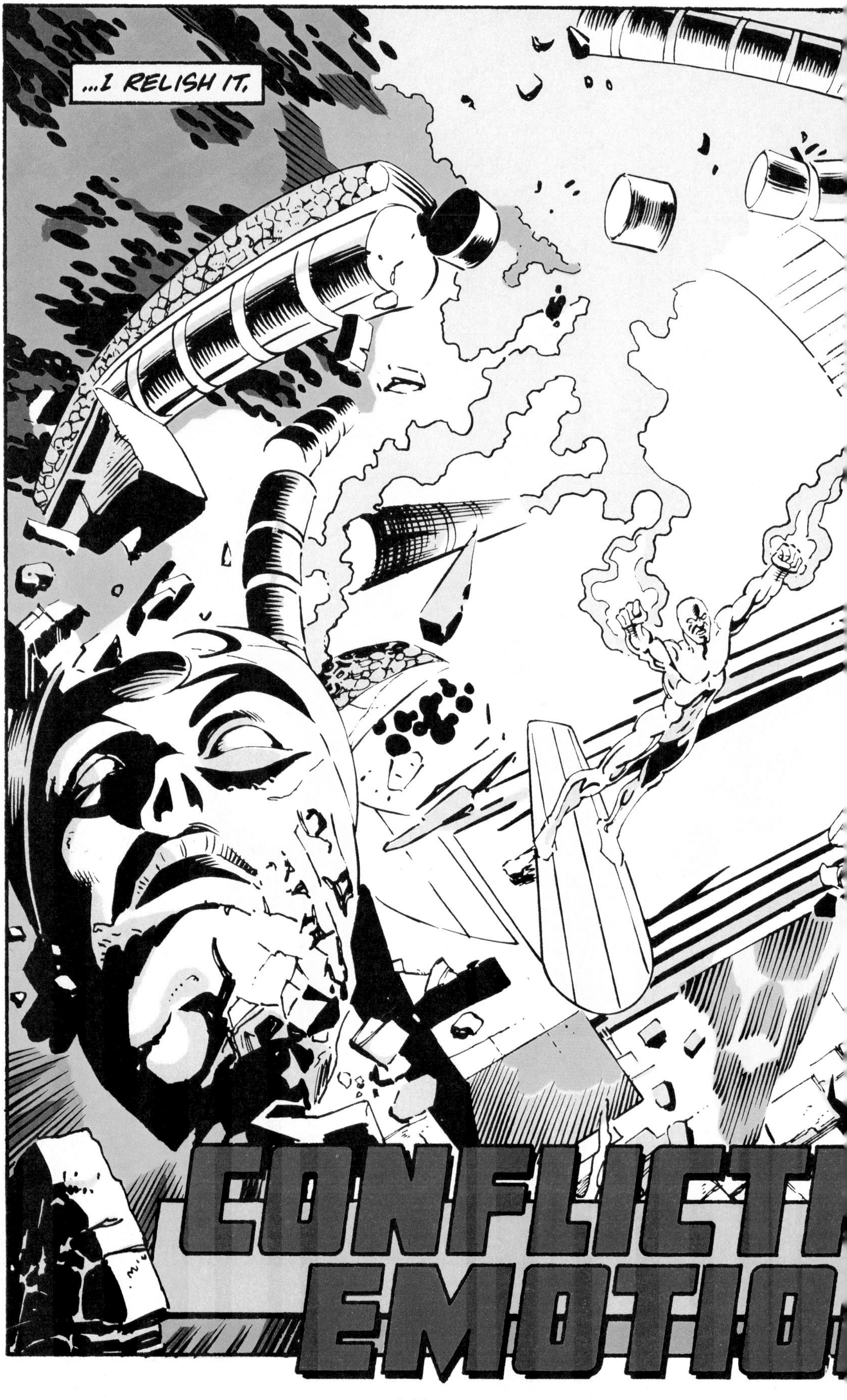
...I RELISH IT.

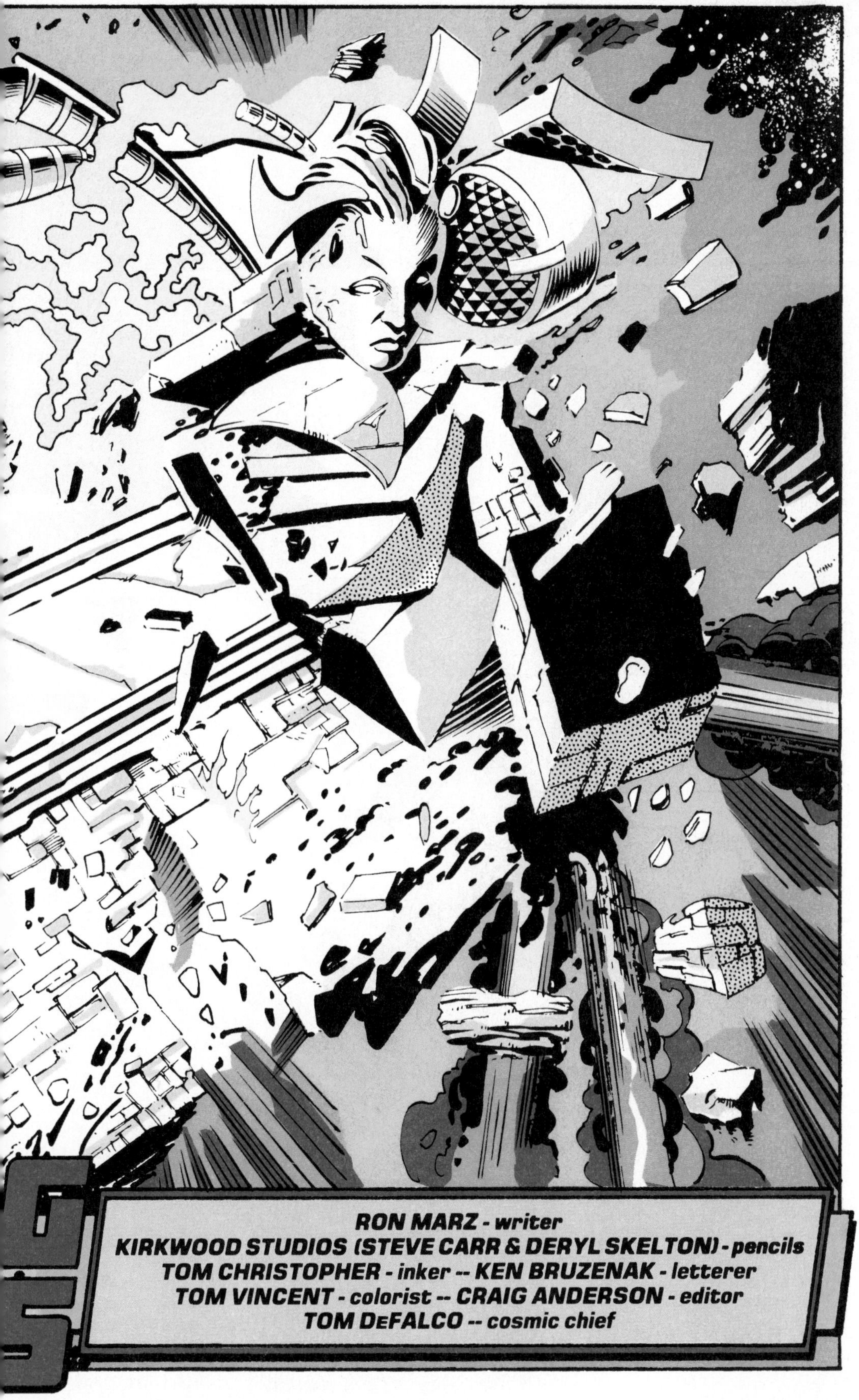
RON MARZ - writer
KIRKWOOD STUDIOS (STEVE CARR & DERYL SKELTON) - pencils
TOM CHRISTOPHER - inker -- KEN BRUZENAK - letterer
TOM VINCENT - colorist -- CRAIG ANDERSON - editor
TOM DeFALCO -- cosmic chief

JUST AS THANOS IS NO MORE, THE MONUMENT HE ERECTED TO HIMSELF* IS ALSO DESTROYED.

*IN INFINITY GAUNTLET #1, OF COURSE.—CRAIG

THIS EVIL CHAPTER OF HISTORY IS WELL AND TRULY CLOSED.

FREE OF THIS DESPOT'S HAND, THE FUTURE RIGHTLY UNFOLDS TO NO DESIGN SAVE ITS OWN.

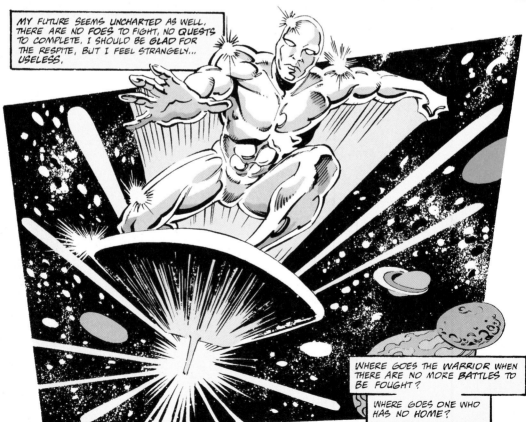

MY FUTURE SEEMS UNCHARTED AS WELL. THERE ARE NO FOES TO FIGHT, NO QUESTS TO COMPLETE. I SHOULD BE GLAD FOR THE RESPITE, BUT I FEEL STRANGELY... USELESS.

WHERE GOES THE WARRIOR WHEN THERE ARE NO MORE BATTLES TO BE FOUGHT?

WHERE GOES ONE WHO HAS NO HOME?

THRONEWORLD OF THE KHARTA'EEN EMPIRE.

ROYAL BEDCHAMBERS OF THE PRINCESS ALAISA.

I'VE NEVER BEEN SO HUMILIATED.

I PRACTICALLY *THROW MYSELF* AT HIM, AND WHAT DOES HE SAY?

"*I'M NO LONGER EVEN MORTAL, WHILE YOU ARE SIMPLY HUMAN.*" THE ARROGANCE!

DOESN'T HE KNOW WHO I *AM*?

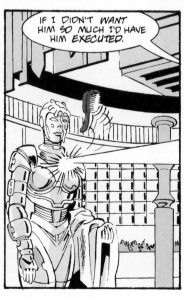

IF I DIDN'T WANT HIM SO MUCH I'D HAVE HIM *EXECUTED.*

Perhaps the reason you want him at all is due to your inability to attract *him?*

Your emotional manipulations apparently have no *effect on the Silver Surfer.*

THAT HAS *NOTHING* TO DO WITH IT.

I WANT HIM FOR MY CONSORT BECAUSE HE'S PERFECT.

IT'S JUST A QUESTION OF HOW I GET HIM.

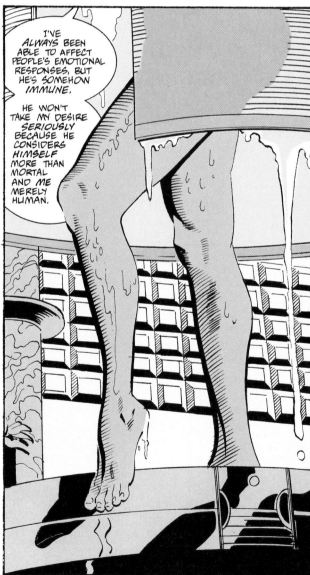

I'VE ALWAYS BEEN ABLE TO AFFECT PEOPLE'S EMOTIONAL RESPONSES, BUT HE'S SOMEHOW IMMUNE.

HE WON'T TAKE MY DESIRE SERIOUSLY BECAUSE HE CONSIDERS HIMSELF MORE THAN MORTAL AND ME MERELY HUMAN.

SO I HAVE TO BECOME MORE THAN MORTAL AS WELL.

I HAVE TO BECOME TRANSCENDENT.

THERE MUST BE A WAY TO GET THE KIND OF POWER THAT WILL MAKE ME THE SILVER SURFER'S EQUAL.

I WANT EVERYTHING RELEVANT IN YOUR DATA BANKS.

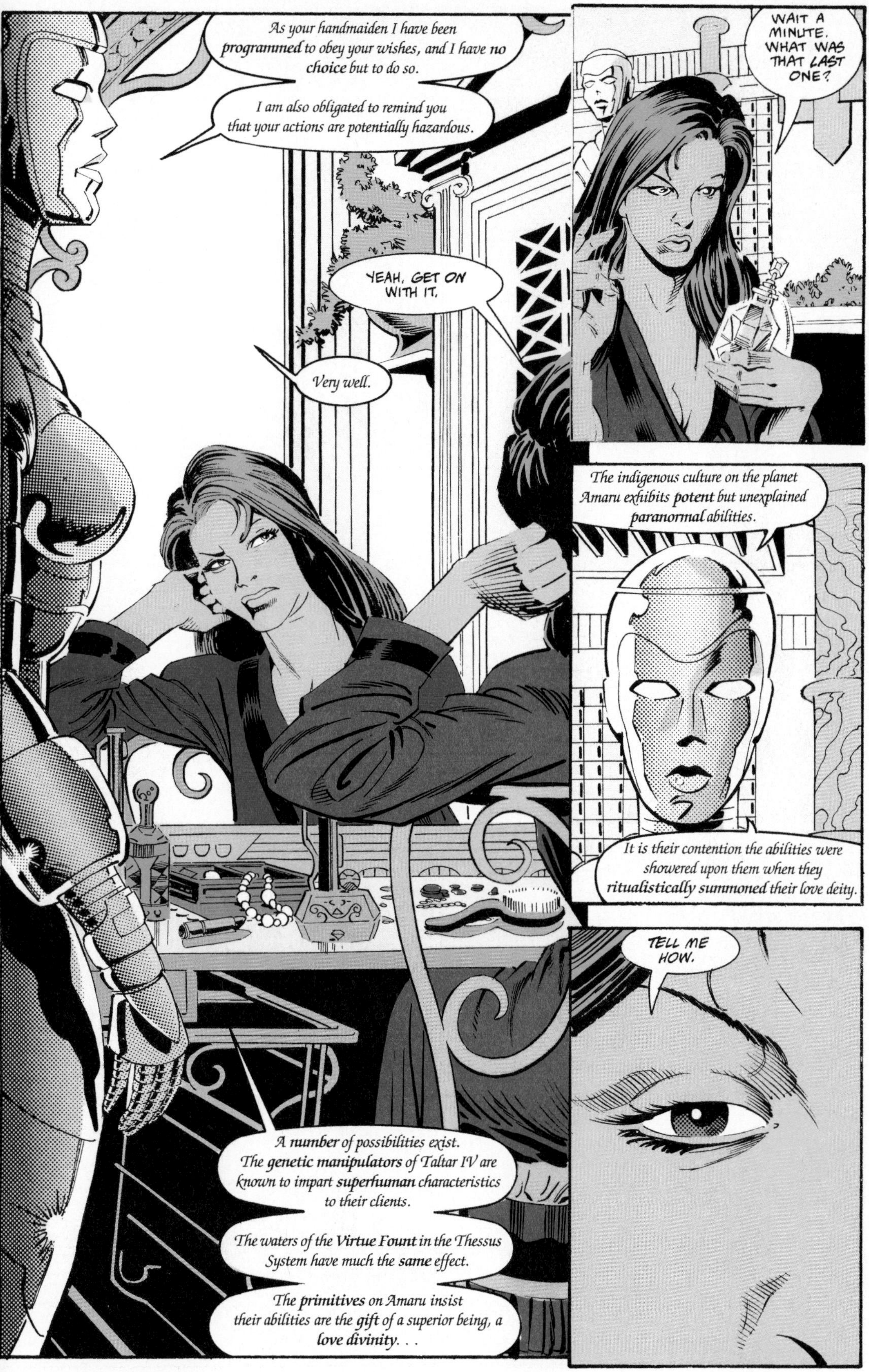

As your handmaiden I have been programmed to obey your wishes, and I have no choice but to do so.
I am also obligated to remind you that your actions are potentially hazardous.
YEAH, GET ON WITH IT.
Very well.
A number of possibilities exist. The genetic manipulators of Taltar IV are known to impart superhuman characteristics to their clients.
The waters of the Virtue Fount in the Thessus System have much the same effect.
The primitives on Amaru insist their abilities are the gift of a superior being, a love divinity. . .
WAIT A MINUTE. WHAT WAS THAT LAST ONE?
The indigenous culture on the planet Amaru exhibits potent but unexplained paranormal abilities.
It is their contention the abilities were showered upon them when they ritualistically summoned their love deity.
TELL ME HOW.

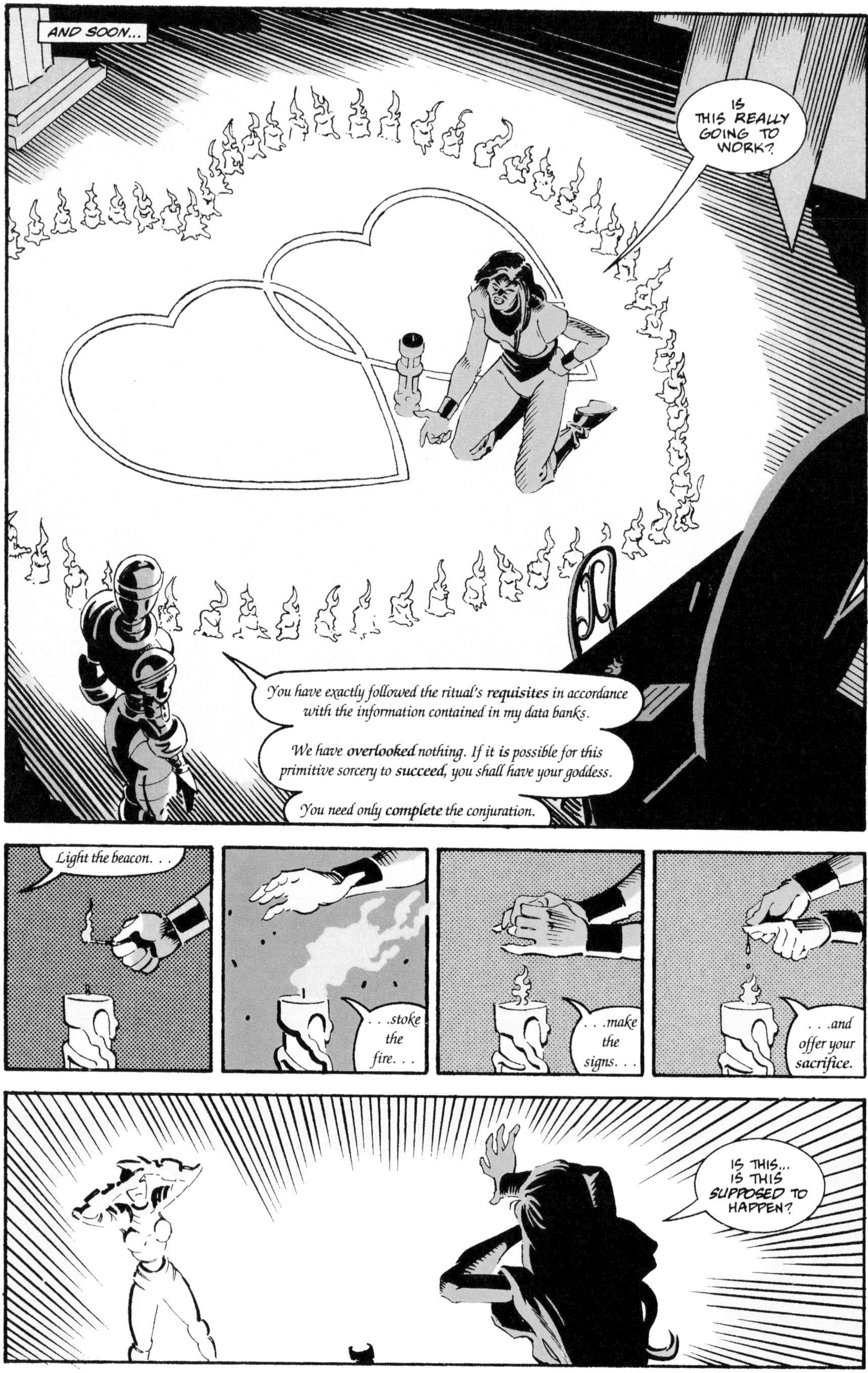
AND SOON...
IS THIS REALLY GOING TO WORK?
You have exactly followed the ritual's requisites in accordance with the information contained in my data banks.
We have overlooked nothing. If it is possible for this primitive sorcery to succeed, you shall have your goddess.
You need only complete the conjuration.
Light the beacon. . .
. . .stoke the fire. . .
. . .make the signs. . .
. . .and offer your sacrifice.
IS THIS... IS THIS SUPPOSED TO HAPPEN?

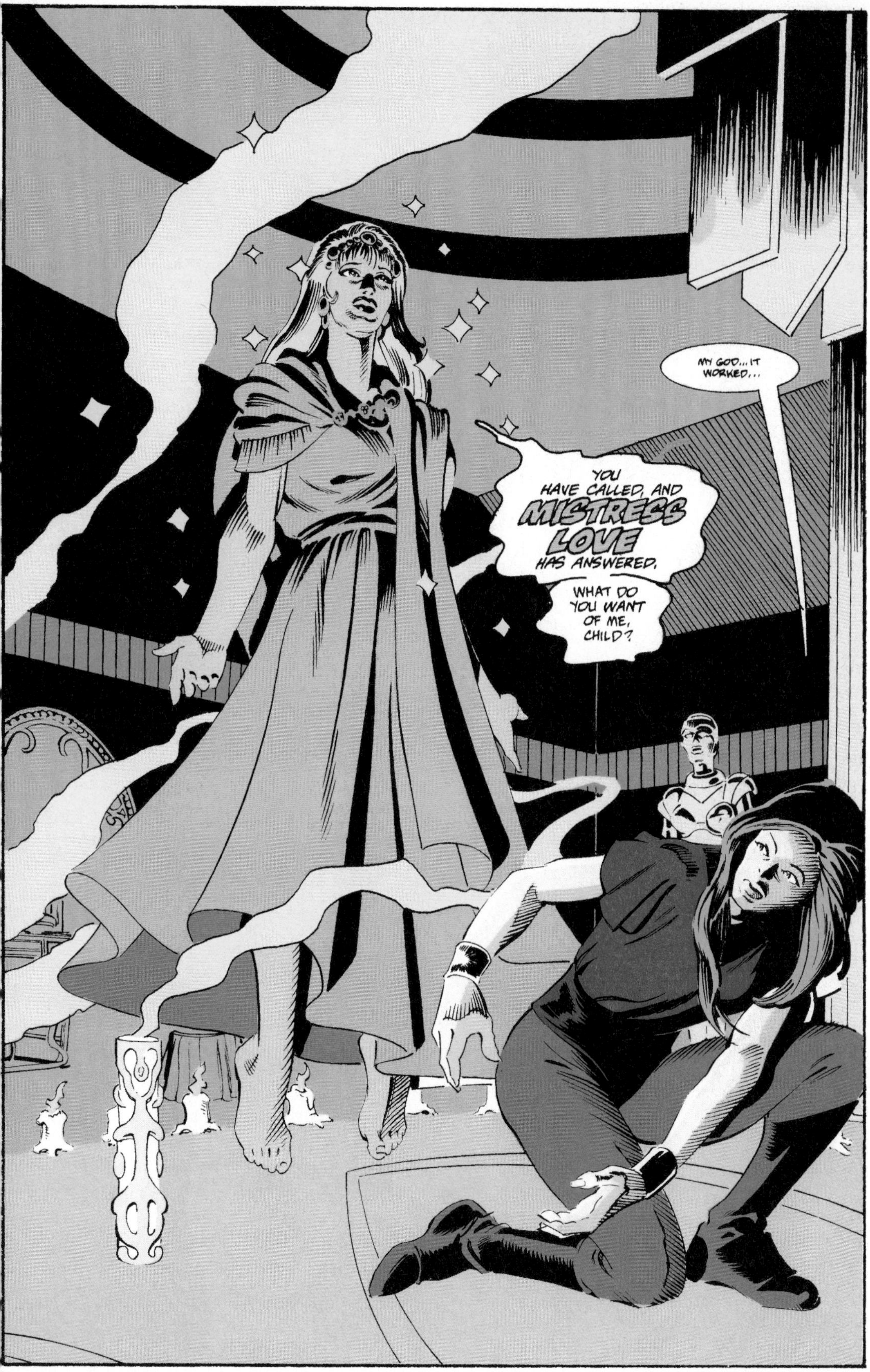
MY GOD... IT WORKED...
YOU HAVE CALLED, AND MISTRESS LOVE HAS ANSWERED.
WHAT DO YOU WANT OF ME, CHILD?

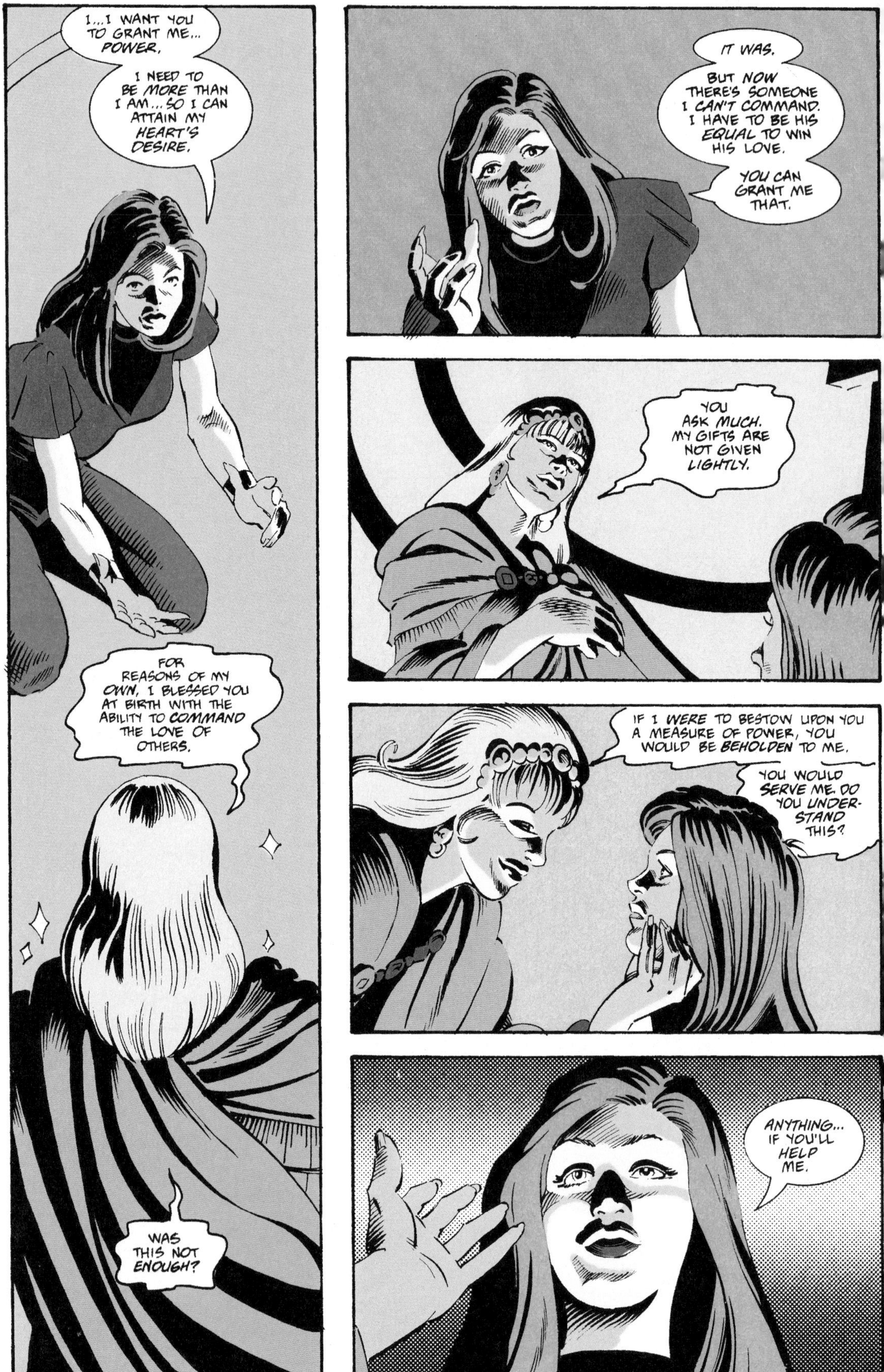
I...I WANT YOU TO GRANT ME... POWER.
I NEED TO BE MORE THAN I AM...SO I CAN ATTAIN MY HEART'S DESIRE.
FOR REASONS OF MY OWN, I BLESSED YOU AT BIRTH WITH THE ABILITY TO COMMAND THE LOVE OF OTHERS.
WAS THIS NOT ENOUGH?
IT WAS.
BUT NOW THERE'S SOMEONE I CAN'T COMMAND. I HAVE TO BE HIS EQUAL TO WIN HIS LOVE.
YOU CAN GRANT ME THAT.
YOU ASK MUCH. MY GIFTS ARE NOT GIVEN LIGHTLY.
IF I WERE TO BESTOW UPON YOU A MEASURE OF POWER, YOU WOULD BE BEHOLDEN TO ME.
YOU WOULD SERVE ME. DO YOU UNDERSTAND THIS?
ANYTHING... IF YOU'LL HELP ME.

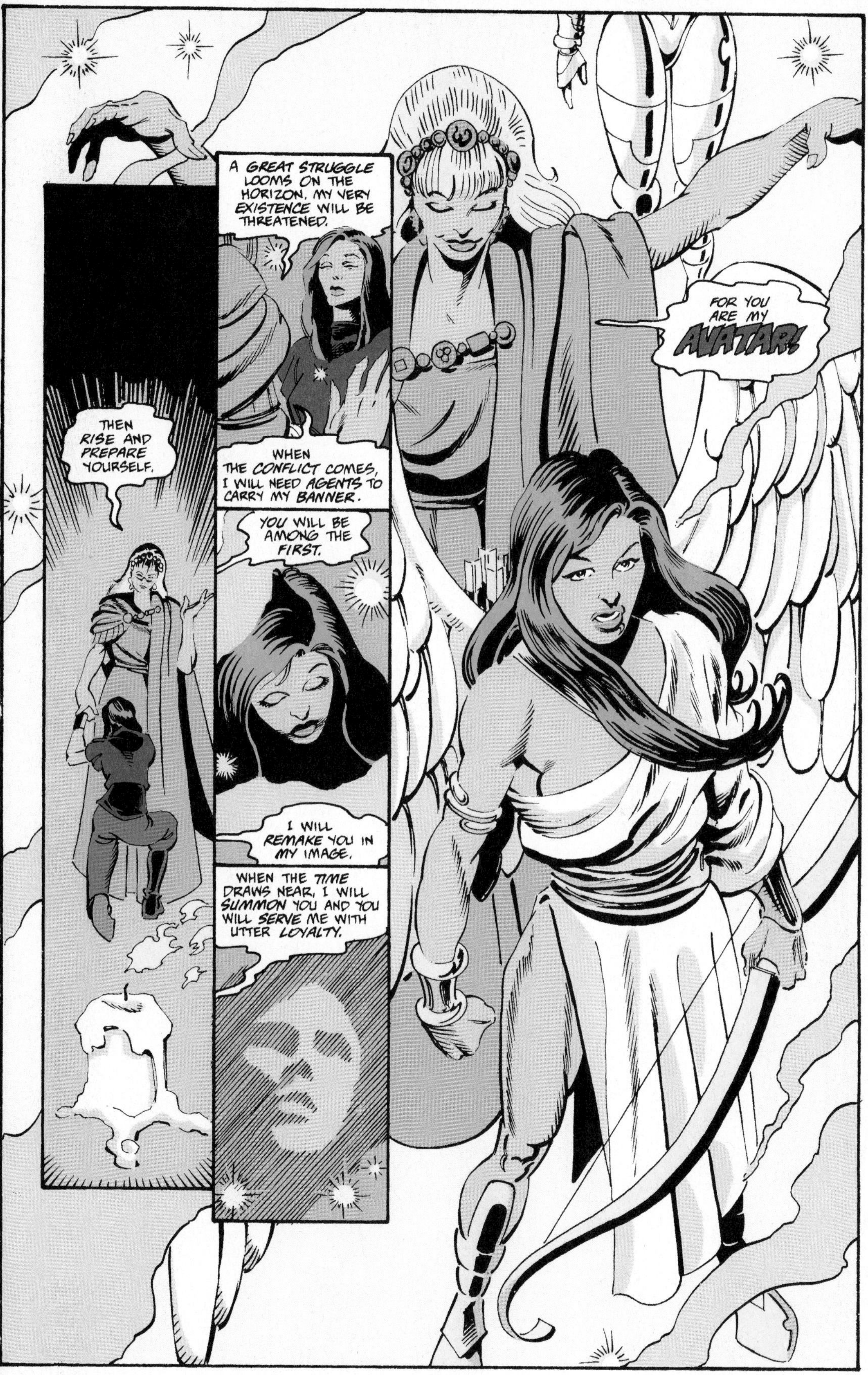
A GREAT STRUGGLE LOOMS ON THE HORIZON. MY VERY EXISTENCE WILL BE THREATENED.
FOR YOU ARE MY AVATAR!
THEN RISE AND PREPARE YOURSELF.
WHEN THE CONFLICT COMES, I WILL NEED AGENTS TO CARRY MY BANNER.
YOU WILL BE AMONG THE FIRST.
I WILL REMAKE YOU IN MY IMAGE.
WHEN THE TIME DRAWS NEAR, I WILL SUMMON YOU AND YOU WILL SERVE ME WITH UTTER LOYALTY.

LOOK AT ME!

LOOK AT ALL MY BEAUTY, ALL MY POWER, MY--

I UNDERSTAND YOUR EUPHORIA. BUT REMEMBER, THE POWER YOU WIELD IS MINE, NOT YOURS.

OF COURSE, LADY. I'M SORRY.

IN TIME, I WILL CALL FOR YOU, BUT FOR NOW YOU ARE FREE.

USE THE GIFTS I HAVE GIVEN YOU. USE THEM LOVINGLY, AND WITHOUT MALICE.

I GO TO NURTURE MY INTERESTS ELSEWHERE.

I LEAVE YOU WITH A WARNING: REMAIN TRUE. RESIST THE TEMPTATION POSED BY THE DARKER SIDE OF LOVE.

FOR THAT WAY LIES ONLY DESPAIR...

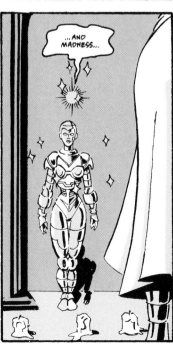

...AND MADNESS...

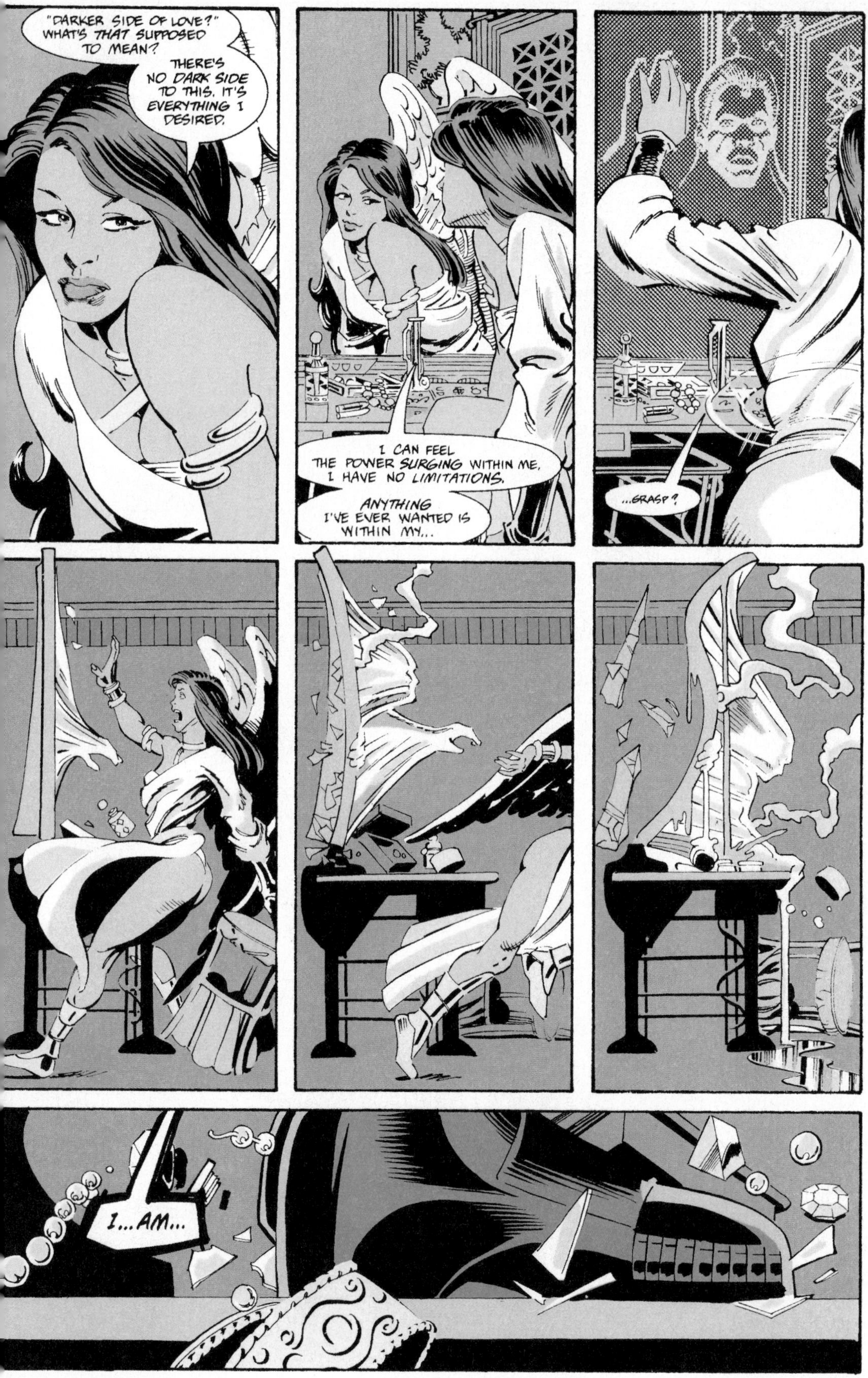
"DARKER SIDE OF LOVE?" WHAT'S THAT SUPPOSED TO MEAN?
THERE'S NO DARK SIDE TO THIS. IT'S EVERYTHING I DESIRED.
I CAN FEEL THE POWER SURGING WITHIN ME. I HAVE NO LIMITATIONS.
ANYTHING I'VE EVER WANTED IS WITHIN MY...
...GRASP?
I...AM...

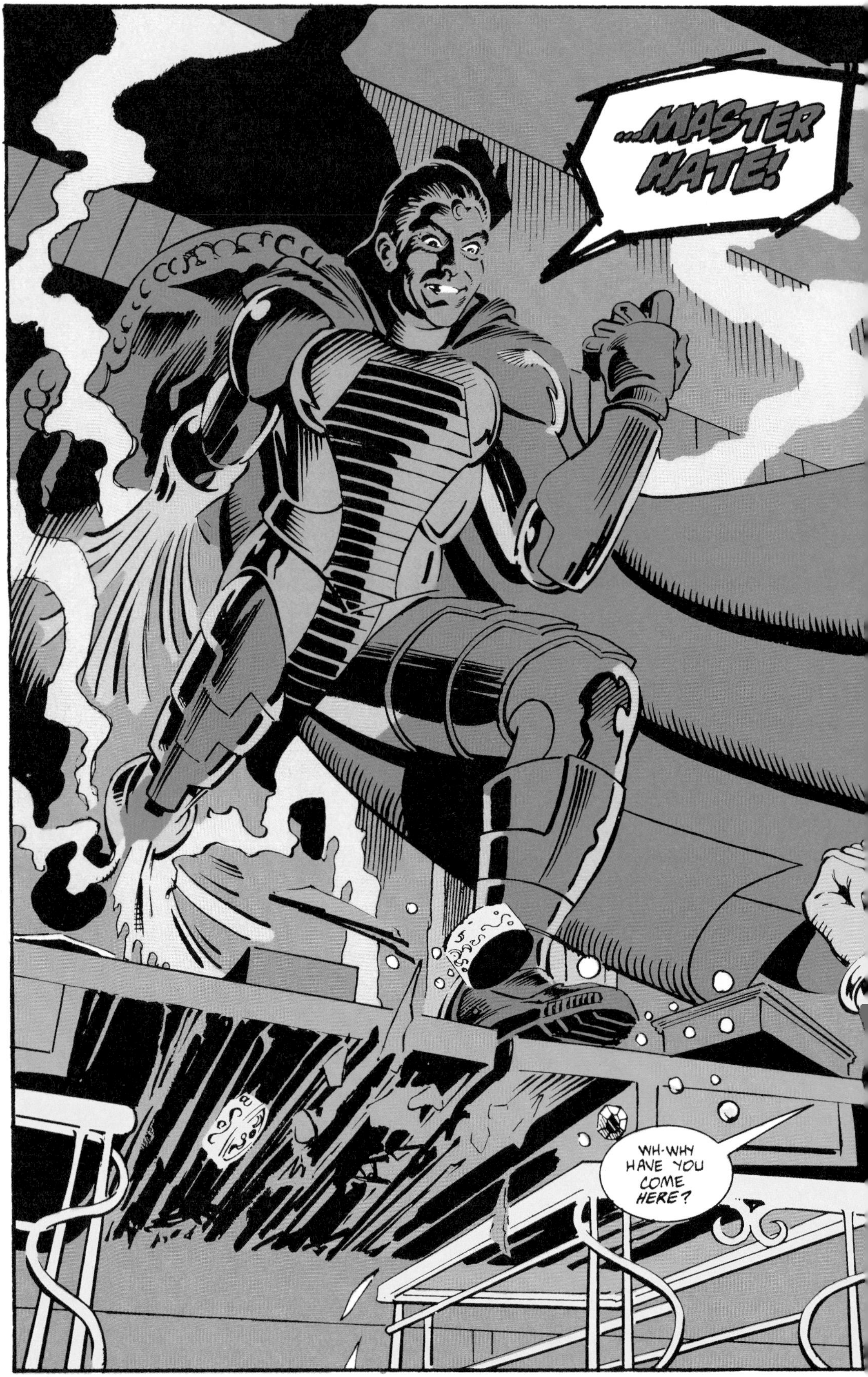
...MASTER HATE!
WH-WHY HAVE YOU COME HERE?

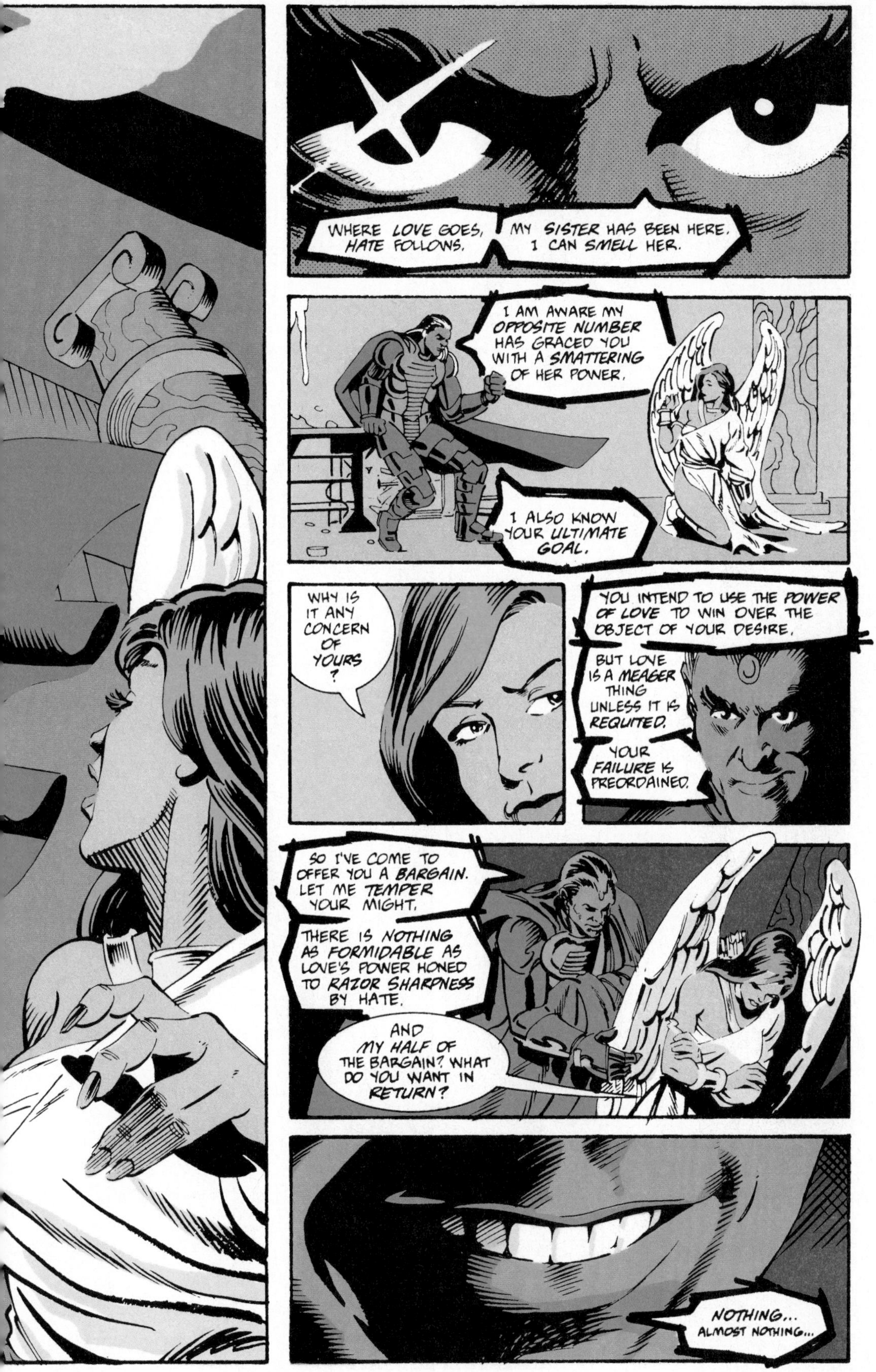
WHERE LOVE GOES, HATE FOLLOWS.
MY SISTER HAS BEEN HERE. I CAN SMELL HER.
I AM AWARE MY OPPOSITE NUMBER HAS GRACED YOU WITH A SMATTERING OF HER POWER.
I ALSO KNOW YOUR ULTIMATE GOAL.
WHY IS IT ANY CONCERN OF YOURS?
YOU INTEND TO USE THE POWER OF LOVE TO WIN OVER THE OBJECT OF YOUR DESIRE.
BUT LOVE IS A MEAGER THING UNLESS IT IS REQUITED.
YOUR FAILURE IS PREORDAINED.
SO I'VE COME TO OFFER YOU A BARGAIN. LET ME TEMPER YOUR MIGHT.
THERE IS NOTHING AS FORMIDABLE AS LOVE'S POWER HONED TO RAZOR SHARPNESS BY HATE.
AND MY HALF OF THE BARGAIN? WHAT DO YOU WANT IN RETURN?
NOTHING... ALMOST NOTHING...

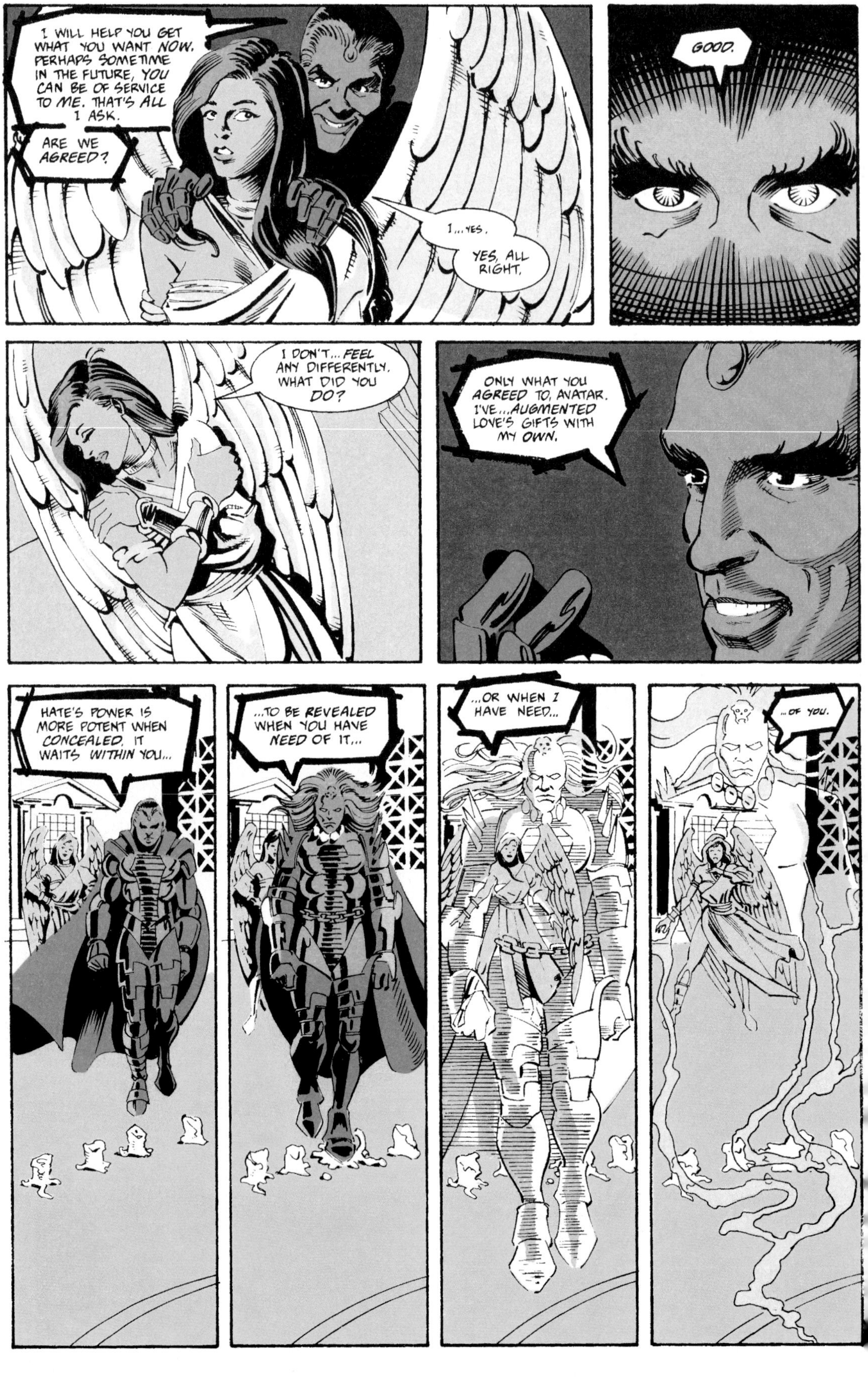
I WILL HELP YOU GET WHAT YOU WANT NOW. PERHAPS SOMETIME IN THE FUTURE, YOU CAN BE OF SERVICE TO ME. THAT'S ALL I ASK.
ARE WE AGREED?
I... YES.
YES, ALL RIGHT.
GOOD.
I DON'T... FEEL ANY DIFFERENTLY. WHAT DID YOU DO?
ONLY WHAT YOU AGREED TO, AVATAR. I'VE... AUGMENTED LOVE'S GIFTS WITH MY OWN.
HATE'S POWER IS MORE POTENT WHEN CONCEALED. IT WAITS WITHIN YOU...
...TO BE REVEALED WHEN YOU HAVE NEED OF IT...
...OR WHEN I HAVE NEED...
...OF YOU.

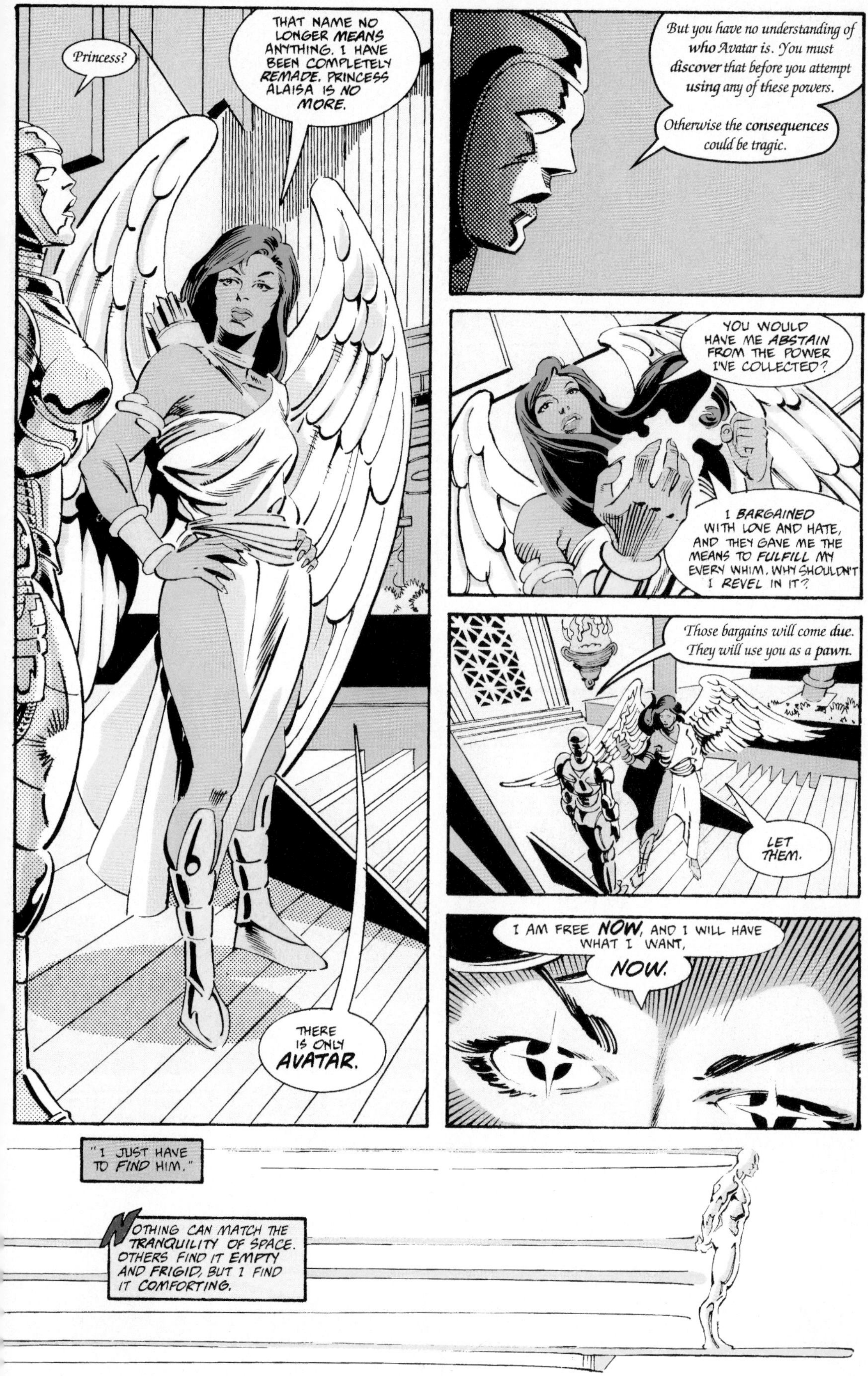

Princess?
THAT NAME NO LONGER MEANS ANYTHING. I HAVE BEEN COMPLETELY REMADE. PRINCESS ALAISA IS NO MORE.
THERE IS ONLY AVATAR.
But you have no understanding of who Avatar is. You must discover that before you attempt using any of these powers.
Otherwise the consequences could be tragic.
YOU WOULD HAVE ME ABSTAIN FROM THE POWER I'VE COLLECTED?
I BARGAINED WITH LOVE AND HATE, AND THEY GAVE ME THE MEANS TO FULFILL MY EVERY WHIM. WHY SHOULDN'T I REVEL IN IT?
Those bargains will come due. They will use you as a pawn.
LET THEM.
I AM FREE NOW, AND I WILL HAVE WHAT I WANT,
NOW.
"I JUST HAVE TO FIND HIM."
NOTHING CAN MATCH THE TRANQUILITY OF SPACE. OTHERS FIND IT EMPTY AND FRIGID, BUT I FIND IT COMFORTING.

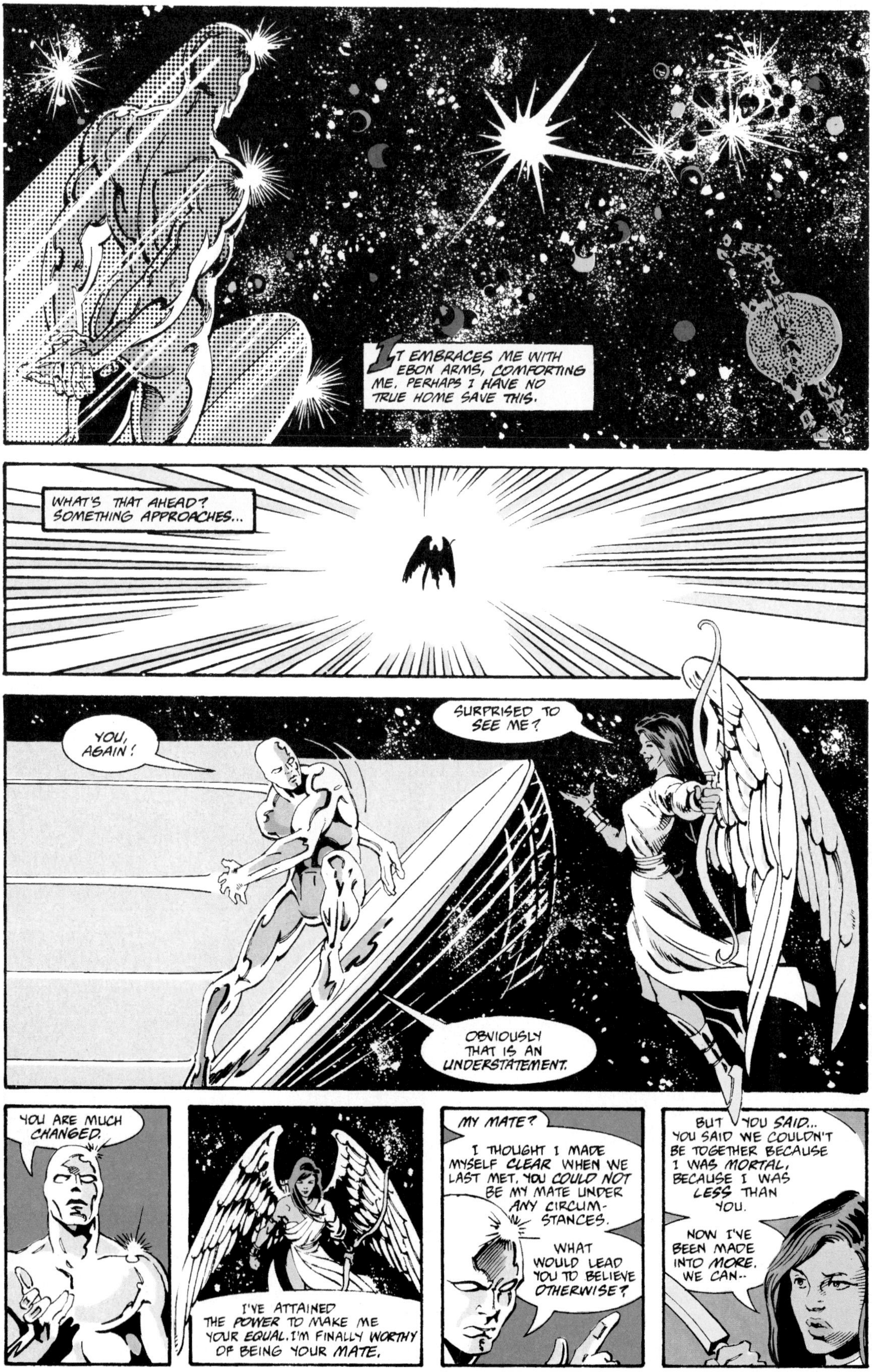
IT EMBRACES ME WITH EBON ARMS, COMFORTING ME. PERHAPS I HAVE NO TRUE HOME SAVE THIS.
WHAT'S THAT AHEAD? SOMETHING APPROACHES...
YOU, AGAIN!
SURPRISED TO SEE ME?
OBVIOUSLY THAT IS AN UNDERSTATEMENT.
YOU ARE MUCH CHANGED.
I'VE ATTAINED THE POWER TO MAKE ME YOUR EQUAL. I'M FINALLY WORTHY OF BEING YOUR MATE.
MY MATE?
I THOUGHT I MADE MYSELF CLEAR WHEN WE LAST MET. YOU COULD NOT BE MY MATE UNDER ANY CIRCUM-STANCES.
WHAT WOULD LEAD YOU TO BELIEVE OTHERWISE?
BUT YOU SAID... YOU SAID WE COULDN'T BE TOGETHER BECAUSE I WAS MORTAL, BECAUSE I WAS LESS THAN YOU.
NOW I'VE BEEN MADE INTO MORE. WE CAN..

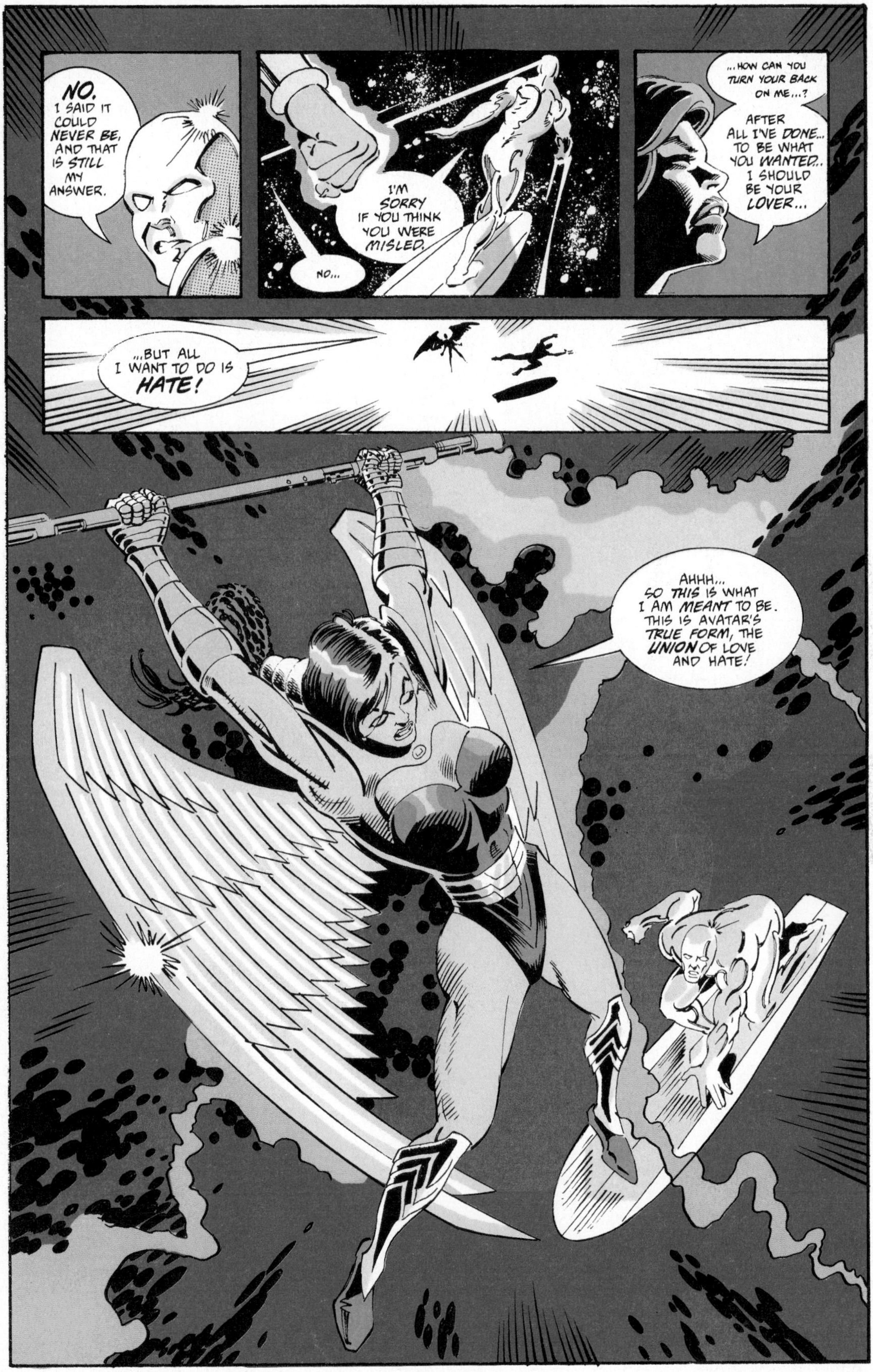

NO. I SAID IT COULD NEVER BE, AND THAT IS STILL MY ANSWER.
I'M SORRY IF YOU THINK YOU WERE MISLED.
NO...
...HOW CAN YOU TURN YOUR BACK ON ME...?
AFTER ALL I'VE DONE... TO BE WHAT YOU WANTED... I SHOULD BE YOUR LOVER...
...BUT ALL I WANT TO DO IS HATE!
AHHH... SO THIS IS WHAT I AM MEANT TO BE. THIS IS AVATAR'S TRUE FORM, THE UNION OF LOVE AND HATE!

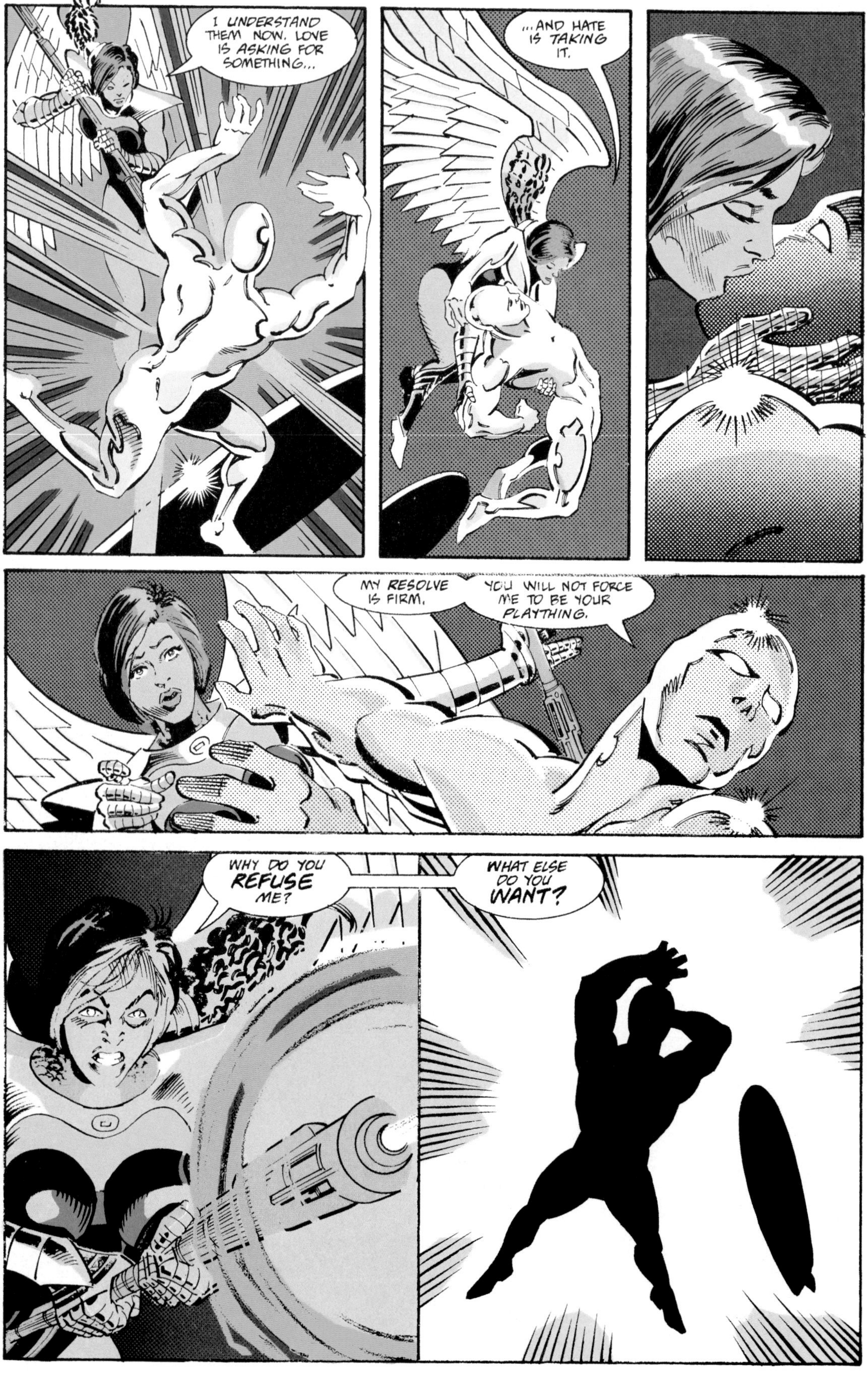
I UNDERSTAND THEM NOW. LOVE IS ASKING FOR SOMETHING...
...AND HATE IS TAKING IT.
MY RESOLVE IS FIRM.
YOU WILL NOT FORCE ME TO BE YOUR PLAYTHING.
WHY DO YOU REFUSE ME?
WHAT ELSE DO YOU WANT?

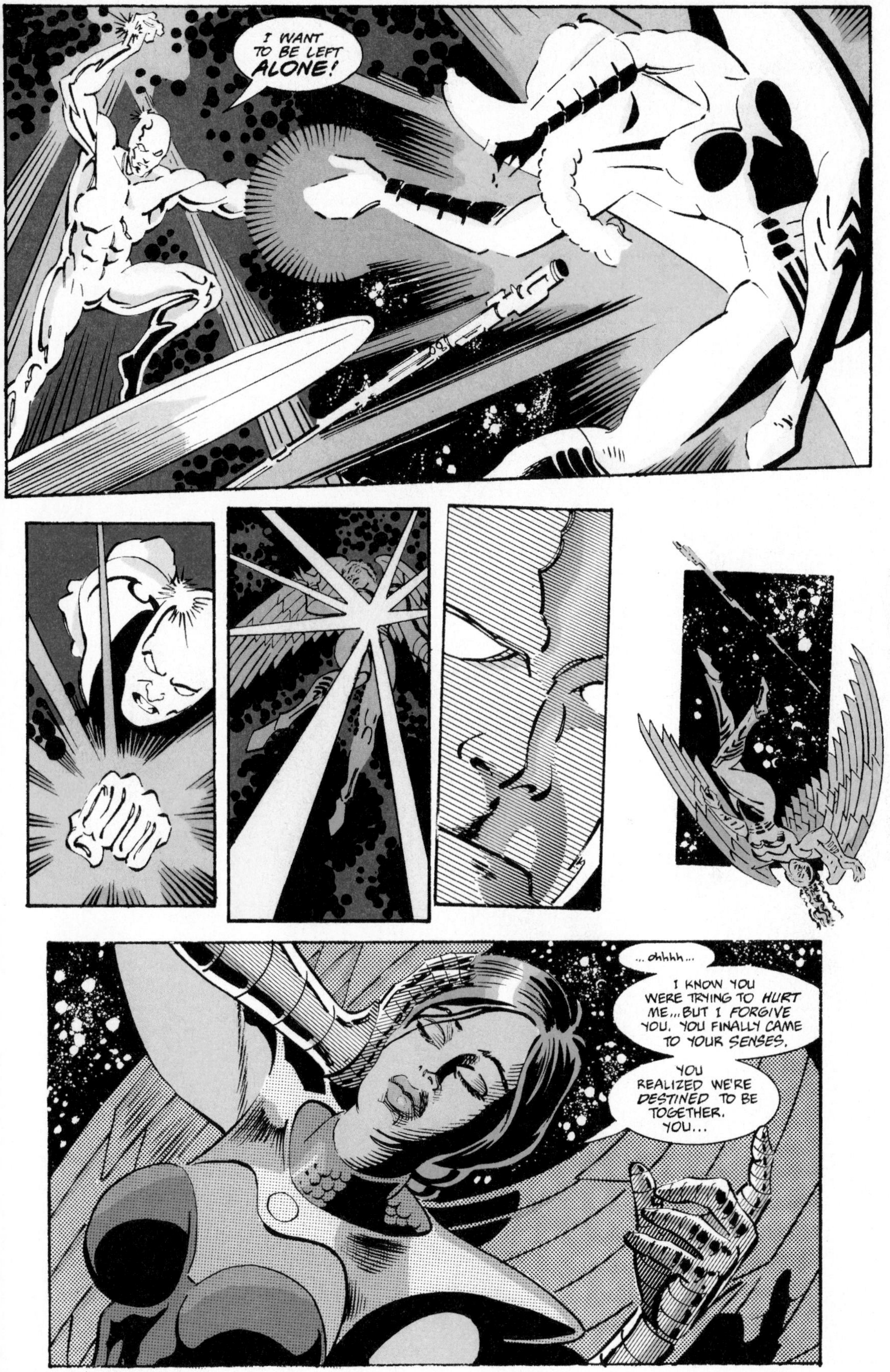
I WANT TO BE LEFT ALONE!
...ohhhh...
I KNOW YOU WERE TRYING TO HURT ME...BUT I FORGIVE YOU. YOU FINALLY CAME TO YOUR SENSES.
YOU REALIZED WE'RE DESTINED TO BE TOGETHER. YOU...

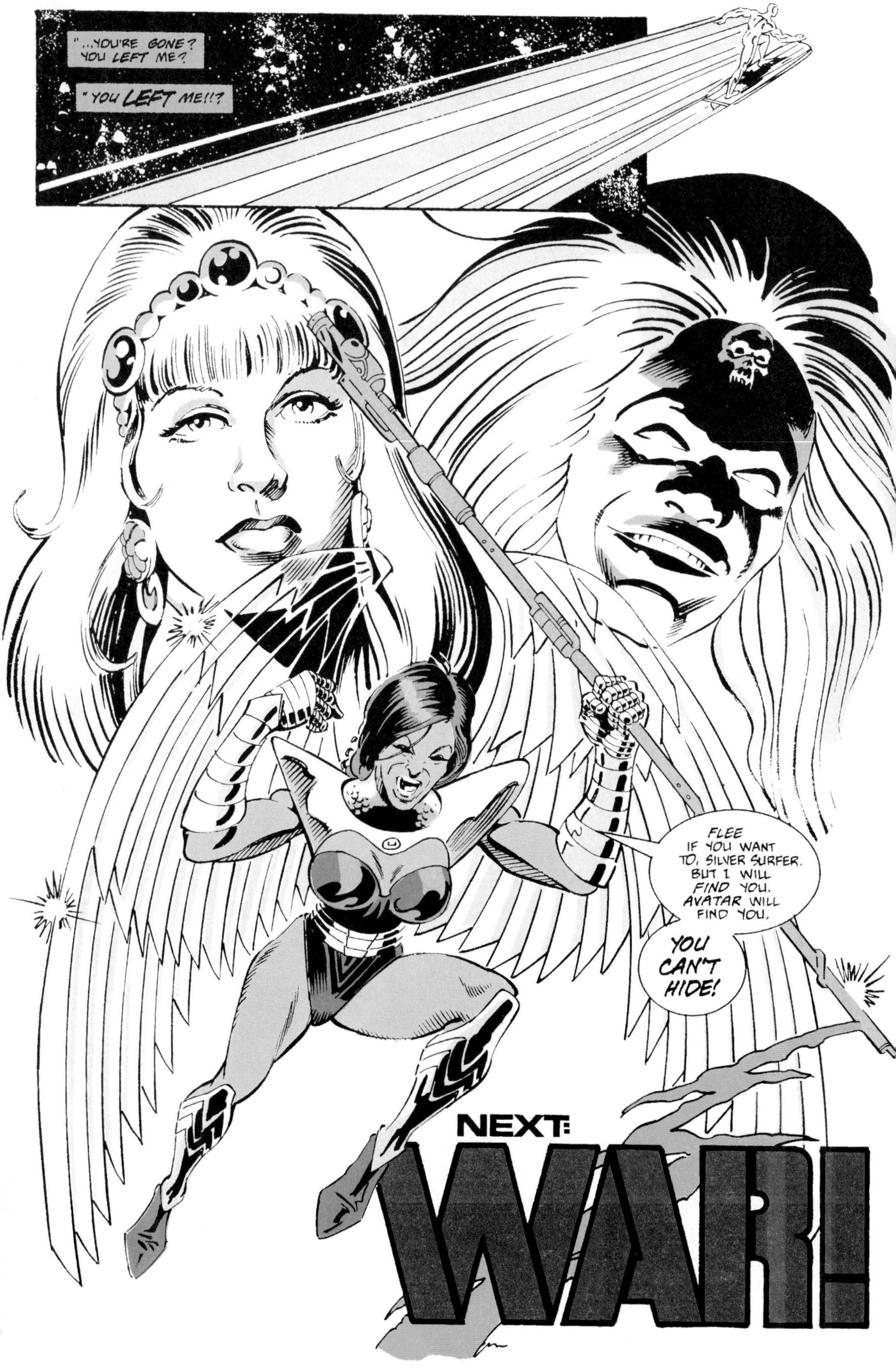
"...YOU'RE GONE? YOU LEFT ME?
"YOU LEFT ME!!?
FLEE IF YOU WANT TO, SILVER SURFER. BUT I WILL FIND YOU. AVATAR WILL FIND YOU.
YOU CAN'T HIDE!
NEXT:
WAR!

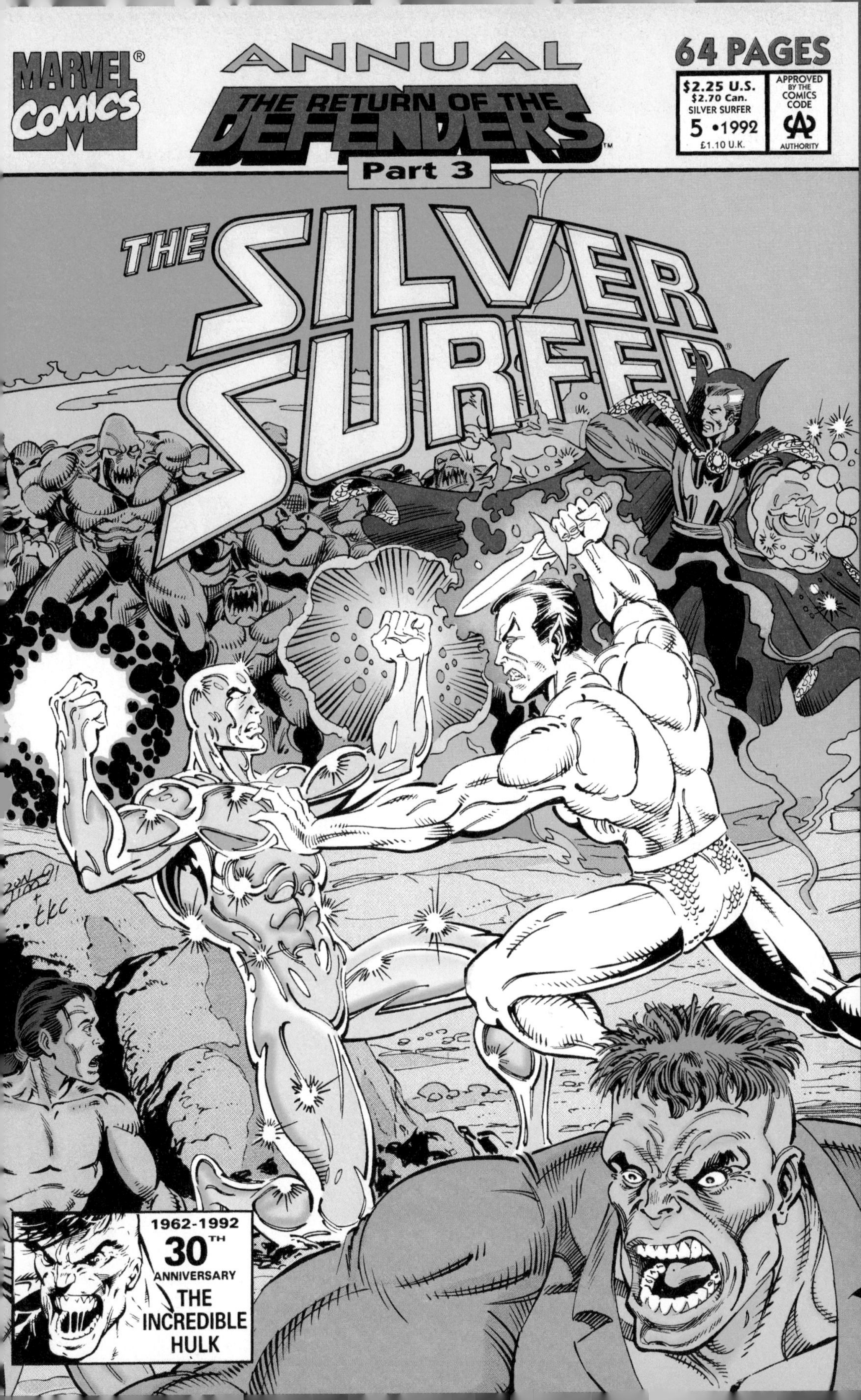
MARVEL COMICS
ANNUAL
THE RETURN OF THE DEFENDERS
Part 3
THE SILVER SURFER
64 PAGES
$2.25 U.S.
$2.70 Can.
SILVER SURFER
5 •1992
£1.10 U.K.
APPROVED BY THE COMICS CODE AUTHORITY
1962-1992
30TH ANNIVERSARY
THE INCREDIBLE HULK

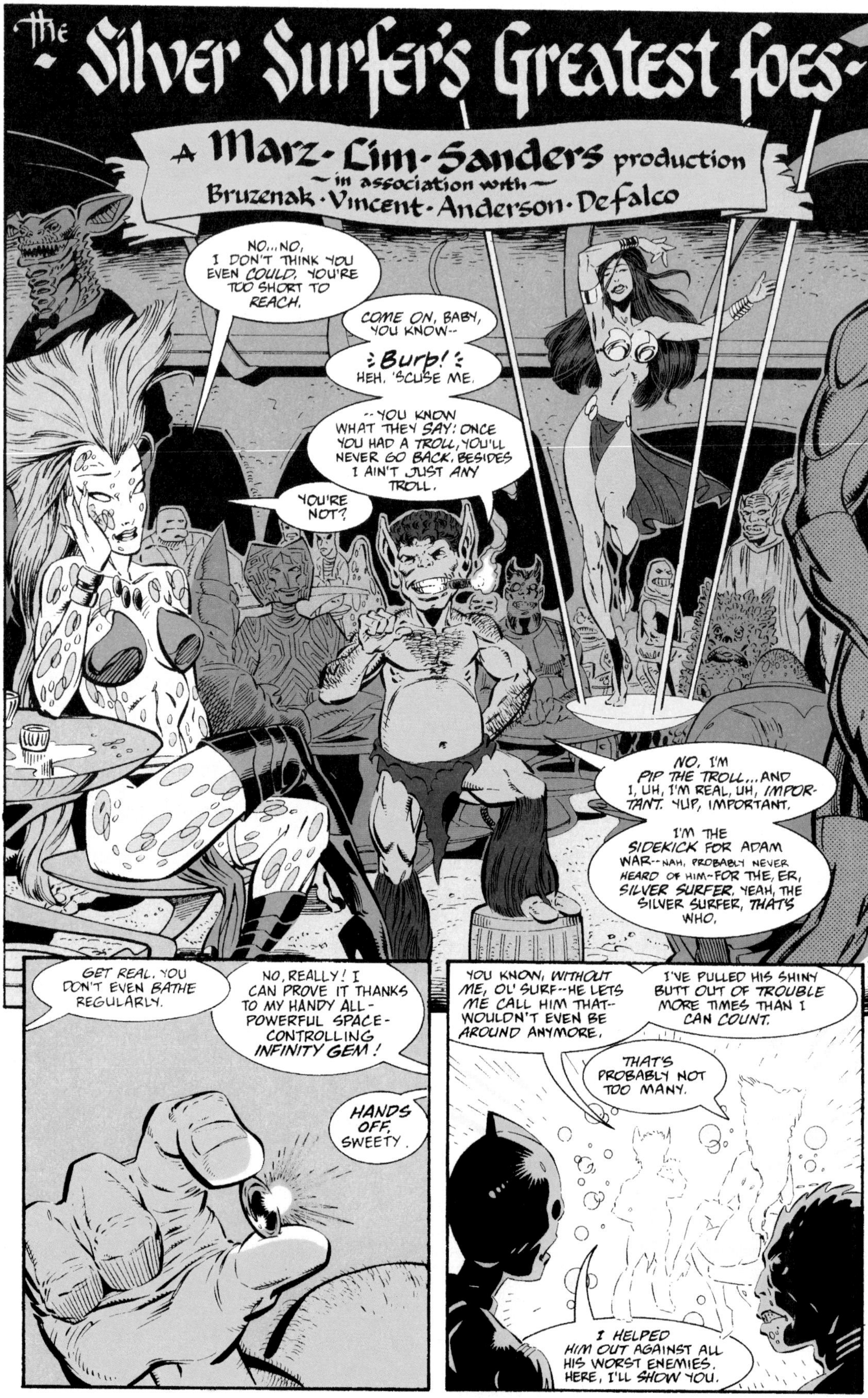
The Silver Surfer's Greatest Foes
A Marz-Lim-Sanders production
in association with
Bruzenak·Vincent·Anderson·DeFalco
NO...NO, I DON'T THINK YOU EVEN COULD. YOU'RE TOO SHORT TO REACH.
COME ON, BABY, YOU KNOW--
Burp! HEH. 'SCUSE ME.
--YOU KNOW WHAT THEY SAY: ONCE YOU HAD A TROLL, YOU'LL NEVER GO BACK. BESIDES I AIN'T JUST ANY TROLL.
YOU'RE NOT?
NO. I'M PIP THE TROLL...AND I, UH, I'M REAL, UH, IMPORTANT. YUP, IMPORTANT.
I'M THE SIDEKICK FOR ADAM WAR--NAH, PROBABLY NEVER HEARD OF HIM--FOR THE, ER, SILVER SURFER. YEAH, THE SILVER SURFER, THAT'S WHO.
GET REAL. YOU DON'T EVEN BATHE REGULARLY.
NO, REALLY! I CAN PROVE IT THANKS TO MY HANDY ALL-POWERFUL SPACE-CONTROLLING INFINITY GEM!
HANDS OFF, SWEETY.
YOU KNOW, WITHOUT ME, OL' SURF--HE LETS ME CALL HIM THAT--WOULDN'T EVEN BE AROUND ANYMORE.
I'VE PULLED HIS SHINY BUTT OUT OF TROUBLE MORE TIMES THAN I CAN COUNT.
THAT'S PROBABLY NOT TOO MANY.
I HELPED HIM OUT AGAINST ALL HIS WORST ENEMIES. HERE, I'LL SHOW YOU.

HUH? GEM MUST BE ON THE *FRITZ.*

DON'T KNOW WHO THAT BROAD IS. *

*BUT YOU CAN FIND OUT IN *SILVER SURFER* #66, ON SALE IN TWO WEEKS! -- CRAIG

THAT'S MORE LIKE IT.

THIS BUNCH IS THE *COLLECTION AGENCY,* MERCENARIES OF THE WORST SORT.

AND THAT'S *THE COLLECTOR.*

THEY USED TO *WORK* FOR HIM BEFORE GOING FREE-LANCE

HE'S *CHAMPION.*

REAL *BRUISER,* TILL WE TOOK HIS POWER GEM AND MAROONED HIM HERE.

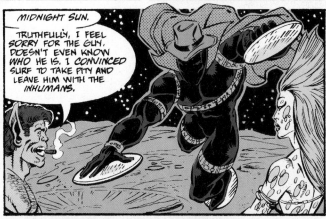

MIDNIGHT SUN.

TRUTHFULLY, I FEEL SORRY FOR THE GUY. DOESN'T EVEN KNOW WHO HE IS. I CONVINCED *SURF* TO TAKE PITY AND LEAVE HIM WITH THE *INHUMANS.*

OH. *THIS* GUY.

USED TO BE A REAL *GEEK,* BUT HE STARTED *WORKING OUT* AND BULKED UP. WANTS TO BE CALLED *REPTYL PRIME* NOW.

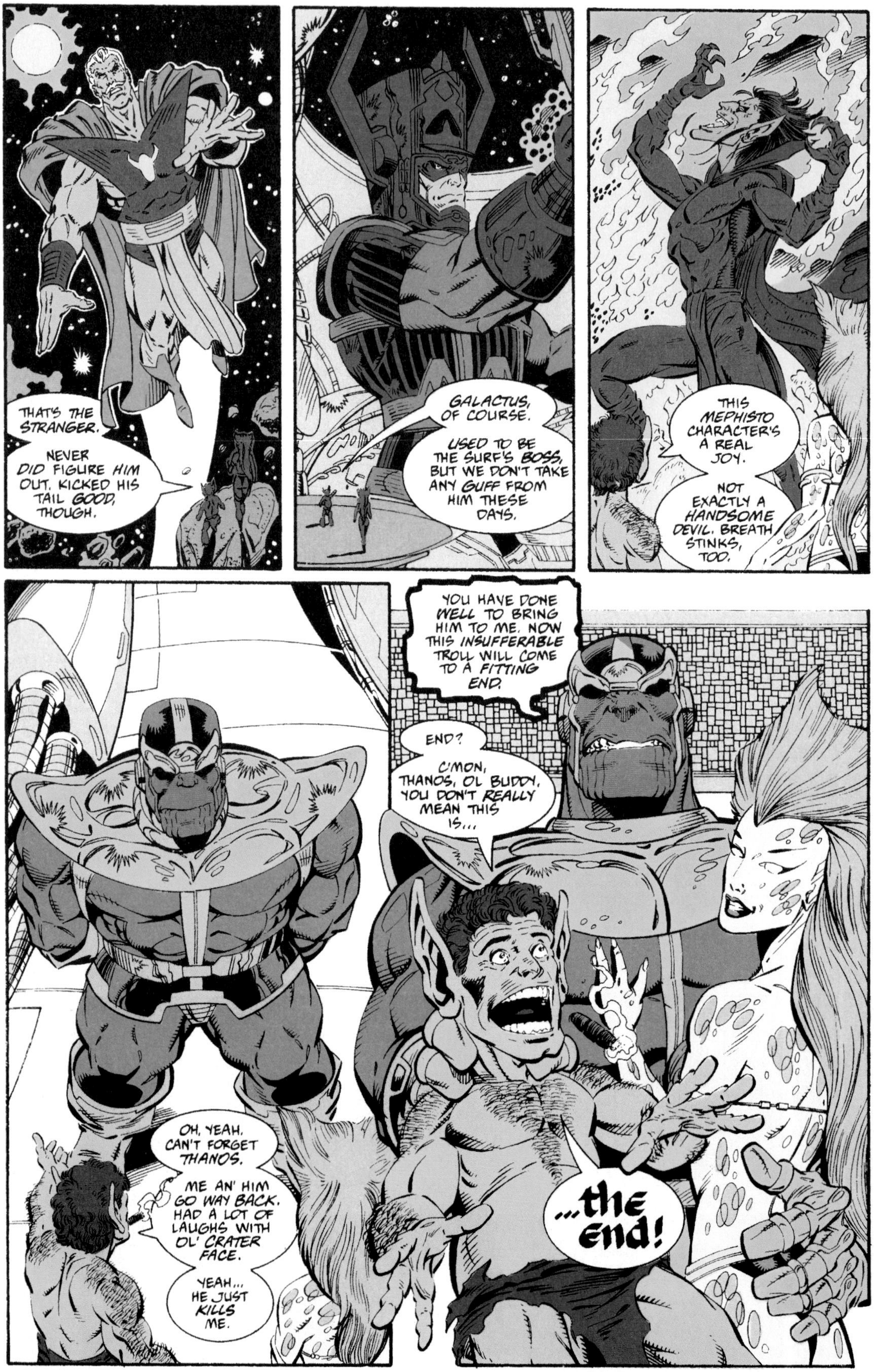
THAT'S THE STRANGER.
NEVER DID FIGURE HIM OUT. KICKED HIS TAIL GOOD, THOUGH.
GALACTUS, OF COURSE.
USED TO BE THE SURF'S BOSS, BUT WE DON'T TAKE ANY GUFF FROM HIM THESE DAYS.
THIS MEPHISTO CHARACTER'S A REAL JOY.
NOT EXACTLY A HANDSOME DEVIL. BREATH STINKS, TOO.
OH, YEAH, CAN'T FORGET THANOS.
ME AN' HIM GO WAY BACK. HAD A LOT OF LAUGHS WITH OL' CRATER FACE.
YEAH... HE JUST KILLS ME.
YOU HAVE DONE WELL TO BRING HIM TO ME. NOW THIS INSUFFERABLE TROLL WILL COME TO A FITTING END.
END?
C'MON, THANOS, OL BUDDY, YOU DON'T REALLY MEAN THIS IS...
...the End!

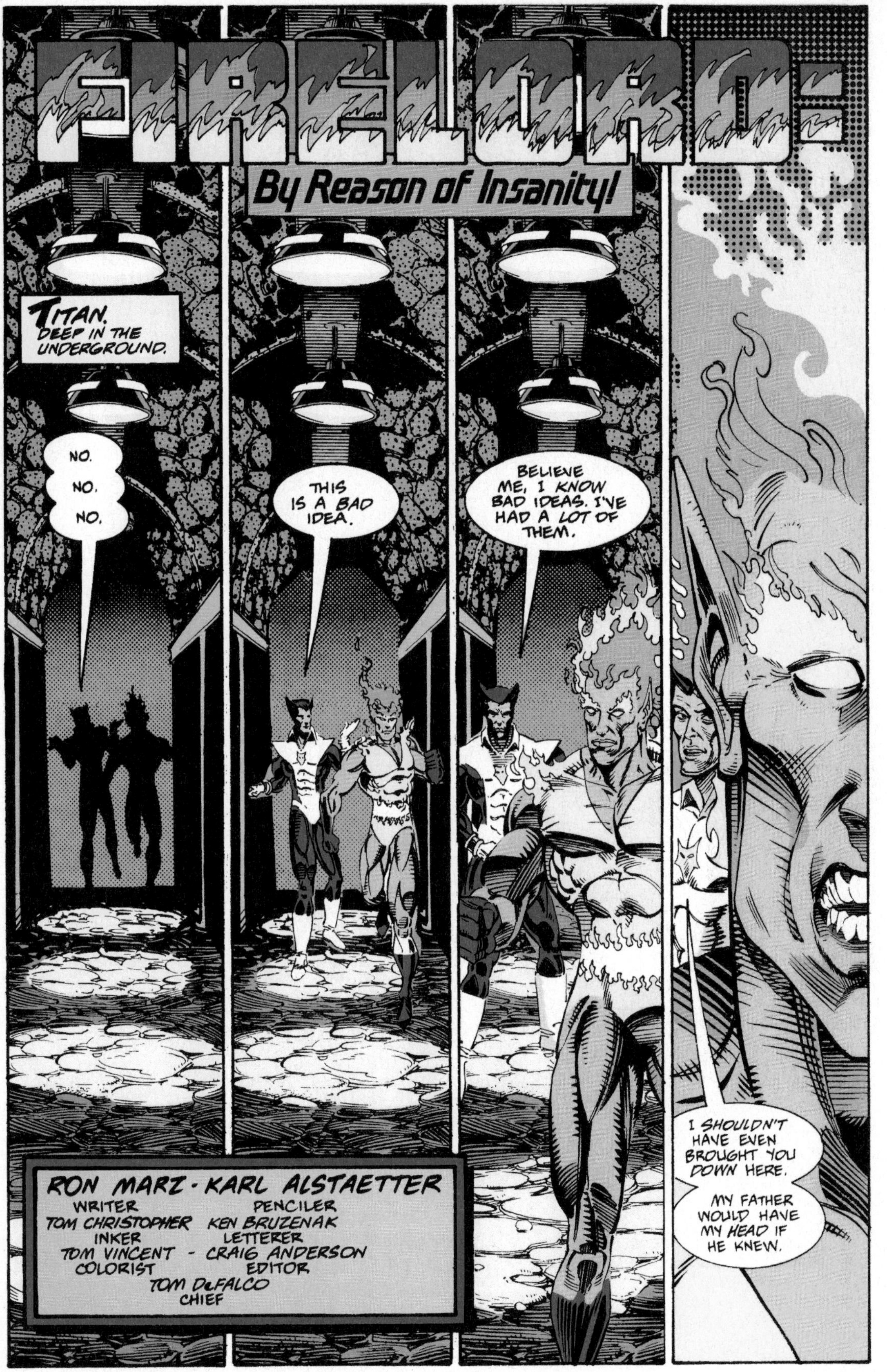
FIRELORD:
By Reason of Insanity!
TITAN. DEEP IN THE UNDERGROUND.
NO. NO. NO.
THIS IS A BAD IDEA.
BELIEVE ME, I KNOW BAD IDEAS. I'VE HAD A LOT OF THEM.
I SHOULDN'T HAVE EVEN BROUGHT YOU DOWN HERE.
MY FATHER WOULD HAVE MY HEAD IF HE KNEW.
RON MARZ - KARL ALSTAETTER
WRITER PENCILER
TOM CHRISTOPHER KEN BRUZENAK
INKER LETTERER
TOM VINCENT - CRAIG ANDERSON
COLORIST EDITOR
TOM DeFALCO
CHIEF

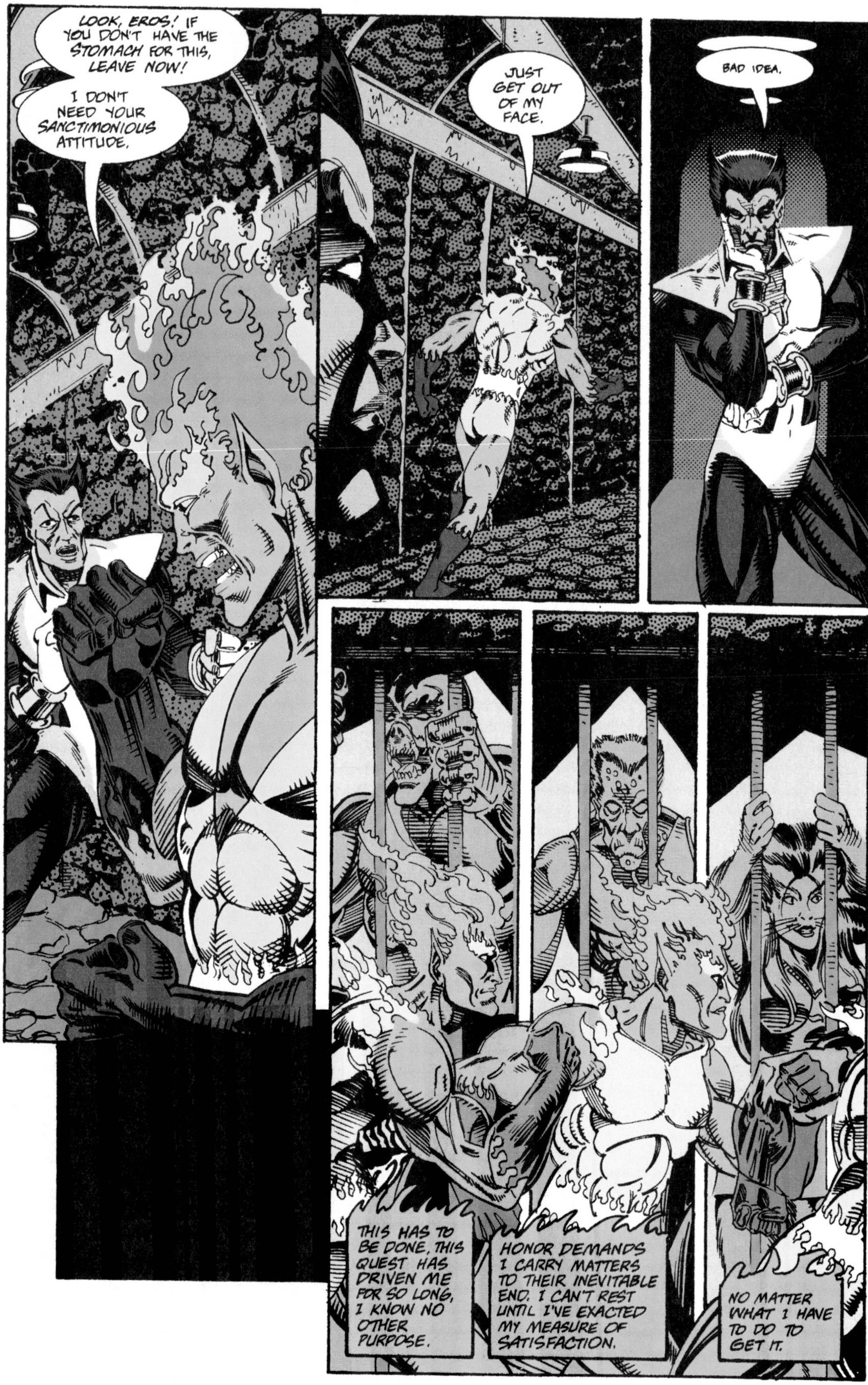
LOOK, EROS! IF YOU DON'T HAVE THE STOMACH FOR THIS, LEAVE NOW!
I DON'T NEED YOUR SANCTIMONIOUS ATTITUDE.
JUST GET OUT OF MY FACE.
BAD IDEA.
THIS HAS TO BE DONE. THIS QUEST HAS DRIVEN ME FOR SO LONG, I KNOW NO OTHER PURPOSE.
HONOR DEMANDS I CARRY MATTERS TO THEIR INEVITABLE END. I CAN'T REST UNTIL I'VE EXACTED MY MEASURE OF SATISFACTION.
NO MATTER WHAT I HAVE TO DO TO GET IT.

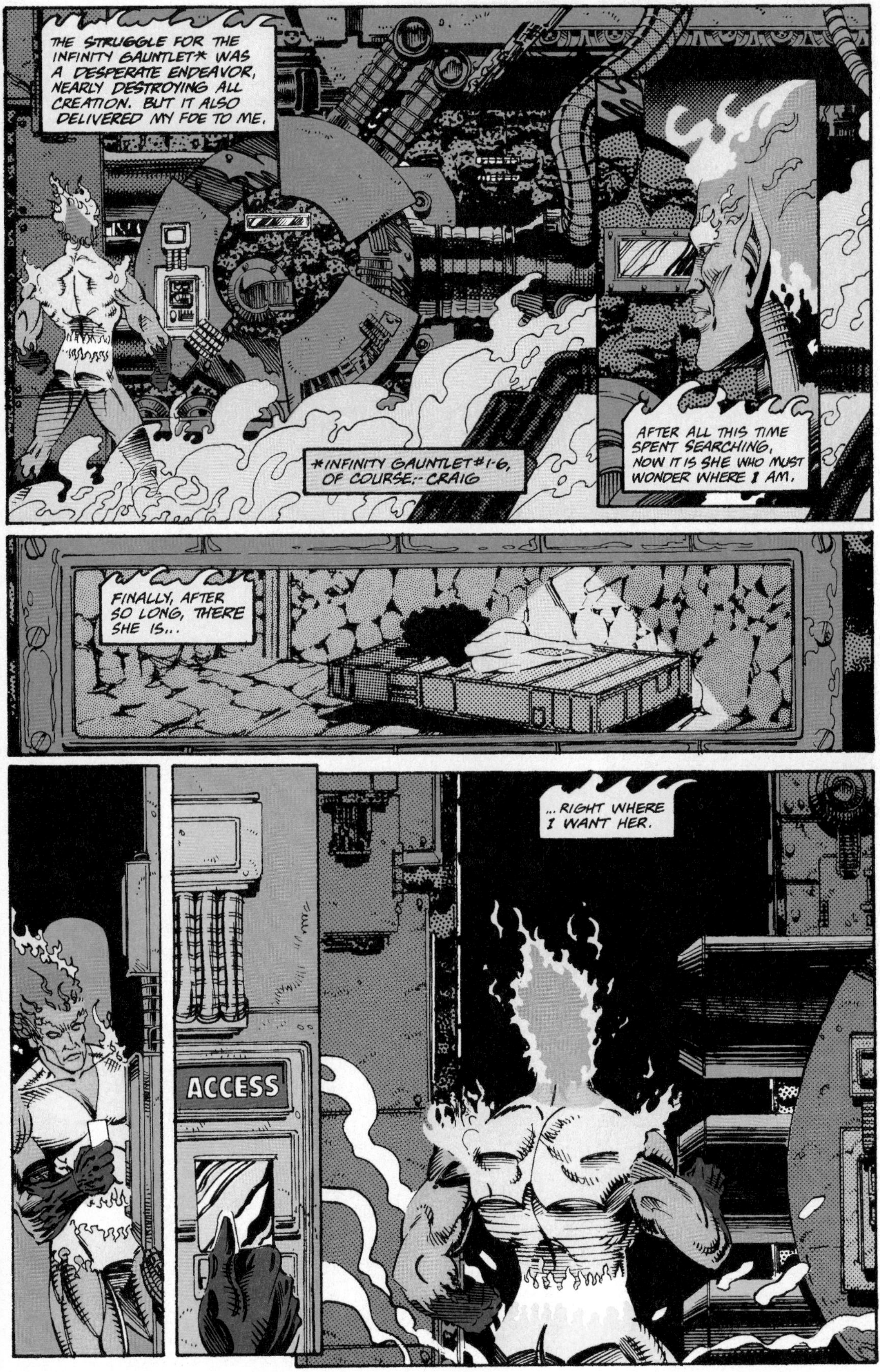
THE STRUGGLE FOR THE INFINITY GAUNTLET* WAS A DESPERATE ENDEAVOR, NEARLY DESTROYING ALL CREATION. BUT IT ALSO DELIVERED MY FOE TO ME.
*INFINITY GAUNTLET #1-6, OF COURSE.- CRAIG
AFTER ALL THIS TIME SPENT SEARCHING, NOW IT IS SHE WHO MUST WONDER WHERE I AM.
FINALLY, AFTER SO LONG, THERE SHE IS...
...RIGHT WHERE I WANT HER.
ACCESS

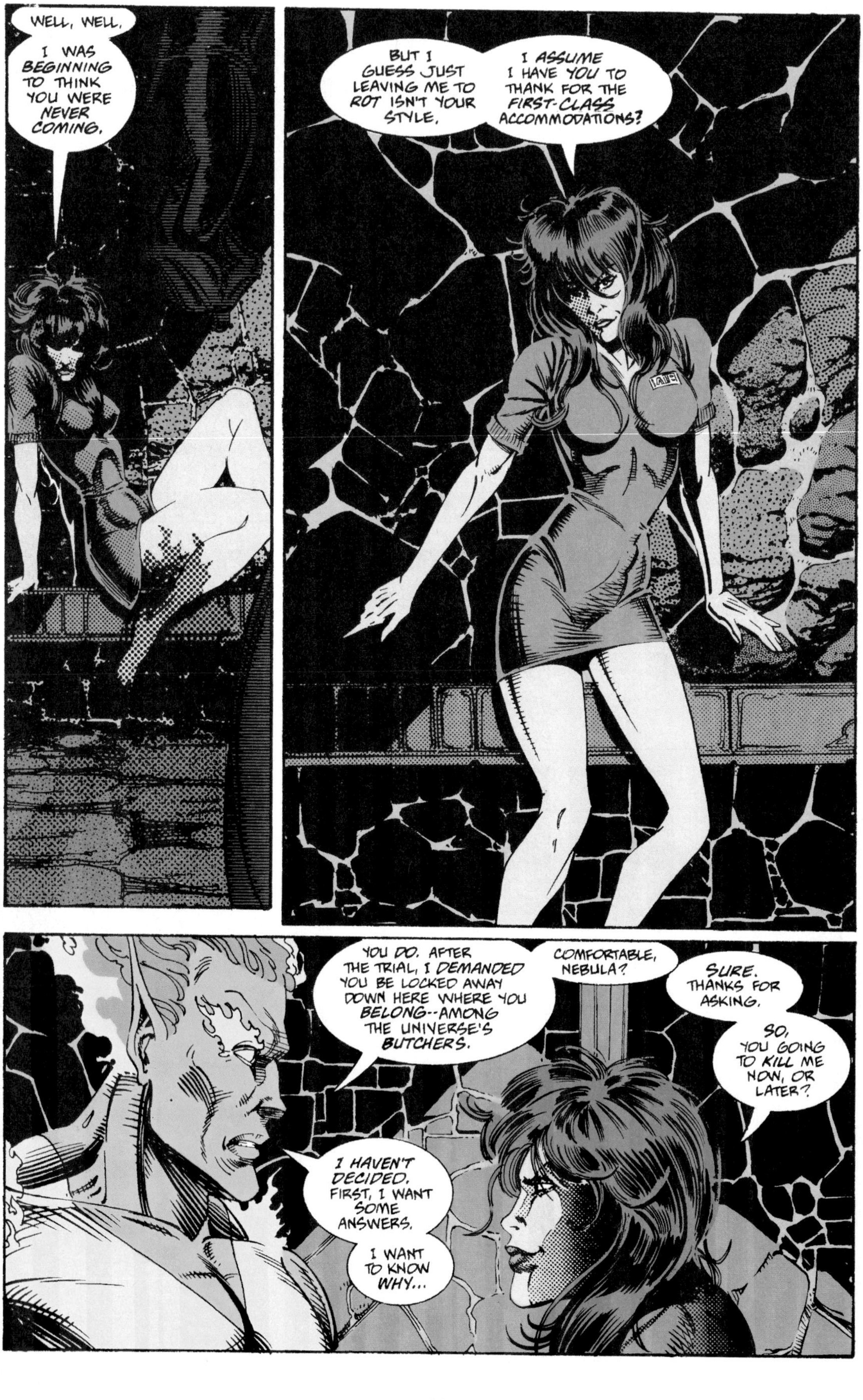
WELL, WELL.
I WAS BEGINNING TO THINK YOU WERE NEVER COMING.
BUT I GUESS JUST LEAVING ME TO ROT ISN'T YOUR STYLE.
I ASSUME I HAVE YOU TO THANK FOR THE FIRST-CLASS ACCOMMODATIONS?
YOU DO. AFTER THE TRIAL, I DEMANDED YOU BE LOCKED AWAY DOWN HERE WHERE YOU BELONG--AMONG THE UNIVERSE'S BUTCHERS.
COMFORTABLE, NEBULA?
SURE. THANKS FOR ASKING.
SO, YOU GOING TO KILL ME NOW, OR LATER?
I HAVEN'T DECIDED. FIRST, I WANT SOME ANSWERS.
I WANT TO KNOW WHY...

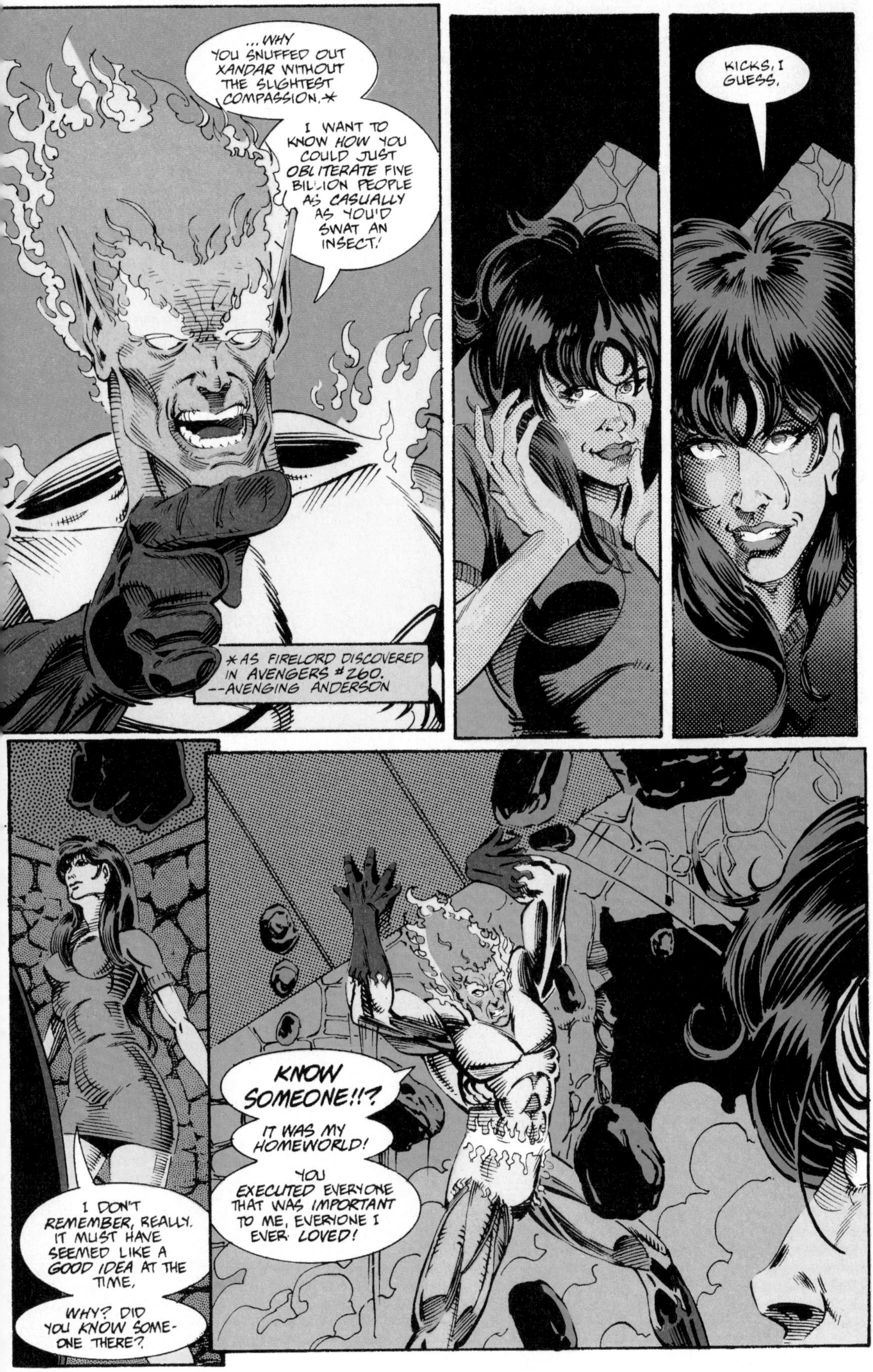
...WHY YOU SNUFFED OUT XANDAR WITHOUT THE SLIGHTEST COMPASSION.*
I WANT TO KNOW HOW YOU COULD JUST OBLITERATE FIVE BILLION PEOPLE AS CASUALLY AS YOU'D SWAT AN INSECT!
*AS FIRELORD DISCOVERED IN AVENGERS #260. --AVENGING ANDERSON
KICKS, I GUESS.
I DON'T REMEMBER, REALLY. IT MUST HAVE SEEMED LIKE A GOOD IDEA AT THE TIME.
WHY? DID YOU KNOW SOME-ONE THERE?
KNOW SOMEONE!!?
IT WAS MY HOMEWORLD!
YOU EXECUTED EVERYONE THAT WAS IMPORTANT TO ME, EVERYONE I EVER LOVED!

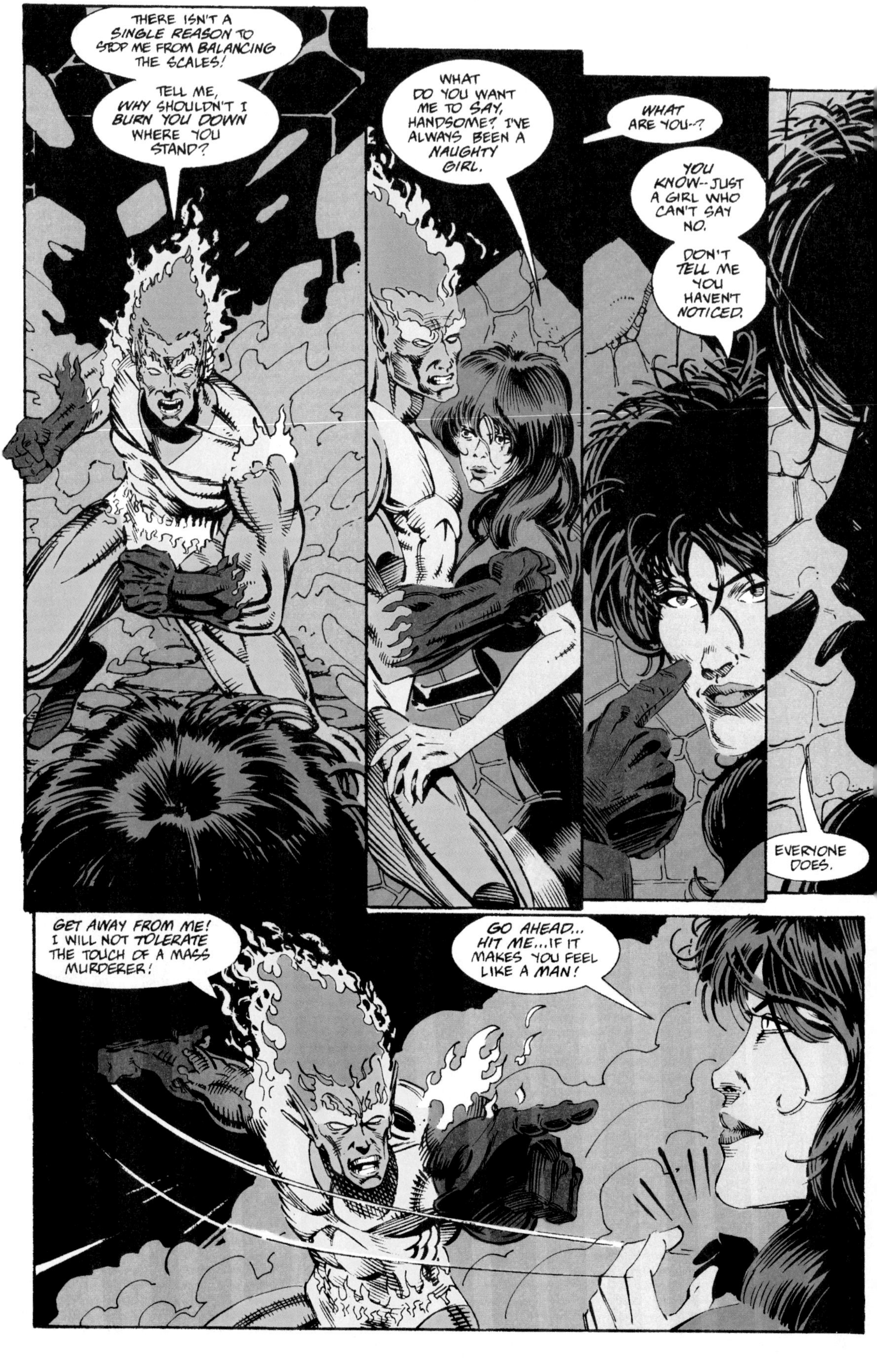
THERE ISN'T A SINGLE REASON TO STOP ME FROM BALANCING THE SCALES!
TELL ME, WHY SHOULDN'T I BURN YOU DOWN WHERE YOU STAND?
WHAT DO YOU WANT ME TO SAY, HANDSOME? I'VE ALWAYS BEEN A NAUGHTY GIRL.
WHAT ARE YOU--?
YOU KNOW--JUST A GIRL WHO CAN'T SAY NO.
DON'T TELL ME YOU HAVEN'T NOTICED.
EVERYONE DOES.
GET AWAY FROM ME! I WILL NOT TOLERATE THE TOUCH OF A MASS MURDERER!
GO AHEAD... HIT ME...IF IT MAKES YOU FEEL LIKE A MAN!

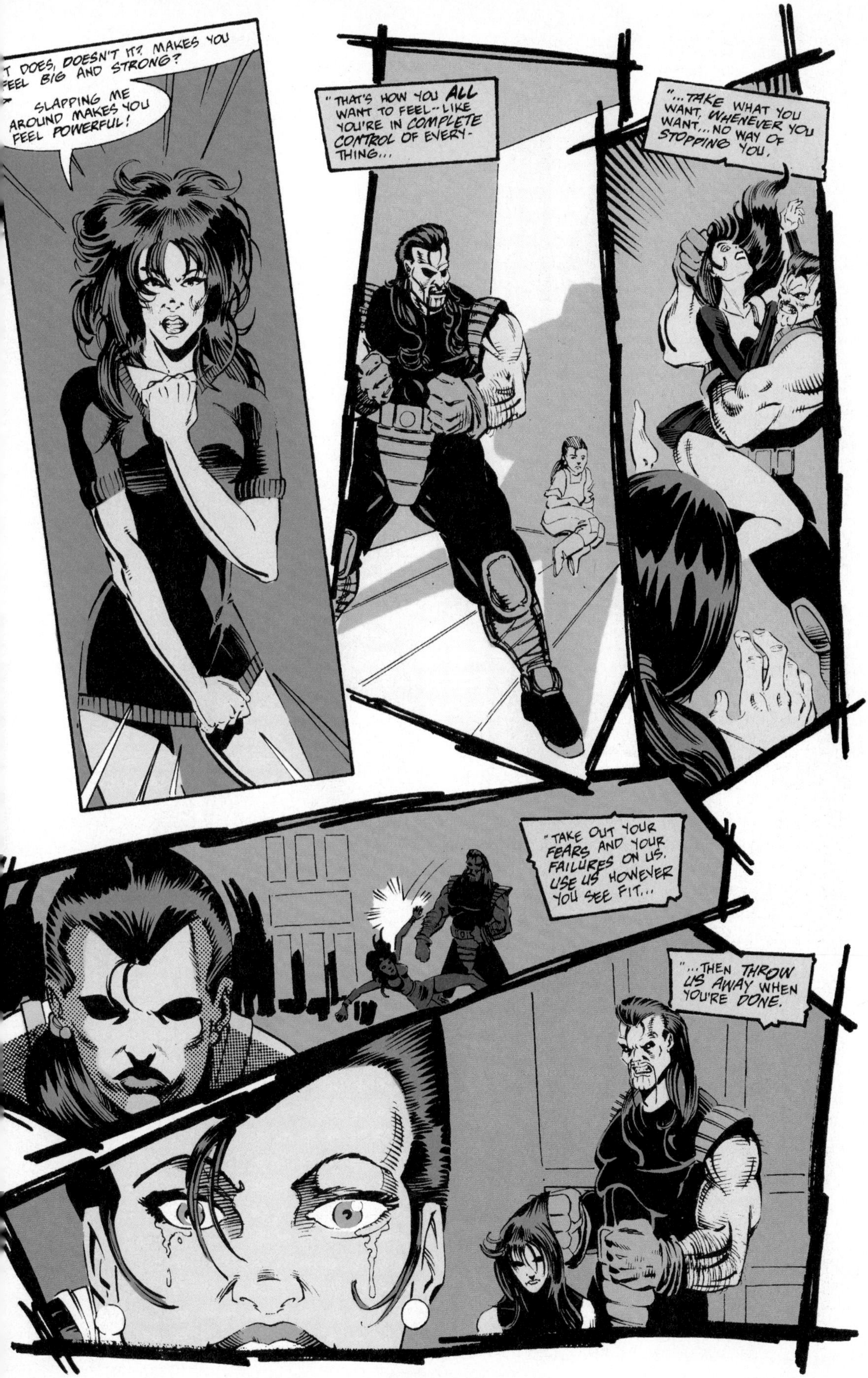

IT DOES, DOESN'T IT? MAKES YOU FEEL BIG AND STRONG?
SLAPPING ME AROUND MAKES YOU FEEL POWERFUL!
"THAT'S HOW YOU ALL WANT TO FEEL--LIKE YOU'RE IN COMPLETE CONTROL OF EVERY-THING...
"...TAKE WHAT YOU WANT, WHENEVER YOU WANT... NO WAY OF STOPPING YOU.
"TAKE OUT YOUR FEARS AND YOUR FAILURES ON US. USE US HOWEVER YOU SEE FIT...
"...THEN THROW US AWAY WHEN YOU'RE DONE.

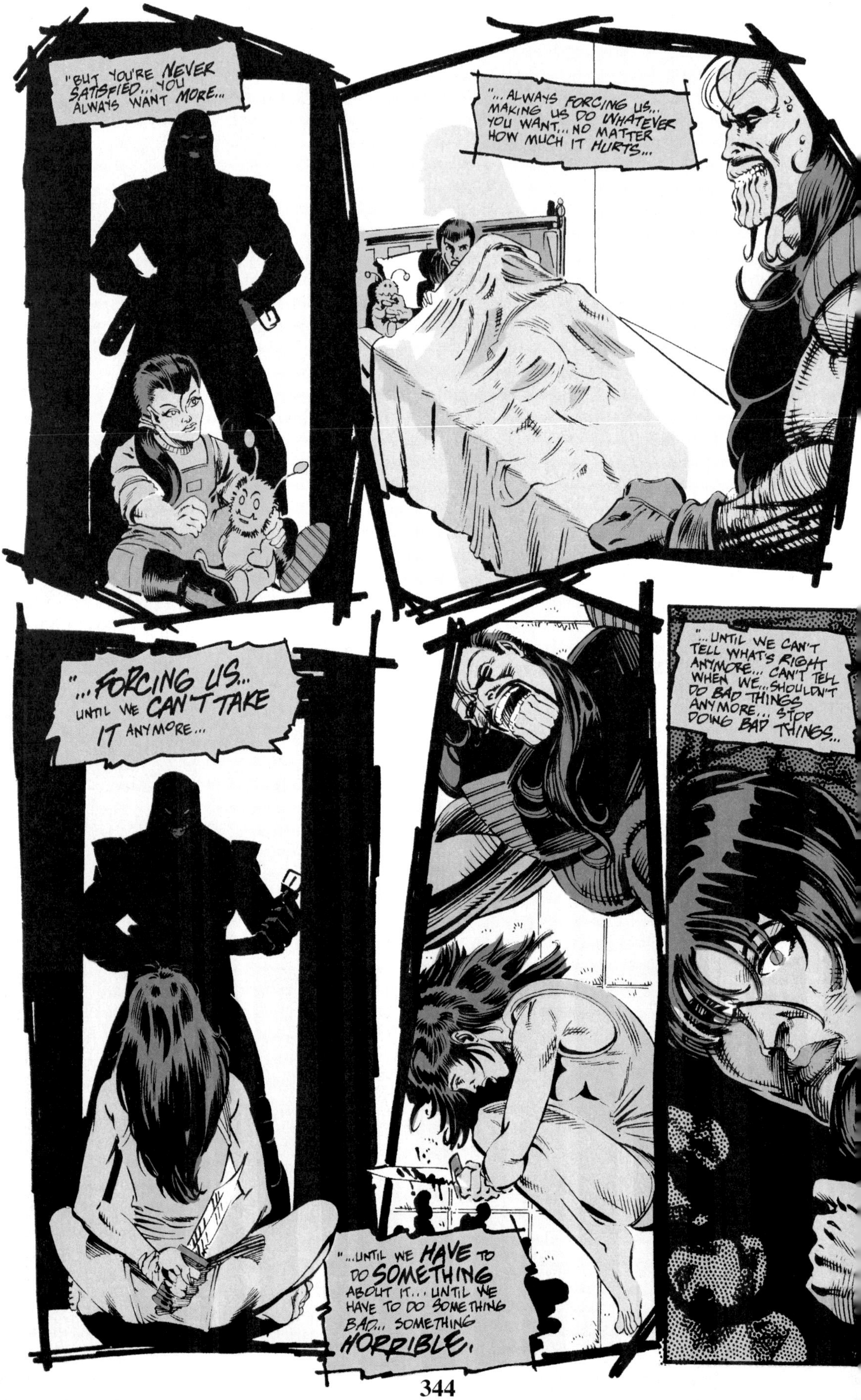
"BUT YOU'RE NEVER SATISFIED... YOU ALWAYS WANT MORE...
"...ALWAYS FORCING US... MAKING US DO WHATEVER YOU WANT... NO MATTER HOW MUCH IT HURTS...
"...FORCING US... UNTIL WE CAN'T TAKE IT ANYMORE...
"...UNTIL WE HAVE TO DO SOMETHING ABOUT IT... UNTIL WE HAVE TO DO SOMETHING BAD... SOMETHING HORRIBLE.
"...UNTIL WE CAN'T TELL WHAT'S RIGHT ANYMORE... CAN'T TELL WHEN WE... SHOULDN'T DO BAD THINGS ANYMORE... STOP DOING BAD THINGS...

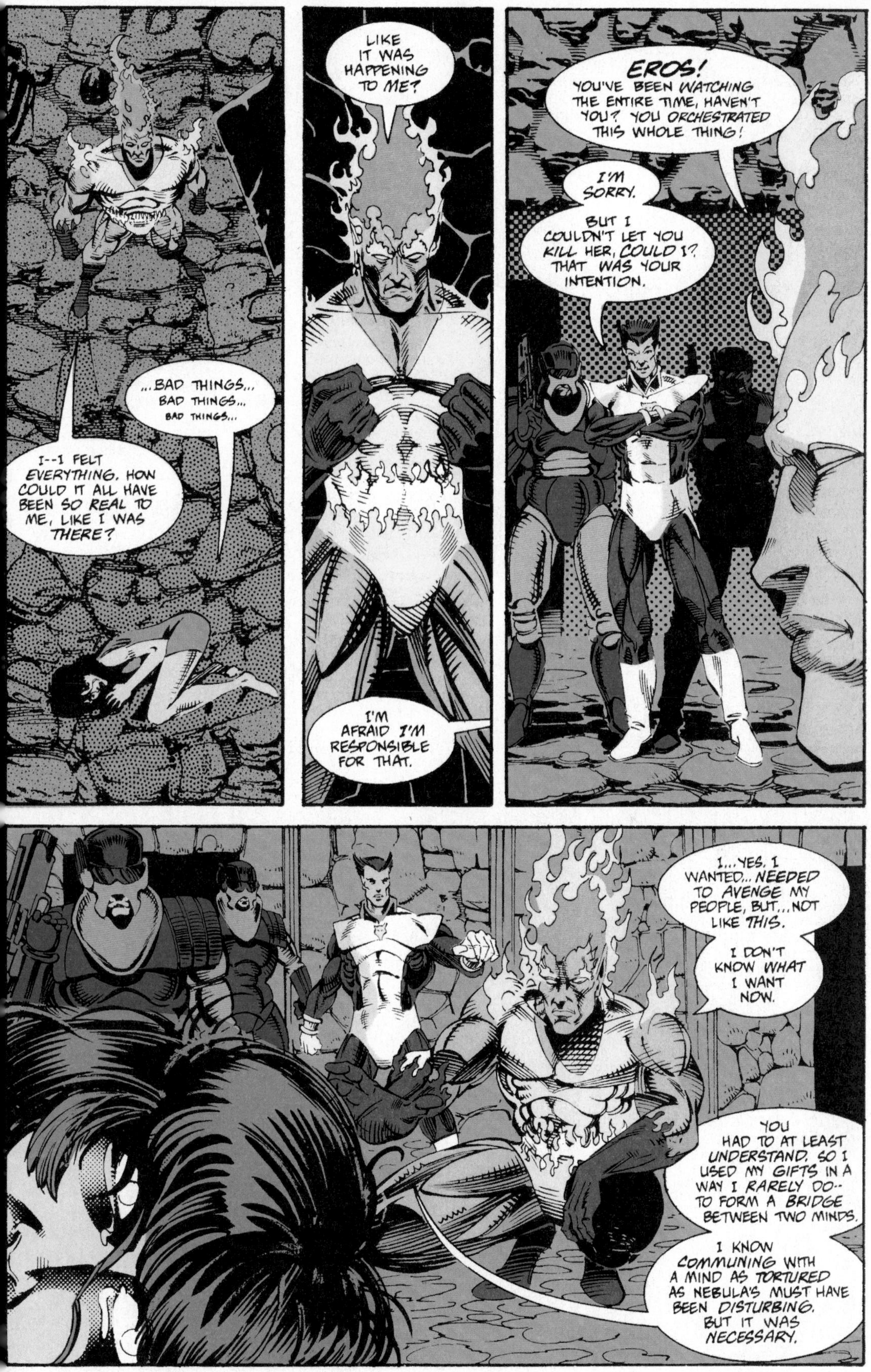
...BAD THINGS...
BAD THINGS...
BAD THINGS...
I--I FELT EVERYTHING. HOW COULD IT ALL HAVE BEEN SO REAL TO ME, LIKE I WAS THERE?
LIKE IT WAS HAPPENING TO ME?
I'M AFRAID I'M RESPONSIBLE FOR THAT.
EROS! YOU'VE BEEN WATCHING THE ENTIRE TIME, HAVEN'T YOU? YOU ORCHESTRATED THIS WHOLE THING!
I'M SORRY.
BUT I COULDN'T LET YOU KILL HER, COULD I? THAT WAS YOUR INTENTION.
I... YES. I WANTED... NEEDED TO AVENGE MY PEOPLE, BUT... NOT LIKE THIS.
I DON'T KNOW WHAT I WANT NOW.
YOU HAD TO AT LEAST UNDERSTAND, SO I USED MY GIFTS IN A WAY I RARELY DO-- TO FORM A BRIDGE BETWEEN TWO MINDS.
I KNOW COMMUNING WITH A MIND AS TORTURED AS NEBULA'S MUST HAVE BEEN DISTURBING. BUT IT WAS NECESSARY.

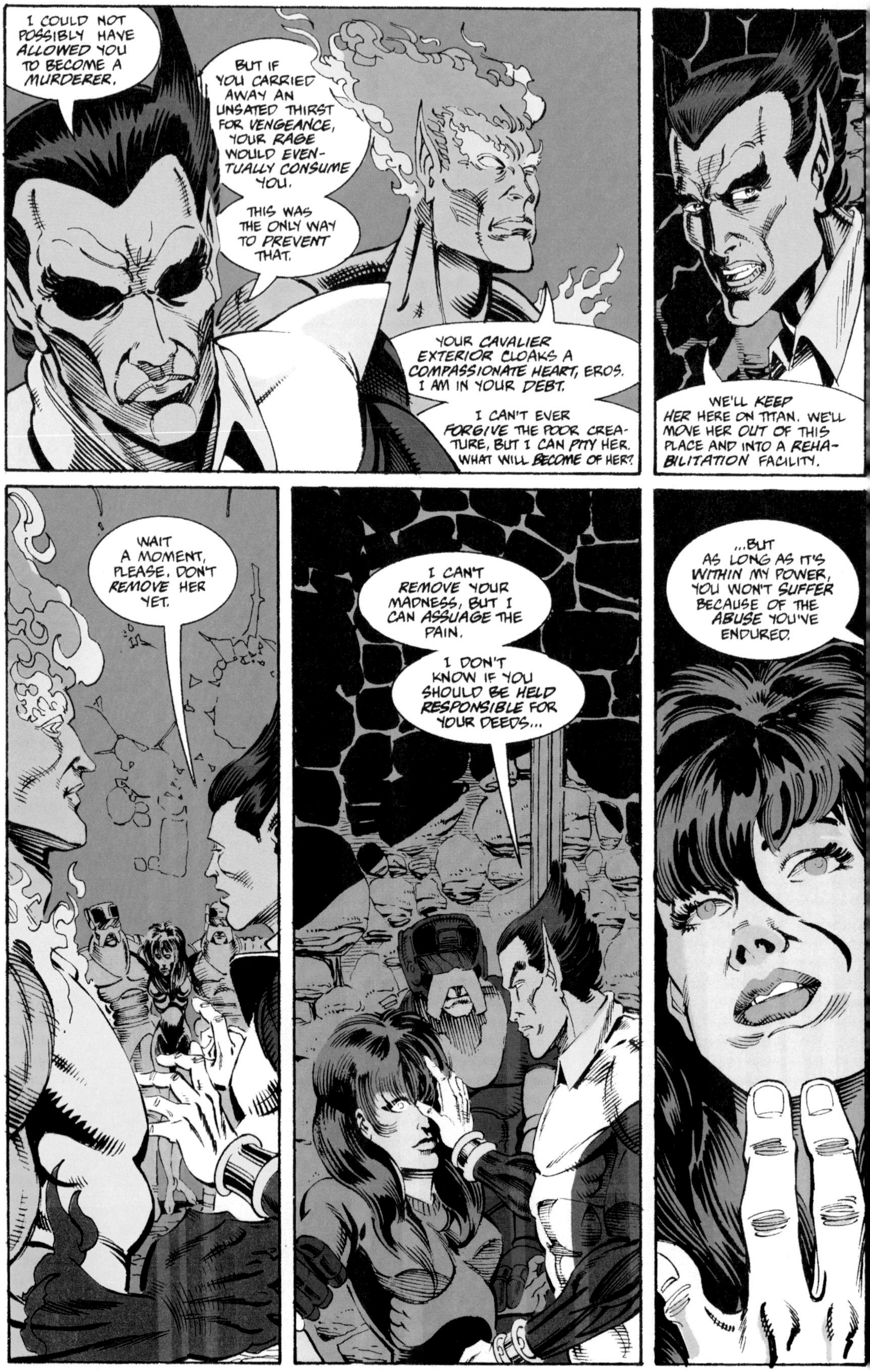

I COULD NOT POSSIBLY HAVE ALLOWED YOU TO BECOME A MURDERER.
BUT IF YOU CARRIED AWAY AN UNSATED THIRST FOR VENGEANCE, YOUR RAGE WOULD EVENTUALLY CONSUME YOU.
THIS WAS THE ONLY WAY TO PREVENT THAT.
YOUR CAVALIER EXTERIOR CLOAKS A COMPASSIONATE HEART, EROS. I AM IN YOUR DEBT.
I CAN'T EVER FORGIVE THE POOR CREATURE, BUT I CAN PITY HER. WHAT WILL BECOME OF HER?
WE'LL KEEP HER HERE ON TITAN. WE'LL MOVE HER OUT OF THIS PLACE AND INTO A REHABILITATION FACILITY.
WAIT A MOMENT, PLEASE. DON'T REMOVE HER YET.
I CAN'T REMOVE YOUR MADNESS, BUT I CAN ASSUAGE THE PAIN.
I DON'T KNOW IF YOU SHOULD BE HELD RESPONSIBLE FOR YOUR DEEDS...
...BUT AS LONG AS IT'S WITHIN MY POWER, YOU WON'T SUFFER BECAUSE OF THE ABUSE YOU'VE ENDURED.

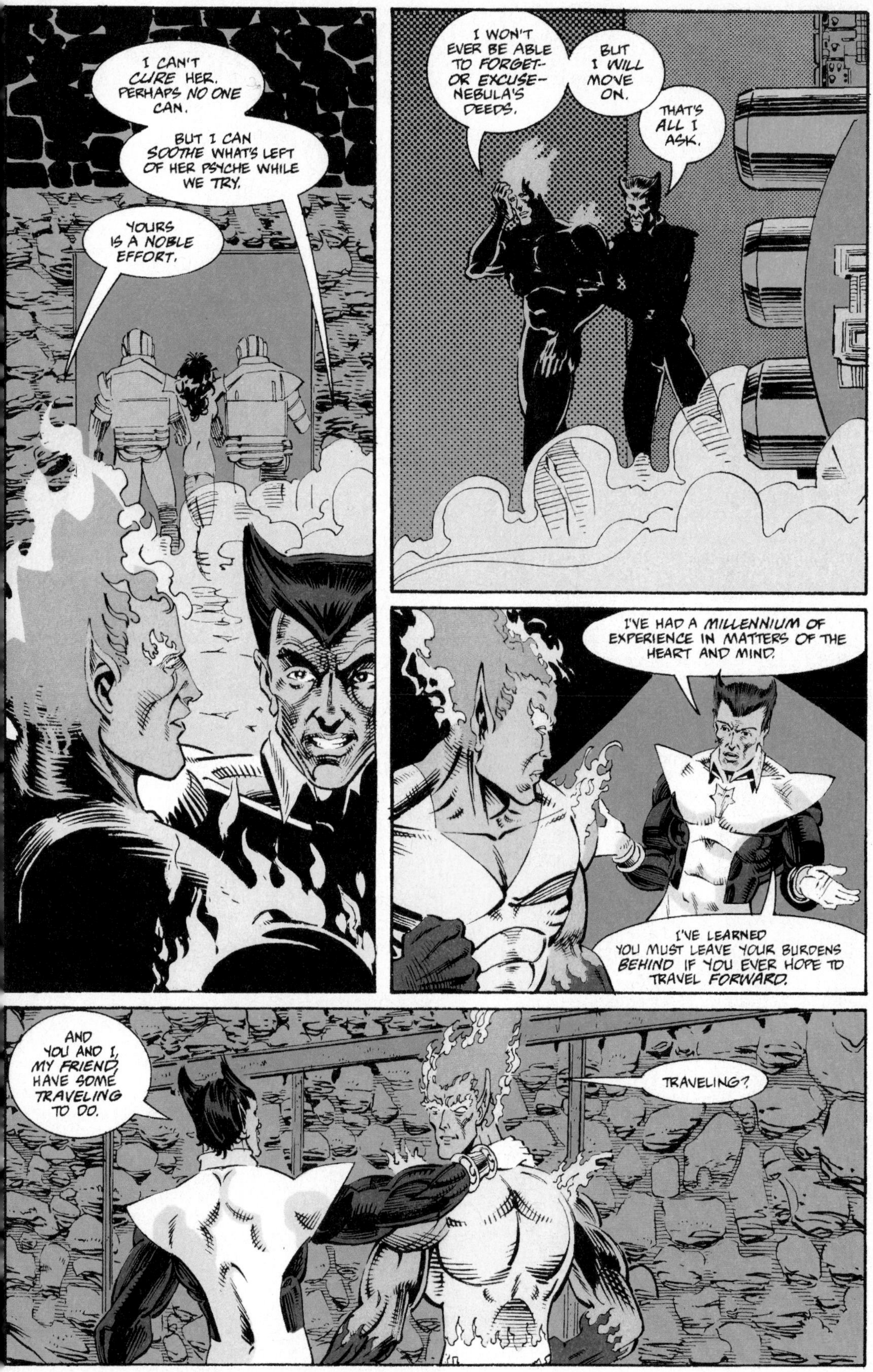

I CAN'T CURE HER. PERHAPS NO ONE CAN.
BUT I CAN SOOTHE WHAT'S LEFT OF HER PSYCHE WHILE WE TRY.
YOURS IS A NOBLE EFFORT.
I WON'T EVER BE ABLE TO FORGET-- OR EXCUSE-- NEBULA'S DEEDS.
BUT I WILL MOVE ON.
THAT'S ALL I ASK.
I'VE HAD A MILLENNIUM OF EXPERIENCE IN MATTERS OF THE HEART AND MIND.
I'VE LEARNED YOU MUST LEAVE YOUR BURDENS BEHIND IF YOU EVER HOPE TO TRAVEL FORWARD.
AND YOU AND I, MY FRIEND, HAVE SOME TRAVELING TO DO.
TRAVELING?

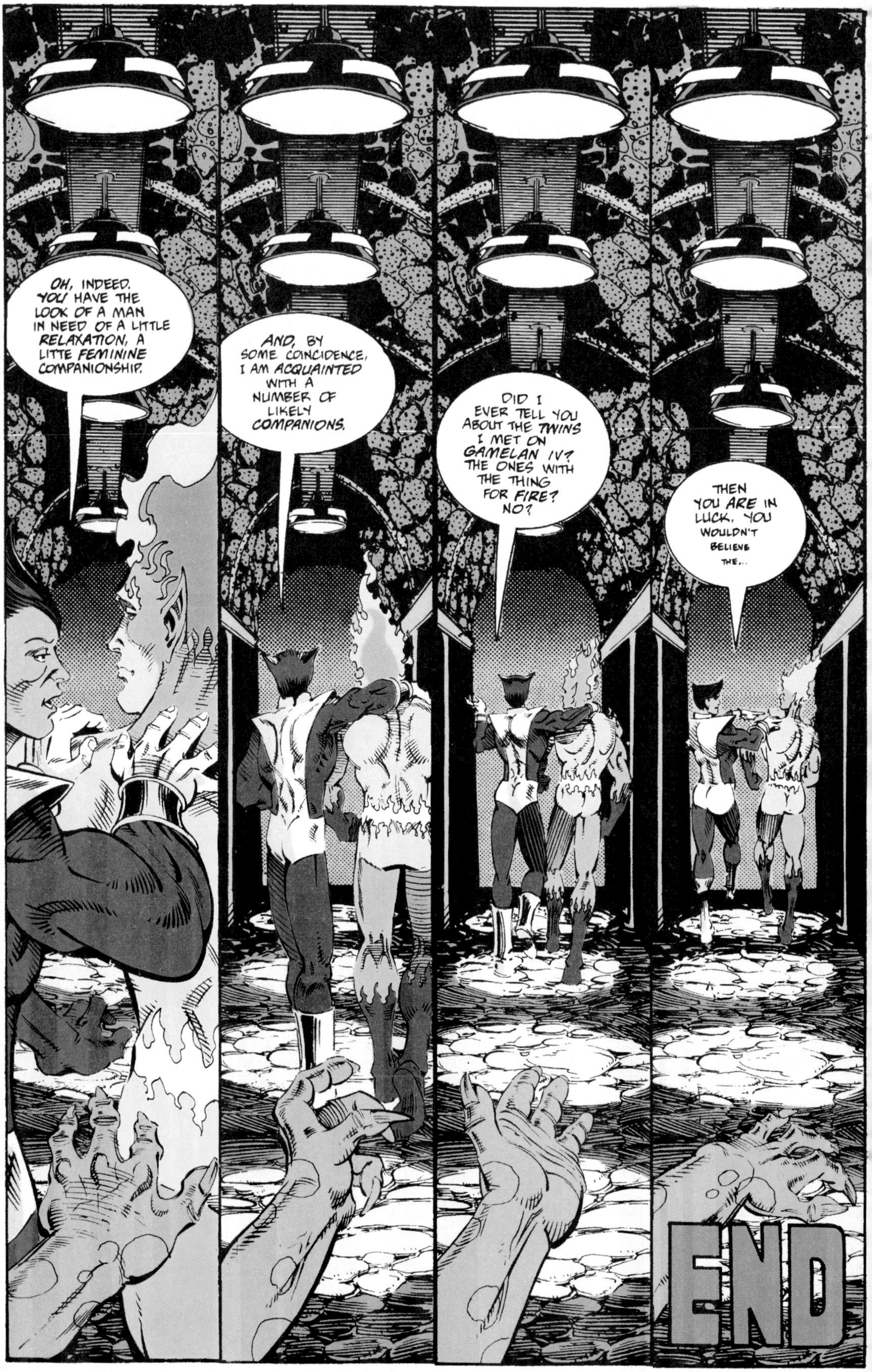
OH, INDEED. YOU HAVE THE LOOK OF A MAN IN NEED OF A LITTLE RELAXATION, A LITTE FEMININE COMPANIONSHIP.
AND, BY SOME COINCIDENCE, I AM ACQUAINTED WITH A NUMBER OF LIKELY COMPANIONS.
DID I EVER TELL YOU ABOUT THE TWINS I MET ON GAMELAN IV? THE ONES WITH THE THING FOR FIRE? NO?
THEN YOU ARE IN LUCK. YOU WOULDN'T BELIEVE THE...
END

WARLOCK and the INFINITY WATCH

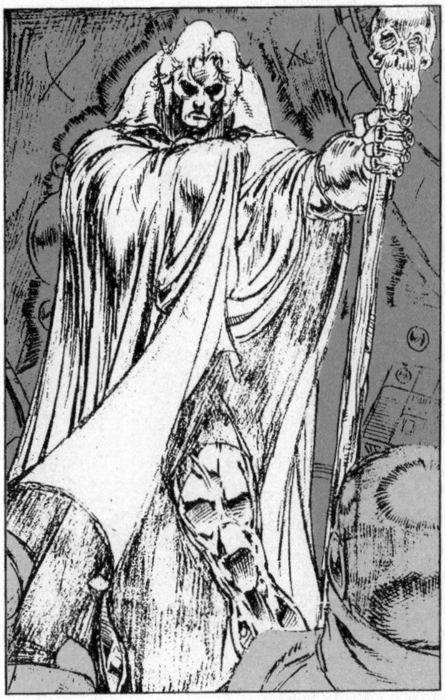

Following the events of the INFINITY GAUNTLET, Adam Warlock inds himself in possession of the Infinity Gems, a situation that causes he cosmic beings (such as Eternity, the Celestials and the Living Tri-ounal) more than a little concern.

The solution, for Warlock to form The Infinity Watch, a group who will divide the power of the gems, and will use the power to keep the cosmos free of the danger such as they faced againstThe Infinity Gauntlet.

ADAM WARLOCK AND THE INFINITY WATCH will star Warlock, Pip the Troll, Gamora, Drax the Destroyer, Moondragon, and a really startling sixth member. Their first mission will be to face the return of he High Evolutionary.

This series will contain the kind of cosmic adventure readers have come to expect from Jim Starlin, and there will be a fair dose of humor. With guys like Pip and Drax, hanging around with women like Moon-dragon and Gamora, the possibilities range from the ironic to the slap-stick.

And, of course, Warlock & Co. will play a pivotal role in THE NFINITY WAR limited series.

WRITER
Jim Starlin

INKER
Al Williamson

IMPRINT
Marvel

FORMAT
Newsprint offset

PAGE COUNT
32

PENCILERS
Angel Medina
and Rick Leonardi

EDITOR
Craig Anderson

SHIPPING
Ongoing

FREQUENCY
Monthly

COVER PRICE
$1.25

Silver Surfer letters-page logo

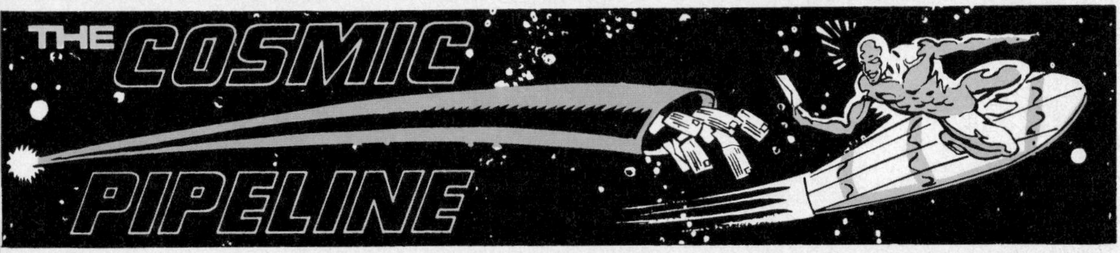
THE COSMIC
PIPELINE

Warlock and the Infinity Watch letters-page logo

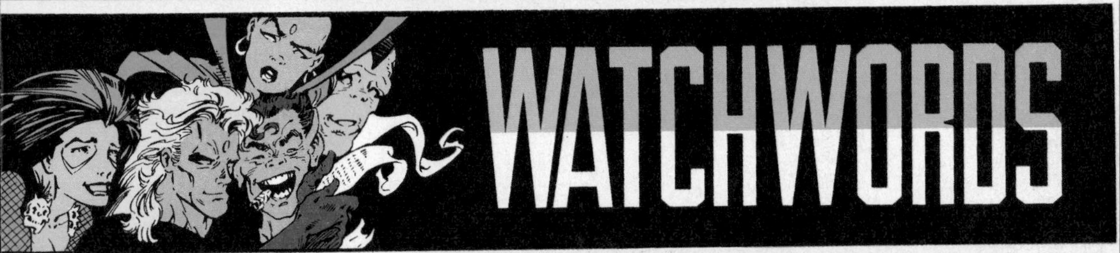
WATCHWORDS

Silver Surfer #60, page 13 art by Ron Lim & Jim Sanders III

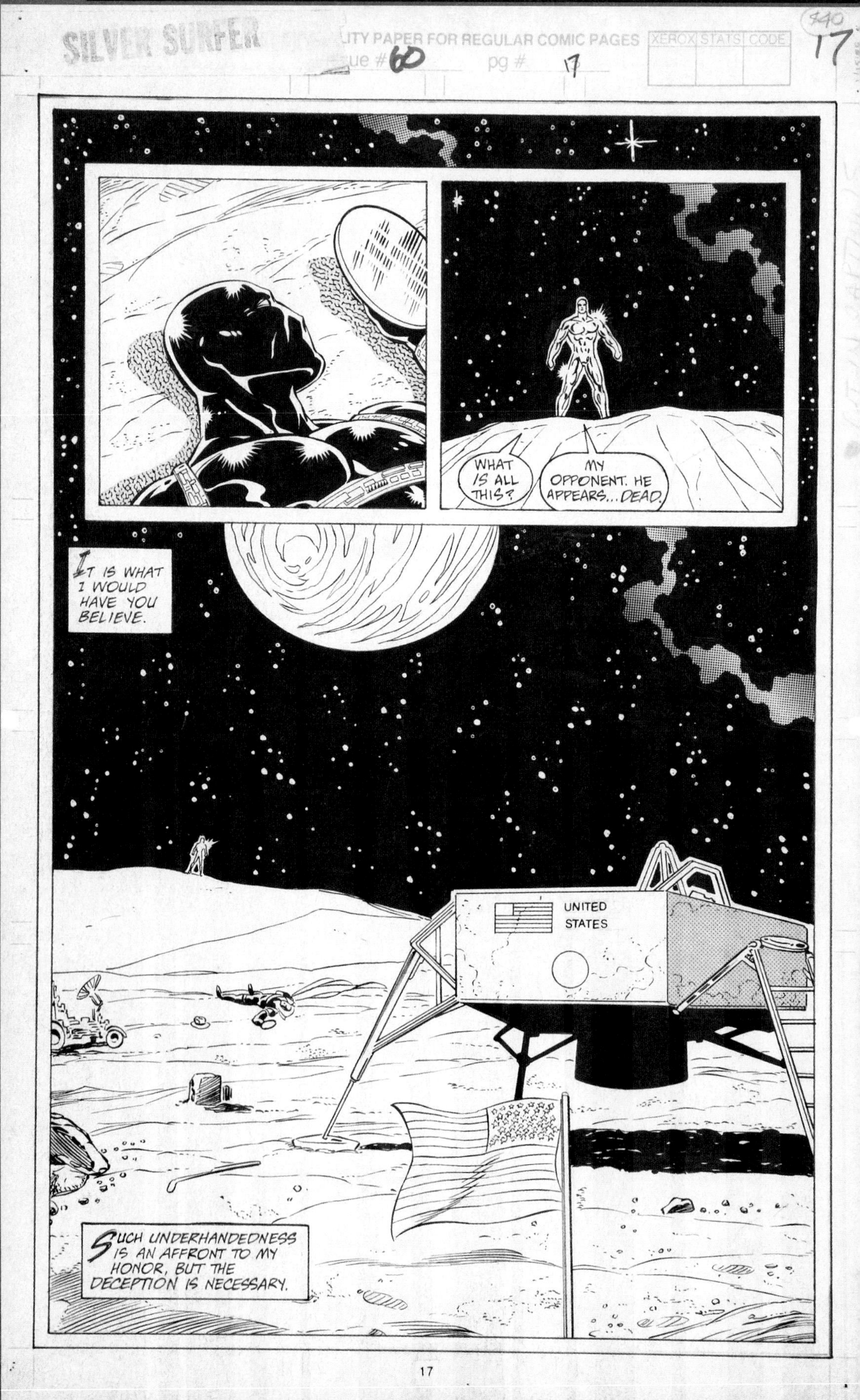
SILVER SURFER
LITY PAPER FOR REGULAR COMIC PAGES
XEROX STATS CODE
ue # 60
pg # 17
$40
17
WHAT IS ALL THIS?
MY OPPONENT. HE APPEARS... DEAD.
IT IS WHAT I WOULD HAVE YOU BELIEVE.
UNITED STATES
SUCH UNDERHANDEDNESS IS AN AFFRONT TO MY HONOR, BUT THE DECEPTION IS NECESSARY.
17

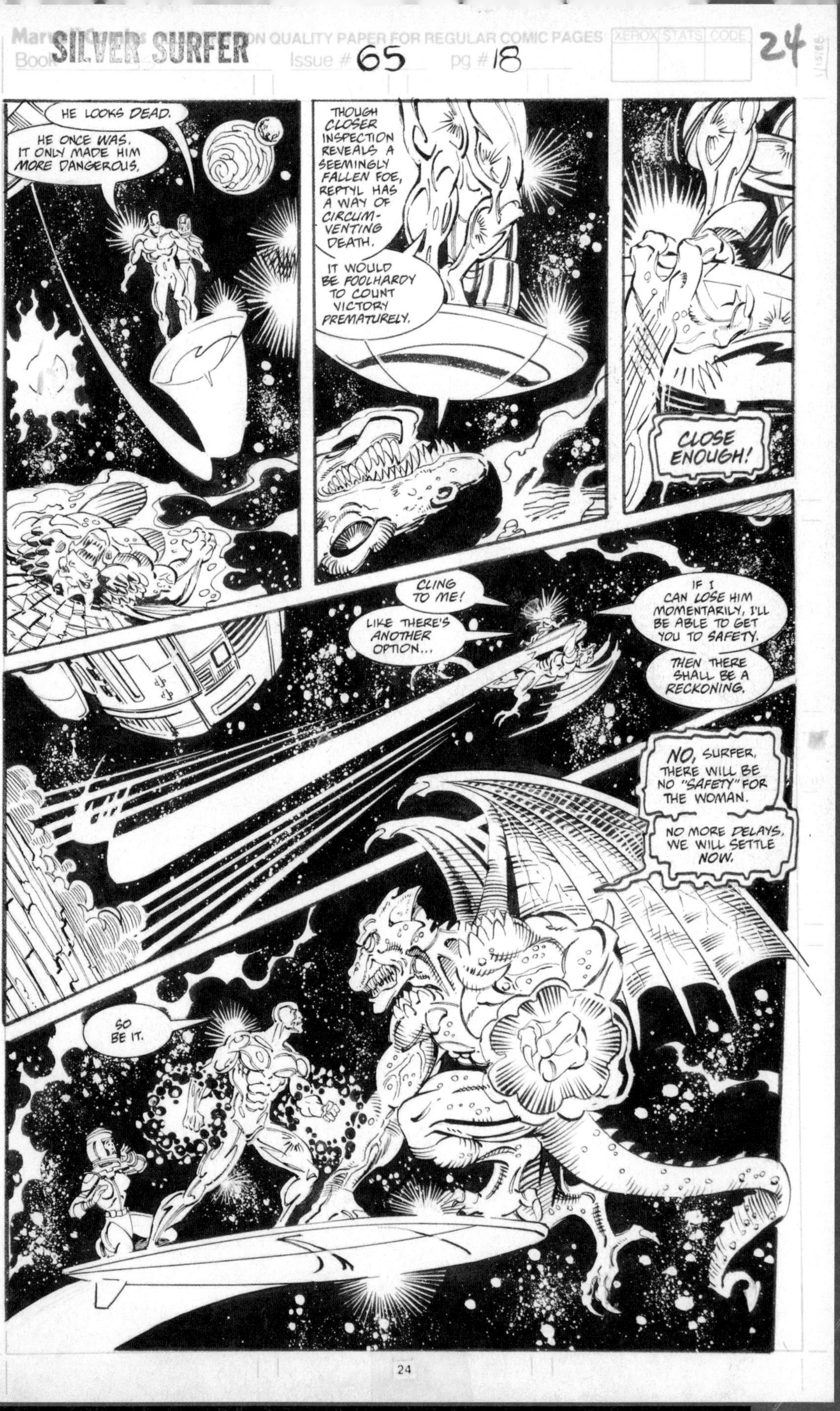
SILVER SURFER
Issue # 65
pg # 18
24
HE LOOKS DEAD.
HE ONCE WAS. IT ONLY MADE HIM MORE DANGEROUS.
THOUGH CLOSER INSPECTION REVEALS A SEEMINGLY FALLEN FOE, REPTYL HAS A WAY OF CIRCUMVENTING DEATH.
IT WOULD BE FOOLHARDY TO COUNT VICTORY PREMATURELY.
CLOSE ENOUGH!
CLING TO ME!
LIKE THERE'S ANOTHER OPTION...
IF I CAN LOSE HIM MOMENTARILY, I'LL BE ABLE TO GET YOU TO SAFETY.
THEN THERE SHALL BE A RECKONING.
NO, SURFER, THERE WILL BE NO "SAFETY" FOR THE WOMAN.
NO MORE DELAYS. WE WILL SETTLE NOW.
SO BE IT.
24

Wizard: The Guide to Comics #5 cover by Ron Lim

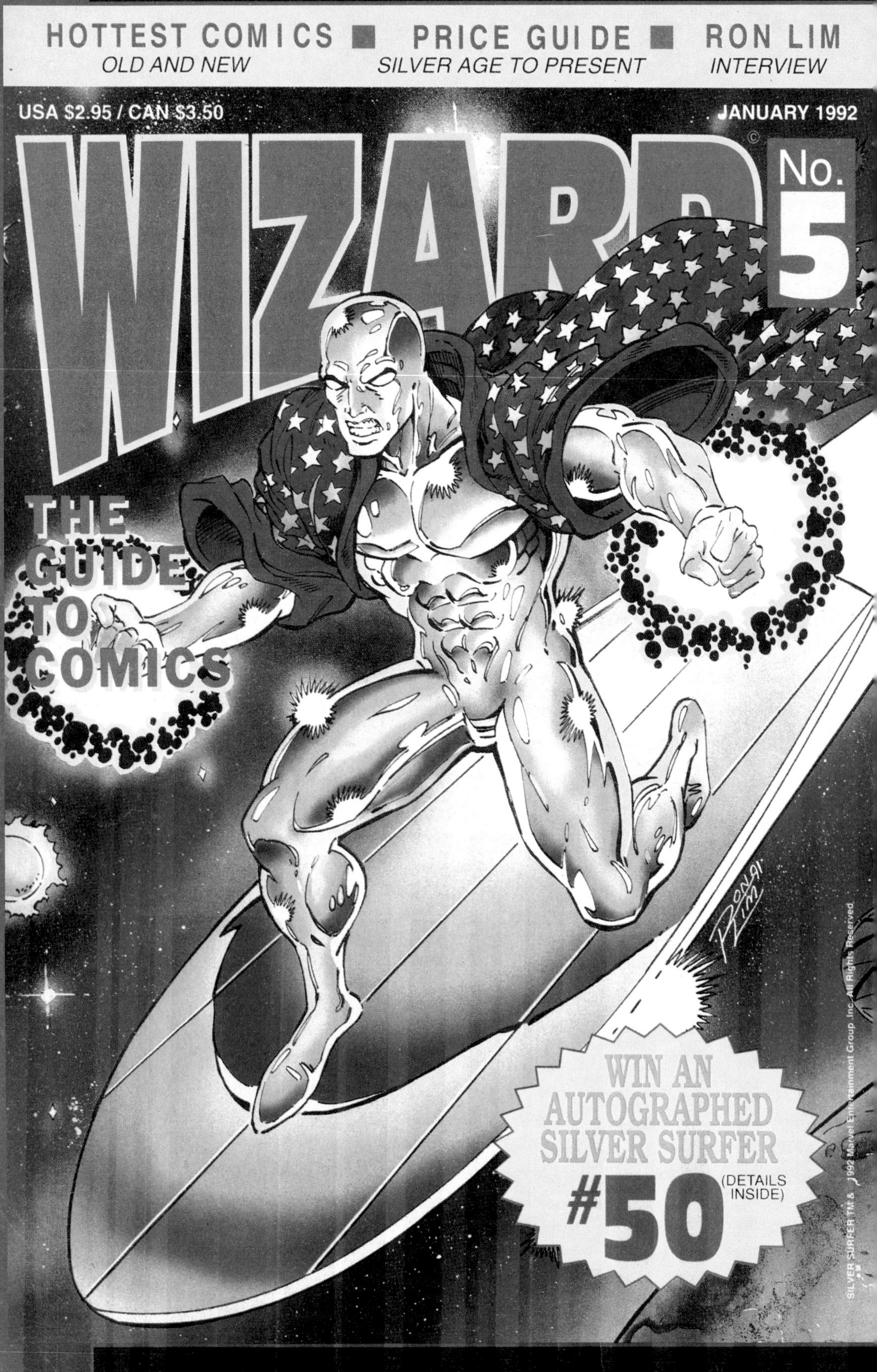
HOTTEST COMICS
OLD AND NEW
PRICE GUIDE
SILVER AGE TO PRESENT
RON LIM
INTERVIEW
USA $2.95 / CAN $3.50
JANUARY 1992
WIZARD
No. 5
THE GUIDE TO COMICS
WIN AN AUTOGRAPHED SILVER SURFER #50
(DETAILS INSIDE)
SILVER SURFER TM & © 1992 Marvel Entertainment Group, Inc. All Rights Reserved